The Long and Winding Road to Equality and Inclusion for Persons with Disabilities

The United Nations Convention on the Rights of Persons with Disabilities

School of Human Rights Research Series, Volume 74

The titles published in this series are listed at the end of this volume.

The Long and Winding Road to Equality and Inclusion for Persons with Disabilities

The United Nations Convention on the Rights of Persons with Disabilities

Andrea Broderick

intersentia
Cambridge – Antwerp – Portland

Intersentia Ltd
Sheraton House | Castle Park
Cambridge | CB3 0AX | United Kingdom
Tel.: +44 1223 370 170 | Email: mail@intersentia.co.uk

Distribution for the UK:
NBN International
Airport Business Centre, 10 Thornbury Road
Plymouth, PL6 7PP
United Kingdom
Tel: +44 1752 202 301 | Fax: +44 1752 202 331
Email: orders@nbninternational.com

Distribution for the USA and Canada:
International Specialized Book Services
920 NE 58th Ave Suite 300
Portland, OR 97213
USA
Tel.: +1 800 944 6190 (toll free)
Email: info@isbs.com

Distribution for Austria:
Neuer Wissenschaftlicher Verlag
Argentinierstraße 42/6
1040 Wien
Austria
Tel.: +43 1 535 61 03 24
Email: office@nwv.at

Distribution for other countries:
Intersentia Publishing nv
Groenstraat 31
2640 Mortsel
Belgium
Tel.: +32 3 680 15 50
Email: mail@intersentia.be

The Long and Winding Road to Equality and Inclusion for Persons with Disabilities.
The United Nations Convention on the Rights of Persons with Disabilities
Andrea Broderick

ISBN 978-1-78068-358-4
D/2015/7849/141
NUR 828

British Library Cataloguing in Publication Data. A catalogue record for this book is available from the British Library.

Acknowledgments

This book is the culmination of two and a half years of hard work, all of which I thoroughly enjoyed. The process of writing was made easier by the support and encouragement of several people.

I am indebted to Lisa Waddington, as my main supervisor, for her many words of wisdom, her generous support and her careful work in checking through all aspects of this book. Lisa has gone far beyond what I could have expected from a supervisor and has dedicated a lot of time to reading drafts of this Ph.D., as well as helping me along the way with other academic work. For that, I am truly grateful. I am also deeply grateful for the support and dedication of my co-supervisor, Fons Coomans. He has provided me with inspiration for several aspects of this thesis and his door was always open to discuss concerns and new ideas. I am also thankful to him for the time he spent checking through the drafts of this thesis and for his wise feedback on those drafts.

In addition, I am grateful to the members of the Reading Committee, who took the time to read this thesis and provided helpful comments and insight: Aalt Willem Heringa, Jenny Goldschmidt, Liesbeth Lijnzaad, Oddný Mjöll Arnardóttir and Theresia Degener.

I would also like to thank the European Commission for the financial support and impetus provided in the framework of the DREAM (Disability Rights Expanding Accessible Markets) network, through which this research project was made possible.

In addition, a special word of thanks is due to Gerard Quinn, Professor of Law at the National University of Ireland, Galway, for introducing me to disability rights scholarship. I am also indebted to Anna Lawson, Shivaun Quinlivan and Mary Keys for their invaluable support and advice.

To my many colleagues at Maastricht University, I also owe special thanks. You have become great friends along the way and I will always hold you very dear.

Last but certainly not least, I dedicate this book to my parents, Madge and Tom. Their unwavering support and love has helped me enormously. I owe them much gratitude for encouraging me along my chosen career path and helping me at any stumbling blocks I encountered.

Where, after all, do universal human rights begin? In small places, close to home – so close and so small that they cannot be seen on any maps of the world. Yet they are the world of the individual person; the neighborhood he lives in; the school or college he attends; the factory, farm, or office where he works.

Such are the places where every man, woman, and child seeks equal justice, equal opportunity, equal dignity without discrimination. Unless these rights have meaning there, they have little meaning anywhere. Without concerted citizen action to uphold them close to home, we shall look in vain for progress in the larger world.[1]

1 Excerpt from a speech by Eleanor Roosevelt at the presentation of 'In Your Hands: A Guide for Community Action for the Tenth Anniversary of the Universal Declaration of Human Rights' (United Nations, New York, March 27, 1958).

Contents

Acknowledgments v
List of Abbreviations xix

Chapter 1.
Introductory Chapter 1

1. Introduction 1
2. Research Objectives and Research Questions 3
3. Methodology 5
   3.1. Normative Analysis: Treaty Interpretation 5
      3.1.1. The Vienna Convention on the Law of Treaties 7
      3.1.2. The Purpose of Treaty Interpretation 8
      3.1.3. Approaches to Treaty Interpretation in the VCLT 10
         3.1.3.1. The Literal (Textual) Interpretative Approach 10
         3.1.3.2. The Systematic (Contextual) Approach 10
         3.1.3.3. The Teleological (Functional) Approach 12
         3.1.3.4. The Historical Interpretative Approach 12
   3.2. Traditional Doctrinal Methodology 13
   3.3. Comparative Methodology 14
4. Structure 15
5. Existing Research Gaps 17
6. Research Limitations 18
7. Conclusion 19

Chapter 2.
Disability Equality: An Evolving Journey 21

1. Introduction 21
2. Theoretical Models of Disability 22
   2.1. Introduction to Theoretical Models of Disability: The Medical Model *versus* the Social Model 22
   2.2. A Consideration of Theoretical Models of Disability 25
      2.2.1. The Minority Rights Approach to Disability 25
      2.2.2. The Universalist Approach to Disability 26
      2.2.3. The Human Rights-Based Approach to Disability 26
      2.2.4. The Capabilities Approach 28
3. Theoretical Models of Equality and their Relationship to Disability Rights 31

3.1. Introduction to Theoretical Models of Equality 31
3.2. Formal Equality 31
3.2.1. Formal Equality and the Medical Model of Disability 33
3.2.2. The Shift Away from Formal Equality Towards Substantive Equality 34
3.3. Substantive Equality 35
3.4. Transformative Equality (Equality as Transformation) 36
3.5. The Objectives of Substantive and Transformative Equality Models. . 38
3.5.1. Equality of Opportunity 38
3.5.2. Equality of Results (Outcome) 40
3.6. The Development of the Equality Norm in International Human Rights Law: Substantive Difference *versus* Substantive Disadvantage Equality 41
3.6.1. Substantive/Specific Difference Equality 42
3.6.2. Substantive Disadvantage (Diversity) Equality 44
3.7. Conclusion on Theoretical Models of Equality 46
4. The International Framework for the Protection of Disability Rights 46
4.1. Disability Rights in Soft-Law Human Rights Instruments (1945–1980) 46
4.2. Disability Rights in Soft-Law Human Rights Instruments (1980–1990) 49
4.3. Disability Rights in Soft-Law Human Rights Instruments (1990-Present Day) 51
4.4. The Protection of the Rights of Persons with Disabilities under Binding International and Regional Human Rights Law before the Adoption of the CRPD 56
4.4.1. The Protection of Disability Rights under the Core International Human Rights Treaties 56
4.4.2. The Regional Framework for the Protection of the Rights of Persons with Disabilities 61
4.5. The Final Steps in the Journey towards the Adoption of the CRPD. . . 63
5. The Link between 'Equality' and 'Participation and Inclusion' in Society for Persons with Disabilities 68
5.1. Introduction to the Concepts of Participation and Inclusion in Society for Persons with Disabilities: Their Link to the Equality Norm 68
5.2. The Dilemma of Difference: Inclusion *versus* Integration in Society . 71
6. Conclusion 73

Chapter 3.
Treaty Interpretation: The Equality and Non-Discrimination Provisions in the CRPD 75

1. Introduction 75
2. Research Methodology 76
3. The Conceptual Understanding of Disability in the CRPD 77

3.1. The Social-Contextual Model of Disability 77
3.2. The Human Rights-Based Understanding of Disability 79
4. Legal Interpretation of Article 5 of the CRPD 80
4.1. The Tripartite Typology of States' Obligations under International Human Rights Law 80
4.2. Article 5(1) of the CRPD 82
4.2.1. The Guarantee of 'Equality Before the Law' and 'Equal Protection of the Law' Without Discrimination 83
4.2.2. The Requirements of 'Equality Under the Law' and 'Equal Benefit of the Law' 86
4.3. Article 5(2) of the CRPD 90
4.3.1. Introduction to Article 5(2) of the CRPD 90
4.3.2. The Definition of Discrimination in the CRPD 90
4.3.2.1. Enjoyment of Rights 'On an Equal Basis with Others' 92
4.3.2.2. Direct *versus* Indirect Discrimination 95
4.3.2.3. Discrimination 'on the Basis of Disability' 96
4.3.3. The Prohibition of Disability-Based Discrimination 98
4.3.4. The Guarantee of 'Equal and Effective Legal Protection against Discrimination' 100
4.3.4.1. The Requirement of 'Equal and Effective Legal Protection against Discrimination' under the CRPD: An Analogy with Similar Obligations in the Core Human Rights Treaties and Observations from the Drafting History of the CRPD 100
4.3.4.2. The Obligation to Protect against Discrimination in the Private Sector 103
4.3.4.3. Equal and Effective Protection against Discrimination 'on all grounds' 104
4.4. Article 5(3) of the CRPD 105
4.4.1. Introduction to Article 5(3) of the CRPD 105
4.4.2. The Elements of the Duty to Accommodate 107
4.4.2.1. What is Meant by the Term 'Accommodation?' 107
4.4.2.2. The Limitation to the Duty to Accommodate: 'Disproportionate or Undue Burden' 109
4.4.2.3. The Duty to Accommodate as Part of the Equality and Non-Discrimination Norms in the Convention . . 111
4.4.3. The Objective of the Duty to Accommodate 112
4.4.3.1. The Duty to Accommodate and the Promotion of Equality 113
4.4.3.2. The Duty to Accommodate and the Elimination of Discrimination 115
4.5. Article 5(4) of the CRPD 115
4.5.1. Introduction to Positive Action Measures under Article 5(4) of the CRPD 115

4.5.2. General Observations on Special Measures in the Core Human Rights Treaties 117
4.5.2.1. Temporary *versus* Permanent Special Measures 117
4.5.2.2. The Importance of a Clear Delineation of the Types of Measures Adopted by States 117
4.5.2.3. 'Specific Measures:' An Exception to the Equality and Non-Discrimination Norms? 120
4.5.2.4. The Participation of Marginalised Groups in the Adoption of Specific Measures 121
4.5.3. Observations from the Drafting History of Article 5(4) of the CRPD 122
4.5.4. Comparison of the Positive Action Clause in the CRPD with CERD and CEDAW 125
4.5.5. Examples of Temporary and Permanent Specific Measures under the CRPD 128
4.5.6. Positive Action under the CRPD: Obligatory or Optional? . . . 130
4.5.6.1. The Nature of Temporary Specific Measures under the CRPD 131
4.5.6.2. The Nature of Permanent Specific Measures under the CRPD 134
4.5.7. Conclusion on the Interpretation of Article 5(4) of the CRPD 135
5. The Model of Equality in the CRPD: A Theoretical and Comparative Perspective 136
5.1. A Consideration of the Theoretical Framework of Equality in the CRPD 136
5.1.1. A Substantive Conception of Equality 136
5.1.2. A Transformative Approach to Equality 138
5.1.3. Substantive Disadvantage Equality 140
5.2. The CRPD's Approach to Disability 141
5.3. A Comparative Perspective on the CRPD's Equality Provisions 142
6. Conclusion 148

Chapter 4.
The Duty to Accommodate Persons with Disabilities 151

1. Introduction 151
2. The Duty to Accommodate 152
2.1. The Origins and Theoretical Underpinning of the Duty to Accommodate 152
2.2. What is Meant by the Term 'Accommodation?' 154
3. The Duty to Accommodate in the CRPD 154
3.1. The Key Strengths of the Duty to Accommodate in the CRPD 154
3.2. The Weaknesses of the Duty to Accommodate as a Facilitator of Substantive Equality 156
4. The Outer Limits of the Duty to Accommodate in the CRPD 158

4.1. Introduction to the Outer Limits of the Duty to Accommodate 158
4.2. The Outer Limits of the Duty to Accommodate in the CRPD: The Concept of 'Reasonableness' 158
4.3. The Outer Limits of the Duty to Accommodate in the CRPD: The Requirements of Necessity and Effectiveness 159
4.4. The Outer Limits of the Duty to Accommodate in the CRPD: A Consideration of the Objective of the Accommodation Duty and the Inherent Dignity of Persons with Disabilities 162
4.5. The Outer Limits of the Duty to Accommodate in the CRPD: The Defence of 'Disproportionate or Undue Burden' 163
4.5.1. Financial and Other Resource Considerations 164
4.5.2. Third-Party Benefits and Negative Impacts of the Requested Accommodation 170
4.5.3. Non-Financial Considerations 174
5. Conclusion 175

Chapter 5.
A Proposed Framework for the Assessment of the Progressive Realisation of CRPD Rights 177

1. Introduction 177
2. The Progressive Realisation of Human Rights 181
2.1. Introduction to the Concept of Progressive Realisation 181
2.2. The Immediate Duties of States Parties to the CRPD in the Realisation of Economic, Social and Cultural Rights 182
2.2.1. The Obligation to 'Take Steps' to Achieve Progressively the Full Realisation of Rights 183
2.2.2. Deliberately Retrogressive Measures 185
2.2.3. The Obligation to Ensure Non-Discrimination in the Exercise of Economic, Social and Cultural Rights 187
2.2.4. The Obligation to Devote the 'Maximum of Available Resources' to Achieving Progressively the Full Realisation of Rights 187
2.2.5. Minimum Core Obligations 188
2.3. Equality Considerations in the Realisation of Socio-Economic Rights 190
3. Reasonableness Review of Socio-Economic Rights 191
3.1. Introduction to Reasonableness Review of Socio-Economic Rights 192
3.2. Reasonableness Review: The South African Approach to Progressive Realisation of Human Rights 192
3.2.1. South African Reasonableness Review: Delineation of the Test by the Constitutional Court 194
3.2.1.1. The Rationality Test 195
3.2.1.2. The Introduction of the Reasonableness Standard 195
3.2.1.3. The Criteria Inherent in the *Grootboom* Test 196

3.2.1.4. The Development of the Reasonableness Test: The Use of Available Resources, the Equality Limb and Participation of Affected Groups. 200
3.2.1.5. Summary of the South African Approach to Reasonableness Review. 204
3.3. Reasonableness Review: The Standard of Review at the International Level 206
4. A Proposed Framework for Review of the Progressive Realisation of Rights under the CRPD 209
4.1. Introduction to the Proposed Framework. 210
4.2. A Proposed Framework for Review of the Progressive Realisation of CRPD Rights 210
4.3. Proposed Criteria for Assessment of Progressive Realisation under the CRPD 213
4.3.1. The Necessity and Effectiveness of Measures taken by States 213
4.3.2. Disproportionate Burden/Cost Considerations. 215
4.3.3. Equality Considerations 220
4.3.4. Dignity Considerations 224
4.3.5. The Impact of Failure to Take Measures 228
4.3.6. Participatory Processes/Accountability 229
4.3.7. Third-Party Benefits 231
5. Conclusion. 231

Chapter 6.
The Accessibility Obligation in the CRPD. 235

1. Introduction. 235
2. The Accessibility Obligation: Article 9 of the CRPD. 236
2.1. Introduction to Accessibility under Article 9 of the CRPD 236
2.2. The Objective of Article 9 of the CRPD 238
2.3. Accessibility and Access to Rights. 239
3. The Interrelationship Between Accessibility and Equality in the CRPD . . 241
3.1. The Nature of the Link between Accessibility and Equality 242
3.2. Inaccessibility as a Breach of the Non-Discrimination Norm? 244
3.3. Accessibility and Reasonable Accommodation Measures 246
4. The Progressive Realisation of Article 9 of the CRPD. 249
4.1. The Tripartite Obligations of States Parties under Article 9 of the CRPD. 249
4.2. The Progressive Implementation of Disability Accessibility under the CRPD 250
4.3. The Obligation to Ensure Satisfaction of the Minimum Core of Article 9 of the CRPD 252
4.3.1. Priority Areas of Disability Accessibility 252
4.3.2. The Obligation not to Create New Barriers. 253
4.4. Relevant Considerations in the Implementation of Article 9 of the CRPD 254

4.4.1. The Requirement to Adopt Legislation to Ensure Implementation of Article 9 of the CRPD and the Drafting of Accessibility Standards 254
4.4.2. The Obligation to Monitor the Realisation of Disability Accessibility 255
4.4.3. The Provision of Effective Legal Remedies 255
4.4.4. The Provision of Disability Accessibility Training for Stakeholders 256
4.4.5. Accessibility as Part of the Educational Curriculum.... 257
4.4.6. The Continuous Obligation to Improve Conditions of Accessibility 257
4.4.7. The Obligation to Abstain from Taking Deliberately Retrogressive Measures in Realising Disability Accessibility 257
4.4.8. Privatisation of Goods, Products and Services: The Impact on States Parties' Accessibility Obligations 258
4.5. The Criteria for Assessment of Measures taken by States in the Progressive Realisation of Article 9 of the CRPD 258
4.5.1. Disproportionate Burden/Cost Considerations.... 259
4.5.2. The Obligation to Use the Maximum of Available Resources: Resource Prioritisation and Resource Optimisation Efforts of States 260
4.5.3. The Necessity and the Effectiveness of Measures Taken by States.... 261
4.5.4. Equality Considerations 263
4.5.5. Dignity Considerations 265
4.5.6. Participation and Inclusion: The Requirement to Involve Persons with Disabilities in all Aspects of the Implementation and Monitoring of Disability Accessibility .. 266
4.5.7. The Impact of Failure to Take Measures to Ensure Disability Accessibility 268
4.5.8. Benefits to Third Parties.... 269
5. Conclusion.... 271

Chapter 7.
The Right to Education for Persons with Disabilities.... 273

1. Introduction.... 273
2. The Right to Education in International Human Rights Law 275
2.1. The Right to Education in International Human Rights Law and the Development of the Right to Inclusive Education 275
2.2. The Normative Content of the Right to Education in International Human Rights Law 278
3. The Right to Inclusive Education: Article 24 of the CRPD.... 281
3.1. The Concept of Inclusive Education.... 281
3.2. A Legal Interpretation of Article 24 of the CRPD.... 284

3.3. The Obligations of States under Article 24 of the CRPD 289
3.3.1. Non-Discrimination in Education 289
3.3.2. Reasonable Accommodations and Other Individualised Support Measures 293
3.3.3. Appropriate Forms of Communication, Training for Teachers and Lifelong Learning 294
4. Assessment by the CRPD Committee of the Measures Taken by States under Article 24 of the CRPD 296
4.1. Disproportionate Burden/Cost Considerations 296
4.2. Equality Considerations 299
4.3. Dignity Considerations 300
4.4. The Necessity and Effectiveness of Measures Taken to Ensure the Right to Inclusive Education 301
4.5. Participation of Persons with Disabilities in the Provision of Inclusive Education 301
4.6. Third-Party Benefits 302
5. Emerging Trends in Inclusive Education Provision in States Parties to the CRPD 303
5.1. Good Practices in Inclusive Education Provision 303
5.2. Bad Practices in Inclusive Education Provision 305
6. Conclusion 308

Chapter 8.
Case Study: The Influence of the CRPD on the Council of Europe 311

1. Introduction 311
2. Case Study Part 1: The Influence of the CRPD on the Interpretation of the ECHR 313
2.1. Introduction to the Case Study (Part I) 313
2.2. The Relevance of the CRPD to the Interpretation by the European Court of Human Rights of the ECHR 313
2.3. The Interpretation of the Equality Norm in the ECHR 316
3. Case Study Part I: The Influence of the CRPD on the Interpretation of ECHR Rights 320
3.1. A Heightened Standard of Scrutiny of Disability Rights at the ECtHR: The 'Vulnerable Groups Approach' 320
3.1.1. A Positive Step in the Direction of Substantive Equality 322
3.1.2. A Heightened Standard of Scrutiny of Disability Rights 323
3.1.3. A Failure to Recognise Systemic Disadvantage 324
3.1.4. Further Evidence of a Heightened Standard of Scrutiny 326
3.1.5. The Social-Contextual Approach – Steps in the Direction of the Social Model of Disability? 328
3.1.6. Conclusion: Two Steps Forward – One Step Back 332
3.2. *De Facto* Reasonable Accommodation Duties under the ECHR in Limited Circumstances 334

3.2.1. *De Facto* Reasonable Accommodation Duties in Prison Settings: Pre-CRPD 335
3.2.2. Post-CRPD Case Law on Disabled Prisoners 337
3.2.2.1. A Marked Absence of Reference to the CRPD in the ECtHR's Case Law on Disabled Prisoners 337
3.2.2.2. Increased Recognition of the CRPD in the ECtHR's Case Law on Disabled Prisoners 338
3.2.2.3. The Vulnerable Groups Approach: An Obligation to Take 'Reasonable Steps' 341
3.2.2.4. An Inconsistent Approach to International Law as an Interpretative Guide to ECHR Rights 344
3.2.3. Conclusion on *De Facto* Reasonable Accommodations in Institutional Settings 346
4. Case Study Part I: The Potential Influence of the CRPD on the Interpretation of the Right to Equality for Persons with Disabilities under the ECHR 347
4.1. The Explicit Recognition of a Duty to Accommodate under the ECHR's Non-Discrimination Provision? 348
4.2. The Vulnerable Groups Approach as a Facilitator of Substantive Equality in the Context of Disability Rights? 350
4.3. Social-Contextual Analysis and the Social Model of Disability as a Potential Pre-Cursor to a Mainstreaming Approach in the Interpretation of the ECHR? 354
5. Case Study Part II: The CRPD, General Disability Policy of the Council of Europe and the Revised European Social Charter 356
5.1. The CRPD and Council of Europe Policy Instruments on Disability 356
5.1.1. Pre-CRPD: The Council of Europe Disability Action Plan . . . 356
5.1.2. Post-CRPD: Committee of Ministers' Recommendations on Disability 358
5.1.3. Post-CRPD: Council of Europe Issue Papers on Disability . . . 363
5.2. The CRPD and the Revised European Social Charter 366
5.2.1. The Right to Education for Persons with Disabilities under the Revised European Social Charter 369
5.2.2. Pre-CRPD Collective Complaints on the Right to Education . 369
5.2.3. Post-CRPD Collective Complaints on the Right to Education 372
6. Conclusion 374

Chapter 9.
Concluding Chapter: Findings, Conclusions and Recommendations 377

1. Summary of Book's Objectives 377
2. Main Findings and Conclusions 378
2.1. Introduction 378
2.2. Methodology 378
2.3. Findings and Conclusions 379

2.3.1. The Gaps in the Protection of the Rights of Persons with Disabilities Pre-CRPD 380
2.3.2. The Legal Meaning of Equality in the CRPD – A Theoretical and Comparative Framework 380
2.3.3. Lessons Drawn from the Outer Limits of the Duty to Accommodate 384
2.3.4. A Proposed Framework for the Progressive Realisation of Rights in the CRPD 385
2.3.5. The Interrelationship between the Accessibility Obligation and the Equality Norm 388
2.3.6. The Right to Education for Persons with Disabilities 389
2.3.7. The Influence of the CRPD on Council of Europe Disability Law and Policy 391
3. Main Recommendations 393
3.1. Recommendations for the CRPD Committee 393
3.2. Recommendations at the National Level (EU and beyond) 394
3.3. Recommendations for the Council of Europe Mechanisms 394
4. Concluding Remarks 395

Summary in English 397
Valorisation Addendum 411
Curriculum Vitae 415
Bibliography 417

List of Abbreviations

American with Disabilities Act (ADA)
Centre for Studies on Inclusive Education (CSIE)
Court of Justice of the European Union (CJEU)
Early Childhood Care and Education (ECCE)
Education For All (EFA)
Equal Employment Opportunities Commission (EEOC)
European Committee of Social Rights (ECSR)
European Convention on Human Rights (ECHR)
European Court of Human Rights (ECtHR)
European Disability Forum (EDF)
Human Rights Committee (HRC)
Hyper Text Markup Language (HTML)
Information and Communications Technology (ICT)
International Classification of Functioning, Disability and Health (ICF)
International Classification of Impairments, Disabilities and Handicaps (ICIDH)
International Disability Alliance (IDA)
International Disability Caucus (IDC)
International Labour Organization (ILO)
International Law Commission (ILC)
International Year of Disabled Persons (IYDP)
Mental Disability Advocacy Center (MDAC)
National Human Rights Institutions (NHRI)
Non-Governmental Organisations (NGOs)
Office of the High Commissioner for Human Rights (OHCHR)
Optional Protocol to the CRPD (OP-CRPD)
Optional Protocol to the Convention on Economic, Social and Cultural Rights (OP-ICESCR)
Organisations of People with Disabilities (DPOs)
Union of the Physically Impaired Against Segregation (UPIAS)
United Nations (UN)
United Nation's Children's Fund (UNICEF)
United Nations Committee on Economic, Social and Cultural Rights (UNCESCR)
United Nations Committee on the Elimination of Discrimination against Women (CEDAW Committee)
United Nations Committee on the Elimination of Racial Discrimination (CERD Committee)
United Nations Committee on the Rights of the Child (CRC Committee)

United Nations Convention on the Elimination of All Forms of Discrimination Against Women (CEDAW)
United Nations Convention on the Elimination of Racial Discrimination (CERD)
United Nations Convention on the Rights of Persons with Disabilities (CRPD)
United Nations Convention on the Rights of the Child (CRC)
Vienna Convention on the Law of Treaties (VCLT)
World Conference on Education for All (WCEFA)
World Declaration on Education for All (WEA)
World Federation of the Deaf (WFD)
World Health Organisation (WHO)
World Institute on Disability (WID)
World Programme of Action Concerning Disabled Persons (WPA)

Chapter 1
Introductory Chapter

'Human rights are, literally, the rights that one has simply because one is a human being. [...] Human rights are equal rights: one either is or is not a human being, and therefore has the same human rights as everyone else.'[1]

1. Introduction

Persons with disabilities have long been relegated to the margins of society and they have been subjected to discrimination on many levels. This book takes as its point of departure the fundamental premise that persons with disabilities are entitled to enjoy and exercise their human rights on an equal basis with others in society. It also takes as a basic starting point the fact that equality and non-discrimination norms are important facilitators of full and effective participation and inclusion in society for persons with disabilities.

The landscape of disability law and policy has transformed in the last few decades, primarily as a result of a shift in the perception of disability itself, from the out-dated medical model of disability to the social model.[2] According to the social model, disability is now viewed as an interaction between persons with impairments and pervasive societal barriers. By way of contrast, the medical model of disability views functional limitations as a consequence flowing from impairment. In other words, it perceives the inability of disabled people to participate in society as an inevitable result of their own impairment rather than as a consequence of any disabling and discriminatory barriers in society. In addition to the paradigm shift from the medical model to the social model, disability discourse has also moved away from a social welfare perspective towards a human rights-based approach. Under the social welfare model, persons with disabilities were seen as objects of charity. According to the human rights-based approach, disabled people are viewed as holders of rights, entitled to exercise all human rights and fundamental freedoms on an equal basis with others, entailing the provision of material support where necessary.

1 J. Donnelly, *Universal Human Rights in Theory and Practice* (Cornell University Press, Ithaca, New York, Second Edition, 2003), at page 10.

2 For more information on the social model generally and the shift in disability theory from the medical to the social model, see T. Shakespeare (ed.), *Disability Rights and Wrongs* (Routledge, London, 2006), at pages 15–22; See also P. Weller (ed.), *New Law and Ethics in Mental Health Advance Directives: The Convention on the Rights of Persons with Disabilities and the Right to Choose* (Routledge, New York, 2013), at pages 27–38.

The United Nations Convention on the Rights of Persons with Disabilities (CRPD or Convention)[3] is one of the most recent human rights treaties adopted at the international level and it is part of the evolving body of human rights law at the universal level. The provisions of the CRPD are extremely progressive. In particular, its equality and non-discrimination norms go far beyond the substance of international human rights law to date. The Convention encapsulates the paradigm shifts mentioned above. The CRPD embraces a model of equality which seeks to target deep-rooted structural inequalities by advocating legal tools such as positive obligations and reasonable accommodation measures as integral means by which to eradicate barriers which maintain or perpetuate disadvantage. To that extent, the CRPD endeavours to target contextual and asymmetrical structures of oppression and exclusion.

The primary aim of the CRPD was not to create new rights but to ensure that existing human rights were made equally effective for persons with disabilities. The equality and non-discrimination principles are the driving force of the Convention. They apply across the substantive rights and obligations contained therein and breathe new life into human rights for disabled people. Notwithstanding this, there remains a huge gap between the promising equality paradigm contained in the CRPD and the reality which exists for persons with disabilities in their everyday lives. Disabled individuals are victims of glaring inequalities at every level of society. To borrow the words of Gerard Quinn, the CRPD serves as 'a mirror before society:'[4]

> It makes us face up to our own values – to our so-called 'legacy values' of dignity, autonomy equality and social solidarity. It forces us to acknowledge the large gap that still exists between the 'myth system' of our values and the 'operations system' of how these values are in fact dishonoured in daily practice.[5]

The CRPD represents the culmination of major efforts at the international level to ensure that disability equality was enshrined in a binding human rights treaty. The Convention seeks to guarantee participation and inclusion of disabled persons in mainstream society on an equal basis with others. It symbolises a bright light at the end of a long and dark tunnel of exclusion and marginalisation. It provides renewed hope for the future application of the equality and non-discrimination principles for disabled people everywhere. Of course, it remains to be seen whether the progressive norms contained in the CRPD can be translated into practice – into the everyday lives of persons with disabilities.

---

[3] UN Convention on the Rights of Persons with Disabilities, resolution/adopted by the UN General Assembly, 24 January 2007, UN Doc. A/RES/61/106, available at www.refworld.org/docid/45f973632.html, last accessed 26 March 2015.

[4] Comments of Professor Gerard Quinn, The UN Convention on the Human Rights of Persons with Disabilities, Presentation to the Irish Human Rights Commission (Dublin, 19th April, 2007), available at www.ihrc.ie/download/doc/gquinn.doc last accessed 29th May 2014).

[5] Ibid.

2. Research Objectives and Research Questions

The core objectives of this book are three-fold. The first essential aim of this research is to interpret the exact legal meaning of the principles of equality and non-discrimination in the context of the CRPD in order to tease out States' obligations under the Convention. This will facilitate a demonstration of how the non-discrimination tool contained in the Convention can potentially be leveraged to promote lasting reforms and true equality for people with disabilities. A particular focus throughout this book will be on the manner in which the equality and non-discrimination norms in the CRPD can increase the exercise and enjoyment of human rights by persons with disabilities, in particular advancing their participation and inclusion in society. Another aim of this research project is to devise a framework for review of measures adopted by States in the overall context of the progressive realisation of disability rights, with a particular emphasis on how the CRPD's equality norm might strengthen the realisation of socio-economic rights for disabled people. Thirdly, this research seeks to investigate how the equality and non-discrimination norms in the Convention have already influenced, and can potentially influence, the crucial shape of disability equality case law and policy. It also seeks to identify the challenges which lie ahead in the implementation of the Convention. In that connection, a case study will be carried out on the Council of Europe mechanisms. The reason for including that particular case study in this book is to assess whether the CRPD is having an influence on disability law and policy at the regional level. This will facilitate an analysis of whether the equality and non-discrimination norms in the CRPD can be used to expand disability discrimination claims in the Council of Europe.

The overall research question for this book is as follows: To what extent has the CRPD advanced disability equality in theory and how can this potentially advance the participation and inclusion in society of persons with disabilities in practice? Taking this research question as a vital starting point, the paragraphs which follow will delineate the overall schema of this book, highlighting the various sub-research questions that will be answered in each chapter or section of the book.

In order to lay the foundations for this research as a whole, this book will begin by reflecting on various theoretical models of disability and equality which have been outlined by legal scholars to date. That will set the scene for subsequent chapters of this book, in which the CRPD's equality provisions will be examined. The background leading up to the adoption of the CRPD at the international level will then be outlined. The sub-research question to be answered in that regard is as follows: What gaps existed in relation to the protection of the rights of persons with disabilities, which necessitated the adoption of a binding international human rights treaty for disabled people?

The next goal of the research conducted for this book will be to provide a comprehensive legal interpretation of the equality and non-discrimination norms in the Convention (contained in Article 5 and related articles), in order to tease out States' Parties obligations in that regard. This research will also seek to determine the theoretical model(s) of equality contained in the CRPD. In that connection, the following sub-research questions will be answered:

i. What is the legal meaning of the CRPD's equality and non-discrimination norms?; and
ii. How do the concepts of equality and non-discrimination contained in the CRPD fit within the various theoretical models of disability and conceptions of equality which have been elaborated to date by scholars?

The theoretical framework of equality in the CRPD will then be compared to that contained in other international human rights treaties which preceded the Convention. In that regard, the following sub-research questions will be answered:

i. To what extent does the non-discrimination obligation contained in the CRPD go further than previous non-discrimination norms at the international level; and
ii. How can this potentially advance the rights of persons with disabilities to participate and be included in society?

After having analysed the theoretical and comparative framework within which the CRPD's equality provisions operate, a specific component of the equality norm will be examined, namely the duty to accommodate persons with disabilities. The accommodation duty signifies the obligation to alter or modify existing practices or environments which constitute barriers to the participation and inclusion of disabled people in society. The sub-research question to be answered in that particular section of the book is as follows: What are the outer limits of the duty to accommodate? More specifically, can the balancing and sharing of burdens inherent in the accommodation duty (namely, the fact that the covered party is obliged to accommodate the needs of a disabled individual, unless that would amount to a disproportionate burden for the entity concerned) teach us lessons about the overall balancing of burdens and interests implicit in many Convention rights subject to progressive realisation?

Following on from that analysis, this book contains an extensive reflection on the progressive realisation of disability rights. In that regard, several frameworks of review which are used at the national and international levels to assess the measures adopted by States in implementing socio-economic rights will be outlined. Specifically, the framework of reasonableness review adopted by the South African Constitutional Court will be delineated and the emerging notion of reasonableness review envisaged under the Optional Protocol to the International Covenant on Economic, Social and Cultural Rights (OP-ICESCR). The sub-question to be answered in that section of the book is as follows: What are the criteria inherent in already existing frameworks of reasonableness review and how can those criteria be tailored to the specific context of the CRPD in order to advance its equality paradigm? Based on the research carried out for that section of the book, a framework for review of measures will be devised, which can potentially assist the Committee which oversees implementation of the CRPD – the United Nations Committee on the Rights of Persons with Disabilities

(CRPD Committee) – in the difficult task of assessing measures adopted by States under the Convention.

Thereafter the relationship between the equality and non-discrimination norms in the CRPD and some substantive rights and obligations in the Convention will be investigated, in particular those subject to progressive realisation, namely the accessibility obligation and the right to education. In that connection, the following sub-questions will be answered:

i. What kind of criteria might be applied to determine the reasonableness of State action or inaction in the context of the accessibility obligation and the right to education?; and
ii. Can the Convention's equality paradigm advance the realisation of socio-economic rights for persons with disabilities?

The final part of the research conducted for this book will entail a case study on the Council of Europe. The first part of that case study relates to the influence to date, and the potential influence, of the CRPD on disability equality case law of the European Court of Human Rights (ECtHR or Strasbourg Court). The sub-research question to be answered in that regard is as follows: Is the Strasbourg Court evidencing a shift in its approach to disability equality on foot of the entry into force of the CRPD, in terms of adopting a more substantive model of equality, signalled by such indicators as *de facto* reasonable accommodation duties and a social model of disability? Based on the research outcomes of the first part of this case study, the research will go on to consider the influence which the CRPD might have in the future on the interpretation by the Strasbourg Court of the provisions contained in the European Convention on Human Rights (ECHR). In the second part of the case study, the provisions of the Revised European Social Charter (revised Charter) will be considered, as well as the views of the European Committee of Social Rights (ECSR) and the general disability policy of the Council of Europe. In that connection, the following sub-research question will be answered: What influence is the CRPD having on the relevant Council of Europe legal and policy mechanisms?

3. Methodology

3.1. Normative Analysis: Treaty Interpretation

The primary research methodology that will be employed throughout this book will consist of a normative analytical framework. For the most part, that will comprise an analysis of the normative content of rights and obligations, specifically the rights and obligations contained in the CRPD. The specific research methodology that will be employed to interpret the obligations of States Parties under the CRPD will be that of treaty interpretation. Birgit Peters contends that 'treaty interpretation in general, and human rights interpretation in particular, is a complex matter.'[6] The provisions of international human rights treaties are, broadly speaking, ambiguous. As such, they leave significant room for different interpretative accounts. The International Law Commission has stated that 'the interpretation of documents is to some extent an art, not an exact science.'[7] In defining the normative content of a human right, it is often tempting to accede to one's personal preferences with regard to the obligations which the right in question should create. However, as John Tobin observes:

> Simply clothing an assertion about the content of an internationally recognized human right with the apparel of humanity may satisfy a moral or political urge, but it does not necessarily accord with the nature of the *legal* obligations actually assumed by a state under a human rights treaty.[8]

Thus, it is important to employ a solid methodology in order to interpret the CRPD in a coherent manner. The primary point of reference in all aspects of treaty interpretation in this book will be the text of the CRPD itself and the Vienna Convention on the Law of Treaties (VCLT).[9] The VCLT contains a canon of interpretative principles which are accepted at the level of international law as being the appropriate ones for interpreting the substance of international human rights norms. As such, this research does not entail a normative *de lege ferenda* element in the usual sense of the word, in terms of proposing what the law should be or suggesting legislative improvements. Rather, this research enters within the realm of *lex lata*, in that it sets out and analyses the law as it exists, interpreting such law according to an established and reliable framework of interpretation. To that extent, 'new' law is certainly not being proposed in this book. Having said that, at various junctures throughout this book, my own opinions on the meaning of the rights and obligations contained in the CRPD are put forward, at all times adhering to the strict interpretative criteria set out in the VCLT. Furthermore, at times I propose suggestions for the CRPD Committee as to the correct interpretation (in my view) of the rights and obligations contained in the Convention, according to VCLT methodology. However, it is submitted that this in itself does not add a normative *de lege ferenda* element to this research.

In the subsections which follow, the VCLT and its various methodological tools will be introduced. Those tools will be employed throughout this book to interpret the relevant provisions of the CRPD. In addition, the purpose of human rights treaty

---

6 B. Peters, 'Aspects of Human Rights Interpretation by the UN Treaty Bodies,' in H. Keller and G. Ulfstein (eds.), *UN Human Rights Treaty Bodies, Law and Legitimacy* (Cambridge University Press, Cambridge, 2012), at pages 261–319, available at http://ssrn.com/abstract=2013298 last accessed 14 April 2014.

7 International Law Commission, *Report of the Commission to the General Assembly* (Volume 2, Yearbook of the International Law Commission, 1966), at page 218.

8 J. Tobin, 'Seeking to Persuade: A Constructive Approach to Human Rights Treaty Interpretation' (2010) 23(1) *Harvard Human Rights Journal* 1, at page 2.

9 Vienna Convention on the law of treaties (with annex). Concluded at Vienna on 23 May 1969, available at https://treaties.un.org/doc/Publication/UNTS/Volume%201155/volume-1155-I-18232-English.pdf, last accessed 15 April 2014.

interpretation will be reflected upon, as well as the so-called special nature of human rights treaties.

3.1.1. The Vienna Convention on the Law of Treaties

The principles enumerated in the VCLT constitute the legal rules that are accepted widely[10] in the process of interpreting the substance of international human rights treaties. The two provisions that are of paramount importance in interpreting the CRPD are Articles 31 and 32 of the VCLT. Article 31 of the VCLT embodies the general rule of interpretation. It reads as follows:

> 1. A treaty shall be interpreted in good faith in accordance with the ordinary meaning to be given to the terms of the treaty in their context and in the light of its object and purpose.
> 2. The context for the purpose of the interpretation of a treaty shall comprise, in addition to the text, including its preamble and annexes:
>   (a) any agreement relating to the treaty which was made between all the parties in connection with the conclusion of the treaty;
>   (b) any instrument which was made by one or more parties in connection with the conclusion of the treaty and accepted by the other parties as an instrument related to the treaty.
> 3. There shall be taken into account together with the context:
>   (a) any subsequent agreement between the parties regarding the interpretation of the treaty or the application of its provisions;
>   (b) any subsequent practice in the application of the treaty which establishes the agreement of the parties regarding its interpretation;
>   (c) any relevant rules of international law applicable in the relations between the parties.
> 4. A special meaning shall be given to a term if it is established that the parties so intended.[11]

Article 31 must be read in conjunction with Article 32 of the VCLT, which addresses the supplementary means of interpretation. Article 32 of the VCLT provides that:

> Recourse may be had to supplementary means of interpretation, including the preparatory work of the treaty and the circumstances of its conclusion, in order to confirm the meaning resulting from the application of article 31, or to determine the meaning when the interpretation according to article 31:
> (a) leaves the meaning ambiguous or obscure; or
> (b) leads to a result which is manifestly absurd or unreasonable.[12]

---

10 The VCLT is treaty law, which falls within the ambit of customary international law [See, for example, the comments of R.K. Gardiner, *Treaty Interpretation* (Oxford University Press, Oxford, 2008), at pages 12/13].

11 VCLT, Article 31.

12 VCLT, Article 32.

Articles 31 and 32 of the VCLT contain interpretative tools – literal (textual) interpretation, systematic (contextual) interpretation, teleological (functional) interpretation and historical interpretation. Before outlining the main features of the VCLT, it is important to consider firstly the overall purpose of treaty interpretation.

3.1.2. The Purpose of Treaty Interpretation

There are many different theories on the purpose of treaty interpretation.[13] None of these theories are 'mutually exclusive.'[14] The first theory is that the aim of treaty interpretation is to ascertain the intention of the parties. A second proposition advanced by scholars is that the primary goal of treaty interpretation is to determine the ordinary meaning of the text. The concept of 'ordinary meaning' has been described as the 'current and normal, regular and usual meaning'[15] of a term. A further theory of interpretation is that the object and purpose of the treaty is paramount.[16] In the context of human rights treaties, it is often stressed that the drafters' intentions are of lesser importance than they are for general international law treaties.[17] The main emphasis in the interpretation of human rights treaties appears to be on the 'object and purpose' of the treaty or the particular norm under interpretation. Birgit Peters maintains that:

> The interpretation of a treaty in light of its object and purpose is probably the most important rule of article 31(1) of the VCLT, both in general international law and in human rights law. In contrast to the literal and contextual method, an interpretation following the object and purpose touches on the very content of the rule, and, in the human rights context, on the values enshrined in it.[18]

These observations provide support for a dynamic approach to interpretation in the context of the CRPD's equality provisions. It is important to note that the structure of the Convention also champions a dynamic approach to interpretation. The object and purpose of the CRPD, its general principles and its general obligations all seek to contextualise the interpretation of its substantive provisions. Jean Allain points to the fact that 'where the CRPD is concerned, its unique character mandates an approach which turns to the "object and purpose" [of the Convention] as these are given voice,

---

13 See generally, D.B. Hollis (ed.), *The Oxford Guide to Treaties* (Oxford University Press, Oxford, 2012).

14 I. Sinclair (ed.), *The Vienna Convention on the Law of Treaties*, (Manchester University Press, Manchester, 1984), at page 71.

15 M.E. Villiger, 'The Rules on Interpretation: Misgivings, Misunderstandings, Miscarriage? The 'Crucible' Intended by the International Law Commission' in E. Cannizzaro (ed.), *The Law of Treaties: Beyond the Vienna Convention* (Oxford University Press, Oxford, 2011), 105, at page 109.

16 See, for instance, D.S. Jonas and T.N. Saunders, 'The Object and Purpose of a Treaty: Three Interpretive Methods' (2010) 43(3) *Vanderbilt Journal of Transitional Law* 565.

17 For an example of such an opinion, see W. Kälin and J. Künzli, *The Law of International Human Rights Protection* (Oxford University Press, Oxford, 2009), at page 38.

18 B. Peters, 'Aspects of Human Rights Interpretation by the UN Treaty Bodies,' available at http://ssrn.com/abstract=2013298.

in part, through Article 3 which [sets] out the Convention's General Principles.'[19] Article 1 of the CRPD outlines its object and purpose as being to 'promote, protect and ensure the full and equal enjoyment of all human rights and fundamental freedoms by all persons with disabilities, and to promote respect for their inherent dignity.'[20] The purpose of the Convention is also reflected in Article 3 which contains the general principles of the Convention, two of which are 'non-discrimination'[21] and 'equality of opportunity.'[22] It is also mirrored in Article 4, which sets out the general obligations of the Convention. General Obligation 4(1) of the CRPD provides that:

> States Parties undertake to ensure and promote the full realization of all human rights and fundamental freedoms for all persons with disabilities without discrimination of any kind on the basis of disability.[23]

The research methodology employed throughout this book (in all aspects of treaty interpretation) will take into account the relationship between the principles governing conventional treaty law and human rights law and the so-called 'special nature'[24] of human rights treaties. Human rights treaties are considered to be different from ordinary treaties to the extent that they are not intended to benefit State interests but are designed primarily to impose objective obligations on States, with a view to protecting individuals *qua* human beings. Human rights treaties are living instruments and account must be taken of changing social realities in their interpretation. Therefore, the CRPD will be interpreted in a manner which is dynamic and which gives effect to the object and purpose of the treaty as a whole. This approach to interpretation is particularly appropriate, in light of the fact that disability is stated expressly to be an 'evolving concept'[25] in the Preamble of the Convention. As conceptualisations of disability change, so too will the interpretation of equality and non-discrimination norms in the context of persons with disabilities. It is also important to bear in mind that the interpretation of the CRPD should not be overly dynamic, in the sense that it should not be based on wishful thinking. Moreover, any interpretation of the Convention must be rooted firmly in the

---

19 J. Allain, Treaty Interpretation and the United Nations Convention on the Rights of Persons with Disabilities, page 6, available at www.disabilityaction.org/.../legal-report-2-treaty-inte.. last accessed 29 August 2014.

20 UN CRPD, Article 1.

21 UN CRPD, Article 3(b).

22 UN CRPD, Article 3(e).

23 UN CRPD, Article 4(1).

24 The International Court of Justice (ICJ), among others, has noted the special character of human rights treaties. For example, in its Advisory Opinion on Reservations to the Convention on the Prevention and Punishment of the Crime of Genocide, the ICJ stated as follows: 'In such a convention the contracting States do not have any interests of their own; they merely have, one and all, a common interest, namely, the accomplishment of those high purposes which are the raison d'être of the convention. Consequently, in a convention of this type one cannot speak of individual advantages or disadvantages to States, or of the maintenance of a perfect contractual balance between rights and duties. The high ideals which inspired the Convention provide, by virtue of the common will of the parties, the foundation and measure of all its provisions.' [International Court of Justice, Advisory Opinion on Reservations to the Convention on the Prevention and Punishment of the Crime of Genocide, adopted on May 28, 1951(1951 I.C.J. 15), at page 8].

25 UN CRPD, Preamble para. (e).

provisions of the treaty itself and the relevant rules of treaty interpretation. One must ensure not to carve out unrealistic expectations for States Parties to the Convention, especially in the context of developing States under major resource constraints. This is particularly so in light of the stringent obligations imposed by the Convention on States and the fact that many of these obligations will be realised progressively.

3.1.3. Approaches to Treaty Interpretation in the VCLT

In the subsections which follow, the main features of the interpretative tools contained in the VCLT will be outlined.

3.1.3.1. The Literal (Textual) Interpretative Approach

The literal (textual) interpretative approach requires that objective criteria of interpretation are taken into account by the researcher, who must respect the primacy of the text. In that regard, words or phrases 'are to be given their normal, natural, and unstrained meaning.'[26] However, the ordinary meaning of the CRPD will not be determined in the abstract. It will be determined in the context of the treaty as a whole and in light of its object and purpose. This leads neatly onto the next two interpretative tools contained in the VCLT – the systematic (contextual) approach and the teleological (functional approach) to interpretation.

3.1.3.2. The Systematic (Contextual) Approach

The systematic (contextual) approach mandates that the researcher locates the interpretation of any phrases within their broader meaning. The Preamble and Annexes of the CRPD form part of the contextual interpretative framework. In addition, the general principles and general obligations of the CRPD, contained in Articles 3 and 4 of the Convention respectively, provide interpretative context. These are the core values that should guide interpretation and implementation of the Convention as a whole and they will be analysed, where relevant, in order to obtain a broader picture of the scope of the particular rights under interpretation. One must also ensure to interpret each article of the Convention as a whole, where for instance it consists of many sub-sections.

The VCLT also requires account to be taken, where necessary and relevant, of the following: (a) Any agreement relating to the treaty which was made between all the parties in connection with the conclusion of the treaty[27] and; (b) any instrument which was made by one or more parties in connection with the conclusion of the treaty and accepted by the other parties as an instrument related to the treaty.[28] This

---

26 Comment made by Sir Gerald Fitzmaurice, International Law Commission Rapporteur on the Law of Treaties, cited by M. Fitzmaurice, 'The Practical Working of the Law of Treaties' in M. Evans (ed.) *International Law* (Oxford University Press, Oxford, 2nd edition, 2006), at page 198.

27 VCLT, Article 31(2)(a).

28 VCLT, Article 31(2)(b).

would include the Optional Protocol to the CRPD.[29] As outlined above, Article 31(3) of the VCLT also requires consideration of the following items, in conjunction with an analysis of the context of the CRPD: (a) Any subsequent agreement between the parties regarding the interpretation of the treaty or the application of its provisions;[30] (b) any subsequent practice in the application of the treaty which establishes the agreement of the parties regarding its interpretation[31] and; (c) any relevant rules of international law applicable in the relations between the parties.[32] Where the CRPD is concerned, subsequent practice may be manifest in the decisions taken by the CRPD Committee on individual communications, as well as in the general comments and concluding observations of the Committee (if these can be deemed to establish the agreement of the parties regarding the Convention's interpretation). In any event, it is important to consider the general comments and concluding observations of the CRPD Committee as a subsidiary source of interpretation. It is also important to consider the general comments and concluding observations of the other core human rights treaty bodies as they relate to equality and non-discrimination norms in the respective treaties as a subsidiary means of interpretation for the obligations engendered by the CRPD. Anthony Aust confirms that one may look at 'other treaties on the same subject matter adopted either before or after the one in question which use the same or similar terms.'[33] In that respect, the synergistic approach will be applied throughout this chapter. That approach draws on the suggestion of the Office of the United Nations High Commissioner for Human Rights (OHCHR) that all of the international treaties are mutually re-enforcing and that 'rather than being separate, free-standing treaties, the treaties complement each other, with a number of principles binding them together.'[34]

While the comments and observations of the core human rights treaty bodies will be an important secondary source of guidance, it is important to guard against placing too much reliance on them. The treaty bodies have sometimes been accused of overly

---

29 For the purposes of interpreting the equality and non-discrimination norms in the Convention, the Optional Protocol has not revealed any useful material and therefore will not be elaborated on throughout this chapter.

30 VCLT, Article 31(3)(a).

31 VCLT, Article 31(3)(b).

32 VCLT, Article 31(3)(c).

33 A. Aust, *Modern Treaty Law and Practice* (Cambridge University Press, Cambridge, 2nd edition, 2007), at page 248.

34 Office of the High Commissioner for Human Rights, *The United Nations Human Rights Treaty System: An Introduction to the Core Human Rights Treaties and the Treaty Bodies,* at page 20, available at www.ohchr.org/Documents/Publications/FactSheet30en.pdf last accessed 13 August 2014. Indeed, certain observations, such as General Comment 5 of the UNCESCR, shed some light on the manner in which the equality norm in other international treaties has been interpreted in the context of persons with disabilities. As Jean Allain points out: 'that General Comment, though it predates the CRPD by more than a decade, provides some detail as to the obligations flowing from specific rights established by the Covenant Economic, Social and Cultural Rights which are, in turn, reproduced in the Convention on the Rights of Persons with Disabilities.' [J. Allain, Treaty Interpretation and the United Nations Convention on the Rights of Persons with Disabilities, page 13, available at www.disabilityaction.org/.../legal-report-2-treaty-inte.. last accessed 29 August 2014].

expanding the obligations of States and of demonstrating 'a lack of coherence'[35] and 'analytical rigor'[36] in interpreting human rights. Furthermore, it is noteworthy that the general comments and concluding observations of the treaty bodies are not legally binding *per se*. Nonetheless, they carry considerable authoritative weight.

3.1.3.3. The Teleological (Functional) Approach

According to the teleological (functional) approach to interpretation, the object and purpose of a treaty must be taken into account. As stated above, the object and purpose of the treaty plays a major role in interpretation in the context of human rights treaties. The European Court of Human Rights (ECtHR) has stated that the preferred approach to interpretation is one which is 'most appropriate in order to realise the aim and achieve the objective of the treaty, not that which would restrict to the greatest possible degree the obligations undertaken by parties.'[37] Applying the teleological approach in the specific context of a human rights treaty will require that certain additional factors are taken into account to reflect the humanitarian content of the Convention. Article 31 VCLT requires interpretation of a human rights treaty in good faith. This, in turn, requires the interpreter to translate the provisions of treaties in an effective and practical manner for individuals as rights-holders under international law.[38] This is called the principle of effectiveness.[39] It implies that a human rights treaty 'should be interpreted in order to ensure maximum effectiveness in achieving the object and purpose of the treaty.'[40] In accordance with the evolutive nature of human rights treaties, interpretation must also take account of changes and developments in law and society and the general context in which the treaty applies to reflect the fact that international law is evolving constantly.

3.1.3.4. The Historical Interpretative Approach

Article 32 of the VCLT permits recourse to the *travaux préparatoires* (the permanent records of the drafting history and the circumstances of conclusion) of Article 5 of the CRPD and related articles. The documents which are relevant to the negotiation

---

35 On this point see, for example, the arguments of K. Michel, 'Treaty Bodies and the Interpretation of Human Rights' 42 *Vanderbilt Journal of Transitional Law* 905, at page 906.

36 Ibid.

37 ECtHR, *Wemhoff v. Germany*, application no. 2122/64 (1968) 1 EHRR 55, at page 75.

38 Lixinski observes that: 'It has been asserted that the tendency of international law towards literal interpretation aimed at a precise delineation of states' obligations is not applicable in the human rights context. Instead, the interpretation of human rights instruments has the primary aim of promoting the effective application (*effet utile*) of the instrument.' [L. Lixinski, 'Treaty Interpretation by the Inter-American Court of Human Rights: Expansionism at the Service of the Unity of International Law' (2010) 21(3) *European Journal of International Law* 585, 589, citing C. Trindade, 'International Law for Humankind: Towards a New Jus Gentium (II) – General Course on Public International Law' (2006) 317 *Collected Courses of the Hague Academy of International Law* 1, at page 60].

39 See generally, B. Cali, 'Specialised Rules of Treaty Interpretation: Human Rights' in D.B. Hollis (ed.), *The Oxford Guide to Treaties* (Oxford University Press, Oxford, 2012), at page 538; See also ECtHR, *Tyler v. the United Kingdom*, application no. 5856/72, (1978) 2 EHRR 1, at paras. 15–16.

40 M. Dixon, *Textbook on International Law* (Oxford University Press, Oxford, 7th edition, 2013), at page 74.

process and which will be perused in this book as part of the interpretative process include the daily summaries and minutes of the drafting sessions, preliminary drafts of the CRPD, correspondence and public statements of the negotiators, as well as reports of the Ad-Hoc Committee of the Working Group enlisted to draft the Convention.

Unlike the prescriptive rule contained in Article 31 of the VCLT, Article 32 enshrines a supplementary means of interpretation. Notwithstanding this, the drafting history of the CRPD plays an important role in its interpretation, in light of the fact that the Convention has been adopted so recently. As such, there is not yet a catalogue of subsequent practice to rely on. Therefore, in my interpretation of the CRPD's equality and non-discrimination norms, the drafting history of the Convention will often be referred to in the first instance as it provides vital background information to the CRPD's provisions. Having said that, the drafting history will not be resorted to as an 'alternative autonomous'[41] source on the interpretation of the CRPD's equality provisions. In accordance with Article 32 of the VCLT, the drafting history will only be used in order to confirm the meaning resulting from the application of Article 31, or to determine the meaning when the interpretation according to Article 31 'leaves the meaning ambiguous or obscure'[42] or 'leads to a result which is manifestly absurd or unreasonable.'[43] In considering the travaux préparatoires of the CRPD it is necessary to be conscious at all times of the warning issued by the International Law Commission (ILC) when it asserted that 'it is beyond question that the records of treaty negotiations are in many cases incomplete or misleading so that considerable discretion has to be exercised in determining their value as an element of interpretation.'[44] Preparatory work serves merely to provide evidence of the intentions of parties to a treaty, evidence which is to be considered in the context of the text itself and the object and purpose of the treaty as a whole.[45]

3.2. Traditional Doctrinal Methodology

At various junctures throughout this book, and to complement the normative analysis which will be engaged in, the classic form of legal scholarship will be employed – namely, a traditional legal doctrinal approach.[46] The doctrinal approach involves a researcher examining the content of a legal opinion 'to evaluate whether it was

41 T. O'Elias, *The Modern Law of Treaties* (Sijthoff Publishing Company B.V., Leiden, 1974), at page 80.

42 VCLT, Article 32(a).

43 VCLT, Article 32(b).

44 Yearbook of the International Law Commission (1996), Volume II, Page 220, para. 10.

45 The *travaux préparatoires* of a given instrument are merely 'evidence to be weighed against any other relevant evidence of the intentions of the parties, and their cogency depends on the extent to which they furnish proof of the *common* understanding of the parties as to the meaning attached to the terms of the treaty. Statements of individual parties during the negotiations are therefore of small value in the absence of evidence that they were assented to by the other parties '[D. Hollis, *The Oxford Guide to Treaties*, (Oxford University Press, Oxford, 2012), 488, citing R. Waldock, Third Report (No. 4) 58 (21) (emphasis in original, footnotes omitted)].

46 For a review of this form of scholarship generally, see M.H. Redish, 'The Federal Courts, Judicial Restraint, and the Importance of Analyzing Legal Doctrine' (1985) 85 *Columbia Law Review* 1378.

effectively reasoned or to explore its implications for future cases.'[47] Doctrinal analysis, as traditionally understood, is generally descriptive, evaluative and critical. For the purpose of this book, a traditional legal methodology can be defined as one which selects the most relevant legal sources in order to analyse systematically legislative provisions, travaux préparatoires, case law and academic sources in order to clarify the current state of the law, facilitating presentation of that material in a coherent and structured manner. This methodology will be applied, for instance, to the consideration of various theoretical models of disability and equality. The analysis of such theoretical models will be based primarily on academic literature written by legal scholars in the field. Traditional legal methodology will also be applied to the analysis of the protection of disability rights in key documents which preceded the adoption of the CRPD. In that connection, primary sources will be examined, such as the core human rights treaties and soft-law instruments pertaining to disability rights, together with a small selection of international case-law. With regard to secondary sources, relevant statements of UN bodies and those involved in the negotiations of the CRPD will be analysed. Academic literature which examines the various UN instruments will also be considered. A further interpretative aid that will be used throughout this book is secondary academic sources on the equality and non-discrimination norms in the CRPD, together with secondary sources on equality norms in other international human rights treaties. Traditional doctrinal methodology will also be applied in the study of the case law and the legal reasoning of the ECtHR and the views of the ECSR, as well as the disability policy of the Council of Europe.

3.3. Comparative Methodology

The final research methodology that will be employed in this book is a comparative analytical approach. Comparative methodology can be defined generally 'as the act of comparing the law of one country to that of another.' However, 'the comparison can be broader: more than two laws, more than law, more than written words.'[48] Comparative methodology can also extend beyond the national sphere and can consist of a comparison of the judgments of one legal system with those of another system (such as regional systems of law), in order to gain a deeper understanding of how legal organs arrive at legal judgments. Comparative methodology emerged as a discipline by which one could gain an understanding of foreign legal systems and cultures. Comparative law has also sometimes entailed 'a search for universal principles of law that transcend culture, primarily in the field of private law, but with elements transforming public law as well.'[49] The key act of comparison has been deemed to involve 'looking at one mass of legal data in relation to another and then assessing how the two lumps of legal data are similar and how they are

[47] E.H. Tiller and F.B. Cross, 'What is Legal Doctrine' (2006) 100(1) *Northwestern University Law Review* 517, at page 518.

[48] E.J. Eberle, 'The methodology of comparative law' (2011) 16(1) *Roger Williams University law review* 51, at page 52.

[49] Ibid, at page 53/54.

different.'[50] Edward Eberle contends that 'it is not enough simply to compare words on the page. Law sits within a culture.' Thus, one must look at 'the substructural forces that influence the law.'[51] Comparative law assists in discerning commonalities and key differences between legal systems and helps us to understand the cultural and other factors that inform the process of law-making and decision-making in other countries. George Samuel rightly asserts that:

> Without comparing legal systems, we would have no idea of the conceptual differences between systems. [...] Systematic comparison involves the structure and organization of a particular legal area. At the conceptual level, the difference in legal concepts, institutions and solutions is studied.[52]

Comparative international law, in the broad sense, entails comparing how different institutions interpret similar international human rights norms. In this book, the comparative approach will be employed at three junctures. In the first instance, comparative research will be engaged in when analysing the evolution of the equality norm at the international level. This will enable the reader to gain an understanding of how the equality norm has progressed at the level of international human rights law throughout the last few decades, culminating with the adoption of the CRPD. It will also facilitate answering one of the research questions for the book as a whole, namely how the norms contained in the CRPD fit comparatively within various models of disability and theoretical conceptions of equality. In the second instance, comparative methodology will be used when outlining the various frameworks existing at the national and international levels for a review of measures adopted by States in realising progressively human rights. This will allow a determination of whether lessons can be drawn from the various approaches adopted at the national and international levels to aid in a review of measures adopted by States Parties under the CRPD. In the third instance, comparative methodology will be employed in the case study of the Council of Europe mechanisms, when comparing the norms contained in the CRPD to the legal and policy outcomes of the Council mechanisms.

4. Structure

This book is divided into nine chapters as follows:

The present chapter contains a brief introduction to the research project for this book as a whole.

In chapter two of this book the development of various theoretical models of disability and equality will be traced. The background leading up to the adoption of the CRPD

---

50 Ibid.

51 Ibid.

52 G. Samuel, 'Comparative Law and Jurisprudence' (1998) 47(4) *International and Comparative Law Quarterly* 817, 825, citing L. Rayar, 'Translating Legal Texts: A Methodology' (Conference Paper, Euro-forum, April 1993).

will also be laid out, including the principal disability-related developments that have occurred within the human rights division of the United Nations (UN) system in the last few decades. Chapter two will also consist of an analysis of the relevance of the core international and regional human rights treaties to disability rights. The overall aim of chapter two of this book will be to highlight the gaps which existed at the level of international human rights law before the adoption of the CRPD. It will also set the scene for the interpretation and critical analysis of the equality and non-discrimination norms in the CRPD that will follow in chapter three of this book.

Chapter three of this book will contain a legal interpretation of the CRPD's equality and non-discrimination provisions, according to the rules of treaty interpretation contained in the VCLT. Chapter three aims to provide a framework within which to determine the substantive value that the CRPD's equality and non-discrimination paradigm can add to increasing the participation and inclusion of persons with disabilities in society. At the end of chapter three a theoretical and comparative interpretation will be engaged in. This will consist of highlighting the areas in which the CRPD's provisions differ from the existing corpus of international human rights law from an equality perspective.

In chapter four of this book the component elements of, and the intricacies inherent in, the duty to accommodate persons with disabilities under the CRPD will be explored. Specifically, chapter four will reflect on the outer limits of the duty to accommodate and the balancing of needs and interests foreseen under the duty (namely, the fact that the covered party is obliged to accommodate the needs of a disabled individual, subject to the proviso that it must not constitute a disproportionate or undue burden on the entity concerned). One aim of that reflection will be to determine whether lessons can be drawn from such a balancing of needs and interests, which can facilitate a greater understanding of how other provisions of the CRPD can be implemented, specifically those rights and obligations subject to progressive realisation (which also contain an implicit balancing of needs and interests).

In chapter five of this book the outer limits of the concept of progressive realisation of socio-economic rights will be examined. Chapter five will also consist of comparative analysis, highlighting various criteria for reviewing measures taken by States to realise progressively human rights. A focus will be maintained on the criteria inherent in the reasonableness review framework adopted by the South African Constitutional Court and the criteria envisaged for assessing measures adopted under the International Covenant on Economic Social and Cultural Rights (ICESCR). The overall objective of chapter five will be to devise a framework for review of measures adopted by States to realise progressively the socio-economic rights contained in the CRPD. In doing so, the aforementioned criteria will be drawn on and tailored to the values and purposes underlying the CRPD. In order to reflect the spirit and tenor of the CRPD, the research conducted for chapter five of this book will also draw on elements of the balancing of interests inherent in the duty to accommodate.

Chapters six and seven of this book will contain a reflection on certain rights and obligations in the Convention which are subject to progressive realisation. In chapter six, the normative content of the accessibility obligation (contained in Article 9 of the CRPD) will be clarified. In addition, the link between the accessibility obligation and the equality and non-discrimination norms in the Convention will be outlined. Specifically, the interrelationship between accessibility and the duty to accommodate will be explored, as well as the key differences between the two types of measures. In addition, the various criteria outlined in chapter five as being pertinent to the CRPD Committee's assessment of measures taken by States in the progressive realisation of disability rights will be drawn on. Those criteria will be applied to Article 9 of the Convention. In chapter seven of this book, the right to education (as contained in Article 24 of the CRPD) will be examined. That chapter will tie in with chapters five and six of this book in terms of its focus on the progressive realisation of CRPD rights and also in exploring the manner in which the Convention's equality and non-discrimination norms can infuse the right to education for persons with disabilities with added value. A central aim of chapter seven will be to determine the normative content of the right to education and to draw on the various review criteria (outlined in chapter five) to facilitate assessment of measures adopted by States Parties to the CRPD in fulfilling the right to education.

Chapter eight of this book will consist of a case study on the Council of Europe. The main part of that case study will examine the impact which the CRPD is having, and can potentially have, on the case law of the ECtHR related to disability equality. The general disability policy of the Council of Europe will also be considered, as well as the views of the ECSR and the provisions of the Revised European Social Charter.

Finally, chapter nine of this book will contain concluding remarks and a summary of the principal findings and recommendations emerging from this book as a whole.

5. Existing Research Gaps

This book seeks to fill the knowledge gaps which exist with regard to the precise legal interpretation of the equality and non-discrimination norms in the CRPD. While many scholars have written eloquently on the duty to accommodate and miscellaneous aspects of the equality and non-discrimination provisions in the Convention, to date there has been no comprehensive interpretation and critical analysis of all aspects of the CRPD's equality paradigm according to the VCLT methodology. The research conducted for this book aims to bridge that gap by providing an interpretation of the substantive framework of equality within which the provisions of the Convention will operate. It is only within such a comprehensive framework that the precise nature of the legal obligations of States Parties to the Convention can be determined.

In addition, there is certainly room to contribute to the debate on the progressive implementation of disability rights, taking into account equality considerations in particular. Accordingly, attention will be focused in the second half of this book on a potential framework for review of measures taken by States in the progressive realisation of rights contained in the CRPD. While some authors have (briefly) linked existing frameworks of reasonableness review to the standard of review to be adopted by the CRPD Committee,[53] that link has not been expanded on to any great extent to date.

Finally, the case study that will be carried out on the Council of Europe will seek to fill the research gaps in that area by determining the influence, and potential influence, of the CRPD on the legal and policy mechanisms in the Council.

6. Research Limitations

It must be acknowledged that, within the confines of this book, there are certain research limitations. In particular, the prohibition on disability discrimination at the EU level will not be examined, mainly because that area has been covered extensively by leading scholars[54] and I do not feel that I can contribute significantly to the existing scholarship in that area at present. Instead, attention will be focused on the areas in which there are gaps in disability equality scholarship as outlined above.

Due to time constraints it has been impossible to carry out country studies on national jurisdictions detailing the approach to equality taken in domestic jurisdictions and the improvements which the CRPD has already had, or is likely to have in the future, on various aspects of national laws relating to disability equality. Instead, the case study carried out for this book focuses on the Council of Europe. It is envisaged that any influence which the CRPD might have in changing the direction of disability law and policy in the Council of Europe may trickle down slowly into national legislation and policy.

It is also important to point out that, in this book, it is not proposed to provide a framework for actually measuring the increase, or potential increase, in participation and inclusion of persons with disabilities in society on foot of the entry into force of the CRPD. Such a task is outside the ambit of the research agenda for this particular project. Instead, the concepts of participation and inclusion will be used as key

---

53 See, for instance, B. Porter, 'The Reasonableness of Article 8(4) – Adjudicating Claims from the Margins' (2009) 27(1) *Nordisk Tidsskrift for Menneskerettigheter* 39–53, at page 52.

54 See the lengthy writings in this area by such scholars as Lisa Waddington, Gerard Quinn and Anna Lawson, to name but a few [See, for instance, L. Waddington, 'When it is Reasonable for Europeans to Be Confused: Understanding When a Disability Accommodation is "Reasonable" from a Comparative Perspective' (2008) 29(3) *Comparative Labor Law & Policy Journal* 317; See also A. Lawson, 'The EU Rights Based Approach to Disability: Strategies for Shaping an Inclusive Society,' (2005) 6(4) *International Journal of Discrimination and the Law* 269; In addition, see G. Quinn, 'The European Social Charter and EU Anti-discrimination Law in the Field of Disability: Two Gravitational Fields with One Common Purpose' in G. de Búrca, B. de Witte, and L. Ogertschnig (eds.) *Social Rights in Europe* (Oxford University Press, Oxford, 2005)].

threads running through the project as a whole, on account of their link to the overarching themes of equality and non-discrimination for persons with disabilities.

Finally, it must be noted that the cut-off date for this research was January 2015. Therefore, this book does not detail any subsequent developments in the disability equality field after that date.

7. Conclusion

Disabled people have been marginalised and disadvantaged for too long now and deserve to be treated as equals. In the overall context of the struggle for equal rights for persons with disabilities, it is apt to remember the words of former United States Attorney General, Robert F. Kennedy:

> [...] We can perhaps remember – even if only for a time – that those who live with us are our brothers and sisters; that they share with us the same short moment of life; that they seek – as we do – nothing but the chance to live their lives in purpose and happiness, winning what satisfaction and fulfilment they can.[55]

There is no longer any doubt that persons with disabilities are subjects of human rights and are entitled to enjoy and exercise those rights on an equal basis with all other individuals in society. Having said that, the journey towards equality and inclusion for persons with disabilities has been paved with many bumps in the road. Let us now go on to explore that journey.

[55] This quote has been taken from a speech made by former US Attorney General, Robert F. Kennedy, on the South African Day of Affirmation in 1966.

Chapter 2
Disability Equality: An Evolving Journey

'Disability is a human rights issue! I repeat: disability is a human rights issue. Those of us who happen to have a disability are fed up being treated by society and our fellow citizens as if we did not exist [...] We are human beings with equal value, claiming equal rights.'[1]

1. Introduction

The conceptualisation of disability and the protection of the rights of persons with disabilities have evolved significantly in recent decades. Disability is now perceived to be a human rights issue. However, it was not always conceptualised as such. Once perceived as objects of charity and welfare, persons with disabilities are deemed to be holders of rights, entitled to exercise and enjoy human rights guarantees on an equal basis with others. Disability is now viewed through the lens of equality and human dignity. The adoption of the CRPD in 2006 represents the culmination of the evolution of disability rights protection at the international level.

The present chapter will set the scene for this book as a whole. To that end, this chapter will be divided into six sections. In section two several theoretical models that have been linked to disability will be analysed – namely, the minority rights approach, the universalist approach, the human rights-based approach to disability and the capabilities approach. One of the main reasons for exploring theoretical models of disability stems from the fact that the understanding of disability which an instrument endorses is vital in determining the human rights of disabled people. Moreover, it is central to the vantage point that is taken on equality issues. Section three of this chapter will take up the theme of equality by examining various theoretical models of equality that have been delineated by legal scholars to date. This will provide an essential backdrop and a theoretical underpinning for the next chapter of this book, in which the exact meaning of the equality and non-discrimination norms contained in the CRPD will be reflected upon and the manner in which such norms fit comparatively within various models of disability and equality will be analysed. In section four of this chapter, the principal developments that have occurred in

1 Speech by Bengt Lindqvist, Special Rapporteur on Disability of the United Nations Commission for Social Development, at the nineteenth Congress of Rehabilitation International, Rio de Janeiro, 25–30 August 2000, cited by G. Quinn and T. Degener, *Human Rights and Disability: The Current Use and Future Potential of the United Nations Human Rights Instruments in the Context of Disability* (2002), at page 13, available at www.ohchr.org/Documents/Publications/HRDisabilityen.pdf, last accessed 13 January 2014.

the disability context within the human rights division of the UN in the last few decades will be traced. In that connection, several non-binding or soft-law UN instruments which preceded the adoption of the CRPD will be highlighted. Section four will also contain an analysis of the relevance of the core binding international and regional human rights treaties to the rights of persons with disabilities. The aim of that analysis will be to highlight the gaps which existed in the protection of the rights of persons with disabilities before the CRPD came onto the international human rights landscape. Furthermore, it will have as its objective to demonstrate the necessity for the adoption of an integral human rights treaty concerned solely with disability rights. In section five of the present chapter the nature of the relationship between equality and non-discrimination norms, on the one hand, and participation and inclusion in society, on the other hand, will be explored, as this will be a key theme running throughout this book as a whole. Finally, section six of this chapter will contain concluding remarks.

2. Theoretical Models of Disability

In this section various theoretical models of disability will be reflected upon, with a particular focus on their relationship to the equality norm. This will set the backdrop to the analysis in the next section of this chapter of various theoretical models of equality that have been outlined by legal scholars to date. As already stated above, there is an intrinsic link between the model of disability contained in an instrument and the subsequent approach to equality taken by that instrument. Marcia Rioux and Christopher Riddle point to the fact that 'the meaning of equality will vary depending on the perspective of disability adopted.'[2] Therefore, it is important to carve out the link between conceptual models of disability and equality.

2.1. Introduction to Theoretical Models of Disability: The Medical Model *versus* the Social Model

There has been a paradigm shift in the landscape of disability law and policy over the last few decades. There are two main strands to that shift. In the first instance, the paradigm shift is reflected in the move from the medical or welfare model of disability towards the social model of disability.[3] In the past, disability was perceived as a medical or welfare issue according to which functional limitations were deemed to be a direct result of impairment. The medical model of disability focuses on attempts to 'cure' the functional limitations of the disabled person (through rehabilitation and prevention) in order that they can then conform to the non-disabled 'norm.' The

---

2 M.H. Rioux and C.A. Riddle, 'Values in Disability Policy and Law: Equality' in M.H. Rioux, L.A. Basser and M. Jones (eds.), *Critical Perspectives on Human Rights and Disability Policy* (Martinus Nijhoff, The Hague, 2011), at page 42.

3 The social model of disability was labelled originally as such by Michael Oliver – see M. Oliver, 'If I had a Hammer' in C. Barnes and G. Mercer (eds.) *Implementing the Social Model of Disability: Theory and Research* (The Disability Press, Leeds, 2004), at pages 18–31.

focus under the outdated medical model lay on the impairment itself rather than disabling and discriminatory barriers in society and a disabled person's inability to participate in society was seen as a consequence of his or her own impairment. By virtue of the fact that the focus of the medical model was on the biological traits of the individual, there was a distinct lack of focus on structural inequalities and inaccessibility. This brought with it a resultant segregation from mainstream society, as those who were considered 'deviant' from the 'norm' were excluded, due to their 'inability' to cope with mainstream structures.[4] By way of contrast, the social model of disability identifies systemic barriers (in the form of environmental, attitudinal and legislative obstacles, among others) as the main contributory factor in disabling people with impairments. The social model maintains that responsibility lies with national governments and society as a whole to remedy the disadvantage and inequalities faced by persons with disabilities.[5] The social model of disability drew its inspiration from theories of social constructionism. It gained momentum in the 1970s, soon becoming the dominant model advanced by the disability rights movement. The fundamental premises of the social model were developed initially by the Union of the Physically Impaired Against Segregation (UPIAS), a British organisation advocating for the rights of people with physical disabilities. Several scholars and activists – such as Michael Oliver, Paul Hunt, Vic Finkelstein, Paul Abberley and Colin Barnes – played central roles in the development and extension of this model to other forms of disability.[6] In the United States, the passage of the Americans with Disabilities Act (ADA)[7] marked the primary point of departure for a new approach which viewed persons with disabilities through a social model lens.

Kayess and French contend that the social model of disability 'assists to illuminate the limitations of traditional theories of equality in relation to persons with [disabilities].'[8] The equality norm is at the core of the social model. By targeting the barriers that disable individuals with impairments, the social model focuses on the ability (or rather the inability) of societal structures to guarantee equal access to, and enjoyment of, human rights for disabled people. The relevance of the social understanding of disability also lies in its implications for combatting discrimination. The social model requires disability discrimination laws to address the systemic or structural disadvantage caused to people with disabilities by conventional societal structures that are predicated on so called 'able-bodied'

---

4 For further analysis of the medical model of disability, see generally J. Grue (ed.), *Disability and Discourse Analysis* (Ashgate Publishing Limited, England, 2015), page 54 onwards.

5 For further information on the social model, see for instance, M.A Stein, 'Disability Human Rights' (2007) 95 *California Law Review* 75, 88; See also C. Barnes and G. Mercer, 'Theorising and Researching Disability from a Social Model Perspective' in C. Barnes and G. Mercer (eds.) *Implementing the Social Model of Disability: Theory and Research* (The Disability Press, Leeds, 2004).

6 See P. Abberley, 'Work, Utopia and Impairment' in L. Barton (ed.), *Disability and Society: Emerging Issues and Insights* (Longman Publishing, New York, 1996); See also T. Shakespeare, *Disability rights and wrongs* (Routledge, London, 2006).

7 Americans with Disabilities Act of 1990 (ADA), as amended by the Amendments Act of 2008 (P.L. 110–325), which became effective on January 1, 2009, available at www.ada.gov/pubs/adastatute08.htm last accessed 22 June 2014.

8 R. Kayess and P. French, 'Out of Darkness Into Light? Introducing the Convention on the Rights of Persons with Disabilities' (2008) 8(1) *Human Rights Law Review* 1, at page 8.

norms. It is these mainstream structures that hinder the parity of participation and inclusion of people with disabilities in everyday activities. Under the social model, this exclusion is deemed to be a form of discrimination. The social model of disability which underlies the CRPD reinforces a shared experience of inequality, irrespective of the type of individual impairment. It places the focus on the processes by which society marginalises people with disabilities. The renewed focus under the social model is integral to tackling systemic discrimination. In line with the social model, the focus has now shifted away from the disabled individual and his or her differential characteristic towards a broader re-examination of structural disadvantage. Underpinning the human rights of persons with disabilities with the social model has given added value to the equality norm. By focusing on structural inequalities, the social model seeks to increase opportunities for participation and inclusion of persons with disabilities in all aspects of mainstream society. The social model also endorses an increased role for persons with disabilities to express their experiences and views through participatory processes.

Taken in its strictest sense, the social model of disability has been criticised by some scholars for focusing too much on external factors and ignoring the impact of impairment. For instance, Jenny Morris points to the fact that 'while environmental barriers and social attitudes are a crucial part of our experience of disability – and do indeed disable us – to suggest that this is all there is, is to deny the personal experience of physical and intellectual restrictions, of the fear of dying.'[9] At the international level, a model of disability has evolved which focuses both on the individualised impairment, as well as factors external to the disabled person – I will label this a social-contextual model of disability and I will expand on that model later in this chapter and in chapter 3 of this book.[10]

The second limb of the paradigm shift in disability rights lies in the re-conceptualisation of disability as a human rights concern. The human rights-based approach to disability will be discussed in detail below.[11] For present purposes, it is sufficient to note that under the rights-based approach disabled people are now viewed as subjects of the law, entitled to all of the rights and benefits conferred on their non-disabled counterparts by virtue of their inherent dignity. In essence, disabled people are now viewed as equal citizens, capable of contributing to society to the same extent as non-disabled people. Once again, this has served to turn the focus of attention to equality issues, with a view to increasing participation and inclusion in mainstream society. The various elements of this paradigm shift in the disability rights agenda can be seen through an examination of theoretical models of disability.

9 J. Morris, *Pride Against Prejudice: Transforming Attitudes to Disability: A Personal Politics of Disability* (Women's Press, London, 1991), at page 10.

10 See chapter 3.3 of this book.

11 See section 2.2.3 of this chapter.

2.2. A Consideration of Theoretical Models of Disability

Four distinct models of disability will be considered below, namely the minority rights approach, the universalist approach, the human rights-based approach and the capabilities approach. Many elements of those models relate to the broader category of the social model of disability. Each of the approaches below will be contrasted and will be correlated to the equality norm.

2.2.1. The Minority Rights Approach to Disability

The minority rights approach (or minority group analysis) involves the categorisation of classes of individuals into distinct groups in order to determine their entitlement to protection from discrimination and to positive measures to redress the effects of the disadvantage suffered by that class of individuals. The minority rights approach first took hold in the area of race discrimination and it mapped over neatly onto the disability context. Sandra Fredman states that the parallels between race and disability are clear. She states that, much like racial minorities, 'disabled people are also characterised as a discrete and insular minority, who have suffered from a history of discrimination and who are relatively powerless politically and are socially excluded.'[12]

The minority rights approach represents a move away from the medical model of disability to the extent that it places the emphasis on 'the political and social aspect of disability.'[13] However, the minority rights approach has a number of problems associated with it in the disability context. Fredman states that minority rights analysis is 'problematic both legally and socially,'[14] because an individual must prove that they fall into a particular minority category before they can claim protection of the law against discrimination. This can prove challenging for those who do not fall into the legal definition of a particular minority grouping, such definitions often being narrowly construed. Legally this approach is anchored in the identification of people as 'disabled,' which Fredman notes has proven 'notoriously difficult, both in the field of discrimination law and in that of social security.'[15] Fredman also contends that 'one of the biggest legislative stumbling blocks of the minority group analysis has been the definition of disability itself.'[16] A further limitation of minority group analysis stems from the fact that this approach places undue emphasis on difference and deviance from what is deemed 'normal,' rather than placing the emphasis on human diversity. This hinders the ability to overcome unequal power relations between persons with disabilities and their non-disabled counterparts.

---

12 S. Fredman, 'Disability Equality and the Existing Paradigm' in A. Lawson and C. Gooding (eds.) *Disability Rights in Europe: From Theory to Practice* (Hart Publishing, Oxford, 2005), at pages 204/205.

13 Ibid, at page 205.

14 Ibid, at page 206.

15 Ibid.

16 Ibid.

2.2.2. The Universalist Approach to Disability

The minority rights approach contrasts with the universalist approach to disability.[17] The universalist approach endorses the view that disability is not a fixed construction, inherent to one particular group, but is rather a fluid construction and a universal characteristic of the human condition. The universalist approach maintains that impairment can occur at any stage of the life course and it has the potential to affect all individuals equally. The universalist model goes beyond the traditional limitations of equality law as it factors in individual difference and contextual disadvantage. From an equality perspective, the response of the universalist approach to disability is to broaden the range of what might be deemed 'normal' to reflect human diversity and difference. As Bickenbach states, universalist disablement policy is 'not the policy for some minority group, it is policy for all.'[18] This widened norm must be reflected in societal structures and it is given concrete formulation in the mechanism of universal design, which encompasses the idea of maximum accessibility for all individuals.

In a nutshell, the universalist approach emphasises universal access to society for all individuals, regardless of personal characteristics. Laws, policies and social structures based on the universalist maxim should reflect this concept of maximum accessibility. The universalist approach is linked intrinsically with the promotion of full and effective participation and inclusion in society for disabled individuals. Kayess and French are of the view that 'the universalist approach has enormous transformative potential for all persons who experience disadvantage and discrimination.'[19] Nevertheless, they point to the fact that 'its Utopian aspirations may prove impossible to operationalise.'[20]

2.2.3. The Human Rights-Based Approach to Disability

The human rights-based approach is currently predominant in disability discourse. However, it is important to note that its application is not confined to the field of disability. Rather it has been described by the United Nation's Children's Fund (UNICEF) as 'a conceptual framework for the process of human development that is normatively based on international human rights standards and operationally directed to promoting and protecting human rights.'[21] As already noted above, disability was seen traditionally as a medical and social development issue, rather than falling within the confines of human rights law. The shift towards the rights-based approach was a slow and steady one at the international level. The human rights-based approach to disability focuses on the key themes of equal opportunities and non-discrimination

---

17 See generally, J.E. Bickenbach, 'Minority Rights or Universal Participation: The Politics of Disablement' in M. Jones and L.A. Basser (eds.) *Disability, Divers-Ability and Legal Change* (Martinus Nijhoff, The Hague 1999).

18 Ibid, at page 112.

19 R. Kayess and P. French, 'Out of Darkness Into Light? Introducing the Convention on the Rights of Persons with Disabilities' (2008) 8(1) *Human Rights Law Review* 1, at page 10, footnote 43.

20 Ibid.

21 See www.unicef.org/policyanalysis/rights/ last accessed 12 August 2014.

on the basis of disability. It places emphasis on the inherent dignity and autonomy of individuals with disabilities. Other core principles of a human rights-based approach are inclusion, participation, accessibility and respect for difference and diversity. All of these elements of the human rights-based approach can be found in Article 3 of the CRPD.[22] The CRPD Committee has confirmed in a 2014 decision[23] that a human rights-based model of disability requires States 'to take into account the diversity of persons with disabilities [...] as well as the interaction between individuals with impairments and attitudinal and environmental barriers [...].'[24]

It is often recognised that equality as a stand-alone norm is incapable of tackling substantive disadvantage.[25] Underpinning models of equality with human rights-based concepts suffuses them with valuable normative content and increases the scope for promoting and protecting the rights of marginalised groups within the equality framework. By employing the human rights-based conceptualisation of disability, persons with disabilities are empowered. This increased emphasis on participation and empowerment is pivotal in advancing the equality agenda for disabled people.

The human rights model is linked to the universalist approach (outlined above), in the sense that it does not view differential characteristics as being contrary to the so-called 'norm.' Rather, it perceives such characteristics as being a universal component of the human condition and it values diversity and human difference within its framework. Like the social model, the human rights-based approach to disability acknowledges the fact that responsibility lies on the State to redress the disadvantage that disabled people encounter. The human rights-based approach therefore builds on the social model and it advocates the notion that persons with disabilities are entitled to provision 'as a matter of rights to claim, rather than charity to receive.'[26]

---

22 See also Office of the High Commissioner for Human Rights, 'What is Disability?,' available at www.ohchr.org/Documents/.../Disability/.../Module1_WhatDisability.ppt last accessed 20 November 2014.

23 UN Committee on the Rights of Persons with Disabilities, Individual Communication, *S.C. v Brazil*, communication No. 10/2013, decision adopted at the Twelfth Session of the Committee (15 September – 3 October 2014), adopted on 2 October 2014, UN Doc. CRPD/C/12/D/10/2013. [That case concerned a woman who had been demoted after taking more than three months of medical leave in accordance with her employer's policy, following a series of injuries which led to chronic illness and the permanent impairment of her knee. While the Committee found the complaint inadmissible for non-exhaustion of domestic remedies, it nevertheless explored whether the complaint fell within the scope of the Convention. The Committee concluded that the difference between illness and disability is a difference of degree and not a difference of kind, and that a health impairment which is initially conceived of as illness can develop into an impairment in the context of disability because of its duration or its chronic development – para. 6.3].

24 UN Committee on the Rights of Persons with Disabilities, Individual Communication, *S.C. v Brazil*, Communication No. 10/2013, Decision adopted at the Twelfth Session of the Committee (15 September – 3 October 2014), adopted on 2 October 2014, UN Doc. CRPD/C/12/D/10/2013, para. 6.3.

25 See, for instance, the comments of P. Westen, 'The Empty Idea of Equality' (1982) 95(3) *Harvard Law Review* 537.

26 National Council on Disability, *Understanding the Role of an International Convention on the Human Rights of Persons with Disabilities* (White paper, 2002), page 30, available at www.ncd.gov/policy/CRPD last accessed 14 August 2014.

One of the inherent limitations outlined by detractors of the social model in its purest form stems from the fact that it is not well disposed to accommodate disadvantages that result directly from an impairment, as opposed to those which arise from socially constructed barriers.[27] The rights-based approach to disability counteracts this by recognising and accounting for differential characteristics within its framework. It acknowledges that persons with disabilities are entitled to be included fully in the mainstream, not merely accommodated to fit in with the 'norm.' In sum, the human rights-based approach takes account of the manner in which disabled people are different from their non-disabled counterparts, both in terms of their biological capacities and in terms of the socially constructed disadvantages which disabled people encounter relative to non-disabled people.

2.2.4. The Capabilities Approach

The capabilities approach was developed by economist-philosopher Amartya Sen[28] and it was refined significantly by philosopher Martha Nussbaum,[29] among others.[30] It was not developed to apply to the specific context of disability. Nonetheless, many of its inherent premises can be applied to disability.[31] The capabilities approach focuses on the idea of functionings on the one hand (in other words, the various states of human beings and activities that a person can undertake) and capabilities, on the other hand, (that is, the innate potential of each human being). It turns essentially on the idea of 'equality of capabilities' in a wide range of areas that are deemed to be of central importance to the quality of human life. Capabilities are defined as 'what

---

[27] For a critique of this aspect of the social model of disability, see D. Marks 'Dimensions of Oppression: Theorising the Embodied Subject,' (1999) 14(5) *Disability & Society* 661; See also, B. Hughes and K. Paterson, 'The Social Model of Disability and the Disappearing Body: Towards a Sociology of Impairment,' (1997) 12(3) *Disability & Society* 325; See also L. Crow, 'Renewing The Social Model Of Disability (Published in Coalition News; Greater Manchester Coalition of Disabled People, July 1992).

[28] The capabilities approach is deemed to have originated with Amartya Sen's development economics theories. Sen first introduced his theory of 'basic capabilities equality' in his Tanner Lectures on *Equality of What?* (A. Sen, *Equality of What?* Stanford University: Tanner Lectures on Human Value, Delivered at Stanford University, May 22, 1979, available from http://tannerlectures.utah.edu/_documents/a-to-z/s/sen80.pdf). Sen's Tanner lectures were focused on criticising utilitarian and Rawlsian perspectives on well-being and equality. Sen argued as follows: 'I believe what is at issue is the interpretation of needs in the form of basic capabilities. This interpretation of needs and interests is often implicit in the demand for equality. This type of equality I shall call "basic capability equality"' [at page 218]. During the 1980s and 1990s, Sen went on to elaborate in subsequent publications on his capabilities approach. See, for instance, A.K. Sen, 'Development as Capability Expansion' in K. Griffin and J. Knight (eds.), *Human Development and the International Development Strategy for the 1990s* (Macmillan, London, 1990). See also A.K. Sen, 'Development as Capability Expansion,' (1989) *Journal of Development Planning* 19, at page 41. In addition, see A.K. Sen (ed.), *Development as Freedom* (Oxford University Press, Oxford, 1999).

[29] See M.C. Nussbaum, 'Capabilities and Human Rights' (1997) 66(2) *Fordham Law Review*, at page 273; See also M.C. Nussbaum, *Creating Capabilities: The Human Development Approach* (Harvard University Press, Cambridge/London, 2011).

[30] See, for instance, the writings of D.A. Crocker and I. Robeyns, 'Capability and agency' in C. Morris (ed.), *The Philosophy of Amartya Sen* (Cambridge University Press, Cambridge, 2009), at pages 60–90.

[31] The capabilities approach has also been employed in the context of human development, for example, by the United Nations Development Programme, as a broader alternative to economic metrics such as growth in GDP per capita, which are deemed to be quite narrow in focus.

people are actually able to do and to be.'[32] The capabilities approach purports that freedom to achieve well-being is determined by peoples' capabilities and thus the kind of life that they are effectively able to lead.

Although Sen and Nussbaum's accounts of the capabilities approach are often elided, they have significant material differences. While Sen was concerned with producing a general framework for evaluating the quality of lives people can lead, Nussbaum's approach is more concerned with producing a partial normative theory of justice. While Sen's approach is founded on enhancing individual freedom, Nussbaum's theory is founded on respecting human dignity. Furthermore, Sen does not provide an explicit list of central capabilities and, in fact, he was critical of any attempt to provide such a list. Nussbaum, on the other hand, outlines a comprehensive list of 'central human capabilities.'[33]

As stated above, one of the driving forces of Nussbaum's capabilities approach is the recognition of the inherent diversity of human beings (much like the universalist model of disability, outlined above). While Nussbaum and Sen diverge at certain points in their approaches, Sen himself argued that 'diversity is no secondary complication to be ignored, or to be introduced later on; it is a fundamental aspect of our interest in equality.'[34] Woodward and Barbour note that the capabilities approach incorporates 'a notion of the basic heterogeneity of human beings, such that human diversity is essential to [this] approach to equality.[35] In that respect, the links with disability and with the CRPD can be seen clearly. The capabilities approach can be aligned in some respects with the human rights-based approach to disability. The capabilities approach asserts that State responsibility is triggered by an obligation to provide the necessary support in order to ensure that persons with disabilities can develop their capabilities to the same level as their non-disabled counterparts. Caroline Harnacke notes that 'according to the CRPD and the capabilities approach, a society is just if the state guarantees for all citizens the social basis of their

---

32 M.C. Nussbaum, *Women and Human Development* (Cambridge University Press, Cambridge, 2001), at page 5.

33 The list of 'central human capabilities outlined by Nussbaum are as follows: 1.) Life; 2.) Bodily health; 3.) Bodily integrity; 4.) Senses, imagination and thought; 5.) Emotions; 6.) Practical Reason (being able to form a conception of the good and to engage in critical reflection about the planning of one's life); 7.) Affiliation (being able to live with and toward others, to recognize and show concern for other human beings, to engage in various forms of social interaction, having the social bases of self-respect and non-humiliation; being able to be treated as a dignified being whose worth is equal to that of others.); 8.) Other Species (being able to live with concern for and in relation to animals, plants, and the world of nature); 9.) Play; and 10.) Control Over One's Environment (both political control – being able to participate effectively in political choices that govern one's life; having the right of political participation, protections of free speech and association – and material control – having property rights on an equal basis with others; having the right to seek employment on an equal basis with others). [M.C. Nussbaum, *Creating Capabilities: The Human Development Approach* (Harvard University Press, Cambridge/London, 2011), at pages 33–34]. Notably, Nussbaum remarks that this list could be contested and is just a suggestion on her part which is 'subject to ongoing revision and rethinking' – at page 108.

34 A. Sen, *Inequality Re-examined* (Oxford University Press, Oxford 1992).

35 W.R. Woodward and L. Barbour, 'Beyond Universalism: Capabilities Approach for Improving Women's Quality of Life' (2009) 3(2) *Journal of Human Ontogenetics* 75, at page 77.

capabilities, regardless of existing impairments.' She further observes that 'the focus of justice is not on the question of what resources the State has to spend on every person but on the question of what outcome is attained.'[36] Harnacke argues that while 'there is a general agreement on the essential underlying ideas of the capabilities approach and the CRPD,'[37] Nussbaum's capabilities approach 'is unable to guide the implementation process.' Harnacke states that 'this is due to an insufficient grounding of the capabilities which makes a hierarchy among the various capabilities impossible.'[38] Indeed, Nussbaum herself does not provide any guidance as to what should be done when a given State cannot ensure all capabilities immediately at the same time. Nussbaum acknowledges the problem but merely comments as follows:

> In desperate circumstances, it may not be possible for a nation to secure [all capabilities] up to the threshold level, but then it becomes a purely practical question what to do next, not a question of justice. The question of justice is already answered: justice has not been fully done here.[39]

This is a rather unsatisfactory answer. Another criticism of Nussbaum's capabilities approach advanced by certain scholars is that it excludes some individuals with disabilities from its framework and it conditions the inclusion of others.[40] As Chrissie Rogers points out, 'Nussbaum draws from the social contract tradition, which is challenging, largely because it cannot accommodate intellectual disability, due to the fact that agents are said to be independent, free and equal and assume to enter this "contract" for mutual advantage.'[41] On account of these perceived deficiencies in Nussbaum's analytical framework, Michael Stein claims that Nussbaum's approach 'falls short of a comprehensive framework'[42] for assessing disability rights. Notwithstanding this, he does recognise the potential applicability of the capabilities approach to the disability context and, furthermore, suggests that 'amending Nussbaum's capabilities approach to develop the talents of *all* individuals results in a disability human rights paradigm that recognizes the dignity and worth of every person.'[43]

---

36 C. Harnacke, 'Disability and Capability: Exploring the Usefulness of Martha Nussbaum's Capabilities Approach for the UN Disability Rights Convention' (2013) 41 *Journal of Law, Medicine & Ethics* 768, at page 777.

37 Ibid, at page 775.

38 Ibid, at page 777.

39 M.C. Nussbaum, *Frontiers of Justice* (Harvard University Press, Cambridge/London, 2006), at page 175.

40 M.A. Stein, 'Disability Human Rights' (2007) 95 *California Law Review* 75, at page 75.

41 C. Rogers, Inclusive education and intellectual disability: a sociological engagement with Martha Nussbaum, (2013) 17(9) *International Journal of Inclusive Education* 988, 992.

42 M.A. Stein, 'Disability Human Rights' (2007) 95 *California Law Review* 75, at page 75.

43 Ibid [emphasis added].

3. Theoretical Models of Equality and their Relationship to Disability Rights

Having explored the principal theoretical models of disability above, this section will comprise an analysis of various theoretical models of equality that have been delineated by legal scholars to date. The consideration of these conceptual models of equality will be interspersed with reflections on how each model relates to the disability rights agenda generally and to the various models of disability outlined above.

3.1. Introduction to Theoretical Models of Equality

The reason for exploring theoretical conceptions of equality stems primarily from the fact that each model of equality results in different outcomes and practices in the context of persons with disabilities when applied through the medium of legislation and policy. In other words, the trigger and methods for analysing instances of discrimination vary under different models of equality. It is therefore important to disentangle the specificities of each theoretical model, with a view to determining in the next chapter of this book where exactly Article 5 of the CRPD (which contains the Convention's non-discrimination norm) fits within those distinct approaches to equality.

Theoretical conceptions of equality can be described broadly as falling into three main categories, namely (i) Formal or juridical equality; (ii) Substantive equality and; (iii) Equality as transformation. I will consider each of those models in turn in the subsections which follow.

3.2. Formal Equality

The formal model of equality focuses exclusively on equal treatment in the application and enforcement of laws and rights. It requires that individuals are treated in the same manner, if they are situated in a similar situation, and that laws and policies are formulated in a neutral manner. Anna Lawson points to the fact that the formal model of equality 'would insist, for instance, that a university treat identically qualified applicants in the same way regardless of the fact that they might have different genders, racial background, or physical impairments.'[44]

The formal model of equality is encapsulated in the prohibition of direct discrimination[45] and also in the concept of 'equal protection of the law' in (for

44 A. Lawson (ed.), *Disability and Equality Law in Britain: The Role of Reasonable Adjustment* (Hart Publishing, Portland, 2008), at page 19.

45 See for instance, Section 1(1)(a) of the UK Race Relations Act 1976; See also Section 1(2)(a) of the UK Sex Discrimination Act 1975.

instance) the US Constitution[46] and therefore formal equality serves its distinct purposes in protecting human rights. Nonetheless, a formal equality framework has many limitations associated with it, particularly when applied to disability rights. A formal conception of equality results in the enactment of bald non-discrimination proscriptions that do not take account of individual or contextual differences between marginalised and socially privileged groups. Creating neutrality in the playing field is particularly problematic in the disability context as it hampers the equality reform agenda for disabled people, whose differences are varied and multifaceted and must be taken into account in order to engender true equality. Of course, sometimes disabled people will require merely the same measures and the same treatment as everyone else. Often times this will not be the case and, in such instances, application of the formal model alone does not redress inequalities as it contains no procedural mechanism for prohibiting indirect discrimination, accommodating the needs of persons with disabilities or permitting measures such as positive action. The latter measures seek to correct for factual inequalities and imbalances of power.[47]

In order to establish direct discrimination under the formal approach, one must invoke an appropriate comparator. This is problematic in the disability context as it is not always self-evident who the appropriate comparator might be.[48] A further weakness of the formal model of equality is that it requires conformity to an established standard based on the privileged norm. The normative standard under the formal equality model is generally a non-disabled person (although of course the comparator can sometimes be a person with a different disability, depending on the circumstances of the case). In the event that the comparator is a non-disabled person, the formal equality model serves merely to reinforce the dominant paradigm. By virtue of the fact that disabled people often have complex and varied needs and are not similarly situated to their non-disabled counterparts, application of formal equality often does not serve to redress the acute disadvantage already experienced by disabled people and, in fact, it perpetuates disadvantage. In addition, a formal model focuses exclusively on procedural equality, at the expense of the resultant outcome. Oddný Mjöll Arnardóttir states that the focus of the formal model 'is on equal treatment regardless of the possible unequal results that may flow from it.'[49] As a result, this model is normatively indeterminate, in that it demands consistency of treatment but makes no demands on the content of that treatment.[50]

46 Section 1, Fourteenth Amendment to the United States Constitution.

47 See section 4.5 of chapter 3 of this book.

48 This is identified as one of the weaknesses of the formal approach in the context of disability, pregnancy and part-time work by C.J.M. Kimber, 'Equality or Self-Determination' in C. Grearty and A. Tomkins (eds), *Understanding Human Rights* (Mansell Publishing, London, 1996), at pages 268–269.

49 O.M. Arnardóttir, 'A Future of Multidimensional Disadvantage Equality' in O.M. Arnardóttir and G. Quinn, *The UN Convention on the Rights of Persons with Disabilities: European and Scandinavian Perspectives* (Martinus Nijhoff, Leiden, 2009), at page 48.

50 Ibid, referring to C.J.M. Kimber, 'Equality or Self-Determination' in C. Grearty and A. Tomkins (eds), *Understanding Human Rights* (Mansell Publishing, London 1996), at pages 268–269.

3.2.1. *Formal Equality and the Medical Model of Disability*

The formal equality model dominated international human rights law in the period before the mid-1970s.[51] Human rights instruments that were adopted during that period contained open-ended non-discrimination provisions, whose aim was to prohibit distinctions made on the basis of personal attributes, rather than to tackle structural discrimination. The protections against discrimination that were enshrined in legislation during that same period were not free-standing. Instead, they were linked to the substantive provisions of the human rights instruments to which they related and, thus, could be said to be devoid of normative content in and of themselves. An example of the formal approach to equality can be seen in Article 2 of the Universal Declaration of Human Rights (UDHR),[52] which provides *inter alia* that:

> Everyone is entitled to all the rights and freedoms set forth in [the] Declaration, without distinction of any kind, such as race, colour, sex, language, religion, political or other opinion, national or social origin, property, birth or other status.[53]

The formal approach to equality is also evidenced in two further international human rights instruments adopted during the same period. Both Article 2[54] of the International Covenant on Civil and Political Rights (ICCPR)[55] and Article 2[56] of the International Covenant on Economic, Social and Cultural Rights (ICESCR)[57] comprise open-ended provisions whose 'emphasis is on prohibiting distinctions on the grounds of personal characteristics rather than on removing obstacles in society to allow for the full participation of persons with certain characteristics.'[58] Arnardóttir states that open-model non-discrimination clauses are 'generally blunt tools with which to combat discrimination.' She further argues that 'they do not

[51] O.M. Arnardóttir, 'A Future of Multidimensional Disadvantage Equality' in O.M. Arnardóttir and G. Quinn, *The UN Convention on the Rights of Persons with Disabilities: European and Scandinavian Perspectives* (Martinus Nijhoff, Leiden, 2009), at page 47.

[52] UN General Assembly, *Universal Declaration of Human Rights*, 10 December 1948, Paris, General Assembly Resolution, 217 A (III).

[53] Universal Declaration of Human Rights, Article 2.

[54] Article 2 ICCPR provides that: 'Each State Party to the present Covenant undertakes to respect and to ensure to all individuals within its territory and subject to its jurisdiction the rights recognized in the present Covenant, without distinction of any kind, such as race, colour, sex, language, religion, political or other opinion, national or social origin, property, birth or other status.'

[55] UN General Assembly, International Covenant on Civil and Political Rights, adopted by the United Nations General Assembly Resolution 2200A (XXI) of 16 December 1966.

[56] Article 2 ICESCR provides that: 'Each State Party to the present Covenant undertakes to take steps, individually and through international assistance and co-operation, especially economic and technical, to the maximum of its available resources, with a view to achieving progressively the full realization of the rights recognized in the present Covenant by all appropriate means, including particularly the adoption of legislative measures.'

[57] UN General Assembly, International Covenant on Economic, Social and Cultural Rights, adopted by the United Nations General Assembly Resolution 2200A (XXI) of 16 December 1966.

[58] M.V. Liisberg, *Disability and Employment: A Contemporary Disability Human Rights Approach Applied to Danish, Swedish and EU Law and Policy* (Intersentia Publishers, The Netherlands, 2011), at page 26.

automatically recognise the profound differences that exist in reality between the context and situation of socially privileged groups on one hand and marginalised groups on the other.'[59]

The formal model of equality is reflected in international instruments dating from the era when the medical model was the prevailing theoretical model of disability. Gerard Quinn pinpoints the fundamental shortcoming of the formal model as being its failure 'to recognise that the problem resides in the structures (built to reflect and accommodate privileged norms) and not in the person who is judged different.'[60] The formal approach to equality is assimilationist in nature. Its focus on identical treatment leads to the disregard of differential characteristics and, in many cases, will not result in true equality. As the formal model ignores inhibitory societal barriers, there is no requirement on States to make accommodations or to meet the support needs of persons with disabilities. In view of the fact that the formal approach 'does not challenge traditional constructions of equality/sameness and difference/otherness,'[61] Arnardóttir contends that the corresponding era in international human rights law can be termed 'universal sameness.'[62] In other words, the universal equality norm during that era was applied to all, with no regard for accommodation of differences. Accordingly, persons with disabilities were hindered from participating fully and effectively in society and were segregated from the mainstream.[63]

3.2.2. The Shift Away from Formal Equality Towards Substantive Equality

While the formal model of equality has its obvious benefits – most notably the fact that it targets direct discrimination – its limitations are evident in the disability context. Applying a formal approach often results in the perpetuation of inequality rather than in the promotion of equality. There was therefore a concerted shift in emphasis away from formal equality in the context of persons with disabilities. At the level of international human rights law, there was also a concerted move away from the shortcomings of the formal model of equality towards models of substantive and transformative equality. In the subsections which follow, I will analyse both of those

59 O.M. Arnardóttir, 'A Future of Multidimensional Disadvantage Equality' in O.M. Arnardóttir and G. Quinn, *The UN Convention on the Rights of Persons with Disabilities: European and Scandinavian Perspectives* (Martinus Nijhoff, Leiden, 2009), at page 49.

60 G. Quinn, 'The International Covenant on Civil and Political Rights and Disability: A Conceptual Framework' in T. Degener and Y Koster-Dreese (eds.), Human *Rights and Disabled Persons: Essays and Relevant Human Rights Instruments* (Martinus Nijhoff, London, 1995), at page 75/76.

61 O.M. Arnardóttir, 'A Future of Multidimensional Disadvantage Equality' in O.M. Arnardóttir and G. Quinn, *The UN Convention on the Rights of Persons with Disabilities: European and Scandinavian Perspectives* (Martinus Nijhoff, Leiden, 2009), at pages 47/48.

62 Ibid, at page 47.

63 Liisberg outlines the link between formal equality and the medical model of disability as follows: 'Common to the model of formal equality and the medical model of disability is the belief that [...] social structures are a constant and should not be changed. A difference in opportunities for participation in society which is associated with certain personal characteristics must therefore be overcome by disassociating the individual with the personal characteristic or by accepting that there is a difference in opportunities.' [M.V. Liisberg, *Disability and Employment: A Contemporary Disability Human Rights Approach Applied to Danish, Swedish and EU Law and Policy* (Intersentia Publishers, The Netherlands, 2011), at page 24].

models of equality from a disability perspective, before proceeding to delineate the specific theoretical developments regarding the equality norm at the international level.

3.3. Substantive Equality[64]

By way of contrast to the formal model of equality, the substantive or material model of equality does not focus on the same treatment. According to Catharine MacKinnon, a substantive equality approach 'changes not only the outcomes of discrimination cases but, as importantly if not more so, alters the circumstances that are identified as giving rise to equality questions in the first place.'[65] She argues that the core insight of a substantive equality model 'is always a social relation of rank ordering, typically on a group or categorical basis [...] that precedes the legal one.'[66] The UN Committee on Economic Social and Cultural Rights (UNCESCR) highlights the fact that substantive equality is concerned 'with the effects of laws, policies and practices and with ensuring that they do not maintain, but rather alleviate, the inherent disadvantage that particular groups experience.'[67] In other words, it looks to the systematically discriminatory effects of a facially neutral rule. By emphasising the effects of a particular rule, substantive equality includes within its remit instances of indirect discrimination,[68] something that is vital in uncovering covert forms of discrimination against people with disabilities. Substantive equality also requires that States take concrete measures to remove barriers to participation. In order to facilitate this, reasonable accommodations must be put in place.[69] The duty to accommodate signifies alterations to existing facilities, practices and customs, which hinder the participation and inclusion of a disabled individual in mainstream society. While the duty to accommodate cannot result in fundamental structural changes in society, it is nonetheless a key facilitator of substantive equality,[70] as it recognises differential characteristics and caters for the individualised needs of persons with disabilities in specific circumstances. Positive action or affirmative

64 My conceptualisation of substantive equality is based on the authors cited throughout this subsection. My conceptualisation of substantive difference and substantive disadvantage equality (in later subsections of this chapter) is based on the work of Oddný Mjöll Arnardóttir.

65 C.A. Mac Kinnon, 'Substantive Equality: A Perspective' 96 *Minnesota Law Review* 1, 11.

66 Ibid.

67 UNCESCR, General Comment 16 (2005) on the equal right of men and women to the enjoyment of all economic, social and cultural rights (Article 3 of the ICESCR), adopted at the thirty-fourth session of the Committee, Geneva, 25 April-13 May 2005, UN Doc. E/C.12/2005/4 para. 7.

68 See the comments of M.V. Liisberg, *Disability and Employment: A Contemporary Disability Human Rights Approach Applied to Danish, Swedish and EU Law and Policy* (Intersentia Publishers, The Netherlands, 2011), at pages 28/29.

69 J.E. Lord and R. Brown, 'The Role of Reasonable Accommodation in Securing Substantive Equality for Persons with Disabilities: The UN Convention on the Rights of Persons with Disabilities' in M.H. Rioux, L.A. Basser and M. Jones (eds), *Critical Perspectives on Human Rights and Disability Policy* (Martinus Nijhoff, The Hague, 2011), at page 277.

70 Ibid.

action measures are also included within the ambit of substantive equality.[71] This includes, for instance, measures such as quotas which seek to raise the status of a disadvantaged group.

In stark contrast to a formal equality approach (which insists on like treatment regardless of unequal results) substantive equality is concerned with the results that flow from the measures that are taken within its framework and the processes undertaken to achieve equality. Janet Lord and Rebecca Brown contend that the substantive equality framework '[...] compels an inquiry as to whether those efforts taken have adequately involved affected groups and facilitated the actual realization of human rights through the positive measures taken.'[72] Substantive equality addresses many of the shortcomings of formal equality models in the disability context. However, by focusing on the effects of a particular rule, a substantive model of equality often leaves underlying structural causes of discrimination and marginalisation untouched.[73] In addition, while the requirements of reasonable accommodations and positive action go a large way towards ensuring true equality, such measures do not result in fundamental transformation to the established norm. As a result, an even more advanced model of equality emerged in legal discourse, namely transformative equality (equality as transformation). It is to the latter theoretical model that I now turn.

3.4. Transformative Equality (Equality as Transformation)

Transformative equality builds on the elements of a pure substantive model of equality and it can be viewed broadly as an extension of substantive equality. However, it goes further than substantive equality to address the underlying causes of structural inequalities and disadvantage. According to Andrew Byrnes, transformative equality can be seen 'as a form of substantive equality with systemic and structural dimensions.'[74] A transformatory approach to equality seeks to address the socially constructed barriers, stereotypes, negative customs and practices which hinder the full enjoyment of rights by marginalised groups. According to Sandra Fredman, equality as transformation 'requires not only the removal of barriers but also positive measures to bring about change.'[75] Therefore, a model which seeks

---

71 Ibid; See also the comments of M.V. Liisberg, *Disability and Employment: A Contemporary Disability Human Rights Approach Applied to Danish, Swedish and EU Law and Policy* (Intersentia Publishers, The Netherlands, 2011), at pages 28/29.

72 J.E. Lord and R. Brown, 'The Role of Reasonable Accommodation in Securing Substantive Equality for Persons with Disabilities: The UN Convention on the Rights of Persons with Disabilities' in M.H. Rioux, L.A. Basser and M. Jones (eds), *Critical Perspectives on Human Rights and Disability Policy* (Martinus Nijhoff, The Hague, 2011), at page 277.

73 See the comments of A. Timmer, 'Toward an Anti-Stereotyping Approach for the European Court of Human Rights' (2011) 11(4) *Human Rights Law Review* 707, at page 712.

74 A. Byrnes, 'Article 1,' in M.A. Freeman, C. Chinkin, B. Rudolf (eds.), *The UN Convention on the Elimination of All Forms of Discrimination Against Women* (Oxford University Press, New York, 2012), at page 56.

75 S. Fredman, 'Beyond the Dichotomy of Formal and Substantive Equality: Towards a New Definition of Equal Rights' in I. Boerefijn et. al (eds.), *Temporary Special Measures: Accelerating De Facto Equality*

to ensure equality as transformation would require a redistribution of power and resources to nurture the innate capabilities of persons with disabilities and it would also involve the participation of persons with disabilities in every aspect of the reform agenda.[76] Within the framework of transformative equality, positive obligations such as accessibility measures and Universal Design measures assume a central role. Those operational mechanisms seek to alter general structures that maintain or perpetuate disadvantage. In addition, awareness-raising duties fall on States under a transformative equality model. Ensuring that awareness-raising is carried out at all levels of society serves to foster respect for the capabilities of disabled people and their potential contribution to societal processes and it also serves to combat discriminatory stereotypes and deep-rooted attitudinal barriers to participation and inclusion in mainstream society.

Equality as transformation has been described as 'an ambitious project'[77] that challenges the deeply ingrained roles and ideologies on which society is based.[78] The overall aim of a transformative equality framework is to disrupt the hierarchical legal and social status quo.[79] In other words, States must reconsider the various aspects of their social, legal and political systems which impede the full and effective realisation of the equality norm and the recognition of the inherent dignity of individuals. The transformative model of equality can be aligned with the redistributive model of social justice, in so far as it seeks to achieve a more equitable distribution of benefits for all. This involves a reallocation of resources to ensure that all individuals are in a position to access and exercise their rights on an equal basis with others.

It is important to note that some authors[80] and even some human rights treaty bodies[81] have interpreted the substantive equality framework very broadly by

---

of Women under Article 4(1) UN Convention on the Elimination of All Forms of Discrimination against Women (Intersentia, Antwerp, 2003), at page 115.

76 In the context of CEDAW, Fredman notes that 'transformation requires a redistribution of power and resources and a change in the institutional structures which perpetuate women's oppression.' She further contends that equality as transformation 'aims to facilitate the full expression of women's capabilities and choices and the full participation of women in society.' [S. Fredman, 'Beyond the Dichotomy of Formal and Substantive Equality: Towards a New Definition of Equal Rights' in I. Boerefijn et al (eds.), *Temporary Special Measures: Accelerating De Facto Equality of Women under Article 4(1) UN Convention on the Elimination of All Forms of Discrimination against Women* (Intersentia, Antwerp, 2003) 115].

77 A. Timmer, 'Toward an Anti-Stereotyping Approach for the European Court of Human Rights' (2011) 11(4) *Human Rights Law Review* 707, at page 712.

78 Ibid.

79 Ibid, citing E. Bonthuys, 'Institutional Openness and Resistance to Feminist Arguments: The Example of the South African Constitutional Court' (2008) 20 *Canadian Journal of Woman and the Law*, at page 35.

80 See, for example, C. Albertyn and B. Goldblatt, 'Facing the Challenge of Transformation: Difficulties in the Development of an Indigenous Jurisprudence of Equality' (1998) 14 *South African Journal on Human Rights* 248, at page 250. In that article, the authors maintain that 'a commitment to substantive equality involves examining the context of an alleged rights violation and its relationship to systemic forms of domination within a society. It addresses structural and entrenched disadvantage at the same time as it aspires to maximise human development.'

81 The principle of equality embraced by the CEDAW Committee requires States Parties to address the underlying causes and structures of gender inequality ('equality as transformation' or 'transformative

viewing transformative equality as being akin to substantive equality. While there are many overlaps between substantive and transformative equality, conflating the two forms of equality can lead to conceptual confusion. In the context of the CRPD, it is particularly important to distinguish between substantive and transformative equality, as I will demonstrate in the next chapter of this book.

3.5. The Objectives of Substantive and Transformative Equality Models

Both substantive and transformative equality begin from the same starting point (namely that like treatment is often insufficient to ensure true equality). However, they differ in certain key respects (as outlined above). Substantive equality is deemed to have as its twin goals the achievement of equality of opportunity and equality of results. A transformative approach to equality also shares these objectives. Below the concepts of equality of opportunity and equality of results will be reflected upon from a disability perspective.

3.5.1. Equality of Opportunity

Equality of opportunities (traditionally understood) is often taken to mean that people are given merely the same starting point.[82] This understanding of equality of opportunity is not sufficient to guarantee disability rights. As former US President Lyndon Johnson once commented:

> You do not take a person who for years has been hobbled by chains and liberate him, bring him up to the starting line of a race and then say, 'You are free to compete with all others,' and still believe [that you are being fair]. It is not enough just to open the gates of opportunity. All of our citizens must have the ability to walk through those gates.'[83]

In the disability context, equality of opportunity refers to an absence of arbitrary or discriminatory obstacles in society, based on the involuntary personal attribute of impairment. This involuntary aspect of disability is relevant to the extent that it stakes a claim for disabled people to positive measures and increased societal resources. In other words, the responsibility for ensuring equality in the disability context should be a societal responsibility. Under an equal opportunities model every disabled person ought to have the same right of access as their non-disabled counterparts to civil and political and economic, social and cultural rights and, furthermore, they

---

equality'). The Committee has tended to view transformative equality as part of substantive equality rather than as a distinct model of equality [In that regard, see, for instance, paras. 8–10 of CEDAW Committee, General recommendation No. 25, on article 4, paragraph 1, of the Convention on the Elimination of All Forms of Discrimination against Women, on temporary special measures, U.N. Doc. HRI/GEN/1/Rev.7 (2004)].

82 See, for instance, the analysis of equality of opportunity by D. Moeckli, 'Equality and Non-Discrimination' in D. Moeckli, S. Shah, S. Sivakumaran and D. Harris (eds.), International Human Rights Law (Oxford University Press, Oxford, 2014), at page 159.

83 Former United States President Lyndon B. Johnson, Address at Howard University (4 June 1965), cited in S. Fredman, *Discrimination Law* (Oxford University Press, Oxford, 2nd Edition, 2011), at page 16.

should have equal opportunity to exercise those rights. In order to ensure genuine equality of opportunity for persons with disabilities, States are required to eliminate discrimination by taking positive measures to remove barriers, both legal and institutional, in order to pave the way towards increased participation and inclusion in society. To facilitate this, reasonable accommodations must be put in place. This reflects substantive equality of opportunity. Transformative equality of opportunity goes even further to endorse such measures as accessibility measures. In the disability context, an equal opportunities framework involves a redistributive element. Indeed, the *United Nations Standard Rules on the Equalization of Opportunities for Persons with Disabilities*[84] confirms this point. The Standard Rules constitute the most important non-binding instrument adopted by the UN prior to the CRPD in seeking to ensure equal access and participation and inclusion of disabled persons in society. The Standard Rules will be discussed in detail in section four of this chapter but, for present purposes, it is sufficient to note that the Rules recommend that States ensure that all resources are employed 'in such a way as to ensure that every individual has equal opportunity for participation.'[85] Both forms of equality of opportunity (substantive equality of opportunity and transformative equality of opportunity) can be seen in the Standard Rules. Rule 5 of the Standard Rules provides that States 'should recognize the overall importance of accessibility in the process of the equalization of opportunities in all spheres of society. For persons with disabilities of any kind, States should (a) introduce programmes of action to make the physical environment accessible; and (b) undertake measures to provide access to information and communication.'[86] Furthermore, Rule 7 of the Standard Rules acknowledges the importance of reasonable accommodations for the equalisation of opportunities for persons with disabilities.[87]

Under the equal opportunities framework every disabled person should be enabled to develop his/her full potential. Gerard Quinn and Theresia Degener assert that:

> One of the main unarticulated premises of the philosophy of 'equality of opportunity,' in general and in the context of disability, is that every human being has something to contribute to humanity and that social structures should be built inclusively with human empowerment as a key goal.[88]

Everyone should have an equal chance of succeeding under an equal opportunities model. Of course, this will not guarantee equality of results, as that will depend

84 UN Standard Rules on the Equalization of Opportunities for Persons with Disabilities (adopted by the United Nations General Assembly, forty-eighth session, resolution 48/96, annex, of 20 December 1993), available at www.un.org/disabilities/default.asp?id=26 last accessed 3 September 2014.

85 Ibid, para. 25.

86 Ibid, Rule 5.

87 Rule 7 of the *UN Standard Rules on the Equalization of Opportunities for Persons with Disabilities* provides that: 'States should also encourage employers to make reasonable adjustments to accommodate persons with disabilities.'

88 G. Quinn and T. Degener (eds.), *Human Rights and Disability: The Current Use and Future Potential of United Nations Human Rights Instruments in the Context of Disability* (Office of the High Commissioner for Human Rights, United Nations, Geneva 2002), at page 8.

on the number of people who take advantage of the opportunities and those who succeed in a given area. It is to this latter conceptualisation of equality that I will now turn – the notion of equality of results (outcome).

3.5.2. Equality of Results (Outcome)

Equality of results requires that disabled people should be equal in fact – the notion of *de facto* equality (equality in practice). Individual merit does not always[89] play a role in achieving equality of results. Under the equal results model, disabled people are placed in the same position as their non-disabled counterparts, regardless of their ability or input. Theresia Degener and Gerard Quinn assert that equality of results 'is usually taken to mean that each person – by virtue of his/her inherent equal worth and dignity – is entitled to certain minimum rights (particularly economic and social rights) regardless of his/her contribution or capacity to contribute.'[90] This can be contrasted with the equal opportunities framework, in which individual merit plays an integral role – it maintains that persons with disabilities should be provided with the support necessary to enable them to succeed (or indeed to fail), on their own merits. In other words, States should provide the requisite support to ensure that the inherent capabilities or capacities of persons with disabilities are allowed to flourish and that disabled people are in a position to access and exercise opportunities, on an equal basis with others in society. Equality of opportunities may therefore be linked to Sen and Nussbaum's capabilities approach, outlined above.[91] That approach involves enabling people to gain the skills that they need in order to participate in society and in decision-making and to engage in productive activities.

Equality of results requires States to ensure preferential treatment of under-represented groups in society and it manifests itself primarily in the operational mechanism of positive (affirmative) action. Policies such as quotas (specifying the percentage of disabled people who must occupy a position in proportion to non-disabled people) are a good example of measures targeted at achieving equal results. A criticism that is often levelled at proponents of the equal results model is the fact that the model does not take account of the importance of accommodating individual difference or diversity through adaptation of existing social structures. Sandra Fredman contends that the focus on results 'might be misleading.'[92] She states that 'monitoring results does not necessitate any fundamental re-examination of the structures that perpetuate discrimination.'[93] The equal opportunities framework is therefore often the preferred

[89] In some instances, of course, individual merit may play a role e.g. if there is a certain percentage of quota jobs available for persons with disabilities, the most qualified individuals might get them and similarly in the context of educational opportunities.

[90] G. Quinn and T. Degener, *Human Rights and Disability: The Current Use and Future Potential of United Nations Human Rights Instruments in the Context of Disability* (Office of the High Commissioner for Human Rights, United Nations, Geneva 2002), at page 18.

[91] See section 2.2.4 of this chapter.

[92] S. Fredman, *Discrimination Law* (Oxford University Press, Oxford, 2nd Edition, 2011), at page 16.

[93] Ibid.

approach to advancing the equality agenda for disabled people.[94] The reason for this is that the equal opportunities model seeks to tackle discriminatory barriers faced by persons with disabilities so that they can maximise their innate abilities. This contrasts with the equal results model, which instead targets unequal power relations between persons with disabilities and their non-disabled counterparts, without necessarily providing disabled people with the opportunity to use their own potential to attain equality. Notwithstanding this, elements of the equal results model are of particular relevance to the disability reform agenda, particularly in targeting the historical disadvantage experienced by disabled people. For instance, ensuring that persons with disabilities do not experience discrimination in the workplace (under an equal opportunities approach) may not guarantee that disabled people can actually enjoy employment opportunities if they do not possess the skills necessary to compete against other job applicants due to traditional inequalities in education. In order to ensure *de facto* equality in such instances, States may be required to put in place training opportunities for persons with disabilities to redress historical inequalities in education.

3.6. The Development of the Equality Norm in International Human Rights Law: Substantive Difference *versus* Substantive Disadvantage Equality

Leading scholars[95] have traced the development of the equality norm at the level of international human rights law and have elaborated on two further subsets of equality which neatly demonstrate the shift away from the formal model of equality. The first approach has been characterised as the 'substantive difference'[96] or 'specific difference'[97] equality model. That approach to equality can be contrasted with the 'substantive disadvantage'[98] or 'substantive diversity'[99] equality model. Substantive difference and substantive disadvantage equality convey varying theoretical perspectives on the trigger points for analysing instances of discrimination. From a legal perspective, the defining feature of the two models lies in the manner in which a court would examine the particular situation of an applicant, either from the viewpoint of individual differential characteristics (under the substantive difference approach) or from the angle of systemic disadvantage in society (under the substantive disadvantage approach). The substantive difference model represents the beginnings

---

94 While a properly executed equal opportunities model is arguably the most appropriate model in terms of ensuring the substantive equality of persons with disabilities, the equal results model also has a role to play in increasing the participation of disabled people in society through the imposition of quotas and similar measures.

95 See, in particular, O.M. Arnardóttir, 'A Future of Multidimensional Disadvantage Equality' in O.M. Arnardóttir and G. Quinn (eds), *The UN Convention on the Rights of Persons with Disabilities: European and Scandinavian Perspectives* (Martinus Nijhoff, Leiden, 2009), at pages 54–64.

96 O.M. Arnardóttir, 'A Future of Multidimensional Disadvantage Equality' in O.M. Arnardóttir and G. Quinn (eds), *The UN Convention on the Rights of Persons with Disabilities: European and Scandinavian Perspectives* (Martinus Nijhoff, Leiden, 2009), at page 50.

97 Ibid, at page 51.

98 Ibid, at page 50.

99 M.V. Liisberg, *Disability and Employment: A Contemporary Disability Human Rights Approach Applied to Danish, Swedish and EU Law and Policy* (Intersentia, The Netherlands, 2011), at page 47.

of the move away from formal equality towards a more substantive equality framework. Substantive disadvantage equality, on the other hand, falls squarely within the overall models of substantive and transformative equality. Drawing primarily on Oddný Mjöll Arnardóttir's[100] elaboration of substantive difference and substantive disadvantage equality in the disability context, the differences between these two conceptualisations of equality will be explained in the subsections which follow. Firstly, however, it is important to outline the reason for including these final two approaches to equality in this chapter. The principal reason for referring to substantive difference and substantive disadvantage equality is that those models illustrate neatly the development of the equality norm at the level of international human rights law and, furthermore (as pointed out by Arnardóttir), they illustrate the manner in which the equality norm in the CRPD has evolved as a logical progression from previous developments at the international level.[101] This will provide a tidy framework for analysing (in the next chapter of this book) the equality and non-discrimination norms in the CRPD. With that in mind, I will now proceed to analyse the substantive difference and the substantive disadvantage approaches to equality.

3.6.1. Substantive/Specific Difference Equality

The substantive difference approach to equality first made its appearance in international human rights law after the regression of the dominance of the formal equality model in the late 1960s to mid 1970s during the 'specific difference era'[102] of equality. Substantive difference equality moves beyond the limitations of the principle of direct discrimination and it permits the taking of positive measures in order to advance equality. Arnardóttir contends that under the substantive difference model:

> The focus moved from the universal open-model non-discrimination clauses to more concrete and thorough treatment of specific discrimination grounds which were understood as natural and immutable and, thus, generally defined by biological indicators. Hence this era can be characterised by reference to the key terms of specificity and difference.[103]

By contrast with formal equality, the substantive difference model calls for asymmetrical treatment *in certain circumstances*. It acknowledges that some differences, characterised generally by biological factors, must be taken into account in the quest for equality.[104] Notably, however, the substantive difference model of equality does not view special treatment (in other words, the adoption of preferential

[100] See O.M. Arnardóttir, 'A Future of Multidimensional Disadvantage Equality' in O.M. Arnardóttir and G. Quinn (eds), *The UN Convention on the Rights of Persons with Disabilities: European and Scandinavian Perspectives* (Martinus Nijhoff, Leiden, 2009), at pages 49–64.

[101] Arnardóttir argues that 'the CRPD and its approach to equality is the logical result of previous developments in international law and that it represents a substantive and multidimensional disadvantage approach to equality, which is informed by an understanding of disability as a social construct.' [Ibid, at page 42].

[102] Ibid, from page 49–54.

[103] Ibid, at pages 49/50.

[104] Ibid.

or positive measures for disadvantaged or marginalised groups) as desirable but rather as an exception to the mandate of equal treatment. Positive measures and accommodation for differences were only allowed in exceptional circumstances during the specific difference era of equality.[105]

Arnardóttir maintains[106] that the substantive difference model is reflected in the non-discrimination provisions of the Convention on the Elimination of Racial Discrimination[107] (CERD) and the Convention on the Elimination of All Forms of Discrimination Against Women (CEDAW).[108] Both of those treaties view discrimination based on specific identity markers or 'biological'[109] and 'immutable'[110] characteristics – race and sex respectively – as worthy of special attention. The non-discrimination provisions in CERD and CEDAW can be contrasted with the open-ended provisions in the ICCPR and the ICESCR, to the extent that the former treaties incorporate the notion of indirect discrimination[111] in their non-discrimination clauses and also due to the fact that CERD and CEDAW permit the taking of special measures or positive action.[112] However, as Arnardóttir notes, the primary focus under the specific difference era remained 'on negative state obligations and the equal treatment principle.'[113]

The substantive difference model of equality is linked with the minority group approach, in the sense that it emphasises deviance from the 'norm.' Arnardóttir acknowledges the fact that 'the law during [that] era located the "problem" that non-discrimination provisions were supposed to address with the marginalised individual

105 Arnardóttir claims that because the focus of this era was on 'biological or immutable differences,' therefore accommodation for differences were 'generally seen as an exception to the rule of formal equal treatment.' [Ibid, at page 50, referring to Kimber C.J.M., 'Equality or Self-Determination' in Grearty C. and Tomkins A. (eds.), *Understanding Human Rights* (Mansell Publishing, London, 1996), at pages 270–271]. Furthermore, Arnardóttir posits that 'the legitimacy of affirmative action [...] remained highly controversial during this era and all departures from formal and symmetrical equality were conceptualised as exceptions.' [Ibid, at page 53, referring to T. Meron, *Human Rights Law-Making in the United Nations* (Clarendon Press, Oxford, 1986) at page 36].

106 Ibid, at pages 51/52.

107 *International Convention on the Elimination of All Forms of Racial Discrimination* (Adopted and opened for signature and ratification by General Assembly resolution 2106 (XX) of 21 December 1965), entry into force 4 January 1969. Although CERD was adopted in 1965, the specific difference approach was more characteristic of international human rights instruments adopted in the mid-1970s to the 1990s.

108 *International Convention on the Elimination of All Forms of Discrimination against Women* (adopted and opened for signature, ratification and accession by General Assembly resolution 34/180 of 18 December 1979 entry into force 3 September 1981).

109 O.M. Arnardóttir, 'A Future of Multidimensional Disadvantage Equality' in O.M. Arnardóttir and G. Quinn (eds), *The UN Convention on the Rights of Persons with Disabilities: European and Scandinavian Perspectives* (Martinus Nijhoff, Leiden, 2009), at page 50.

110 Ibid.

111 The notion of indirect discrimination is included in the definition of discrimination in Article 1 CERD and Article 1 CEDAW, both of which refer to the 'effect' of discrimination, which is taken to mean indirect discrimination.

112 See Articles 1(4) and 2(2) CERD and Article 4 CEDAW.

113 O.M. Arnardóttir, 'A Future of Multidimensional Disadvantage Equality' in O.M. Arnardóttir and G. Quinn (eds), *The UN Convention on the Rights of Persons with Disabilities: European and Scandinavian Perspectives* (Martinus Nijhoff, Leiden, 2009), at page 53.

herself and her specific natural or biological difference, and not with structural societal factors.'[114] A further related limitation of the substantive difference approach is that, in a similar vein to the formal approach to equality, the emphasis is placed on difference from a comparator. Accordingly, privileged groups in society once again act as the established and unquestioned standard of measure. Arnardóttir points to the fact that international non-discrimination legislation dating from the era when the substantive difference approach was prevalent:

> Could only address the needs of the sub-groups within socially marginalised groups who were most like the prevailing standard. The difference of disability, however, was perceived as so profoundly incomparable to the prevailing standard, that under international law it remained largely unnoticed as an equality issue.[115]

Emphasis was therefore placed on the so-called 'deviant' characteristics of disabled people. Under the substantive difference approach, the dominant 'norm' remained unchanged and existing structures in mainstream society remained unaltered, with the resultant consequence that disabled people were still hindered by structural barriers. This inhibited the full and effective participation and inclusion of persons with disabilities in society on an equal basis with others. The emergence of the substantive difference approach represented a significant development in international human rights law towards a more substantive conceptualisation of equality. Arnardóttir observes that 'ideas about the "inherent emptiness" of the principle of equality and the non-discrimination principle started receding'[116] during the specific difference era. Nonetheless, the cursor of international human rights law had not yet moved to the core of a more substantive and transformative conception of equality. Hence the need for a substantive disadvantage model of equality, which would seek to address deep-seated structural inequalities in society.

3.6.2. Substantive Disadvantage (Diversity) Equality

The substantive disadvantage or substantive diversity approach is predominant in current equality and disability discourse. Arnardóttir describes this model as a 'contextual approach that focuses on the asymmetrical structures of power, privilege and disadvantage that are at work in society.'[117] She notes the fact that the substantive difference approach 'has been elaborated as a response to the weaknesses of the other approaches that frame equality in terms of the comparative concepts of sameness or difference.'[118] Maria Ventegodt Liisberg asserts that under this model 'measures to even out disadvantage between different groups are not seen as an exception to the rule of identical treatment. This model of equality is forward-looking and aims at changing general structures in society so that they reflect the equal rights of different

114 Ibid, at page 54.
115 Ibid.
116 Ibid, at page 51.
117 Ibid, at page 54.
118 Ibid.

groups in society.'[119] The substantive disadvantage model enables the *status quo* of existing societal structures to be questioned and addressed within the framework of equality.

The substantive disadvantage model can be aligned with the universalist model of disability, to the extent that both models emphasise social diversity. By virtue of the fact that the substantive disadvantage model focuses on socially constructed barriers, it is also intertwined with the social model of disability. In addition to the proactive role of States, Sandra Fredman argues that the substantive disadvantage model of equality implies a participatory role for civil society, both in the realm of standard-setting and also with regard to status quo enforcement issues.[120] Fredman states that 'the participation of affected groups increases the likelihood that strategies will succeed as well as democratising the very process of achieving equality.'[121] In the disability context, the substantive disadvantage model focuses on the equal citizenship rights of persons with disabilities as a means to ensuring true equality and inclusion. Included within the ambit of its operational mechanisms are the concepts of indirect discrimination, reasonable accommodation, general positive obligations of States, as well as positive action measures such as quotas. These tools seek to eradicate structures in society that maintain or perpetuate disadvantage. Many of the features of substantive disadvantage equality can be viewed as falling within a substantive equality framework. However, it is argued here that substantive disadvantage equality also takes a step into the realm of transformative equality by seeking to target structural inequalities. The essential point of divergence between the substantive difference approach and the substantive disadvantage approach does not lie in the particular operational mechanisms which come within the ambit of the two approaches. Rather, it lies in the specific trigger for non-discrimination analysis or, as Arnardóttir observes, it lies in 'how the situations that are seen as requiring action and accommodation are perceived.'[122] In other words, while the reasonable accommodation duty may seem to fall exclusively within the substantive difference approach due to its focus on individual differential characteristics, reasonable accommodation measures also fall within the substantive disadvantage equality model. Arnardóttir notes that the disadvantage approach is defined by the 'awareness in legal practice of the social construction of disability and the situated context of the individual in question'.[123]

119 M.V. Liisberg, *Disability and Employment: A Contemporary Disability Human Rights Approach Applied to Danish, Swedish and EU Law and Policy* (Intersentia, The Netherlands, 2011), at page 47.

120 S. Fredman, 'Changing the Norm: Positive Duties in Equal Treatment Legislation' 12(4) *Maastricht Journal of European and Comparative Law* 369, at page 372.

121 S. Fredman, 'Disability Equality, A Challenge to the Existing Anti-Discrimination Paradigm?' in A. Lawson and C. Gooding (eds.), *Disability Rights in Europe: From Theory to Practice* (Hart Publishing, Oxford, 2005), at page 215.

122 O.M. Arnardóttir, 'A Future of Multidimensional Disadvantage Equality' in O.M. Arnardóttir and G. Quinn (eds), *The UN Convention on the Rights of Persons with Disabilities: European and Scandinavian Perspectives* (Martinus Nijhoff, Leiden, 2009), at page 64.

123 Ibid.

3.7. Conclusion on Theoretical Models of Equality

Kayess and French assert that 'the fundamental purpose of equality measures is to challenge the equation of difference with inferiority.'[124] The move away from a formal approach to equality towards more substantive and transformative equality frameworks seeks to live up to this very challenge. The substantive equality framework is not concerned with overcoming innate characteristics and approximating the dominant, apparently 'superior,' paradigm. Rather, it seeks to validate differences from the 'norm' and it endeavours to take those differences into account in its assessment of necessary measures for disadvantaged groups. Transformative equality goes even further than substantive equality by tackling underlying causes of structural discrimination.

The next chapter of this book will assess the extent to which the equality and non-discrimination norms in the CRPD fit within the realm of the different models of equality and theories of disability that have been outlined in the present chapter. The remainder of this chapter will concern itself with an analysis of the level of protection which existed with regard to the rights of disabled people within the UN system in the period leading up to the adoption of the CRPD. Disability rights in the regional framework for human rights protection will also be considered briefly. The objective of that analysis will be to highlight the gaps which existed in human rights protection and to demonstrate the necessity for the adoption of an integral human rights treaty protecting the rights of persons with disabilities.

4. The International Framework for the Protection of Disability Rights

In this section of the chapter, the gaps that existed in disability rights protection in the UN in the period leading up to the adoption of the CRPD will be explored. In addition, this section will contain a brief consideration of the rights of persons with disabilities in regional frameworks for human rights protection. The aim of that will be to demonstrate the necessity for the adoption of a comprehensive and binding human rights framework protecting the rights of persons with disabilities.

4.1. Disability Rights in Soft-Law Human Rights Instruments (1945–1980)

Throughout the first decade of its work in the field of disability, from 1945–1955, the UN addressed disability issues from a decidedly welfare perspective.[125] At that time,

[124] R. Kayess and P. French, 'Out of Darkness Into Light? Introducing the Convention on the Rights of Persons with Disabilities' (2008) 8(1) *Human Rights Law Review* 1, 8.

[125] Information taken from UN Enable website, 'The United Nations and Disabled People – The First Fifty Years', available at www.un.org/esa/socdev/enable/dis50y20.htm, last accessed 18 January 2014. For further information on disability rights in soft-law UN instruments, see O.P. Goyal, 'Understanding and Scouting with Physically Handicapped' (Isha Books, New Delhi, 2005).

the principal bodies dealing with disability-related matters were the UN Secretariat, the Economic and Social Council and its subsidiary organ, the Social Commission. The primary focus of the work of those bodies was on rehabilitation and prevention issues and, as such, consideration of disability issues was steeped in the medical model. During its sixth session in 1950, the Social Commission considered two reports, entitled *Social Rehabilitation of the Physically Handicapped* and *Social Rehabilitation of the Blind.*[126] The focus of those documents was on attempts to 'cure' the functional limitations of the disabled person. At the same session, the Social Commission also examined a report by the International Programme for the Welfare of the Blind, which recommended education, rehabilitation, training and employment of persons with visual disabilities.[127] Some time after this, the Economic and Social Council agreed to establish programmes of rehabilitation for persons with physical disabilities and for the prevention and treatment of blindness.[128] Overall, little attention was paid during that timeframe to factors external to the person which hindered the participation of persons with disabilities in mainstream society.

The next transitional period within the UN human rights system can be viewed as occurring between the late 1950s and the beginning of the 1970s. During that period the focus of the UN machinery shifted from a purely welfare perspective to a social welfare approach.[129] The UN mechanisms re-evaluated their disability policy in the 1960s, leading to a wave of de-institutionalisation and a demand for fuller participation by disabled persons in an integrated society.[130] Another positive development which took place in the late 1960s was the slowly emerging consciousness within the UN of a new social model for dealing with disability matters.[131]

Throughout the 1970s, the failure to mainstream disability on the human rights agenda was rectified, to a certain extent at least. The mainstreaming of disability in the UN system reflected a growing awareness, on a global scale, of the human rights of persons with disabilities. In response to the dearth of disability-specific references at the international level, the UN adopted several declarations[132] and initiated symposiums and world conferences[133] on disability rights. By virtue of those soft law

126 Information taken from UN Enable website, 'The United Nations and Disabled People – The First Fifty Years', available at www.un.org/esa/socdev/enable/dis50y20.htm last accessed 18 January 2014.

127 Ibid.

128 Ibid.

129 Ibid.

130 Information taken from UN Enable website, 'The United Nations and Disabled People – The First Fifty Years', available at www.un.org/esa/socdev/enable/dis50y30.htm last accessed 18 January 2014.

131 Ibid.

132 See, for instance, Declaration on the Rights of Mentally Retarded Persons (Proclaimed by General Assembly resolution 2856 (XXVI) of 20 December 1971), available at www.ohchr.org/EN/ProfessionalInterest/Pages/RightsOfMentallyRetardedPersons.aspx, last accessed 18 January 2014; See also Declaration on the Rights of Disabled Persons, Proclaimed by General Assembly resolution 3447 (XXX) of 9 December 1975, available at www.ohchr.org/EN/ProfessionalInterest/Pages/RightsOfDisabledPersons.aspx last accessed 18 January 2014.

133 In 1981, for instance, experts in the disability field met at the International Symposium on Disabled Persons 27 September–4 October 1981 in Tripoli. Delegates also met in Vienna, Austria 12–23 October 1981 for The World Symposium of Experts on Technical Cooperation Among Developing Countries and Technical Assistance in Disability Prevention and Rehabilitation of Disabled Persons. In addition,

instruments, disability came to be viewed within the UN as a human rights issue. The emergence of a rights-based approach to disability was first evidenced by the adoption of several resolutions by the UN General Assembly recognising the equal rights of disabled persons. For example, the *Declaration on the Rights of Mentally Retarded Persons*[134] provides, *inter alia*, that persons with psychosocial disabilities[135] have, to the degree feasible, the same rights as other human beings.[136] A further resolution adopted by the General Assembly on 9 December 1975, the *Declaration on the Rights of Disabled Persons*,[137] states that disabled persons are entitled to the same civil and political rights as others,[138] including measures designed to enable them to become as self-reliant as possible.[139] Marianne Schulze describes this as one of the 'first indicators of reasonable accommodation'[140] at the international level. Furthermore, the Declaration provides that disabled people shall be protected from treatment of a discriminatory nature.[141] The Declaration identifies a number of economic and social rights of importance to enable persons with disabilities to develop their capabilities and skills to the maximum and to hasten the process of their social integration or reintegration.[142] However, as Michael Stein points out, those instruments 'possessed vestiges of the medical model by assuming individuals are disabled due to "special" medical problems that require segregated social services and institutions as remedies.'[143] In this regard, Stein cites paragraph 8[144] of the *Declaration on the Rights of Disabled Persons*, which he posits underscores the needs of disabled persons with regard to special services.[145] The Declaration was the first international instrument that put forward a definition of disability. However, that definition was based on the medical model of disability.[146] Notwithstanding the

the World Conference on Actions and Strategies on Education, Disability Prevention and Integration of Disabled Persons was held in Spain in 1981. [Information taken from UN Enable website, 'The United Nations and Disabled People – The First Fifty Years', available at www.un.org/esa/socdev/enable/dis50y30.htm last accessed 18 January 2014].

134 Declaration on the Rights of Mentally Retarded Persons (Proclaimed by General Assembly resolution 2856 (XXVI) of 20 December 1971), available at www.ohchr.org/EN/ProfessionalInterest/Pages/RightsOfMentallyRetardedPersons.aspx, last accessed 18 January 2014.

135 The term 'persons with psychosocial disabilities' was not used in the instrument.

136 Declaration on the Rights of Mentally Retarded Persons, para. 1.

137 Declaration on the Rights of Disabled Persons, Proclaimed by General Assembly resolution 3447 (XXX) of 9 December 1975, available at www.ohchr.org/EN/ProfessionalInterest/Pages/RightsOfDisabledPersons.aspx last accessed 18 January 2014.

138 Declaration on the Rights of Disabled Persons, para. 4.

139 Declaration on the Rights of Disabled Persons, para. 5.

140 M. Schulze, *Understanding the UN Convention on the Rights of Persons with Disabilities: A Handbook on the Human Rights of Persons with Disabilities* (July 2010) 17, available at www.equalityhumanrights.com/uploaded_files/humanrights/unconventionhradisabilities.pdf last accessed 24th March 2014.

141 Declaration on the Rights of Disabled Persons, para. 10.

142 Declaration on the Rights of Disabled Persons, para. 8.

143 M.A. Stein, 'Disability Human Rights' (2007) 95 *California Law Review* 75, at page 88.

144 Paragraph 8 of the *Declaration on the Rights of Disabled Persons* provides that: 'Disabled persons are entitled to have their *special* needs taken into consideration at all stages of economic and social planning.' [emphasis added].

145 M.A. Stein, 'Disability Human Rights' (2007) 95 *California Law Review* 75, 88 at Footnote 68.

146 According to the Declaration on the Rights of Disabled Persons, para. 1, the term 'disabled person' means any person unable to ensure by himself or herself wholly or partly, the necessities of a normal individual and/or social life, as a result of a deficiency, either congenital or not, in his or her physical or mental capabilities.

remaining traces of the medical model, the declarations referred to above paved the way for future instruments that would take a more inclusive approach to disability. Those declarations sought ultimately to ensure community integration, where possible. For example, paragraph 4 of the *Declaration on the Rights of Mentally Retarded Persons* states that, 'whenever possible, mentally retarded persons should live with their own families or with foster parents and participate in different forms of community life.'[147] In a similar vein, paragraph 9 of the *Declaration on the Rights of Disabled Persons* provides that 'disabled persons have the right to live with their families or with foster parents and to participate in all social, creative or recreational activities.'[148] In spite of their inherent limitations, those instruments acted as a pre-cursor to future UN instruments designed to foster increased participation and inclusion of persons with disabilities in society.

4.2. Disability Rights in Soft-Law Human Rights Instruments (1980–1990)

The remnants of the medical model were still evident at the beginning of the 1980s when the UN World Health Organisation (WHO) published a document entitled *The International Classification of Impairments, Disabilities and Handicaps* (ICIDH).[149] That document serves as a classification system, providing a framework for the description of health and health-related conditions designed to be used consistently across different countries and settings. It defines disability in accordance with the medical model, stating that the concept of disability encompasses 'any restriction or lack (resulting from an impairment) of ability to perform an activity in the manner or within the range considered normal for a human being.'[150] The ICIDH was criticised heavily for underestimating the role which social and environmental factors play in contributing to disablement.[151] Notwithstanding this, the 1980s provided further impetus for the growth of the rights-based approach to disability issues. Significantly, the UN General Assembly proclaimed 1981 the *International Year of Disabled Persons* (IYDP).[152] The principal objective and overarching theme of IYDP was 'full participation and equality,' defined as the right of persons with disabilities to take part fully in the life and development of their societies, enjoy living conditions equal to those of other citizens, and have an equal share in improved conditions resulting from socio-economic development.[153]

147 Declaration on the Rights of Mentally Retarded Persons, para. 4.

148 Declaration on the Rights of Disabled Persons, para. 9.

149 World Health Organisation, International Classification of Impairments, Disease and Handicaps: A Manual of Classification Relating to the Consequences of Disease (WHO, Geneva 1980).

150 Ibid, at page 28.

151 For an analysis of such criticisms, see J.E. Bickenbach, S. Chatterji, E.M. Badley, & T.B. Üstün, 'Models of disablement, universalism and the international classification of impairments, disabilities and handicaps' (1999) 48 *Social Science & Medicine*, at pages 1173–1187.

152 'The International Year of Disabled Persons' was declared as such by UN General Assembly resolution 31/123. Further information available at www.un.org/esa/socdev/enable/disiydp.htm last accessed 18 January 2014.

153 Defined as such at www.un.org/disabilities/default.asp?id=126 last accessed 25th January 2014.

A major outcome of the IYDP was the formulation of the World Programme of Action Concerning Disabled Persons (WPA), which was adopted by the UN General Assembly in December 1982. The WPA provides a policy framework aimed at promoting 'effective measures for prevention of disability, rehabilitation and the realization of the goals of full participation of [persons with disabilities] in social life and development, and of equality.'[154] The WPA centres on three fields of action as follows: i) prevention ii) rehabilitation and iii) equalisation of opportunities. The first two themes emanate from the medical model stance. However, the third theme on equalisation of opportunities is a central pillar of the document and it signifies the shift within the UN machinery towards the social model of disability. The concept of equalisation of opportunities provided the guiding philosophy of the WPA towards achieving full and effective participation of persons with disabilities in mainstream society. The WPA called on governments to take action to ensure the equalisation of opportunities for disabled people in various spheres, ranging from legislation to education, employment, sports and culture. Quinn and Degener maintain that the inclusion of the rhetoric of equality of opportunities was 'evidence of the slow but sure shift towards a rights-based model.'[155] The WPA has been described by Aart Hendriks as 'an important first step in the global recognition of the equal rights of disabled persons.'[156] It could be said that the WPA was the first international instrument to target the structural roots of exclusion of persons with disabilities from mainstream society. The WPA defines 'equalization of opportunities' as 'the process through which the general system of society, such as the physical and cultural environment, housing and transportation, social and health services, educational and work opportunities, cultural and social life, including sports and recreational facilities, are made accessible to all.'[157] The WPA also acknolwedges the relevance of the social-contextual model of disability, defining 'handicap' as:

> A function of the relationship between disabled persons and their environment. It occurs when they encounter cultural, physical or social barriers which prevent their access to the various systems of society that are available to other citizens. Thus, handicap is the loss or limitation of opportunities to take part in the life of the community on an equal level with others.[158]

This marked a new beginning of sorts – one which recognised the role played by social and environmental barriers in hindering full and effective participation for persons with disabilities. The WPA urged the UN system to make all of its facilities

---

154 World Programme of Action concerning Disabled Persons, adopted by the General Assembly on 3 December 1982, by its resolution 37/52, UN Doc. A/RES/37/52, para. 1.

155 G. Quinn and T. Degener, *Human Rights and Disability: The Current Use and Future Potential of the United Nations Human Rights Instruments in the Context of Disability* (2002), at page 31.

156 A. Hendriks, 'The Significance of Equality and Non-Discrimination for the Protection of the Rights and Dignity of Disabled Persons' in T. Degener and Y. Koster-Dreese (eds.) Human Rights and Disabled Persons Essays and Relevant Human Rights Instruments (Martinus Nijhoff, Dordrecht, 1995), at page 56.

157 World Programme of Action Concerning Disabled Persons, adopted by the General Assembly on 3 December 1982, by its resolution 37/52, UN Doc. A/RES/37/52 para. 12.

158 World Programme of Action Concerning Disabled Persons, para. 7.

'totally barrier-free' in order to achieve the theme of IYDP – full participation and equality.[159] The WPA also established a direct link between the UN human rights machinery and the disability rights agenda.[160] Finally, it is important to note that the decade from 1983 to 1992 was proclaimed the International Decade of Disabled Persons.[161] This provided a timeline for national authorities to implement the framework of the WPA and marked a period of intense reform in international disability activism. One example of disability activism which took place during that period was the publication in 1989 of the *Tallinn Guidelines for Action on Human Resources Development in the Field of Disability*.[162] Those guidelines sought to promote participation, training and employment of persons with disabilities within all government ministries and on all levels of national policy-making in order to equalise opportunities for persons with disabilities.[163] Additionally, in 1998, the UN Commission on Human Rights passed a resolution, entitled *Human Rights of Persons with Disabilities*,[164] acknowledging general responsibility for persons with disabilities under its mandate.

4.3. Disability Rights in Soft-Law Human Rights Instruments (1990-Present Day)

Following in the wake of progress made during the International Decade of Disabled Persons, the 1990s were described as a 'banner period for disability law.'[165] In 1991, a document entitled *Principles for the Protection of Persons with Mental Illnesses and the Improvement of Mental Health Care*[166] was adopted by the UN General Assembly. The twenty-five principles contained therein define fundamental freedoms and basic rights and set detailed standards for the protection of persons with psychosocial disabilities. The principles deal *inter alia*, with the right to life in the community, the determination of mental illness provisions for admission to treatment facilities and the conditions of mental health facilities. They were intended to serve as a guide for national governments, specialised agencies and regional and international organisations, helping them facilitate investigation into problems affecting the

159 World Programme of Action Concerning Disabled Persons, para. 162.

160 The World Programme of Action Concerning disabled persons stated, at para. 164, that 'organizations and bodies involved in the United Nations system responsible for the preparation and administration of international agreements, covenants and other instruments that might have a direct or indirect impact on disabled people should ensure that such instruments fully take into account the situation of persons who are disabled.'

161 Information taken from www.un.org/disabilities/default.asp?id=127 last accessed 19 January 2014.

162 Tallinn Guidelines for Action on Human Resources Development in the Field of Disability, UN Doc.A/RES/44/70, adopted at the 78th plenary meeting 8 December 1989.

163 Information taken from www.un.org/disabilities/default.asp?id=127 last accessed 18 August 2014.

164 UN Commission on Human Rights Resolution 1998/31, 'Human Rights of Persons with Disabilities,' 17 April, 1998 (Geneva).

165 T. Degener, 'International Disability Law – A New Legal Subject on the Rise: The Interregional Experts' Meeting in Hong Kong, December 13–17, 1999' (2000) 18 *Berkley Journal of International Law* 180, 184.

166 Principles for the Protection of Persons with Mental Illness and the Improvement of Mental Health Care (UN Doc. A/RES/46/119, 75th plenary meeting 17 December 1991).

application of fundamental freedoms and basic human rights for persons with mental illness.[167] The document emphasises the fact that all persons have the right to the best available mental health care[168] and that persons with a mental illness shall be treated with humanity and respect for the inherent dignity of the human person.[169] Another instrument relating to the situation of persons with disabilities and adopted by the UN during the same period was the *Guidelines for the Establishment and Development of National Coordinating Committees on Disability or Similar Bodies*,[170] adopted in 1990. Such bodies were intended to serve as a national focal point on disability matters.

The human rights-based approach to disability was evidenced clearly during the UN's Second World Conference on Human Rights, which took place in Vienna on June 25, 1993. That conference linked the rights of persons with disabilities to a human rights model of material equality in its confirmation 'that all human rights and fundamental freedoms are universal and thus unreservedly include persons with disabilities.'[171] The Conference called on all Governments, 'where necessary to adopt or adjust legislation to ensure access to these [life, welfare, education, work, living independently, and active participation in all aspects of society] and other rights for disabled persons.'[172]

Building on the approach taken in the WPA, and on foot of lessons learned during the International Decade of Disabled Persons, the UN adopted the milestone resolution entitled *Standard Rules on the Equalization of Opportunities for Persons with Disabilities*[173] (Standard Rules or Rules) on December 20, 1993. That document has been described by Melinda Jones as 'the most significant instrument'[174] developed prior to the CRPD 'with respect to access and participation of people with disabilities.'[175] The Standard Rules actually came about following several unsuccessful attempts to draft a binding international convention concerning the rights of disabled people. In August 1987, a mid-term review of the United Nations Decade of Disabled Persons had been conducted at a global meeting of experts

---

167 Information taken fromwww.un.org/esa/socdev/enable/dis50y60.htm last accessed 24 August 2014.

168 Principles for the Protection of Persons with Mental Illness and the Improvement of Mental Health Care, adopted by the UN General Assembly at its 75th plenary meeting on 17 December 1991, UN Doc. A/RES/46/119, para. 1.

169 Ibid, para. 2.

170 The Guidelines for the Establishment and Development of National Coordinating Committees on Disability or Similar Bodies (2000) UN Doc. A/C.3/46/4, annex 1.

171 United Nations Vienna Declaration and Programme of Action, Reports of the World Conference at Title II, 63 (1993) UN Doc.A/CONF.157/23.

172 Ibid.

173 UN Standard Rules on the Equalization of Opportunities for Persons with Disabilities, UN Doc.A/RES/48/96, adopted by the General Assembly on 20 December 1993 by its resolution 48/96, 85th Plenary Meeting, available at www.un.org/documents/ga/res/48/a48r096.htm last accessed 20 August 2014.

174 M. Jones, 'Inclusion, Social Inclusion and Participation' in M.H. Rioux, L.A. Basser and M. Jones (eds), *Critical Perspectives on Human Rights and Disability Policy* (Martinus Nijhoff 2011) 78.

175 Ibid.

in Stockholm, Sweden.[176] During that meeting, it was recommended that the UN General Assembly convene a special conference to draft an international convention on the rights of persons with disabilities and that such a convention should be ratified by States by the end of the International Decade of Disabled Persons. A draft outline of the convention was, in fact, prepared by numerous States.[177] However, those efforts to garner support for a disability-specific treaty floundered as many representatives believed that the existing canon of international instruments provided adequate protection for the rights of persons with disabilities. Instead of adopting an international treaty, there was widespread support for the elaboration of another soft-law instrument on disability rights. This consensus led to the drafting of the Standard Rules.

The Rules accentuate the goal of equalisation of opportunities as a pivotal concept in the disability rights agenda and address preconditions for equal participation and target areas for participation, implementation measures and monitoring mechanisms. Furthermore, they highlight the importance of the equality norm for the protection of disability rights and they also view disability from a social-contextual stance. The conceptual framework underlying the Standard Rules hinges on the twin concepts of equality and non-discrimination.[178] The Rules draw a clear distinction between 'disability' and 'handicap' and, thereby, place the emphasis of the process of disablement on environmental factors.[179] The Standard Rules have been described by the UNCESCR as being 'of major importance'[180] and have been further described by one commentator as constituting 'an important change in paradigm,'[181] to the extent that they move away from 'a medical-assistance perspective towards an approach focusing on rights with an interdisciplinary focus, emphasizing the psychosocial,

176 This meeting was entitled the 'Global Meeting of Experts to Review the Implementation of the World Programme of Action concerning Disabled Persons at the Mid-Point of the United Nations Decade of Disabled Persons.'

177 Italy presented a draft convention to the General Assembly at its forty-second session. A further draft convention was presented by Sweden at the forty-fourth session of the Assembly. In addition, Mexico instigated a proposal in the course of the World Conference against Racism, Racial Discrimination, Xenophobia and Related Intolerance in Durban in 2001.

178 The Rules affirm that: 'The principle of equal rights implies that the needs of each and every individual are of equal importance, that those needs must be made the basis for the planning of societies and that all resources must be employed in such a way as to ensure that every individual has equal opportunity for participation.' [UN Standard Rules on the Equalization of Opportunities for Persons with Disabilities, para. 25].

179 The Rules state that the term 'disability' summarises 'a great number of different functional limitations occurring in any population in any country of the world. People may be disabled by physical, intellectual or sensory impairment, medical conditions or mental illness. Such impairments, conditions or illnesses may be permanent or transitory in nature.' [Ibid, para. 17]. By way of contrast, the term 'handicap' is defined in the Standard Rules as 'the loss or limitation of opportunities to take part in the life of the community on an equal level with others. It describes the encounter between the person with a disability and the environment.' [Ibid, para. 18].

180 UNCESCR, General Comment 5 on *Persons with disabilities*: 09/12/94, adopted at the eleventh session of the Committee, UN. Doc E/1995/22, para. 7(b).

181 M.S.C Reyes, 'Standard Rules on Equality of Opportunities for Persons with Disabilities: Legal View of Provisions on Support Services, Auxiliary Resources and Training/View from Latin America' in M.H. Rioux, L.A. Basser and M. Jones (eds.), *Critical Perspectives on Human Rights and Disability Policy* (Martinus Nijhoff, The Hague, 2011), at page 419.

environmental and contextual perspective in its broadest sense.'[182] The Standard Rules are reflective of a strong human rights perspective as they address issues of structural access and promote the inclusion of persons with disabilities in mainstream society. They emphasise the fact that it is the responsibility of States to take action to remove the multifaceted barriers to participation encountered by persons with disabilities.[183] The Standard Rules also contain many provisions targeted at ensuring equal participation through breaking down barriers. They recognise the importance of general accessibility requirements. Rule 5, for example, relates to access to the physical environment, as well as access to information and communications. In addition, the Rules refer to accommodations that States must make, in the context, *inter alia*, of education[184] and employment.[185] They also emphasise a participatory role for persons with disabilities and their representative organisations. They highlight the fact that such groups should play an active role as partners in the process of the removal of obstacles to participation.[186]

It is noteworthy that the Standard Rules are not a binding UN instrument and that they lack direct enforcement mechanisms. Notwithstanding this, their effectiveness has been recognised 'in terms of orientation within national legislation and of public policy'[187] on disability matters. The former UN Special Rapporteur, Bengt Lindqvist, maintains that the Standard Rules 'have clearly defined the functions of the State in the planning of measures aimed at achieving full participation and equality of opportunity, have strengthened aspects related to human rights and have provided a mechanism for active supervision.'[188] At the date of their adoption, the Standard Rules represented the most comprehensive set of human rights standards regarding disability policy and were characterised as implying 'a strong moral

182 Ibid.

183 See para. 15, UN Standard Rules on the Equalization of Opportunities for Persons with Disabilities, which states that: 'In all societies of the world there are still obstacles preventing persons with disabilities from exercising their rights and freedoms and making it difficult for them to participate fully in the activities of their societies. It is the responsibility of States to take appropriate action to remove such obstacles.'

184 See, for example, Rule 6, para. 2, which provides that: 'Education in mainstream schools presupposes the provision of interpreter and other appropriate support services. Adequate accessibility and support services, designed to meet the needs of persons with different disabilities, should be provided.'

185 See, for example, Rule 6, para. 2, which provides that: 'States should also encourage employers to make reasonable adjustments to accommodate persons with disabilities.' Rule 6, Paragraph 3 also provides that: 'States' action programmes should include: Measures to design and adapt workplaces and work premises in such a way that they become accessible to persons with different disabilities; Support for the use of new technologies and the development and production of assistive devices, tools and equipment and measures to facilitate access to such devices and equipment for persons with disabilities to enable them to gain and maintain employment; Provision of appropriate training and placement and ongoing support such as personal assistance and interpreter services.'

186 UN Standard Rules on the Equalization of Opportunities for Persons with Disabilities, para. 15.

187 M.S.C. Reyes, 'Standard Rules on Equality of Opportunities for Persons with Disabilities: Legal View of Provisions on Support Services, Auxiliary Resources and Training/View from Latin America' in M.H. Rioux, L.A. Basser and M. Jones (eds.), *Critical Perspectives on Human Rights and Disability Policy* (Martinus Nijhoff, The Hague, 2011) 419.

188 Comments of Bengt Lindqvist, Final Report of the Special Rapporteur of the UN Commission on Social Development on the application and oversight activities of the Standard Rules on the Equalisation of Opportunities for Persons with Disabilities, at pages 27–28.

and political commitment on behalf of States to take action for the equalization of opportunities for persons with disabilities.'[189] However, they did not plug all of the existing gaps in human rights protection for disabled people. In view of this, a Declaration was adopted at the World NGO Summit on Disability, which took place in Beijing, China on 12 March 2000.[190] That Declaration repeated previous calls for a convention to promote and protect the rights of people with disabilities and enhance equal opportunities for their participation in mainstream society. The signatories highlighted the fact that any convention that might be adopted should address, *inter alia*, the following priority concerns: (a) improvement of the overall quality of life of people with disabilities, and their upliftment from deprivation, hardship and poverty; (b) education, training, remunerative work, and participation in decision-making process levels; (c) elimination of discriminatory attitudes and practices, as well as information, legal and infrastructural barriers and; (d) increased allocations of resources to ensure the equal participation of people with disabilities.[191]

In 2001, shortly before undertaking the drafting of a binding international human rights treaty for persons with disabilities, the UN General Assembly adopted a revised version of the ICIDH. The revised document was entitled the International Classification of Functioning, Disability and Health (ICF). Under the ICF framework, disability is classed as:

> An umbrella term for impairments, activity limitations and participation restrictions. It denotes the negative aspects of the interaction between an individual (with a health condition) and that individual's contextual factors (environmental and personal factors).[192]

The ICF can be viewed as representing an amalgamation of the social model and the medical model. However, many disability rights activists and scholars criticised the ICF on account of the fact that it placed too much emphasis on the medical model of disability. Kayess and French point to the fact that, in the negotiations on the CRPD, the International Disability Caucus (IDC) – which is the network of global, regional and national organisations of persons with disabilities and allied non-governmental agencies – 'vehemently opposed reference to the ICF.'[193] In essence, they viewed it as 'part of the human rights problem faced by persons with disability that the UN CRPD was to overcome through its exposition of the social model of disability.'[194]

---

189 UN Standard Rules on the Equalization of Opportunities for Persons with Disabilities, para. 14.

190 Beijing Declaration on the Rights of People with Disabilities (2000), adopted on 12 March 2000 at the World NGO Summit on Disability, Beijing, People's Republic of China, available at www.lea-test.fi/en/assessme/beijing.html last accessed 16 December 2014.

191 Ibid.

192 World Health Organisation, International Classification of Functioning, Disability and Health (2001) 213. The ICF was endorsed officially by all 191 WHO Member States in the Fifty-fourth World Health Assembly on 22 May 2001(resolution WHA 54.21).

193 R. Kayess and P. French, Out of Darkness into Light? Introducing the Convention on the Rights of Persons with Disabilities (2008) 8(1) *Human Rights Law Review* 25.

194 Ibid.

In light of the obvious shortcomings of the ICF and the other attempts to protect the rights of persons with disabilities, there was clearly a need for the adoption of a binding international disability human rights treaty. As can be seen from the information contained in the present section of this chapter, the main problem regarding the existing human rights framework stemmed from the fact that the human rights instruments which addressed disability issues up to that point (such as the Standard Rules and the other soft law instruments outlined above) were not binding and therefore national governments were not legally required to follow the recommendations contained in those documents. Another concern with the existing corpus of human rights law was the fact that many of the existing human rights instruments conceptualised disability in rather out-dated terms and from a medical stance (at least in part), often resulting in further stereotyping of persons with disabilities.

4.4. The Protection of the Rights of Persons with Disabilities under Binding International and Regional Human Rights Law before the Adoption of the CRPD

The gaps in the soft-law international human rights regime were evident. However, one might question why a binding disability treaty was required in the first place, in light of the fact that persons with disabilities were protected under the universal guarantees of existing binding international human rights treaties. In order to answer that question, and before tracing the final steps towards adoption of the CRPD, I will now turn to an examination of the protection of disability rights under the core international human rights treaties, before analysing briefly protection under regional instruments.

4.4.1. The Protection of Disability Rights under the Core International Human Rights Treaties

Human rights are deemed to be universal and therefore persons with disabilities were protected, in theory at least, under the existing core human rights treaties[195] before the adoption of the CRPD. Notwithstanding this, disabled people have, for the most part, been absent and invisible from human rights discourse at the level of binding international human rights law. The main gap in the protection of the rights of persons with disabilities under the core treaties was that, in order to claim protection, disabled people were forced to rely on universal provisions or to claim protection on a ground other than disability as the existing corpus of human rights

[195] There are nine core human rights treaties: International Convention on the Elimination of all Forms of Racial Discrimination (1965), International Covenant on Civil and Political Rights (1966), International Covenant on Economic, Social and Cultural Rights (1966), UN Convention on the Elimination of All Forms of Discrimination against Women (1979), UN Convention against Torture and other Cruel, Inhumane or Degrading Treatment or Punishment (1984), UN Convention on the Rights of the Child (1989), UN Convention on the Protection of the Rights of All Migrant Workers and Members of Their Families (1990), UN Convention for the Protection of All Persons from Enforced Disappearance (2006), UN Convention on the Rights of the Persons with Disabilities (2006).

law did not mention disability as a covered ground. Thus, the international human rights treaties did not cater for the specific needs of persons with disabilities and certainly did not promote full participation and inclusion in society as a fundamental precept of UN human rights protection. In addition, the core human rights treaty bodies were unwilling to engage with disability issues, whether due to a lack of knowledge concerning such issues or the absence of disability-specific provisions in the treaties.

Disability-based discrimination has, in the past, been described as 'one of the black holes of UN equality law.'[196] The UN Commission on Human Rights had called on the treaty monitoring bodies to take the rights of persons with disabilities into account in carrying out their functions under the core human rights treaties. For example, in its *Resolution on Human Rights and Disability*,[197] the Commission encouraged all of the human rights treaty monitoring bodies 'to respond positively to its invitation to monitor the compliance of States with their commitments under the relevant human rights instruments in order to ensure the full enjoyment of those rights by disabled persons.'[198] In spite of this, the potential of the binding international human rights instruments was under-utilised in protecting the rights of persons with disabilities. Rowena Daw notes that 'disability was, until very recently, the forgotten dimension of human rights and went unacknowledged as a subject for a right to equality.'[199] This stemmed partly from the fact that, within the UN machinery, disability was not considered to be a human rights issue until relatively recently.

Mainstream human rights documents adopted before the 1970s are characterised by a marked absence of any reference to disability. The International Bill of Human Rights – which comprises the UDHR, the ICCPR and the ICESCR – is silent on the issue of disability. Furthermore, there is no reference to disability in the two anti-discrimination treaties adopted at the international level – CERD and CEDAW. In fact, the Convention on the Rights of the Child (CRC) is the only core international human rights treaty to contain an explicit recognition of disability as a ground of discrimination and was the first such treaty to incorporate a specific provision on the rights of disabled children. Article 23 of the CRC acknowledges the fact that disabled children should enjoy 'a full and decent life, in conditions which ensure dignity, promote self-reliance and facilitate the child's active participation in the community.'[200]

---

196 W. Vandenhole, *Non-Discrimination and Equality in the View of the UN Human Rights Treaty Bodies* (Intersentia, Antwerp/Oxford, 2005), at page 2.

197 Office of the High Commission of Human Rights, Resolution 1994/27 on Human Rights and Disability.

198 Office of the High Commission of Human Rights, Resolution 1994/27 on Human Rights and Disability, at para. 6; See also Office of the High Commission of Human Rights, Resolution 1996/27 on the Human Rights of Persons with Disabilities which reiterated this call.

199 R. Daw, *The Impact of the Human Rights Act on Disabled People* (Disability Rights Commission, London, 2000), at page 8.

200 UN Convention on the Rights of the Child (adopted and opened for signature, ratification and accession by General Assembly resolution 44/25 of 20 November 1989 entry into force 2 September 1990, in accordance with article 49) Article 23.

Disability-based discrimination has been recognised as falling under the label of 'other status' by the Human Rights Committee (HRC), the UNCESCR and the UN Committee on the Elimination of Discrimination against Women (CEDAW Committee).[201] In its General Comment 5, the UNCESCR has confirmed that disability-based discrimination falls under the label of 'other status' in the ICESCR.[202] There is no doubt therefore that, in spite of the absence of an explicit reference to disability within the majority of the core human rights treaties, the existing international human rights framework was, and still is, applicable in theory to persons with disabilities in the same manner as it is to their non-disabled counterparts. The fact remained that the rights of disabled people were going largely unnoticed within the UN human rights division of the core treaty bodies. In the past, the HRC has considered a handful of individual disability-related complaints under its Optional Protocol mechanism, under which individuals may call States to account for their actions. In *Hamilton v Jamaica*,[203] for instance, the Committee ruled that the relevant State Party was in breach of Article 10(1) ICCPR (which requires any person deprived of their liberty to be treated with dignity and respect). In that case, poor prison conditions that had a disproportionate effect on the applicant due to his disability were found to be contrary to the Covenant. Additionally, in the case of *Wackenheim v France*,[204] the Committee ruled that differentiation on the grounds of dwarfism fell within Article 26 ICCPR, the Covenant's autonomous equality principle.[205] Furthermore, in the case of *C v Australia*,[206] the Committee held that the State Party was in violation of Article 7 ICCPR (which contains the prohibition of torture, inhuman and degrading treatment), due to the fact that it had deported the applicant (a foreigner who had been granted refugee status) to a country where it was unlikely that he would receive the treatment necessary for his mental illness. In spite of this handful of examples, Colm O'Cinneide points to the fact that in general, 'the case-law of the UN monitoring bodies has yielded little tangible benefits for persons with disabilities, with the exception of the odd decision.'[207]

---

201 Information taken from W. Vandenhole, *Non-Discrimination and Equality in the View of the UN Human Rights Treaty Bodies* (Intersentia, Antwerp/Oxford, 2005), at page 185.

202 UNCESCR, General Comment 5 on Persons with Disabilities, adopted on 09/12/94 at the Eleventh Session of the Committee, U.N. Doc E/1995/22, at para. 5, states as follows: 'Since the Covenant's provisions apply fully to all members of society, persons with disabilities are clearly entitled to the full range of rights recognized in the Covenant. In addition, insofar as special treatment is necessary, States parties are required to take appropriate measures, to the maximum extent of their available resources, to enable such persons to seek to overcome any disadvantages, in terms of the enjoyment of the rights specified in the Covenant, flowing from their disability. Moreover, the requirement contained in article 2 (2) of the Covenant that the rights 'enunciated [...] will be exercised without discrimination of any kind' based on certain specified grounds 'or other status' clearly applies to discrimination on the grounds of disability.'

203 Human Rights Committee, *Hamilton v Jamaica*, Communication No. 616/1995 of 28 July 1999.

204 Human Rights Committee, *Wackenheim v France*, Communication No 854.1999 of 26 July 2002.

205 However, in that case, the differentiation in question was found to be based on objective and reasonable grounds.

206 Human Rights Committee, *C v Australia*, Communication No. 900/1999 of 13 November 2002, para. 8.5.

207 C. O'Cinneide, 'Extracting Protection for the Rights of Persons with Disabilities from Human Rights Frameworks: Established Limits and New Possibilities,' in O.M. Arnardóttir and G. Quinn (eds.), *The*

The UNCESCR is the only one of the core human rights treaty bodies that has adopted a general comment specifically on the rights of persons with disabilities. General Comment 5 (1994) of the Committee refers at several junctures to the UN Standard Rules. It maintains that the Rules 'are of major importance and constitute a particularly valuable reference guide in identifying more precisely the relevant obligations of States parties under the [ICESCR].'[208] This bridges core treaty provisions to soft law instruments in the context of persons with disabilities. General Comment 5 details the manner in which the ICESCR should be interpreted in order to ensure the equal enjoyment of the rights specified therein by persons with disabilities. It takes a social constructionist perspective on disability issues by acknowledging the fact that the rights of disabled people cannot be realised properly if discriminatory barriers continue to exist in society.[209] The Committee also acknowledges the fact that 'it is particularly important that artificial barriers to integration in general, and to employment in particular, be removed.'[210] General Comment 5 of the UNCESCR acknowledges explicitly the link between equality norms on the one hand, and participation and inclusion in society for persons with disabilities, on the other hand.[211] It also underscores the emphasis which the Standard Rules place on accessibility measures[212] and reasonable accommodations.[213] Significantly, it also includes within the definition of disability-based discrimination a denial of reasonable accommodation.[214]

It is noteworthy that, through its General Comment 5, the Committee explains the reason for the absence of an explicit disability-related provision in the ICESCR, attributing this 'to the lack of awareness of the importance of addressing this

---

UN Convention on the Rights of Persons with Disabilities: European and Scandinavian Perspectives (Martinus Nijhoff Publishers, The Netherlands, 2009) 174.

208 UNCESCR, General Comment No. 5 on persons with disabilities (adopted at the eleventh session of the Committee, 1994), U.N. Doc E/1995/22 at 19 (1995), para. 7.

209 For example, the Committee notes that ensuring that disabled people can work will require the elimination of 'prominent and persistent' discrimination, as well as 'the physical barriers that society has erected in areas such as transport, housing and the workplace.' [Ibid, para. 22].

210 Ibid.

211 General Comment 5 of the UNCESCR states at para. 5: 'Through neglect, ignorance, prejudice and false assumptions, as well as through exclusion, distinction or separation, persons with disabilities have very often been prevented from exercising their economic, social or cultural rights *on an equal basis* with persons without disabilities. The effects of disability-based discrimination have been particularly severe in the fields of education, employment, housing, transport, cultural life, and access to public places and services' [emphasis added].

212 It recommends that States 'should promote the accessibility to and availability of places for cultural performances and services.' [General Comment 5 of the UNCESCR, para. 36]. It also emphasises the fact that 'the right to adequate housing includes the right to accessible housing for persons with disabilities.' [Ibid, para. 33].

213 With regard to reasonable accommodation measures, General Comment 5 reiterates Rule 4 of the Standard Rules by stating that it is also necessary to ensure that support services, including assistive devices are available for persons with disabilities, to assist them to increase their level of independence in their daily living and to exercise their rights. [Ibid, citing the UN Standard Rules, Rule 4.].

214 Para. 15 of General Comment 5 reads that, for the purposes of the ICESCR 'disability-based discrimination' may be defined as including 'any distinction, exclusion, restriction or preference, or denial of reasonable accommodation based on disability which has the effect of nullifying or impairing the recognition, enjoyment or exercise of economic, social or cultural rights.'

issue explicitly, rather than only by implication, at the time of the drafting of the Covenant over a quarter of a century ago.'[215] The Committee goes on to state that it is now 'very widely accepted that the human rights of persons with disabilities must be protected and promoted through general, as well as specially designed laws, policies and programmes.'[216] Alongside this one disability-specific general comment, the CEDAW Committee adopted a general recommendation on disabled women. General Recommendation 18[217] (1991) of the Committee calls on States to provide information on disabled women in their periodic reports, specifically relating to measures taken to deal with their particular situation, including special measures to ensure that they have equal access to education and employment, health services and social security and to ensure that they can participate in all areas of social and cultural life.[218] General Recommendation 24 (1999) of the CEDAW Committee also refers specifically to women with disabilities. Paragraph 6 thereof urges States to give special attention to the health needs and rights of women belonging to vulnerable and disadvantaged groups such as [...] women with physical or mental disabilities.[219] The HRC also issued a General Comment[220] in 1982, which included a reference to persons with psychosocial disabilities. The Committee states therein that the right to liberty and security of the person applies to 'all deprivations of liberty, whether in criminal cases or in other cases, such as, for example, mental illness, vagrancy, drug addiction, educational purposes.'[221] Moreover, in its General Comment 9, the UN Committee on the Rights of the Child (CRC Committee) notes that children with disabilities experience difficulties and barriers to the full enjoyment of the rights enshrined in the CRC and recommends that those barriers should be removed by States.[222]

Finally, it is worth noting that one of the specialised UN organs, the International Labour Organisation (ILO), put disability rights firmly on its agenda by adopting key instruments designed to create equal opportunities for disabled people in the spheres of employment and vocational rehabilitation. The UNCESCR has acknowledged that the ILO documents constitute 'valuable and comprehensive instruments with respect to the work-related rights of persons with disabilities.'[223] The non-binding

215 UNCESCR, General Comment No. 5 on persons with disabilities (adopted at the eleventh session of the Committee, 1994), U.N. Doc E/1995/22 at 19 (1995), para. 6.

216 Ibid, para. 6.

217 UN Committee on the Elimination of all Forms of Discrimination against Women, General Recommendation No. 18 on disabled women (adopted at the Tenth Session, UN Doc. A/46/38).

218 Ibid.

219 UN Committee on the Elimination of all Forms of Discrimination Against Women, General Recommendation No. 24 (Article 12 of the Convention) on Women and Health, (adopted at the twentieth session of the Committee, 1999), U.N. Doc. A/54/38.

220 Human Rights Committee, General Comment 8 on Liberty and security of the person (Article 9) (adopted at the sixteenth session of the Committee, June 1982).

221 Ibid, para. 1.

222 UN Committee on the Rights of the Child, General Comment 9 on the Rights of Children with Disabilities (2006) (adopted by the Committee at its Forty-third session Geneva, 11–29 September 2006), U.N. Doc. CRC/C/GC/9, para. 5.

223 UNCESCR, General Comment No. 5 on persons with disabilities (adopted at the eleventh session of the Committee, 1994), U.N. Doc E/1995/22, para. 27.

Recommendation concerning Vocational Rehabilitation of the Disabled[224] adopted in 1955, was the first ILO instrument adopted in respect of persons with disabilities. Two further instruments supplement the provisions of the 1955 Recommendation. The Convention concerning Vocational Rehabilitation and Employment (Disabled Persons),[225] adopted in 1983, provides for vocational rehabilitation measures for all categories of disabled persons and for the promotion of employment opportunities and equal treatment of disabled men and women. In addition, the ILO Recommendation concerning Vocational Rehabilitation and Employment (Disabled Persons), adopted in 1983,[226] applies to all disabled workers.

The preceding paragraphs demonstrate the existing gaps in the protection of disability rights under the core international human rights treaties pre-CRPD. Before outlining the final steps in the journey towards the adoption of the CRPD, the extent to which the human rights of persons with disabilities are protected under regional human rights law will be discussed briefly, specifically under American law, within the Council of Europe and in the EU.

4.4.2. The Regional Framework for the Protection of the Rights of Persons with Disabilities

During the period of increased recognition of the rights of disabled people at the international level, several regional human rights instruments also increased their references to persons with disabilities. Some of the most important instruments concerning the protection of the rights of persons with disabilities in regional human rights law will be explored below.

In the context of the Americas, the Additional Protocol to the American Convention on Human Rights[227] states that 'everyone affected by a diminution of his physical or mental capacities is entitled to receive special attention designed to help him achieve the greatest possible development of his personality.'[228] In 1999, the Organization of American States went even further in their recognition of the rights of disabled people by adopting the Inter-American Convention on the Elimination of All Forms of Discrimination Against Persons with Disabilities.[229] That convention calls on States to facilitate the full integration of disabled people into mainstream society

[224] International Labour Organization, Recommendation No. 99 Concerning Vocational Rehabilitation (Disabled), adopted in Geneva on 22 June 1955.

[225] International Labour Organization, International Labour Convention No. 159 Concerning Vocational Rehabilitation and Employment (Disabled Persons), adopted in Geneva on 20 June 1983.

[226] International Labour Organization, Recommendation No. 168 Concerning Vocational Rehabilitation and Employment (Disabled Persons) (1983), adopted in Geneva on 20 June 1983.

[227] Additional Protocol to the American Convention on Human Rights in the Area of Economic, Social and Cultural Rights "Protocol of San Salvador" Adopted in San Salvador on November 17, 1988.

[228] Ibid, Article 18.

[229] The Inter-American Convention on the Elimination of All Forms of Discrimination against Persons with Disabilities, O.A.S. AG/Res. 1608, 7 June 1999 (entered into force 14 September 2001), available at www.oas.org/juridico/english/treaties/a-65.html last accessed 19 September 2014.

through a variety of means, including legislation, educational programmes and social initiatives.

Within the Council of Europe, disability rights were not recognised widely in the period before the adoption of the CRPD. The European Convention on Human Rights (ECHR),[230] was adopted under the auspices of the Council of Europe in 1950 to protect human rights and fundamental freedoms. It was adopted at a time when the formal model of equality prevailed. The ECHR does not contain any specific rights for the protection of persons with disabilities. The only provision in the ECHR that even mentions disability is Article 5(e), which refers to 'persons of unsound mind' in the context of a justified deprivation of liberty for the purposes of administering medical treatment. This reflects the medical conceptualisation of disability that was prevalent at the time of the adoption of the ECHR. The ECHR does not mention disability as a characteristic covered by its non-discrimination provision, Article 14. Notwithstanding this, the list of grounds of discrimination in that article is not exhaustive and it is evident that the rights contained in the ECHR apply equally to all human beings, including persons with disabilities. This has been confirmed by the European Court on Human Rights (ECtHR) in the case of *Glor v Switzerland*,[231] which was decided in 2009. Nonetheless, it must be noted that it took the ECtHR a long time to hand down an Article 14 judgment concerning disability.

In a similar vein to Article 14 ECHR, disability does not feature as a ground of discrimination in Protocol 12[232] to the ECHR. Protocol 12 expands the scope of the prohibition of discrimination under the ECHR by guaranteeing equal treatment in the enjoyment of any right (including rights under national law). By way of contrast, Article 14 ECHR cannot be invoked independently. It is accessory to the substantive rights contained in the Convention.[233] The explanatory report to the drafting of Protocol 12 explains the absence of disability (among other grounds of discrimination, such as sex and age) in the following terms, namely that it was:

> Not because of a lack of awareness that such grounds have become particularly important in today's societies as compared with the time of drafting of Article 14 of the Convention, but because such an inclusion was considered unnecessary from a legal point of view since the list of non-discrimination grounds is not exhaustive, and because inclusion of any

---

230 Convention for the Protection of Human Rights and Fundamental Freedoms, Rome, 4.XI.1950.

231 *Glor v Switzerland*, application no. 13444/04, Judgment 30 April 2009, EHRC 2009/79. In that case, the Court found disability discrimination contrary to Article 14 ECHR, in conjunction with Article 8 ECHR, by virtue of the fact that the State in question had failed to carve out exemptions to a rule which imposed a penalty tax on persons deemed unfit to perform military service on grounds other than severe disability.

232 Protocol No. 12 to the Convention for the Protection of Human Rights and Fundamental Freedoms (ETS No. 177) is an anti-discrimination treaty of the Council of Europe. Protocol 12 was adopted on November 4, 2000, in Rome and entered into force on April 1, 2005.

233 The accessory nature of Article 14 ECHR has been confirmed, *inter alia*, in *Abdul-Aziz, Cables and Balkandali v UK,* application nos. 9214/80, 9473/81, 9474/81, judgment 28 May 1985 (1985) 7 EHRR 471, para. 71; See also *Inze v Austria,* application no. 8695/79, judgment 28 October 1987 (1987) 10 EHRR 394, para. 36.

> particular additional ground might give rise to unwarranted *a contrario* interpretations as regards discrimination based on grounds not so included.[234]

The other major human rights instrument adopted within the Council of Europe – the European Social Charter of 1961 – does contain a provision pertaining specifically to the rights of disabled people. Article 15 of the original Charter elaborates the right to 'vocational, training, rehabilitation and resettlement.'[235] Article 15 of the original Charter was replaced with a right to 'independence, social integration and participation in the life of the community'[236] in the Revised European Social Charter (revised Charter), adopted in 1996. Gerard Quinn has summarised the difference between the formulation of Article 15 in the original Charter and the version contained in the revised Charter. He states that the provision in the original Charter can be characterised as constituting a provision on 'rehabilitation with a nod toward equality,'[237] whereas the provision in the revised Charter can be viewed as one which has a predominant emphasis on equality with merely 'a nod toward rehabilitation.'[238] The revised Charter therefore brought disability equality more to the forefront.

Finally, in terms of EU law, it is worth noting that the Charter of Fundamental Rights of the European Union[239] incorporates a provision on the rights of persons with disabilities. Article 26 thereof (on the integration of persons with disabilities) provides that 'the Union recognises and respects the right of persons with disabilities to benefit from measures designed to ensure their independence, social and occupational integration and participation in the life of the community.'[240] There are also several Directives[241] at the EU level aimed at protecting the rights of persons with disabilities. Notwithstanding these disability-specific provisions, overall it could be said that disability rights were not prominent within the regional human rights framework pre-CRPD.

4.5. The Final Steps in the Journey towards the Adoption of the CRPD

It has been illustrated above that while, in theory, persons with disabilities were protected under the core international human rights treaties, there were huge gaps in practice in the protection of the rights of persons with disabilities at the international level. While the cross-cutting obligations of equality and non-discrimination

---

234 Protocol No. 12 to the Convention for the Protection of Human Rights and Fundamental Freedoms, Explanatory Report, CETS No. 177 (2000), para. 20, available at http://Conventions.coe.int/Treaty/en/Reports/Html/177.html last accessed 12 September 2014.

235 European Social Charter, CETS No. 35 (1961), Article 15.

236 European Social Charter (Revised), CETS No. 163 (1996), Article 15.

237 G. Quinn, 'The European Social Charter and EU Anti-Discrimination Law in the Field of Disability: Two Gravitational Fields with One Common Purpose' in G. De Búrca and B. De Witte (eds.), *Social Rights in Europe* (Oxford University Press, Oxford, 2005) 279.

238 Ibid.

239 Charter of Fundamental Rights of the European Union (2000) OJ C 364/01.

240 Charter of Fundamental Rights of the European Union (2000) OJ C 364/01, Article 26.

241 See, for instance, Council Directive 2000/78/EC of 27 November 2000 establishing a general framework for equal treatment in employment and occupation, OJ L 303, 2.12.2000, pages 16–22.

in the core treaties applied equally to disabled people (as they did to every other marginalised group), the reality was quite different. A vacuum existed with regard to the protection of the rights of disabled people under both the existing soft law instruments and the binding international treaties. As a result of these deficiencies, there was consensus among the international human rights community regarding the fact that a binding international human rights instrument was required that would reflect a social-constructionist and a human rights-based approach to disability. The CRPD emerged from that consensus. Below the final steps in the journey towards the adoption of the CRPD will be traced.

In 1993, an insightful report[242] was prepared by Leandro Despouy, the then Special Rapporteur appointed by the UN Sub-Commission on Prevention of Discrimination and Protection of Minorities. That report was endorsed by the UN Commission on Human Rights and the UN General Assembly. It chronicled the extent to which disabled people were subject to human rights abuses on a global scale. As a result of that report, and all the other developments at the international level, there were numerous calls for the adoption of a disability-specific international treaty during the 1990s.[243] Responding to the calls for a disability-specific treaty, the UN Consultative Expert Group held a Meeting on International Norms and Standards relating to Disability at the University of California, Berkeley, in December 1998, in cooperation with the World Institute on Disability (WID).[244] Delegates at the Berkeley meeting put forward the idea that a new convention should be drafted which would afford 'the opportunity to revise or discard existing standards or statements of rights which were inconsistent with current thinking about the human rights of persons with disabilities or which were unsatisfactory in other respects.'[245] The Despouy Report reiterated this call by indicating that, in the absence of a thematic convention on disability rights, disabled people would find themselves at a 'legal disadvantage'[246] when compared with other vulnerable groups. It was against this background that proposals for a convention on the rights of persons with disabilities garnered support. The UN General Assembly established an Ad-Hoc Committee,

---

242 L. Despouy, *Human Rights and Disabled Persons* (United Nations publication 1993) UN Sales No. E.92.XIV.4, available at www.un.org/esa/socdev/enable/dispaperdes0.html last accessed 20 February 2014.

243 For instance, the World Conference against Racism, Racial Discrimination, Xenophobia and Related Intolerance, which was held in South Africa in September 2001, recommended that the UN General Assembly would consider drafting an integral and comprehensive international convention to protect and promote the rights and dignity of persons with disabilities. The World Conference recommended, in particular, the inclusion of provisions that would address discriminatory practices and treatment affecting persons with disabilities. See UN Doc. A/CONF.189/12, chapter I, para. 180.

244 United Nations Consultative Expert Group Meeting on International Norms and Standards relating to Disability, hosted by the Boalt Hall School of Law, University of California at Berkeley, in cooperation with the World Institute on Disability (WID) (8–12 December 1998).

245 Information taken from G. Quinn and T. Degener, *Human Rights and Disability: The Current Use and Future Potential of the United Nations Human Rights Instruments in the Context of Disability* (2002), at page 43, available at www.ohchr.org/Documents/Publications/HRDisabilityen.pdf, last accessed 13 January 2014.

246 L. Despouy, *Human Rights and Disabled Persons* (1993), United Nations publication, Sales No. E.92. XIV.4, available at www.un.org/esa/socdev/enable/dispaperdes0.html last accessed 20 September 2014, at paras. 280–281.

by General Assembly resolution 56/168 of 19 December 2001, to consider the enactment of such a convention. At its second session, held from 16 to 27 June 2003, the Ad-Hoc Committee decided to form a Working Group with the aim of preparing and presenting a draft text, which would form the basis for negotiations by Member States and observers. The Working Group was composed of twenty-seven governmental representatives designated by regional groups, twelve representatives from non-governmental organisations and one representative of national human rights institutions.[247] The Working Group of the AD-Hoc Committee met initially from 5 to 16 January 2004, during which time it produced a draft comprehensive and integral international convention on the protection and promotion of the rights and dignity of persons with disabilities. The Ad-Hoc Committee considered the draft text of the Working Group at its third session, which was held from 24 May to 4 June 2004 and the Committee began negotiating a convention on the basis of the draft text. In December 2001, the UN General Assembly adopted a resolution on a Comprehensive and Integral International Convention to Promote and Protect the Rights and Dignity of Persons with Disabilities.[248] That resolution acknowledged the fact that 'previous efforts made to increase cooperation and integration and increasing awareness of and sensitivity to disability issues [...] have not been sufficient to promote full and effective participation by and opportunities for persons with disabilities in economic, social, cultural and political life.'[249]

As already stated, the reason for the failure of previous efforts to ensure full and effective participation and inclusion of disabled people in society stemmed partly from the fact that the application of a universal human rights system and, thereby, a universal equality norm, to particular marginalised groups fails to take into account the lived experiences of such groups. In other words, none of the previous international human rights instruments were tailored to the requirements of persons with disabilities and could not therefore cater for their specific needs. The Ad-Hoc Committee was tasked with developing a human rights treaty that would ensure full and effective enjoyment of all existing human rights, ensuring equal access to those rights for disabled people. The mandate that came from the General Assembly was that no new rights were to be created. Indeed, the Chairman characterised the CRPD

---

247 The Working Group of the Ad-Hoc Committee was comprised of representatives of the following Governments, non-governmental organizations and national human rights institution: Cameroon, Canada, China, Colombia, Comoros, Ecuador, Germany, India, Ireland, Jamaica, Japan, Lebanon, Mali, Mexico, Morocco, New Zealand, Philippines, Republic of Korea, Russian Federation, Serbia and Montenegro, Sierra Leone, Slovenia, South Africa, Sweden, Thailand, Uganda, Venezuela Disability Australia Limited, Disabled Peoples' International, Disabled Peoples' International (Africa), European Disability Forum, Inclusion International, Inter-American Institute on Disability, Landmine Survivors Network, Rehabilitation International, World Blind Union, World Federation of the Deaf, World Federation of the Deafblind, World Network of Users and Survivors of Psychiatry South African Human Rights Commission (representing national human rights institutions).

248 UN General Assembly resolution 56/168 of 19 December 2001, on a Comprehensive and integral international convention to promote and protect the rights and dignity of persons with disabilities, available at www.un.org/esa/socdev/enable/disA56168e1.html. last accessed 18 February 2013.

249 Ibid.

as 'an implementation convention.'[250] He stated that 'without creating for the most part new rights, the convention sets out a detailed code of implementation and spells out how individual rights should be put into practice.'[251]

The CRPD was adopted by the UN General Assembly on December 13, 2006 and entered into force on May 3, 2008. As well as the Convention itself, an Optional Protocol to the CRPD (OP-CRPD) was established. It also came into force on May 3, 2008. In line with the Optional Protocol, States Parties to the Convention recognise the competence of the CRPD Committee to receive and consider communications from or on behalf of individuals or groups of individuals subject to its jurisdiction who claim to be victims of a violation by that State Party of the provisions of the CRPD. This should add considerable protection for disabled people seeking to exercise and enjoy their human rights on an equal basis with others. The adoption of the Convention at the UN level triggered the process of signing and ratifying the treaty by UN Member States. On 23 December 2010, the EU ratified the CRPD. As such, it was the first regional integration organisation to become a party to a UN human rights treaty.

The CRPD is unique among international treaties, not least by virtue of the high number of signatures and ratifications that it attracted within a short period of time, both within the Council of Europe[252] and on a global stage.[253] The adoption of the Convention was the result of a participatory process, whereby an unprecedented level of civil society organisations, including persons with disabilities and their representative organisations, took part in the Convention's negotiation process. The participation of civil society in the drafting of international human rights treaties is not a new phenomenon.[254] However, the difference in the case of the CRPD arose from the fact that record numbers participated in the drafting process and also from the fact that the official documents of the Ad-Hoc Committee were made available to representatives of Non-Governmental Organisations (NGOs) during the negotiations.[255] This participatory process is relevant to the vision of equality

---

250 R. Kayess and P. French, Out of Darkness into Light? Introducing the Convention on the Rights of Persons with Disabilities (2008) 8(1) *Human Rights Law Review* 1, 20, quoting the words of the Chairman of the Ad-Hoc Committee, Mr. Don Mc Kay.

251 UN Press Releases, 'Chairman says draft convention sets out detailed code of implementation and spells out how individual rights should be put into practice,' 15 August 2005, SOC/4680, available at www.un.org/News/Press/docs/2005/soc4680.doc.htm last accessed 13 March 2014.

252 Of the 47 Council of Europe States, 45 have signed the UN CRPD (Switzerland and Liechtenstein have not signed) and 41 have ratified the UN CRPD (Finland, Iceland, Ireland, Liechtenstein, Monaco and The Netherlands have not yet ratified), available at www.un.org/disabilities/countries.asp?id=166 last accessed 19 August 2014.

253 As at August 2014, the UN CRPD has 146 ratifications, while the Optional Protocol (OP) has 82 ratifications. The number of signatories to the UN CRPD is 159 while the OP has 91 signatures.

254 The drafting of the Convention on the Elimination of Discrimination against Women and the Convention on the Rights of the Child both benefitted from the input of the relevant cohorts.

255 In the report of its first session (UN Doc. A/57/357), the Ad Hoc Committee set modalities for participation of accredited NGOs in its open meetings. The Ad Hoc Committee decided that representatives from accredited NGOs may participate in the work of the Committee by: Attending any public meetings of the Committee, making oral statements (subject to availability of time and in accordance with United Nations practice), as well as submitting written statements and receiving

advanced by the Convention. Organisations of People with Disabilities (DPOs) were particularly influential in the drafting process and many of the suggestions made by the DPOs were incorporated into the final text of the Convention. The Mental Disability Advocacy Center (MDAC) contends that, by virtue of the fact that disabled people and their representative organisations were 'a key part of negotiating and drafting the Convention, the resultant text seeks to ensure that a high level of participation is maintained at the domestic level as the Convention is implemented.'[256] In that regard, Article 4(3) of the CRPD[257] is a crucial provision. It requires close consultation with and active involvement of persons with disabilities in the development and implementation of legislation and policies and in decision-making processes concerning issues relating to persons with disabilities. In addition, Article 33(3) of the CRPD provides that 'civil society, in particular persons with disabilities and their representative organizations, shall be involved and fully participate in the monitoring process.'[258] Disabled people must be among those who monitor the Convention and their voices must also be listened to as experts. Finally, Article 34(4) of the CRPD provides that, in electing the CRPD Committee, States must ensure that due regard is given to 'participation of experts with disabilities.'[259] These articles require full participation rather than mere consultation with people with disabilities. This is vital to unlocking the structural inequalities that disabled people face in society.

The CRPD represents the first binding normative framework that seeks to ensure the promotion and protection of the human rights of persons with disabilities on an equal basis with others. The adoption of the CRPD was welcomed with fanfare. The UN Secretary-General stated that it 'heralded the dawn of a new era – an era in which disabled people will no longer have to endure the discriminatory practices and attitudes that have been permitted to prevail for all too long.'[260] Frédéric Mégret

copies of the official documents, as well as making written or other presentations. Furthermore, in the annex III of the report of its fourth session (UN Doc. A/59/360), the Ad Hoc Committee set modalities for the participation of accredited NGOs and National Human Rights Institutions in its informal consultations closed meetings during the fourth and fifth session. The Ad Hoc Committee decided to invite intergovernmental organizations, NGOs and National Human Rights Institutions to be present. The Committee, however, also made provisions for the fact that meetings closed to those organisations might be required at some point.

256 Mental Disability Advocacy Center, *Building the Architecture for Change: Guidelines on Article 33 of the UN Convention on the Rights of Persons with Disabilities* (March 2011).

257 Article 4(3) of the UN CRPD provides that: 'In the development and implementation of legislation and policies to implement the present Convention, and in other decision-making processes concerning issues relating to persons with disabilities, States Parties shall closely consult with and actively involve persons with disabilities, including children with disabilities, through their representative organizations.'

258 UN CRPD, Article 33(3).

259 UN CRPD, Article 34(3).

260 Official Statement of the UN Secretary-General, Kofi Annan, 'Secretary General Hails Adoption of Landmark Convention on Rights of People with Disabilities,' 13 December 2006 (SG/SM/ 10797, HR/4911, L/T/4400), available at: www.un.org/News/Press/docs/2006/sgsm10797.doc.htm Last accessed 13 September 2014. Furthermore, the Secretary-General expressed the hope that it would 'usher in an age when all those living with disabilities around the world become fully fledged citizens of their societies.'

refers to the CRPD as an instance of the 'pluralisation of human rights,'[261] a situation whereby the international human rights regime is adapted to the specific rights of vulnerable or marginalised groups. However, as Mégret points out, the CRPD 'is about more than making sure that existing human rights are applied to persons with disability. It also subtly reformulates and extends existing human rights to take into account the specific experience of persons with disability.'[262] Before the adoption of the CRPD, it was evident that the UN human rights machinery had endorsed a human rights-based approach for persons with disabilities. This in itself was an important step, as the concept of human dignity is integral to treatment as equals and the recognition and celebration of diversity and difference. The UN system had also clearly recognised the importance of full and effective participation and inclusion of disabled people in society on an equal basis with others. During several UN world conferences[263] which took place during the 1990s, the UN bodies had emphasised the need for a 'society for all,' advocating the participation of all citizens, including persons with disabilities, in every sphere of society. This shift in emphasis was cemented by the adoption of the CRPD. Accordingly, it is important to reflect more closely on the link between equality and non-discrimination norms, on the one hand, and participation and inclusion of persons with disabilities in society, on the other hand. In the next section of this chapter, that link will be examined.

5. The Link between 'Equality' and 'Participation and Inclusion' in Society for Persons with Disabilities

In the subsections which follow, the concepts of participation and inclusion in society for persons with disabilities will be analysed, in particular their link to the equality norm. The aim of that analysis will be to provide a backdrop for subsequent chapters of this book, which will reflect on the manner in which the CRPD's equality paradigm advances the disability rights agenda by providing scope for increased participation and inclusion of persons with disabilities in society.

5.1. Introduction to the Concepts of Participation and Inclusion in Society for Persons with Disabilities: Their Link to the Equality Norm

International human rights law is premised upon the ideal that 'all human beings are born free and equal in dignity and rights.'[264] Furthermore, it takes as its starting point the notion that everyone is entitled to rights and freedoms without distinction of

---

261 F. Mégret, 'The Disabilities Convention: Human Rights of Persons with Disabilities or Disability Rights?' (2008) 30 *Human Rights Quarterly* 494, 495.

262 Ibid, at page 494.

263 For instance, The Rio de Janeiro Conference on Environment and Development (Rio de Janeiro, 1992), The World Conference on Human Rights (Vienna, 1993), The International Conference on Population and Development (Cairo, 1994), The United Nations World Summit for Social Development (Copenhagen, 1995) and the Fourth World Conference on Women (Beijing, 1995).

264 Universal Declaration of Human Rights, Article 1.

any kind.[265] While those sentiments are laudable, people with disabilities have been subjected to numerous forms of discriminatory treatment as a result of their perceived deviation from the so-called 'norm.' Disabled people have been excluded routinely and segregated from general societal structures, on account of their differential characteristics.[266] They face countless barriers to participation at all levels of society. These barriers take many forms and can relate to the physical environment, to provisions in domestic legislation and policy or to attitudinal barriers in the form of the perpetuation of stereotypes. The corollary of such barriers is the denial of equal access to substantive rights and, thereby, to participation and inclusion in mainstream society.[267]

Equality and non-discrimination norms are linked intrinsically to the notions of participation and inclusion in society. Participation is an increasingly important construct for persons with disabilities. Depending on the type of impairment involved, the kind of participation enjoyed by persons with disabilities may vary widely. According to the ICF, participation is defined as 'a person's involvement in a life situation.'[268] A restriction in participation is determined by comparing an individual's participation profile to 'that which is expected of an individual without disability in that culture or society.'[269] The definition of participation in the ICF includes the notion of involvement, which is defined as 'taking part, being included or engaged in an area of life, being accepted or having access to needed resources.'[270] The ICF definition of participation is somewhat vague, particularly in light of the conceptual ambiguity inherent in the notion of 'life situation.' Certain researchers have criticised the fact that the ICF places so much emphasis on individual performance as a defining characteristic of participation.[271] Leading authors within the disability movement argue that the idea of living independently and participating freely is linked intrinsically with access to resources and support measures, rather than the ability to actually perform a particular activity or task.[272]

---

265 Universal Declaration of Human Rights, Article 2.

266 On this point, see among others, R. Kayess and P. French, Out of Darkness into Light? Introducing the Convention on the Rights of Persons with Disabilities (2008) 8(1) *Human Rights Law Review* 1.

267 See UN CRPD, Preamble para. (k) which recognises that 'persons with disabilities continue to face barriers in their participation as equal members of society and violations of their human rights in all parts of the world;' See also UN CRPD, Preamble para. (y) which states that 'a comprehensive and integral international convention to promote and protect the rights and dignity of persons with disabilities will make a significant contribution to redressing the profound social disadvantage of persons with disabilities and promote their participation in the civil, political, economic, social and cultural spheres with equal opportunities, in both developing and developed countries.'

268 World Health Organization, International Classification of Functioning, Disability and Health (Geneva, Switzerland, 2001), at page 213.

269 Ibid,

270 Ibid, at page 15.

271 See, for instance, R.J.M Perenboom and A.M.J Chorus, 'Measuring participation according to the International Classification of Functioning, Disability and Health (ICF)' (2003) 25 *Journal of Disability Rehabilitation* 577.

272 See, for example, J. Morris, *Independent lives? Community Care and Disabled People* (The Macmillan Press, London, 1993).

Academic scholars have also carried out research into the meaning of participation in society for persons with disabilities, from which the general consensus emerges that participation must naturally be defined from the point of view of persons with disabilities themselves. As Hammel et al. point out:

> There continues to remain a critical need for participatory research that involves people with diverse disabilities and participation experiences in the grounded conceptualization of participation 'from within', and in the development and refinement of participation assessment tools that emerge from this grounded approach.[273]

One particular group of researchers has carried out a qualitative, multi-site study that sought to gain an insider perspective from people with disabilities as to what participation means, how to characterise it, and the barriers to and supports necessary for participation.[274] To that end, the researchers carried out qualitative research with focus groups comprised of persons with various types of impairment. The disabled participants described several values that exemplified participation for them. Several themes related to core participation values emerged across the focus groups as follows: (i) active and meaningful engagement/being a part of; (ii) choice and control; (iii) access and opportunity/enfranchisement; (iv) personal and societal responsibilities; (v) having an impact and supporting others; and (vi) social connection, societal inclusion, and membership. Respect and dignity were identified repeatedly as a critical feature of participation across all themes.[275] The outcome of the study was that participation was deemed to be both a right and a responsibility 'influenced by and ascribed to the person and to the society.'[276] The disabled people who took part in the study 'viewed participation as a right that is predicated upon access, opportunity, respect and inclusion.' They also described participation 'as a personal and societal responsibility that required determination, advocacy and empowerment.'

From the above, it is obvious that the notion of inclusion in society is linked intrinsically to the concept of participation for persons with disabilities. Drawing on the words of Jürgen Habermas, Melinda Jones contends that inclusion is the principle that says that 'whatever benefits accrue to members of society are the heritage of all people, not just those that are able-bodied. Inclusion means that all people are entitled to full membership of the human family.'[277] Jones links the concepts of participation and inclusion in society in her assertion that inclusion means that:

---

273 J. Hammel, S Magasi, A. Heinemann, G. Whiteneck, J. Bogner and E. Rodriguez, 'What does Participation Mean: An Insider Perspective from People with Disabilities' (2008) 30(19) *Disability and Rehabilitation* 1445, 1446.

274 Ibid, at pages 1445–1460.

275 Ibid, at pages 1449/1450.

276 Ibid, at page 1445.

277 M. Jones, 'Inclusion, Social Inclusion and Participation' in M.H. Rioux, L.A. Basser and M. Jones (eds.), *Critical Perspectives on Human Rights and Disability Policy* (Martinus Nijhoff, The Hague 2011) 57, citing J. Habermas, *The Philosophical Discourse of Modernity* (F.G. Lawrence Translation) (Polity Press, Cambridge, 1987).

> We are all entitled to participate fully in all aspects of society; that we all have the same rights and responsibilities; that we all have something to contribute. It is the principle which demands valued recognition of all people and the entitlement of all to meaningful interaction, involvement and engagement in every part [of society].[278]

Viewed in that light, inclusion is a means to facilitating full and effective participation in society as it requires that barriers which impede participation are removed. Jones argues that there are three interlinking components to inclusionary structures and that, in order for people with disabilities to be included in society, each of the three dimensions of inclusion must be operational:

i. A non-discriminatory attitude towards people with disabilities;
ii. The guarantee of access to participation in every area of life; and
iii. The facilitation of people with disabilities to limit the impact of disability.[279]

Each of these components of inclusionary structures may be linked to the principles of equality and non-discrimination. The concepts of participation and inclusion in society are both an end in themselves but also a means to an end (namely the fulfilment of equality). For instance, the inclusion and participation of disabled people in decision-making processes and in legislative and social changes results in their needs and concerns setting the disability rights agenda. It results in empowerment and ultimately in a more effective realisation of the principles of equality and non-discrimination. It has been acknowledged that the most efficient way for States 'to update their understanding of the nature and forms of disability and the ways in which social barriers to participation can be removed'[280] is to consult with people with disabilities and their representative organisations. This is key to bolstering equal rights for people with disabilities. There is, however, a line of distinction to be drawn between full and effective inclusion in society, as opposed to merely integrating persons with disabilities into the mainstream. This distinction is relevant to the fulfilment of the equality norm for persons with disabilities.

5.2. The Dilemma of Difference: Inclusion *versus* Integration in Society

Disabled people are set apart from their non-disabled counterparts by differential characteristics, whether physical, intellectual or otherwise. Rioux et al. argue that 'where people are differently situated, it is essential to establish the extent to which the difference needs to be taken into account if equality is to be [realised fully].'[281]

278 M. Jones, 'Inclusion, Social Inclusion and Participation' in M.H. Rioux, L.A. Basser and M. Jones (eds), *Critical Perspectives on Human Rights and Disability Policy* (Martinus Nijhoff, The Hague, 2011) 57.

279 Ibid, at page 58.

280 United Nations Enable, *Handbook for Parliamentarians on the Convention on the Rights of Persons with Disabilities,* Page 59, available at www.un.org/disabilities/default.asp?id=236 last accessed 8th October 2014.

281 M.H. Rioux, L.A. Basser and M. Jones (eds), *Critical Perspectives on Human Rights and Disability Policy* (Martinus Nijhoff, The Hague, 2011), at pages 7–8.

This raises the important issue of the so-called 'dilemma of difference.'[282] Ignoring differences often serves to perpetuate discrimination and inequality, yet focusing on differences can, in certain circumstances, result in keeping stigmatisation alive. Martha Minow summarises the difficulties inherent in contending with human differences when she poses the following questions: 'When does treating people differently emphasize their differences and stigmatize or hinder them on that basis? And when does treating people the same become insensitive to their difference and likely to stigmatize or hinder them on that basis.'[283]

The tensions inherent in the 'dilemma of difference' are an important backdrop to any consideration of the equality and non-discrimination norms in the context of the CRPD. The recognition of difference is a vital component in ensuring true equality for disabled people. Unlike other grounds of discrimination, such as colour and race, the difference of disability and the root causes of disability discrimination cannot be neutralised fully by remedying past discrimination. Disabled people cannot avail of equal opportunities to participate in a meaningful way in the absence of individualised accommodations and other supports, as well as structural change in mainstream society.

Prior to the advent of the CRPD, the language used in disability discourse was that of 'integration' and 'mainstreaming.' The CRPD, on the other hand, mandates 'full and effective participation and inclusion for persons with disabilities in society.'[284] Inclusion requires the adaptation of existing societal structures and a universal design approach that accepts diversity and difference. If such an approach were followed, there would be no need (or at least much less need) for accommodations *per se*. By way of contrast, integration requires that the individual with differential characteristics adapts to the so-called 'norm.' Reasonable accommodations can be deemed to fall under an integrationist approach as they seek to ensure that existing practices and structures are modified to allow disabled people to fit in with mainstream structures. The duty to accommodate does not result in structural changes to the 'norm.' According to the integrationist approach, the disabled individual is merely 'accepted' within mainstream society. However, there is no claim to, or focus on, equality. Inclusion is linked intrinsically to the equality norm as it insists on equal structures and takes account of differential characteristics in refashioning what may be deemed 'normal.' As Jones states, 'inclusion ultimately depends on the acceptance of difference and the willingness to celebrate diversity.'[285]

---

282 See M. Minow, Learning to Live with the Dilemma of Difference: Bilingual and Special Education' (1985) 48 *Law and Contemporary Problems* 157, 202.

283 M. Minow, *Making All the Difference: Inclusion, Exclusion and American Law* (Cornell University Press, Ithaca, 1990) 20.

284 UN CRPD, General Principle 3(c).

285 M. Jones, 'Inclusion, Social Inclusion and Participation' in M.H. Rioux, L.A. Basser and M. Jones (eds.), *Critical Perspectives on Human Rights and Disability Policy* (Martinus Nijhoff, The Hague, 2011) 58.

It is worth noting that some authors argue that an inclusionary approach to equality accords with the 'liberal idea of inclusion into the *status quo*.'[286] Albertyn, for instance, aligns inclusionary equality more or less with the notion of integration outlined above. She also distinguishes inclusionary equality from transformative equality, which she argues dislodges 'the underlying norms and structures that create and reinforce a rigid and hierarchical *status quo*.'[287] For the purposes of this book, the understanding that is being put forward of inclusion is, in fact, linked to substantive and transformative equality. The reason for putting forward this understanding of inclusion is that it fits best with the norms contained in the CRPD. In the next chapter of this book, it will be demonstrated that the provisions of the Convention go far beyond an integrationist approach to endorse a substantive and transformative approach to equality. Indeed, it will be shown in chapter three of this book that the equality norm in the CRPD seeks to dismantle the *status quo* and underlying systemic disadvantages that stand in the way of the exercise of rights by persons with disabilities on an equal basis with others.

6. Conclusion

The primary objective of this chapter was to set the scene for the interpretation in the next chapter of this book of the equality and non-discrimination norms contained in the CRPD. In order to do that, various theoretical models of disability and conceptualisations of equality have been examined, with a view to analysing how those theoretical models relate to the disability rights agenda and also how they relate to the precise model(s) of equality which the CRPD espouses. In order to enable the reader to gain an insight into the extent to which the CRPD surpasses previous instruments in terms of its progressive equality and non-discrimination norms, the development of disability rights at the international level has been traced, both in binding and in non-binding instruments. A brief outline of the protection of disability rights in regional instruments has also been sketched. This serves to place the CRPD in context.

This chapter forms a pivotal backdrop to chapter three of this book, in which a definitive interpretation of the equality and non-discrimination norms in the CRPD will be provided. The overall aim of chapter three is to provide a normative framework within which to determine the substantive value that the equality and non-discrimination norms in the Convention can add to enhancing the rights of persons with disabilities, in particular by increasing their participation and inclusion in all aspects of society. To that end, the present chapter has also outlined the connection between equality and non-discrimination norms and the notions of participation and inclusion in mainstream society.

---

286 See, for instance, C. Albertyn, 'Substantive Equality and Transformation in South Africa' (2007) 23 *South African Journal on Human Rights* 253, 256.

287 Ibid.

It has been a long and winding road towards ensuring that disability equality and inclusion came to the forefront of the binding international human rights landscape. Throughout the remaining chapters of this book, the question as to whether the CRPD can truly be defined as the bright light at the end of the long and dark tunnel of exclusion and marginalisation will be explored.

Chapter 3
Treaty Interpretation: The Equality and Non-Discrimination Provisions in the CRPD

'Application of any rules on treaty interpretation, and in particular the [rules in the Vienna Convention on the Law of Treaties] is not a purely mechanical process; but their proper application is the correct procedure and the best assurance of reaching the correct interpretation.'[1]

1. Introduction

In chapter two of this book, the background leading up to the adoption of the CRPD was laid out in order to determine the gaps that existed in relation to the protection of the rights of persons with disabilities before the adoption of the CRPD. Various theoretical models of disability and equality were also analysed. One of the purposes of that analysis was to provide a benchmark against which to assess the equality and non-discrimination norms in the CRPD. Following on from the conclusions reached in chapter two, the present chapter will consist of a thorough interpretation of Article 5 of the CRPD and related articles. The overall aim of this chapter is to analyse the extent to which the Convention's equality paradigm can potentially advance the rights of persons with disabilities, facilitating their participation and inclusion in society. The present chapter will reflect on the manner in which the CRPD tackles issues of structural or systemic discrimination, seeking to ensure that disabled people are included in society's mainstream and are no longer relegated to its margins.

This chapter will contain a theoretical and comparative analysis of the CRPD's equality and non-discrimination provisions. The equality and non-discrimination norms in the Convention will be interpreted according to VCLT methodology, in order to define States' obligations and to determine the precise theoretical model(s) of equality contained in the CRPD. To that end, the following sub-research questions will be answered:

i. What is the legal meaning of the equality and non-discrimination norms contained in the CRPD?; and
ii. How do the concepts of equality and non-discrimination in the CRPD fit within the various theoretical models of disability and conceptions of equality and non-discrimination that have been elaborated to date by scholars?

---

1 R.K. Gardiner, *Treaty Interpretation* (Oxford University Press, Oxford, 2008), at page 29.

Thereafter, the theoretical framework of equality in the CRPD will be compared to that contained in other human rights treaties which preceded the Convention. In that regard, the following sub-research questions will be addressed:

i. To what extent does the non-discrimination obligation contained in the CRPD go further than previous non-discrimination norms at the international level; and
ii. How can this potentially advance the rights of persons with disabilities to participate and be included in society?

In order to answer the foregoing questions, this chapter will be structured as follows: Section two will provide a brief overview of the methodology that will be employed in interpreting the CRPD. In section three of this chapter the conceptual framework of disability in the CRPD will be outlined, as that forms a vital backdrop to a substantive interpretation of the Convention's equality and non-discrimination norms. Section four of this chapter will consist of an analysis of the constituent elements of Article 5 of the Convention, together with Article 2. To that end, the documents related to those articles will be examined, together with the Preamble of the CRPD (where relevant and necessary) and the general principles and general obligations of the Convention, which are contained in articles 3 and 4 respectively. This will aid in the determination of the precise model(s) of equality which informs the Convention in section five of this chapter. In section five, the Convention's equality paradigm will be analysed, from a theoretical and comparative perspective. In that regard, the various theoretical models of equality and disability that have been outlined by scholars to date will be drawn on, in order to determine how the CRPD's equality provisions fit comparatively within already existing models. Furthermore, the areas in which the CRPD differs from the existing corpus of international human rights law will be highlighted, from an equality perspective. Finally, section six of this chapter will contain concluding remarks.

2. Research Methodology

The opening quotation in this chapter draws attention to the fact that the best assurance of reaching the correct interpretative outcome depends on the proper application of the relevant rules and principles. This chapter seeks to ensure a coherent and transparent interpretative process, in order to extract an appropriate meaning from the equality and non-discrimination provisions in the CRPD. Of course, the CRPD Committee will provide its own interpretation of the provisions of the Convention. The Committee's general comments, concluding observations and recommendations have a non-binding status but are nonetheless authoritative.

In terms of the specific research methodology that will be employed in this chapter, the VCLT will be the primary point of reference in interpreting Article 5 of the CRPD and related articles. The VCLT and its specific methodological tools were expanded on in detail in chapter one of this book. The research that will be undertaken in this chapter will endeavour to guard against an overly subjective interpretation of the equality and non-discrimination norms in the CRPD. By grounding this research in a stable methodological framework, the risk of misguided conclusions will be reduced substantially.

3. The Conceptual Understanding of Disability in the CRPD

Before embarking upon a definitive interpretation of the equality and non-discrimination norms in the CRPD, the conceptual understanding of disability endorsed by the Convention will be considered below as this provides an essential backdrop to a thorough interpretation of Article 5 of the CRPD and related articles.

3.1. The Social-Contextual Model of Disability

During the second session of the Ad-Hoc Committee, before negotiations on the CRPD got underway, a panel of disability experts was convened to discuss the concept of disability that was to be enshrined in the Convention. The panel stated that the aim of the discussion was:

> Not to derive an international definition for disability that would be employed as a mechanism for determining who is covered under a disability/human rights convention. Rather, the purpose of examining concepts of disability was to aid in the systematic determination of the Convention's scope, because the viewpoint of what disability is may determine the actual rights that are conferred.[2]

The focus of that panel mirrors the outcome of the negotiations on the CRPD, whereby the delegates eventually came to the realisation that the formulation of a conceptual understanding of disability was more important to the determination of substantive rights than agreeing on an actual definition of disability.[3] Consensus was reached during the negotiations that if a definition of disability was to be included in the Convention, it must be based on the social model of disability, rather than the out-dated medical model. The desire to formulate a conception of disability which reflected the changing understanding of disability at the international level is borne out by the information contained in the *travaux préparatoires*. The Ad Hoc Committee of the CRPD recognised at an early stage of the negotiation process that:

---

[2] Second Session of the Ad Hoc Committee on a Comprehensive and Integral International Convention on Protection and Promotion of the Rights and Dignity of Persons with Disabilities New York, 16–27 June 2003, Report of the Committee, UN Doc. A/58/118 & Corr.13 July 2003, available at www.un.org/esa/socdev/enable/rights/ahc2panel3.htm last accessed 5 October 2014.

[3] Stefan Trömel states that 'it was clear from the start of the negotiation process that to try to arrive at an internationally agreed definition of disability would be an almost impossible task.' [S. Trömel, 'A Personal Perspective on the Drafting History of the United Nations Convention on the Rights of Persons with Disabilities' in G. Quinn and L. Waddington (eds.) *European Yearbook of Disability Law: Volume 1* (Intersentia, Antwerp, 2009), at page 121].

> There is a range of definitions of disability adopted at the international level. This reflects different purposes as well as changes in the understanding of disability. [...] The Convention should contain a definition of disability that reflects an understanding of disability as something which is the result of social and environmental factors.[4]

During the negotiations, the Australian delegate pointed to the fact that while the social model of disability is important, 'disability seen purely as a function of the environment would render a definition unworkable.'[5] As alluded to in chapter two above, it can be argued that the primary weakness of the social model of disability, in its strictest form, is its lack of focus on impairment itself.[6] In other words, one of the inherent limitations of a strict version of the social model stems from the fact that it cannot accommodate disadvantages that result directly from an impairment, as opposed to those which arise from a socially constructed barrier. In view of this, delegates were of the opinion that the Convention should endorse a conceptualisation of disability which stems from the social model theoretical framework but which also works on the concept of impairment and disability. Paragraph (e) of the Preamble of the CRPD recognises that:

> Disability is an evolving concept and that disability results from the interaction between persons with impairments and attitudinal and environmental barriers that hinders their full and effective participation in society on an equal basis with others.[7]

The Preamble must be read in conjunction with Article 1[8] of the CRPD, which has been termed a 'non-definition of disability.'[9] It provides as follows:

---

4 Ad Hoc Committee on a Comprehensive and Integral International Convention on Protection and Promotion of the Rights and Dignity of Persons with Disabilities (New York), 16–27 June 2003 Compilation of proposals for a Comprehensive and Integral International Convention to Promote and Protect the Rights and Dignity of Persons with Disabilities, available at www.un.org/esa/socdev/enable/rights/a_ac265_2003_crp13.htm accessed 6th October 2014.

5 Fourth Session of the Ad Hoc Committee on Article 2 CRPD, Volume 5(1), August 23 2004, available at www.un.org/esa/socdev/enable/rights/ahc4sumart03.htm, last accessed 6 October 2014.

6 For a critique of this aspect of the social model of disability, see D. Marks 'Dimensions of Oppression: Theorising the Embodied Subject,' (1999) 14(5) *Disability & Society* 611; See also, B. Hughes and K. Paterson, 'The Social Model of Disability and the Disappearing Body: Towards a Sociology of Impairment,' (1997) 12(3) *Disability & Society* 325.

7 UN CRPD, preamble para. (e).

8 One might question whether the unique positioning of the concept of disability in Article 1, which outlines the purpose of the CRPD, is significant from the point of view of the obligations engendered by the Convention. The simple answer is that it has ramifications for State Parties, due to the fact that States cannot declare a reservation to Article 1. Article 46 of the CRPD provides that reservations incompatible with the object and purpose of the Convention are not permitted. By implication, the concept of disability enshrined in Article 1 of the CRPD must be adhered to by all State Parties which have ratified the Convention. This has important implications for disability discrimination laws on a global scale as it means that States will find it extremely difficult to limit the application of the provisions of the Convention.

9 M. Schulze, *Understanding The UN Convention On The Rights Of Persons With Disabilities: A handbook on the human rights of persons with disabilities: A Handbook on the Human Rights of Persons with Disabilities* (July 2010), at page 39, available at www.hrea.org/erc/Library/display_doc.php?url=http%3A%2F%2Fwww.hiproweb.org%2Fuploads%2Ftx_hidrtdocs%2FHICRPDManual2010.pdf&external=N last accessed 24 June 2014.

> Persons with disabilities include those who have long-term physical, mental, intellectual or sensory impairments, which in interaction with various barriers may hinder their full and effective participation in society on an equal basis with others.[10]

Article 1 of the CRPD is open-ended, in so far as the category of persons with disabilities intended to be covered by the wording of that provision is not exhaustive. The interactional nature of the concept of disability contained in Article 1 is mirrored in the Preamble, as both provisions acknowledge the role of societal barriers in the process of disablement. However, the CRPD does not view disability as being entirely socially constructed. Rather, it recognises the relevance of individual impairments. The CRPD acknowledges that it is the interactional relationship between people with impairments and the wider environment which brings about disability. This might suggest that while the overall conception of disability is based on the social model, a strict social model approach was not intended to be adopted by the drafters. Instead, a social-contextual model of disability prevailed.

3.2. The Human Rights-Based Understanding of Disability

It is important to note that the CRPD goes beyond conceptualising disability in terms of a social-contextual framework. The concept of disability contained in the Convention is also grounded in the core notion of human dignity[11] and it acknowledges the fact that disability should be addressed from the perspective of human rights rather than from a social welfare perspective. It recognises the fact that persons with disabilities are holders of rights on an equal basis with others and that they are not objects of charity. A point which sets the human rights model apart from the social and medical models of disability is the fact that the human rights model recognises that 'failing to counteract the unequal position of people with disabilities perpetuates their social stigma and the attitudes that maintain subordination.'[12] Thus, States must take all necessary measures to remove barriers which hinder participation and inclusion of persons with disabilities in society in order that they are in a position to enjoy human rights on an equal basis with their non-disabled counterparts.

The conceptual framework of the CRPD is clearly very progressive. In conjunction with its equality and non-discrimination norms, the Convention has the potential to effect far-reaching changes in the protection of the rights of persons with disabilities. It is to the CRPD's equality and non-discrimination provisions that I now turn.

---

10 UN CRPD, Article 1.

11 The object and purpose of the CRPD contained in Article 1 (which also contains the elaboration on the meaning of 'persons with disabilities') includes promotion of respect for the inherent dignity of persons with disabilities in the purpose of the Convention. The concept of dignity also features throughout some of the substantive articles of the Convention [see, for instance, Article 8(1)(a), Article 16(4), Article 24(1)(a) and Article 25(d), as well as in the General Principles of the CRPD (see Article 3(a)].

12 M.A. Stein & P.J.S. Stein, 'Beyond Disability Civil Rights' (2007) 58 *Hastings Law Journal* 1203, at page 1209.

4. Legal Interpretation of Article 5 of the CRPD

The subsections which follow will comprise an in-depth legal interpretation and critical analysis of the equality and non-discrimination norms in the CRPD, contained primarily in Article 5. The analysis of those norms will be conducted, in part, using the tripartite typology of States' obligations under international human rights law.

4.1. The Tripartite Typology of States' Obligations under International Human Rights Law

The obligations of States Parties under international human rights treaties have been categorised into a tripartite typology. The concept of a tripartite typology of human rights was first introduced by Henry Shue, who highlighted the fact that States have an obligation under international human rights law 'to avoid depriving,' 'to protect from deprivation' and 'to aid the deprived.'[13] Asbjørn Eide characterised State responsibility as arising at three levels, namely obligations to respect, to protect and to fulfil. With regard to the passive obligation to respect, Eide maintains that it:

> Requires the State, and thereby all its organs and agents, to abstain from doing anything that violates the integrity of the individual or infringes on his or her freedom, including the freedom to use the material resources available to that individual in the way he or she finds to satisfy basic needs.[14]

Eide notes that the obligation to *protect* 'requires from the State and its agents the measures necessary to prevent other individuals or groups from violating the integrity, freedom of action or other human rights of the individual – including the prevention of infringements of his or her material resources.'[15] He further observes that the obligation to *fulfil* 'requires the State to take the measures necessary to ensure for each person opportunities to obtain satisfaction of those needs, recognized in the human rights instruments, which cannot be secured by personal efforts.'[16]

The tripartite typology has also been employed by the UNCESCR and the Committee's version of the typology has been endorsed by Eide.[17] In a similar vein to Eide's typology of State obligations, the typology adopted by the UNCESCR has

13 H. Shue, *Basic Rights, Substinence, Affluence and U.S. Foreign Policy* (Princeton University Press, Princeton, 2nd edition, 1996), at page 160.

14 A. Eide, 'Realisation of Social and Economic Rights and the Minimum Threshold Approach' (1989) 10(1–2) *Human Rights Law Journal* 36, at page 37.

15 Ibid.

16 Ibid.

17 A. Eide, 'Economic, Social and Cultural Rights as Human Rights' in A. Eide, C. Krause and A. Rosas (eds.), *Economic, Social and Cultural Rights: A Textbook* (Martinus Nijhoff, Dordrecht/London, 2nd edition, 2001), at pages 9–28.

three levels – obligations to protect, to respect and to fulfil.[18] The latter obligation is further broken down by the Committee into obligations to facilitate, to provide and to promote.[19] The Committee has stated that the obligation to fulfil (facilitate) 'requires States to take positive measures that enable and assist individuals and communities to enjoy'[20] a particular right. The Committee observes that States are obliged to fulfil (provide) a specific right in the Covenant 'when an individual or group is unable, for reasons beyond their control, to realize the right themselves by the means at their disposal [...].'[21] The obligation to fulfil (promote) is related essentially to education and awareness-raising duties for States.

In the context of persons with disabilities, the obligation to respect is an immediate obligation which requires States Parties to the CRPD to abstain from discrimination or, otherwise stated, to refrain from interfering with the right of people with disabilities to equality. For example, States must not engage in any discriminatory act, custom or practice or enact laws, policies or institutional structures that create discriminatory barriers for people with disabilities. The obligation to protect persons with disabilities is also an immediate duty. It requires States to take active measures to prevent and eliminate discrimination and violations of the right to equality by third parties, both State and non-State actors, including by private individuals, organisations and private enterprises or other non-State actors, as well as other States and inter-governmental organisations. States Parties must prevent, investigate, punish and ensure redress for the harm caused by abuses of disability rights by third parties. Under the CPRD, the obligation to protect is particularly important as a considerable degree of discrimination against disabled people stems from the private sphere of society. The obligation to fulfil (facilitate) requires States to take all necessary measures, including positive action measures, to enable and assist individuals and communities to enjoy their rights in practice. The obligation to fulfil (provide) requires states to ensure access to the right in question in instances where the particular individual or group cannot realise the right by themselves. In order to meet the obligation to fulfil (facilitate and provide), States Parties to the CRPD must ensure *de jure* and *de facto* equality. This will involve the adoption of legislative, administrative, policy, programmatic and positive action measures to implement the rights of persons with disabilities. Finally, the obligation to fulfil (promote) requires States to engage in awareness-raising and educational measures with regard to the rights of persons with disabilities.

The tripartite typology of State obligations has been deemed to provide a helpful analytical tool,[22] to the extent that this framework of classification clarifies the nature and scope of relevant State obligations. It points to the fact that the implementation of

---

18 UNCESCR, General Comment 14, The right to the highest attainable standard of health (article 12 of the International Covenant on Economic, Social and Cultural Rights), para. 33., (adopted on 11 August 2000 Twenty-second session, 2000), U.N. Doc. E/C.12/2000/4 (2000).

19 Ibid.

20 UNCESCR, General Comment No. 13: The Right to Education (Article 13 of the Covenant), para. 47 (adopted on 8 December 1999) U.N. Doc. E/C.12/1999/10.

21 Ibid.

22 Ibid, at page 12.

human rights requires more than mere non-interference on the part of States. Rather, it ascribes an active role to States. Magdalena Sepúlveda argues that such typologies 'have contributed to overcoming the simplified view that each set of human rights falls into a neat category [...] The typologies are analytical frameworks that explain that the complete fulfilment of each human right requires the performance of multiple kinds of duties.' Moreover, she claims that:

> By analysing the different levels of State duties imposed by each human right (civil, political, economic, social or cultural), it is easier to assess what specific State behaviours are necessary or compulsory for the implementation of a right, thereby increasing the understanding of its content.[23]

Having said that, the typology framework has its inherent limitations. Henry Shue (the 'father' of the tripartite typology) himself observed that 'typologies are at best abstract instruments for temporarily fending off the complexities of concrete reality that threaten to overwhelm our circuits.'[24] As such, the tripartite typology of State obligations will only be referred to occasionally below (where necessary) in order to facilitate the interpretation of the equality and non-discrimination norms in the Convention. I will now turn to an examination of the constituent elements of Article 5 of the CRPD. I will interpret each of the subsections of Article 5 in turn.

4.2. Article 5(1) of the CRPD

> **States Parties recognize that all persons are equal before and under the law and are entitled without any discrimination to the equal protection and equal benefit of the law.**

The text highlighted above represents the final text of Article 5(1) of the CRPD. It differs from the original suggestion of the Working Group of the Convention, which was formulated as follows: 'States Parties recognise that all persons are equal before the law and are entitled without any discrimination to the equal protection of the law.' As we can see, the guarantees of equality under the law and equal benefit of the law were added to the final text of Article 5(1). In light of the differences between the two texts, it is important to appraise the original terms chosen by the Working Group and to go on to interpret the additional terms that made it into the final text of Article 5(1). This will allow a determination of the substantive value which they add, if any, to the rights of persons with disabilities.

---

23 Ibid.

24 H. Shue, *Basic Rights, Substinence, Affluence and U.S. Foreign Policy* (Princeton University Press, Princeton, 2nd Edition, 1996), at page 160.

4.2.1. The Guarantee of 'Equality Before the Law' and 'Equal Protection of the Law' Without Discrimination

The terms 'equality before the law,' 'equal protection of the law' and 'non-discrimination by way of the law' are deemed to express 'related but distinct ideas.'[25] A perusal of the drafting history of the CRPD reveals little information regarding the interpretation of the term 'equality before the law.' The Mexican delegate pointed to the fact that 'equality before the law is formal, requiring equal treatment.'[26] It was also distinguished clearly from the concept of equality of opportunities in the negotiations.[27] Apart from this, the information which can be gleaned from the drafting history is sparse. However, it is notable that the right to 'equality before the law' is guaranteed by several provisions in international human rights treaties, including Article 14(1) and Article 26 of the ICCPR, Article 5(a) CERD and Article 15 CEDAW. Article 26 of the ICCPR has been interpreted widely by legal scholars. It reads as follows:

> All persons are equal before the law and are entitled without any discrimination to the equal protection of the law. In this respect, the law shall prohibit any discrimination and guarantee to all persons equal and effective protection against discrimination on any ground such as race, colour, sex, language, religion, political or other opinion, national or social origin, property, birth or other status.[28]

Manfred Nowak offers a respected interpretation of the phrase 'equality before the law' under Article 26 of the ICCPR in his assertion that it 'does not give rise to a claim of whatever nature to substantive equality but instead solely to a formal claim that existing laws be applied in the same manner to all those subject to them.'[29] In other words, it is aimed exclusively at the application and enforcement of the law. It means that judges and administrative officials must not act arbitrarily in enforcing laws. This interpretation is consolidated by the UNCESCR in its General Comment 16 (2005) on the equal rights of men and women, wherein the Committee states as follows: 'the principle of equality before the law must be respected by administrative agencies, and courts and tribunals, and implies that those authorities must apply the law equally to men and women.'[30]

---

25 A. Eide & T. Opsahl, 'Equality and Non-Discrimination' (Written communication presented in Proceedings of the 7th International Colloquy on the European Convention on Human Rights) at page 103, cited by L. Weiwei, 'Equality and Non-Discrimination under International Human Rights Law,' (Norwegian Centre for Human Rights, University of Oslo, 2004), Page 20, available at www.mittendrinundaussenvor.de/fileadmin/bilder/0304.pdf, last accessed 14 October 2014.

26 Third Session of the Ad Hoc Committee of Article 5 CRPD, May 25 2004, volume 4(2), available at www.un.org/esa/socdev/enable/rights/ahc3sum7.htm, accessed 9th October 2012.

27 See, for example, Comments of Australia, Fifth Session of the Ad Hoc Committee on, volume 5(3), August 25, 2004, available at www.un.org/esa/socdev/enable/rights/adhocmeetings.htm, accessed 14 October 2014.

28 ICCPR, Article 26.

29 M. Nowak, *UN Covenant on Civil and Political Rights: CCPR commentary* (N.P. Engel Publisher, Kehl, 2nd Edition, 2005), at page 605.

30 UNCESCR, General Comment 16 (2005) on the equal right of men and women to the enjoyment of all economic, social and cultural rights (art. 3 of the International Covenant on Economic, Social and

An analysis of the *travaux préparatoires* of the CRPD reveals little information about the interpretation of the phrase 'equal protection of the law.' Therefore, it is useful to turn once again to Nowak's account of the interpretation of the same phrase in the context of the ICCPR. In contrast to the notion of 'equality before the law,' Nowak asserts that the phrase 'equal protection of the law' in the ICCPR is directed at the national legislature, which is bound to protect the right to equality without any discrimination.[31] In a similar vein, Lester et al. contend that 'the requirement of "equal protection of the law" is directed at the national legislator, who should not adopt or maintain discriminatory legislative standards.'[32] Lester states that the guarantee of 'equal protection of the law' 'secures *de jure* equality (or equality in law) so that the law itself dispenses rights and benefits to all equally.'[33] This interpretation of Article 26 ICCPR accords with the interpretation of the same provision by the HRC. In its General Comment 18 (1989), the Committee maintains that Article 26 ICCPR is concerned 'with the obligations imposed on States parties in regard to their legislation and the application thereof. Thus, when legislation is adopted by a State party, it must comply with the requirement of article 26 that its content should not be discriminatory.'[34]

– 'Equality Before the Law' and 'Equal Protection of the Law' in the CRPD: Obligations to Respect and Protect

The obligation to ensure 'equality before the law' falls under the typology of State obligations known as the duty to respect the right to equality. This so-called negative obligation of respect requires States to abstain from engaging in any discriminatory act or practice. In the context of the CRPD and, on an ordinary reading of the term, the obligation to ensure 'equality before the law' requires that no person should be discriminated against by the judiciary or law-enforcement officers in the application or enforcement of the law on account of their disability.

The phrase 'equal protection of the law' in Article 5(1) of the CRPD imposes an obligation on national legislatures to refrain from any discrimination against disabled people when enacting laws and policies. This represents the so-called negative aspect of the obligation of non-discrimination imposed by Article 5(1). On a contextual reading of the term, it is argued that the entitlement to 'equal protection of the law without any discrimination' also imposes positive duties on States, in

---

Cultural Rights), adopted at the thirty- fourth session of the Committee, 2005, U.N. Doc. E/C.12/2005/3, para. 9.

31 M. Nowak, *UN Covenant on Civil and Political Rights: CCPR commentary* (N.P. Engel Publishers, Kehl, 2nd Edition 2005), at page 607.

32 Lord Lester of Herne Hill QC and S. Joseph, 'Obligations of Non-Discrimination' in D. Harris and S. Joseph (eds.), *The International Covenant on Civil and Political Rights and United Kingdom Law* (Clarendon Press, Oxford, 1995), at page 566.

33 Lord Lester of Herne Hill QC, 'Non Discrimination in International Human Rights Law,' in *Developing Human Rights Jurisprudence* (Volume 6: Sixth Judicial Colloquium on the Domestic Application of International Human Rights Norms: Bloemfontein, South Africa, 3–5 September 1993), at page 11.

34 Human Rights Committee, General Comment 18 on Non Discrimination (adopted at the thirty seventh session of the Human Rights Committee on 10 November 1989), para. 12.

light of the fact that it must be read in conjunction with Article 4(b) of the CRPD. Article 4(b) is a general obligation of the Convention which requires States 'to take all appropriate measures, including legislation, to modify or abolish existing laws, regulations, customs and practices that constitute discrimination against persons with disabilities.'[35] In short, the requirement of 'equal protection of the law' appears to mandate that domestic legislatures do not maintain laws that discriminate against people with disabilities and that they also take steps, in line with Article 4(b), to modify or abolish existing laws that constitute discrimination against persons with disabilities.

All of the core human rights treaty bodies make a distinction between *de jure* discrimination (discrimination in law) and *de facto* discrimination (discrimination in fact). The treaty bodies consider the elimination of *de jure* discrimination to be an essential pre-requisite for the attainment of *de facto* equality. Vandenhole points to the fact that the CEDAW Committee, in particular, has drawn attention to the importance of eliminating *de jure* discrimination.[36] In order to comply with the obligations inherent in the right to equal protection of the law, the CEDAW Committee has declared that States Parties are required to review all existing laws and amend discriminatory provisions in consultation with women's groups[37] in order that they are compatible with CEDAW.[38] In its concluding observations to Gabon, the CEDAW Committee urged the State Party concerned 'to accelerate the process of legal reform to eliminate discriminatory provisions,' as well as 'to establish a concrete programme and timetable for such a reform process and to activate fully the [...] committee established for the purpose of reviewing the discriminatory aspects of the various codes.'[39] The Committee also encouraged Gabon 'to step up its efforts to increase awareness about the importance of legal reform for achieving *de jure* and *de facto* equality for women in accordance with its obligations under the Convention.'[40] These observations are important in terms of the obligations of States Parties to the CRPD. Article 4(3) of the CRPD requires that States consult closely with and involve actively people with disabilities in the development and implementation of non-discrimination legislation. It is therefore imperative that States Parties to

---

35 UN CRPD, Article 4(b).

36 Vandenhole observes that 'strong emphasis is put on the elimination of discriminatory legislation in the CEDAW Committee's concluding observations. As *de jure* equality is considered a necessary prerequisite for achieving de facto equality of women, detailed recommendations have been given [by the CEDAW Committee] to review discriminatory legislation in all fields of life.' [W. Vandenhole, *Non-Discrimination and Equality in the View of the UN Human Rights Treaty Bodies* (Intersentia, Antwerp/Oxford, 2005), at page 271].

37 UN Committee on the Elimination of Discrimination against Women, Report of the Committee, Twenty-seventh session, UN Doc. A/57/38 (Part II), para. 191 [cited by W. Vandenhole, *Non-Discrimination and Equality in the View of the UN Human Rights Treaty Bodies* (Intersentia, Antwerp/Oxford, 2005), at page 242].

38 UN Committee on the Elimination of Discrimination against Women, Concluding Observations to Turkey, Un Doc. CEDAW/C/TUR/CC/4–5, para. 26, cited by W. Vandenhole, *Non-Discrimination and Equality in the View of the UN Human Rights Treaty Bodies* (Intersentia, Antwerp/Oxford, 2005), at page 242.

39 UN Committee on the Elimination of Discrimination against Women, Concluding Observations to Gabon, UN Doc., CEDAW/C/GAB/CC/2–5, para. 23.

40 Ibid.

the Convention consult with people with disabilities, through their representative organisations, at all stages of the legal reform process. This participatory process is a vital means by which States can work towards the creation of inclusive societies, in which people with disabilities can participate on an equal basis with others.

To the extent that the obligations of 'equality before the law' and 'equal protection of the law' require abstention from discrimination, they are deemed to be obligations of immediate effect.[41] In its General Comment 11 (1999), the UNCESCR states that 'non-discrimination must be implemented fully and immediately.'[42] It is submitted that national authorities will not be permitted to delay in the initiation of the law reform process and will be required to establish, as soon as possible, a concrete programme for reform of discriminatory legislation and policies, in line with the observations of the CEDAW Committee above.

4.2.2. The Requirements of 'Equality Under the Law' and 'Equal Benefit of the Law'

In this subsection it is proposed to examine the additional phrases that were added to the final text of Article 5(1) of the CRPD by delegates – namely the guarantees of 'equality under the law' and 'equal benefit of the law.' Those human rights guarantees are unique to the CRPD and are not contained in non-discrimination clauses in other international human rights treaties. Therefore, there are no sources from which to draw inspiration at the level of international human rights law. It is important to investigate how these amendments to the CRPD came about and the implications, if any, of those additional terms with regard to the rights of persons with disabilities.

During the negotiations on the CRPD, it was the Canadian delegate who suggested that the text of the Working Group should be amended by adding in these additional guarantees of equality.[43] The amendments reflect the wording of Section 15(1) of the Canadian Charter of Rights and Freedoms[44] and they gained widespread support among delegates during the negotiation process. In the Canadian context, the guarantee of 'equal benefit of the law' in particular has been accorded a wide interpretation and has been aligned with a positive or substantive right to equality

41 Vandenhole states that all of the Committees overseeing the implementation of the human rights treaties 'have emphasised the immediate character of the obligation to abstain from discrimination. This obligation is subject to neither progressive realisation nor the availability of resources.' [W. Vandenhole, *Non-Discrimination and Equality in the View of the UN Human Rights Treaty Bodies* (Intersentia, Antwerp/Oxford, 2005), at page 188/189].

42 UNCESCR, General Comment 11 on Article 14: Plans of Action for Primary Education, (1999) (adopted at the twentieth session of the Committee, 1999), UN Doc. E/2000/22, para. 10.

43 Third Session of the Ad Hoc Committee on Article 5 CRPD, May 25 2004 available at www.un.org/esa/socdev/enable/rights/adhocmeetings.htm, accessed 9 October 2013.

44 Section 15(1) of the Canadian Charter of Rights and Freedoms provides that 'every individual is equal before and under the law and has the right to equal protection and equal benefit of the law without discrimination based on race, national or ethnic origin, colour, religion, sex, age, or mental or physical disability.'

in a few cases.[45] Before reflecting on the Canadian interpretation of this particular guarantee below, I will look briefly to the drafting history of the CRPD.

Unfortunately, there is little information contained in the *travaux préparatoires* which might help in the interpretation of the guarantees of 'equality under the law' and equal benefit of the law. During the negotiation sessions, it was stated that equality under the law is achieved 'through strict respect for non-discrimination'[46] and therefore it would not appear to have been aligned with a right to substantive equality by the drafters of the Convention. At first glance, it would appear that the phrase 'equality under the law' comes under the umbrella framework of formal equality, together with the term 'equality before the law.' However, it is argued that 'equality under the law' differs somewhat from 'equality before the law,' despite the fact that these terms are often used interchangeably in practice.[47] As stated above, 'equality before the law' requires that no person should be discriminated against by the judiciary or law-enforcement officers in the application or enforcement of the law on account of their disability. The phrase 'equality under the law,' taken on its ordinary meaning, implies that the substance of the law should be equal, to the extent that all groups in society are treated equally and fairly under the law. This interpretation is confirmed by academic commentary. William Lacy contends that the requirement of 'equality under the law' would insist 'that legal standards be general in the sense, first, that their content is the same for all to whom they apply, and second, that their range of application should be as broad as possible, normally including all citizens or all in a jurisdiction.'[48]

The interpretation of the phrase 'equal benefit of the law' is particularly interesting on account of the fact that it has been given a broad interpretation in the Canadian context. It is proposed to look briefly to that context, bearing in mind that it is a specific interpretation, confined to Canadian jurisprudence.[49] Nonetheless, it is worthwhile to build a picture of this novel term in international human rights law. In the landmark case of *Eldridge v British Colombia (Attorney General)*,[50] the Canadian Supreme Court ruled that when the government or its agents provide a service or benefit to the public, it must make special efforts to ensure that all persons have an equal opportunity to take advantage of that service or benefit. The central issue in

[45] See, for example, *Eldridge v. British Columbia (A.G.)*, [1997] 3 S.C.R. 624 and *Vriend* v. *Alberta* (1998) 132 D.L.R. (4th) 595 (Alta. C.A.).

[46] Fifth Session of the Ad Hoc Committee, January 24, 2005, volume 6(1), available at www.un.org/esa/socdev/enable/rights/adhocmeetings.htm, accessed 16 October 2014.

[47] In that regard, William Lacy states that 'both notions, frequently to the fore in judicial and various other statements of and about the law, are so familiar that we tend not to regard them as separate, running both together because – another common assumption, this – they are surely simply part of, or reducible to, or derivable from, the 'rule of law' ideal.' [W. Lacy, 'Equality Under and Before the Law' (2011) 61(3) *University of Toronto Law Journal* 411, at page 412.].

[48] W. Lacy, 'Equality Under and Before the Law' (2011) 61(3) *University of Toronto Law Journal* 411, at page 415.

[49] It is interesting to note that Section 9(1) of the South African Constitution also contains the phrase 'equal benefit of the law.' It states that: 'Everyone is equal before the law and has the right to equal protection and benefit of the law.'

[50] *Eldridge v. British Columbia (A.G.)* [1997] 3 S.C.R. 624.

the *Eldridge* case was the refusal of the government of British Columbia to provide sign language interpretation to deaf patients through provincial legislation[51] (which provided free medical services to citizens) in order to enable them to communicate effectively with their health care providers. The key question in the case was whether the appellants had been afforded equal benefit of the law without discrimination within the meaning of Article 15 of the Canadian Charter. The respondent argued that the legislation in question afforded free medical services equally to both the hearing and deaf populations and therefore that the legislation was not discriminatory on its face. However, the Supreme Court ruled that the failure to ensure equality of opportunity in the *Eldridge* case constituted adverse effects (indirect) discrimination against deaf persons.[52] In essence, the Court ruled that the failure of the Medical Services Commission and hospitals to provide sign language interpretation where it is necessary for effective communication denied the deaf patients of the equal benefit of the law and discriminated against them in comparison with persons of full hearing.[53] The Court held that 'the principle that discrimination can accrue from a failure to take positive steps to ensure that disadvantaged groups benefit equally from services offered to the general public is widely accepted in the human rights field.' The Court stated that it is also 'a cornerstone of human rights jurisprudence that the duty to take positive action to ensure that members of disadvantaged groups benefit equally from services offered to the general public is subject to the principle of reasonable accommodation.'[54] The Court also remarked that the notion that governments should be entitled to provide benefits to the general population without ensuring that disadvantaged members of society have the resources to take full advantage of those benefits 'bespeaks a thin and impoverished vision of [Section 15(1)].'[55] As Colm O'Cinneide notes, the positive provision required of the State in *Eldridge* was 'a question of reasonable accommodation to enable individuals to access, on an equal basis, services which were open to all.'[56]

Of course, there is no implication that this particular interpretation will translate automatically to Article 5(1) of the CRPD or that the CRPD Committee would even be inclined towards such an interpretation. In the absence of specific guidance in the

---

51 The relevant pieces of legislation were the Medical and Health Care Services Act [S.B.C. 1992, c. 76 (now the Medicare Protection Act, R.S.B.C. 1996, c. 286), ss. 1 , 4(1)(c), (j), 6, 8)] and the Hospital Insurance Act [R.S.B.C. 1979, c. 180 (now R.S.B.C. 1996, c. 204), ss. 3(1), 5(1), 9, 10(1), 29(b)].

52 *Eldridge v. British Columbia (A.G.)*, [1997] 3 S.C.R. 624.

53 The Court stated as follows: 'Although the standard set is broad, this is not to say that sign language interpretation will have to be provided in every medical situation. The "effective communication" standard is a flexible one, and will take into consideration such factors as the complexity and importance of the information to be communicated, the context in which the communications will take place and the number of people involved. For deaf persons with limited literacy skills, sign language interpretation can be surmised to be required in most cases.' [Ibid, at para. 625].

54 Ibid.

55 *Eldridge v. British Columbia (A.G.)*, [1997] 3 S.C.R. 624.

56 C. O'Cinneide, 'Extracting Protection for the Rights of Persons with Disabilities from Human Rights Frameworks: Established Limits and New Possibilities' in O.M. Arnardottir and G. Quinn (eds.), *The UN Convention on the Rights of Persons with Disabilities: European and Scandinavian Perspectives* (Martinus Nijhoff, Leiden, 2009), at page 177. In the words of the Court, the 'appellants [...] ask only for equal access to services that are available to all.' [*Eldridge v. British Columbia (A.G.)*, [1997] 3 S.C.R. 624, para. 92].

drafting history of the Convention and also in the absence of guidance at the level of international human rights law, it is difficult to come to a definitive conclusion on the possible interpretation of the guarantee of 'equal benefit of the law.' Nonetheless, it is argued here that an examination of that term, according to the rules of interpretation in the VCLT, leads to much more than a guarantee of mere formal equality. Benefiting from the law implies that citizens will be able to enjoy the rights guaranteed by legislation in practice. In order to facilitate the enjoyment of rights guaranteed by legislation to persons with disabilities on an equal basis with others (in other words, in order to guarantee the equal benefit of the law to persons with disabilities), this will require positive measures on the part of States in certain circumstances. For example, if domestic legislation guarantees a right to free primary education for all its citizens, the implementation of that right would necessitate the adoption of additional measures to enable persons with disabilities to avail of the right or to enable them to benefit equally from it. Such measures might include accessibility measures or putting in place reasonable accommodations or individualised supports. In the absence of such measures, the right itself would be negated in the context of many people with disabilities who would not be able to enjoy and exercise the right to education due to their particular impairments. Interpreting the phrase in any other manner would not do justice to the spirit and tenor of the Convention as a whole. Reading the phrase 'equal benefit of the law' in its broader context, the interpretation above would appear to be confirmed. The general principles of the Convention include the guiding tenets of 'equality of opportunity'[57] and 'accessibility,'[58] both of which require the elimination of barriers to the enjoyment of rights proscribed by legislation. Breaking down barriers to ensure the equal benefit of the law to disabled people may require that additional resources are accorded to persons with disabilities so that they can take advantage of the rights which are available to others. A contextual interpretation of Article 5 of the CRPD also confirms the fact that ensuring the equal benefit of the law to persons with disabilities will require States to take positive measures in certain instances. In that regard, the other sub-sections of Article 5 must be considered. The inclusion of the duty to accommodate within the equality and non-discrimination paradigm provides concrete support for the interpretation presented above. In addition, the general obligation on States in Article 4(1)(a) of the CRPD to 'adopt all appropriate legislative, administrative *and other measures* for the implementation of the rights'[59] [emphasis added] contained in the CRPD strengthens the contention that ensuring the equal benefit of the law to persons with disabilities may require positive measures. In order that disabled people (and all other citizens) can benefit from the law, the rights in question must not merely be enshrined in legislation but must actually be implemented and, according to Article 4(1)(a) of the CPRD, all necessary measures must be taken to ensure that disabled people can benefit from the law on an equal basis with others. Finally, turning to the purpose of the CRPD in Article 1, this legitimates the taking of positive measures in certain circumstances to ensure the full and equal enjoyment

57 UN CRPD, Article 3(e).
58 UN CRPD, Article 3(f).
59 UN CRPD, Article 4(1)(a).

or benefit of rights to disabled people, those rights being proscribed by legislation and being available to the general population.

It remains to be seen whether the guarantee of 'equal benefit of the law' will be interpreted by the CRPD Committee as reflecting a more substantive or even transformative version of equality for people with disabilities. In other words, will the Committee deem that this additional term in Article 5(1) of the CRPD (over and above that contained in non-discrimination clauses in other international human rights treaties) provides greater protection for disabled people? If so, has that provision potential to carry added meaning for persons with disabilities? To date, there is no information which we can garner from the Committee's concluding observations on the interpretation of the phrase 'equal benefit of the law' but it is argued here that the inclusion of the phrase in the CRPD is significant, in the sense that it can potentially serve to tackle invidious and systemic forms of discrimination that are often at the core of the disadvantage faced by disabled people in society. It has the potential to ensure that disabled people can, in fact, exercise and enjoy the rights which are enshrined in legislation, on an equal basis with others.

4.3. Article 5(2) of the CRPD

> **States Parties shall prohibit all 'discrimination on the basis of disability' and guarantee to persons with disabilities equal and effective legal protection against discrimination on all grounds.**

4.3.1. Introduction to Article 5(2) of the CRPD

Article 5(2) of the CRPD sets out the legal requirements necessary for the facilitation of the equality norm. It imposes a positive duty of protection on States Parties to the Convention. Below each of the discrete elements of Article 5(2) of the CRPD will be looked at in turn. The definition of disability-based discrimination in the CRPD will be examined, in the first instance. Thereafter, the prohibition of disability-based discrimination will be considered, followed by an analysis of the obligation to guarantee to persons with disabilities 'equal and effective legal protection against discrimination on all grounds.'

4.3.2. The Definition of Discrimination in the CRPD

The CRPD contains a broad definition of discrimination. In order to consider the various elements of Article 5(2) of the CRPD, it is necessary to refer to Article 2 of the Convention which contains the definition of 'discrimination on the basis of disability.' Article 2 reads as follows:

> Any distinction, exclusion or restriction on the basis of disability which has the purpose or effect of impairing or nullifying the recognition, enjoyment or exercise, on an equal basis with others, of all human rights and fundamental freedoms in the political, economic,

social, cultural, civil or any other field. *It includes all forms of discrimination, including denial of reasonable accommodation.*[60]

The wording of the definition of discrimination contained in Article 2 of the CRPD is mirrored in the definitions contained in other human rights treaties at the international level, notably the definitions contained in CEDAW[61] and CERD.[62] However, there are certain additions to the definition of 'discrimination on the basis of disability' in the CRPD, over and above those contained in other international human rights treaties. In particular, the last line of Article 2, highlighted above in italics, constitutes a significant advancement on traditionally understood discrimination at the level of existing international human rights law. It makes it clear that a duty to accommodate is included as a distinct element of the non-discrimination norm. Denial of reasonable accommodation is not included in other international human rights treaties as a form of discrimination. In that respect, the CRPD goes further than any other UN human rights instrument and, for that reason, the Convention adds considerable value to the equality reform agenda for people with disabilities.

The inclusion of the duty to accommodate within the non-discrimination norm in the CRPD is significant for many reasons, not least due to the fact that it obliges States to take positive measures, tailored to the individualised needs of persons with disabilities. Jenny Goldschmidt contends that by making reasonable accommodations part of the prohibition of discrimination and not merely an exception to the principle of equal treatment 'the whole legal definition of the case is thereby transformed.' She states that one is 'not asked anymore whether it was possible to hire [a] person in a situation where necessary accommodations were not already available; on the contrary, [one has to] demonstrate that the accommodations were *not* possible. This is a fundamental shift.'[63] The duty to accommodate under the CRPD will be discussed in further detail below[64] and in the next chapter of this book. For now, I will concentrate on other discrete aspects of the definition of discrimination on the basis of disability.

---

60 UN CRPD, Article 2 [emphasis added].

61 Article 1 CEDAW defines discrimination against women as: 'Any distinction, exclusion or restriction made on the basis of sex which has the effect or purpose of impairing or nullifying the recognition, enjoyment or exercise by women, irrespective of their marital status, on a basis of equality of men and women, of human rights and fundamental freedoms in the political, economic, social, cultural, civil or any other field.'

62 Article 1(1) CERD defines the term 'racial discrimination' as: 'Any distinction, exclusion, restriction or preference based on race, colour, descent, or national or ethnic origin which has the purpose or effect of nullifying or impairing the recognition, enjoyment or exercise, on an equal footing, of human rights and fundamental freedoms in the political, economic, social, cultural or any other field of public life.'

63 J. Goldschmidt (interviewed by J. Anderson and J. Philips), 'Shifting the Burden of Proof: How the CRPD is Transforming our Understanding of Discrimination, Intersectionality and Priorities' in J. Anderson and J. Philips (eds.), *Disability and Human Rights: Legal, Ethical and Conceptual Implications of the Convention on the Rights of Persons with Disabilities* (Netherlands Institute of Human Rights, SIM Special 35, 2012), at page 57 [emphasis in original].

64 See Section 4.4 of this chapter.

4.3.2.1. Enjoyment of Rights 'On an Equal Basis with Others'

Another noteworthy component of the definition of discrimination in Article 2 of the CRPD is the inclusion of the phrase 'on an equal basis with others.' That phrase is not confined to the definition of 'discrimination on the basis of disability.' Rather, it permeates the CRPD on the whole, appearing thirty-one times throughout the text of the Convention. It is important to examine what is intended by this phrase in the context of the equality and non-discrimination norms in the Convention. The original draft Article 7 of the Working Group contained the following definition of discrimination:

> Discrimination shall mean any distinction, exclusion or restriction which has the purpose or effect of impairing or nullifying the recognition, enjoyment or exercise by persons with disabilities, *on an equal footing*, of all human rights and fundamental freedoms.[65]

It can be observed from the draft definition above that the phrase 'on an equal footing' was replaced by the phrase 'on an equal basis with others' in the final definition of discrimination contained in Article 2 of the CRPD. This was as a result of a proposal made by the Canadian delegate, to which there was general agreement among other delegates.[66] The reason for the amendment would appear, in the words of the Coordinator of the fourth session of the Ad-Hoc Committee, Ambassador Don MacKay (New Zealand), to be due to the fact that the phrase 'on an equal footing' has 'no legal meaning.'[67] This leads to the implication that, by changing the phrase to 'on an equal basis with others,' it was intended that it would have legal meaning. The only international human rights treaty to contain a similar phrase is CEDAW in Articles 1[68] and 3[69] thereof. It is interesting to examine the manner in which the phrase 'on a basis of equality' has been interpreted by the CEDAW Committee. In its General Recommendation 24 (1999) regarding access to health care, the Committee asserts that the duty of States to ensure access to health care services, information and education, *on a basis of equality* between men and women, 'implies an obligation to respect, protect and fulfil women's rights to health care.'[70] The Committee notes

---

65 Original Draft Article 7 of the Working Group to the CRPD, available atwww.un.org/esa/socdev/enable/rights/ahcstata5tscompilation.htm, last accessed 27 October 2014. [emphasis added].

66 Fourth Session of the Ad Hoc Committee on Article 5 CRPD, August 25, 2004, available at www.un.org/esa/socdev/enable/rights/adhocmeetings.htm, accessed 10 October 2014.

67 Fourth Session of the Ad Hoc Committee on Article 5 CRPD, Volume 5(10), September 3, 2004 available at www.un.org/esa/socdev/enable/rights/adhocmeetings.htm, accessed 10 October 2014.

68 Article 1 CEDAW defines the term 'discrimination against women' as: 'Any distinction, exclusion or restriction made on the basis of sex which has the effect or purpose of impairing or nullifying the recognition, enjoyment or exercise by women, irrespective of their marital status, *on a basis of equality* of men and women, of human rights and fundamental freedoms in the political, economic, social, cultural, civil or any other field.' [emphasis added].

69 Article 3 CEDAW provides that: States Parties shall take in all fields, in particular in the political, social, economic and cultural fields, all appropriate measures, including legislation, to ensure the full development and advancement of women, for the purpose of guaranteeing them the exercise and enjoyment of human rights and fundamental freedoms *on a basis of equality* with men [emphasis added].

70 UN Committee on the Elimination of all Forms of Discrimination Against Women, General Recommendation No. 24 on Article 12: Women and Health (1999) (adopted at the Committee's

that States 'have the responsibility to ensure that legislation and executive action and policy comply with these three obligations.'[71] It is evident therefore that the duty to accord rights to women on a basis of equality with men imposes significant obligations on States, which must ensure that they respect, protect and fulfil the substantive rights of women to the same extent as the rights of men are respected, protected and fulfilled. The CEDAW Committee has stated that the obligation to fulfil can entail positive action measures, requiring States Parties to 'take a wide variety of steps to ensure that women and men enjoy equal rights *de jure* and *de facto*, including, where appropriate, the adoption of temporary special measures [...].'[72] In that regard, the Committee notes that 'States parties should consider that they have to fulfil their legal obligations to all women through designing public policies, programmes and institutional frameworks that are aimed at fulfilling the specific needs of women leading to the full development of their potential on an equal basis.'[73] The CEDAW Committee further elaborated on the meaning of the phrase 'on a basis of equality' in its concluding observations on Ireland's second and third periodic reports, in which the Committee urged the Irish Government to ensure that 'legislation and policies create the structural and systemic framework that will lead to women's long-term participation in the labour force on a basis of equality with men.'[74] Those observations serve to highlight the fact that the CEDAW Committee appears to equate the phrase 'on a basis of equality' with *de facto* equality (or equality in practice). The UNCESCR also equates the phrase 'on a basis of equality' with *de facto* equality. In the context of Article 3 of the Covenant, the UNCESCR stated, in its General Comment 16 (2005), that the term 'on a basis of equality' is 'a concept that carries substantive meaning.'[75] The Committee went on to align it with *de facto* equality when it observed that the enjoyment of human rights on the basis of equality between men and women 'must be understood comprehensively. Guarantees of non-discrimination and equality in international human rights treaties mandate both *de facto* and *de jure* equality.'[76]

Controversy arose during the negotiation process leading up to the adoption of the CRPD with regard to the level of protection that might be afforded to people with disabilities under the Convention. Several delegates feared that disabled people would be accorded rights over and above those afforded to other segments of the population.

---

twentieth session, 1999), U.N. Doc. A/54/38, para. 13.

71 Ibid.

72 UN Committee on the Elimination of all Forms of Discrimination Against Women, General Recommendation 28: The Core Obligations of States Parties under Article 2 of the Convention on the Elimination of All Forms of Discrimination against Women (adopted on 16 December 2010), UN Doc. CEDAW/C/GC/28, para. 9.

73 Ibid.

74 Concluding comments of the UN Committee on the Elimination of Discrimination against Women to Ireland (Combined second and third periodic report), comments adopted at the Twenty-first session, 7–25 June 1999 Excerpted from: Supplement No. 38 (A/54/38/Rev.1) at para. 182, available at www.un.org/.../cedaw/cedaw25years/.../Ireland/Ireland-CO-2–3.pdf last accessed 24 September 2014.

75 UNCESCR, General Comment 16 (2005) on the equal right of men and women to the enjoyment of all economic, social and cultural rights (Article 3 of the ICESCR), adopted at the thirty-fourth session of the Committee, Geneva, 25 April-13 May 2005, UN Doc. E/C.12/2005/ (2005), para. 6.

76 Ibid, para. 7.

In fact, this appears to be the reason that the phrase 'on an equal basis with others' was included in the CRPD in the first instance. Marianne Schulze argues that the phrase was intended to act as 'a guarantee that persons with disabilities are not given more protection than others in a Member State.'[77] Notwithstanding the rationale underlying the insertion of the phrase 'on an equal basis with others' in the CRPD (as evidenced by the drafting history), an examination of the ordinary meaning of the phrase, in its context, allows for a more expansive interpretation. Some people might argue that the ordinary meaning of the phrase means that disabled people must not be granted additional measures of protection. I would disagree with that interpretation. I will argue in the next section of this chapter that the overall model of equality contained in the Convention is both a substantive and transformative equality model, which seeks to ensure equality in practice for persons with disabilities. If one reads the phrase 'on an equal basis with others' in conjunction with the purpose of the CRPD, this would indicate that an interpretation of the phrase as giving effect to *de facto* equality is not inconsistent with that purpose. The purpose of the Convention is stated expressly in Article 1 as being, *inter alia*, to 'promote, protect and *ensure the full and equal enjoyment* of all human rights and fundamental freedoms by all persons with disabilities.'[78] Furthermore, under the general obligations of the Convention, States Parties have undertaken 'to ensure and promote the *full realization* of all human rights and fundamental freedoms for all persons with disabilities without discrimination of any kind on the basis of disability.[79] Ensuring the full and equal enjoyment of rights for persons with disabilities will, in certain instances, require additional measures of protection, going beyond equality of opportunity and aiming at securing *de facto* equality. States will be required to implement measures to accelerate or achieve equality in fact, where necessary and appropriate. Indeed, reading the phrase 'on an equal basis with others' together with Article 5(4) of the CRPD confirms this point. That particular provision will be expanded on below.[80] For present purposes, it is sufficient to note that Article 5(4) legitimates the taking of measures aimed at accelerating or achieving *de facto* equality.

In sum, it is argued here that the phrase 'on an equal basis with others' falls clearly within the realm of substantive and transformative equality. By stating that disabled people must be accorded rights on an equal basis with others, there is an implicit acknowledgment that disabled people do not enjoy the same level of rights as their non-disabled peers at present – in other words, there is a situation of *de facto* inequality which must be remedied by the taking of all measures to ensure equality in practice, where such measures are deemed necessary and appropriate. The circumstances in which such measures may be deemed necessary and appropriate will no doubt be elaborated on by the CRPD Committee in its general comments and concluding observations. The inclusion of the phrase 'on an equal basis with others' in several articles of the CRPD should have a major impact on the substantive

77 M. Schulze, *A Handbook on the Human Rights of Persons with Disabilities: Understanding the UN Convention on the Rights of Persons with Disabilities* (July 2010), at page 43.

78 UN CRPD, Article 1 [emphasis added].

79 UN CRPD, Article 4(1) [emphasis added].

80 See section 4.5 of this chapter.

and transformative potential of the Convention. Marianne Schulze contends that a Convention 'guaranteeing all human rights to all persons with disabilities "on an equal basis with others" means that the promotion, protection, monitoring and evaluation of human rights will be on a par with mainstream conditions.'[81] In the disability context, ensuring the protection of human rights on a par with mainstream conditions may sometimes involve taking measures to ensure equality in fact. States must adopt and implement measures, including positive measures where necessary, to give full effect to the principles of equality and non-discrimination. This will clearly involve a redistributive element.

4.3.2.2. Direct *versus* Indirect Discrimination

The definition of 'discrimination on the basis of disability' (outlined above) was arrived at after heated debate regarding many aspects of its wording. The first bone of contention arose over the EU's proposal to include a specific reference to direct and indirect discrimination in the text of the CRPD.[82] Those terms were included originally in the draft proposed by the Working Group. However, their inclusion in the final text was resisted by a majority of delegates. Gerard Quinn points to the fact that 'some, especially civil society groups, were fearful that the notion of indirect discrimination (which permits some limited defences) would open a Pandora's box.'[83] Others supported a specific reference to direct and indirect discrimination but opposed defining the concepts within the Convention. The United States and Canadian delegates pointed to the fact that 'attempts to give disparate legal definitions and disparate consequences to direct *versus* indirect discrimination could lead to tremendous confusion in implementation for those States who do not have this sort of jurisprudence in their national law.'[84] The Canadian delegate made the point that 'definitions are best left to the jurisprudence to develop, given the difficulty in distinguishing between these concepts in practice.'[85] This viewpoint seemed to garner support among delegates and the final outcome of the negotiations was that there would be no explicit reference to the concepts of 'direct discrimination' and 'indirect discrimination' in the CRPD. However, the concept of indirect discrimination is implicit in Article 2 of the Convention. The inclusion of the word 'effect' in the definition leaves no doubt in this respect. The HRC includes, within the definition of discrimination, certain acts that have a discriminatory 'purpose or effect' in its General Comment 18. Lester maintains that 'the reference to "effect" makes it unnecessary to prove a discriminatory intention or purpose and indicates

---

81 M. Schulze, *A Handbook on the Human* Rights *of Persons with Disabilities: Understanding the UN Convention on the Rights of Persons with Disabilities* (July 2010), at page 177.

82 The EU delegate did, however, abandon this proposal in the end and admitted that a specific reference to direct and indirect discrimination was not necessary.

83 G. Quinn, 'A Short Guide to the United Nations Convention on the Rights of Persons with Disabilities,' in G. Quinn and L. Waddington (eds.), *European Yearbook of Disability Law: Volume 1* (Intersentia, Antwerp, 2009), at page 100.

84 Fourth Session of the Ad Hoc Committee, volume 5(8), September 1, 2004, available at www.un.org/esa/socdev/enable/rights/ahc4sumart07.htm, accessed 9 October 2014.

85 Fourth Session of the Ad Hoc Committee, volume 5(9), September 2, 2004, available at www.un.org/esa/socdev/enable/rights/ahc4sumart07.htm, last accessed 9 October 2014.

that indirect discrimination is also forbidden under the Covenant.'[86] Joseph et al. contend that the 'clearest enunciation by the HRC of the proscription of indirect discrimination comes from *Althammer v Austria*'[87] in which the Committee stated that 'a violation of Article 26 can also result from the discriminatory effect of a rule or measure that is neutral at face value or without intent to discriminate.'[88] The CERD Committee has confirmed that Article 1(1) of CERD, which contains the same reference to 'effect' as the CRPD, proscribes indirect discrimination.[89]

This interpretation is also borne out by the *travaux préparatoires* of the CRPD. Delegates felt that there was no need to refer specifically to the concept of indirect discrimination as it was covered adequately by the clarification in the last line of Article 2 of the Convention that 'discrimination on the basis of disability' includes *all* forms of discrimination. Furthermore, the Coordinator of the fourth session, Ambassador Don MacKay (New Zealand), pointed out that 'as a matter of legal interpretation, it is clear that any reference to discrimination alone would imply its broadest sense and therefore include direct and indirect [discrimination].'[90] Indeed, the CRPD Committee has confirmed that the Convention proscribes indirect discrimination. In its concluding observations to China, the Committee encouraged the State Party 'to provide a legal definition of discrimination against persons with disabilities and include in such a definition the prohibition of indirect discrimination.'[91]

4.3.2.3. Discrimination 'on the Basis of Disability'

Another vital aspect of the definition of discrimination is the fact that it has a broad remit in terms of its personal scope. This is evidenced by the inclusion of the phrase 'on the basis of disability' in Article 2 of the CRPD. During the negotiation process, delegates expressed the view that a broad definition of discrimination was essential and that the categories of those who were to be covered under the non-discrimination provision should be as wide as possible. The phrase 'on the basis of disability' can be construed as including not only those who have, in fact, an impairment but also

---

86 Lord Lester of Herne Hill QC, 'Non Discrimination in International Human Rights Law,' in *Developing Human Rights Jurisprudence* (Volume 6: Sixth Judicial Colloquium on the Domestic Application of International Human Rights Norms: Bloemfontein, South Africa, 3–5 September 1993), at page 13.

87 S. Joseph, J. Schultz and M. Castan, *The International Covenant on Civil and Political Rights: Cases, Materials, and Commentary* (Oxford University Press, Oxford, 2nd Edition, 2005), at page 694.

88 Human Rights Committee, *Rupert Althammer et al. v Austria*, Communication No. 998/2001, U.N. Doc. CCPR/C/78/D/998/2001 (2003), para. 10.2.

89 In its General Recommendation 14 (1993), the CERD Committee states that 'in seeking whether an action has an effect contrary to the Convention, it will look to see whether that action has an unjustifiable disparate impact upon a group distinguished by race, colour, descent or ethnic or national origin.' [UN Committee on the Elimination of Racial Discrimination, General Recommendation No. 14 on definition of racial discrimination (Article 1, para. 1) (1993), adopted at the forty-second session of the Committee on 22 March 1993, U.N. Doc. A/48/18, at para. 2].

90 Fourth Session of the Ad Hoc Committee on Article 5 CRPD, Volume 5(9), September 2, 2004, available at www.un.org/esa/socdev/enable/rights/ahc4sumart07.htm, accessed 9 October 2014.

91 UN Committee on the Rights of Persons with Disabilities, Concluding Observations to China, para. 12, UN Doc. CRPD/C/CHN/CO/1, adopted 15 October 2012, available at www.ohchr.org/EN/HRBodies/CRPD/Pages/CRPDIndex.aspx last accessed 20 October 2014.

those who are discriminated against as a result of their association with a person with a disability or those who encounter discrimination on account of a perceived impairment. Several references were made throughout the negotiations to such aspects of the non-discrimination norm.[92]

Furthermore, the original text of the Working Group included the notion of perceived disability in its definition of discrimination.[93] In the final text of the CRPD, none of these distinct aspects of the non-discrimination norm were referred to specifically. However, a comment made by the EU delegate during the negotiations is instructive, namely that not mentioning such elements does not mean that they are not included in the definition of discrimination put forward by the Convention.[94] The CRPD Committee confirms the expansive interpretation of 'discrimination on the basis of disability.' In its concluding observations to Spain, the Committee urged the State Party in question to expand the protection of discrimination on the grounds of disability to cover explicitly:

> Multiple disability, perceived disability and association with a person with a disability, and to ensure the protection from denial of reasonable accommodation, as a form of discrimination, regardless of the level of disability.[95]

As Stefan Trömel points out, the incorporation of the phrase 'on the basis of disability' will have implications for UN Member States 'when implementing the Convention and, in particular, when drafting national anti-discrimination legislation' and should not be overlooked.[96] He further acknowledges that legislation prohibiting discrimination on the basis of disability 'has to put the focus not on whether the person who has been discriminated [against] has or has not a (legally certified) disability, but on whether the situation faced by the person is a discriminatory situation based

---

92 The Chair of the Ad-Hoc Committee presented Draft Elements for a Comprehensive and Integral International Convention to Promote and Protect the Rights and Dignity of Persons with Disabilities to the Working Group, in which discrimination was defined as including: 'The less favourable treatment of an associate of a person with a disability because of that other person's disability or because of the association, and a reference to disability includes a suspected, imputed, assumed or possible future disability, perceived disability, a past disability or the effects of a past disability, or the characteristics of a disability.' [Draft Elements for a Comprehensive and Integral International Convention to Promote and Protect the Rights and Dignity of Persons with Disabilities to the Working Group, Proposed by the Chair of the Ad Hoc Committee (December 2003), available at www.un.org/esa/socdev/enable/rights/wgcontrib-chairl.htm. last accessed 17 October 2014].

93 Draft Article 7(2) of the Working Group stated that: 'Discrimination shall include all forms of discrimination, including direct, indirect and systemic, and shall also include discrimination based on an actual or perceived disability.'

94 Fourth Session of the Ad Hoc Committee, volume 5(9), September 02, 2004, available at www.un.org/esa/socdev/enable/rights/ahc4sumart07.htm, accessed 10 October 2014.

95 UN Committee on the Rights of Persons with Disabilities, Concluding Observations to Spain, adopted at the 6th session (19–23 September 2011), UN Doc. CRPD/C/ESP/CO/1, para. 20, available at http://tbinternet.ohchr.org/_layouts/treatybodyexternal/TBSearch.aspx?TreatyID=4&DocTypeID=5 last accessed 20 October 2014.

96 S. Trömel, 'A Personal Perspective on the Drafting History of the United Nations Convention on the Rights of Persons with Disabilities' in G. Quinn and L. Waddington (eds.) *European Yearbook of Disability Law: Volume 1* (Intersentia, Antwerp, 2009), at page 124.

on disability.'[97] States Parties to the CRPD will therefore have to consider the impact of this expansive understanding of disability-based discrimination for all those who are not protected by non-discrimination statutes at present.

4.3.3. The Prohibition of Disability-Based Discrimination

Under Article 5(2) of the CRPD, States are under a specific obligation to prohibit 'all discrimination on the basis of disability.' The prohibition of disability-based discrimination mandated by the CRPD is broad in its material scope in several respects. In the first instance, the prohibition of discrimination must be read in conjunction with General Obligation 4(e) of the Convention which provides that States must 'take all appropriate measures to eliminate discrimination on the basis of disability by any person, organization or private enterprise.'[98] Therefore, national authorities must regulate both the public and private sectors of society in order to eliminate discrimination. The UNCESCR has underlined the importance of the regulation of discrimination in the private sphere in the context of persons with disabilities in its General Comment 5 (1994).[99] The UNCESCR emphasises the 'obligation to protect' which is incumbent on States and notes, in that regard, that States are required to ensure that the enjoyment of rights by persons with disabilities is not hampered by third-party actors in the private sphere. The Committee emphasises the fact that 'it is essential that private employers, private suppliers of goods and services, and other non-public entities be subject to both non-discrimination and equality norms in relation to persons with disabilities.'[100] The Committee has acknowledged that if States fall short of this obligation:

> The ability of persons with disabilities to participate in the mainstream of community activities and to realize their full potential as active members of society will be severely and often arbitrarily constrained.[101]

The issue also arises as to whether the prohibition of discrimination in the purely private sphere (in other words, discrimination between private individuals) falls within the sphere of responsibility of States Parties to the CRPD. As already outlined above, Article 4(e) of the CRPD requires States 'to take all appropriate measures to eliminate discrimination on the basis of disability by any *person*, organization or private enterprise.'[102] A similar reference to eliminating discrimination in the

---

97 Ibid.

98 UN CRPD, General Obligation 4(e).

99 In that general comment, the UNCESCR observes that there is a 'need to ensure that not only the public sphere, but also the private sphere, are, within appropriate limits, subject to regulation to ensure the equitable treatment of persons with disabilities.' UNCESCR General Comment No. 5 on Persons with disabilities, adopted at the eleventh session of the Committee on 9 December 1994, U.N. Doc E/1995/22 at 19 (1995), para. 11.

100 Ibid.

101 Ibid.

102 UN CRPD, Article 4(e) [emphasis added].

private sphere can be found in Article 2(1)(d) of CERD.[103] Vandenhole points to the fact that the CERD Committee 'has emphasised the importance of adequately prohibiting and penalising acts of racial segregation, whether they are committed by individuals or associations.'[104] There would appear to be little doubt therefore that the CRPD obliges States to regulate discrimination against persons with disabilities by private individuals. States must prohibit such discrimination explicitly if they are to fulfil their obligations of protection under the Convention. Frederic Mégret argues that '[...] because much of the assistance that persons with disabilities need will be provided by family members and/or within the home, they will be particularly at risk of their rights being obstructed in this context.'[105] He also points out that State involvement in preventing negative encroachments occurring in the private sphere covers an 'important dimension of the experience of persons with disabilities.'[106]

A second element of the prohibition of discrimination on the basis of disability under the CRPD stems from the fact that a specific prohibition should be included not only in general non-discrimination laws but also in all laws governing the substantive rights of persons with disabilities. This argument is supported by the concluding observations of the CRPD Committee which, as outlined above, have a non-binding status but carry legal weight. In its concluding observations to Tunisia, for example, the Committee recommended that the State Party in question should act with urgency to include an explicit prohibition of disability-based discrimination 'in an anti-discrimination laws, as well as ensure that disability-based discrimination is prohibited in all laws, particularly those governing elections, labour, education, and health, among others.'[107]

Thirdly, Article 5(2) of the CRPD mandates the prohibition of *all* forms of discrimination on the basis of disability. Accordingly, States will be required to incorporate in their laws all forms of prohibited discrimination under the Convention. As already mentioned above, this includes direct and indirect discrimination, as well as a denial of reasonable accommodation. In line with the concluding observations of the CRPD Committee to Spain outlined above, States should also expand the prohibition of disability-based discrimination to cover multiple disabilities, perceived disability and discrimination by association with a person with a disability.

---

103 Article 2(1)(d) CERD provides that 'each State Party shall prohibit and bring to an end, by all appropriate means, including legislation as required by circumstances, racial discrimination by any *persons*, group or organization' [Emphasis added].

104 UN Committee on the Elimination of Racial Discrimination, Concluding Observations to Liberia, UN Doc.A/56/18, para. 434 and Concluding Observations to Ukraine, UN Doc.A/56/18, para. 369 [cited by W. Vandenhole, *Non-Discrimination and Equality in the View of the UN Human Rights Treaty Bodies* (Intersentia, Antwerp/Oxford, 2005), at page 193].

105 F. Mégret, 'The Disabilities Convention: Towards a Holistic Concept of Rights' 12 *The International Journal of Human Rights* 261, at page 266.

106 Ibid.

107 UN Committee on the Rights of Persons with Disabilities, Concluding Observations to Tunisia, adopted at the 8th session of the Committee on 17–28 September 2012, UN Doc. C/TUN/CO/1, para. 13, available at http://tbinternet.ohchr.org/_layouts/treatybodyexternal/TBSearch.aspx?Lang=en&TreatyID=4&DocTypeID=5 last accessed December 2014.

4.3.4. The Guarantee of 'Equal and Effective Legal Protection against Discrimination'

In addition to the prohibition of discrimination contained in Article 5(2) of the Convention, that subsection also includes a guarantee of equal and effective legal protection against discrimination, which is an obligation of result (or an obligation to attain a particular outcome through unspecified means).[108] Furthermore, it falls within the obligation to protect. It will be shown below how the obligation in Article 5(2) of the CRPD to guarantee equal and effective legal protection against discrimination differs from the prohibition of discrimination, to the extent that it imposes a positive duty of protection on States to take active measures to combat discrimination. In other words, States must ensure that the prohibition of discrimination which they enshrine in legislation is effective in practice. The types of positive measures required of States under that provision will be expanded upon in the subsections which follow.

4.3.4.1. The Requirement of 'Equal and Effective Legal Protection against Discrimination' under the CRPD: An Analogy with Similar Obligations in the Core Human Rights Treaties and Observations from the Drafting History of the CRPD

Article 26 of the ICCPR contains a duty 'to guarantee to all persons equal and effective protection against discrimination on any ground.'[109] The wording in Article 26 ICCPR[110] is similar[111] to that contained in Article 5(2) of the CRPD. Manfred Nowak contends that the specific meaning of the duty to ensure equal and effective protection against discrimination in Article 26 ICCPR is 'even more disputed in literature and practice than the negative prohibition of discrimination.'[112] Notwithstanding the disputed nature of the provision, Nowak offers his own respected interpretation of its meaning when he states that it embodies 'a positive obligation on States Parties to take steps to protect against discrimination.'[113] Nowak argues that protection against

---

108 Obligations of result can be distinguished from obligations of conduct, the latter obligations specifying the means by which human rights standards must be reached.

109 ICCPR, Article 26.

110 Article 26 of the ICCPR states as follows: 'All persons are equal before the law and are entitled without any discrimination to the equal protection of the law. *In this respect*, the law shall prohibit any discrimination and guarantee to all persons *equal and effective protection against discrimination on any ground* such as race, colour, sex, language, religion, political or other opinion, national or social origin, property, birth or other status.' [emphasis added].

111 The principal difference between Article 26 ICCPR and Article 5(2) of the CRPD is that the latter provision imposes an obligation to guarantee 'equal and effective *legal* protection against discrimination' [emphasis added], whereas the word 'legal' is not contained in the obligation outlined in Article 26 ICCPR. However, Manfred Nowak asserts that the obligation to guarantee 'equal and effective protection against discrimination' in the ICCPR is connected to the right to 'equal protection *of the law*' [emphasis added] by the words 'in this respect.' [M. Nowak, *UN Covenant on Civil and Political Rights: CCPR commentary* (N.P. Engel, Kehl, 2nd Edition 2005) 607.] Therefore, both provisions relate to equal and effective legal protection, which facilitates comparison of the interpretation of Article 5(2) of the CRPD with Article 26 ICCPR.

112 M. Nowak, *UN Covenant on Civil and Political Rights: CCPR commentary* (N.P. Engel, Kehl, 2nd Edition 2005), at page 630.

113 Ibid.

discrimination calls for positive State measures and he states that this conclusion 'follows from the wording of [Article 26 ICCPR] and the logical difference between it and the mere prohibition of discrimination.'[114]

An analysis of the CRPD's duty to ensure equal and effective legal protection against discrimination, pursuant to the general rule of treaty interpretation codified in Article 31 of the VCLT, confirms these observations. According to a respected dictionary, the adjective 'effective' means 'producing the desired effect' and the term 'equal' means 'like for each member of a class, group or society.'[115] It is important to read these adjectives in light of the object and purpose of the Convention. A contextual and teleological reading of the word 'effective' signifies that the prohibition of non-discrimination enacted by States must contribute to the elimination and prevention of discrimination. In other words, it must be sufficient, *inter alia*, to 'promote, protect and ensure the full and equal enjoyment of all human rights and fundamental freedoms by all persons with disabilities.'[116] This would support the conclusion that the adoption of positive measures to combat discrimination in the context of the guarantee of equal and effective legal protection against discrimination is not inconsistent with the purpose of the CRPD. This interpretation is confirmed by academic scholars. Arnardóttir, for instance, observes that '[...] positive obligations are a necessary component of effective protection against discrimination.'[117]

By placing the requirement to ensure equal and effective legal protection against discrimination directly beside the prohibition of discrimination, it is evident that the drafters of the CRPD intended that the two obligations should be distinct. The duty to ensure equal and effective legal protection against discrimination means that the legal prohibition of discrimination enacted by States, pursuant to the first part of Article 5(2) of the CRPD, should produce the intended result – namely, effective protection against discrimination for disabled people in order that they can exercise their human rights and fundamental freedoms on an equal basis with their non-disabled counterparts. This will entail positive measures on the part of States and a consequent reallocation of resources. This interpretation is also confirmed by the views expressed by delegates throughout the negotiation sessions. In the course of the negotiations on the CRPD, the EU sought to streamline the original text of Article 5(2) (which was repetitive and disjointed) in order to make the obligation contained therein clearer. While delegates did not oppose the attempt to streamline

114 Ibid.

115 Merriam-Webster's Dictionary of Law, Merriam-Webster, 1996, available at www.merriam-webster.com last accessed 2 October 2014.

116 UN CRPD, Article 1.

117 O.M. Arnardóttir, 'A Future of Multidimensional Disadvantage Equality' in O.M. Arnardóttir and G. Quinn (eds.), *The UN Convention on the Rights of Persons with Disabilities: European and Scandinavian Perspectives* (Martinus Nijhoff, Leiden, 2009), at page 61. [In support of this view, Arnardóttir cites General Comment 28 of the Human Rights Committee on the Equality of Rights between Men and Women (Article 3) (2000), para. 3 and also General Recommendation 25 of the UN Committee on the Elimination of Discrimination against Women on Article 4, paragraph 1 of the Convention on the Elimination of All Forms of Discrimination against Women on temporary special measures, para. 24].

that provision, several countries urged the retention of the phrase 'equal and effective protection.' The reason given by the delegate from Liechtenstein was that its retention was necessary in order 'to remind States that including non-discrimination in laws is not sufficient and that active measures are required,'[118] over and above bald non-discrimination provisions.

Under the guarantee of equal and effective protection against discrimination, it is also submitted that States Parties to the CRPD will be required to establish effective redress mechanisms and sanctions in the event that people with disabilities are discriminated against. This appears to be confirmed by the drafting history of the Convention. During the negotiations, Chile drew attention to the fact that the punitive consequences of discrimination should be addressed in Article 5(2) of the CRPD. Chile proposed the extension of the provision so that it would read that States should 'guarantee sanctions against those responsible for such discriminations, with those sanctions to be determined by national legislation.'[119] The Russian delegate stated that the provision was essential to ensure the link between norms and penalties for discrimination.[120] In the same session, delegates argued that the word 'legal' should be added to qualify the original phrase 'equal and effective protection,' which appeared in the draft text of the Working Group. In light of such comments, it is argued that the word 'legal' may have been added to further emphasise the necessity to have effective remedies and sanctions for discriminatory acts. Effective remedies and sanctions should be established through criminal, civil or administrative processes, as necessary. In practice, this would mean the removal of all forms of barriers encountered by disabled people in accessing justice following a discriminatory act – environmental, legal and structural barriers. In addition, States will be required to eradicate attitudinal barriers in the judicial system through awareness-raising programmes and training sessions for law enforcement officers. Removing such barriers will necessitate the use of positive measures. The UN Committee on the Elimination of Racial Discrimination (CERD Committee) has elaborated on the obligation to ensure protection against discrimination, stating that 'guarantees of non-discrimination laid down in law, without mechanisms to monitor their application, do not on their own ensure the enjoyment of non-discrimination.'[121] The UNCESCR has affirmed the fact that non-discrimination legislation is to be monitored effectively.[122] In view of these comments, States Parties to the CRPD may be required to adopt a range of measures that will ensure the proper application of, and effective compliance with, any non-discrimination legislation which they enact, in both the public and in the private sector. Bearing that in mind, I will now turn to a brief consideration of the obligation to protect against discrimination in the private sector.

---

118 Seventh Session of the Ad Hoc Committee on Article 5 CRPD, January 16, 2006, available at www.un.org/esa/socdev/enable/rights/ahc7sum16jan.htm, last accessed 10 October 2014.

119 Ibid.

120 Ibid.

121 See UN Committee on the Elimination of Racial Discrimination, Concluding Observations to Saudi-Arabia, UN Doc., CERD/C/62/CO/8, para. 11; See also UN Committee on the Elimination of Racial Discrimination, Concluding Observations to Nepal, UN Doc. CERD/C/304/Add.108, para. 10.

122 See UNCESCR, Concluding Observations to Norway, UN Doc. E/C.12/1/Add.109, para. 27.

4.3.4.2. The Obligation to Protect against Discrimination in the Private Sector

Manfred Nowak contends that 'the primary significance of protection against discrimination lies in the obligation on States Parties to provide effective protection against discrimination by private parties to those subject to their laws.'[123] The CEDAW Committee has elaborated on the measures to be taken by States to meet the obligation to protect against discrimination in the context of Article 2 CEDAW. The Committee notes that States must:

> Protect women from discrimination by private actors and take steps directly aimed at eliminating customary and all other practices that prejudice and perpetuate the notion of inferiority or superiority of either of the sexes, and of stereotyped roles for men and women.[124]

There would appear to be a particular onus on States Parties to the CRPD to ensure effective legal protection against discrimination by private actors, in light of the grave consequences for persons with disabilities of discrimination encountered in the private sector. States should establish appropriate and effective safeguards to prevent discrimination and to eliminate customs and practices in the private sector that are prejudicial to people with disabilities. The UNCESCR has confirmed, in its General Comment 20 (2009), that States' obligations in ensuring effective protection against discrimination are not confined to the enactment of legislative measures. In that General Comment, the Committee underlines the fact that States must 'adopt measures, *which should include* legislation, to ensure that individuals and entities in the private sphere do not discriminate on prohibited grounds.'[125] States Parties to the CRPD will likely be required to go beyond formal legal measures to enact strategies, plans of action and policy measures targeted at addressing discrimination in the private sector and at removing discriminatory barriers that are preventing the participation and inclusion of people with disabilities in the private sphere of society. As already outlined above,[126] under the CRPD the obligation on the State to protect against discrimination in the private sector extends as far as protecting against discrimination between private individuals. In practice, of course, this form of discrimination will be difficult to regulate but would, at a minimum, include the establishment of effective remedies and sanctions in private or criminal law, as appropriate, to deter discriminatory acts by private individuals.

---

123 M. Nowak, *UN Covenant on Civil and Political Rights: CCPR commentary* (N.P. Engel, Kehl, 2nd Edition 2005), at page 632.

124 UN Committee on the Elimination of all Forms of Discrimination against Women, General Recommendation 28 on The Core Obligations of States Parties under Article 2 of the Convention on the Elimination of All Forms of Discrimination against Women (2010), UN Doc. CEDAW/C/GC/28, para. 9.

125 UNCESCR General Comment 20: Non-Discrimination in Economic, Social and Cultural Rights (art. 2, para. 2) (2009), para. 11 [Emphasis added].

126 See Section 4.3.3 of this chapter.

4.3.4.3. Equal and Effective Protection against Discrimination 'on all grounds'

It must be remembered that States Parties to the CRPD are required to ensure equal and effective protection against discrimination on *all* grounds. The original text of the Working Group of the Ad-Hoc Committee listed the 'other' grounds on which States had to prohibit discrimination,[127] in recognition of the fact that people with disabilities may experience discrimination on multiple and intersecting grounds.[128] However, delegates at the negotiations decided to delete that list in Article 5(2) and to refer instead to 'discrimination on all grounds' on account of 'the difficulties inherent in including lists in treaties.'[129] The Coordinator of the fourth session of the Ad-Hoc Committee on Article 5 of the CRPD, Ambassador Don MacKay (New Zealand), summed up the general agreement between delegates that there should not be a list in the text of the equality and non-discrimination provision and, furthermore, if there was to be a list, that it should be in the Preamble, in which case it should not go beyond existing human rights Conventions.[130] Therefore, Article 5(2) of the CRPD must be read in conjunction with the list contained in paragraph (p) of the Preamble of the Convention. That paragraph expresses concern:

> About the difficult conditions faced by persons with disabilities who are subject to multiple or aggravated forms of discrimination on the basis of race, colour, sex, language, religion, political or other opinion, national, ethnic, indigenous or social origin, property, birth, age or other status.[131]

The guarantee of equal and effective protection against discrimination on all grounds strengthens States' obligations to cover invidious forms of multiple or intersectional discrimination[132] against people with disabilities. Multiple discrimination refers to situations whereby 'individuals or groups of individuals face discrimination on more than one of the prohibited grounds.'[133] Intersectional discrimination has been described by Aart Hendriks as exemplifying 'the reality in which two or more protected grounds can interact concurrently, cumulatively or otherwise cross-cut to

---

127 These were as follows: 'race, colour, sex, language, religion, political or other opinion, national or social origin, property, birth, source or type of disability, age, or any other status.'

128 See the comments of the Canadian delegate, Fourth Session of the Ad Hoc Committee, Volume 5(3), August 2 2,004, available at www.un.org/esa/socdev/enable/rights/adhocmeetings.htm, accessed 10 October 2014.

129 Comments of the Holy See, Fourth Session of the Ad Hoc Committee, Volume 5(3), August 24, 2004, available at http://www.un.org/esa/socdev/enable/rights/adhocmeetings.htm, last accessed 10 October 2014.

130 Fourth Session of the Ad Hoc Committee, Volume 5(9), September 2, 2004, available at www.un.org/esa/socdev/enable/rights/adhocmeetings.htm, last accessed 10 October 2014.

131 UN CRPD, Preamble, para. (p).

132 For an in-depth analysis of the concept of multiple or intersectional discrimination, see for instance, A. Hendriks, 'The UN Disability Convention and (Multiple) Discrimination: Should EU Non-Discrimination Law Be Modelled Accordingly?' in G. Quinn and L. Waddington (eds.), *European Yearbook of Disability Law*, Volume 2 (Intersentia, Antwerp, 2010).

133 UNCESCR, General Comment No. 20 (2009), Non-Discrimination in Economic, Social and Cultural Rights, UN Doc E/C.12/GC/20, at para. 17.

constitute a new – real or perceived – "identity."'[134] Article 5(2) of the CRPD seeks to counteract such nefarious forms of discrimination experienced by disabled people.

4.4. Article 5(3) of the CRPD

In order to promote equality and eliminate discrimination, States Parties shall take all appropriate steps to ensure that reasonable accommodation is provided.

4.4.1. Introduction to Article 5(3) of the CRPD

Article 5(3) of the CRPD links the equality and non-discrimination norms with the duty to accommodate – an integral part of ensuring disability equality under the CRPD. Article 5(3) should be read together with the definition of reasonable accommodation in Article 2, which provides as follows:

> "Reasonable accommodation" means necessary and appropriate modification and adjustments not imposing a disproportionate or undue burden, where needed in a particular case, to ensure to persons with disabilities the enjoyment or exercise on an equal basis with others of all human rights and fundamental freedoms.[135]

Based on this definition, taken in conjunction with Article 5(3), one can summarise the key features of the duty to accommodate as follows:

- The identification and removal of barriers that impact on the enjoyment of human rights for persons with disabilities;
- The 'necessity and appropriateness' of modifications or adjustments to address barriers specific to a particular individual;
- The adoption of modifications or adjustments that do not impose a disproportionate or undue burden on the duty-bearer;
- The requirement to find a response or solution which is tailored to the individual circumstances of the person with a disability; and
- The fact that accommodations have as their essential objective the promotion of equality and the elimination of discrimination, by means of the enjoyment of all human rights by persons with disabilities on an equal basis with others.

The duty to accommodate imposes a positive obligation of result on States, which are required to meet the high burden of ensuring[136] that reasonable accommodations

---

134 A. Hendriks, 'The UN Disability Convention and (Multiple) Discrimination: Should EU Non-Discrimination Law Be Modelled Accordingly?' in G. Quinn and L. Waddington (eds.), *European Yearbook of Disability Law*, Volume 2 (Intersentia, Antwerp, 2010), at page 17.

135 UN CRPD, Article 2.

136 In the draft text of the Working Group, the duty to accommodate read as follows: 'In order to secure the right to equality for persons with disabilities, States Parties undertake to take all appropriate steps, including by legislation, to *provide* reasonable accommodation.' [emphasis added] Therefore, in the earlier drafts of the Convention the obligation being imposed on State Parties was framed in terms of an obligation to 'provide' reasonable accommodation. However, the Netherlands made a valid point

are actually provided to people with disabilities in order that they may exercise their rights without discrimination and on the basis of equality with their non-disabled peers. The HRC has stated that the obligation to 'ensure' to all individuals the rights recognised in the ICCPR:

> Requires that State parties take *all necessary steps* to enable every person to enjoy those rights. These steps include the removal of obstacles to the equal enjoyment of such rights, the education of the population and of state officials in human rights and the adjustment of domestic legislation so as to give effect to the undertakings set forth in the Covenant.[137]

In the context of the CRPD, this will require that States oversee the implementation of the duty to accommodate by public and private entities, who will be required to engage in a constructive dialogue with the disabled individual in order to determine the most appropriate accommodation in the circumstances of a particular case. States will also be required to ensure that they educate all those involved in the implementation of the duty to accommodate and the manner in which this contributes to disability equality, as well as educating the judiciary and State officials on the promotion of equality and the elimination of discrimination via the duty to accommodate. In addition, national authorities will be required to ensure that their legislative frameworks comply with the obligations engendered by the CRPD. In accordance with the Employment Equality Directive,[138] EU Member States will already have in place legislative provisions requiring entities to provide reasonable accommodations in the areas of employment and occupation. The Employment Equality Directive is a major part of EU labour law, which aims to combat discrimination on grounds of disability, sexual orientation, religion or belief and age in the workplace. However, the CRPD creates a broader, more far-reaching duty to accommodate, which spans all human rights. Under the Convention, it falls on States to ensure that a wide array of social actors, including employers, schools, health care providers and those supplying goods and services, accommodate persons with disabilities. Therefore, EU Member States will be obliged to expand their legal provisions relating to reasonable accommodation for people with disabilities to cover areas outside employment and occupation.

---

as to who the real duty-bearers of the accommodation duty were in its assertion that: 'States Parties cannot provide reasonable accommodation as they are obligated to do in the Working Group text. In most cases it will be private enterprises that will be thus obligated, and not the State. The State's role therefore is to 'ensure that reasonable accommodation is provided.'

[Comments of the Netherlands, Fourth Session of the Ad Hoc Committee, volume 5(10), September 03, 2004, available at www.un.org/esa/socdev/enable/rights/ahc4sumart07.htm last accessed 20 December 2014].

137 Human Rights Committee, General Comment 28 on Equality of rights between men and women (article 3), adopted on 29 March 2000, U.N. Doc. CCPR/C/21/Rev.1/Add.10 (2000), para. 3 [emphasis added].

138 Council Directive 2000/78/EC of 27 November 2000 establishing a general framework for equal treatment in employment and occupation (Official Journal L 303, 02/12/2000 P. 0016–0022), available at http://eur-lex.europa.eu/LexUriServ/LexUriServ.do?uri=CELEX:32000L0078:en:HTML last accessed 26 June 2014.

4.4.2. The Elements of the Duty to Accommodate

Before analysing the distinct components of the duty to accommodate, it is proposed to reflect firstly on the meaning of the term accommodation itself.

4.4.2.1. What is Meant by the Term 'Accommodation?'

The term 'accommodation' is understood generally to mean adjustments or modifications to existing policies, practices or environments in order to facilitate the participation and inclusion of the disabled person in society. In light of the individualised nature of the duty to accommodate, it is not possible to provide an exhaustive list of the types of accommodations that might be appropriate in any given scenario. The drafting history of Article 5 does not reveal much information about the meaning of the term 'accommodation.' However, national legislation provides several examples of suitable accommodations. In that regard, the United Kingdom's Disability Discrimination Act of 1995[139] is illustrative. Although that Act has now been repealed and replaced by the Equality Act 2010,[140] the new act does not give concrete examples of reasonable adjustments (the British equivalent term for reasonable accommodations). The 1995 Act legislated the duty of employers to make reasonable adjustments and many of the examples contained in paragraph 6(3) of the 1995 Act can be deemed to carry over to the new Act. The 1995 Act provided specific examples of steps an employer could take in order to comply with the duty to accommodate as follows:

- making adjustments to premises;
- allocating some of the disabled person's duties to another person;
- transferring the disabled person to fill an existing vacancy;
- alteration of working hours;
- assigning the disabled person to a different place of work;
- allowing the individual in question to be absent during working hours for rehabilitation, assessment or treatment;
- giving the disabled individual (or arranging for him/her to be given) training;
- acquiring or modifying equipment;
- modifying instructions or reference manuals;
- modifying procedures for testing or assessment;
- providing a reader or interpreter;
- providing supervision.[141]

The ADA reiterates many of the examples above and defines the term 'reasonable accommodation' in the context of employment as including the following: making existing facilities used by employees readily accessible to and usable by individuals

---

139 UK Disability Discrimination Act [1995], available at www.legislation.gov.uk/ukpga/1995/50/contents last accessed 15 October 2014. Before being repealed and replaced by the Equality Act [2010], the Disability Discrimination Act [1995] was amended by the 2005 Disability Discrimination Act.

140 UK Equality Act [2010], available at www.legislation.gov.uk, last accessed 15 October 2014.

141 UK Disability Discrimination Act (1995), para. 6(3).

with disabilities,[142] job restructuring, part-time or modified work schedules, reassignment to a vacant position, acquisition or modification of equipment or devices, appropriate adjustment or modifications of examinations, training materials or policies, the provision of qualified readers or interpreters and other similar accommodations for individuals with disabilities.[143] Recital 20 of the (non-binding) Preamble to the Employment Equality Directive provides the following examples of types of measures that could amount to a reasonable accommodation: adapting premises and equipment, patterns of working time, the distribution of tasks or the provision of training or integration resources.[144] In the case of *Ring and Skouboe Werge*,[145] the Court of Justice of the European Union (CJEU) had to answer the question, *inter alia*, as to whether a reduction in working hours could be regarded as a reasonable accommodation measure. The Court observed that a reduction in working hours may be deemed an appropriate accommodation measure in a case in which the reduction makes it possible for the worker to continue in his employment. The Court held, however, that it was for the national court to assess whether a reduction in working hours, as an accommodation measure, represents a disproportionate burden on employers.

While the accommodations listed above are not exhaustive, they illustrate the types of measures that may be considered as appropriate accommodations for persons with disabilities in the context of employment and occupation. Accommodations under the CRPD are likely to take a similar form. However, as we have seen, the duty to accommodate in the CRPD goes far beyond the field of employment to extend to all of the rights contained in the Convention, imposing significant obligations on private and public entities. In non-employment fields, examples of reasonable accommodations include the granting of extra time for students with disabilities in exams, the provision of readers for disabled students, the provision of lecture notes in advance or the facilitation of part-time study.

It is important to mention that there was widespread agreement in the Working Group of the CRPD negotiation process on the need to keep the reasonable accommodation duty in the Convention both 'general and flexible in order to ensure that it could be adapted [readily] to different sectors (e.g., employment, education, etc.) and in order

142 Title 42, Chapter 126, Sub-chapter 1 on Employment, Section 12111, Subsection 9(a), Americans with Disabilities Act (1990), as amended by the Americans with Disabilities Amendments Act (2008) (effective as of 1 January 2009).

143 Title 42, Chapter 126, Sub-chapter 1 on Employment, Section 12111, Subsection 9(b), Americans with Disabilities Act (1990), as amended by the Americans with Disabilities Amendments Act (2008) (effective as of 1 January 2009).

144 Recital 20, Preamble, Council Directive 2000/78/EC of 27 November 2000 establishing a general framework for equal treatment in employment and occupation.

145 European Court of Justice, Joined Cases C-335/11 and C-337-11, *HK Danmark, acting on behalf of Jette Ring v Dansk almennyttigt Boligselskab and HK Danmark, acting on behalf of Lone Skouboe Werge v Dansk Arbejdsgiverforening acting on behalf of Pro Display A/S*, judgment of the Court (Second Chamber) of 11 April 2013.

to respect the diversity of legal traditions.'[146] It is also worth noting that there was general agreement that the process of determining what amounted to a 'reasonable accommodation' should be both 'individualised'[147] and 'interactive,'[148] in the sense that it should address consciously the individual's specific need for accommodation and that it should be the result of a constructive dialogue between both parties. The individualised nature of the accommodation duty is mirrored in the words 'where needed in a particular case' in the final text of Article 2 of the CRPD. Having reflected on what might constitute an accommodation under the CRPD, it is apt to consider the defence of 'disproportionate or undue burden.'

4.4.2.2. The Limitation to the Duty to Accommodate: 'Disproportionate or Undue Burden'

The wording of the so-called limitation to the duty to accommodate (namely the proviso that reasonable accommodations will only be mandatory where they do not entail a disproportionate or undue burden for entities) was the subject of heated debate during the negotiation sessions leading to the adoption of the CRPD. A perusal of the drafting history of the Convention reveals that many delegates were confused about the necessity for the use of qualifying language in light of what they felt was already existing qualifying language in the form of the term 'reasonable.' Indeed, confusion has arisen in this regard in the EU,[149] whereby many EU Member States have interpreted the word 'reasonable' itself as a limitation to the duty to accommodate.[150] According to the *travaux préparatoires* of the Convention, the Coordinator of the fourth session of the Ad-Hoc Committee, Ambassador Don MacKay (New Zealand) expressed the view that 'reasonable accommodation' is a single term that is being defined and that the word 'reasonable' was not intended to be an exception clause in and of itself.[151] There was also considerable disquiet amongst delegates regarding the use of the term 'disproportionate burden' that was proposed by the Working Group. The delegate appearing on behalf of National Human Rights Institutions (NHRI) suggested the deletion of the term because they felt that it would be easier for States to renege on their obligations if disproportionate burden was the applicable standard.[152] In general, delegates felt that the term disproportionate burden set a threshold that was too low. Many delegates also expressed the view that the term

146 Footnotes to Annex I, Draft articles for a Comprehensive and Integral International Convention on the Protection and Promotion of the Rights and Dignity of Persons with Disabilities, Article 7, available at www.un.org/esa/socdev/enable/rights/ahcwgreporta7.htm last accessed 13 October 2014.

147 Ibid.

148 Ibid.

149 For further analysis on this issue, see L. Waddington, 'When is it Reasonable for Europeans to be Confused: Understanding when a Disability Accommodation is 'Reasonable' from a Comparative Perspective,' (2008) 29(3) *Comparative Labor Law and Policy Journal* 101.

150 This point will be expanded on in chapter 4 of this thesis which concerns the duty to accommodate and the progressive realisation of human rights contained in the CRPD.

151 Fourth Session of the Ad Hoc Committee, volume 5(10), September 03, 2004 www.un.org/esa/socdev/enable/rights/ahc4sumart07.htm, accessed 12 October 2014.

152 Third Session of the Ad Hoc Committee, volume 4(2) May 25, 2004, available at www.un.org/esa/socdev/enable/rights/ahc3sum7.htm, accessed 13 October 2014.

disproportionate burden was unclear[153] and underdeveloped.[154] In particular, there was a fear as to who would determine what amounted to a disproportionate burden when applying this defence in a national setting. The Australian delegate elaborated on that point in a Position Paper submitted during the eight session of the Ad-Hoc Committee. In that paper, the Australian delegate noted that although the standard of disproportionate burden is used in Article 5 of the EU Employment Equality Directive, 'generally there is no clear understanding or jurisprudence of what the standard means in practice.'[155] Accordingly, the Australian delegate submitted that the term disproportionate burden has the 'very real potential for subjective application and for States Parties to the Convention to set their own standards on what constitutes a disproportionate burden.'[156] The general consensus during the negotiations was that the language used in the draft of the Working Group needed to be strengthened to protect the rights of people with disabilities. Australia proposed alternative language in the form of the term 'unjustifiable hardship.'[157] The Australian delegate submitted that 'the preferred test' must be that of 'unjustifiable hardship' or 'undue hardship' as 'these are tests that are a common feature in the domestic anti-discrimination laws of a number of States Parties and this has led to the extensive development of jurisprudence around these tests.'[158] The majority[159] of the delegates agreed with the Australian proposal, pointing out that the phrases 'unjustifiable hardship' or 'undue hardship' were preferable to 'disproportionate burden' as the former terms represent better the interests of people with disabilities, as well as entities.[160] It is interesting to note that the final text of the CRPD employs two terms to limit the duty to accommodate somewhat. Article 2 of the Convention states that the denial of reasonable accommodation may be justified if it constitutes a 'disproportionate

[153] See, for example, the comments of China in the Third Session of the Ad Hoc Committee, volume 4(2) May 25, 2004, available at www.un.org/esa/socdev/enable/rights/ahc3sum7.htm, accessed 13 October 2014.

[154] For example, the Australian delegate commented that the standard of disproportionate burden is underdeveloped and does not have the clarity and depth of interpretation that is provided by better developed standards, such as 'unjustifiable hardship' and 'undue hardship.' [Position Paper of People with Disability Australia (Incorporated) and the Australian National Association of Legal Centres, available at www.un.org/esa/socdev/enable/rights/ahc8docs/ahc8naclc2.do last accessed 13 October 2014].

[155] Position Paper of People with Disability Australia (Incorporated) and the Australian National Association of Legal Centres, Eighth Session of the Ad Hoc Committee on a Comprehensive and Integral International Convention on the Protection and Promotion of the Rights and Dignity of Persons with Disabilities, available at www.un.org/esa/socdev/enable/rights/ahc8docs/ahc8naclc2.doc, last accessed 14 October 2014.

[156] Ibid.

[157] Third Session of the Ad Hoc Committee, volume 4(2) May 25, 2004, available at www.un.org/esa/socdev/enable/rights/ahc3sum7.htm, last accessed 13 October 2014.

[158] Position Paper of People with Disability Australia (Incorporated) and the Australian National Association of Legal Centres, Eighth Session of the Ad Hoc Committee on a Comprehensive and Integral International Convention on the Protection and Promotion of the Rights and Dignity of Persons with Disabilities, available at www.un.org/esa/socdev/enable/rights/ahc8docs/ahc8naclc2.doc, last accessed 14 October 2014.

[159] Some delegates, however, felt that the threshold set by the term 'undue hardship' was too high.

[160] Comments of the Lebanese delegate, Fourth Session of the Ad Hoc Committee, Volume 5(10), September 3, 2004, www.un.org/esa/socdev/enable/rights/ahc4sumart07.htm, accessed 13 October 2014.

or undue burden.'[161] There is little information contained in the drafting history as to why delegates opted for those particular terms or what the terms actually mean. The concepts of disproportionate and undue burden will be explored in chapter four of this book, drawing on already existing national legislation incorporating similar terms. For the moment, I will move on to the intrinsic link between the duty to accommodate and disability equality.

4.4.2.3. The Duty to Accommodate as Part of the Equality and Non-Discrimination Norms in the Convention

The proposal to include the duty to accommodate within Article 5 of the CRPD aroused grave concerns during the negotiation process. Gerard Quinn asserts that the view was apparently taken by many delegates 'that if the notion of reasonable accommodation were tied to the notion of non-discrimination, then it could become a Trojan horse for the enforceability of more and more slices of social and economic rights.'[162] In other words, delegates feared the resource implications of its inclusion on account of the fact that non-discrimination is an obligation of immediate effect and that the duty to accommodate in the CRPD spans all rights – both civil and political and economic, social and cultural rights. This provoked the fear among delegates at the negotiation sessions that the non-discrimination norm could result in increased judicial enforceability of economic, social and cultural rights.[163] Many delegates did, however, recognise the intrinsic link between the duty to accommodate and the equality and non-discrimination norms. For example, the representative speaking on behalf of NHRI noted that the intimate connection between the two concepts was 'one of the most visible and positive accomplishments in modern non-discrimination law in the context of disability.'[164] The delegate was of the view that the absence of this innovative aspect of comparative disability discrimination law would be conspicuous in the Convention.[165] General Comment 5 (1994) of the UNCESCR was drawn on by many national representatives in order to forge a link in the CRPD between the duty to accommodate and the equality and non-discrimination norms. That general comment includes a denial of reasonable accommodation in the

---

161 An examination of the drafting history of the CRPD shows that there is no apparent different between the term 'hardship' proposed by delegates and the term 'burden' which made it into the final text of the CRPD.

162 G. Quinn, 'A Short Guide to the United Nations Convention on the Rights of Persons with Disabilities,' in G. Quinn and L. Waddington (eds.) *European Yearbook of Disability Law: Volume 1* (Intersentia, Antwerp, 2009), at page 100.

163 Ibid.

164 Seventh Session of the Ad Hoc Committee, volume 8(12), January 31, 2006, available at www.un.org/esa/socdev/enable/rights/ahc7sum31jan.htm, accessed 16 October 2014.

165 Ibid.

definition of disability-based discrimination.[166] The EC Presidency[167] opposed the link between reasonable accommodation and non-discrimination initially. However, that opposition was dispelled by advice from the EC Commission,[168] who Gráinne de Búrca states was the 'main advocate'[169] of the inclusion of an accommodation duty within the realm of the non-discrimination norm. She contends that this was 'an attempt to transpose the EU [anti-discrimination] model to the international domain.'[170] In other words, 'the Commission – which positioned itself as guardian of the then EC treaties and existing EC legislation – insisted that the failure to achieve reasonable accommodation constituted discrimination.'[171] In the end, the EC maintained the position that the inclusion of a duty to accommodate in Article 5 of the CRPD was 'on solid ground'[172] pursuant to General Comment 5 of the UNCESCR.

The non-discrimination provision in the CRPD is of general and cross-cutting application and it underpins the substantive rights in the Convention. By tying the duty to accommodate into the equality norm, it is clear that the drafters intended that it would apply across the whole spectrum of civil and political rights, as well as economic, social and cultural rights. Janet Lord and Rebecca Brown assert that this version of substantive equality '[...] undermines the untenable and increasingly rejected position that civil and political rights are 'negative' and require little positive action or investment of resources on the part of the State.'[173]

4.4.3. The Objective of the Duty to Accommodate

There were several attempts to bolster the language of Article 5(3) of the CRPD during the negotiation process. Delegates expressed the desire to move the duty to

166 General Comment 5 of the UNCESCR provides at para. 15 that: 'For the purposes of the Covenant, "disability-based discrimination" may be defined as including any distinction, exclusion, restriction or preference, or *denial of reasonable accommodation* based on disability which has the effect of nullifying or impairing the recognition, enjoyment or exercise of economic, social or cultural rights.' [emphasis added].

167 The Presidency of the Council of the EU rotates between each of the 27 Member States every six months. During its six month term the hosting Member State is Chair of the Council of the European Union meeting. The Presidency organises these meetings and has the responsibility of moving Council work forward as much as possible by helping Member States reach agreement and by formulating compromise proposals that support the interests of the EU as a whole when differences in opinion emerge.

168 The European Commission is the executive arm of the European Union. It is responsible, inter alia, for legislative proposals and implementing decisions of the Union. It is the guardian of the treaties and it is responsible for upholding them, as well as looking after the day-to-day affairs of the Union.

169 G. de Búrca, 'The EU in the Negotiation of the Disability Convention' *Fordham Law Legal Studies Research Paper No. 1525611*, available at http://papers.ssrn.com/sol3/papers.cfm?abstract_id=1525611 last accessed 20 April 2013.

170 Ibid.

171 Ibid.

172 Fourth Session of the Ad Hoc Committee, volume 5(9), September 2, 2004. Available at www.un.org/esa/socdev/enable/rights/ahc4sumart07.htm, accessed 16 October 2014.

173 J.E. Lord and R. Brown, 'The Role of Reasonable Accommodation in Securing Substantive Equality for Persons with Disabilities: The UN Convention on the Rights of Persons with Disabilities' in M. Rioux, L.A. Basser and M. Jones, *Critical Perspectives on Human Rights and Disability Law* (Martinus Nijhoff, The Hague, 2011), at page 280.

accommodate closer to the equality norm.[174] In the final text of Article 5(3) of the CRPD, the objective of the duty to accommodate is clear – the aim of the provision is to promote equality and to eliminate discrimination. The link between the duty to accommodate and the equality norm in the CRPD highlights the fact that there is both a negative and a positive aspect to the right to equality. This is vital in terms of the redistributive effect of Article 5(3).[175] States will be obliged to ensure the assignment of financial support and expertise to entities in order to support the provision of reasonable accommodation and, thereby, to support the promotion of substantive equality. The CRPD Committee has already acknowledged the need for positive measures on the part of States. For example, in its concluding observations to Spain, the Committee recommended that the State Party increase its efforts to ensure the provision of reasonable accommodation in education 'by allocating sufficient financial and human resources to implement the right to inclusive education.'[176] The CEDAW Committee has stated that the elimination of discrimination and the promotion of equality are 'two different but equally important goals in the quest for women's empowerment.'[177] Unfortunately, the Committee has not elaborated any further on the distinction between the two concepts. Notwithstanding this, some information can be gleaned from the general comments and the concluding observations of the core human rights treaty bodies regarding the content of these distinct but complementary obligations. Those comments and observations will be drawn on in the subsections which follow.

4.4.3.1. The Duty to Accommodate and the Promotion of Equality

Aart Hendriks states that the 'active promotion of equality [...] goes further than mere prohibition of less favourable treatment of individuals or groups.'[178] Thus, positive

---

[174] The original Working Group text stated simply that 'discrimination on the grounds of disability' includes a failure to make reasonable accommodation. The Kenyan delegate proposed linking reasonable accommodation with the equality norm by adding the phrase 'so that persons with disabilities may exercise all human rights and fundamental freedoms on an equal basis with others' to Article 5(3). The delegate observed that 'the effect of this is to go further than simply stating a need to provide reasonable accommodation by framing reasonable accommodation within the context of equality and the elimination/prevention of discrimination.' Seventh Session of the Ad Hoc Committee on Article 5, volume 8(1), January 16, 2006, available at www.un.org/esa/socdev/enable/rights/ahc7sum16jan.htm, last accessed 16 October 2014.

[175] During the negotiation sessions leading to the adoption of the CRPD, the International Disability Alliance (IDA) stated that 'the right to equality entails not only the right to be free from discrimination by the State or private persons, but also the right to reasonable accommodation, which may in some cases require the State or others to allocate resources for that purpose.' [International Disability Alliance, Interactive Roundtable on Legislative Measures to Implement the CRPD, with a Focus on Accessibility and Reasonable Accommodation, available at www.un.org/.../IDA%20Draft%20Background%20Note_Roundtable, last accessed 15 October 2014].

[176] UN Committee on the Rights of Persons with Disabilities, Concluding Observations to Spain, UN Doc. CRPD/C/ESP/CO/1 (2011), para. 44(a).

[177] UN Committee on the Elimination of All Forms of Discrimination Against Women, Concluding Observations to Belgium, UN Doc. A/57/38 (Part II), para. 146, available at http://daccess-dds-ny.un.org/doc/UNDOC/GEN/N02/614/17/PDF/N0261417.pdf?OpenElement last accessed 24 August 2014.

[178] A. Hendriks, 'Disabled Persons and their Right to Equal Treatment: Allowing Differentiation while Ending Discrimination' (1995) 1(2) *Health and Human Rights* 152, at page 157.

steps will be required to promote equality by means of the duty to accommodate. According to the human rights treaty bodies, an obligation 'to promote' (which is derived from the obligation to fulfil) imposes duties on States to raise awareness and to establish educational campaigns. Under the umbrella framework of the obligation to promote, the UNCESCR has stated that awareness about international anti-discrimination standards is to be increased among judges and other members of the legal profession.[179] The HRC has also stated that education which is provided with regard to discrimination must be directed towards the population at large[180] and towards the public service[181] (law enforcement officers, the legal profession and the judiciary). In the context of the CRPD, the 'promotion of equality' indicates (according to its ordinary meaning), that awareness must be raised, amongst the judiciary, other members of the legal profession and also amongst all relevant stakeholders, about the equal rights of persons with disabilities and how the duty to accommodate can contribute to equalising opportunities and outcomes for persons with disabilities. In its concluding observations to Tunisia, the CRPD Committee recommended that the State party should make greater efforts to raise awareness of non-discrimination among members of the legal profession, particularly the judiciary, and persons with disabilities themselves, including through training programmes on the concept of reasonable accommodation.[182] This can be linked to Article 8 of the CRPD, according to which States are required to take measures to 'raise awareness throughout society, including at the family level, regarding persons with disabilities, and to foster respect for the rights and dignity of persons with disabilities.'[183] This awareness-raising should be designed to foster a climate of understanding, tolerance and respect for the equal rights of persons with disabilities. States may also be required to raise awareness amongst the public at large and within private entities of the potential of persons with disabilities to contribute to society and the means by which the provision of reasonable accommodation can facilitate this. The promotion of equality will require that an equality focus is embedded in all practices, procedures and policies, as well as in decision-making processes. In that regard, States may be required to develop codes of practice and guidelines in respect of the duty to accommodate.

---

179 UNCESCR, Concluding Observations to Serbia and Montenegro, UN Doc. E/C.12/1/Add.108, para. 39.

180 Human Rights Committee, Concluding Observations to Togo, UN Doc. CCPR/CO/76/TGO, para. 22; Human Rights Committee, Concluding Observations to Georgia, UN Doc. CCPR/CO/74/GEO, para. 13 [cited by W. Vandenhole, *Non-Discrimination and Equality in the View of the UN Human Rights Treaty Bodies* (Intersentia, Antwerp/Oxford, 2005), at page 202].

181 Human Rights Committee, Concluding Observations to Philippines, UN Doc. CCPR/CO/79/PHL, para. 13; Human Rights Committee, Concluding Observations to United Kingdom, UN Doc. CCPR/C/79/Add.55, para. 26 [cited by W. Vandenhole, *Non-Discrimination and Equality in the View of the UN Human Rights Treaty Bodies* (Intersentia, Antwerp/Oxford, 2005), at page 202].

182 UN Committee on the Rights of Persons with Disabilities, Concluding Observations to Tunisia, UN Doc. CRPD/C/TUN/CO/1 (2011), para. 13.

183 UN CRPD, Article 8(a).

4.4.3.2. The Duty to Accommodate and the Elimination of Discrimination

The second objective of the duty to accommodate is stated in Article 5(3) of the CRPD as being the elimination of discrimination. In their endeavours to eliminate discrimination, States must bear in mind several other provisions of the Convention as the duty to eliminate discrimination features heavily in the general obligations of the CRPD. Specifically, Article 4(1)(b) of the CRPD requires States to 'take *all appropriate measures*, including legislation, to modify or abolish existing laws, regulations, customs and practices that constitute discrimination against persons with disabilities.'[184] This will entail, in the first instance, ensuring that the unjustified denial of reasonable accommodation is included as a distinct form of discrimination in national legislation and that national policy documents give express recognition to this new form of discrimination under international human rights law. Furthermore, national legislation and policy documents must not contain any provisions that would inhibit fulfilment of the duty to reasonably accommodate or the duty to eliminate discrimination. General Obligation 4(e) of the CRPD requires States Parties 'to take *all appropriate measures* to eliminate discrimination on the basis of disability by any person, organization or private enterprise.'[185] This will include ensuring that private entities remove all discriminatory barriers which result in a denial of the right to reasonable accommodation. In order to eliminate discrimination, States will also be required to put in place effective legal remedies for persons with disabilities who have been discriminated against by means of denial of reasonable accommodation.

It is evident that the duty to accommodate is an important component of any State policy to ensure the promotion of equality and the elimination of discrimination. However, the duty to accommodate should form part of a wider legal and policy framework by States targeted at ensuring *de facto* equality. Other subsections of Article 5 also require States to take active steps to secure *de facto* equality for persons with disabilities, beyond the provision of reasonable accommodations. One such measure required by States is that of positive action, contained in Article 5(4) of the Convention. I will now turn to an examination of Article 5(4).

4.5. Article 5(4) of the CRPD

> **Specific measures which are necessary to accelerate or achieve *de facto* equality of persons with disabilities shall not be considered discrimination under the terms of the present Convention**

4.5.1. Introduction to Positive Action Measures under Article 5(4) of the CRPD

Positive action (affirmative action) clauses are no stranger to international human rights treaties. Such clauses are found in varying formats in several provisions at

---

184 UN CRPD, Article 4(1)(b) [emphasis added].

185 UN CRPD, Article 4(e) [emphasis added].

the international level. Examples can be seen in Article 1 CERD[186] and Article 4 CEDAW,[187] both of which address what are known as 'special measures,' a term which is used widely in international human rights law to denote provisions targeted at rectifying disadvantages attributable to past or current discriminatory laws, policies and practices. Article 5(4) of the CRPD can be termed a positive action clause, which endorses 'specific measures' aimed at equalising opportunities and accelerating *de facto* equality for people with disabilities. There is a reason why the measures endorsed by the CRPD are entitled 'specific measures' rather than the more commonly used term 'special measures.' This point will be expanded upon below.[188]

Positive action means adopting or maintaining certain advantages in favour of an under-represented or marginalised group. Lizzie Barmes describes positive action as activity 'designed to improve the position, in terms of the distribution of benefits or dis-benefits, of a given social group or sub-group (or of several such groups), on the basis that its members suffer systematic disadvantage in that regard.'[189] Positive action is linked to the substantive model of equality as it seeks to 'correct or compensate for past or present discrimination [... and ...] prevent discrimination from recurring in the future.'[190] Positive action has obvious benefits in the disability context. However, it must be noted from the outset that such measures should form part of a broader policy initiative aimed at achieving true equality and wider structural change for people with disabilities. In other words, positive action can only guarantee a certain level of equality of outcome for persons with disabilities. Such measures do not target the underlying root causes of entrenched discrimination and dominant ideologies.

The core human rights treaty bodies and legal scholars have made some general observations regarding the adoption of special measures under the respective human rights treaties. These observations can potentially be applied to the types of measures to be taken by States under Article 5(4) of the CRPD. Before looking at the specificities of the positive action clause in Article 5(4), I will pen some general

186 Article 1(4) CERD provides that: 'Special measures taken for the sole purpose of securing adequate advancement of certain racial or ethnic groups or individuals requiring such protection as may be necessary in order to ensure such groups or individuals equal enjoyment or exercise of human rights and fundamental freedoms shall not be deemed racial discrimination, provided, however, that such measures do not, as a consequence, lead to the maintenance of separate rights for different racial groups and that they shall not be continued after the objectives for which they were taken have been achieved.'

187 Article 4 CEDAW provides that (1) 'Adoption by States Parties of temporary special measures aimed at accelerating de facto equality between men and women shall not be considered discrimination as defined in the present Convention, but shall in no way entail as a consequence the maintenance of unequal or separate standards; these measures shall be discontinued when the objectives of equality of opportunity and treatment have been achieved.' (2) Adoption by States Parties of special measures, including those measures contained in the present Convention, aimed at protecting maternity shall not be considered discriminatory.'

188 See subsection 4.5.3 below.

189 L. Barmes, 'Equality law and experimentation: The positive action challenge' (2009) 68 *Cambridge Law Journal*, 623, at page 623.

190 J. O'Brien, 'Affirmative Action, Special Measures and the Sex Discrimination Act' (2004) 27(3) *University of New South Wales Law Journal* 840.

observations on special measures in the core human rights treaties in the next subsection of this chapter.

4.5.2. General Observations on Special Measures in the Core Human Rights Treaties

In the subsections which follow, the most pertinent observations made by the core human rights treaty bodies and also by legal scholars will be outlined, with regard to the adoption of special measures at the international level.

4.5.2.1. Temporary *versus* Permanent Special Measures

It is well established that special measures are usually temporary in nature. The use of temporary special measures is recognised by the HRC as a means to 'diminish or eliminate conditions which cause or help to perpetuate discrimination.'[191] The objective of such measures has been stated by the CERD Committee as being the 'advancement of effective equality.'[192] Rebecca Cook elaborates on this and, furthermore, links temporary special measures to participation in society in her assertion that:

> Generally speaking, temporary special measures are time-limited positive measures intended to enhance opportunities for historically and systematically disadvantaged groups, with a view to bringing group members into the mainstream of political, economic, social, cultural and civil life.[193]

There are, however, some instances in which permanent positive action measures may be deemed necessary under international human rights law. This point will be expanded on below[194] in the context of the provisions of CEDAW and the CRPD.

4.5.2.2. The Importance of a Clear Delineation of the Types of Measures Adopted by States

There is a clear difference between positive action measures and other measures of a more general nature that seek to eliminate discrimination and to redress disadvantage. As already noted above, temporary positive action measures seek to accelerate or

191 Human Rights Committee, General Comment 18 on Non-Discrimination (1989), (adopted at the thirty-seventh session, 1989), U.N. Doc. HRI/GEN/1/Rev.1 at 26 (1994), para. 10.

192 UN Committee on the Elimination of Racial Discrimination, General Recommendation 32 on The meaning and scope of special measures in the International Convention on the Elimination of Racial Discrimination (2009), adopted at the seventy-fifth session of the Committee on 24 September 2009, UN Doc. CERD/C/GC/32, para. 11.

193 R. Cook, 'Obligations to Adopt Temporary Special Measures under the Convention on the Elimination of All Forms of Discrimination Against Women' in I. Boerefijn, F. Coomans, J. Goldschmidt, R. Holtmaat and R. Wolleswinkel (eds.), *Temporary Special Measures: Accelerating de facto Equality of Women under Article 4(1) UN Convention on the Elimination of All Forms of Discrimination Against Women* (Intersentia, Antwerp, 2003), at page 119.

194 See section 4.5.4 of this chapter.

achieve *de facto* equality of disadvantaged groups due, *inter alia*, to historical and ongoing discrimination. In that sense, they are different from, and much narrower than, general measures taken to alter environmental and other structures in order to tackle the root causes of discrimination and structural inequalities. States will be required to take many active measures to promote *de facto* equality and, thereby, to promote participation and inclusion of persons with disabilities in society. The types of measures to be taken by States include, but are not limited to, positive action. Lisa Waddington and Mark Bell distinguish clearly between positive action measures and other measures of a more general nature aimed at promoting social inclusion. The authors state that measures which are closer to positive action share some or all of the following characteristics:[195]

i. Firstly, they are 'targeted at a well-defined social group;'[196]
ii. Secondly, they 'seek to redress disadvantages in a specific setting, such as access to education or employment.'[197] The authors state that positive action schemes 'will typically be designed for those pursuing a particular job or career where there is evidence of past and/or present disadvantage. The initiative may be open to any potential jobseeker, but it is normally not aimed at everyone in the labour market possessing a particular characteristic;'[198]
iii. Thirdly, the authors state that 'the necessity for positive action will be subject to periodic review.'[199] However, 'this does not mean that positive action must be time-limited, but it is not automatically assumed to be indefinite.' In contrast, the authors note that 'many of the social benefits extended on the basis of disability are not assumed to have any preordained time-limit.'[200]

The awareness-raising duties of States in Article 8 and the accessibility obligation in Article 9 of the CRPD do not fall within the concept of positive action. Rather, they are general measures aimed at eliminating discrimination and promoting participation and inclusion through transformation of social and environmental structures, as well as entrenched ideologies. In addition to those measures, social benefits linked to ensuring increased access for persons with disabilities to social protection, including social security, social assistance and healthcare, education and certain goods or services which are available to the public also do not fall within the net of positive action *per se*, although they may appear to be similar in nature. Those types of social benefits are targeted simply at promoting the economic, social or cultural participation and inclusion of persons with disabilities. Positive action can also be distinguished from the broader framework of positive duties designed to promote equality and to ensure participation of persons with disabilities in decision-

195 L. Waddington and M. Bell, 'Exploring the Boundaries of Positive Action under EU Law: A Search for Conceptual Clarity' (2011) 48(5) *Common Market Law Review* 1503, at pages 1523/1524.
196 Ibid, 1523.
197 Ibid, 1523/1524.
198 Ibid.
199 Ibid, 1524.
200 Ibid.

making processes and in the adoption of legislation and policies which affect their rights.[201]

A clear line of distinction must also be drawn between positive action and the duty to accommodate. A handful of authors[202] have argued that reasonable accommodation measures lie within the framework of positive action. Brian Doyle, for example, opines that the duty to make a reasonable adjustment in the British context 'is an example of legally mandated positive action rather than a requirement of reverse or positive discrimination.'[203] The conceptual confusion surrounding the two concepts is not confined to legal scholars. Waddington and Bell refer to the case of *Coleman* v. *Attridge Law and Law*[204] as exhibiting a lack of clarity on the issue. The authors state that in that case, the (then) European Court of Justice, when considering the provisions of the Employment Equality Directive, seems to 'lump both [reasonable accommodations and positive action] together, referring to them as "provisions concerning positive discrimination measures."'[205] Notwithstanding this conceptual confusion, it is submitted that the two forms of measures are separate and distinct. The text of the CRPD itself distinguishes between the two measures by including positive action as a sub-category of measures in Article 5(4), clearly separate from the duty to accommodate in Articles 2 and 5(3) of the Convention. The distinction between the two types of measures is confirmed by the fact that positive action is not stated to be mandatory on the face of the Convention.[206] Reasonable accommodations, on the other hand, are mandated clearly by Articles 2 and 5(3) of the CRPD. Another distinguishing feature of the duty to accommodate, as opposed to positive action measures, lies in the individualised nature of the former, when compared with the group dimension inherent in the latter measures. The duty to accommodate has the advantage of being tailored specifically to meet the needs of the disabled individual in question. The crux of the duty to accommodate involves 'an individual assessment and a tailored individual solution,'[207] both in terms of the actual accommodation requested and the assessment as to whether the accommodation constitutes a disproportionate or undue burden on an entity. By way of contrast, positive action

---

201 Waddington and Bell state that: 'Positive duties aim to incorporate the promotion of equality into decision-making and service delivery. To this end, they advocate a change in the mindset of policy-makers and the method of policy-making so that improved equality outcomes are achieved. This manifests itself in a range of responses, many of which are not positive action.' [Ibid, at page 1524].

202 See, for example, the views of P.S. Karlan and G. Rutherglen, 'Disabilities, Discrimination, & "reasonable accommodation,"' (1996) 46(1) *Duke Law Journal* 1; See also B.P. Tucker, 'The ADA's Revolving Door: Inherent Flaws in the Civil Rights Paradigm' (2001) 62 *Ohio State Law Journal* 335.

203 B. Doyle, 'Enabling Legislation or Dissembling Law? The Disability Discrimination Act 1995,' (1997) 60 *Modern Law Review*, 64, 74.

204 European Court of Justice, Case C-303/06, *Coleman* v. *Attridge Law and Law* [2008] ECR I-5603.

205 L. Waddington and M. Bell, 'Exploring the Boundaries of Positive Action Under EU Law: A Search for Conceptual Clarity' (2011) 48 *Common Market Law Review* 1503, at page 1504.

206 However, it will be argued later in this chapter that positive action measures in the CRPD may, in fact, be required in certain instances.

207 E.U. Network of Experts on Disability Discrimination, *Implementing and Interpreting the Reasonable Accommodation Provision of the Framework Employment Directive: Learning from Experience and Achieving Best Practice* (Report Prepared by Lisa Waddington in collaboration with Lee Ann Basser, Robert L. Burgdorf, Jeremy Cooper, Shivaun Quinlivan, and members of the European Commission Expert Group on Disability Discrimination) 2004, at page 8.

is targeted generally at members of socially disadvantaged groups. The aims of reasonable accommodation and positive action are similar, to the extent that both types of measures seek to increase the participation and inclusion of persons with disabilities in society. However, unlike positive action measures, the aim of the duty to accommodate is not to repair historical inequalities. Rather, its aim is to *ensure* to persons with disabilities the enjoyment or exercise *on an equal basis with others* of all human rights and fundamental freedoms.[208] The duty to accommodate is focused on current discriminatory obstacles to the enjoyment of rights by persons with disabilities, whereas positive action seeks to target the present effects of past discrimination. While in practice it may be difficult to draw a clear line of distinction in practice, States Parties to the Convention must at least seek to distinguish in their laws and policies between positive action measures and other measures of a more general nature which are taken to ensure that the underlying structural inequalities against persons with disabilities are addressed. This is in line with the observations of the core human rights treaty bodies.[209]

4.5.2.3. 'Specific Measures:' An Exception to the Equality and Non-Discrimination Norms?

Positive action is often perceived as being controversial, to the extent that it appears to be *prima facie* incompatible with the non-discrimination principle.[210] Olivier de Schutter states that an important contribution of General Recommendation 25 of the CEDAW Committee 'is that, far from being presented as [a] derogation from the requirement of (formal) equality, the adoption of such positive action measures is seen as a contribution to the implementation of the principles of equality and non-discrimination.'[211] This is evident from the remarks of the CEDAW Committee in paragraph 14 of that recommendation, which is formulated as follows: 'The

208 UN CRPD, Article 2 [emphasis added].

209 The UNCESCR has observed that temporary special measures 'should be distinguished from *permanent* policies and strategies undertaken towards equality of men and women.' [UNCESCR, General Comment No. 16 on the equal right of men and women to the enjoyment of all economic, social and cultural rights (Article 3) (2005), adopted at the thirty-fourth session, 2005, UN Doc. E/C.12/2005/4, para. 35]. In its General Recommendation 25 (2004), the CEDAW Committee calls for a differentiation between the two types of measures. The Committee states that: 'Not all measures that potentially are, or will be, favourable to women are temporary special measures. The provision of general conditions in order to guarantee the civil, political, economic, social and cultural rights of women and the girl child, designed to ensure for them a life of dignity and non-discrimination, cannot be called temporary special measures.' [UN Committee on the Elimination of All Forms of Discrimination Against Women, General Recommendation 25, on article 4, paragraph 1, of the Convention on the Elimination of All Forms of Discrimination against Women, *On Article 4, Paragraph 1, – Temporary Special Measures* (2004), UN Doc. HRI/GEN/1/Rev.7, para. 19].

210 Kitching notes that positive action appears to run counter to the formal conception of equality as it tends 'to privilege group over individual rights when in many systems individual rights are paramount. The right to equal treatment is an individual right; preferential treatment concerns group rights.' [K. Kitching (ed.), *International Discrimination Law: A Handbook for Practitioners* (Interights, London, January 2005)].

211 O. de Schutter, 'Positive Action' in D. Schiek, L. Waddington and M. Bell (eds.), *Cases, Materials and Text on National, Supranational and International Non-Discrimination Law* (Hart Publishing, Oxford, 2007), at page 785.

application of temporary special measures in accordance with the Convention is one of the means to realize *de facto* or substantive equality for women, rather than an exception to the norms of non-discrimination and equality.'[212] In the context of persons with disabilities, the UNCESCR has stressed that positive action does not constitute a violation of the principle of non-discrimination. Rather, the Committee notes that positive action is a legitimate means by which to eliminate past discrimination and to achieve equalisation of opportunities.[213] The HRC has also acknowledged the compatibility of special measures with the general prohibition of discrimination in *Stalla Costa v. Uruguay*[214] and *Jacobs v Belgium*.[215] In line with these observations, States Parties to the CRPD must bear in mind that specific measures under Article 5(4) of the Convention are an integral component of the equality norm for people with disabilities and they should not be viewed as an exception thereto. The obligation to take positive action must be implemented as a matter of priority, along with other general measures mandated by the Convention, in order to ensure *de facto* equality for people with disabilities.

4.5.2.4. The Participation of Marginalised Groups in the Adoption of Specific Measures

In its General Recommendation 32 (2009), the CERD Committee notes that 'States parties should ensure that special measures are designed and implemented on the basis of prior consultation with affected communities and the active participation of such communities.'[216] Article 4(3) of the CRPD already requires States to consult closely with and to involve actively persons with disabilities, including children

212 UN Committee on the Elimination of All Forms of Discrimination Against Women, General recommendation 25, on article 4, paragraph 1, of the Convention on the Elimination of All Forms of Discrimination against Women, *On Article 4, Paragraph 1, – Temporary Special Measures,* UN Doc. HRI/GEN/1/Rev.7, para. 14.

213 In its General Comment 5 (1994) on persons with disabilities, the UNCESCR observes that: '[B]ecause appropriate measures need to be taken to undo existing discrimination and to establish equitable opportunities for persons with disabilities, such actions should not be considered discriminatory in the sense of article 2(2) of the ICESCR as long as they are based on the principle of equality and are employed only to the extent necessary to achieve that objective.' [UNCESCR, General Comment 5 on persons with disabilities (1994) para. 18. See also UNCESCR, General Comment No. 13 on the right to education (1999), para. 32, which reads as follows: '[t]he adoption of temporary special measures intended to bring about de facto equality for men and women and for disadvantaged groups is not a violation of the right to non-discrimination with regard to education [...].'

214 Human Rights Committee, Communication No. 198/1985, *Stalla Costa v Uruguay* (1987). [In that case, the Committee held that the preferential treatment granted to certain public officials in gaining admission to the public service was a permissible positive action measure. – UN Doc. CCPR/C/30/D/198/1985, para. 10].

215 Human Rights Committee, Communication No. 943/2000, *Guido Jacobs v Belgium* (2004) [In that case, the Committee found the adoption of positive measures aimed at increasing the representation and participation of women in the public service was an objective and reasonably justifiable measure pursuant to several articles of the Covenant, namely Articles 2, 3, 25(c) and 26 – UN Doc. CCPR/C/81/D/943/2000, para. 9.3].

216 UN Committee on the Elimination of Racial Discrimination, General Recommendation 32 on the meaning and scope of special measures in the International Convention on the Elimination of Racial Discrimination (2009), adopted at the seventy-fifth session, UN Doc. CERD/C/GC/32, para. 18.

with disabilities, through their representative organisations[217] in the 'development and implementation of legislation and policies to implement the present Convention, and in other decision-making processes concerning issues relating to persons with disabilities.'[218] DPOs should therefore be involved fully in the design, implementation and monitoring of specific measures under Article 5(4) of the CRPD. In practice, this might mean involving DPOs in the drafting of policies related to positive action measures in order to determine the most appropriate types of measures to be taken in a given context. Examples of this consultative process in the overall context of implementation and monitoring of the CRPD is evidenced in Article 9 of the Austrian Disabled Persons Act.[219] Cypriot law contains similar provisions regarding consultation with persons with disabilities.[220]

All of the general features of positive action clauses that have been outlined above map over to the context of persons with disabilities. Nonetheless, there are certain features of the positive action clause in Article 5(4) of the CRPD which merit particular attention. As such, it is important to analyse the drafting history of Article 5(4). After having analysed the drafting history of the CRPD, I will then embark on a comparison of the positive action clause contained in the CRPD with those contained in CERD and CEDAW in order to draw analogies between the various positive action clauses existing at the international level. Finally, I will outline several types of specific measures that may be taken by States under the CRPD, before going on to reflect on whether the adoption of positive action measures is merely optional or whether it is, in fact, obligatory.

4.5.3. Observations from the Drafting History of Article 5(4) of the CRPD

Notwithstanding the fact that the notion of 'special measures' is already contained in several international human rights treaties, its inclusion in the CRPD provoked lengthy debate. One of the reasons for disconcertion arose from the fact that, in the disability context, the term 'special' has sometimes had a derogatory meaning, as pointed out by the Working Group of the Ad-Hoc Committee.[221] Delegates at

---

217 UN CRPD, Article 4(3).

218 Ibid.

219 That Act establishes a Federal Disability Board consisting of seven representatives of disabled persons, which is consulted during the process of policy-making and the drafting of laws. [Bundesrecht konsolidiert: Gesamte Rechtsvorschrift für Bundesbehindertengesetz, Fassung vom 11.12.2014, available at www.ris.bka.gv.at/GeltendeFassung.wxe?Abfrage=Bundesnormen&Gesetzesnummer=10008713 last accessed 11 December 2014].

220 The Law on the Consultation Process between the Government and other Services for issues concerning Persons with Disabilities in Cyprus provides that the government must consult with the Confederation of Organisations of the Disabled (as the social partner of the State) on decisions that directly or indirectly affect persons with disabilities. The confederation is made up of nine DPOs. This demonstrates the types of consultative processes that States Parties to the CRPD will be required to engage in related, *inter alia*, to the adoption of positive measures. Available at www.kysoa.org.cy/kysoa/page.php?pageID=17&langID=13 last accessed 11 December 2014.

221 Footnote 28, Report of the Working Group to the Ad Hoc Committee, Annex I: Draft articles for a Comprehensive and Integral International Convention on the Protection and Promotion of the Rights and Dignity of Persons with Disabilities, available at www.un.org/esa/socdev/enable/rights/wgcontrib-chair1.html last accessed 17 December 2014.

the negotiation sessions echoed the fear of the Working Group regarding the inappropriate use of the term 'special' in the context of an equality provision in a disability convention. The Canadian delegate proposed the use of the term 'positive measures' as an alternative. This appeared to have strong support among non-governmental organisations. However, the Austrian delegate stated that a reference to positive measures might cause concern for some government delegations and it suggested instead the insertion of the word 'specific.'[222] The term 'specific measures' was retained in the final text of Article 5(4) of the CRPD.

The CEDAW Committee has stated that 'the real meaning of "special" in the formulation of article 4, paragraph 1 of the Convention, is that the measures are designed to serve a specific goal.'[223] There is no information contained in the *travaux préparatoires* of the CRPD regarding the exact interpretation of the term 'specific' but it is noteworthy that many delegates supported the inclusion of the term 'measures' with no qualifier such as 'special' or 'positive.' Therefore, it is likely that the term 'specific measures' was chosen merely as a neutral alternative to the other proposals. It is apt to look at the ordinary meaning of the word in question. According to a respected legal dictionary, the adjective 'specific' means 'having a special application, bearing or reference' or something which is 'explicit or definite.'[224] The measures to be taken under Article 5(4) of the CRPD must therefore be designed to serve an explicit or definite goal. This interpretation is borne out by the text of Article 5(4) itself, which elaborates on the particular goal of specific measures, namely the achievement or acceleration of *de facto* equality for disabled people.

There was lengthy debate about various other aspects of Article 5(4) of the CRPD. The original wording of Article 5(4) read as follows:

> Special measures aimed at accelerating *de facto* equality of persons with disabilities shall not be considered discrimination as defined in the present Convention, *but shall in no way entail as a consequence the maintenance of unequal or separate standards; those measures shall be discontinued when the objectives of equality of opportunity and treatment have been achieved.*[225]

The second part of the provision, highlighted above in italics, stirred intense deliberations among delegates. Several delegates argued for the deletion of the

---

222 Seventh Session of the Ad Hoc Committee, Volume 8(1), 16 January 2006 available at www.un.org/esa/socdev/enable/rights/ahc7sum16jan.htm, last accessed 17 October 2014.

223 UN Committee on the Elimination of All Forms of Discrimination Against Women, General recommendation 25: Article 4, paragraph 1, of the Convention on the Elimination of All Forms of Discrimination against Women - Temporary Special Measures (2004), para. 21.

224 Merriam-Webster's Dictionary of Law, Merriam-Webster, 1996 available at www.dictionary.com last accessed 27 June 2014.

225 Draft Article 2(4) of the Working Group Chair's Draft Elements of a Comprehensive and Integral International Convention on Protection and Promotion of the Rights and Dignity of Persons with Disabilities, available at www.un.org/esa/socdev/enable/rights/wgcontrib-chair1.htm. last accessed 17 October 2014 [emphasis added].

second part of the provision in its entirety, for two reasons. The first reason was that some delegates felt that 'unequal or separate standards' may be required in certain contexts in order to facilitate *de facto* equality for people with disabilities.[226] Secondly, the Japanese delegate pointed to the fact that, if the second part of the draft Article 7(5) was to remain as written above, then this could be 'misinterpreted as obliging States to abolish all specific measures, regardless of justification, within a given time span.'[227] It was argued that the provision on 'specific measures' in the CRPD should not be subject to a 'sunset clause.'[228]

The section highlighted above in italics was, in fact, removed from the final text of the CRPD. This supports two conclusions. The first of those is that States would appear to have a wide latitude with regard to the types of specific measures which they can incorporate in their national disability regimes, even where the measures adopted entail different criteria for persons with disabilities. States would presumably be allowed to modify criteria that constitute entrance barriers to an educational facility or a particular job for persons with disabilities (in instances where such criteria would not lower academic or employment standards). Some might argue that modifying criteria for persons with disabilities could be deemed to constitute a form of discrimination vis-à-vis non-disabled people. On this point, it has already been demonstrated above that ensuring *de facto* equality for persons with disabilities and ensuring the exercise and enjoyment of rights on an equal basis with others will require the adoption of different or additional measures in the disability context, separate and distinct from measures adopted for other marginalised groups. This is on account of the particular nature of the disadvantage faced by disabled individuals. This might mean that entrance requirements for a particular position or educational facility may need to be modified for persons with disabilities to take account of the historical disadvantage to which disabled people have been subjected and to enable them to gain equal access to the right to employment or the right to education, among others. The Coordinator of the Fifth Session of the Ad-Hoc Committee, Ambassador Don MacKay (New Zealand), noted that 'in the employment context, lower standards in some jobs to accelerate employment of people with disabilities could lead to positive outcomes.'[229] The Irish Equality Authority has stated that, among the main barriers for disabled people that may be identified at recruitment level in the public service, is the specification of a minimum educational requirement, which disabled people are often not in a position to comply with. As a result, the Equality Authority claims that 'employers may need to examine whether there are suitable alternative means of assessing future job suitability and performance.'[230] As this demonstrates, differential treatment of persons with disabilities may be required in

226 Fifth Session of the Ad Hoc Committee, volume 6(1), January 24, 2005 available at www.un.org/esa/socdev/enable/rights/ahc5sum24jan.htm, last accessed 17 October 2014.

227 Ibid.

228 Fourth Session of the Ad Hoc Committee, Volume 5(8), September 1, 2004, available at www.un.org/esa/socdev/enable/rights/ahc4sumart07.htm, last accessed 19 October 2014.

229 Fifth Session of the Ad Hoc Committee, volume 6(1), January 24, 2005 available at www.un.org/esa/socdev/enable/rights/ahc5sum24jan.htm, last accessed 17 October 2014.

230 The Irish Equality Authority, Department of Justice, Equality and Law Reform, *Positive Action for People with Disabilities: Assisting Public Sector Bodies to Achieve the 3% Employment Target,*

some instances to further the object and purpose of the Convention and the overall goal of substantive equality.

The second conclusion to be drawn from the drafting history of the CRPD is that States Parties to the Convention will not be under a temporal limitation with regard to the specific measures which they put in place. While temporary specific measures fall under this provision, ongoing or permanent specific measures are also permissible under Article 5(4) of the CRPD. Indeed, it has been recognised that 'both types of [specific] measures might be necessary in order to achieve equality and therefore a State party will be obliged to adopt a range of [specific] measures across different areas of social life'[231] During the negotiation sessions, the Japanese delegate argued that 'as with the protection of maternity in Article 4(2) of CEDAW[232] – which is not considered a temporary measure – there are similarly valuable measures in disability policy that should be maintained.'[233] The European Disability Forum (EDF), amongst others, replicated this argument by stating that:

> Special measures may need to be dealt with differently for people with disabilities than for other groups. While some positive action measures, such as quotas, may be short term, there are many measures which are not temporary. For example assistive technology and respite care are not temporary, and do lead to equality.[234]

4.5.4. Comparison of the Positive Action Clause in the CRPD with CERD and CEDAW

As we have seen already, CERD and CEDAW are among the international human rights treaties which contain positive action clauses. Article 5(4) of the CRPD can be distinguished from Article 1(4) CERD on account of the fact that both temporary and permanent specific measures are permissible under Article 5(4). By way of contrast, Article 1(4) CERD highlights the temporary character of the measures envisaged by that provision. It provides that special measures 'shall not be continued after the objectives for which they were taken have been achieved.'[235] Article 5(4) of the CRPD does not contain this temporal limitation and it is therefore akin to Article 4 CEDAW, under which both temporary special measures and permanent protective measures are permissible. Article 4(2) CEDAW provides that permanent special measures may be taken by States in the context of maternity-related matters. By

available at www.equality.ie/Files/Positive%20Action%20for%20People%20with%20Disabilities.pdf last accessed 20 October 2014.

231 United Nations Enable, *Handbook for Parliamentarians on the Convention on the Rights of Persons with Disabilities*, available at www.un.org/disabilities/default.asp?id=236, last accessed 8 October 2012.

232 Article 4(2) CEDAW states that the 'adoption by States Parties of special measures, including those measures contained in the present Convention, aimed at protecting maternity shall not be considered discriminatory.'

233 Fifth Session of the Ad Hoc Committee, volume 6(1), January 24, 2005 available at www.un.org/esa/socdev/enable/rights/ahc5sum24jan.htm, accessed 17 October 2014.

234 Third Session of the Ad-Hoc Committee, volume 4(2), May 25, 2004, available at www.un.org/esa/socdev/enable/rights/ahc3sum7.htm, last accessed 17 October 2014.

235 CERD, Article 1(4).

way of contrast, Article 4(1) CEDAW allows for measures aimed at accelerating *de facto* equality between men and women, such measures to be discontinued when the objectives of equality of opportunity and treatment have been achieved.[236] In order to determine whether analogies can be drawn between the rationale for allowing permanent positive action measures under the CRPD and CEDAW, I will now examine the interpretation of special measures in Article 4 CEDAW.

The CEDAW Committee has distinguished clearly between the purpose of temporary special measures in Article 4(1), on the one hand, and permanent special measures in Article 4(2) of CEDAW, on the other hand. In its General Recommendation 25 (2004), the Committee states that:

> The purpose of article 4, paragraph 1, is to accelerate the improvement of the position of women to achieve their de facto or substantive equality with men, and to effect the structural, social and cultural changes necessary to correct past and current forms and effects of discrimination against women, as well as to provide them with compensation. These measures are of a temporary nature.[237]

In the same general recommendation, the Committee distinguishes the foregoing measures from the permanent measures envisaged by Article 4(2), in its assertion that:

> Article 4, paragraph 2, provides for non-identical treatment of women and men due to their biological differences. These measures are of a permanent nature, at least until such time as the scientific and technological knowledge referred to in article 11, paragraph 3,[238] would warrant a review.[239]

The Committee has also drawn attention to the distinction between the two forms of special measures in its concluding observations.[240] From these sources, it can be deduced that the temporary special measures envisaged by Article 4(1) CEDAW are corrective in nature, designed to redress past and present inequalities and unequal power relations between men and women. According to the Committee, temporary special measures are designed to achieve a 'specific goal,'[241] in so far as they are

236 CEDAW, Article 4(1).

237 UN Committee on the Elimination of All Forms of Discrimination Against Women, General recommendation 25 on Article 4, paragraph 1, of the Convention on the Elimination of All Forms of Discrimination against Women, on temporary special measures (adopted at the thirtieth session of the Committee 2004), UN Doc. HRI/GEN/1/Rev.7, para. 15.

238 Article 11, para. 3 CEDAW provides that: 'Protective legislation relating to matters covered in this article shall be reviewed periodically in the light of scientific and technological knowledge and shall be revised, repealed or extended as necessary.'

239 UN Committee on the Elimination of All Forms of Discrimination Against Women, General recommendation 25, para. 16.

240 See, for example, the concluding observations of the CEDAW Committee to Peru in UN Doc. A/53/38/Rev.1 (Part II), para. 321.

241 UN Committee on the Elimination of All Forms of Discrimination Against Women, General recommendation No. 25, at para. 21, where it is stated that 'the real meaning of "special" in the formulation of article 4, paragraph 1, is that the measures are designed to serve a specific goal.'

'part of a necessary strategy by States Parties directed towards the achievement of *de facto* or substantive equality of women with men in the enjoyment of their human rights and fundamental freedoms.'[242] This objective has been elaborated on by the Committee as encompassing an obligation to accelerate the modification and elimination of cultural practices and stereotypical attitudes and behaviour that discriminate against or are disadvantageous for women[243] and to ensure the redistribution of power and resources.[244] The Committee has also noted that measures taken by States under Article 4(1) should aim to accelerate the equal participation of women in the political, economic, social, cultural, civil or any other field.'[245] With regard to the duration of temporary special measures, the Committee has stated that this should be determined by [the] 'functional result [of the measure] in response to a concrete problem and not by a predetermined passage of time.'[246]

By way of contrast, the permanent special measures envisaged by Article 4(2) CEDAW are aimed specifically at protecting women during the maternity period. The rationale for the adoption of such measures is the biological differences which exist between men and women. This rationale has been delineated clearly by the CEDAW Committee in its General Recommendation 25 as follows:

> Women's biologically determined permanent needs and experiences should be distinguished from other needs that may be the result of past and present discrimination against women by individual actors, the dominant gender ideology, or by manifestations of such discrimination in social and cultural structures and institutions.[247]

In light of the fact that the CRPD is the only other international human rights treaty that also permits permanent positive action measures, it is apt to draw an analogy between positive action measures in CEDAW and the CRPD. The reasons for doing this are twofold. In the first instance, an explicit link was made between the permanent measures envisaged under Article 5(4) of the CRPD and those envisaged under Article 4(2) CEDAW during the negotiations of the CRPD.[248] The second reason for comparing the two provisions is that the rationale underlying the adoption of permanent special measures under CEDAW can be aligned (to some extent) with the rationale underlying the adoption of permanent specific measures in the CRPD. Maternity cannot, of course, be equated with impairment, in the sense that pregnancy generally represents an individual choice, whereas impairment does not. Additionally, maternity is a temporary state, as opposed to impairment, which

---

242 Ibid, para. 18.

243 Ibid, para. 38.

244 Ibid, paras. 18 and 39.

245 Ibid, para. 18.

246 Ibid, para. 20.

247 Ibid, para. 11.

248 As outlined earlier in this chapter (in section 4.5.3), the Japanese delegate argued during the negotiation sessions that 'as with the protection of maternity in Article 4(2) of CEDAW – which is not considered a temporary measure – there are similarly valuable measures in disability policy that should be maintained.' [Fifth Session of the Ad Hoc Committee, volume 6(1), January 24, 2005 available at www.un.org/esa/socdev/enable/rights/ahc3sum7.htm, accessed 17 October 2014].

is usually a more permanent condition. However, as outlined above, the permanent measures which are called for under Article 4(2) CEDAW are necessary and justified on account of women's biologically determined permanent needs and experiences. It is argued that this logic can be applied to persons with disabilities, who also have biologically determined, and of course mentally/intellectually determined, permanent needs and experiences. This inherent aspect of impairment may in certain circumstances necessitate the adoption of permanent positive action measures. By virtue of the particular nature of some impairments, disadvantage and exclusion from society becomes so systemic that it can only be remedied by permanent or long-term positive action measures. This is the case particularly with certain types of intellectual or developmental disabilities, where the very nature of the impairment itself often leads to a permanent and ongoing reduction in equal opportunities and possibilities for participation and inclusion in society, whether in the employment, educational or other fields of activity. In such instances, permanent positive action schemes can be justified as long as they are proportionate to the aim to be achieved by the measures.

The incorporation of permanent specific measures in Article 5(4) of the CRPD demonstrates quite clearly that the conceptualisation of disability in the Convention is not solely a social construct. Disability is a partly biologically determined experience and, as such, biologically determined factors must be taken into account in accelerating or achieving substantive equality. The understanding of disability endorsed by the CRPD seeks to redress, *inter alia*, the inequalities which result from biological (mental/intellectual) needs by placing ultimate responsibility on national governments to tackle the disadvantage arising from the interaction of impairment with societal barriers.[249]

Having considered the rationale for the adoption of both temporary and permanent specific measures under the CRPD, the next question to be addressed concerns the types of measures that might be deemed to constitute positive action under the Convention.

4.5.5. Examples of Temporary and Permanent Specific Measures under the CRPD

The CEDAW Committee has stated that positive action 'encompasses a wide variety of legislative, executive, administrative and other regulatory instruments, policies and practices.'[250] The CEDAW Committee gives various examples of the types of positive measures that States can take to ensure substantive equality as follows: 'outreach or support programmes; allocation and/or reallocation of resources;

249 Interestingly, the reason for not dividing temporary and permanent specific measures in the CRPD into two separate paragraphs (as under Article 4 CEDAW) may reflect the fact that the concept of disability contained in the Convention is viewed as being both socially constructed and biologically determined. Therefore, it would seem more appropriate to amalgamate temporary and permanent specific measures into the one paragraph.

250 UN Committee on the Elimination of All Forms of Discrimination Against Women, General Recommendation 25, para. 22.

preferential treatment; targeted recruitment, hiring and promotion; numerical goals connected with time frames; and quota systems.'[251] Specific measures adopted under Article 5(4) of the CRPD will seek to ensure the full and effective participation and inclusion of people with disabilities in society. Temporary specific measures will be required, *inter alia*, to address the historical and ongoing inequality of power between disabled people and their non-disabled counterparts. An example of a temporary specific measure might be the setting of quotas in employment or political institutions specifying the number or percentage of disabled people to be included in such institutions. Another example might be the preferential treatment of candidates with disabilities in the employment or education sector, even where the qualifications of the disabled candidate are not equal to those of the non-disabled candidate.[252] A concrete example[253] of temporary positive action measures can been seen in Birmingham University in the United Kingdom. That university has established a scheme which provides financial awards to students with disabilities, including students who have dyslexia, to help them with their studies. The money does not have to be spent on disability specific aids. Instead, the award recognises that students with a disability often find it difficult to supplement their income through part-time work whilst they are studying. A further example of a temporary specific measure in the disability context might entail setting and reporting on goals and timetables for the advancement of people with disabilities in social and political institutions or helping persons with disabilities to gain further educational qualifications. In addition, a targeted recruitment campaign raising awareness about employment opportunities amongst persons with disabilities would qualify as a type of temporary specific measure under the CRPD. Temporary specific measures may also be taken to increase the participation of persons with disabilities in political and public life under Article 29 of the CRPD. The amendment of electoral procedures has been alluded to by the CEDAW Committee as a form of temporary special measure[254] taken by States in the context of increasing the participation of women in political and public life. The CEDAW Committee has elaborated on the types of temporary measures that have been adopted by States Parties to that Convention with a view to increasing *de facto* equality in political and public life, including the following: recruiting, financially assisting and training women candidates, amending electoral procedures, developing campaigns directed at equal participation, setting numerical goals and quotas and targeting women for appointment to public positions.'[255] Some

---

251 Ibid.

252 As outlined earlier in this section, the drafting history of the CRPD supports the conclusion that States will have a wide latitude with regard to the types of specific measures that they endorse, even where those measures result, for instance, in modifying criteria or requirements for persons with disabilities.

253 This example is taken from M. Bell and L. Waddington, Annotation to the Legal Definition of Positive Action used in the PAMECUS Project (International perspectives on positive action measures: a comparative analysis in the European Union, Canada, the United States and South Africa, Office for Official Publications of the European Communities, 2009), available at www.brad.ac.uk/T4-health/new.../Definition_of_Positive_Action.doc, last accessed 10 December 2014.

254 UN Committee on the Elimination of Discrimination against Women, General Recommendation 23 on Political and Public Life (1997), adopted at the 16th session of the Committee, 1997, para. 15, available at www.un.org/womenwatch/daw/cedaw/recommendations/recomm.htm#recom23 last accessed 12 December 2014.

255 Ibid.

of those measures may translate to the context of increasing participation for persons with disabilities in political and public life.

As shown above in the preceding subsection of this chapter, certain individuals will require permanent positive action measures to equalise opportunities and outcomes on account of the particular nature of their impairment. Without such measures, the exercise of many rights will be hindered in respect of persons with intellectual or developmental disabilities, for instance. Permanent positive action in respect of those individuals might include respite care or assistive technology to overcome the disadvantage accruing to such persons and flowing from their impairment, in circumstances where the disadvantage is particularly embedded. The UNCESCR gives examples of measures to achieve non-discrimination in the disability context that may need to be of a permanent nature, such as interpretation services for linguistic minorities and persons with sensory impairments in health care facilities.[256]

On the whole, the two types of measures envisaged by Article 5(4) of the CRPD constitute a powerful means by which the participation and inclusion of people with disabilities in society can be increased. The obvious differences between people with disabilities and non-disabled people, whether based on socially created differences (arising from discriminatory norms, structures and practices) or biological differences (arising from impairment) results in the asymmetrical experience of disadvantage. Article 5(4) of the CRPD seeks to counter both forms of differences through its endorsement of temporary and permanent specific measures. However, it must be borne in mind that positive action measures, taken alone, cannot ensure substantive equality. It is important that such measures are adopted in tandem with the array of other measures in the Convention designed to tackle individual and structural disadvantage.

4.5.6. Positive Action under the CRPD: Obligatory or Optional?

The pivotal question arises as to whether the adoption of specific measures under the CRPD is obligatory or optional? Unlike the duty to accommodate under the Convention, positive action measures are not stated expressly to be mandatory. In other words, on the face of the CRPD there is no obligation to take the types of measures envisaged by Article 5(4). Arnardóttir states that it remains to be seen how the CRPD Committee:

> [...] Will construe the dividing line between the clearly justiciable individual rights claim of denial of reasonable accommodation under the Convention and the more elusive constituency of affirmative action.[257]

---

256 UNCESCR, General Comment 20 on non-discrimination in economic, social and cultural rights (2009), para. 9.

257 O.M. Arnardóttir, 'A Future of Multidimensional Disadvantage Equality' in O.M. Arnardóttir and G. Quinn (eds.), *The UN Convention on the Rights of Persons with Disabilities: European and Scandinavian Perspectives* (Martinus Nijhoff, Leiden, 2009) 60.

While the ultimate decision in this regard will remain with the Committee, it is argued that despite the lack of clarity on the face of the text, there may be circumstances in which the adoption of temporary and permanent specific measures under Article 5(4) of the CRPD will be required (although it will be extremely difficult to assert an individual claim to positive action measures under Article 5(4) of the CRPD). The reasoning underlying this argument will be outlined in the subsections which follow.

4.5.6.1. The Nature of Temporary Specific Measures under the CRPD

From a textual interpretation of Article 5(4) of the CRPD, there does not appear to be a specific obligation on States to implement temporary specific measures. Rather, such measures are optional. However, it is submitted that reading the Convention as a whole, and taking a dynamic or teleological approach to interpretation, one is led to the conclusion that the adoption of temporary specific measures may, in fact, be required by States Parties to the CRPD in certain circumstances. A dynamic approach is justified on account of the fact that the preamble of the CRPD notes at paragraph 'e' thereof that disability is 'an evolving concept.'[258] Accordingly, the types of positive action measures that States will be required to take under Article 5(4) will vary over time depending on evolving definitions of disability and also according to the context in which disability is experienced. Therefore, it is important to depart from a mere textual interpretation of the CRPD. It has already been established that all articles of the CRPD must be read in light of the object and purpose of the Convention. The adoption and implementation of positive action must not be viewed in isolation but should be viewed as an extension of achieving the objectives of the treaty as a whole. A dynamic approach to interpretation in the context of Article 5(4) of the CRPD would also appear to be consolidated by the views of the core human rights treaty bodies, which have elaborated on the circumstances in which the adoption of temporary special measures is required in other international treaties. The CEDAW Committee has pointed to the fact that:

> The practice of treaty monitoring bodies, including the Committee on the Elimination of Racial Discrimination, the Committee on Economic, Social and Cultural Rights, and the Human Rights Committee, shows that these bodies consider the application of temporary special measures as *mandatory* to achieve the *purposes of the respective treaties*.[259]

By way of reminder, Article 1 of the CRPD outlines the purpose of the Convention as being, *inter alia*, 'to promote, protect and ensure the full and equal enjoyment of all human rights and fundamental freedoms by all persons with disabilities.'[260] This will involve an obligation to eliminate discrimination, as a guarantee of equal rights implies the enjoyment of rights without discrimination. The purpose of the CRPD is mirrored in Article 3, which enumerates the general principles of the Convention. It is argued here that the overall aim of the Convention, as outlined above, mandates

---

[258] UN CRPD, Preamble, para. e.

[259] UN Committee on the Elimination of All Forms of Discrimination Against Women, General recommendation 25, at Footnote 3 [emphasis added].

[260] UN CRPD, Article 1.

that temporary specific measures will be required of States in circumstances where discrimination must be eliminated at a structural level. In other words, temporary specific measures should not be deemed to be obligatory in every instance which requires the elimination of discrimination. However, such measures will be mandatory to achieve the purpose of the CRPD, with a view to eliminating discrimination on the basis of disability in instances where discrimination is a structural or systemic feature of a society. Manfred Nowak confirms this interpretation when he states that 'in the event of *traditional, structural discrimination*, protection against discrimination also includes temporary special measures (privileges) aimed at accelerating the attainment of *de facto* equality'[261] In the words of Oliver de Schutter, the 'defining characteristic'[262] of structural discrimination would be that:

> It cuts across different spheres (education, employment, housing and access to health care in particular), resulting in a situation where the prohibition of discrimination in any one of these spheres or, indeed, in all of them, will not suffice to ensure effective equality.[263]

In cases where structural discrimination is rife, the full enjoyment of the human rights of persons with disabilities would be impaired and therefore the overall object and purpose of the CRPD would be obstructed. It is submitted that this, in itself, would mandate the adoption of temporary specific measures in the context of the CRPD in order to ensure that the object and purpose of the Convention is fulfilled.

The foregoing observations regarding the mandatory nature of Article 5(4) of the CRPD in relation to the elimination of discrimination would appear to be confirmed by the comments of the core human rights treaty bodies. Lester observes that 'the Human Rights Committee has confirmed in its general comments that positive action is sometimes *required* by States in order to combat discrimination.'[264] In that regard, he cites General Comment 18 (1989) of the HRC wherein it is stated that 'the principle of equality sometimes *requires* States parties to take affirmative action in order to diminish or eliminate conditions which cause or help to perpetuate discrimination prohibited by the Covenant.'[265] The Committee goes on to observe, for example that:

> In a state where the general conditions of a certain part of the population *prevent or impair their enjoyment of human rights*, the State should take specific action to correct those conditions. Such action may involve granting for a time to the part of the population

261 M. Nowak, *UN Covenant on Civil and Political Rights: CCPR commentary* (N.P. Engel, Kehl, 2nd Edition 2005) 631 [emphasis in original].

262 O. de Schutter, 'Positive Action' in D. Schiek, L. Waddington, M. Bell (eds.), *Cases, Materials and Text on National, Supranational and International Non-Discrimination Law* (Hart, Oxford, 2007) 793.

263 Ibid.

264 Lord Lester of Herne Hill QC, 'Non Discrimination in International Human Rights Law,' in *Developing Human* Rights Jurisprudence (Volume 6: Sixth Judicial Colloquium on the Domestic Application of International Human Rights Norms: Bloemfontein, South Africa, 3–5 September 1993) 17 [emphasis added].

265 Human Rights Committee, General Comment No. 18 on non-discrimination (1989), adopted at the thirty-seventh session, 1989), U.N. Doc. HRI/GEN/1/Rev.1 at 26 (1994), para. 10 [emphasis added].

> concerned certain preferential treatment in specific matters as compared with the rest of the population.[266]

Moreover, in its General Comment 4 (1981) on gender equality, the HRC has confirmed that the '*prevention of discrimination* on a number of grounds, among which sex is one, *requires* not only measures of protection but also *affirmative action* designed to ensure the positive enjoyment of rights'[267] In its General Comment 20 (2009), the UNCESCR elaborates on the circumstances in which the adoption of 'special measures' may be deemed obligatory. The Committee notes that 'in order to eliminate substantive discrimination, States parties may be, and in some cases are, under *an obligation* to adopt special measures to attenuate or suppress conditions that perpetuate discrimination.'[268]

In sum, the realisation of *de facto* equality for persons with disabilities will require the elimination of discrimination in the form of the removal of barriers to the equal enjoyment of rights through the adoption of temporary positive action measures, among other measures. States Parties to the CRPD will not be required to take temporary specific measures in every instance relating to the elimination of discrimination. However, States will be required to adopt temporary specific measures where they are deemed 'necessary' to 'accelerate or achieve *de facto* equality,'[269] particularly where discrimination is structural in nature.[270] National authorities will most likely be accorded discretion to decide which measures might be deemed most appropriate in any given situation in their endeavours to eliminate discrimination. However, the CRPD Committee will maintain its supervisory role by considering State Party reports and making recommendations as to the appropriateness of 'the measures taken to give effect to [a State's obligations]' under the Convention.[271] Rebecca Cook points to the fact that there is generally a 'margin of appreciation or discretion'[272] for States. However, she contends that in circumstances where it is proven that temporary special measures 'are particularly effective in achieving

---

266 Ibid, para. 10 [emphasis added].

267 Human Rights Committee, General Comment 4 on equality between the sexes (Article 3) (adopted at the thirteenth Session, 1981), U.N. Doc. HRI/GEN/1/Rev.6 at 126 (2003), para. 2 [emphasis added].

268 UNCESCR, General Comment 20 on non-discrimination in economic, social and cultural Rights on Article 2, Paragraph 2 of the International Covenant on Economic, Social and Cultural Rights, (2009), UN Doc. E/C.12/GC/20 (adopted at the forty-second session of the Committee) para. 9.

269 UN CRPD, Article 5(4).

270 In that regard, Rebecca Cook remarks that: 'Obligations to adopt temporary measures in particular fields will depend on the cause and the consequences of each particular form of discrimination and the context in which it takes place. If the discrimination is embedded in the nature of the society and culture, it could well take more than a change in the law that prohibits both direct and indirect discrimination.' [R. Cook, 'Obligations to Adopt Temporary Special Measures under the Convention on the Elimination of all Forms of Discrimination against Women' in I. Boerefijn, F. Coomans, J. Goldschmidt, R. Holtmaat and R. Wolleswinkel (eds.), *Temporary Special Measures: Accelerating de facto Equality of Women under Article 4(1) UN Convention on the Elimination of All Forms of Discrimination Against Women* (Intersentia, Antwerp, 2003) 134].

271 UN CRPD, Article 35.

272 R. Cook, 'Obligations to Adopt Temporary Special Measures under the Convention on the Elimination of All Forms of Discrimination Against Women' in I. Boerefijn, F. Coomans, J. Goldschmidt, R. Holtmaat and R. Wolleswinkel (eds.), *Temporary Special Measures: Accelerating de facto Equality*

a treaty objective, the latitude left to States parties in choosing remedial measures, particularly where they are demonstrably less effective, might be narrower.'[273]

4.5.6.2. The Nature of Permanent Specific Measures under the CRPD

With regard to the adoption of permanent specific measures under Article 5(4) of the CPRD, it is also submitted that such measures may be deemed obligatory in certain circumstances. As outlined above, the permanent specific measures envisaged by Article 5(4) are linked to the biological element of disability. In other words, they may be deemed to be justified on account of impairment *per se*. The biological dimension of disability is structural and general in nature – it is an involuntary attribute. Accordingly, it is the responsibility of national governments to eliminate the disadvantage that is associated with impairment under the Convention. This conclusion is supported by General Comment 5 (1994) of the UNCESCR, in which the Committee reiterates the words contained in the World Programme of Action concerning Disabled Persons, namely that 'the ultimate responsibility for remedying the conditions that lead to impairment and for dealing with the consequences of disability rests with Governments.'[274] It is argued here that permanent specific measures may be mandatory in circumstances where the failure to rectify the structural disadvantage flowing from impairment would result in the negation of the human rights of persons with disabilities. Taking the example of persons with certain kinds of intellectual or developmental disabilities, one can argue that a failure to put in place permanent positive action measures with respect to the right to participation in political and public life (among others) would negate the exercise of that right for such individuals as their disadvantage has become so embedded that they may never have the opportunity to participate equally in political life (as well as in many other areas). It is important to point out that the conclusion reached in this regard is not tantamount to a proposition that permanent specific measures will be required every time an individual claims a right to such measures as a result of a particular impairment. Of course, States will not be required to provide every disabled person with, for instance, access to assistive technology on demand. It would not be realistic to expect States to provide immediate access to costly assistive technologies for all persons with disabilities. According to General Comment 20 of the UNCESCR (2009), positive action measures may 'exceptionally'[275] need to be of a permanent nature in the disability context. Of course it is difficult to determine what might amount to an exceptional case but one might surmise that permanent

of Women under Article 4(1) UN Convention on the Elimination of All Forms of Discrimination Against Women (Intersentia, Antwerp, 2003) 132.

273 Ibid.

274 UNCESCR, General Comment 5 on Persons with Disabilities, adopted on 09/12/94 at the eleventh Session of the Committee, U.N. Doc E/1995/22, para. 12. The UNCESCR goes on in General Comment 5 to note that: 'In so far as special treatment is necessary, States parties are *required* to take appropriate measures, to the maximum extent of their available resources, to enable [persons with disabilities] to seek to overcome any disadvantages, in terms of the enjoyment of the rights specified in the Covenant, flowing from their disability.' [Ibid, para. 5].

275 UNCESCR, General Comment 20 on non-discrimination in economic, social and cultural rights (2009), UN Doc. E/C.12/GC/20, adopted at the forty-second session of the Committee, para. 9.

specific measures may be deemed mandatory in instances where the essence of protection of a human right would be rendered meaningless in the absence of such measures and, thereby, the object and purpose of the Convention would be hindered irremediably. This would certainly be the case in the context of persons with certain kind of intellectual or developmental disabilities, as highlighted above.

4.5.7. Conclusion on the Interpretation of Article 5(4) of the CRPD

It is clear from the general comments of the international human rights treaty bodies, and from an analysis of academic commentary, that the principle of equality under the CRPD will sometimes *require* a state to take positive action in order to diminish or eliminate conditions that cause or help to perpetuate discrimination. In his report to the UN Sub-Commission for the Promotion and Protection of Human Rights, Mr. Marc Bossuyt (former Special Rapporteur) summed up the status of positive action measures under international human rights law. He stated that

> A persistent policy in the past of systematic discrimination of certain groups of the population may justify – *and in some cases even require* – special measures intended to overcome the sequels of a condition of inferiority which still affects members belonging to such groups.[276]

There is no concrete positive obligation on States to take temporary or permanent specific measures on the face of Article 5(4) of the CRPD. However, it has been argued above that such an obligation is, in fact, derived from the general interpretative framework of the CRPD, including Article 1 which enshrines the object and purpose of the Convention, as well as Articles 3 and 4 which contain the general principles and general obligations of the Convention, respectively. Notwithstanding the apparent mandatory nature of positive action measures in certain defined circumstances, it may be very difficult, even impossible, for individuals seeking to benefit from such measures to assert an individual justiciable claim to those measures, when compared with the justiciable nature of reasonable accommodations, for example. Nonetheless, it is argued that any failure by States Parties to the CRPD to implement positive action, where necessary, will be subject to strict scrutiny from the CPRD Committee. Whether this failure alone would amount to an actual breach of the Convention is unlikely, given the fact that there is no stated duty to adopt positive action measures on the face of the Convention. However, States will be required to adopt an active approach to eliminating systemic discrimination on the basis of disability and to ensuring substantive equality. Their endeavours in that regard should include, but are not limited to, the adoption of positive measures.

---

276 M. Bossuyt, 'The Concept and Practice of Affirmative Action,' Final Report submitted by the former Special Rapporteur, in accordance with resolution 1998/5 of the Sub-Commission for the Promotion and Protection of Human Rights, UN Doc. E/CN.4/Sub.2/2002/21, 17 June 2002, para. 101 [emphasis added].

5. The Model of Equality in the CRPD: A Theoretical and Comparative Perspective

Having interpreted and analysed the constituent elements of Article 5 of the CRPD above (and related articles), the aim of this section is to reflect on the precise theoretical model(s) of equality that the CRPD embodies and to consider the extent to which the equality and non-discrimination norms in the CRPD go beyond those in other international human rights treaties. The equality norm contained in the CRPD will therefore be examined from a theoretical and comparative perspective at the level of international human rights law.

5.1. A Consideration of the Theoretical Framework of Equality in the CRPD

It is clear from the preceding section of this chapter that Article 5 of the CRPD goes beyond a formal approach to equality and endorses a substantive approach. Having established that much, it is important to consider the provisions of the Convention as a whole (Article 5 itself and beyond) in order to determine the exact theoretical model(s) of equality which the CRPD embodies. The following subsections of this chapter will reflect on that very issue.

5.1.1. A Substantive Conception of Equality

The principle of equality has been described as the 'leitmotif'[277] of the CRPD. The non-discrimination norm features heavily throughout the text of the Convention. Non-discrimination is a general principle in Article 3. Pursuant to Article 4, one of the general obligations of States is to 'ensure and promote the full realization of all human rights and fundamental freedoms for all persons with disabilities without discrimination of any kind on the basis of disability.'[278] In addition, the Preamble of the CRPD refers to the need for persons with disabilities to be guaranteed their full enjoyment of all human rights and fundamental freedoms without discrimination[279] and, furthermore, stresses that 'discrimination against any person on the basis of disability is a violation of the inherent dignity and worth of the human person.'[280] It is clear that the principles of equality and non-discrimination lie at the very heart of the CRPD. They are cross-cutting provisions of general application which permeate the substantive rights in the Convention.

Aside from the substantive conception of equality contained in Article 5 of the CRPD, the provisions of the Convention on the whole go far beyond a formal model of equality to endorse a substantive approach to equality. The substantive conception

277 O.M. Arnardóttir, 'A Future of Multidimensional Disadvantage Equality' in O.M. Arnardóttir and G. Quinn, *The UN Convention on the Rights of Persons with Disabilities: European and Scandinavian Perspectives* (Martinus Nijhoff, Leiden, 2009), at page 41.

278 UN CRPD, Article 4(1).

279 UN CRPD, Preamble, para. (c).

280 UN CRPD, Preamble, para. (h).

of equality is evidenced at numerous junctures throughout the Convention. The definition of discrimination in Article 2 of the Convention covers the concept of indirect discrimination, as well as direct discrimination. The duty to accommodate is also included as a distinct component of the definition of discrimination on the basis of disability. Furthermore, the general principles of the CRPD mirror the substantive conception of equality in their call for 'full and effective participation and inclusion in society'[281] and 'respect for difference and acceptance of persons with disabilities as part of human diversity and humanity.'[282] One of the general principles[283] of the CRPD is stated explicitly as being equality of opportunity, which falls within the substantive equality paradigm.

The Convention envisages more than mere token participation and inclusion of disabled people in society. In fact, a concrete vision of participation and inclusion is embedded in the substantive articles of the CRPD.[284] The Convention aims to achieve this inclusionary vision through the elimination of discrimination and through the removal of barriers to participation. Article 5 of the CRPD lies at the heart of the process of barrier removal and the equality and non-discrimination norms underlie the substantive provisions of the Convention. The duty to accommodate forms part of the process of barrier removal. It acts as a facilitator for substantive equality to the extent that it seeks to ensure the equalisation of opportunities for persons with disabilities. The duty to accommodate is embedded explicitly in several of the substantive articles of the Convention.[285] Moreover, it forms an implicit component of the majority of the articles of the CRPD, by virtue of the fact that the non-discrimination norm is a cross-cutting one which spans the breadth of the Convention. By including the individualised concept of reasonable accommodation in the definition of discrimination, the Convention tailors the non-discrimination norm to the individual, lived experiences of persons with disabilities rather than viewing the rights of disabled people within a neutral, universal equality framework.

---

281 UN CRPD, Article 3(c).

282 UN CRPD, Article 3(d).

283 UN CRPD, Article 3(e).

284 The majority of the substantive rights in the CRPD are facilitators of participation and inclusion of persons with disabilities in mainstream society. Indeed, numerous provisions of the Convention mention the concepts of inclusion and participation explicitly or implicitly. For example, Article 19 of the CRPD (on the right to live independently and be included in the community) provides that States shall recognise 'the equal right of all persons with disabilities to live in the community, with choices equal to others, and shall take effective and appropriate measures to facilitate full enjoyment by persons with disabilities of this right and their full inclusion and participation in the community.' Furthermore, Article 24 enshrines the core concept of inclusive education in the Convention. In that regard, Article 24(3) provides that 'States Parties shall enable persons with disabilities to learn life and social development skills to facilitate their full and equal participation in education and as members of the community.' Moreover, Article 29 of the Convention relates to participation in political and public life and Article 30 concerns participation of disabled people in cultural life, recreation, leisure and sport. Another article which recognises the importance of participation and inclusion for persons with disabilities, such as Article 27 (on employment), which refers to the right of persons with disabilities to have the opportunity to gain a living by work in a labour market which is 'open, inclusive and accessible to persons with disabilities.'

285 See, for example, Article 14(2) CRPD, Article 17(1)(i) CRPD, Article 24(2)(c) CRPD, Article 24(5) CRPD.

The fact that the conception of disability in the Convention does not concentrate solely on environmental factors is vital to the equality reform agenda for people with disabilities. The Convention recognises that society must be fine-tuned to the individual needs of people with disabilities. By that token, the CRPD engages in an expansion of traditionally understood inequalities. The Supreme Court of Canada neatly summarised the core of the issue related to disability equality in its famous case of *Eaton v Brant County Board of Education*[286] when it stated that by not allowing for the condition of a disabled individual, one:

> Ignores his or her disability and forces the individual to sink or swim within the mainstream environment. It is recognition of the actual characteristics, and reasonable accommodation of these characteristics which is the central purpose of [non-discrimination in the disability context].[287]

The CRPD certainly fulfils this central purpose of the non-discrimination inquiry by adopting a substantive approach to equality, which covers within its ambit the notions of indirect discrimination, reasonable accommodation and positive action. While the duty to accommodate is an essential component of substantive equality, accommodations are linked with an integrationist approach rather than an inclusive approach to equality. As outlined in chapter two of this book,[288] the notion of inclusion takes account of diversity and requires the adaptation of existing societal structures. Integration, on the other hand, requires that the individual with differential characteristics adapts to the so-called 'norm' and fits in with mainstream structures. The duty to accommodate does not result in structural changes to the 'norm.' By accommodating a disabled person, it requires that the individual in question fits in with existing norms. It does not seek to challenge systemic barriers and inequalities. The duty to accommodate is therefore deemed to be linked to the difference model of discrimination. As Lisa Waddington and Mark Bell point out, this model recognises that 'individuals who possess the relevant characteristic are different in a relevant respect from individuals who do not, and that treating them similarly can lead to discrimination.'[289] While the duty to accommodate is an important facilitator of substantive equality, it cannot result in fundamental transformation in society. Therefore, it is important to determine whether the CRPD goes further than integrationist equality to endorse a more transformative approach to equality.

5.1.2. A Transformative Approach to Equality

The transformative model of equality seeks to tackle deep-seated structural inequalities in society and to target the root causes of exclusion of marginalised groups. It goes beyond requiring the removal of barriers to require widespread

[286] Supreme Court of Canada, *Eaton v Brant County Board of Education* (1998) 1 S.C.R. 241.
[287] Ibid, para. 67.
[288] See chapter 2, section 5.2.
[289] L. Waddington and M. Bell, 'Exploring the Boundaries of Positive Action under EU Law: A Search for Conceptual Clarity' (2011) 48(5) *Common Market Law Review* 1503, at page 1518.

positive measures to bring about change.[290] A basic premise of the CRPD is the fact that societal structures should be altered fundamentally. The equality norm in the CRPD is buttressed by the social-contextual approach to disability, which recognises the relevance of individual impairments and their interaction with systemic barriers. By endorsing the social construction of disability, the CRPD requires disability discrimination laws to go beyond targeting discrimination caused by prejudice or stereotypical attitudes in society. It requires States to delve deeper into the realm of equality law to grant disabled citizens a right of equal access to all areas of life that are open to their non-disabled counterparts by ensuring fundamental transformations of structures and processes. The CRPD imposes numerous positive obligations on States targeted at removing discriminatory barriers and altering structures that are at the core of the disadvantage experienced by disabled people. The Convention imposes a human rights mandate on States Parties to make the necessary changes to ensure fully inclusive societies and to ensure reallocation of resources for that purpose. Beyond the duty to reasonably accommodate, the accessibility obligation in Article 9 of the CRPD goes much further in seeking to ensure that mainstream societal barriers that stand in the way of the full and effective participation and inclusion of disabled people are dismantled. The duty to ensure accessible structures can be aligned with what has traditionally been described as transformative equality. The accessibility obligation requires States to take appropriate measures to ensure to person with disabilities access, *on an equal basis with others*, to the physical environment, to transportation, to information and communication [...] and to other facilities and services open or provided to the public.[291] The obligations imposed on States under Article 9 of the Convention are part of the holistic human rights-based approach to disability which seeks to ensure widespread structural change in society and increased participation and inclusion for persons with disabilities. In addition, the concept of 'universal design' contained in the Convention envisages inclusionary structures that facilitate full and effective participation in society. The premise behind universal design is the development of structures that enhance participation (to the maximum) for all individuals – those who are disabled and also non-disabled users. It is based on the concept that societal structures should 'benefit all, not merely accommodate the few.'[292] According to Article 2 of the Convention, the objective of universal design is to ensure the 'design of products, environments, programmes and services to be usable by all people, to the greatest extent possible, without the need for adaptation or specialized design.'[293] Universal design goes far beyond an accommodation mandate to recognise the inherent diversity of individuals.

---

290 S. Fredman, 'Beyond the Dichotomy of Formal and Substantive Equality: Towards a New Definition of Equal Rights' in I. Boerefijn, F. Coomans, J. Goldschmidt, R. Holtmaat and R. Wolleswinkel (eds.), *Temporary Special Measures: Accelerating de facto Equality of Women under Article 4(1) UN Convention on the Elimination of All Forms of Discrimination Against Women* (Intersentia, Antwerp, 2003), at page 115.

291 Article 9, CRPD [emphasis added].

292 R.M. Jackson, 'National Centre on Accessing the General Curriculum, Curriculum Access for Students with Low-Incidence Disabilities: The Promise of Universal Design for Learning (2011), at page 2, available at http://aim.cast.org/learn/disabilityspecific last accessed 20 October 2014.

293 UN CRPD, Article 2.

As well as ensuring transformation of environmental structures, a transformative approach to equality also seeks to address the socially constructed stereotypes, prejudices and negative customs and practices which hinder the full enjoyment of rights by marginalised groups. Article 8 of the CRPD is illustrative of a transformative approach to equality. Pursuant to that article, States are under an obligation 'to combat stereotypes, prejudices and harmful practices.'[294] Awareness-raising duties are embedded in several of the substantive articles of the CRPD.[295] For instance, Article 13 of the Convention (on access to justice) imposes both accommodation duties on States, as well as a proactive duty to raise awareness by promoting 'appropriate training for those working in the field of administration of justice, including police and prison staff.'[296]

Both substantive and transformative equality require the participation of affected groups in every aspect of decision making that concerns them. Article 4(3) of the CRPD requires States to consult closely with and to involve actively disabled people and their representative organisations 'in the development and implementation of legislation and policies to implement the present Convention, and in other decision-making processes concerning issues relating to persons with disabilities.'[297] This increased participation and inclusion of persons with disabilities and their representative organisations in the reform agenda is key to unlocking the transformatory potential of the CRPD.

5.1.3. Substantive Disadvantage Equality

The CRPD moves far beyond the specific difference approach. Indeed, it has been deemed to fall squarely within the substantive disadvantage model of equality by academic scholars, such as Arnardóttir.[298] Under that model, measures to even out disadvantage are considered to be an essential means of achieving equality. The CRPD views reasonable accommodation measures as intrinsic to the achievement of substantive equality for persons with disabilities. Article 2 of the Convention includes a failure to reasonably accommodate as a vital component of the definition of discrimination on the basis of disability. Article 5(3) of the CRPD reinforces the importance of the duty to accommodate in ensuring disability equality. That article confirms that accommodations should be viewed as an integral element of the equality norm rather than as an exception thereto and that the objective of accommodations is 'to promote equality and eliminate discrimination.'[299] The CRPD also makes it clear that positive action measures are not to be viewed as an exception to the achievement of substantive equality but rather as an integral part of ensuring *de facto* equality. This can be seen from the text of Article 5(4) of the Convention

294 UN CRPD, Article 8(1)(b).
295 See, for example, CRPD Articles 24(4) and 13(2).
296 UN CRPD, Article 13(2).
297 UN CRPD, Article 4(3).
298 See generally, O.M. Arnardóttir, 'A Future of Multidimensional Disadvantage Equality' in O.M. Arnardóttir and G. Quinn, *The UN Convention on the Rights of Persons with Disabilities: European and Scandinavian Perspectives* (Martinus Nijhoff, Leiden, 2009).
299 UN CRPD, Article 5(3).

which states that 'specific measures which are *necessary* to accelerate or achieve *de facto* equality of persons with disabilities shall not be considered discrimination under the terms of the present Convention.'[300] Under the substantive disadvantage model of equality, the focus is not on the differential characteristics *per se* but on the wider disadvantage encountered by disabled people in society. The substantive disadvantage approach to equality is evident in the Preamble of the CRPD, which notes the 'profound social disadvantage'[301] and the barriers which people with disabilities continue to encounter in their endeavours to participate 'as equal members of society.'[302] In addition, the wide-ranging positive obligations imposed on States by the CRPD make it abundantly clear that the substantive disadvantage encountered by persons with disabilities is the driving force of the equality norm in the Convention.

5.2. The CRPD's Approach to Disability

Having established that the CRPD endorses both substantive and transformative equality models (and specifically a substantive disadvantage approach to equality), it is apt to consider the approach to disability embodied in the CRPD. I have already demonstrated the fact that the CRPD endorses a social-contextual model of disability, which recognises the relevance of impairments and structural barriers in society in creating disability. However, the Convention goes even further than that to embody a human rights-based approach to disability, according to which disabled people are viewed as subjects of the law, entitled to all of the rights and benefits conferred on their non-disabled counterparts. As already outlined in chapter two of this book, the rights-based approach to disability focuses on the inherent dignity and autonomy of individuals with disabilities. The key underlying principles of a human rights-based approach to disability are equal opportunities and non-discrimination on the basis of disability, as well as inclusion, participation, accessibility and respect for difference and diversity.[303] The human rights model empowers citizens to claim their rights and it acknowledges the fact that responsibility lies on the state to redress the disadvantage that disabled people encounter. Under that model, human rights ought to be integrated into policy-making and practices at all levels.

Beyond the human rights-based approach, I would argue that the CRPD also endorses vital elements of Martha Nussbaum's version of the capabilities approach,[304] an approach that is based on the inherent dignity of each individual. The Convention's equality norm is built on the foundational notion of human dignity and the importance of human dignity resonates in the duty to accommodate. The Convention embraces an inclusive approach to disability equality rather than an integrationist approach.

300 UN CRPD, Article 5(4) [emphasis added].
301 UN CRPD, preamble, para. (y).
302 UN CRPD, preamble, para. (k).
303 Office of the High Commissioner for Human Rights, 'What is Disability?,' available at www.ohchr.org/Documents/.../Disability/.../Module1_WhatDisability.ppt last accessed 10 January 2015.
304 The essential elements of the capabilities approach were outlined in chapter two of this book.

It mandates that the inherent capabilities, the innate potential and the equal moral worth of each disabled individual is valued and taken into account in the formulation of appropriate measures to counteract disadvantage. The principle of 'equality of opportunities' runs through the Convention like a red thread. This entails that State responsibility is triggered by an obligation to provide the resources that each individual requires in order to ensure that persons with disabilities can develop their capabilities or potential to the same threshold level as their non-disabled counterparts. The CRPD clearly recognises the responsibility of States Parties to overcome the structural disadvantage and exclusion engendered by impairment and disability. Furthermore, it mandates that national authorities provide the resources necessary to rectify this disadvantage in all areas – related simultaneously to the exercise of civil and political rights, as well as economic, social and cultural rights.

Underpinning the foregoing approaches to disability, the CRPD also endorses a universalist approach to disability. As outlined in chapter two of this book, the universalist model views disability as a fluid conception and as 'a universal feature of the human condition.'[305] The CRPD demonstrates a clear 'respect for difference and acceptance of persons with disabilities as part of human diversity and humanity'[306] through its general principles and requires national authorities to cater for such diversity. The universalist approach to disability can be seen most clearly in the CRPD's universal design provisions contained in Article 2 and in Article 4(f) of the Convention. Overall, the Convention emphasises the diverse nature of humanity and the fact that social structures must be fully inclusive.

The theoretical models of equality and disability which the CRPD endorses are far-reaching and have the potential to have a major impact on the participation and inclusion of persons with disabilities in society, if translated correctly into national, European and international legislative and policy contexts. These models underline the necessity to mainstream disability into laws and policies to reflect diversity and difference. While the overall theoretical framework of equality and non-discrimination in the CRPD is clearly very progressive, the question arises as to how it compares with other equality frameworks at the level of international human rights law. The next subsection of this chapter will address that very question.

5.3. A Comparative Perspective on the CRPD's Equality Provisions

The understanding of the equality norm has evolved greatly in recent years, both at the level of international human rights law and in the disability context. International human rights law has progressed from embodying the formal model of equality to endorsing a more substantive conception of equality. The CRPD represents the culmination of previous steps in the direction of the substantive disadvantage

305 J.E. Bickenbach, 'Minority Rights or Universal Participation: The Politics of Disablement' in M. Jones and L.A. Basser (eds.) *Disability, Divers-Ability and Legal Change* (Martinus Nijhoff, London, 1999) 112.

306 UN CRPD, General Principle 3(d).

and transformative models of equality. Oddný Mjöll Arnardóttir categorises the non-discrimination provisions in the core human rights instruments into three distinct eras.[307] She states that the period dating from the 1950s to the 1970s can be defined as the era of 'universal sameness,'[308] in the sense that the open-ended non-discrimination provisions in the ICCPR and the ICESCR are representative of the formal or symmetrical approach to equality. During that era, there was no accommodation for difference and the open-ended non-discrimination provisions and universal equality norm applied to everyone in the same manner, regardless of difference. Arnardóttir contends that:

> It seems clear that a genuine and benign belief in the utility of universal human rights norms and their potential to provide the same protection to everyone lay behind the international law adopted during this era.[309]

Arnardóttir characterises the next era, which runs from the 1970s to the 1990s, as the 'specific difference'[310] equality era. She states that the 'specific difference' approach was based on the premise that 'the law intervenes in an otherwise simple and neutral situation where the two individuals compared are alike in all relevant respects other than with regard to the one specific identity marker singled out as the "difference" to be corrected for.'[311] She notes that the 'correction for a specific difference could, depending on the context, take the form of strict scrutiny of invidious differentiations or the form of reasonable accommodations and affirmative action to facilitate inclusion.'[312] She argues that the specific difference model of equality forms the basis of the non-discrimination provisions in both CERD and CEDAW.[313] As outlined in chapter two above, those treaties view discrimination based on specific identity markers or biological and immutable characteristics – race and sex respectively – as being worthy of special attention, but only in certain circumstances. Both treaties incorporate the notion of indirect discrimination[314] in their non-discrimination clauses and they also permit the taking of special measures or positive action.[315] For instance, CEDAW endorses a substantive conception of equality. It devotes attention to the legal status of women, voicing concern about the basic civil and political rights of women. It affirms women's rights to non-discrimination in education, employment and economic and social activities, among others. Aside from civil rights issues, CEDAW also devotes attention to women's reproductive rights. Accordingly, provisions for maternity protection and child-

---

307 O.M. Arnardóttir, 'A Future of Multidimensional Disadvantage Equality' in O.M. Arnardóttir and G. Quinn, *The UN Convention on the Rights of Persons with Disabilities: European and Scandinavian Perspectives* (Martinus Nijhoff, Leiden, 2009), at pages 47–64.

308 Ibid, at page 47.

309 Ibid, at page 49.

310 Ibid.

311 Ibid, at page 53.

312 Ibid.

313 Ibid.

314 The notion of indirect discrimination is included in the definition of discrimination in Article 1 CERD and Article 1 CEDAW, both of which refer to the 'effect' of discrimination, which is taken to mean indirect discrimination.

315 See Articles 1(4) and 2(2) CERD and Article 4 CEDAW.

care are proclaimed as essential rights and are incorporated into all areas of the Convention, whether dealing with employment, family law, health care or education. Notably, positive action measures are recommended for maternity protection in Article 4 of CEDAW and are not considered to be discriminatory.

Mirroring the move in international human rights law to a more substantive conception of equality, the human rights treaty bodies have gradually interpreted the various non-discrimination provisions in the respective treaties as embodying more than mere formal equality and have included within their ambit indirect discrimination.[316] Arnardóttir notes that the HRC and the ECtHR began to mirror the theme-specific developments of the specific difference era by singling out certain discrimination grounds 'for more thorough treatment [... and ...] asserting the strict scrutiny of discrimination based on specific "suspect" discrimination grounds.'[317] In addition, the inclusion of reasonable accommodation in the definition of discrimination in General Comment 5 of the UNCESCR provides further evidence of a move away from a formal interpretation of the principle of equality. These developments all paved the way for the adoption of the CRPD and its progressive equality provisions.

In spite of the positive developments seen in the ground-specific treaties such as CERD and CEDAW (in particular their call for accommodation for difference and positive action in appropriate cases), Arnardóttir contends that the primary focus under the specific difference era (to which those treaties belong) remained on 'negative state obligations and the equal treatment principle.'[318] By way of contrast, the CRPD has been described by Arnardóttir as representing the substantive disadvantage model of equality.[319] It adopts a contextual approach that focuses on asymmetrical disadvantage experienced by individuals or groups in society. Arnardóttir characterises the era culminating with the adoption of the CRPD, as embracing 'multidimensional disadvantage' equality. She claims that this era epitomises:

> The strengthening of protection against discrimination, an increased awareness of the complex structural social factors that intervene in the playing field that the law previously

316 For example, the Human Rights Committee includes within the definition of discrimination certain acts which have a discriminatory 'purpose or effect' in its General Comment 18. In addition, in the case of *Simunek et al. v the Czech Republic*, the State Party in question contended that there was no violation of the Covenant because the Czech and Slovak legislators had no discriminatory intent at the time of the adoption of a particular legislative act. However, the HRC rebutted that argument and affirmed that Article 26 ICCPR covers indirect discrimination. The Committee stated its view as follows: 'The intent of the legislature is not alone dispositive in determining a breach of article 26 of the Covenant. A politically motivated differentiation is unlikely to be compatible with article 26. But an act which is not politically motivated may still contravene article 26 if its effects are discriminatory.' [Human Rights Committee, *Simunek et al. v. the Czech Republic*, Communication No. 516/1992, Views of 19 July 1995, para. 11.7].

317 O.M. Arnardóttir, 'A Future of Multidimensional Disadvantage Equality' in O.M. Arnardóttir and G. Quinn, *The UN Convention on the Rights of Persons with Disabilities: European and Scandinavian Perspectives* (Martinus Nijhoff, Leiden, 2009) at page 52.

318 Ibid, at page 53.

319 Ibid.

> presumed was neutral and an increased awareness of how individual and group identities that create vulnerabilities to discrimination are multidimensional.[320]

The CRPD embodies all of the above elements. It strengthens the non-discrimination norm in numerous respects. The inclusion of the duty to accommodate within the non-discrimination provision ensures an individualised application of the equality paradigm and has increased the potential for ensuring substantive equality. The CRPD does not reject the universal approach to equality that was characteristic of previous eras. Instead, it refashions the universal equality norm and recognises that it must be tailored to the specific needs of disabled people. It applies the equality and non-discrimination paradigm across the substantive provisions of the Convention and, thereby, breathes new life into specific provisions in accordance with the lived realities of disabled people. By acknowledging the fact that disability is an evolving concept, which results from the interactional relationship between persons with impairments and complex societal barriers, the Convention seeks to target asymmetrical structures of disadvantage and oppression. It shifts the target of non-discrimination laws onto deeply unequal structures in society. Finally, the CRPD rejects an analysis of discrimination that is based on only one ground of discrimination at any given time. It seeks to overcome the limitations of traditional non-discrimination laws by embracing a multidimensional or intersectional approach to non-discrimination analysis. That approach recognises the fact that discrimination which arises from a number of grounds in combination produces a unique discriminatory experience for the individual concerned. In that connection, Article 6(1) of the CRPD recognises that 'women and girls with disabilities are subject to multiple discrimination.'[321] Furthermore, paragraph (p) of the Preamble of the CRPD expresses its concern about:

> The difficult conditions faced by persons with disabilities who are subject to multiple or aggravated forms of discrimination on the basis of race, colour, sex, language, religion, political or other opinion, national, ethnic, indigenous or social origin, property, birth, age or other status.[322]

While the CEDAW Committee has addressed the issue of multiple or intersectional discrimination on a handful of occasions and has begun to elucidate its meaning,[323] the CRPD refers specifically to intersectional discrimination within its text. The Convention recognises the complexity of remedying structural discrimination and it

---

320 Ibid, at page 54.
321 UN CRPD, Article 6(1).
322 UN CRPD, Preamble, para (p).
323 See, for example, UN Committee on the Elimination of Discrimination Against Women, General Recommendation No. 28 on the core obligations of States' parties under article 2 of the Convention on the Elimination of All Forms of Discrimination against Women, para. 18, adopted on 16 December 2010, UN Doc. CEDAW/C/GC/28; See also UN Committee on the Elimination of Discrimination Against Women, Concluding observations to Norway's 8th periodic report, UN Doc. CEDAW/C/NOR/8l; Furthermore, see the comments of the UNCESCR, General Comment 20, para. 17.

acknowledges the fact that disabled people are defined not only by their disability but by the other aspects of their human identity, such as gender, race and age.[324]

The CRPD also goes further than previous human rights treaties in seeking to ensure a transformative approach to equality. The CEDAW Convention can be described as endorsing, to some extent, a transformative approach to equality[325] when compared with previous international human rights instruments. Article 2(f) CEDAW requires States 'to take all appropriate measures, including legislation, to modify or abolish existing laws, regulations, customs and practices which constitute discrimination against women.'[326] In addition, Article 5(a) CEDAW requires States to:

> Take all appropriate measures to modify the social and cultural patterns of conduct of men and women, with a view to achieving the elimination of prejudices and customary and all other practices which are based on the idea of the inferiority or the superiority of either of the sexes or on stereotyped roles for men and women.[327]

The general thrust of CEDAW 'gives formal recognition to the influence of culture and tradition on restricting women's enjoyment of their fundamental rights' and it acknowledges the stereotypes, customs and norms that 'give rise to the multitude of legal, political and economic constraints on the advancement of women.'[328] Noting this interrelationship, the Preamble of the Convention stresses 'that a change in the traditional role of men as well as the role of women in society and in the family is needed to achieve full equality of men and women.'[329] The introduction to CEDAW affirms that:

> Cultural patterns which define the public realm as a man's world and the domestic sphere as women's domain are strongly targeted in all of the Convention's provisions that affirm the equal responsibilities of both sexes in family life and their equal rights with regard to education and employment.[330]

The CEDAW Committee also takes up this theme of transformative equality in its general recommendations. For instance, in its General Recommendation 25 (2004), the CEDAW Committee notes that 'the lives of women and men must be considered in a contextual way' and, furthermore, recommends that States adopt measures tailored towards ensuring 'a real transformation of opportunities, institutions

---

324 In addition to CRPD, Article 6 and Preamble para. (p), see CRPD, Preamble para. (q).

325 See, for example, the views of S. Fredman on this point in 'Beyond the Dichotomy of Formal and Substantive Equality: Towards a New Definition of Equal Rights' in I. Boerefijn, F. Coomans, J. Goldschmidt, R. Holtmaat and R. Wolleswinkel (eds.), *Temporary Special Measures: Accelerating de facto Equality of Women under Article 4(1) UN Convention on the Elimination of All Forms of Discrimination Against Women* (Intersentia, Antwerp, 2003), at pages 115–118.

326 CEDAW, Article 2(f).

327 CEDAW, Article 5(a).

328 For elaboration on this point, see CEDAW, 'Introduction' to the Convention.

329 CEDAW, Preamble.

330 See CEDAW, 'Introduction' to the Convention.

and systems so that they are no longer grounded in historically determined male paradigms of power and life patterns.'[331]

The text of the CPRD goes further into the realm of transformative equality than CEDAW by requiring States not only to eliminate prejudices and customs based on the inferior notion of persons with disabilities but to target, in addition, all socially constructed barriers that stand in the way of *de facto* equality. The era of 'multidimensional disadvantage' to which the CRPD belongs therefore goes further in recognising that positive measures are central to disability equality. By virtue of its accessibility obligation, its awareness raising-duties and also by tying the equality norm (via the reasonable accommodation duty) to all of the substantive rights in the Convention (including the socio-economic rights), the CRPD aims to target deep-seated inequalities and to ensure participation and inclusion of persons with disabilities in every aspect of mainstream society on an equal basis with others.

In the respects outlined above, the CRPD moves beyond the protections granted by previous international human rights instruments. The Convention has been described by Jenny Goldschmidt as 'a major advance,'[332] when compared with the existing corpus of international human rights law relating to equality and non-discrimination provisions. Goldschmidt summarises the changes that have taken place at the level of international human rights law. She argues that the shift in approach at the international level began with CERD, 'which focused on non-discrimination in the way of not treating people differently,'[333] and claims that CEDAW went 'one step further – in particular by including Article 5, which urges States to end stereotypes in traditional practices.'[334] Goldschmidt asserts that the CRPD goes further still to the extent that discrimination is being viewed increasingly 'as a bilateral phenomenon'[335] on account of its recognition that the conceptualisation of disability 'depends not only on the characteristics of the disabled person but also on the barriers that exist in society and in peoples' behaviours.'[336]

---

331 UN Committee on the Elimination of All Forms of Discrimination Against Women, General Recommendation 25, on article 4, paragraph 1, of the Convention on the Elimination of All Forms of Discrimination against Women - Temporary Special Measures (2004), UN Doc. HRI/GEN/1/Rev.7, para. 10.

332 J. Goldschmidt (interviewed by J. Anderson and J. Philips), 'Shifting the Burden of Proof: How the CRPD is Transforming our Understanding of Discrimination, Intersectionality and Priorities' in J. Anderson and J. Philips (eds.), *Disability and Human Rights: Legal, Ethical and Conceptual Implications of the Convention on the Rights of Persons with Disabilities* (Netherlands Institute of Human Rights, SIM Special 35, 2012), at page 51, referring to an important working paper by H. Bielefeldt, Zum Innovationspotential der UN-Behindertenrechtskonvention, Berlin: Deutsches Institut fur Menschenrechte (2009).

333 J. Goldschmidt (interviewed by J. Anderson and J. Philips), 'Shifting the Burden of Proof: How the CRPD is Transforming our Understanding of Discrimination, Intersectionality and Priorities' in J. Anderson and J. Philips (eds.), *Disability and Human Rights: Legal, Ethical and Conceptual Implications of the Convention on the Rights of Persons with Disabilities* (Netherlands Institute of Human Rights, SIM Special 35, 2012), at pages 51/52.

334 Ibid.

335 Ibid, at page 52.

336 Ibid.

Notwithstanding the strides made by the CRPD in increasing the potential for realising *de facto* equality for persons with disabilities, States Parties to the Convention will face great challenges in unlocking this potential. Many difficulties lie ahead in translating the progressive equality and non-discrimination norms into tangible change on the ground. In that regard, a note of caution has been sounded by Arnardóttir in her assertion that 'there remain quite a few difficulties in transforming the multidimensional disadvantage approach into hard non-discrimination law and individually justiciable rights.'[337] Among the concerns that Arnardóttir cites in that regard is the fact that 'some of the issues raised by multidimensional situations may [...] be too complex for the law as it is an inherent tendency of the law to simplify and compartmentalise complex issues.'[338] Another issue which she identifies relates to the fact that the social construction analysis of disability 'is of a different nature from that which [international courts and monitoring bodies] traditionally encounter.'[339] This may cause problems in translating rights effectively through legal or quasi-legal mechanisms. Notwithstanding these impediments, there is no doubt that the CRPD holds great promise for the future application of the equality and non-discrimination norms in relation to the rights of persons with disabilities, but only if its transformative potential is unlocked.

6. Conclusion

The equality and non-discrimination norms form the twin pillars of the CRPD. The Convention is informed by a pressing need to ensure equal rights and equal opportunities for disabled people. It is evident that the application of a formal model of equality at the international level was not sufficient to tackle the many forms of structural disadvantage encountered by persons with disabilities. By requiring symmetrical treatment, formal equality served only to perpetuate existing inequalities. During the era when formal equality was the dominant paradigm, the universal equality norm was applied in the same manner to everyone, regardless of individual difference. This emphasis on 'sameness' proved to be particularly problematic in the realm of disability rights, where individual differences are pivotal to the full realisation of substantive equality. The evolution in international human rights law from a purely formal approach to equality towards a more substantive version of equality has had major implications on the rights of disabled people. It is now acknowledged that covert forms of discrimination must be unearthed and that the full and effective participation and inclusion of people with disabilities can only be achieved through the realisation of a barrier-free society. The evolution in disability theory from a medical model to a social model of disability[340] has also had

337 O.M. Arnardóttir, 'A Future of Multidimensional Disadvantage Equality' in O.M. Arnardóttir and G. Quinn, *The UN Convention on the Rights of Persons with Disabilities: European and Scandinavian Perspectives* (Martinus Nijhoff, Leiden, 2009), at page 65.

338 Ibid.

339 Ibid.

340 For more information on the shift in disability theory from the medical to the social model, see T. Shakespeare (ed.), *Disability Rights and Wrongs* (Routledge, London, 2006), at pages 15–22; See also P. Weller (ed.), *New Law and Ethics in Mental Health Advance Directives: The Convention on*

a colossal impact on the understanding of equality and non-discrimination norms in the context of persons with disabilities. The CRPD's endorsement of the social-constructionist model of disability has resulted in the reconfiguration of the equality norm for persons with disabilities. For the purposes of non-discrimination laws, the pivotal issues requiring attention are no longer viewed as lying with the specific differential characteristics of the disabled individual. Rather, a broader examination of structural disadvantage is mandated.

It has been illustrated throughout this chapter that the CRPD embodies a substantive and transformative equality framework, which takes into account the multifaceted ways in which disabled people differ from their non-disabled counterparts. Under the CRPD, individual differences and structural inequalities are acknowledged and responded to by positive measures designed to accelerate and to achieve equality in fact. The full realisation of equality for disabled people presupposes, in the first instance, the elimination of all forms of discrimination on the basis of disability. However, true equality requires the adoption of positive measures, such as reasonable accommodations, accessibility and awareness-raising measures, as well as positive action to correct for entrenched prejudices and past inequalities.

The Convention endorses a holistic human rights-based model whose focus is on the full realisation of the equality norm. It seeks to ensure the application of all human rights to disabled people on an equal basis with their non-disabled counterparts. The equality paradigm in the CRPD is pivotal in seeking to achieve increased participation and inclusion of persons with disabilities in society. In its mandate of full and effective participation and inclusion, the CRPD goes far beyond traditional approaches to the rights of persons with disabilities that are based on an accommodation mandate. The overall scheme of the Convention aims at creating a barrier-free society, in which disabled people will be able to participate effectively and be included at all levels of society – at the economic, social, cultural, as well as at the civil and political levels.

From a theoretical and comparative perspective, it can be said with certainty that the CRPD goes further in its approach to equality than previous international human rights instruments. The CRPD has been described as 'an extraordinarily far-reaching Convention'[341] and it has also been termed 'unique in its complexity.'[342] Its far-reaching provisions and its complexity are translated mainly through the foundational principles of equality and non-discrimination which span the Convention's substantive rights. The full realisation of the human rights of persons with disabilities cannot occur in circumstances where these principles are obstructed.

the Rights of Persons with Disabilities and the Right to Choose (Routledge, New York, 2013), at pages 27–38.

341 Press conference on the adoption of the UN Convention on the Rights of Persons with Disabilities, UN Headquarters, New York, 6 December 2006.

342 J. Allain, 'Treaty Interpretation and the United Nations Convention on the Rights of Persons with Disabilities,' 17, available at www.disabilityaction.org/.../legal-report-2-treaty-inte.. last accessed 29 August 2014.

One particular aspect of the equality and non-discrimination paradigm in the CRPD – the duty to accommodate – is worthy of special consideration due to its novel appearance in an international human rights treaty. In the next chapter of this book, the various elements of the duty to accommodate will be explored, including its outer limits. The balancing of needs and interests inherent in the outer limits of the duty to accommodate can potentially teach us something about the balancing of needs and interests that is implicit in other rights and obligations contained in the CRPD, specifically those subject to progressive realisation.

Chapter 4
The Duty to Accommodate Persons with Disabilities

'Exclusion from the mainstream of society results from the construction of a society based solely on mainstream attributes to which disabled persons will never be able to gain access.'[1]

1. Introduction

By virtue of the fact that the duty to accommodate persons with disabilities has never before been included in an international human rights treaty, as well as the fact that it applies across the substantive rights and obligations in the CRPD (including socio-economic rights), it is important to explore the constituent elements of the duty. This chapter has two related goals. The first objective of this chapter will be to analyse the components of the duty to accommodate. The second aim of this chapter will be to draw lessons from the outer limits of the duty to accommodate which can potentially be applied to the progressive realisation of CRPD rights. The outer limits of the accommodation duty seek to define the test under the CRPD for balancing the needs and interests of a disabled person, on the one hand, and a duty-bearer, on the other hand. While this reflects an individual balancing of needs and interests, it is envisaged that the outer limits of the accommodation duty may nonetheless provide some degree of insight into the balancing of interests that is implicit in the implementation of other rights and obligations in the Convention which are subject to progressive realisation.

The two obligations – the duty to accommodate and the duty to realise rights progressively – are subject to different criteria and objectives, as well as to different timeframes in terms of the steps to be taken by entities or States. Another difference between the two obligations is that progressive realisation is an obligation incumbent solely on States, while it is private or public entities that will be taking steps to accommodate disabled people, subject to supervision by States who will be required to ensure fulfilment of the duty. Notwithstanding the many differences between the duty to accommodate and the obligation to realise disability rights progressively, the outer limits of both obligations reflect, on the one hand, the needs of persons with disabilities and, on the other hand, resource limitations and other non-financial considerations, as well as the balancing exercise to be undertaken in the implementation of CRPD rights. In chapter five of this book, the concept of progressive realisation will be analysed generally, including its outer limits. In

1 Supreme Court of Canada, *Eaton v Brant County Board of Education* (1998) 1 S.C.R. 241, para. 67.

that chapter, various frameworks will be analysed, which are designed to assess the measures taken by States to realise progressively human rights. The criteria or factors inherent in those frameworks will then be drawn on in order to tailor them to the specific context of the CRPD and to draft a framework of review of State measures under the Convention. In drafting such a framework of review, elements of the CRPD's equality norm, specifically the outer limits of the duty to accommodate highlighted in the present chapter, will be drawn on.

The present chapter is divided into five sections. In section two, the duty to accommodate will be considered generally, including its origins and the theoretical basis of the duty, as well as the precise meaning of the term 'accommodation.' In section three of this chapter, the meaning of the duty to accommodate will be reflected on in the specific context of the CRPD, including a consideration of its key features – the innate strengths and weaknesses of the duty to accommodate as a facilitator of substantive equality. In section four of this chapter, the outer limits of the duty to accommodate will be analysed, with a view to teasing out the primary factors which make up the balancing test related to the needs and interests of disabled individuals, on the one hand, and duty bearers, on the other hand. Finally, section five of this chapter will contain some concluding remarks.

2. The Duty to Accommodate

This section of the chapter will reflect briefly on the origins and theoretical underpinning of the duty to accommodate in the CRPD, as well the meaning of the term 'accommodation' itself.

2.1. The Origins and Theoretical Underpinning of the Duty to Accommodate

Although the concept of reasonable accommodation is associated most frequently with disability rights, it is interesting to note that the term did not, in fact, originate in the disability context. It was employed originally in the United States Civil Rights Act[2] with respect to discrimination on the grounds of religious practice. That Act requires employers to reasonably accommodate an employee or potential employee's religious observance or practice unless an accommodation would amount to an undue hardship in respect of the employer's business. The concept of reasonable accommodation was first applied to the field of disability rights in the United States Rehabilitation Act of 1973.[3] The first explicit statutory embodiment of the duty to accommodate in the context of employment can be seen in Title I of the ADA.[4]

[2] The US Civil Rights Act of 1964 prohibits religious discrimination in the employment context. It was amended in 1972 to impose a reasonable accommodation requirement on employers, subject to the proviso that this should not constitute an undue hardship to the employer.

[3] See Section 504 of the United States Rehabilitation Act of 1973.

[4] The Americans with Disabilities Act (1990) as amended by the Americans with Disabilities Amendment Act (2008) (effective as of 1 January 2009).

With regard to the influential role which the ADA had in promoting the obligation to accommodate on a global scale, Lisa Waddington states that 'it is probably no exaggeration to say that this statute brought the issue of reasonable accommodations for individuals with disabilities to the attention of policy-makers and disability activists on a global scale, including those within the EU.'[5] At the European level, the duty to accommodate is embedded in the Employment Equality Directive,[6] Article 5 of which requires employers to reasonably accommodate persons with disabilities.[7] At the level of international human rights law, the concept of reasonable accommodation first made its appearance in General Comment 5 of the UNCESCR regarding persons with disabilities.[8] The CRPD cements the well-established trend of requiring the provision of reasonable accommodations for disabled people. Indeed, it goes further than previous international and European instruments by imposing duties on States to ensure that accommodations are provided by a wide array of social actors and also by including the duty to accommodate within the non-discrimination paradigm.

The principal objective of the duty to accommodate is to ensure equality of opportunity for persons with disabilities. In the context of the CRPD, it seeks to ensure that States prevent a broad faction of social actors from denying people with disabilities the opportunity to participate in society on an equal basis with others, by failing to accommodate their differential characteristics. Individual difference is incorporated into the equality and non-discrimination norms in the CRPD via the reasonable accommodation requirement. This constitutes a departure from the general premise of non-discrimination law, according to which personal characteristics should not be a relevant factor. The duty to accommodate takes into account the specific characteristics of people with disabilities in order to counteract the disadvantage and social exclusion which would result from ignoring such differential characteristics.[9]

---

5 L. Waddington, 'Reasonable Accommodation' in D. Schiek, L. Waddington and M. Bell (eds.), *Cases, Materials and Text on National, Supranational and International Non-Discrimination Law* (Hart Publishing, Oxford, 2007), page 631.

6 Council Directive 2000/78/EC of 27 November 2000 establishing a general framework for equal treatment in employment and occupation (Official Journal L 303, 02/12/2000 Pp0016–0022). Article 5 of the Directive provides that: 'In order to guarantee compliance with the principle of equal treatment in relation to persons with disabilities, reasonable accommodation shall be provided. This means that employers shall take appropriate measures, where needed in a particular case, to enable a person with a disability to have access to, participate in, or advance in employment, or to undergo training, unless such measures would impose a disproportionate burden on the employer. This burden shall not be disproportionate when it is sufficiently remedied by measures existing within the framework of the disability policy of the Member State concerned.'

7 However, it does not state that failure to provide reasonable accommodation is a form of discrimination.

8 UNCESCR, General Comment No. 5 states specifically, at paragraph 15 thereof, that: 'For the purposes of the Covenant, "disability-based discrimination" may be defined as including any distinction, exclusion, restriction or preference, or denial of reasonable accommodation based on disability which has the effect of nullifying or impairing the recognition, enjoyment or exercise of economic, social or cultural rights.' [UNCESCR, General Comment No. 5 on *Persons with Disabilities* (1994), adopted on 9/12/1994, UN Doc. E/1995/22].

9 Some scholars argue that the concept of 'reasonable accommodation' does not recognise diversity and merely requires persons with disabilities to conform to established non-disabled norms. This point will be expanded on in section 3.2 below.

2.2. What is Meant by the Term 'Accommodation?'

The term 'accommodation' is generally uncontroversial, to the extent that it is understood to mean adjustments or modifications to existing policies, practices or environments in order to facilitate the participation and inclusion of the disabled person in the social sphere. We have seen already in chapter three of this book examples of the types of measures which constitute accommodations in national legislation. By way of reminder, the ADA defines the term 'reasonable accommodation' in the context of employment as including the following: making existing facilities used by employees readily accessible to and usable by individuals with disabilities,[10] job restructuring, part-time or modified work schedules, reassignment to a vacant position, acquisition or modification of equipment or devices, appropriate adjustment or modifications of examinations, training materials or policies, the provision of qualified readers or interpreters and other similar accommodations for individuals with disabilities.[11] Furthermore, Recital 20 of the (non-binding) Preamble to the Employment Equality Directive provides the following examples of types of measures that could amount to a reasonable accommodation: adapting premises and equipment, patterns of working time, the distribution of tasks or the provision of training or integration resources.[12] While the accommodations listed above are not exhaustive, they illustrate the types of measures that may be deemed an 'accommodation' for persons with disabilities in the context of employment and occupation. Accommodations under the CRPD are likely to take a similar form. However, the duty to accommodate in the CRPD goes far beyond the field of employment. In the next section of this chapter, the duty to accommodate in the CRPD will be explored.

3. The Duty to Accommodate in the CRPD

This section of the present chapter will comprise an analysis of the duty to accommodate in the CRPD, including a consideration of the key strengths and weaknesses of the duty as a facilitator of substantive equality for persons with disabilities.

3.1. The Key Strengths of the Duty to Accommodate in the CRPD

The duty to accommodate in the CRPD holds significant promise for advancing the rights of persons with disabilities and ensuring their full and effective participation

---

10 Title 42, Chapter 126, Sub-chapter 1 on Employment, Section 12111, Subsection 9(a), Americans with Disabilities Act (1990), as amended by the Americans with Disabilities Amendments Act (2008) (effective as of 1 January 2009).

11 Title 42, Chapter 126, Sub-chapter 1 on Employment, Section 12111, Subsection 9(b), Americans with Disabilities Act (1990), as amended by the Americans with Disabilities Amendments Act (2008) (effective as of 1 January 2009).

12 Recital 20, Preamble, Council Directive 2000/78/EC of 27 November 2000 establishing a general framework for equal treatment in employment and occupation(Official Journal L 303, 02/12/2000 pp. 0016–0022).

and inclusion in all spheres of life. The reasonable accommodation duty mandates differential treatment for persons with disabilities in order that they are not placed at a disadvantage when compared with their non-disabled counterparts. It requires the removal of discriminatory barriers to ensure equalisation of opportunities and effective access to, and enjoyment of, rights for persons with disabilities on an equal basis with others. Under the CRPD, the notion of 'reasonable accommodation' is defined in Article 2 as:

> Necessary and appropriate modification and adjustments not imposing a disproportionate or undue burden, where needed in a particular case, to ensure to persons with disabilities the enjoyment or exercise on an equal basis with others of all human rights and fundamental freedoms.[13]

Article 5(3) of the CRPD outlines the role of States in ensuring the provision of reasonable accommodations to persons with disabilities. It reads as follows: 'In order to promote equality and eliminate discrimination, States Parties shall take all appropriate steps to ensure that reasonable accommodation is provided.'[14] To that end, States have undertaken to ensure that the duty to accommodate is actually followed through by entities in practice. For the first time in a UN human rights treaty, a denial of reasonable accommodation is included as a distinct form of discrimination. Article 2 of the CRPD includes a failure to reasonably accommodate as an integral component of the definition of discrimination on the basis of disability. This strengthens considerably the protection provided to persons with disabilities under international human rights law. The duty to accommodate in the Convention is embedded explicitly or implicitly across the substantive rights. This again strengthens the rights of persons with disabilities as it cements equality as a key component of the realisation of all CRPD rights. Reasonable accommodation duties are mentioned specifically in the context of such rights as the right to employment,[15] the right to education[16] and the right to liberty and security of the person.[17] In addition, the accommodation duty is an implicit element of almost all of the provisions of the Convention by virtue of the cross-cutting nature of Articles 2 and 5 of the CRPD. Persons with disabilities are therefore holders of a fundamental right to be accommodated in a variety of contexts and by a wide array of entities.

Reasonable accommodations have certain key strengths over and above other measures taken to ensure *de facto* equality. For instance, the duty to accommodate has the advantage of being tailored specifically to meet the needs of the disabled individual and, thereby, avoids (for instance) the controversial aspects of positive action measures, which often hinge on stereotypes[18] and generalised assumptions

---

13 UN CRPD, Article 2.
14 UN CRPD, Article 5(3).
15 UN CRPD, Article 27.
16 UN CRPD, Article 24.
17 UN CRPD, Article 14.
18 On this point, see, for example, S. Coate and G.C. Loury, 'Will Affirmative-Action Policies Eliminate Negative Stereotypes?' (1993) 83(5) *The American Economic Review* 1220.

regarding marginalised groups. Certain weaknesses of the duty to accommodate have also been highlighted by scholars, as will be demonstrated below.

3.2. The Weaknesses of the Duty to Accommodate as a Facilitator of Substantive Equality

While the duty to accommodate has been welcomed warmly by many commentators[19] as a means of facilitating substantive equality, it has also been criticised, to some extent, by others who believe that it simply reifies difference and militates against structural change. Accommodating a person with a disability requires that person to fit into a pre-existing social pattern based on the dominant norm – the non-disabled norm. It does not tackle wider issues of structural disadvantage for persons with disabilities. This view is taken by Bronagh Byrne, for example, who states that the duty to accommodate 'does not challenge the legitimacy of prevailing ways of being and doing, focusing only on the need to instigate change where necessary.'[20] In a similar vein, Oliver de Schutter contends that the duty to provide reasonable accommodations obliges the collectivity to:

> Make certain adjustments, here and there, to do what [is] needed in order to avoid excluding particular disabled people but disabled people generally [...] remain inhabitants of structures conceived by and made for others – structures which, by their very nature, [...] render them forever strangers and outsiders.[21]

These arguments mirror the remarks of Shelagh Day and Gavin Brodsky in their highly influential article on the duty to accommodate,[22] in which they argue that the framework of reasonable accommodations can neither address inequalities nor foster inclusive institutions. They further contend that the reasonable accommodation norm is flawed on account of the fact that it is embedded in the notion that dominant groups should determine the social 'norm' and that concessions should be made for

---

19 See, for example, the views of J.E. Lord and R. Brown, 'The Role of Reasonable Accommodation in Securing Substantive Equality for Persons with Disabilities: The UN Convention on the Rights of Persons with Disabilities' in M.H. Rioux, L.A. Basser and M. Jones (eds.), *Critical Perspectives on Human Rights and Disability Law* (Martinus Nijhoff, The Hague, 2011), at pages 273–307; See also the views expressed by A. Lawson, 'The UN Convention on the Rights of Persons with Disabilities and European Disability Law: A Catalyst for Cohesion?' in O.M. Arnardóttir and G. Quinn (eds.) *The UN Convention on the Rights of Persons with Disabilities: European and Scandinavian Perspectives* (Martinus Nijhoff 2009), at pages 81–109.

20 B. Byrne, 'Minding the Gap? Children with Disabilities and the United Nations Convention on the Rights of Persons with Disabilities in M. Freeman (ed.), *Law and Childhood Studies* (Oxford University Press, Oxford, 2012), at page 433.

21 O. De Schutter, 'Reasonable Accommodation and Positive Obligations in the European Convention on Human Rights' in A. Lawson and C. Gooding (eds.), *Disability Rights in Europe: From Theory to Practice* (Oxford and Portland, Oregon, 2005) 63.

22 S. Day and G. Brodsky, 'The Duty to Accommodate: Who Will Benefit?' (1996) 75 *Canadian Bar Review* 433 [That article was quoted at length in an influential judgment of the Supreme Court of Canada - *British Columbia (Public Service Employee Relations Commission) v BCGSEU* [1999] 3 SCR 3 – at para. 41 thereof, in particular].

those who are 'different.'[23] Day and Brodsky assert that accommodation, conceived in this way, 'appears to be rooted in the formal model of equality.'[24] As a result, they argue that:

> Accommodation does not go to the heart of the equality question, to the goal of transformation, to an examination of the way institutions and relations must be changed in order to make them available, accessible, meaningful and rewarding for the many diverse groups of which our society is composed [...].[25]

These arguments are highly plausible. Viewed in this light, reasonable accommodations do result in an inadequate facilitation of substantive equality. As against these arguments, one might say that the facilitation of participation and inclusion of persons with disabilities in society cannot be achieved without incorporating some element of reasonable accommodation. Existing structures cannot be transformed immediately. As such, the duty to accommodate fills an essential gap in ensuring the participation of persons with disabilities in mainstream society while rights and obligations are being realised progressively. In the long-term, it is hoped that other mechanisms, such as the accessibility obligation in the CRPD, can create truly inclusive societies.

While the duty to accommodate itself is realisable immediately (falling within the non-discrimination norm), it also forms part of an overall schema of other measures in the CRPD that are designed to achieve *de facto* equality in a progressive fashion. In that regard, the CRPD Committee will be tasked with defining criteria for assessing State action or inaction in the progressive realisation of the rights and obligations under the Convention. As outlined at the outset of this chapter, the outer limits of the duty to accommodate represent the balancing of needs and interests of disabled individuals, on the one side, and duty-bearers, on the other side. This balancing act is also reflected implicitly in several rights subject to progressive realisation. The outer limits of the duty to accommodate may tell us something about the implicit balancing act that underlies the progressive implementation of many CRPD rights and obligations. The next section of this chapter will consist of an examination of those outer limits.

23 Ibid.

24 Ibid.

25 Ibid.

4. The Outer Limits of the Duty to Accommodate in the CRPD

4.1. Introduction to the Outer Limits of the Duty to Accommodate

Anna Lawson comments on the 'peculiar bridging role played by the concept of reasonable accommodation in the context of human rights law.'[26] She states that while it is technically situated within the realm of civil and political rights, the function of the duty to accommodate is to 'ensure that rights of all kinds – whether they are classified as economic, social and cultural rights or civil and political ones – become available, in a meaningful sense, to disabled people.'[27] The provision of reasonable accommodations requires positive measures to address the unique needs of persons with disabilities in order to ensure that they can exercise the right to work, education and health, among many others, on an equal basis with non-disabled persons. Bruce Porter notes that the CRPD offers an exceptional model of 'convergent paradigms of rights and remedies'[28] on account of the 'convergence of the right to equality and non-discrimination and the economic, social and cultural rights'[29] of persons with disabilities in the Convention. He emphasises the importance of the standard adopted by the CRPD Committee 'in reviewing the right to positive measures in light of available resources in the context of both equality rights and [economic, social and cultural] rights.'[30] As stated above, the duty to accommodate and the concept of progressive realisation are subject to outer limits. In the subsections which follow, I will tease out the limits to the duty to accommodate. In the next chapter of this book I will reflect on the progressive realisation of CRPD rights, seeking (among other things) to determine if any lessons can be drawn from the CRPD's equality norm, and more specifically the outer limits of the reasonable accommodation duty, to be applied to the assessment of measures taken by States under the Convention.

4.2. The Outer Limits of the Duty to Accommodate in the CRPD: The Concept of 'Reasonableness'

It is worth noting that confusion has arisen at the EU level with regard to the concept of 'reasonableness' on account of the fact that divergent meanings have been attributed to the word 'reasonable' in several European countries. Lisa Waddington has summarised the various meanings into three categories.[31] This tripartite categorisation will now be drawn on in order to clarify whether we can draw any

[26] A. Lawson, 'Duties to Make Adjustments and Human Rights' in A. Lawson (ed.), *Disability and Equality Law in Britain: The Role of Reasonable Adjustment* (Hart Publishing, Oxford, 2008), at page 32.

[27] Ibid.

[28] B. Porter, 'The Reasonableness of Article 8(4) – Adjudicating Claims from the Margins' (2009) 27(1) *Nordisk Tidsskrift for Menneskerettigheter* 39, at page 42.

[29] Ibid.

[30] Ibid.

[31] See L. Waddington, 'Reasonable Accommodation' in D. Schiek, L. Waddington and M. Bell (eds.), *Cases, Materials and Text on National, Supranational and International Non-Discrimination Law* (Hart Publishing, Oxford, 2007), at page 635.

lessons from the concept of 'reasonableness' under the CRPD's accommodation duty.

Waddington has observed that, in certain European jurisdictions, the term 'reasonable' under the Employment Equality Directive[32] is taken to mean an accommodation that does not result in excessive difficulties or costs for the employer. This is separate and distinct from the defence of disproportionate burden. Waddington states that 'this approach implies that an accommodation can be regarded as *prima facie* "unreasonable," and therefore not required, in which case the stricter disproportionate burden test will not be considered at all.'[33] Waddington categorises the second approach as encompassing situations in which 'an accommodation will be regarded as "reasonable" if it is effective in allowing the individual in question to carry out the necessary (employment-related) tasks.'[34] The final approach described by Waddington is one which defines the term 'reasonable' as conveying both the requirement that 'the accommodation must be effective and that it must not impose significant inconvenience or cost on the employer or covered party.'[35] In the context of the CRPD, it is worth recalling that, according to the drafting history of the Convention, it was not intended that the term 'reasonable' should act as a qualifier in and of itself, such as to modify or weaken the provision of accommodations.[36] The drafting history also reveals that the term 'reasonable accommodation' is a single concept that is being defined.[37] We can conclude from this information that the concept of 'reasonableness' *per se* does not form part of the outer limits of the duty to accommodate in the CRPD. One must look at the definition of reasonable accommodation in its entirety to extract the other factors that will be relevant in defining the outer limits of the duty to accommodate.

4.3. The Outer Limits of the Duty to Accommodate in the CRPD: The Requirements of Necessity and Effectiveness

When looking at the process of balancing needs and interests, it is imperative to examine the definition of reasonable accommodation contained in Article 2 of the Convention. The interests of disabled people are captured by the following phrase taken from Article 2: 'necessary and appropriate adjustments and modifications [...] to ensure to persons with disabilities the enjoyment or exercise on an equal

32 Council Directive 2000/78/EC of 27 November 2000 establishing a general framework for equal treatment in employment and occupation,Official Journal L 303, 02/12/2000 P. 0016–0022, available at http://eur-lex.europa.eu/LexUriServ/LexUriServ.do?uri=CELEX:32000L0078:en:HTML last accessed 14 April 2014.

33 L. Waddington, 'Reasonable Accommodation' in D. Schiek, L. Waddington and M. Bell (eds.), *Cases, Materials and Text on National, Supranational and International Non-Discrimination Law* (Hart Publishing, Oxford, 2007), at page 669/670.

34 Ibid, at page 669.

35 Ibid, at page 670.

36 Fourth Session of the Ad Hoc Committee, Volume 5(10), September 03, 2004, available at www.un.org/esa/socdev/enable/rights/ahc4sumart07.htm, last accessed 12 April 2014.

37 Ibid.

basis with others of all human rights and fundamental freedoms.'[38] The interests of duty bearers, on the other hand, are spelt out within the phrase 'not imposing a disproportionate or undue burden.'[39] The disproportionate burden defence will be considered below[40] but for now, it is proposed to concentrate on the interests of disabled people as contained in the 'necessary and appropriate' requirement.

In the context of the duty to accommodate in the CRPD, satisfying the needs and interests of persons with disabilities will require duty-bearers to take the steps which are *necessary* to ensure that the disabled person in question can enjoy their human rights and fundamental freedoms on an equal basis with others and which are *appropriate* in resulting in the realisation of the rights contained in the Convention. On a literal interpretation of Article 2 of the CRPD, and according to the ordinary meaning of the terms contained therein, 'necessary' signifies something which is 'essential, needed to be done, achieved or present' and 'appropriate' means 'suitable or proper in the circumstances.'[41] The necessity criterion signifies the requirement to take all essential measures to ensure access to, and enjoyment of, CRPD rights for persons with disabilities. There is no duty incumbent on States to ensure the provision by entities of every requested accommodation and indeed some accommodations may not be necessary to ensure enjoyment of Convention rights. However, entities must provide those accommodations which are essential for persons with disabilities to benefit from the substantive rights contained in the Convention. It is submitted that the use of the word 'appropriate' in the definition of reasonable accommodation implies that accommodations must be effective in ensuring that persons with disabilities can exercise their human rights on an equal basis with others. This interpretation of the word 'appropriate' is confirmed by other sources relating to the provision of reasonable accommodations. In the Employment Equality Directive, 'appropriate measures' are defined as '*effective and practical measures* to adapt the workplace to the disability.'[42] Furthermore, Article 5 of the Directive defines the objective of 'appropriate measures' as enabling a person with a disability 'to have access to, participate in, or advance in employment, or to undergo training [...].'[43] The Employment Equality Directive therefore links the notion of 'appropriateness' to the effectiveness of measures taken in increasing participation and inclusion in employment. The reading of the word 'appropriate' as meaning effective measures is reinforced by the use of that term in the Irish Employment Equality Act 1998–2004.[44] Furthermore, Dutch legislation[45] uses the term 'effective' accommodation,

---

38 UN CRPD, Article 2.

39 Ibid.

40 See section 4.5 of this chapter.

41 See the following website: www.oxforddictionaries.com/ last accessed 08 April 2014.

42 Preamble, Recital 20, Council Directive 2007/78/EC of 27 November 2000 establishing a general framework for equal treatment in employment and occupation [Emphasis added].

43 Article 5, Council Directive 2007/78/EC of 27 November 2000 establishing a general framework for equal treatment in employment and occupation).

44 See Section 9(b)(a) of the Irish Employment Equality Act 2004, which provides that 'appropriate measures; in relation to a person with a disability means 'effective and practical measures, where needed in a particular case, to adapt the employer's place of business to the disability concerned.'

45 Article 2 of the Dutch Act on Equal Treatment on the Grounds of Disability or Chronic Illness (2003).

as opposed to 'reasonable' accommodation. Interestingly, Section 6(4) of the (now repealed) UK Disability Discrimination Act listed effectiveness as a key factor to be considered in determining whether it is reasonable for an employer to take a particular step in order to comply with his or her paragraph 6(1) duty to make reasonable adjustments.[46]

If a disabled person requests an accommodation in an employment context, one must consider the extent to which the requested accommodation will contribute to ensuring participation in the workforce. In that regard, it is interesting to note that in a 2014 individual communication, *Jungelin v Sweden*,[47] a joint dissenting opinion issued by five dissenting members of the CRPD Committee[48] referred implicitly to the concept of the effectiveness of accommodation measures in the realisation of disability rights. That case concerned a woman with visual impairment who alleged discrimination on the basis of her disability in a recruitment procedure because the public agency employer had failed to provide reasonable accommodation, in the form of reasonable support and adaptation measures, to guarantee her right to employment on an equal basis with others. The applicant also alleged that insufficient consideration had been given by the domestic labour court to alternatives that would allow her to carry out the tasks assigned to the post, in violation of Articles 5 and 27 of the Convention. While the Committee ultimately concluded that the author's rights had not been violated,[49] it is interesting to note that the dissenting Committee members stated that 'the reasonableness and proportionality of the measures of accommodation proposed must be assessed in the view of the context in which they are requested.'[50] In the instant case, the measures were requested in a professional context. Therefore, the dissenting Committee members remarked that:

> The test of reasonableness and proportionality should therefore ensure, *inter alia*, that [...] the measures of accommodation were requested to promote the employment of a person with disability, with the professional capacity and experience to perform the functions corresponding to the position [for which] he or she applied.[51]

This certainly reflects considerations of the effectiveness of measure adopted in the realisation of Convention rights.

---

46 In that connection, Section 6(4)(a) of the UK Disability Discrimination Act (1995) states that regard shall be had, *inter alia*, to 'the extent to which taking the step would prevent the effect in question.'

47 *Marie-Louise Jungelin (represented by the Swedish Association of Visually Impaired Youth (US) and the Swedish Association of the Visually Impaired (SRF) v Sweden,* Communication No. 5/2011, views adopted by the Committee at its twelfth session (15 September–3 October 2014), adopted 2 October 2014.

48 Joint opinion of Committee members Mr. Carlos Rios Espinosa, Ms. Theresia Degener, Mr. Munthian Buntan, Ms. Silvia Judith Quan-Chang and Ms. Maria Soledad Cisternas Reyes (dissenting).

49 Referring to the State's margin of appreciation, the Committee concluded that the author's rights had not been violated because it found that the domestic court had thoroughly and objectively assessed the alternatives.

50 Joint opinion of Committee members Mr. Carlos Rios Espinosa, Ms. Theresia Degener, Mr. Munthian Buntan, Ms. Silvia Judith Quan-Chang and Ms. Maria Soledad Cisternas Reyes (dissenting), para. 4.

51 Ibid, para. 4.

4.4. The Outer Limits of the Duty to Accommodate in the CRPD: A Consideration of the Objective of the Accommodation Duty and the Inherent Dignity of Persons with Disabilities

In order to determine the effectiveness of measures adopted under the duty to accommodate, it is vital that one also considers the object and purpose of the duty itself. As outlined in chapter three above, the specific objective of the duty to accommodate is to promote equality and to eliminate discrimination. Measures taken to accommodate persons with disabilities must contribute to fulfilling those purposes. Equality considerations will therefore be paramount in determining the effectiveness of measures taken to accommodate disabled individuals. Linked to the equality guarantee and the overall requirement of effectiveness that has been examined above, it is also submitted that dignity interests will play an integral role in determining the reasonableness of measures taken under the duty to accommodate. The overall link between equality and dignity is clear from the case of *Law v. Canada* (*Minister of Employment and Immigration*).[52] In that case, the Supreme Court of Canada noted in its articulation of the purpose of Section 15(1) of the Canadian Charter of Rights and Freedoms[53] (which contains the guarantee of equality) that 'a focus is quite properly placed upon the goal of assuring human dignity by the remedying of discriminatory treatment.'[54] The dignity interests of persons with disabilities can be deemed to form part of the outer limits of the duty to accommodate in the sense that an accommodation that is not effective (or indeed failure to provide any accommodation at all) will not cater for the inherent dignity of a disabled individual. It will impede access to the substantive human rights to which persons with disabilities are entitled under the Convention and it will result in marginalisation and exclusion from society. It is argued here that the benefits of inclusion and the stigmatisation costs of not providing accommodations, or of providing ineffective accommodations, should be a relevant criterion for the CRPD Committee in its assessment of measures taken by States or entities. Indeed, the idea of effectiveness in the context of the duty to accommodate has been defined by one author as including 'the prevention and elimination of segregation, humiliation and stigma,'[55] which mirrors a consideration of dignity interests. This link between dignity and marginalisation is also reflected in the jurisprudence of the Canadian Supreme Court, which states that:

> Dignity is harmed when individuals and groups are marginalized, ignored, or devalued, and is enhanced when laws recognize the full place of all individuals and groups within [society].[56]

---

52 *Law v Canada* (*Minister of Employment and Immigration*) [1999] 1 S.C.R. 497.

53 Section 15(1) of the Canadian Charter of Rights and Freedoms provides that: 'Every individual is equal before and under the law and has the right to the equal protection and equal benefit of the law.'

54 *Law v Canada* (*Minister of Employment and Immigration*) [1999] 1 S.C.R. 497, para. 52.

55 L. de Campos Velho Martel, 'Reasonable Accommodation: The New Concept from an Inclusive Constitutional Perspective' (2007) *International Journal on Human Rights*, available at www.surjournal.org/eng/conteudos/getArtigo14.php?artigo=14 last accessed 12 April 2014.

56 *Law v Canada* (*Minister of Employment and Immigration*) [1999] 1 S.C.R. 497, para. 53.

Notably, the CRPD Committee has already recognised in its General Comment 2 (on accessibility) that dignity is an essential component of the duty to accommodate. In that connection, the Committee states that 'reasonable accommodation seeks to achieve individual justice in the sense that non-discrimination or equality is assured, taking the dignity, autonomy and choices of the individual into account.'[57] Taking dignity into account as part of the outer limits of the accommodation duty will include not only consideration of the manner in which the accommodation is provided but also the level of participation of the disabled individual in the process of accommodation. Human dignity is concerned with integrity, empowerment and self-respect. In considering the extent to which a particular accommodation promotes full participation and maximises inclusion in society, account must be taken of such factors as privacy, autonomy, comfort and self-esteem.

4.5. The Outer Limits of the Duty to Accommodate in the CRPD: The Defence of 'Disproportionate or Undue Burden'

In the preceding subsections, certain outer limits of the duty to accommodate have been highlighted, namely the requirement that any measures taken to fulfil the duty must be necessary and effective, as well as furthering the equality principle and the inherent dignity of disabled people. In this section, the second part of the definition of reasonable accommodation – the notion of disproportionate or undue burden[58] – will be reflected upon, as this establishes another outer limit of the duty to accommodate. In other words, we can discern from the test of disproportionate burden the types of measures that might be deemed adequate or reasonable on the part of public or private entities or States Parties to the CRPD in fulfilment of the duty to accommodate.

The essential question rests on what actually constitutes a disproportionate or undue burden? These concepts have not been defined anywhere in the Convention. There is little guidance contained in the *travaux préparatoires* on the meaning of the terms 'disproportionate' and 'undue burden.' During the drafting sessions leading up to the adoption of the CRPD, it was clear that most States associated the notion of disproportionate burden with addressing the resource implications of the duty to accommodate.[59] Furthermore, the European Disability Forum (EDF) stated that the duty to accommodate 'needs to be qualified by type of entity, size of entity, financial

[57] UN Committee on the Rights of Persons with Disabilities, General Comment No. 2 on Article 9 (Accessibility), adopted at the eleventh session of the Committee (30 March–11 April 2014) on 11 April 2014, UN Doc. CRPD/C/GC/2, para. 26.

[58] In this section, the concepts of disproportionate and undue burden will be considered together under the overall heading of 'disproportionate burden.'

[59] See, for example, the comments of Israel in the Fourth Session of the Ad Hoc Committee on Article 5 CRPD, Volume 5(10), September 3, 2004, available at www.un.org/esa/socdev/enable/rights/ahc4sumart07.htm, last accessed 14 October 2014. Israel commented that 'different entities have different levels of resources and there is a need to match the obligations of the employer/service provider with the level and extent of its resources and with the person with a disability.'

capacity and the cost of the reasonable accommodation.'[60] While none of these criteria made it into the final text, it would appear that cost will be the primary factor to be taken into account in determining what amounts to a disproportionate or undue burden. There was general agreement among delegates that the availability of State funding should limit the use of the concept of 'disproportionate burden' as a reason by employers and service providers not to provide reasonable accommodations.[61] The CRPD Committee commented on the duty to accommodate in the first individual communication brought before the Committee in *HM v Sweden*.[62] However, it did not elaborate on the precise meaning of the terms 'disproportionate' or 'undue burden.' Domestic and European legislation incorporating accommodation duties employ many terms to delimit the duty to accommodate, including the expressions 'disproportionate burden,'[63] 'undue burden,'[64] 'undue hardship'[65] and 'unjustifiable hardship.'[66] It is instructive to examine relevant national legislation and case law incorporating those terms, with a view to unravelling the various components of the defence that can be invoked by entities in order to justify a failure to reasonably accommodate a disabled individual. The various elements of the defence of disproportionate burden can be categorised broadly as follows:

4.5.1. Financial and Other Resource Considerations

Sandra Fredman notes that one of the major themes in equality law concerns costs which 'constitute the hidden but powerful agenda behind much of equality policy

60 Third Session of the Ad Hoc Committee, volume 4(2), May 25, 2004, available at www.un.org/esa/socdev/enable/rights/ahc3sum7.htm, last accessed 12 October 2014.

61 Report of the Working Group to the Ad Hoc Committee, Footnotes to Annex I: Draft articles for a Comprehensive and Integral International Convention on the Protection and Promotion of the Rights and Dignity of Persons with Disabilities, available at www.un.org/esa/socdev/enable/rights/wgcontrib-chair1.html last accessed 13th October 2014.

62 UN CRPD Committee, Individual Communication, *HM v Sweden*, UN Doc CRPD/C/7/D/3/2011 (21 May 2012), views adopted at the 7th session of the Committee (16 to 20 April 2012, Geneva). [At issue in that individual communication was the refusal of the domestic authorities to depart from a development plan in order to allow the building of a hydrotherapy pool, which was essential for the rehabilitation of a disabled Swedish citizen. The Committee held that the refusal was disproportionate and produced a discriminatory effect that affected the individual's access, as a person with a disability, to the health care and rehabilitation required for her specific health condition. The Committee found, *inter alia*, a breach of Article 5(3) of the CRPD and noted that the legislation in question allowed for departure from a building development plan, and that it could thus accommodate, where necessary in a particular case, an application for reasonable accommodation. On the basis of the information before it, the Committee concluded that the approval of a departure from the development plan in the author's case would not impose a 'disproportionate or undue burden' on the State party].

63 See Council Directive 2000/78/EC of 27 November 2000.

64 See the Israeli Equal Rights for People with Disabilities Law 5758 (1998).

65 See the American with Disabilities Act (1990), which employs the term 'undue hardship;' See also the Canadian Human Rights Act (1985).

66 See, for instance, the use of the term 'unjustifiable hardship' in the Australian Disability Discrimination Act [1992], Act No. 135 of 1992 as amended, available at www.comlaw.gov.au/Details/C2013C00022 last accessed 25 July 2014; See also the use of this term in the South African Employment Equality Act No. 55 of 1998, available at www.ilo.org/dyn/natlex/docs/WEBTEXT/51169/65139/E98ZAF01.htm last accessed 25 July 2014.

and legislation.'[67] She states that 'the ideals of equality and fairness are always tempered by a strong sense, among policy-makers, that equality should not impose burdens on business.'[68] Lisa Waddington[69] outlines the fact that the cost[70] of a requested accommodation is the primary factor that has been taken into account in national legislation and case law in determining whether the accommodating party can avail of a defence to the duty to accommodate. In the context of the ADA, the test of 'undue hardship' includes considerations such as the nature and cost of the accommodation, the overall financial resources of the facility or facilities involved in the provision of the reasonable accommodation and the effect on expenses and resources.[71] The matter of costs also features heavily in Preamble, paragraph 21 of the Employment Equality Directive and has been deemed 'the primary factor in determining whether a disproportionate burden exists.'[72] The relevant part of the Directive reads as follows:

> To determine whether the measures in question give rise to a disproportionate burden, account should be taken in particular of the financial and other costs entailed, the scale and financial resources of the organisation or undertaking and the possibility of obtaining public funding or any other assistance.[73]

In a similar vein, Bulgarian law provides that an employer:

> Shall be obliged to adapt the workplace to the needs of persons with disabilities at their employment or when the disability occurs after the beginning of employment, unless the

---

67 S. Fredman, 'Disability Equality and the Existing Paradigm' in A. Lawson and C. Gooding (eds.), *Disability Rights in Europe: From Theory to Practice* (Hart Publishing, Oxford, 2005), at page 208.

68 Ibid.

69 L. Waddington, 'Reasonable Accommodation' in D. Schiek, L. Waddington and M. Bell (eds.), *Cases, Materials and Text on National, Supranational and International Non-Discrimination Law* (Hart Publishing, Oxford, 2007), at page 731.

70 Michael Stein conceptualises the potential costs arising from the duty to accommodate as falling into one or both of two categories. He defines the first category of costs as 'hard' costs, meaning that they involve 'readily quantifiable out-of-pocket expenses.' This category of costs, he asserts, requires the alteration or provision of a physical plant. As an example of such costs he cites the provision of a ramp to accommodate the needs of an employee who uses a wheelchair, the purchase and installation of which is usually 'a one-time expenditure with a fixed and knowable cost.' Stein contends that the second type of accommodation involves the alteration of the way in which a job is performed and this brings into play 'soft' costs, which he rightly asserts are more difficult to quantify. An example of such a cost, according to Stein, might involve not requiring a wheelchair-using store clerk to stack high shelves and instead requiring a fellow worker to stack the high shelves while the disabled employee staffs the register. The 'soft' costs in that case might also extend to requiring the human resource manager to meet with other employees to explain the change in their daily duties, or to requiring a supervisor to learn how to take these alterations into consideration when evaluating overall job performance. [M.A. Stein, 'The Law and Economics of Disability Accommodations' (2003) 53(1) *Duke Law Journal* 79, at pages 88–89].

71 Title 42, Chapter 126, Subchapter 1 on Employment, Section 12111, Subsection 10(b), Americans with Disabilities Act (1990), as amended by the Americans with Disabilities Act (2008) (effective as of 1 January 2009).

72 K. Wells, The Impact of the Framework Employment Directive on UK Disability Discrimination Law (December 2003) 32(4) *Industrial Law Journal* 253, at page 264.

73 Council Directive 2000/78/EC of 27 November 2000 establishing a general framework for equal treatment in employment and occupation, Preamble para. 21.

> costs of such adaptation are unreasonably high and would cause serious difficulties to the employer.[74]

In considering the financial burden placed on an employer by the accommodation in question, the non-binding Belgian Guide to Reasonable Accommodations for Persons with a Disability at Work also takes into account human resources by stating that 'certain adjustments require human investment. The financial cost associated with this generally coincides with the staff costs and will also have to be taken into account.'[75] The Guide provides an example of such staff costs, whereby it states that 'the recruitment of an additional person to support or monitor a person with a disability could by nature be an unreasonable accommodation if the additional cost cannot be offset.'[76]

The size of the accommodating party might be relevant to a determination of the entity's ability to bear the costs and make the required adjustment, as larger firms will generally have more resources than smaller firms. The Belgian Guide, referred to above, states that when considering whether an accommodation is reasonable or not, the financial capabilities and organisational potential of the business or the employer must be taken into account. In doing so, it states that the size or extent of the business will play an important role. Moreover, it notes that while expensive reconstruction may be reasonable for large firms or multinationals, the same accommodations could mean a disproportionate burden for a small or medium-sized business.[77] The Guide states, for example, that it may be unreasonable in certain cases to expect a firm with four employees to have various doors widened to permit access by a person in a wheelchair. On the other hand, it may be reasonable for a small or medium-sized business to have a ramp installed to make the workplace accessible.[78]

With regard to the scale of an entity's operations, the nature of the entity is relevant in determining the extent of the burden. In the context of public employment, it will be much more difficult for an employer to argue that resources do not allow for the provision of a requested accommodation, in comparison with a (usually smaller-scale) private employer. This is evident from the U.S. decision of *Nelson v. Thornburgh*,[79] which sets a high threshold for the test of undue hardship in the field of public employment. The Court in that case held that the accommodations requested by employees with visual impairments would not impose an undue

---

74 Article 16, *Bulgarian Protection Against Discrimination Act* (effective as of 1 January 2004) [State Gazette (SG) No. 86/30.09.2003, effective 1.01.2004, supplemented, SG No. 70/10.08.2004, effective 1.01.2005, amended, SG No. 105/29.12.2005, effective 1.01.2006, SG No. 30/11.04.2006, effective 12.07.2006], available at www.refworld.org/docid/44ae58d62d5.html last accessed 14 October 2014.

75 Belgian Guide to Reasonable Accommodations for Persons with a Disability at Work [March 2005], para. 3.1.2. [[Information taken from L. Waddington, 'Reasonable Accommodation' in D. Schiek, L. Waddington, M. Bell (eds.), *Cases, Materials and Text on National, Supranational and International Non-Discrimination Law (*Hart Publishing, Oxford, 2007), at page 730].

76 Ibid.

77 Ibid, at para. 3.1.1.

78 Ibid.

79 *Nelson v. Thornburgh*, United States Court of Appeals, Third Circuit. - 732 F.2d 146 3/6/84567 F. Supp. 369 (E.D.Pa. 1983).

hardship on the employer, which was a State agency. The requested accommodations were comprised, *inter alia*, of readers, braille forms and a computer that could store and retrieve data in Braille and were cost-intensive. Nonetheless, the Court held that the monetary burden of the accommodations would represent only a small fraction of the $300 million administrative budget of the agency in question.[80] That case demonstrates neatly the balanced assessment or weighing up of various factors in determining the extent of the monetary burden placed on an entity. Interestingly, the nature of the entity in question was a relevant factor in the joint dissenting opinion of five CRPD Committee members in the 2014 individual communication of *Jungelin v Sweden*.[81] The Committee members raised the failure of the domestic courts to consider, when assessing the 'reasonableness and proportionality' of requested accommodation measures under the Convention, the profile (including the role and functions) of the Social Insurance Agency, one of the State's main public institutions in charge of implementing the national policy on persons with disabilities.[82]

In outlining the balancing act which occurs in assessing whether a duty to accommodate should fall on an entity, Lisa Waddington refers[83] to the analysis of the final regulation[84] which accompanied the original Regulations under Section 504 of the American Rehabilitation Act.[85] The analysis describes the relative approach to be taken in determining whether an accommodation constitutes an undue hardship for an entity. It states, for instance, that a small day-care centre might not be required to spend more than a nominal sum, such as that necessary to equip a telephone for use by a secretary with impaired hearing. On the other hand, a large school district might be required to make available a teacher's aide to a blind applicant for a teaching job. Furthermore, it might be considered appropriate to require a State welfare agency to accommodate a deaf employee by providing an interpreter, while it could constitute an undue hardship to impose such a requirement on a provider of foster home care services.[86] In light of the foregoing, arguments raised in relation to costs by States Parties to the CRPD or by public entities will be less sympathetically received by the CRPD Committee than those raised by private entities.

---

80 Ibid at 382.

81 *Marie-Louise Jungelin (represented by the Swedish Association of Visually Impaired Youth (US) and the Swedish Association of the Visually Impaired (SRF) v Sweden*, Communication No. 5/2011, views adopted by the Committee at its twelfth session (15 September–3 October 2014). [Joint opinion of Committee members Mr. Carlos Rios Espinosa, Ms. Theresia Degener, Mr. Munthian Buntan, Ms. Silvia Judith Quan-Chang and Ms. Maria Soledad Cisternas Reyes (dissenting)].

82 Ibid, para. 5.

83 L. Waddington, 'Reasonable Accommodation' in D. Schiek, L. Waddington and M. Bell (eds.), *Cases, Materials and Text on National, Supranational and International Non-Discrimination Law* (Hart Publishing, Oxford, 2007), at page 632.

84 Analysis of Final Regulation, 42 Fed. Reg. 22,688, No. 16 (1977) (codified as reissued at 45 C.F.R. 375 (app. A to pt. 84) [commentary on § 84.12(c)) (1993)].

85 Section 504 of the Rehabilitation Act is published in the United States Code at 29 U.S.C. § 794.; EPA's Section 504 implementing regulations are published in the Code of Federal Regulations at 40 C.F.R. Part 7.

86 Information taken from the report of the E.U. Network of Experts on Disability Discrimination, *Implementing and Interpreting the Reasonable Accommodation Provision of the Framework Employment Directive: Learning from Experience and Achieving Best Practice* (2004), available at http://antidiscriminare.ro/pdf/ImplInterprReason.pdf last accessed 8 May 2014, at pages 68/69.

It is noteworthy that the costs element of the defence to the duty to accommodate has been deemed to set a high threshold in some jurisdictions. For example, the test of 'undue burden' in the Canadian Human Rights Act,[87] was considered to give rise to a high standard of proof in the case of *British Columbia (Public Service Employee Relations Commission) v BCGSEU.*[88] It is also interesting to note that cost does not refer exclusively to the financial aspect of an accommodation. It also takes into account the level of disruption that an accommodation might wreak on an entity or the extent to which a requested accommodation would alter the nature of an entity's business. In that regard, the ADA cites as relevant factors the impact of an accommodation upon the operation of the facility and also the type of operation or operations of the covered entity.[89] The U.S. federal Equal Employment Opportunities Commission (EEOC) has issued interpretative Enforcement Guidelines on the ADA. Those guidelines elaborate on the definition of 'undue hardship' contained in the ADA by explaining that 'an action requiring significant difficulty or expense' means 'an action that is unduly costly, extensive, substantial, disruptive, or that will fundamentally alter the nature of the program.'[90] Additionally, Section 6(4) of the (now repealed) UK Disability Discrimination Act[91] listed key factors that must be considered in determining whether it is reasonable for an employer to take a particular step in order to comply with his or her paragraph 6(1) duty to make reasonable adjustments, including the level of disruption arising to the employer. The Act states that regard shall be had, in particular, to the extent to which it is practicable for the employer to take the step and the extent to which taking it would disrupt any of his activities.

The availability of public subsidies or the possibility of finding support from other sources is also a relevant consideration under the umbrella heading of costs. The accommodating party may be compensated in respect of the duty to accommodate in the form of State immunities, exemptions, subsidies or grants. Such compensatory measures will be relevant in determining whether the overall cost of the accommodation imposes a disproportionate or undue burden on the accommodating party. In *Jungelin v Sweden*,[92] the joint dissenting opinion of several Committee members points to the relevance and the possibility of accessing wage subsidies and

87 Canadian Human Rights Act (R.S.C., 1985, c. H-6).

88 *British Columbia (Public Service Employee Relations Commission) v BCGSEU* [1999] 3 SCR 3.

89 Title 42, Chapter 126, Subchapter 1 on Employment, Section 12111, Subsection 10(b), Americans with Disabilities Act (1990), as amended by the Americans with Disabilities Act (2008) (effective as of 1 January 2009).

90 U.S. Federal Equal Employment Opportunities Commission's (EEOC) *ADA Enforcement Guidelines: Reasonable Accommodation and Undue Hardship Under the Americans with Disabilities Act*, available atwww.eeoc.gov/policy/docs/accommodation.html last accessed 20 October 2014, citing 42 U.S.C. § 12111(10) (1994); 29 C.F.R. § 1630.2(p) (1997); 29 C.F.R. pt. 1630 app. § 1630.2(p) (1997).

91 UK Disability Discrimination Act [1995].

92 UN Committee on the Rights of Persons with Disabilities, *Marie-Louise Jungelin (represented by the Swedish Association of Visually Impaired Youth (US) and the Swedish Association of the Visually Impaired (SRF) v Sweden*, Communication No. 5/2011, views adopted by the Committee at its twelfth session (15 September–3 October 2014).

assistance benefits to implement measures to ensure the author's employment.[93] The availability of public subsidies or funding from other sources is also acknowledged as a relevant factor at the national level. In that regard, Lisa Waddington points to Section 5 of the Finnish Non-Discrimination Act,[94] which states that 'in assessing what constitutes "reasonable" accommodations, particular attention shall be devoted to the costs of the steps, the financial position of the person commissioning work or arranging training and the possibility of support from public funds or elsewhere towards the costs involved.'[95] As outlined above, the Employment Equality Directive also cites the possibility of obtaining public funding or any other assistance[96] as a relevant factor in determining the reasonableness of the requested accommodation. In addition, legislation adopted in several European countries includes the availability of public funding as a pertinent consideration.[97] Of course, each country will have differing levels of resources to offset the cost of reasonable accommodations.

It is evident that cost is a major factor in determining the outer limits of the accommodation duty. In other words, a determination will be made as to whether or not a requested accommodation is in proportion to the resources of the entity in question, both in financial terms and in terms of manpower or institutional capacity. Certain requested accommodations will, by their very nature, be too costly relative to the individualised circumstances of the entity in question. In such circumstances, the provision of the requested accommodation will not be realistic, unless State funding is available to alleviate the burden on the entity. Other accommodations will constitute cost-free alterations, which carry no obvious burden for the entity in question, such as allowing a person with a visual impairment to bring a guide dog into a venue. A concrete example of such cost-free accommodations may be seen in the Irish case, *A Company v A Worker*,[98] in which it was held that an employer's failure to provide reasonable accommodation to an employee with cerebral palsy grounded an action for constructive dismissal. In that case, it was found that the tasks that were allocated to the employee were not suited to her disability. The Equality Officer ruled that the employer had not responded sufficiently to the difficulties raised by the employee and, furthermore, that the employer could have addressed the problems at no cost through an existing policy of task rotation.

---

93 Ibid, joint opinion of Committee members Mr. Carlos Rios Espinosa, Ms. Theresia Degener, Mr. Munthian Buntan, Ms. Silvia Judith Quan-Chang and Ms. Maria Soledad Cisternas Reyes (dissenting), para. 5.

94 Finnish Non-Discrimination Act 21 (2004), as amended by several acts, including No. 84/2009, available at www.finlex.fi/en/laki/kaannokset/2004/en20040021.pdf last accessed 21 November 2014.

95 *Finnish Non-Discrimination Act 21* (2004), Section 5.

96 Council Directive 2000/78/EC of 27 November 2000 establishing a general framework for equal treatment in employment and occupation, Preamble para. 21.

97 The availability of public funding to defray certain costs involved in the provision of reasonable accommodations is required according to the legislation in Portugal, Slovakia, Austria, Denmark, Cyprus, Ireland, Malta, France, Luxembourg, The Netherlands, Sweden, Spain and the United Kingdom. [Information taken from the report of the E.U. Network of Experts on Disability Discrimination, *Implementing and Interpreting the Reasonable Accommodation Provision of the Framework Employment Directive: Learning from Experience and Achieving Best Practice* (2004), at page 78].

98 *A Company v A Worker* (EED021).

Other alterations will be not be cost-free but will be low-cost. There are several examples from national case law of circumstances which were not considered to constitute an 'unjustifiable hardship' in the employment context. In the Australian case of *Woodhouse v Wood Coffill Funerals Pty Ltd*,[99] the Human Rights and Equal Opportunity Commission found that had the employee, a pallbearer with a prosthetic foot, been given a small amount of training, he would have been able to carry out the inherent requirements of the job and that the provision of such training would not have imposed an unjustifiable hardship on his employer. Similarly, in *Daghlian v Australia Post*,[100] the provision of a simple stool to accommodate a postal worker was held not to have amounted to an unjustifiable hardship on the employer. In that case, the Federal Court of Australia found that the employer had discriminated against an employee with degenerative back problems by not allowing her to use a stool because of a perceived risk of tripping over the stool when there was no evidence of such risk. Furthermore, the Court found that the employer had not investigated the cost of remodelling the employee's desk to enable her to use the stool comfortably at the counter. It is also instructive to examine domestic legislation which incorporates the term 'unjustifiable hardship.' In the Australian case of *Hills Grammar School v Human Rights and Equal Opportunity Commission*,[101] it was held that the phrase 'unjustifiable hardship' implies a high threshold that anticipates a degree of hardship in making adjustments.

It is also important to set out the meaning accorded to the phrase 'undue burden,' as this is one of the two terms used in the CRPD (alongside disproportionate burden). In the context of the ADA (1990), the test is that of 'undue burden.' Section 101(10) of the Act includes considerations such as the nature of the accommodation, the financial resources available to the provider and the overall impact on the operation of the provider. The Canadian Human Rights Act (1985) also incorporates the test of undue burden. In that jurisdiction, the costs element of the undue burden test has been deemed to set a high threshold in *British Columbia (Public Service Employee Relations Commission) v BCGSEU*.[102] An interpretation of the phrase 'undue burden,' according to its ordinary meaning, would indicate that it refers to situations where the request for a particular accommodation causes excessive hardship to a private entity. Whether an accommodation causes excessive hardship will presumably be determined in the context of the overall resources available to an entity, in a similar fashion to the term 'disproportionate burden.' Therefore, it would appear that there is no difference in meaning between the terms undue and disproportionate burden in the context of the CRPD's reasonable accommodation duty.

4.5.2. Third-Party Benefits and Negative Impacts of the Requested Accommodation

In considering the boundaries of the CRPD's duty to accommodate set by the disproportionate burden defence, other factors may be relevant in assessing the

99 *Woodhouse v Wood Coffill Funerals Pty Ltd* [1998] HREOCA 12.
100 *Daghlian v Australia Post* [2003] FCA 759.
101 *Hills Grammar School v Human Rights and Equal Opportunity Commission* [2000] 100 FCR 206.
102 *British Columbia (Public Service Employee Relations Commission) v BCGSEU* [1999] 3 SCR 3.

burden to an entity, such as the potential benefits to, and negative impact on, persons other than the disabled person requesting the accommodation. Dealing firstly with third-party benefits, such benefits may accrue not only to the accommodating party (such as an employer) but also to other parties, such as fellow disabled employees (with a comparative disability) or non-disabled employees (who may nevertheless benefit in some way from the measures adopted). Jenny Goldschmidt draws attention to the fact that many of the provisions of the Convention, including reasonable accommodations 'not be regarded as costs only; they may lead to profit as well.'[103] Peter Blanck refers to the 'ripple effects' which can result from the provision of accommodations to disabled individuals.[104] Lisa Waddington contends that, from the point of view of an employer, for instance, an accommodation 'may pay for itself in the greater productivity of the worker with a disability.'[105] She also asserts that an accommodation 'may have externalities beyond that particular worker, by, for example, enabling other workers to be more productive, or by attracting customers who would otherwise not have been able or inclined to patronise the firm.'[106] In the context of the ADA, Elizabeth Emens acknowledges the potential benefits of accommodations to third parties. She states as follows:

> Numerous accommodations – from ramps to ergonomic furniture to telecommuting initiatives – can create benefits for co-workers, both disabled and non-disabled, as well as for the growing group of employees with impairments that are not limiting enough to constitute disabilities under the ADA.[107]

However, Waddington notes that 'not all accommodations can be justified by this model [as] some accommodations are simply economically inefficient.[108] Certainly, Waddington is correct – not all accommodations can be justified by a consideration of third-party benefits. Nonetheless, it is arguable that, in certain instances (as highlighted above), a consideration of the reasonableness of requested measures may be influenced by the potential benefits which might accrue to the entity itself or to third parties. In fact, in the field of employment, the (then) EU Network of Experts on Disability Discrimination advised that, in considering the disproportionate burden

[103] J. Goldschmidt (interviewed by J. Anderson and J. Philips), 'Shifting the Burden of Proof: How the CRPD is Transforming our Understanding of Discrimination, Intersectionality and Priorities' in J. Anderson and J. Philips (eds.), *Disability and Human Rights: Legal, Ethical and Conceptual Implications of the Convention on the Rights of Persons with Disabilities* (Netherlands Institute of Human Rights, SIM Special 35, 2012), at page 52.

[104] P.D. Blanck, *Communicating the Americans with Disabilities Act, Transcending Compliance: 1996 Follow-up Report on Sears, Roebuck and Co.* (Iowa City, Iowa, 1996). available at www.annenberg.nwu.edu/pubs/sears/ last accessed 22 July 2014.

[105] L. Waddington, 'Reasonable Accommodation' in D. Schiek, L. Waddington and M. Bell (eds.), *Cases, Materials and Text on National, Supranational and International Non-Discrimination Law* (Hart Publishing, Oxford, 2007), at page 727.

[106] Ibid.

[107] E.F. Emens, 'Integrating Accommodation' (2008) 156(4) *University of Pennsylvania Law Review* 839, at page 840.

[108] L. Waddington, 'Reasonable Accommodation' (2007) in D. Schiek, L. Waddington and M. Bell (eds.), *Cases, Materials and Text on National, Supranational and International Non-Discrimination Law* (Hart Publishing, Oxford, 2007), at page 727.

defence, specific account should be taken of any external benefit resulting to the employer, such as enhanced access for disabled customers.[109]

It is worth noting that very few European legislative provisions refer to the potential benefits to an employer or other individuals of making a reasonable accommodation. Lisa Waddington[110] refers to the non-binding Belgian Guide to Reasonable Accommodations for Persons with a Disability at Work[111] as one of the few examples of European instruments which take into consideration the potential benefits arising from the adoption of accommodation measures. The guide refers, at paragraph 3.1.4 thereof, to the 'direct and indirect consequences' of a reasonable accommodation. Under that heading, the Guide acknowledges the fact that, beyond facilitating the disabled individual in question, 'certain accommodations may offer support for a larger group of employees and/or for external visitors.'[112] In that regard, it provides specific examples as follows:

- Widening the entrance to a business to permit access by an employee in a wheelchair also offers greater ease to other employees and visitors (persons in wheelchairs, persons with prams, large persons etc.); and
- Installing a lift improves accessibility for persons in a wheelchair but also makes life easier for other employees and visitors.[113]

The same paragraph of the Belgian guide elaborates on other potential benefits of making a reasonable accommodation, stating that 'an accommodation that was originally intended for one person can also ultimately assist future employees with a comparable disability.'[114] It goes on to highlight the fact that an adjusted telephone switchboard for a deaf employee would benefit the hard of hearing generally and that the conversion of work documents or courses in Braille or audiotape would have multilateral effects if more than one blind person is employed by the firm.[115] The provision of reasonable accommodations (through the alteration, for instance, of a work system or practice) may therefore result in increased accessibility for others.

From the perspective of the outer limits of the duty to accommodate, it is interesting to note that, in the individual communication of *Jungelin v Sweden*[116] the five CRPD

---

109 E.U. Network of Experts on Disability Discrimination, *Implementing and Interpreting the Reasonable Accommodation Provision of the Framework Employment Directive: Learning from Experience and Achieving Best Practice* (2004), at page 74.

110 L. Waddington, 'Reasonable Accommodation' (2007) in D. Schiek, L. Waddington and M. Bell (eds.), *Cases, Materials and Text on National, Supranational and International Non-Discrimination Law* (Hart Publishing, Oxford, 2007), at page 727.

111 Belgian Guide to Reasonable Accommodations for Persons with a Disability at Work [March 2005]. [Information taken from L. Waddington, 'Reasonable Accommodation' (2007)].

112 Belgian Guide to Reasonable Accommodations for Persons with a Disability at Work [March 2005], para. 3.1.4.

113 Ibid.

114 Ibid.

115 Ibid.

116 UN Committee on the Rights of Persons with Disabilities, *Marie-Louise Jungelin (represented by the Swedish Association of Visually Impaired Youth (US) and the Swedish Association of the Visually*

Committee members who issued a joint dissenting opinion referred to the issue of third-party benefits. The dissenting Committee members highlighted the failure of the domestic court to consider the potential impact of the alternative measures 'on the future employment of other persons with visual impairments as an additional positive criterion to assess the requested measures.'[117] They[118] stated that even if reasonable accommodations are in principle an individual measure, 'the benefit for other employees with disabilities must also be taken into account when assessing reasonableness and proportionality in compliance with Articles 5, 9 and 27.'[119] It seems that, under the CRPD, benefits to third parties might increase the likelihood that a particular accommodation may not be deemed to impose a disproportionate or undue burden on the duty-bearer, particularly if the benefit accrues to a person with a comparative disability. If adopting a particular accommodation measure would result in tangential benefits to third parties, especially those with comparative disabilities – a consideration which would then be taken into account in the assessment of the reasonableness of measures – then this could potentially facilitate the implementation of the Convention's socio-economic rights and obligations. This particular point will be expanded on in subsequent chapters of this book.

The counter-side of benefits is the potential negative impact which an accommodation might have on others.[120] Providing accommodations in schools or university settings may, for instance, have effects on other students, on the educational programme itself or they may (exceptionally) pose unusual risks for staff or other students with disabilities. Australian legislation promotes a balancing act which entails assessing the costs of the accommodation to the employer and the benefits to the person with a disability, as well as taking account of the impact on others in the workplace. Section 11 of the Australian Disability Discrimination Act[121] utilises the term 'unjustifiable hardship' and includes among the criteria for assessing that standard the nature of the benefit or detriment for all people concerned. Australian case law also illustrates

Impaired (SRF) v Sweden, Communication No. 5/2011, views adopted by the Committee at its twelfth session (15 September–3 October 2014), decision adopted 2 October 2014.

117 UN Committee on the Rights of Persons with Disabilities, Joint opinion of Committee members Mr. Carlos Rios Espinosa, Ms. Theresia Degener, Mr. Munthian Buntan, Ms. Silvia Judith Quan-Chang and Ms. Maria Soledad Cisternas Reyes (dissenting), para. 5.

118 See the Opinion of Committee member, Mr. Damjan Tactic, at para. 10 of the dissenting opinion in which he concurs partially with the joint opinion of the dissenting Committee members 'with the exception of the issue of the need to take into account the potential effects of the reasonable accommodation on the future employment of persons with disabilities in the Swedish Agency as elaborated in the first and second sentence of paragraph 5.'

119 Joint opinion of Committee members Mr. Carlos Rios Espinosa, Ms. Theresia Degener, Mr. Munthian Buntan, Ms. Silvia Judith Quan-Chang and Ms. Maria Soledad Cisternas Reyes (dissenting), para. 5.

120 In a similar vein to third-party benefits, consideration of the negative consequences which making an accommodation may have on others gives rise to a difficult balancing of conflicting interests. For example, granting a disabled employee an accommodation may result in reduced funds being available for third parties within an entity or restructuring a work schedule may result in heavier duties on non-disabled employees. In such instances, it is difficult to adjudicate on whether the duty to accommodate should be weakened to take into account such third-party impacts and that task will be left to the CRPD Committee. It is submitted that, as with all other aspects of the reasonable accommodation duty, an individual assessment will be necessary.

121 Australian Disability Discrimination Act [1992], Act No. 135 of 1992 (as amended).

the tendency to consider not merely the benefits to the requesting party but rather the wider benefits to, and negative impact on, third parties and society in general. In the Australian case of *Access for All Alliance (Hervey Bay) v Hervey Bay City Council*,[122] the Court stated that consideration of whether a requested accommodation constitutes an unjustifiable hardship goes beyond individual circumstances and that one must look to the benefits and costs generally in making a determination as to whether a measure constitutes such a hardship. In the context of the Australian Disability Discrimination Act, the Australian Human Rights and Equal Opportunity Commission has stated that, in addition to the financial costs and benefits of making the adjustment and the benefit of providing equal opportunity, treatment or participation to the person with a disability directly concerned, consideration may be required, *inter alia*, of 'any benefit, or detriment, of the adjustment concerned for access or opportunity for other employees or potential employees, customers or clients or other persons who would possibly be affected.'[123] Case law in Canada illustrates a similar emphasis on third-party impacts. In that jurisdiction, the duty to accommodate is contained in paragraph 5(b) of the Employment Equity Act.[124] In determining whether an accommodation would impose undue hardship on an entity, the Supreme Court of Canada ruled in *Central Alberta Dairy Pool v Alberta (Human Rights Commission)*[125] that the list of relevant considerations is not exhaustive but includes problems of morale of other employees in the workforce. In the Canadian case of *British Columbia (Public Service Employee Relations Commission) v. British Columbia Government Service Employees' Union*,[126] the Court had regard (in defining the undue hardship test) to the issue of whether a requested accommodation demonstrated the potential to interfere substantially with the rights of other employees.

4.5.3. Non-Financial Considerations

In the context of employment, there are some examples from national legislation which demonstrate that financial cost is not the only matter that may justify a failure to accommodate a disabled person. For example, in Canada, the Ontario Human Rights Code[127] lists health and safety requirements as a consideration relevant to establishing that a requested accommodation would constitute an 'undue hardship.' Lisa Waddington cites[128] the German Social Law Code on the Rehabilitation and

---

122 *Access for All Alliance (Hervey Bay) v Hervey Bay City Council* [2004] FMCA 915 [87].

123 Australian Human Rights Commission, *Guidance and Information, Employment and the Disability Discrimination Act. Part* 1, available at www.humanrights.gov.au/employment-and-disability-discrimination-act-part-1#adjustment last accessed 23 October 2014.

124 Employment Equity Act 1986, as amended in 1995.

125 *Central Alberta Dairy Pool v Alberta (Human Rights Commission)* (1990) 72 D.L.R. 4th 417.

126 *British Columbia (Public Service Employee Relations Commission) v. British Columbia Government Service Employees' Union* [1999] 3 S.C.R. 3, 1999 SCC 48.

127 First enacted in 1962, the Code is a provincial law and it is available at www.e-laws.gov.on.ca/html/statutes/english/elaws_statutes_90h19_e.htm last accessed 15 June 2014.

128 L. Waddington, 'Reasonable Accommodation' in D. Schiek, L. Waddington and M. Bell (eds.), *Cases, Materials and Text on National, Supranational and International Non-Discrimination Law* (Hart Publishing, Oxford, 2007), at page 730, citing the German Social Law Code, Book Nine 9 (SGB IX), Rehabilitation and Participation of Disabled Persons, of 19 June 2001, Section 81(4) SGB IX.

Participation of disabled persons as evidencing a similar factor. That code takes into account, *inter alia*, health and safety rules laid down by national law in determining whether a requested accommodation imposes a disproportionate burden on an employer. Waddington also cites[129] the Preparatory Works to the Finnish Non-Discrimination Act,[130] which state that an 'arrangement' might be unreasonable if it could 'endanger compliance with workplace safety legislation.'[131] Other non-financial considerations have been cited by Waddington,[132] who refers to Slovakian[133] and Austrian[134] statutes as enacting the principle that an employer or other covered party cannot argue that an accommodation would amount to a disproportionate burden if the accommodation or adaptation is required under separate legislation.[135]

5. Conclusion

The duty to accommodate in the CRPD is a highly individualised and context-sensitive notion, infused with the foundational principle of the inherent dignity of human beings and grounded in substantive equality. It entails a balancing of interests and burdens between the disabled individual and the duty-bearer. In this chapter, the duty to accommodate has been broken down into its various constituent elements and the outer limits of the duty have been delineated. The scope and application of the duty to accommodate, and, in particular, the parameters of the disproportionate/undue burden test, continue to evolve and are not settled in the various jurisdictions which have been examined for the purposes of this chapter. Nonetheless, it is submitted that there are several common denominators underlying the provision of accommodations. In the first instance, any requested accommodation must be necessary and effective in allowing the disabled person in question to participate in the required activity and in contributing to the realisation of the substantive rights in the Convention. Linked to the criterion of the effectiveness of measures taken under the duty to accommodate is the core notion of the inherent dignity of persons with disabilities. The duty to accommodate is based on the values underlying the Convention as a whole – human dignity and respect for difference. Those values, together with a consideration of the object and purpose of the duty – the promotion of equality and the elimination of discrimination – will be essential to any determination of whether measures taken by entities are effective. In addition,

129 Ibid, 737.

130 Preparatory Works to the Finnish Non-Discrimination Act, HE 44/2003 [Government Proposal 44/2003] concerning Section 5 of the Act.

131 Ibid.

132 L. Waddington, 'Reasonable Accommodation' in D. Schiek, L. Waddington and M. Bell (eds.), *Cases, Materials and Text on National, Supranational and International Non-Discrimination Law* (Hart Publishing, Oxford, 2007), at page 737/738.

133 Section 7(3), Slovakian Anti-Discrimination Act No. 365/2004 Coll. On Equal Treatment in Certain Areas and Protection against Discrimination, amending and supplementing certain other laws (Anti-Discrimination Act) of 20 May 2004.

134 Austrian Act on the Employment of People with Disabilities (effective as of 1 January 2006).

135 L. Waddington, 'Reasonable Accommodation' in D. Schiek, L. Waddington and M. Bell (eds.), *Cases, Materials and Text on National, Supranational and International Non-Discrimination Law* (Hart Publishing, Oxford, 2007), at page 738.

the decision as to whether to grant an accommodation in a given case will rest on an underlying proportionality test, which seeks to balance the rights of, and burdens and benefits to, all persons affected by the proposed accommodation. It has been outlined above that several factors will be relevant to a determination of whether an accommodation amounts to a disproportionate or undue burden, on the facts of a particular case. The primary consideration under the CRPD will be a detailed balancing of the costs and benefits of the proposed measure to the entity providing it. Costs will not merely be financial in nature and will extend to a consideration of the manner in which the accommodation alters the nature of the entity's business or causes excessive difficulties for an entity. In addition, it has been argued above that third-party benefits should be considered as a tangential consideration in the assessment of the reasonableness of measures adopted under the CRPD.

The outer limits of the duty to accommodate, as detailed in this chapter, are intended to uncover some information about the types of criteria that may be taken into account in determining the overall balancing of needs and interests in the progressive realisation of CRPD rights. All of the criteria highlighted above as being relevant to the outer limits of the duty to accommodate may potentially translate to the progressive realisation by States of the substantive rights and obligations contained in the Convention. In a similar manner to private/public entities, States face resource and capacity constraints, as well as institutional limitations. In allocating resources and in deciding on priorities, States also have to balance the rights of disabled people against the rights of other individuals in society. The next chapter of this book will reflect on the complex issue of the progressive realisation of disability rights. The aim of that chapter will be to devise a framework for assessment of the reasonableness of measures adopted by States in the realisation of socio-economic rights under the Convention. The proposed framework will draw on already existing frameworks of review at the national and international levels and also on elements of the CRPD's equality norm, specifically the outer limits of the duty to accommodate highlighted in this chapter. It is hoped that the criteria outlined in chapter five of this book as forming part of a review framework can add to the CRPD Committee's existing body of work under the Convention. This should serve to ensure that the assessment of measures adopted by States in the progressive realisation of CRPD rights remains grounded in the human rights-based approach to disability, rather than in an abstract and mechanical review of the programmes and policies devised by States.

Chapter 5
A Proposed Framework for the Assessment of the Progressive Realisation of CRPD Rights

'The obligation of States [...] to promote progressive realization of the relevant rights to the maximum of their available resources clearly requires Governments to do much more than merely abstain from taking measures which might have a negative impact on persons with disabilities.'[1]

1. Introduction

At the level of international human rights law, there is a divide between rights that are subject to immediate implementation and those that are to be realised progressively. Civil and political rights are viewed traditionally as negative or first-generation rights, to the extent that States have a duty to respect those rights and not to take any action that would interfere with them. They are the customary preserve of non-discrimination legislation, among other types of legislation, and they seek to ensure equal treatment. They have been associated traditionally with minimal cost implications and are deemed to be effective immediately and, furthermore, justiciable. By way of contrast, economic, social and cultural rights (socio-economic rights) are viewed traditionally as positive or second-generation rights which require States to take specific action to ensure that an individual's entitlement to those rights is secured. This involves an allocation of significant resources. As a result, such rights are subject to progressive implementation. Quintessential examples of civil and political rights in the CRPD are, among others, the right to participation in political and public life[2] and the right to liberty and security of the person.[3] Examples of economic, social and cultural rights in the CRPD include the right to education,[4] the right to employment[5] and the right to an adequate standard of living and social protection.[6]

The traditional dichotomy of rights into civil and political rights, on the one hand, and economic, social and cultural rights, on the other hand, and the justifications underpinning that dichotomy, have been increasingly eroded in scholarly discourse. It is now acknowledged that implementation of civil and political rights can also

---

1 UNCESCR, General Comment 5 on Persons with Disabilities, adopted on 09/12/94 at the Eleventh Session of the Committee, U.N. Doc E/1995/22, para. 9.

2 UN CRPD, Article 29.

3 UN CRPD, Article 14.

4 UN CRPD, Article 24.

5 UN CRPD, Article 27.

6 UN CRPD, Article 28.

require significant expenditure on the part of States.[7] It is also recognised that both sets of rights may give rise to positive duties.[8] In its preamble, the CRPD reaffirms 'the universality, indivisibility, interdependence and interrelatedness of all human rights and fundamental freedoms.'[9] The CRPD also blurs the dividing lines between civil and political rights and economic, social and cultural rights by incorporating immediately realisable reasonable accommodation duties into many of the Convention's socio-economic rights. For that reason, the inclusion of the reasonable accommodation duty within the non-discrimination norm was controversial during the negotiation sessions of the CRPD, as there was a fear among delegates, specifically the EU Presidency, that the non-discrimination norm could become 'a Trojan horse for the judicial enforceability of economic, social and cultural rights'[10] Notwithstanding that fear, it is vitally important to recognise the indivisibility of human rights for the protection of persons with disabilities. Gerard Quinn states that 'there can be few more obvious areas than the field of disability in which to emphasize the inter-connectedness of the civil and political rights tradition with the more avowedly egalitarian social & economic rights tradition.'[11] Among other things, the proper implementation of socio-economic rights is an essential pre-requisite in ensuring the full and effective participation and inclusion of disabled people in society on an equal basis with others.

By virtue of the fact that socio-economic rights are subject to progressive realisation, this incorporates the resource and capacity limitations of States into the implementation framework of human rights. In its General Comment 3 on the nature of States Parties' obligations, the UNCESCR observes that the notion of progressive realisation 'constitutes a recognition of the fact that full realization of all economic, social and cultural rights will generally not be able to be achieved in a short period of time.'[12] The principle of progressive realisation has often been invoked to support

---

7 See, for example, the views of Sandra Fredman – S. Fredman, *Human Rights Transformed: Positive Rights and Positive Duties* (Oxford University Press, Oxford, 2008), in which the author argues forcefully that all human rights impose negative and positive obligations. See also the views expressed by María Magdalena Sepúlveda Carmona, *The Nature of the Obligations Under the International Covenant on Economic, Social and Cultural Rights*, School of Human Rights Research Series, Volume 18 (Intersentia, Antwerpen, 2003) 127. See also the opinions of Ida Elizabeth Koch in the context of the traditional hierarchy of human rights and the cost implications of rights in the UN CRPD – I.E. Koch, 'From Invisibility to Indivisibility: The International Convention on the Rights of Persons with Disabilities' in O.M. Arnardóttir and G. Quinn (eds.) *The UN Convention on the Rights of Persons with Disabilities: European and Scandinavian Perspectives* (Martinus Nijhoff, Leiden, 2009).

8 See, for example, S. Fredman, *Human Rights Transformed: Positive Rights and Positive Duties* (Oxford University Press, Oxford, 2008).

9 Preamble, para.(c) of the CRPD.

10 Comments of Professor Gerard Quinn, The UN Convention on the Human Rights of Persons with Disabilities, Presentation to the Irish Human Rights Commission (Dublin, 19th April, 2007), available at www.ihrc.ie/download/doc/gquinn.doc last accessed 29 May 2014.

11 G. Quinn, 'The International Covenant on Civil and Political Rights and Disability: A Conceptual Framework,' in T. Degener and Y. Koster-Dreese (eds.), *Human Rights and Disabled Persons: Essays and Relevant Human Rights Instruments* (Martinus Nijhoff Publishers, Leiden, 1995), at page 70.

12 UN Committee on Economic, Social and Cultural Rights (UNCESCR), General Comment No. 3 on the nature of States Parties obligations (Article 2, para. 1) adopted on 14 December 1990, UN Doc. E/1991/23, para. 9.

a view of ICESCR rights 'as aspirational policy objectives, which do not impose precise legal obligations on states.'[13] It must be recognised, however, that national authorities are not given a comforting escape clause (by virtue of progressive realisation clauses) from their obligations under international human rights treaties. There are limitations to the extent to which the concept of progressive realisation can be relied on by States in defence of their non-implementation of socio-economic rights. Just like some of the outer limits of the duty to accommodate (applying to entities), the outer limits of the progressive realisation norm will generally[14] be adjudicated upon in accordance with the availability of resources and priorities set by States, among other considerations. However, national authorities have an obligation to take all necessary steps to realise rights within available resources.

The limits to the progressive realisation norm also include the concept of a minimum threshold for adjudicating on socio-economic rights provision.[15] Minimum thresholds seek to ensure the satisfaction of 'basic rights, capabilities and needs.'[16] This point will be expanded upon in the next section of this chapter. For now, it suffices to note that, while a definition of the minimum threshold of rights is essential in terms of setting out concrete State obligations and ensuring accountability, some scholars[17] have criticised the idea of minimum threshold levels of human rights as being inconsistent with the fundamental principle of equality. In other words, the notion of a minimum threshold ignores the cumulative economic and social inequalities experienced by marginalised or disadvantaged groups. Acknowledging such inequalities is deemed vital to ensuring the full and effective implementation of socio-economic rights for disadvantaged groups. Equality considerations will be particularly important in ensuring the full and effective realisation of CRPD guarantees for persons with disabilities in light of the significant cumulative material and social disadvantage which persons with disabilities have faced in the past and, indeed, continue to face. The principle of equality is also a relevant concern in light of the fact that the duty to accommodate spans the substantive rights and obligations contained in the Convention. While the accommodation duty falls within the non-discrimination norm and is therefore categorised primarily as a civil and political right, by its cross-cutting application it seeks to breathe life into the Convention's

---

13 UK Parliament, Joint Committee On Human Rights Twenty-First Report (2004), para. 45, available at www.publications.parliament.uk/pa/jt200304/jtselect/jtrights/183/18307.htm last accessed 12 November 2014.

14 The concept of minimum core obligations (which will be expanded on in the next section of this chapter) is not deemed to be subject to the availability of resources.

15 For further information on minimum thresholds of socio-economic rights, see generally, G. Mc Naughton, 'Beyond a Minimum Threshold: The Right to Social Equality' in Lanse Minkler (ed.), *The State of Economic and Social Human Rights: A Global Overview* (Cambridge University Press 2013), at page 279 onwards.

16 G. Mc Naughton, 'Beyond a Minimum Threshold: The Right to Social Equality' in L. Minkler (ed.), *The State of Economic and Social Human Rights: A Global Overview* (Cambridge University Press 2013), at page 279.

17 See, for instance, G. Mc Naughton, 'Beyond a Minimum Threshold: The Right to Social Equality' in L. Minkler (ed.), *The State of Economic and Social Human Rights: A Global Overview* (Cambridge University Press, Cambridge, 2013), at page 279 onwards.

socio-economic guarantees. This injects a substantial equality dimension into the progressive realisation of rights under the CRPD.

One must be realistic about the types of measures that States can take in the implementation of the socio-economic rights in the CRPD, particularly developing States. A certain margin of discretion will be left to national authorities to decide on priorities with regard to the quantum and proper allocation of resources, subject to supervision by the CRPD Committee. In examining the measures taken by national authorities, the Committee will have to assess State action or inaction based not only on the needs of persons with disabilities but also in light of resource and institutional or capacity constraints, as well as the needs and interests of others, including other marginalised groups in society. In that regard, it is necessary to place a normative framework around the progressive implementation of CRPD rights (both in terms of resource allocation and programme and policy design), to ensure the appropriate balancing of needs between duty-bearers and rights-holders. There are numerous sources which the CRPD Committee may draw upon in order to determine the most relevant criteria to be taken into account in assessing the measures adopted by States to ensure compliance with their obligations under the CRPD. It will be argued in this chapter that the principal sources which the Committee may look to are already existing frameworks of so-called 'reasonableness review' at the national and international levels, such as the reasonableness standard emerging under the Optional Protocol to the ICESCR (OP-ICESCR) and under South African Constitutional jurisprudence. Those frameworks set down certain criteria which seek to define, in the words of the UNCESCR, the reasonableness or adequacy[18] of measures taken by States to ensure compliance with their obligations under international human rights law. While such frameworks can arguably provide some level of guidance for the CRPD Committee, the provisions of the CRPD itself may inject a further element for consideration in the context of positive equality claims via the reasonable accommodation duty, and in particular via the outer limits of the duty outlined in chapter four above.

The present chapter will be broken down into five principal sections. In section two of this chapter, the general contours and outer limits of the progressive realisation norm will be highlighted. Section three of this chapter will contain an overview of established models of reasonableness review in the progressive implementation of human rights. In section four of this chapter, a proposed framework for the assessment of measures taken by States in fulfilling socio-economic rights under the CRPD will be put forward. In that regard, I will 'borrow' some of the elements from the review mechanisms established under the OP-ICESCR and under South African Constitutional jurisprudence in order to tailor them to the specific context of the CRPD. I will also reflect, at various junctures, on whether the balancing of

[18] In its 2007 Statement, entitled *An Evaluation of the Obligation to Take Steps to the 'Maximum of Available Resources' Under an Optional Protocol to the Covenant*, the Committee lays out the general considerations which it deems relevant to assessing whether measures taken by States are 'reasonable or adequate.' [UN Doc. E/C.12/2007/1, para. 8].

interests and burdens foreseen under the accommodation duty can facilitate a greater understanding of how CRPD provisions can be implemented progressively. Section five of this chapter will contain concluding remarks

2. The Progressive Realisation of Human Rights

In this section of the chapter, the general contours of the progressive realisation norm, including its outer limits, will be traced and the interaction between the equality norm and the progressive realisation of human rights will be reflected upon.

2.1. Introduction to the Concept of Progressive Realisation

The concept of progressive realisation is an express acknowledgment of the fact that lack of resources – whether financial, human or technical resources – or competing priorities can hamper the full realisation of economic, social and cultural rights in certain States, particularly in developing countries. Progressive realisation clauses are enshrined in numerous international human rights treaties. Article 2[19] of the ICESCR[20] and Article 4[21] of the CRC[22] require States to realise progressively the rights contained therein. Article 23(2) of the CRC[23] refers specifically to the progressive realisation of rights relating to children with disabilities. The CRPD contains a progressive realisation clause in Article 4(2) thereof. It reads as follows:

> With regard to economic, social and cultural rights, each State Party undertakes to take measures to the maximum of its available resources and, where needed, within the framework of international cooperation, with a view to achieving progressively the full realization of these rights, without prejudice to those obligations contained in the present Convention that are immediately applicable according to international law.[24]

The very notion of progressive realisation implies that States are being facilitated on account of certain onerous human rights obligations that would otherwise impose

---

19 Article 2 of the ICESCR provides that: 'Each State Party to the present Covenant undertakes to take steps, individually and through international assistance and co-operation, especially economic and technical, to the maximum of its available resources, with a view to achieving progressively the full realization of the rights recognized in the present Covenant by all appropriate means, including particularly the adoption of legislative measures.'

20 [1966].

21 Article 4 of the UN CRC provides that "With regard to economic, social and cultural rights, State Parties shall undertake measures to the maximum extent of their available resources and, where needed, within the framework of international cooperation."

22 [1989].

23 Article 23(2) of the UN CRC provides that 'State Parties recognise the right of the disabled child to special care and shall encourage and ensure the extension, subject to available resources, to the eligible child and those responsible for his or her care, of assistance for which application is made and which is appropriate to the child's condition and to the circumstances of the parents or others caring for the child.'

24 UN CRPD, Article 4(2).

a disproportionate burden on them if they were subject to immediate enforcement. The OHCHR has stated that progressive realisation is 'a practical device that acknowledge(s) the real world challenges'[25] and 'helps to avoid overburdening [S]tates, employers and other duty-bearers.'[26] In a similar vein to the concept of disproportionate burden under the accommodation duty (which takes into account the constraints weighing on private and public entities), the progressive realisation norm entails a balancing of burdens and interests and takes account of financial, institutional and other constraints encountered by States in realising human rights. Nonetheless, it is recognised by the core human rights treaty bodies that certain State obligations are achievable immediately. This defines what might be termed the outer limits of progressive realisation. The notion of the 'reasonableness' of measures adopted by States seeks to place a framework of review around those outer limits and around the realisation of socio-economic rights generally. In the subsections which follow, the immediate duties of States Parties to the CRPD will be outlined.

2.2. The Immediate Duties of States Parties to the CRPD in the Realisation of Economic, Social and Cultural Rights

While the rationale underlying progressive implementation of socio-economic rights is to avoid overburdening duty-bearers, States are required to take certain steps immediately in the actualisation of rights. The UNCESCR has confirmed this in its General Comment 13.[27] As such, it can be said that there are inherent limitations or outer boundaries to the concept of progressive realisation of human rights generally and States cannot rely on progressive realisation as a justification for complete inaction following their accession to or ratification of the CRPD. The general contours of the concept of progressive realisation can be derived from Article 2(1) of the ICESCR. That article reads as follows:

> Each State Party to the present Covenant undertakes to *take steps*, individually and through international assistance and co-operation, especially economic and technical, *to the maximum of its available resources*, with a view to achieving progressively the full realisation of the rights recognised in the present Covenant by all appropriate means, including particularly the adoption of legislative measures.[28]

The formulation of the obligation to realise progressively socio-economic rights in the ICESCR is similar to that contained in Article 4(2) of the CRPD, cited above. Therefore, in the sub-sections which follow, academic commentary and general

---

25 Office of the High Commissioner of Human Rights, *From Vision to Action: The Road to Implementation of the Convention* (2007) 5.

26 Ibid.

27 In its General Comment No. 3, the UNCESCR observes that 'while the Covenant provides for progressive realization and acknowledges the constraints due to the limits of available resources, it also imposes on States Parties various obligations which are of immediate effect.' [UNCESCR, General Comment 13 on the right to education (Article 13 of the Covenant), adopted at the twenty-first session of the Committee on 8 December 1999, UN Doc. E/C.12/1999/10, para. 43].

28 ICESCR, Article 2(1). [emphasis added].

comments related to the ICESCR will be drawn on in determining some of the outer limits of the concept of progressive realisation of socio-economic rights in the CRPD.

2.2.1. *The Obligation to 'Take Steps' to Achieve Progressively the Full Realisation of Rights*

The UNCESCR has stated that the notion of progressive realisation imposes an obligation on States to move 'as expeditiously and effectively as possible'[29] towards the goal of full realisation of rights. The Committee has elaborated on this by noting that steps towards the goal of full realisation of the relevant rights must be taken within a 'reasonably short time'[30] after the Covenant's entry into force for the States concerned and, moreover, that such steps should be 'deliberate, concrete and targeted'[31] as clearly as possible towards meeting the obligations in the Covenant. The steps envisaged under Article 2(1) of the ICESCR should include 'all appropriate means, including particularly the adoption of legislative measures.'[32] In addition to legislation, the UNCESCR has interpreted the term 'appropriate means' to include the provision of judicial or other remedies, where appropriate, as well as 'administrative, financial, educational and social measures'[33] The OHCHR has provided the following examples of steps that might be considered 'deliberate, concrete and targeted' towards the full realisation of human rights:

a. Assessing the state of enjoyment of economic, social and cultural rights, including ensuring adequate mechanisms to collect and assess relevant and suitably disaggregated data;
b. Formulating strategies and plans, incorporating indicators and time-bound targets, which should be realistic, achievable and designed to assess progress in the realization of these rights;
c. Adopting the necessary laws and policies, and making adequate funds available to put the plans and strategies into practice;
d. Regularly monitoring and assessing the progress made in the implementation of the plans and strategies; and
e. Establishing grievance mechanisms so that individuals can complain if the State is not meeting its responsibilities.[34]

The General Comments of the UNCESCR mirror these examples of immediate steps to be taken by States in the realisation of socio-economic rights. For instance, in its General Comment 1, the Committee notes that the obligation to 'take steps' in

---

29 UNCESCR, General Comment 3 on the nature of States Parties obligations (Article 2, para. 1) adopted on 14/12/1990, UN Doc. E/1991/23, para. 9.

30 Ibid, para. 2.

31 Ibid.

32 ICESCR, Article 2(1).

33 UNCESCR, General Comment 3 on the nature of States Parties obligations (Article 2, para. 1) adopted on 14/12/1990, UN Doc. E/1991/23, para. 7.

34 Office of the High Commissioner of Human Rights, *Frequently Asked Questions on Economic, Social and Cultural Rights: Factsheet 33*, page 16, available at www.ohchr.org/Documents/Publications/FactSheet33en.pdf last accessed 10 May 2013.

Article 2(1) clearly implies an obligation on States 'to work out and adopt a detailed plan of action for the progressive implementation of each of the rights contained in the Covenant.'[35] At the very least, therefore, States Parties to the CRPD must devise and put in place plans of action and targeted strategies immediately to ensure the progressive implementation of Covenant rights.

The UNCESCR places great weight on the obligation to monitor the realisation of human rights. In its General Comment 5 on Persons with Disabilities, the Committee states that, irrespective of the level of development pertaining in a State, there is an obligation 'to ascertain, through regular monitoring, the nature and scope of the problems existing within the State [...].'[36] The *Maastricht Guidelines on Violations of Economic, Social and Cultural Rights*[37] specify that a 'failure to monitor the realisation of economic, social and cultural rights, including the development of criteria for assessing compliance' is a violation of the ICESCR.[38] The Maastricht Guidelines are an important (albeit non-binding) secondary legal source on socio-economic rights. The Guidelines seek to identify the legal implications of acts and omissions which constitute violations of socio-economic rights. They build on the Limburg Principles on the Implementation of the International Covenant on Economic, Social and Cultural Rights.[39] The Maastricht Guidelines have been used extensively by the UN as an interpretative tool for establishing violations of socio-economic rights. Both documents will be referred to throughout this chapter, where relevant.

The UNCESCR has also highlighted the importance of identifying appropriate national benchmarks and indicators in ensuring the realisation of the substantive rights in the Covenant.[40] Where the realisation of a right is particularly complex, benchmarks have been developed in respect of three types of indicators necessary for the realisation of rights, namely 'structural indicators' (which monitor mechanisms and key structures), 'process indicators' (which monitor activities, programmes and interventions) and 'outcome indicators' (to measure outcomes).[41] The UNCESCR

---

35 UNCESCR, General Comment No. 1 on reporting by State Parties (1989), adopted at the third session of the Committee, 1989, UN Doc. E/1989/22, para. 4.

36 UNCESCR, General Comment No. 5 on *Persons with Disabilities* (1994), UN Doc. E/1995/22, para. 13.

37 *Maastricht Guidelines on Violations of Economic, Social and Cultural Rights*, adopted in Maastricht, January 22–26, 1997, reprinted as the *Maastricht Guidelines on Violations of Economic, Social and Cultural Rights* (1998) 20(3) *Human Rights Quarterly* 691–704, available at www1.umn.edu/humanrts/instree/Maastrichtguidelines_.html last accessed 12 December 2014.

38 *Maastricht Guidelines on Violations of Economic, Social and Cultural Rights*, Maastricht, January 22–26, 1997, Guideline No. 15 (f).

39 *Limburg Principles on the Implementation of the International Covenant on Economic, Social and Cultural Rights* (1987), adopted by the Commission on Human Rights at the 43rd session, UN doc. E/CN.4/1987/17, reprinted as the *Limburg Principles on the Implementation of the International Covenant on Economic, Social and Cultural Rights* (1987) 9 *Human Rights Quarterly* 121–135.

40 See, for example, UNCESCR, General Comment No. 14 on The Right to the Highest Attainable Standard of Health (Article 12 ICESCR), adopted 11 August 2000, UN Doc. EC 12/2000/4, at paras. 57 and 58.

41 In 1998, Paul Hunt, the UN Special Rapporteur on the right to health, developed right to education indicators, which had to be disaggregated by vulnerable groups. He later developed a comprehensive set of indicators relating to the right to health. [See, for example, P. Hunt, *State Obligations, Indicators,*

has clarified that the methods to be used by States in seeking to implement their obligations under the Covenant towards persons with disabilities are essentially the same as those available in relation to other groups. Based on the observations of the UNCESCR, it is submitted that all States Parties to the CRPD must monitor and identify the nature of the human rights gaps within the given State and devise strategies, benchmarks and indicators immediately to bridge the gaps and to respond to the requirements thus identified. States will also be required to legislate where necessary and to eliminate any existing discriminatory legislation. In addition, national authorities must make appropriate budgetary provisions or, where necessary, seek international cooperation and assistance.[42]

2.2.2. Deliberately Retrogressive Measures

There is a strong presumption regarding the impermissibility of adopting any retrogressive measures in the implementation of human rights. This means that States must not permit the existing protection of socio-economic rights to be weakened unless there are very strong justificatory reasons for such deterioration. In its General Comment 4, the UNCESCR gave an indication of what might be termed a deliberately retrogressive measure when it stated that 'a general decline of living and housing conditions, *directly attributable* to policy and legislative decisions by State Parties, and in the absence of accompanying compensatory measures, would be inconsistent with the obligations under the Covenant.'[43] Magdalena Sepúlveda Carmona contends that it is therefore possible to argue that a deliberately retrogressive measure means 'any measure that implies a step back in the level of protection accorded to the rights contained in the [ICESCR] which is the consequence of an intentional decision by the State.'[44] She provides several examples[45] of what might be deemed retrogressive measures, as follows:

a. If a State Party were to adopt any legislation or policy with a direct collateral negative effect on the enjoyment of the rights by individuals or if it introduces legislation which discriminates in the enjoyment of the Covenant rights;[46]

Benchmarks and the Right to Education (Background paper submitted to the UNCESCR), 16 July 1998, UN Doc. E/C. 12/1998/11; See also, P. Hunt, *Report of the Special Rapporteur on the Right of Everyone to the Enjoyment of the Highest Attainable Standard of Physical and Mental Health*, 3 March 2006, UN Doc. E/CN.4/2006/48, Annex; In addition, see P. Hunt and G. Mac Naughton, 'A Human Rights-Based Approach to Health Indicators', in M. Baderin and R. McCorquodale (eds.), *Economic, Social and Cultural Rights in Action* (Oxford University Press, Oxford, 2007) 303–330, Annex]. Hunt's proposal to divide human rights indicators into three types, structural, process and outcome was subsequently adopted by the OHCHR.

42 UNCESCR, General Comment No. 5 on persons with disabilities (1994), adopted at the eleventh session of the Committee, UN Doc. E/1995/22, para. 13.

43 UNCESCR, General Comment No. 4 on the right to adequate housing (1991), adopted at the sixth session of the Committee, U.N. Doc. E/1992/23, para. 59.

44 M.M. Sepúlveda Carmona, *The Nature of the Obligations Under the International Covenant on Economic, Social and Cultural Rights*, School of Human Rights Research Series, Volume 18 (Intersentia, Antwerpen, 2003), at page 321.

45 Ibid, at page 323.

46 In that regard, Sepúlveda cites General Comment 13 on the right to education (Article 13 ICESCR), adopted on 8 December 1999, UN Doc. E/C.12/1999/10, para. 59.

b. If a State Party were to abrogate any legislation or policy consistent with these rights, unless obviously outdated or replaced with equally or more consistent laws or compensatory measures;[47]
c. If a State Party makes an unjustified reduction in public expenditure devoted to implementing economic, social and cultural rights, in the absence of adequate compensatory measures aimed at protecting the injured individuals;[48] and
d. If a State Party adopts regional measures for the protection of human rights, without integrating economic, social and cultural rights.[49]

In order to justify retrogressive measures, States Parties to the CRPD will have to meet a very high threshold. The UNCESCR has listed a number of issues that it would consider relevant when assessing retrogressive social security measures, *inter alia*:

- Whether there was reasonable justification for the action;
- Whether alternatives were comprehensively examined;
- Whether there was genuine participation of affected groups in examining the proposed measures and alternatives;
- Whether the measures will have a sustained impact on the realisation of the right or whether an individual or group is deprived of access to the minimum essential level of social security.[50]

If a State Party decides that it must adopt retrogressive measures, then according to the UNCESCR it has the high burden of proving that they have been introduced after:

> The most careful consideration of all alternatives and that they are duly justified by reference to the totality of the rights provided for in the Covenant in the context of the full use of the State party's maximum available resources.[51]

---

47 Sepúlveda cites Maastricht Guideline 14(a) in this respect, according to which a violation of rights would occur through an act of the State when it makes a 'formal removal or suspension of legislation necessary for the continued enjoyment of an economic, social and cultural right that is currently enjoyed.'

48 Sepúlveda cites the UNCESCR Concluding Observations to Zimbabwe, wherein the Committee expressed its 'concern about cutbacks in education expenditure which result in non-compliance with Article 13(2)(a) requiring free compulsory and universal primary education.' [UN Doc. E/1998/22, para. 77].

49 In that regard, Sepúlveda rightly points to the fact that the UNCESCR has already expressly noted that this would constitute a retrogressive measure. In its Statement to the Convention to draft a Charter of Fundamental Rights of the European Union, the Committee stated that if economic, social and cultural rights were not integrated into the draft Charter on an equal footing with civil and political rights, this 'would have to be regarded as a retrogressive step contravening the existing obligations of member States of the European Union under the International Covenant on Economic, Social and Cultural Rights.' [UN Doc. E/2001/22, Annex VIII, para. 4].

50 UNCESCR, General Comment No 19 on the right to social security (2008), adopted at the thirty-ninth session of the Committee, UN doc E/C12/GC/19, para. 42.

51 UNCESCR, General Comment 14 on the right to the highest attainable standard of health (article 12 of the International Covenant on Economic, Social and Cultural Rights) (2000), adopted at the twenty-second session of the Committee, UN Doc. E/C.12/2000/4, para. 32.

2.2.3. *The Obligation to Ensure Non-Discrimination in the Exercise of Economic, Social and Cultural Rights*

States have an immediate obligation stemming from Article 2(2) of the ICESCR to 'guarantee that the rights enunciated in the Covenant will be exercised without discrimination of any kind.' This has been confirmed by the UNCESCR on many occasions, including in its General Comment 3.[52] The immediacy of the obligation to ensure non-discrimination is also reflected in Principle 22 of the Limburg Principles, which highlights the fact that States must 'eliminate *de jure* discrimination by abolishing without delay any discriminatory laws, regulations and practices (including acts of omission as well as commission) affecting the enjoyment of economic, social and cultural rights.'[53] The Limburg Principles also note that '*de facto* discrimination occurring as a result of the unequal enjoyment of economic, social and cultural rights, on account of a lack of resources or otherwise, should be brought to an end as speedily as possible.'[54] This is also reflected in the general comments of the UNCESCR.[55] In the context of the CRPD, the elimination of discrimination will be achieved *inter alia* through the duty to accommodate. This injects a substantial equality dimension into the outer limits of the progressive realisation of rights under the Convention.

2.2.4. *The Obligation to Devote the 'Maximum of Available Resources' to Achieving Progressively the Full Realisation of Rights*

Under international human rights law, States have an obligation to devote the maximum of their available resources to achieving the full realisation of rights in a progressive manner. The concept of the 'maximum of available resources' is somewhat vague and can give rise to assessment difficulties. Determining which parts of the normative content of a right should receive priority in the allocation of State resources is not an easy task. Notwithstanding its vague nature, benchmarks have been developed over time to assess the content of the obligation to realise rights to the maximum of available resources. In her summary of a report[56] detailing the duty to use the maximum of available resources, Sandra Fredman has stated that three elements of government appropriations are highlighted as being capable of concrete assessment, namely (a) the sufficiency of government spending/investment;

---

52 UNCESCR, General Comment 3 on the nature of States Parties obligations (Article 2, paragraph 1), adopted at the fifth session of the Committee on 14 December 1990, UN Doc. E/1991/23, para. 1.

53 *Limburg Principles on the Implementation of the International Covenant on Economic, Social and Cultural Rights*, Principle No. 37.

54 Ibid, Principle No. 38.

55 In that regard, see, for example, UNCESCR General Comment 13, para. 37, in which the Committee commented as follows: 'States parties must closely monitor education – including all relevant policies, institutions, programmes, spending patterns and other practices – so as to identify and take measures to redress any *de facto* discrimination.'

56 S. Fredman, *Human Rights Transformed: Positive Rights and Positive Duties* (Oxford University Press, Oxford, 2008), at page 82, citing H. Hofbauer, A. Blyberg and W. Krafchik, *Dignity Counts: A guide to using budget analysis to advance human rights,* (Fundar, IBP, IHRIP) (2004), available at www.internationalbudget.org/files/Dignity_Counts_english1.pdf. last accessed 12 October 2013.

(b) the equity of expenditure patterns; and (c) the efficiency of expenditure.[57] These points are relevant to a determination of the reasonableness of State action. Of course, budgetary allocations will be essential in ensuring that States realise rights to the maximum of available resources. The UNCESCR has noted that the phrase 'to the maximum of its available resources' was intended to refer to both the resources existing within a State and those available from the international community through international cooperation and assistance.[58] The obligation to seek assistance, where needed, through the framework of international cooperation is provided for specifically in Article 4(2) of the CRPD. This will be a particularly important aspect of the progressive realisation of rights in developing countries that are party to the CRPD.

2.2.5. Minimum Core Obligations

In addition to the categories listed above, there are certain obligations stemming from the ICESCR which are deemed to take effect immediately in order to meet minimum essential levels of economic, social and cultural rights. These are termed the 'minimum core obligations' resulting from human rights or the 'minimum core content' of human rights. These two concepts are related[59] but it is notable that the UNCESCR speaks in terms of minimum core obligations, while scholars often refer to the minimum core content. The concept of the minimum core obligations resulting from human rights is a relatively recent one. The UNCESCR referred to minimum core obligations in its General Comment 3 on Article 2(1).[60] Audrey Chapman and Sage Russell assert that the minimum core content is:

---

57 Fredman explains that 'sufficiency is assessed by comparing actual expenditure with a benchmark figure, such as the proportion of GDP, or of total government spending.' Also of importance, she asserts, is: 'The way in which budgeting has changed over time. If government spending has been dropping, relative to GDP or other government spending, it strongly suggests that there are available resources but the duty has not been prioritized. This is particularly true where a government reduces spending on realization of a right but increases its budget overall.' Regarding the second criterion of equity, Fredman states that 'if spending is inequitable between genders, classes, regions or ethnic groupings, the government would be in breach of its duty.' Fredman also claims that 'efficiency of spending is more difficult to assess. But where a sum has been clearly budgeted and not used, a very strong argument can be made to compel a government to fulfil its obligations.' [S. Fredman, *Human Rights Transformed: Positive Rights and Positive Duties* (Oxford University Press, Oxford, 2008), at page 82].

58 UNCESCR, General Comment No. 3 on the nature of States Parties obligations (Article 2, para. 1) adopted at the fifth session of the Committee on 14 December 1990, UN Doc. E/1991/23, para. 13.

59 See the comments of G. Mc Naughton 'Beyond a Minimum Threshold: The Right to Social Equality' in L. Minkler (ed.), *The State of Economic and Social Human Rights: A Global Overview* (Cambridge University Press, Cambridge, 2013), at page 279.

60 In its General Comment no. 3 on Article 2(1), the UNCESCR refers (at para. 10) to the minimum core obligations resulting from human rights in the following terms: (...) The Committee is of the view that a minimum core obligation to ensure the satisfaction of, at the very least, minimum essential levels of each of the rights is incumbent upon every State Party. Thus, for example, a State party in which any significant number of individuals is deprived of essential foodstuffs, or essential primary health care, of basic shelter and housing, or of the most basic forms of education is, prima facie, failing to discharge its obligations under the Covenant [...].

> Often defined as the nature or essence of a right, that is the essential elements without which it loses its substantive significance as a human right and in the absence of which a State party should be considered to be in violation of its international obligations.[61]

The minimum core represents the basic standard of provision of socio-economic rights designed to meet the survival needs of the most disadvantaged in society, namely those who cannot access this fundamental level on their own. It lays a claim to priority on a given State's resources and represents the beginnings of the progressive realisation of rights. David Bilchitz observes that States have an obligation to realise immediately a minimum level of provision of a right and then to improve the level of provision beyond the minimum on a progressive basis.[62] He explains that progressive realisation acknowledges the fact that what governments are required to do is to provide core services to everyone without delay that will meet their survival needs and then to increase those services qualitatively so as ultimately to meet the maximal interests that the State is required to protect.[63] Such core obligations must be accorded a degree of priority or urgency in budgetary allocations. Even in times of scarce resources, a State must make continuous efforts for the improvement of human rights and must attend, as a matter of utmost priority, to the core obligations of the rights in question. The UNCESCR has confirmed this and has, on several occasions, highlighted the fact that the minimum core obligations of States are non-derogable.[64] Thus, even if a State has clearly inadequate resources at its disposal, the Government bears an increased justificatory burden to show that it has introduced low-cost and targeted programmes to assist those most in need. The minimum core of a given human right is deemed to be universal in nature and not resource-dependent. Even in developing countries, governments must take steps immediately to realise the minimum core of rights. As Fons Coomans states, 'a country-dependent core would undermine the concept of the universality of human rights.'[65] The Maastricht Guidelines confirm this – they state that 'minimum core obligations apply irrespective of the availability of resources of the country concerned or any other factors and difficulties.'[66]

---

61 A. Chapman and S. Russell (eds.), *Core Obligations: Building a Framework for Economic, Social and Cultural Rights* (Intersentia, Antwerp, 2002), at page 9.

62 D. Bilchitz 'Towards a Reasonable Approach to the Minimum Core: Laying the Foundations for Future Socio-Economic Rights Jurisprudence' (2003) *South African Journal of Human Rights* 1, at page 11.

63 Ibid, at page 12.

64 See, for instance, UNCESCR, General Comment No. 14, on the right to the highest attainable standard of health, UN Doc. E/C.12/2000/4 (2000) para. 47; See also UNCESCR, General Comment No. 15, on the right to water (Article 11 and 12) U.N.Doc E/C.12/2002/11 (2002) paragraph 40; In addition, see UNCESCR, Statement on Poverty and the ICESCR, UN Doc. E/C.12/2001/10, 4 May 2001, at para. 18.

65 F. Coomans, 'In Search of the Core Content of the Right to Education' in D. Brand and S. Russell (eds.) *Exploring the Core Content of Socio-Economic Rights: South African and International Perspectives* (Protea Book House, Pretoria, 2002), at page 167.

66 *Maastricht Guidelines on Violations of Economic, Social and Cultural Rights*, Maastricht, January 22–26, 1997, Guideline No. 8.

The concept of minimum core obligations is controversial in certain academic quarters.[67] Certain scholars argue that, because the minimum core focuses on survival needs and appears to create a hierarchy of rights, it is 'inconsistent with both human dignity and the holistic framework of the International Bill of Human Rights.'[68] It has also been rejected by the South African Constitutional Court,[69] which has identified the problem of defining the minimum core, on account of the fact that different groups have varying social needs and also by virtue of the differing economic and social history and circumstances of a country.[70] While the minimum core of human rights is important from the perspective of ensuring that disadvantaged groups are brought above the so-called poverty line and also in attempting to delineate State obligations and in holding States accountable for fundamental violations of human rights, it is certainly true that the minimum core threshold does not really factor in equality (or more advanced dignity) considerations and that it ignores cumulative disadvantage and inequalities in the enjoyment of socio-economic rights. It will be argued below, and at various junctures throughout this chapter, that the right to equality has a greater role to play within socio-economic rights adjudication and, in particular, that there is further scope for infusing already existing frameworks of reasonableness review with equality considerations. This could potentially serve to strengthen the protection of the rights of disadvantaged groups, such as persons with disabilities.

2.3. Equality Considerations in the Realisation of Socio-Economic Rights

The full realisation of socio-economic rights in the context of marginalised groups requires that, in addition to considering the core content of a given right, equality concerns are given more prominence. This rings particularly true in the specific context of the CRPD. The equality and non-discrimination norms are the beating heart of the CRPD and must necessarily be taken into account in any assessment of the measures taken by States under the Convention. The integration of equality with socio-economic rights under the CRPD is justified and indeed mandated, in large part, by the application of the non-discrimination norm (via the duty to accommodate) to the Convention's socio-economic provisions. It is argued here that the outer limits of the accommodation duty have the potential to infuse the CRPD Committee's assessment of State measures with added value to boost *de facto* equality. The

67 See, for instance, the work of Katherine Young – 'The Minimum Core of Economic and Social Rights: A Concept in Search of Content' (2008) 33(1) *Yale Journal of International Law* 113, in which Young states that: '[T]he focus on biological survival can set the interpretations of economic and social rights on the wrong ground. A focus on needs may disclose little about the ranking of alternative strategies designed to save lives, and is unhelpful in a mature recognition of the inevitability of death. Similarly, the emphasis on minimalism behind the core becomes suggestive, when attached to life, of a more scientific, needs-based assessment of the commodities necessary for biological survival.'

68 See, for instance, G. Mc Naughton, 'Beyond a Minimum Threshold: The Right to Social Equality' in L. Minkler (ed.) *The State of Economic and Social Human Rights: A Global Overview* (Cambridge University Press, Cambridge, 2013), at page 282.

69 This point will be discussed in section 3 of this chapter.

70 *Government of the Republic of South Africa and Others v Grootboom and Others* (2001) (1) SA 46 (CC). 2000 (11) BCLR 1169 (CC), paras. 32–33.

reasonableness review frameworks which have been delineated at the national and international levels provide a complementary method of reviewing the implementation of socio-economic rights, which can potentially act alongside a consideration of the minimum core of CRPD rights and equality considerations. Reasonableness review frameworks are deemed to be context-sensitive and they generally seek to assess the measures taken by States relative to the values and principles underlying the particular right or rights in question. Where these reasonableness review frameworks are infused with equality considerations, they are particularly effective. Sandra Liebenberg and Beth Goldblatt argue that a framework of reasonableness review which integrates a substantive equality perspective would incorporate an inquiry as to 'whether the socio-economic deprivation in question prevents the claimant group from developing to their full potential and participating as equals in society.'[71] Liebenberg and Goldblatt also claim that where reasonableness review is infused with equality concerns, such a framework would ask whether denial of access to the particular rights has the effect of 'entrenching and perpetuating systemic patterns of racial, gender and other forms of discrimination and subordination in our society.'[72]

In sum, a reasonableness review framework incorporating substantive equality concerns (primarily through a consideration of the outer limits of the duty to accommodate), in conjunction with minimum core analysis, could provide an appropriate means of reviewing State compliance with the obligations contained in the CRPD. This unique blend has the potential to ensure a framework of review that is tailored to the underlying values and norms contained in the Convention and that is not just based on an abstract mechanical review of indicators and benchmarks. To provide the building blocks for this proposed framework for review of State measures, the next section of this chapter will highlight the various criteria inherent in reasonableness review frameworks at the national and international levels.

3. Reasonableness Review of Socio-Economic Rights

The immediate obligations of States outlined above in the context of the ICESCR represents a rigid framework that does not necessarily take into account contextual factors and the situation existing at the domestic level. Partly to counteract this, the notion of reasonableness review of socio-economic rights has evolved at both the national level and the international level. In this section of the chapter the various components of, and criteria inherent in, such reasonableness review frameworks will be delineated.

---

71 S. Liebenberg and B. Goldblatt, 'The Interrelationship between Equality and Socio-Economic Rights under South Africa's Transformative Constitution' (2007) 23 *South African Journal on Human Rights*, at page 357.

72 Ibid.

3.1. Introduction to Reasonableness Review of Socio-Economic Rights

The reasonableness review model first evolved in South African jurisprudence. It came to the fore at the international level when the UNCESCR created a 'reasonableness standard' under Article 8(4) of the OP-ICESCR. In 2006, during the Open-Ended Working Group sessions leading to the drafting of the Optional Protocol, the UN High Commissioner for Human Rights, Louise Arbour, picked up on the theme of reasonableness in the realisation of socio-economic rights. She remarked that the ICESCR requires States to use limited resources reasonably and that States should be held accountable for the manner in which they use their resources in the implementation of socio-economic rights.[73] Before considering the framework of review at the international level, it is proposed to outline the key components of the South African framework of reasonableness review.

3.2. Reasonableness Review: The South African Approach to Progressive Realisation of Human Rights

The South African Constitutional Court has established a reasonableness test as a normative standard for reviewing government action, and indeed inaction, in the implementation of socio-economic rights guaranteed by the South African Constitutional Bill of Rights. The concept of 'reasonableness' is inherent in Sections 26 and 27 of the South African Constitution. Section 26(1) of the Constitution provides that 'everyone has the right to have access to adequate housing.'[74] In that regard, Section 26(2) provides that 'the state must take *reasonable* legislative and other measures, within its available resources to achieve the progressive realisation of this right.'[75] In a similar vein, Section 27 of the Constitution requires the State to take *reasonable* legislative and other measures, within its available resources to achieve the progressive realisation of the rights to health care, food, water and social security.

Reasonableness review in the South African context devolved partly from the challenges inherent in balancing the protection of fundamental rights, on the one hand, and overseeing policy and resource allocation choices, on the other hand. It seeks to give States a certain latitude to make policy choices, within boundaries. The South African reasonableness approach has many features that would fit well

---

[73] UN High Commissioner for Human Rights, Louise Arbour, has stated that: 'The concept of 'reasonableness' of State action is a well-known legal concept and long used in adjudication of civil and political rights. The growing body of jurisprudence at the national and regional levels illustrates that it can be similarly employed to assess the extent to which States respect their obligations in the area of economic, social and cultural rights.' Statement by Ms. Louise Arbour, High Commissioner for Human Rights to the third session of the Open-Ended WG OP ICESCR (Third session, 2006), available at www.ohchr.org/EN/NewsEvents/Pages/DisplayNews.aspx?NewsID=6011&LangID=E last accessed last accessed 10 December 2014.

[74] Section 26(1) of the South African Constitution – see www.gov.za/documents/constitution/chapter-2-bill-rights#26, last accessed 16 December 2014.

[75] Section 26(2) of the South African Constitution [emphasis added].

in reviewing the implementation of the rights and obligations contained in the CRPD. The South African Constitution is a 'transformative'[76] one, endorsing a constitutional commitment to substantive equality, akin to the approach taken to equality in the CRPD. The South African Constitutional framework embraces the foundational values of human dignity, equality and freedom.[77] It was designed to overcome the legacy of disadvantage owing to the Apartheid regime and to transform South African society into a democratic and egalitarian one, creating better living conditions for all citizens. It advocates substantive equality measures, such as positive action and other measures designed to redress historical injustices, racial segregation and marginalisation during the Apartheid regime. The South African Constitution contains a Bill of Rights, which codifies fundamental human rights and spells out, in broad terms, the steps to be taken by the South African government to achieve transformative constitutionalism. The South African courts, in particular the Constitutional Court, are empowered to adjudicate on alleged breaches of rights and they do so by means of 'reasonableness review.'

The approach of the South African Constitutional Court to reasonableness review is highly context-sensitive. It seeks to apply general values and principles to the assessment of the content of rights in particular circumstances.[78] In other words, it seeks to make a value-laden judgment by assessing claims to positive measures on the basis of the values and principles underlying the South African Constitutional Bill of Rights. Sandra Liebenberg points to the fact that South African jurisprudence indicates that the reasonableness of State conduct will be assessed in light of the 'social, economic and historical context of the State'[79] and that consideration will be given to the capacity of institutions responsible for implementing the programmes in question.[80] She further asserts that 'reasonableness review enables the Court to adjust the stringency of its review standard informed by factors such as the position of the

76 Several authors refer to the South African Constitution as a transformative one. See, for instance, the seminal article by K. Klare, 'Legal Culture and Transformative Constitutionalism' (1998) 14 *South African Journal of Human Rights* 146; See also C. Albertyn and B. Goldblatt, 'Facing the Challenge of Transformation: Difficulties in the Development of an Indigenous Jurisprudence of Equality' (1998) 14 *South African Journal on Human Rights* 248. In relation to socio-economic rights generally, see S. Liebenberg, 'Needs, Rights and Transformation: Adjudicating Social Rights' (2006) 17 *Stellenbosch Law Review* 5.

77 See Section 7(1) of the South African Constitutional Bill of Rights. See also Sections 9 and 10 of the Bill of Rights.

78 B. Porter and S. Liebenberg, 'Consideration of Merits under the OP-ICESCR: Reasonableness Review under 8(4) and the Maximum of Available Resources Standard' (Notes for Discussion at the Workshop on Strategic Litigation under the OP-ICESCR), at page 5, available at www.escr-net.org/sites/default/files/Porter_and_Liebenberg,_Reasonableness_0.pdf last accessed 7 May 2014.

79 S. Liebenberg, 'Adjudicati.ng Social Rights Under a Transformative Constitution' in M. Langford (ed.), *Social Rights Jurisprudence: Emerging Trends in International and Comparative Law* (Cambridge University Press, Cambridge, 2008), at page 84.

80 Ibid.

claimant group in society,[81] the nature of the resource or service claimed[82] and the impact of the denial of access to the service or resource in question on the claimant group.'[83] The assessment of compliance with Constitutional requirements under the South African reasonableness test is undertaken from the human rights perspective of the inherent dignity of individuals and the needs of the most disadvantaged groups in society. For all of these reasons, it is argued here that the reasonableness approach would provide a good starting point from which to assess measures taken by States under the CRPD. It provides a flexible and context-sensitive tool with which to assess the measures taken by States in varying socio-economic arenas and could serve to give effect to the substantive and transformative framework of the CRPD as a whole.

An overview of key case law decided by the South African courts using the reasonableness approach will be provided below. The cases essentially concern two types of claims. The first of these can be viewed through the lens of an equality claim, namely that particular disadvantaged groups are excluded from a governmental programme of support, the result of which is a ruling that the government must extend the reach of the benefits in question to the disadvantaged group. The second set of claims decided in the South African courts under the reasonableness review model has not been viewed through an equality lens *per se*. Those cases concern the argument that a given State is not providing appropriate or reasonable programmes to ensure the realisation of socio-economic rights. While those cases were not necessarily argued from an equality perspective, it is submitted that such claims would benefit from a closer integration of equality and socio-economic rights jurisprudence. In the next section of this chapter, it will be argued that the equality norm can be integrated more comprehensively within a reasonableness review model to strengthen socio-economic rights provision for persons with disabilities. Bearing that in mind, I will now turn to South African case law in order to outline the development and content of the so-called reasonableness test in that jurisdiction.

3.2.1. South African Reasonableness Review: Delineation of the Test by the Constitutional Court

The South African Constitutional Court has developed its approach to reasonableness review in a gradual manner, on a case-by-case basis. Hereunder the major developments and key criteria inherent in the South African reasonableness review framework will be outlined.

---

81 Ibid at page 89, citing the South African *Grootboom, TAC* and *Khosa* judgments (all outlined in section 3.2 of this chapter), in which the Court emphasised, in its consideration of the merits of the cases at hand, the fact that the affected groups in question were disadvantaged.

82 Ibid, at page 89, citing the *Soobramoney* judgment (outlined in section 3.2 of this chapter). Liebenberg notes that, in that case, a more tertiary and expensive form of medical treatment was claimed leading the Constitutional Court to apply a deferential standard of review based on rationality. In contrast, Liebenberg cites the *Grootboom, TAC* and *Khosa* cases (all detailed in section 3.2 of this chapter), in which the standard of review was stricter and involved a more searching scrutiny of the government's justifications for denying the applicants access to a basic level of service provision.

83 Ibid, at page 89/90 citing the *Grootboom, TAC* and *Khosa* cases (outlined in section 3.2 of this chapter), in which the Court emphasised the severe impact on the claimants of the deprivation in question.

3.2.1.1. The Rationality Test

The first noteworthy case to be decided by the Court in this context was *Soobramoney v Minister of Health*[84] [hereafter referred to simply as *Soobramoney*]. That case related to an applicant who required renal dialysis treatment for his survival. He was refused such treatment on account of the fact that the hospital in question did not have sufficient resources to provide treatment to all patients. Instead, patients were assessed according to strict criteria and were given treatment only if they were eligible for a kidney transplant, eligibility for which depended on the absence of 'significant vascular or cardiac disease.'[85] As Mr. Soobramoney did not satisfy that requirement, he was denied access to the requested treatment.[86] The applicant challenged the denial of treatment in the South African Constitutional Court, claiming, *inter alia*, that the Court should order the State to provide the necessary funds.[87] The Court introduced a rationality test as the relevant standard of review of governmental action. It ruled that 'a court will be slow to interfere with rational decisions taken in good faith by the political organs and medical authorities whose responsibility it is to deal with such matters.'[88] The Court in *Soobramoney* adopted a deferential approach to State interests and did not undertake a strict review of the State's positive obligations to ensure the realisation of socio-economic rights. In cases decided after *Soobramoney*, the Court moved away from the notion of rationality to the idea of reasonableness review.[89] In those later cases, the Court elaborated upon the constitutional requirements of reasonable measures in the South African context. The subsequent line of case law will be explored below.

3.2.1.2. The Introduction of the Reasonableness Standard

The concept of 'reasonableness' was first introduced in the case of *Government of the Republic of South Africa and Others, v Grootboom and Others*[90] [hereafter referred to simply as *Grootboom*]. The applicants in *Grootboom*, a group of homeless individuals, had been evicted from private land on which they were squatting. They contended that while the State was implementing (progressively) a programme to

---

84 Constitutional Court of South Africa, *Soobramoney v Minister of Health (Kwazulu-Natal) (CCT32/97) [1997] ZACC 17; 1998 (1) SA 765 (CC); 1997 (12) BCLR 1696* (27 November 1997) [hereafter referred to simply as *Soobramoney*].

85 *Soobramoney*, para. 4.

86 See *Soobramoney*, paras. 1–4.

87 Ibid, at para. 23, which reads as follows: 'The respondent has conclusively proved that there are no funds available to provide patients such as the applicant with the necessary treatment. This finding was not disputed by the appellant, but it was argued that the state could make additional funds available to the renal clinic and that it was obliged to do so to enable the clinic to provide life saving treatment to the appellant and others suffering from chronic renal failure.'

88 Ibid, at para. 29.

89 For further elaboration on the case law outlined in this section generally, see F. Coomans, 'Reviewing Implementation of Social and Economic Rights: An Assessment of the "Reasonableness" Test as Developed by the South African Constitutional Court' (2005) 65(1) *Heidelberg Journal of International Law* 175, at pages 173–174.

90 Constitutional Court of South Africa, *Government of the Republic of South Africa and Others v Grootboom and Others* (2001) (1) SA 46 (CC). 2000 (11) BCLR 1169 (CC) [hereafter referred to simply as *Grootboom*].

provide access to adequate housing, it should provide them, *inter alia*, with some form of temporary shelter or housing.[91] The group brought an action to the Cape of Good Hope High Court under sections 26 (the right of access to adequate housing) and 28 (children's right to basic shelter) of the South African Constitution demanding action by various levels of government. When the case came before the High Court, it relied on the principle of judicial deference outlined by the Constitutional Court in the *Soobramoney* case. The High Court found that the South African government had taken reasonable measures within available resources to achieve the progressive realisation of the right to have access to adequate housing, as required by Section 26(2) of the Constitution. The High Court cited the State's limited resources and their efforts to implement a housing program. However, the High Court did rule that there had been a violation of Section 28(a)(c) of the Constitution, by virtue of the fact that every child has the unequivocal right to shelter and that such right was not subject to available resources. Thus, where parents could not provide for their children, the State must step in and therefore the applicants were entitled to be provided with basic shelter. On appeal, the Constitutional Court found no violation of Section 28 of the Constitution but found instead a violation of the right to adequate housing in Section 26 thereof. The Constitutional Court outlined its reasonableness test in order to evaluate whether the legislative and other measures taken by the Government in relation to its own housing policy were reasonable with regard to the situation of the squatters in question. The Constitutional Court emphasised the fact that:

> A court considering reasonableness will not enquire whether other more desirable or favourable measures could have been adopted [...] It is necessary to recognise that a wide range of possible measures could be adopted by the state to meet its obligations.[92]

The Court outlined several criteria for assessing the notion of reasonable measures. The types of criteria inherent in the *Grootboom* standard of reasonableness will be outlined below.

3.2.1.3. The Criteria Inherent in the *Grootboom* Test

The Constitutional Court conceptualised the notion of 'reasonableness' as begging the question as to whether the measures chosen actually facilitate the realisation of the socio-economic right at issue.[93] In other words, measures will only be reasonable if they actually result in the facilitation of human rights. Interestingly, this ties back to the notion of the effectiveness of measures elaborated on in the previous chapter of this book with regard to the duty to accommodate. The various other elements of the *Grootboom* standard of reasonableness are as follows: Firstly, the Court stated that for a programme to be reasonable, it must allocate responsibilities among different spheres of government (at the national, provincial and local levels) and provide each

---

91 The applicants requested the Cape of Good Hope High Court to provide them with adequate temporary shelter or housing until they could find permanent homes as well as adequate basic nutrition, healthcare, and social services as guaranteed by the South African constitution.

92 *Grootboom*, at para. 41.

93 Ibid.

sphere of government with the necessary financial and human resources to carry out their respective legal obligations.[94] Secondly, the Court acknowledged the fact that legislation must be complemented by policies and programmes that are reasonable in conception and implementation. Such policies and programs should be coordinated, coherent and comprehensive.[95] Thirdly, the Court outlined the fact that reasonable measures must take account of the 'social, economic and historical context' and the background of the situation which the policy aims to address. Additionally, the Court stated that a reasonable program must be flexible and cater for the alleviation of needs over the short, medium and long term and must not exclude a significant segment of society.[96]

The *Grootboom* test of reasonableness is linked inherently to the notion of human dignity. The Court stated that this underlying principle of human rights must be taken into account in the evaluation of the reasonableness of State action.[97] The Court in *Grootboom* commented that, in order for measures to be reasonable, they cannot:

> Leave out of account the degree and extent of the denial of the right they endeavour to realize. Those whose needs are the most urgent and whose ability to enjoy all rights therefore is most in peril, must not be ignored by the measures aimed at achieving realization of the right [...].[98]

The Constitutional Court held that, although the programme satisfied all the other requirements of the reasonableness test, the programme was nonetheless unreasonable because no provision had been made for relief in respect of those groups in most desperate need. The State was therefore found to be in violation of Section 26(2) of the Constitution. Accordingly, a declaratory order was made requiring the government to act to meet the obligations imposed on it by Section 26(2). This entailed an obligation to devise, fund, implement and supervise measures aimed at providing relief to those in desperate need. As well as incorporating the core norm of human dignity, the Grootboom standard of reasonableness touched, to a small extent, on equality concerns. The Court outlined the fact that the appropriate standard of review must be based on the values and principles underlying the instrument under interpretation, stating that 'reasonableness must [...] be understood in the context of the Bill of Rights as a whole.'[99] By situating the claim against the backdrop of inequality resulting from the apartheid regime and by affirming that reasonableness review must necessarily take into account the historical, social and economic context of the claim at hand, the Court in *Grootboom* took equality as an important starting point. As Bruce Porter maintains, the *Grootboom* standard of reasonableness

94 Ibid, at paras. 39 and 40.
95 Ibid, at para. 42.
96 Ibid, at para. 43.
97 Ibid, at para. 83.
98 Ibid, at para. 44.
99 Ibid, at para. 44.

'emphasises the transformative dimension of socio-economic rights,'[100] to the extent that core human rights values (such as human dignity and equality) should inform socio-economic rights claims rather than mechanical standards or quantitative norms. However, the Court did not delve deeper into the interaction between the equality norm and socio-economic rights adjudication in the *Grootboom* case.

It is important to note that the types of reasonable measures outlined by the Court in *Grootboom* are essentially all process requirements which the State must meet, rather than setting minimum essential levels of rights provision or according direct relief to individuals. In fact, the Court in *Grootboom* rejected the contention that the socio-economic provisions of the South African Constitution[101] created a minimum core obligation to provide basic shelter enforceable immediately upon demand. The amici curiae[102] in *Grootboom* had argued[103] that the Constitution should be interpreted in line with General Comment 3 of the UNCESCR, in which the Committee sets out the notion of minimum core obligations. The Constitutional Court did not accept this approach, however, and identified the problem of defining the minimum core, on account of the fact that different groups have varying social needs, according to income, (un)employment, availability of land and poverty and also on account of the economic and social history and circumstances of a country.[104] The Constitutional Court held that detailed information is required to determine the needs and opportunities for the enjoyment of a given right and that this kind of detailed information was not available to the Court in order to determine what the notion of minimum core obligations would entail in the context of the right to housing under the South African Constitution.[105] Thus, the right to positive measures in *Grootboom* was determined by the sole criterion of reasonableness. Notably, however, the Constitutional Court stated that there may be cases that come before the Court in the future in which 'it may be possible and appropriate to have regard to the content of a minimum core obligation' to determine whether the measures taken by the State were reasonable,' provided that sufficient detailed information is available to determine the minimum core in a given context.[106]

A further notable aspect of the *Grootboom* judgment concerns the interpretation of the phrase 'within available resources' in sections 26(2) and 27(2) of the South African Constitution. That phrase was interpreted in *Grootboom* to mean that 'both

---

100 B. Porter, 'Reasonableness and Article 8(4)' in M. Langford, B. Porter, R. Brown and J. Rossi (eds.), The Optional Protocol to the International Covenant on Economic, Social and Cultural Rights: A Commentary (Forthcoming 2014), available at http://papers.ssrn.com/sol3/papers.cfm?abstract_id=2481712 last accessed 12 December 2014; On this point see also, S. Liebenberg, 'The value of human dignity in interpreting socio-economic rights', 21 South *African Journal on Human Rights*' (2005) at pages 1–31; See also S. Liebenberg, 'Towards a transformative adjudication of socio-economic rights' (2007) 21 *Speculum Juris*, at pages 41–59.

101 Specifically Section 26(1) of the South African Constitution.

102 The South African Human Rights Commission and the Community Law Centre of the University of the Western Cape.

103 *Grootboom,* at para. 29.

104 Ibid, at paras. 32–33.

105 Ibid, at paras. 31–33.

106 Ibid, at para. 33.

the content of the obligation in relation to the rate at which it is achieved as well as the reasonableness of the measures employed to achieve the result are governed by the availability of resources.'[107] Thus, within the *Grootboom* test, the availability of resources becomes the key indicator in determining what is reasonable or not. As Fons Coomans observes, the Court 'seems to be of the view that neither rights nor obligations have an independent meaning, but that they are subject to and ultimately determined by the availability of resources.'[108] Coomans illustrates the fallacy of the Court's reasoning when he points to the fact that:

> The availability of resources affects the rate and the extent to which a right can be realized in practice and that this process is subject to the test of reasonableness. The content of rights, however, as well as the content of obligations result independently of the availability of resources; they cannot be subject to reasonableness review. Otherwise one would risk stepping onto a downward slope.[109]

In other words, the starting point of the enquiry of any human rights treaty body (which is quasi-judicial) should always be the content of the right or rights at issue and tangential State obligations. From then on, the relevant consideration becomes whether the State in question is acting reasonably in accordance with its obligations, in terms of the speed at which it is realising human rights and the types of measures undertaken, in light of contextual factors pertaining to that State.

Notably, equality concerns were not raised explicitly as an argument in either the *Soobramoney* case or the *Grootboom* case. Both cases focused on the content of the positive obligation on the State to fulfil the rights in question – the right to health services in *Soobramoney* and the right to housing in *Grootboom*. The next major socio-economic rights case in South African Constitutional jurisprudence – *Minister of Health and Others v Treatment Action Campaign and Others (No 2)*[110] – provided the first occasion on which an equality argument was raised as a subsidiary claim. However, that argument was overlooked by the Court for the most part. Shortly thereafter, another case – *Khosa* and *Mazibuko and Others v City of Johannesburg and Others*[111] – provided a further opportunity to invoke an equality argument in a socio-economics rights case concerning the right of access to water. In the next subsection of this chapter, the aforementioned cases will be considered.

---

107 Ibid, at para. 46.

108 F. Coomans, 'Reviewing Implementation of Social and Economic Rights: An Assessment of the "Reasonableness" Test as Developed by the South African Constitutional Court' (2005) 65(1) *Heidelberg Journal of International Law*, at page 180.

109 F. Coomans, 'In Search of the Core Content of the Right to Education' in D. Brand and S. Russell (eds.) *Exploring the Core Content of Socio-Economic Rights: South African and International Perspectives* (Protea Book House, Pretoria 2002), at page 192.

110 Constitutional Court of South Africa, *Minister of Health and Others v Treatment Action Campaign and Others (No 2) (CCT8/02) [2002] ZACC 15; 2002 (5) SA 721; 2002 (10) BCLR 1033* (5 July 2002).

111 Constitutional Court of South Africa, *Khosa and Others v Minister of Social Development and Others, Mahlaule and Another v Minister of Social Development (CCT 13/03, CCT 12/03) [2004] ZACC 11; 2004 (6) SA 505 (CC); 2004 (6) BCLR 569 (CC)* (4 March 2004).

3.2.1.4. The Development of the Reasonableness Test: The Use of Available Resources, the Equality Limb and Participation of Affected Groups

The next case incorporating reasonableness review in the South African context is *Minister of Health and Others v Treatment Action Campaign and Others (No. 2)*[112] [hereafter referred to simply as *TAC*]. That case was brought as an appeal by the Government to the South African Constitutional Court against the decision of the High Court of Pretoria in *Treatment Action Campaign and Others v Minister of Health and Others.*[113] The original High Court case concerned allegations that the State had failed to take reasonable measures to prevent mother-to-baby transmission of HIV. The South African Government had refused to provide medication (Nevirapine) which was proven to restrict mother-to-baby HIV transmission beyond a number of pilot training and research sites in the public health sector, failing to ensure access to health care for all, in alleged violation of Section 27 of the South African Constitution.[114] The State raised a number of arguments in defence of its decision not to roll-out a comprehensive programme throughout the public health sector, such as lack of resources and lack of capacity. The High Court dismissed those arguments and made an order[115] requiring the respondent to make Nevirapine available to pregnant women with HIV who give birth in the public health sector and to their babies in public health facilities.[116] Therefore, the government was obliged to make Nevirapine available in medical facilities beyond the pilot sites where there was capacity to administer the drug, in particular where the women concerned could be appropriately tested and counselled. The High Court also ruled that the Minister of Health had a positive duty to devise and implement progressively in a reasonable manner a comprehensive programme to reduce mother-to-baby transmission of HIV and ordered the Minister to submit reports to the court outlining the governmental programme and the steps taken to comply with the Court order.

It is interesting to note that the appellants in the original High Court case had raised the argument that the Government's actions were in breach of the right to equality under Section 9 of the South African Constitution on account of the fact that the policy of the Government discriminated unfairly against poor women (and thus black women) by allowing the relevant medication to be available in the private health care system and not allowing it to be available widely in the public health care system. The Government argued that equality should not be defined in terms of access to the same resources but as the ability to achieve the same result (in that case, to secure the health of children). The Government further claimed that the safety and efficacy

---

112 Constitutional Court of South Africa, *Minister of Health and Others v Treatment Action Campaign and Others (No 2) (CCT8/02) [2002] ZACC 15; 2002 (5) SA 721; 2002 (10) BCLR 1033* (5 July 2002). [hereafter referred to simply as *TAC*].

113 High Court of South Africa, *Treatment Action Campaign and Other v Minister of Health and Others (2002) 4BCLR 356.*

114 Section 27(2) of the Constitution obliges the government to take 'reasonable measures' in providing for the right to healthcare.

115 Per Botha J.

116 Where in the opinion of the attending medical practitioner, acting in consultation with the medical superintendent of the facility concerned, this is medically indicated.

of the medication, over the long term in particular, was unknown and therefore they argued that it could not be deemed discriminatory to refuse to provide the medication to some groups. The equality argument was not taken into account by the Court in its consideration of the merits of the case. Nonetheless, the Court did comment generally on equality issues in socio-economic rights jurisprudence. Botha J. noted that the phased implementation of a health care programme was 'discriminating, that it causes inequality and that it denies access to those who find themselves outside the reach of the sites where implementation is being effected.'[117] However, he did not rule on whether this phased implementation actually breached the right to equality guaranteed under Section 9 of the South African Bill of Rights.

It is also interesting to note that the civil society group in the original High Court case argued that the South African Government was failing to use the maximum of available resources to secure the rights in question. The Government countered this argument by stating that it did not have enough resources to fund a full roll-out of the programme to prevent mother-to-child transmission of HIV. Rebuking that argument, the High Court ruled that the programme in question was affordable for the Government and that it had failed to take reasonable steps to provide access to programmes preventing HIV transmission from mother to child. The Court ruled (per Botha J.) that there was 'incontrovertible evidence that there is a residual of latent capacity in the public sector'[118] outside of the 18 pilot sites to prescribe the relevant medication and, moreover, that allowing doctors to prescribe the medication without restraint would not cause too much strain on the health care budget. The High Court ruled that the Government simply had to make additional resources available and that proper planning would make full coverage possible. The Court ordered the Government to draw up a plan that would ensure that the relevant medication would cover the groups that were currently excluded from provision and noted that the Government's failure to plan coherently was an unjustified barrier to the progressive realisation of the right to health care.

When the case reached the Constitutional Court on appeal by the Government, the Court made most of the same determinations as the High Court and demonstrated once again that socio-economic rights are justiciable. Employing the reasonableness approach, the Constitutional Court enjoined the State to distribute the medicine beyond the testing sites, in light of the fact that the additional costs involved in extending its reach to other sites were negligible and that training on the use of the drug was 'not a complex task,'[119] in particular given the benefits that the provision of the drug offered to those in need.[120] As Sandra Liebenberg observes, 'the costs and capacity arguments did not have sufficient cogency to outweigh the impact on a particularly

117 Judgment of Botha J., High Court of South Africa, *Treatment Action Campaign and Other v Minister of Health and Others (2002)* 4BCLR 356.

118 High Court of South Africa, *Treatment Action Campaign v Minister of Health* (2002) 4 BCLR 356 (T) 148, at 383.

119 *TAC,* para. 95.

120 For evidence of the benefits of the medication in question, see *TAC* para. 22.9, para. 48 and para. 57.

vulnerable group of the denial of a basic life-saving medical intervention.'[121] The Constitutional Court did, however, reject the minimum core approach to progressive realisation,[122] in a similar vein to its rejection of that approach in *Grootboom*.[123] The Court pointed to the fact that 'it is impossible to give everyone access even to a "core" service immediately'[124] and ruled that all that can be expected of the State is that it acts reasonably to provide access to the socio-economic rights identified in the Constitution[125] on a progressive basis.[126] It is disappointing that the Court failed to integrate the minimum core into its reasonableness review. As Fons Coomans points out, the question may be raised as to 'whether a governmental program can be reasonable if it does not provide for the realization of the core elements of a right.' He states that in circumstances where it does not provide for such, 'it may be said that a right would lose its meaning as a human right.'[127] Incorporating minimum core considerations into a framework for reasonableness review would essentially require a higher justification from a given State in respect of its failure to meet the basic needs of the most destitute in society.[128]

In spite of its regrettable failure to incorporate minimum core obligations into its case law, the Constitutional Court in *TAC* demonstrated once again that reasonableness review has the potential to provide a useful vehicle for increased judicial enforceability of socio-economic rights. In the subsequent case of *Khosa* and *Mazibuko and Others v City of Johannesburg and Others*,[129] [hereafter referred to

---

121 S. Liebenberg, 'Adjudicating Social Rights Under a Transformative Constitution' in M. Langford (ed.), *Social Rights Jurisprudence: Emerging Trends in International and Comparative Law* (Cambridge University Press, Cambridge, 2008), at page 86.

122 Notwithstanding its failure to consider a minimum core approach to socio-economic rights in the *Grootboom* and *TAC* cases, the Constitutional Court did acknowledge that 'there may be cases where it may be possible and appropriate to have regard to the content of a minimum core obligation to determine whether the measures taken by the State are reasonable,' provided that sufficient information is available to the Court in that regard. [*Grootboom* judgment, para. 33].

123 The amici curiae in *TAC* had argued that Section 27(1) of the Constitution has an independent status, giving rise to a minimum core to which everyone in need is entitled and that this minimum level is not subject to available resources or to progressive realisation. The Constitutional Court rejected this interpretation of the South African Constitution and, in doing so, rejected the notion of the minimum core. *TAC*, paras. 26 and 28.

124 Ibid, para. 35.

125 Specifically Sections 26 and 27 of the South African Constitution.

126 *TAC*, para. 35.

127 F. Coomans, Reviewing Implementation of Social and Economic Rights: An Assessment of the "Reasonableness" Test as Developed by the South African Constitutional Court (2005) 65 *Max-Planck-Institut für ausländisches öffentliches Recht und Völkerrecht* 167–196, at page 189.

128 This is recognised by the UNCESCR in its General Comment 3, in which the Committee envisages situations where States may not be able to fulfil the minimum core of their obligations under international human rights law. In that regard, the Committee has held that in order for a government 'to be able to attribute its failure to meet at least its minimum core obligations to a lack of available resources it must demonstrate that every effort has been made to use all resources that are at its disposition in an effort to satisfy, as a matter of priority, those minimum obligations. [UNCESCR, General Comment 3 on the nature of States Parties' obligations (Art. 2, Para. 1, of the Covenant), (1990), adopted at the fifth session of the Committee on 14 December 1990, UN Doc. E/1991/23, para. 10].

129 Constitutional Court of South Africa, *Khosa and Others v Minister of Social Development and Others, Mahlaule and Another v Minister of Social Development (CCT 13/03, CCT 12/03) [2004] ZACC 11; 2004 (6) SA 505 (CC); 2004 (6) BCLR 569 (CC) (4 March 2004)* [hereafter referred to simply as *Khosa*].

simply as *Khosa*] the Court's reasonableness test was expanded by the introduction of a proportionality limb, taking into account equality concerns. *Khosa* concerned the disqualification of a number of Mozambican citizens from entitlement to social assistance under national laws due to the fact that they did not have South African citizenship. The applicants argued, *inter alia*, that their exclusion on the grounds of lack of citizenship did not comply with the State's obligations under the South African Constitution[130] to provide social security to everyone. In addition, the applicants contended that their exclusion was contrary to the right to equality guaranteed under the Constitution.[131] The Court in *Khosa* considered the resource justifications advanced by the Government but ultimately viewed the applicant's exclusion from the socio-economic rights at issue through the lens of equality, ruling that the State must allocate resources to cover the excluded (disadvantaged) group. In considering the reasonableness or otherwise of the measure in question, the Court examined the impact of the exclusion of Mozambican nationals on the non-discrimination norm in Article 9 of the South African Constitution, specifically the right to equal protection and equal benefit of the law. Coomans describes this as:

> A proportionality test [... scrutinising ...] the reasonableness of the measure, an assessment in which the dignity of people and equality among people as constitutional values requiring protection played a crucial role.[132]

In applying the proportionality test, the Court held that the denial to non-nationals of the right of access to social security (guaranteed to everyone under Section 27 of the South African Constitution) was unfair,[133] disproportionate and had a grave effect on the life and dignity of the individuals concerned. The Court also noted that the impact of the exclusion from social assistance on the life and dignity of permanent residents outweighed the financial and immigration arguments which the State had raised and relied on.[134] Thus, it was deemed[135] not to constitute a reasonable measure under the relevant provision[136] of the Constitution. In its proportionality analysis, the Court held that there were other less drastic measures which could have been taken by the State to reduce the risk of permanent residents becoming a burden on the State rather than excluding them from gaining access to social assistance.[137] As Sandra Liebenberg observes, 'the stringent standard of review applied in this case should be understood in the context of the denial of a basic social benefit to a vulnerable group, and the intersecting breaches of a socio-economic right and the right against unfair

130 Section 27(1)(c) of the South African Constitution.

131 Section 9 of the South African Constitution.

132 F. Coomans, 'Reviewing Implementation of Social and Economic Rights: An Assessment of the "Reasonableness" Test as Developed by the South African Constitutional Court' (2005) 65(1) *Heidelberg Journal of International Law*, at page 179.

133 The Court in *Khosa* held that: 'As far as the applicants are concerned, the denial of the right is total and the consequences of the denial are grave. They are relegated to the margins of society and are deprived of what may be essential to enable them to enjoy other rights vested in them under the Constitution.' [*Khosa*, para. 77].

134 *Khosa*, para. 82.

135 Ibid, para. 82.

136 Section 27(2) of the South African Constitution.

137 *Khosa*, paras. 64–65.

discrimination.'[138] Liebenberg contends that 'the intersection of equality rights and socio-economic rights offers much untapped potential to challenge inequalities in access to resources and services that are based on, for example, gender, sexual orientation, and HIV status.'[139]

Finally, it is important to note that the South African Constitutional Court has also added another limb to its reasonableness test, namely that to be considered reasonable, any measures taken must involve 'meaningful engagement' with those affected by the measures, especially if they are marginalised or vulnerable.[140] This emphasises the need, under reasonableness review, for participatory processes in the realisation of human rights.

3.2.1.5. Summary of the South African Approach to Reasonableness Review

The reasonableness standard used by the South African Constitutional Court to assess the right to positive measures in the context of socio-economic rights adjudication seeks to recognise the prerogative of governments to make choices with regard to the types of measures that will be appropriate in their particular national context. At the same time, it acknowledges that governmental choices must be subject to certain criteria or requirements to ensure compliance with wider human rights norms. The South African reasonableness model contains many strands. Hereunder the most important of those will be summarised, in order to determine (in the next section of this chapter) if these criteria can be tailored to the specific context of the CRPD.

The first important strand of reasonableness review in the South African context is the application of the dignity norm to socio-economic rights adjudication. The core importance of human dignity in advancing socio-economic claims can be seen clearly in the *Grootboom* case, as highlighted above. A central element of a reasonable governmental programme is the notion that the needs of those who are most disadvantaged should be catered for as a matter of priority. State choices are subject to the threshold requirement that any measures taken must provide short-term relief for those whose needs are most urgent. Of course, the importance of catering to the needs of those in most dire circumstances is also an important consideration at the international level, a point which will be expanded upon in the next subsection of this chapter.

In addition to dignity considerations, the South African model demonstrates the potential role which the equality norm can play in reinforcing socio-economic rights adjudication. As illustrated above, the *Khosa* case related to a claim by a disadvantaged group to entitlement to existing social programmes provided to

---

138 S. Liebenberg, 'Adjudicating Social Rights Under a Transformative Constitution' in M. Langford (ed.), *Social Rights Jurisprudence: Emerging Trends in International and Comparative Law* (Cambridge University Press, Cambridge, 2008), at page 89.

139 Ibid.

140 Constitutional Court of South Africa, *Occupiers of 51 Olivia Road, Berea Township and 197 Main Street Johannesburg v City of Johannesburg and Others* (2008) ZACC 1 at para. 15.

other groups. The Court in *Khosa* outlined a proportionality test which sought to scrutinise the so-called reasonableness of measures adopted by States in light of the inherent dignity of people, and also in light of the fundamental precept of equality amongst individuals. In the *Khosa* judgment, the Court ruled that the governmental programme in question unreasonably and unfairly excluded a particular marginalised group. The effect of this was a finding by the Court that the equality norm had been breached in the circumstances. It will be argued in the next subsection of this chapter that the intersection of equality and socio-economic rights in the CRPD may provide a key to unlocking the structural inequalities which disabled people have encountered for too long now.

Another important element of reasonableness review in the South African context is the principle of the effectiveness of measures adopted by States, as seen above in *Grootboom*. In that case, the Court highlighted the fact that measures will only be reasonable if they actually result in the facilitation of human rights. Additionally, the notion of the least restrictive alternative, outlined by the Court in *Khosa*, is instructive. In that case, the Court held that there were other less drastic measures which could have been taken by the State to achieve its aims. The final strand of the South African reasonableness standard that is of relevance for present purposes is that of participatory processes and inclusiveness, namely the obligation to consult closely with and involve marginalised groups in policy-making and programme implementation.

It is important to note that while certain scholarly voices have welcomed the reasonableness approach elaborated by the South African Constitutional Court,[141] other commentators[142] have drawn attention to the weaknesses of any mechanism of reasonableness review of the progressive realisation of socio-economic rights. These criticisms will be elaborated on in the next section of this chapter as they are relevant to the proposed framework for review of measures taken by States in realising progressively the rights contained in the CRPD. Coomans, for instance, notes that reasonableness is an 'inherently vague'[143] and 'elastic'[144] notion. In addition, many scholars have been critical of the fact that the reasonableness approach in South Africa does not include a consideration of the minimum core obligations of human rights. Accordingly, various voices in South African scholarship for social rights promote

141 See, for instance, C.R. Sunstein, 'Social and Economic Rights? Lessons from South Africa' 11(4) *Constitutional Forum* (2001) at page 23; See also P. De Vos, 'Grootboom, The Right of Access to Housing and Substantive Equality as Contextual Fairness' (2001) 17 *South African Journal of Human Rights* at pages 258 and 259.

142 See, in particular F. Coomans, 'Reviewing Implementation of Social and Economic Rights: An Assessment of the "Reasonableness" Test as Developed by the South African Constitutional Court' (2005) 65(1) *Heidelberg Journal of International Law* 187; See also D. Bilchitz, 'Giving socio-economic rights teeth: the minimum core and its importance' (2002) 119 *South African Law Journal* 484; See also D. Bilchitz, 'Towards a reasonable approach to the minimum core: laying the foundations for future socio-economic rights jurisprudence (2003) 18 *South African Journal on Human Rights* 1.

143 F. Coomans, 'Reviewing Implementation of Social and Economic Rights: An Assessment of the "Reasonableness" Test as Developed by the South African Constitutional Court' (2005) 65(1) *Heidelberg Journal of International Law* 187.

144 Ibid.

a model which combines reasonableness review with a core contents approach.[145] In spite of the foregoing criticisms, the *Grootboom* standard of reasonableness has had some influence on the development of a similar standard of review at the international level under the OP-ICESCR.[146] The latter standard of reasonableness review will be examined below, before turning to the CRPD itself.

3.3. Reasonableness Review: The Standard of Review at the International Level

In 2008, an Optional Protocol was drafted to the ICESCR. The drafting of this Optional Protocol was the culmination of lengthy negotiations relating, in particular, to proposals to insert a standard of review of measures taken by States to realise socio-economic rights. According to Brian Griffey, the insertion of this standard of review in the OP-ICESCR stemmed from some States' 'ongoing discomfort with the adjudication of economic, social and cultural rights.'[147] The negotiations led to the drafting of Article 8(4) of the OP-ICESCR, which contains a form of reasonableness review. Article 8(4) provides as follows:

> When examining communications under the present Protocol, the Committee shall consider the *reasonableness* of the steps taken by the State Party in accordance with part II of the Covenant. In doing so, the Committee shall bear in mind that the State Party may adopt a range of possible policy measures for the implementation of the rights set forth in the Covenant.[148]

The concept of 'reasonableness' delineated by the South African Constitutional Court, and specifically the test elaborated in the *Grootboom* case,[149] influenced the

---

145 Bilchitz, for instance, observes that in order to work out 'which considerations are relevant to a determination of reasonableness in each context, it is necessary to have a prior understanding of the general obligations government is under by virtue of having to realise the rights in question.' [D. Bilchitz, 'Towards a Reasonable Approach to the Minimum Core: Laying the Foundations for Future Socio-Economic Rights Jurisprudence' (2003) 18 *South African Journal on Human Rights* 1, at page 10]; See also D. Bilchitz, 'Giving Socio-Economic Rights Teeth: The Minimum Core and its Importance' (2002) 119 *South African Law Journal* 484; See also S. Liebenberg, *Socio-economic rights: Adjudication under a Transformative Constitution* (Juta & Co Ltd Publishers, Claremont, 2010).

146 See the comments of B. Griffey, 'The 'Reasonableness' Test: Assessing Violations of State Obligations under the Optional Protocol to the International Covenant on Economic, Social and Cultural Rights' 11(2) *Human Rights Law Review* (2011) 275, at page 277; See also B. Porter, 'The Reasonableness of Article 8(4) – Adjudicating Claims from the Margins' (2009) 27(1) *Nordisk Tidsskrift for Menneskerettigheter* 39.

147 B. Griffey, 'The 'Reasonableness' Test: Assessing Violations of State Obligations under the Optional Protocol to the International Covenant on Economic, Social and Cultural Rights' 11(2) *Human Rights Law Review* (2011) 275, at page 302.

148 ICESCR, Optional Protocol, Art 8(4) [emphasis added].

149 It is noteworthy that it was merely the *Grootboom* decision that was the key frame of reference for the drafters of Article 8(4) of the OP-ICESCR and not the later jurisprudence of the South African Court. Accordingly, the various elements of *Grootboom* reasonableness are likely to be more influential on the UNCESCR in developing its own standard of review. However, the Committee would also do well to keep a keen eye on other emerging developments related to reasonableness in the South African context beyond the *Grootboom* standard.

standard of review contained in Article 8(4) of the ICESCR. The drafting history[150] of the OP-ICESCR demonstrates the fact that the final sentence of Article 8(4) was taken directly from the *Grootboom* judgment. This illustrates the interconnectedness of approaches to reviewing socio-economic rights provision at the national and international levels and the possibility for cross-fertilisation of the various approaches, most notably in the context of the CRPD. Of course, the UNCESCR will develop its own distinct approach to reasonableness review. Nonetheless, the fact that the wording of Article 8(4) was adopted from the text of the *Grootboom* decision can certainly be deemed relevant to the application of the standard of review under the OP-ICESCR (although of course the UNCESCR will not be bound to follow the jurisprudence of the Constitutional Court of South Africa in that regard).

Numerous queries were brought forward at the Working Group sessions with regard to the standard of review that would be adopted by the UNCESCR under Article 8(4). The UNCESCR sought to answer those questions by adopting a guidance statement[151] in 2007 designed to clarify how it might consider States Parties' obligations of progressive realisation in the context of an individual communications procedure under the OP-ICESCR. Although that statement is non-binding and was drafted before the actual insertion of Article 8(4) in the OP-ICESCR, the statement was written with a view to future implementation of the reasonableness standard and it is therefore important to consider it here. In evaluating the obligation to take steps to the 'maximum of available resources' under the OP-ICESCR, the UNCESCR recognises (in the 2007 Statement) the fact that resource constraints may limit the ability of States to take extensive measures. Notwithstanding such constraints, the Committee notes that States are under a duty to protect the most vulnerable groups in society – those in dire need.[152] Beyond protecting those in dire need, the Committee recognises the fact that measures taken by States to fulfil socio-economic rights must be 'adequate or reasonable'[153] and lays down the following general considerations which it deems relevant to assessing whether measures taken by States fulfil this adequacy or reasonableness criterion:

a. The extent to which the measures taken were deliberate, concrete and targeted towards the fulfilment of economic, social and cultural rights;
b. Whether the State Party exercised its discretion in a non-discriminatory and non-arbitrary manner;

150 For a review of the evolution of the text of Article 8(4) Optional Protocol to the ICESCR, see B. Porter, 'The Reasonableness of Article 8(4) – Adjudicating Claims from the Margins' (2009) 27(1) *Nordisk Tidsskrift for Menneskerettigheter* 39, at pages 48–50.

151 UNCESCR Statement, *An evaluation of the obligation to take steps to the 'Maximum of Available Resources' Under an Optional Protocol to the Covenant* (2007), U.N. Doc. E/C.12/2007/1, adopted at the thirty-eighth session of the Committee on 10 May 2007, para. 3.

152 The Committee notes that: 'The obligation remains for a State party to ensure the widest possible enjoyment of economic, social and cultural rights under the prevailing circumstances. The Committee has already emphasized that, even in times of severe resource constraints, States parties must protect the most disadvantaged and marginalized members or groups of society by adopting relatively low-cost targeted programmes.' [Ibid, para. 4].

153 Ibid, para. 8.

c. Whether the State Party's decision (not) to allocate available resources was in accordance with international human rights standards;
d. Where several policy options are available, whether the State Party adopted the option that least restricts Covenant rights;
e. The time frame in which the steps were taken; and
f. Whether the steps had taken into account the precarious situation of disadvantaged and marginalized individuals or groups, whether they were non-discriminatory, and whether they prioritized grave situations or situations of risk.[154]

The criteria set forth by the UNCESCR in the foregoing statement are somewhat reflective of the standard of reasonableness developed by the South African Constitutional Court. Both standards of review (the South African standard and that contained in Article 8(4) of the OP-ICESCR, as elaborated on by the UNCESCR in the above statement) place a high priority on the protection of vulnerable groups and the overall compliance of measures with wider human rights norms, specifically the non-discrimination norm. Griffey points to the fact that 'the most novel additions' to State obligations are those contained in clauses (b) and (d) above, which he argues recognises and restricts States' discretion in their selection of 'appropriate measures.'[155] In particular, clause (b) above highlights the importance of the equality and non-discrimination norms in assessing the reasonableness of measures taken by States. Furthermore, clause (d) above presumes that States will opt for the least restrictive alternative in the progressive realisation of rights. This ties in with the notion that appropriate or reasonable measures are those which result in the effective realisation of human rights. The principle of effectiveness was also outlined in chapter four of this book as one of the criteria inherent in the outer limits of the accommodation duty. In addition to the criteria listed above, the UNCESCR has also stated that emphasis should be placed on 'transparent and participatory decision-making at the national level'[156] and links this to a margin of discretion for States allowing them 'to take steps and adopt measures most suited to their specific circumstances.'[157] This element of participatory processes or inclusiveness was also highlighted above in the South African line of jurisprudence.

In the context of the ICESCR, it has been stated that any policies or decisions adopted by States should be reviewed 'for both procedural and substantive compliance with the rights, purposes and values of the ICESCR, in the context of available resources and the needs and rights of others.'[158] Such review will be based not only on the types of measures outlined in the general comments and concluding observations

154 Ibid.

155 B. Griffey, 'The "Reasonableness" Test: Assessing Violations of State Obligations under the Optional Protocol to the International Covenant on Economic, Social and Cultural Rights' (2011) 11(2) *Human Rights Law Review* 275, at page 322.

156 UNCESCR Statement, *An Evaluation of the Obligation to Take Steps to the 'Maximum of Available Resources' Under an Optional Protocol to the Covenant*, UN Doc. E/C.12/2007/1, adopted at the thirty-eighth session of the Committee on 10 May 2007, at para. 11.

157 Ibid.

158 B. Porter and S. Liebenberg, 'Consideration of Merits under the OP-ICESCR: Reasonableness Review under 8(4) and the Maximum of Available Resources Standard' (Notes for Discussion at the Workshop

of the UNCESCR, but also on the criteria outlined in the Committee's 2007 Statement, outlined above. In terms of requirements of procedural compliance with the Article 8(4) reasonableness standard, Bruce Porter and Sandra Liebenberg note that this will include, for example, meaningful engagement with stakeholders in both the design and implementation of programmes (including in budgeting and resource allocation). Porter and Liebenberg also contend that it will include participatory rights and effective remedies for rights-holders (including affirmative measures for marginalised groups, built into program design and legislation as well as measures to ensure that more powerful interest groups do not adversely affect fair decision-making). Lastly, they argue that procedural review of measures taken under Article 8(4) will entail ensuring that meaningful goals and timetables are put in place, with independent monitoring, review and complaints mechanisms to ensure progress in fulfilling rights.[159] These overall requirements of participation and effectiveness mirror the criteria employed by the South African Constitutional Court. Furthermore, Porter and Liebenberg argue that reasonable measures which comply substantively with State obligations will include, as a basic starting point, 'provision for those in the most desperate or precarious circumstances' and 'universal access to basic levels of entitlements.'[160] They highlight the importance of 'protection of equality, non-discrimination, dignity, autonomy and other human rights in program design and implementation.'[161] Most of these criteria overlap, to some extent, with the types of criteria inherent in the South African line of case law. It is interesting to note that, around the same time as the adoption of the OP-ICESCR, the CRPD entered into force. On account of the fact that the CRPD incorporates its very own standard of so-called 'reasonableness' via the reasonable accommodation duty and applies that duty to the substantive rights and obligations in the Convention which are subject to progressive realisation, it is important to consider the types of criteria that might be employed by the CRPD Committee in assessing the measures adopted by States Parties to the Convention.

4. A Proposed Framework for Review of the Progressive Realisation of Rights under the CRPD

In this section of the chapter, a proposed framework for assessing the measures adopted by States to realise socio-economic rights under the CRPD will be put forward. The various sources that will be drawn upon in devising that framework will be highlighted below. In addition, the types of criteria that might be adopted by the CRPD Committee in adjudicating on the right to positive measures in the realisation of socio-economic rights (both under the Convention itself and under the OP-CRPD) will be outlined. Attention will also be drawn to the interaction of

---

on Strategic Litigation under the OP-ICESCR), at page 7, available at www.escr-net.org/sites/default/files/Porter_and_Liebenberg,_Reasonableness_0.pdf last accessed 7 April 2014.

159 Ibid.

160 Ibid, at page 8.

161 Ibid.

the proposed framework with the minimum core obligations resulting from human rights.

4.1. Introduction to the Proposed Framework

The idea of developing a framework for review of socio-economic rights under the CRPD is not intended to serve the interests of entities or States alone, by acting as a defence to non-implementation of Convention rights. Nor is it intended solely to benefit persons with disabilities. In fact, it is meant to act as an intermediary between the interests of both parties and all other stakeholders involved. It is designed to ensure that there is an appropriate balancing of interests and burdens in the assessment of measures taken to ensure compliance with State obligations under the CRPD. It is also designed to ensure consistency with broader values underlying the Convention. States Parties to the CRPD will have difficult policy and budgetary choices to make, often in the context of limited resources. The CRPD Committee will be required to assess the measures taken by States to give effect to disability rights in light of competing claims on States' financial and institutional resources. If the Committee decides that there has been a failure to take 'reasonable' measures, it will issue a recommendation for remedial action to be adopted. However, it will generally be left to the discretion of the relevant State Party to determine, through its own domestic processes, the means by which any breach of Convention rights will be remedied. The CRPD Committee will nonetheless undertake the important task of assessing the measures taken by States both in determining compliance with treaty obligations under the State reporting procedure and also in its consideration of alleged violations under the OP-CRPD. In the sub-sections below it will be argued that the best manner in which claims under the CRPD can be assessed is according to a framework of reasonableness review, incorporating substantive equality concerns, combined with a minimum core obligations approach.

4.2. A Proposed Framework for Review of the Progressive Realisation of CRPD Rights

Invoking a reasonableness test to assess alleged violations of CRPD rights under the State reporting procedure will mean that the Committee can take into account the specific national circumstances. Higher levels of protection will be required in developed States when compared with developing countries and the Committee will be compelled to tailor its assessment to the specific context at issue and the socio-economic disadvantage faced by persons with disabilities in that context. The unique nature of reasonableness review under the OP-CRPD will be the determination of the realisation of the right in question in the particular circumstances of the individual's lived experience.

It is argued here that the assessment of measures taken by States under the CRPD should be informed and guided by three intertwining 'reasonableness' standards. In the first instance, the various elements of the standard of reasonableness set out in the *Grootboom* line of case law might influence the Committee's views. The reasons why the Committee might draw on the South African standard of reasonableness are twofold. Firstly, the CRPD (akin to the South African Constitution) is based on the core norm of human dignity, as well as substantive and transformative equality. The South African model of review seeks to balance the justifications advanced by States for failing to fulfil rights with a consideration of the inherent values and objectives underpinning the rights in question and, furthermore, the consequences of denial of the right in question on the claimant group. Basing its assessment on similar standards of review would enable the CRPD Committee to give full effect to the purpose and values underlying the CRPD. Secondly, it is argued that because the *Grootboom* standard has influenced the development of the reasonableness standard of review at the international level – under Article 8 OP-ICESCR – the *Grootboom* standard (and even later elaborations by the South African Constitutional Court on reasonableness) may also be relevant to socio-economic claims under the CRPD.

The second standard of review which the CRPD Committee can use to draw some guidance from is that contained in Article 8 of the OP-ICESCR, together with the statements made by the UNCESCR on what constitute 'reasonable or adequate' measures, as well as decisions of the Committee in which it adjudicates on socio-economic rights. One should not underestimate the importance of the manner in which reasonableness review of socio-economic rights claims evolves at the level of other human rights treaty bodies. The assessment of claims by the CRPD Committee under the OP-CRPD will naturally be influenced by the standard of reasonableness adopted in claims under the OP-ICESCR. Likewise, the UNCESCR would do well to keep a keen eye on the pronouncements of the CRPD Committee with regard to its assessment of socio-economic rights and equality claims. As Janet Lord and Rebecca Brown point out, the OP-CRPD taken in conjunction with the OP-ICESCR 'provide new entry points for claimants with disabilities and their representative organizations with the opportunity to enrich human rights advocacy through the application of reasonable accommodation across all spheres of life.'[162] Both of these mechanisms can provide fertile ground for advancing socio-economic claims and for harmonising disability rights at the level of the human rights treaty bodies.

The two intertwining standards of reasonableness above can provide some level of guidance to the CRPD Committee in its assessment of claims under the Convention and its Optional Protocol. However, the lessons which may be drawn from those review standards must be tempered to fit the obligations contained in the CRPD. The Convention incorporates its very own standard for the assessment of positive equality claims via the reasonable accommodation obligation. Therefore, the third standard of review that I will draw upon in this context is the outer limits of the accommodation duty. Those outer limits reflect, to a certain extent, some of the

162 J. Lord and R. Brown, 'The Role of Reasonable Accommodation in Securing Substantive Equality for Persons with Disabilities: The UN Convention on the Rights of Persons with Disabilities' in M.H. Rioux, L.A. Basser and M. Jones (eds.) *Critical Perspectives on Human Rights and Disability Law* (Martinus Nijhoff, The Hague, 2011), at page 273.

elements emerging from the frameworks of reasonableness review outlined above. Moreover, the accommodation duty very clearly incorporates dignity and equality considerations, together with cost considerations into its outer limits. Its application to socio-economic rights in the Convention seeks to challenge instances of systemic inequality in the enjoyment of such rights by persons with disabilities. Therefore, the equality norm and the outer limits of the accommodation duty must necessarily inform the standard of review which will be adopted by the CRPD Committee. This will serve to ensure that any criteria based on reasonableness remain grounded in a substantive equality framework.

It is vital to point out that the notion of reasonableness review alone will not result in the effective implementation of CRPD rights. In order to give teeth to the underlying principles and obligations in the Convention, the CRPD Committee should consider the various elements of reasonableness review in conjunction with a minimum core obligations approach. The immediacy of core obligations has been confirmed by Craig Mokhiber, Chief of Development and Economic and Social Issues Branch at the OHCHR, who has stated that the core obligations of the CRPD are to be implemented immediately by those countries that have ratified the Convention and 'are not to be implemented as money becomes available.'[163] Irrespective of the resources available to States, they should, as a matter of priority, seek to ensure, at the very least, that all persons with disabilities have access to minimum levels of the rights which are contained in the Convention. Identification of the minimum core obligations of States Parties to the CRPD must stem from the information which exists already at the level of the international human rights treaty bodies, such as the general comments of the UNCESCR.[164] Fons Coomans points to the fact that this core should be translated or operationalised at the national, regional and local levels into carefully targeted policies and programmes that duly implement obligations.[165] The availability of resources should not alone be determinant in the assessment of measures taken by States Parties to the CRPD. In assessing the actions of national authorities, the normative content of the particular right at issue must first be analysed, followed by a consideration of the reasonableness of measures adopted. Having said that, it is important that the CRPD Committee would not bifurcate the assessment of minimum core obligations under the CRPD from a review of reasonableness, as reasonable policies and programs include universal core minimum entitlements. Coomans argues 'that the [...] values of human dignity and substantive equality imply that a reasonable governmental program must include provision to cater for the [...] needs of vulnerable and needy groups on a priority basis.'[166]

163 Opinion of Craig Mokhiber, Chief of Development and Economic and Social Issues Branch at the Office of the High Commissioner for Human Rights, cited at http://globalaccessibilitynews.com/2012/09/12/ohchr-says-the-core-crpd-obligations-to-be-immediately-implemented-not-implemented-only-as-money-becomes-available last accessed 7 May 2014.

164 The UNCESCR has elaborated on the content of such minimum core obligations in relation to the right to food, the right to health, the right to employment and the right to education, among others.

165 F. Coomans, 'In Search of the Core Content of the Right to Education' in D. Brand and S. Russell (eds.) *Exploring the Core Content of Socio-Economic Rights: South African and International Perspectives* (Protea Book House, Pretoria 2002), at page 189.

166 Ibid, at page 190.

4.3. Proposed Criteria for Assessment of Progressive Realisation under the CRPD

While States Parties to the CRPD will have a certain margin or discretion with regard to the types of measures they take in the progressive implementation of rights contained in the Convention, one thing is certain – any measures taken by States must be in compliance with Convention requirements and the values underlying the CRPD. Drawing on the various sources highlighted above, I will outline hereunder what I propose to be the most relevant criteria to be taken into account by the CRPD Committee in its assessment of States' obligations to realise rights progressively under the CRPD. These criteria are only illustrative and are certainly not exhaustive. The CRPD Committee will no doubt enunciate its own criteria over time and the suggestions below are merely intended as a starting point for the Committee, which will be the ultimate arbitrator on the review criteria that it deems most appropriate to CRPD rights realisation. The observations below are general in nature (not attaching to any specific socio-economic right(s) in the Convention). In chapters six and seven of this book, the criteria below will be tailored to two substantive rights and obligations under the Convention, namely the accessibility obligation and the right to education.[167] Each factor will be outlined in turn and its adoption will be justified in the context of the CRPD:

4.3.1. The Necessity and Effectiveness of Measures taken by States

One of the outer limits of the duty to accommodate is the requirement that duty-bearers must take steps which are 'necessary and appropriate.'[168] National authorities will be required to take necessary measures to give effect, at the very least, to the minimum core of the right(s) in question in order to ensure that the basic needs and capabilities of persons with disabilities are catered for. States are also required to take all necessary steps to realise rights fully within available resources and the measures taken by States in that regard should be adjudged according to their reasonableness. The reasonableness of measures may be assessed by the Committee according to many criteria. In chapter four above it was highlighted that any accommodation provided by an entity must be appropriate – in other words, it must be effective in terms of resulting in the realisation of Convention rights for disabled individuals. Under the accommodation duty, a relevant consideration is the anticipated effects of measures taken on the requesting party's ability to exercise their rights. It is argued here that the criterion of the effectiveness of general measures taken by States in the realisation of socio-economic rights under the CRPD will be a vital criterion for consideration by the CRPD Committee. Measures adopted by national authorities must produce tangible outcomes which are compatible with the requirements of the Convention. When choosing between measures to facilitate Convention obligations, States will also be required to consider the least restrictive options for persons with

167 Minimum core obligations will not be elaborated on to any great extent in the present chapter. Instead, they will be considered in respect of the Convention's accessibility obligation and the right to education in chapters six and seven of this book.

168 UN CRPD, Article 2.

disabilities. In other words, when States choose measures to attain their policy goals, they must choose the measures which cause the least disruption to the human rights of persons with disabilities as laid down in the Convention and which also ensure effectiveness in rights realisation.[169] The criterion of effectiveness is confirmed by a contextual reading of the Convention. Taken in the overall scheme of the CRPD, the term 'appropriate' implies that measures adopted by States must result in the effective realisation of the rights contained in the Convention. This is borne out by General Obligation 4(1), which links the word 'appropriate' with the full realisation of rights.[170] The UNCESCR has confirmed this understanding of the term 'appropriate measures' as meaning measures resulting in the effective implementation of rights (or measures which give effect to human rights) in its General Comment 9.[171] The criterion of 'appropriateness' is repeated at numerous junctures throughout the substantive rights in the CRPD which are subject to progressive realisation. It features, for instance, in the right to education,[172] the right to health,[173] the right to work and employment[174] and the right to an adequate standard of living and protection.[175] It is evident that the effectiveness of measures will change over time and therefore the measures expected of States Parties to the CRPD will alter as time goes on. A given State may take effective measures to fulfil one part of the accessibility obligation, for instance. Once it has done so, it must move on to the next target and take equally effective measures in order to ensure the full realisation of the accessibility obligation.

The requirement of effectiveness has also been affirmed in the *Grootboom* judgment, in which the Court stated that reasonable policies 'must be capable of facilitating the realisation of the right [in question].'[176] Notably, the requirement of effectiveness has already been taken into account by the CRPD Committee in an individual communication on the accessibility of banking facilities for persons with disabilities.[177] Finally, it is argued that the substantive and transformative equality framework of the CRPD actually requires consideration of the effectiveness of

---

169 The link between effectiveness and the least restrictive alternative has been stated by Eva Brems as follows: 'The obligation to chose the least rights-restrictive option applies only to alternatives that are comparable in terms of effectiveness towards realising the goal.' [E. Brems, 'Human Rights: Minimum and Maximum Perspectives' (2009) 9(3) *Human Rights Law Review* 349, at page 360].

170 General Obligation 4(1) of the CRPD reads as follows: 'States Parties undertake to ensure and promote the *full realization* of all human rights and fundamental freedoms for all persons with disabilities without discrimination of any kind on the basis of disability. To this end, States Parties undertake: a) To adopt all *appropriate* legislative, administrative and other measures for the implementation of the rights recognized in the present Convention.' [emphasis added].

171 See UNCESCR, General Comment No 9 on the domestic application of the Covenant (adopted at the nineteenth session of the Committee, 3 December 1998), UN Doc. E/C.12/1998/24, at para. 2.

172 See UN CRPD, Article 24(3) and 24(4).

173 See UN CRPD, Article 25.

174 See UN CRPD, Article 27.

175 See UN CRPD, Article 28(2).

176 *Grootboom*, para. 41.

177 UN CRPD Committee, Individual Communication taken by Szilvia Nyusti and Péter Takács (represented by counsel, Tamás Fazekas, Hungarian Helsinki Committee), Communication No. 1/2010, views adopted by the Committee at its ninth session (15–19 April 2013) [I will examine this decision of the Committee in the next chapter of this book].

measures taken in the realisation of Convention rights. Janet Lord and Rebecca Brown contend that the CRPD's equality framework requires one to address the question as to whether States have 'facilitated the actual realization of human rights through the positive measures taken.'[178]

4.3.2. Disproportionate Burden/Cost Considerations

The South African reasonableness review model does not provide much guidance on financial considerations. The Court views rights and obligations as being 'subject to and ultimately determined by the availability of resources'[179] and this factors into the Constitutional Court's assessment of the reasonableness of measures taken by States. The Court touches briefly on financial considerations in some of its case law[180] but does not give much guidance about the competing constraints on limited resources. International human rights law begins from the fundamental premise that the starting point in the progressive realisation of rights is that where governmental resources are severely constrained, States must accord high priority to the needs of the most destitute, vulnerable members of society, particularly their subsistence rights.[181] This is also reflected in the reasonableness standard outlined by the Court in the *Grootboom* case. Once a State has catered for the needs of the most destitute (both disabled and non-disabled persons), it must seek to implement disability rights to the fullest, as well as the socio-economic rights of all other disadvantaged groups.

Any analysis by the CRPD Committee of measures taken by States Parties to the Convention must entail a balancing of burdens and interests. Translating the notion of disproportionate burden to progressive realisation, the Committee will be required to set out various criteria designed to assess whether States have done everything in their power to facilitate the enjoyment of the socio-economic rights in the Convention, in light of resource, capacity and institutional constraints, as well as a lack of political

[178] J.E. Lord and R. Brown. 'The Role of Reasonable Accommodation in Securing Substantive Equality for Persons with Disabilities: The UN Convention on the Rights of Persons with Disabilities' in M.H. Rioux, L.A. Basser and M. Jones (eds.), *Critical Perspectives on Human Rights and Disability Policy* (Martinus Nijhoff, The Hague, 2011), at page 277.

[179] F. Coomans, 'Reviewing Implementation of Social and Economic Rights: An Assessment of the "Reasonableness" Test as Developed by the South African Constitutional Court' (2005) 65(1) *Heidelberg Journal of International Law* 175, at page 180.

[180] In *TAC*, for instance, the Constitutional Court noted that 'budgetary constraints' were not an impediment and that 'problems of financial incapacity' could be addressed in light of the fact that the government had made substantial additional funds available for the treatment of HIV. [*TAC*, para. 120]. Furthermore, in *Khosa*, the Court simply remarks that the cost of including permanent residents in the system of social grants constituted a 'small proportion' of the total expenditure on social grants. [*Khosa*, para. 62].

[181] In this regard, see UNCESCR, General Comment 3 on the nature of States Parties' obligations (1990), para. 12; See also Principle 28 of the Limburg Principles on the Implementation of the International Covenant on Economic, Social and Cultural Rights (1987) 9 HRQ, 122–135, which states that: 'In the use of the available resources due priority shall be given to the realization of the rights recognized in the Covenant, mindful of the need to assure to everyone the satisfaction of subsistence requirements as well as the provision of essential services;' See also Principle 25 of the Limburg Principles which provides that 'States parties are obligated regardless of the level of economic development to ensure respect for minimum subsistence rights for all.'

will. The primary factor taken into account under the disproportionate burden test related to the duty to accommodate is the cost of measures to be undertaken. Under the broad heading of costs, an entity's economic circumstances and its right to organise the operation of its business as it sees fit must be taken into account. The ability of the entity in question to bear the costs and the impact on the operation of the provider with respect to undertaking the measures (such as decreased efficiency and how quickly the measures can be undertaken) can all be considered as relevant factors under the duty to accommodate. The availability of outside sources of support, such as public subsidies, is also a pertinent consideration. Similar criteria will apply to States Parties to the Convention in the implementation of rights and obligations under the CRPD. The Committee will obviously require more advanced measures to be taken by developed States in the realisation of socio-economic rights when compared with developing countries. In the case of a large private entity with substantial resources, the duty to provide a reasonable accommodation will be much greater than that owed by a small entity. In a similar vein, greater assistance will be required of large States (with sizeable financial and other resources at their disposal) in the progressive realisation of rights.

Resources must be allocated carefully by States, taking account of the fact that the rights of all vulnerable and disadvantaged groups must be realised to an equal degree as persons with disabilities. In other words, in the overall consideration of whether measures constitute a disproportionate burden, the Committee must consider the impact of limited resources on the enjoyment of socio-economic rights by non-disabled persons who are also in need. David Bilchitz asserts that this 'will usually mean under conditions of scarcity that each specific individual cannot claim their full entitlements under the right; but it also implies that each individual will be provided equally with some access to what resources allow [...].'[182] While the rights of disabled people will not take priority over those of other marginalised groups, States must recognise that the full realisation of socio-economic rights in the disability context will most likely require additional resources, as recognised by the UNCESCR in its General Comment 5 on Persons with Disabilities.[183]

There is no doubt that the division of resources between all groups in society will be a tricky one. That is where priority-setting comes into play. Although it is maintained that human rights should have equal priorities, one must acknowledge that States will make their own decisions regarding priority issues in a national context. Many important questions will arise in the context of priority-setting by States in implementation of the CRPD. In that regard, Jos Philips summaries the

---

182 D. Bilchitz, 'Towards a Reasonable Approach to the Minimum Core: Laying the Foundations for Socio-Economic Rights Jurisprudence' (2003) 19 *South African Journal on Human Rights* 1, at page 22.

183 In General Comment No. 5, the UNCESCR states that: 'The obligation in the case of such a vulnerable and disadvantaged group [as persons with disabilities]' is to take positive action to reduce structural disadvantages and to give appropriate preferential treatment to people with disabilities in order to achieve the objectives of full participation and equality within society for all persons with disabilities. This almost invariably means that additional resources will need to be made available for this purpose and that a wide range of specially tailored measures will be required.' [UNCESCR, General comment 5 on persons with disabilities: (1994) para. 9].

potential concerns that might arise into three categories.[184] The first question, he claims, 'is whether principled priority should be given to *certain human rights*, or general principles' over others?[185] One might question whether, for instance, certain rights which are preconditions for exercising other rights should be given ultimate priority. A second question that Philips poses in the overall context of priority-setting is whether it is possible to provide 'second-best specifications' of rights? He asks whether it would 'be (possible and) acceptable, say in situations of extreme resource limitations, to single out certain forms of communication and information, access to which is to receive priority?'[186] In other words, he asks whether a second-best threshold should be specified which tells us when a certain right counts as being minimally fulfilled? A third way to identify priorities in rights implementation according to Philips concerns 'not the priorities within human rights, but the priority that human rights *as a whole* ought to receive vis-a-vis other policy goals that a state may have.'[187] These are all critical questions, to which there is no definitive answer among scholars and human rights advocates alike. Indeed, without principled guidelines, one might argue that 'priority setting risks becoming an ad-hoc exercise, which may harm the cause of disabled persons as well as the cause of human rights'[188] more generally. It is argued here that it is essential to have some principles guiding human rights implementation. Hence the importance, among other things, of the minimum core of CRPD rights. At the same time, it is important not to adhere to rigid frameworks of implementation, given the diverse socio-economic contexts which are involved in implementing the Convention. This is why the types of criteria inherent in reasonableness review frameworks can serve to focus attention on the particular national context at issue and to allow the CRPD Committee to judge the diverging priority choices of States according to their overall reasonableness.

In the process of resource allocation, States must ensure transparency and cost-effectiveness. Under the overall heading of cost considerations, the CRPD Committee must look to the resource prioritisation and resource optimisation efforts of States. A review of resource prioritisation efforts will involve ensuring that States have done all in their power to safeguard necessary resources to implement disability rights. In order to ensure open and transparent resource allocation and expenditure in the realisation of socio-economic rights for all groups, national authorities should develop performance-based budgets.[189] Performance budgets seek to allocate resources for the achievement of certain objectives. Geoffrey Segal and Adam Summers define

184 J. Philips, 'Human Rights, the CRPD, and Priority-Setting' in J. Anderson and J. Philips (eds.), *Disability and Human Rights: Legal, Ethical and Conceptual Implications of the Convention on the Rights of Persons with Disabilities* (Netherlands Institute of Human Rights, SIM Special 35, 2012), at page 150/151.

185 Ibid, at page 150 [emphasis in original].

186 Ibid, at page 151.

187 Ibid, at page 151.

188 Ibid, at page 147.

189 For further information on performance-based budgets, see generally, R.D. Young, 'Performance-Based Budget Systems' Public Policy and Practice USC Institute for Public Service and Policy Research (2003); See also M. Robinson (ed.), *Performance Budgeting: Linking Funding and Results* (Palgrave Macmillan, New York, 2007).

performance budgeting as comprising three elements, namely: (i) the result (final income); (ii) the strategy (the different ways in which the final outcome can be achieved); and (iii) activity outputs (the activities conducted to achieve the final outcome).[190] Performance-based budgeting is result-oriented. By tying the rationale for specific activities to the end result, it is possible to assess the cost-effectiveness of measures taken relative to achieving the desired result for all those in need. States Parties to the CRPD should develop performance-based budgets to facilitate the realisation of all socio-economic rights and obligations under the Convention. States should also examine performance-based budgets corresponding to other areas of government expenditure in order to determine which areas of expenditure are not cost-effective. This will enable them to direct the necessary funds to socio-economic rights-related areas pertaining not only to disabled people but to all other groups. With regard to resource optimisation efforts, General Comment 3 of the UNCESCR (1990) highlights the fact that there should be 'an active programme of international assistance and cooperation on the part of all those States that are in a position to undertake one.'[191] In the case of a shortfall of funding, States Parties to the CRPD must, where necessary, have recourse to international assistance, as mandated by Article 32 of the Convention. Failure to do so would be indicative of a State not having taken appropriate or reasonable measures in the implementation of Convention rights.

Human rights treaty bodies cannot direct States as to how exactly they must allocate their resources. However, they can certainly assess the actions or inactions of States according to defined criteria. Moellendorf argues that a broad meaning must be given to the term 'available resources' if socio-economic rights 'are to guide policy rather than depend on it.'[192] The CRPD Committee should investigate the extent to which national authorities, in their efforts to use *all* available resources, reallocated resources from one segment of governmental expenditure to another (subject to their competency to do so) in order to ensure maximum efficiency in spending on socio-economic rights. Fons Coomans points to the fact that 'it is also possible to move resources from one sector within a governmental department to another, for example from higher education to primary education.'[193] Another option, he asserts, 'would be to move resources among social welfare budgets, say more resources for housing, less for social assistance.'[194]

190 G. Segal and A. Summers, Citizens' Budget Reports: Improving Performance and Accountability in Government, Reason Public Policy Institute, Policy Study No. 292 (March 2002), at page 4.

191 UNCESCR, General Comment 3 on the nature of States Parties' obligations (Article 2, para. 1, of the Covenant), (1990), adopted at the fifth session of the Committee on 14 December 1990, UN Doc. E/1991/23, para. 20.

192 D. Moellendorf, 'Reasoning About Resources: Soobramoney and the Future of Socio-Economic Rights Claims' (2008) 14 *South African Journal on Human Rights* 327, at page 332.

193 F. Coomans, 'Reviewing Implementation of Social and Economic Rights: An Assessment of the "Reasonableness" Test as Developed by the South African Constitutional Court' (2005) 65(1) *Heidelberg Journal of International Law* 175, at page 191.

194 Ibid.

Magdalena Sepúlveda Carmona notes that the requirement to realise rights to the maximum of available resources does not require a State 'to devote all the resources at its disposal, nor, obviously, does it require a State to devote resources that it does not have in order to fulfil these rights.'[195] Nevertheless, she states that 'it does impose limitations on a State's freedom to allocate resources.'[196] In the context of limited resources, the CRPD Committee will have to consider the extent to which States have used resources reasonably or wisely. In particular, the Committee must consider whether States have acted in a non-discriminatory or non-arbitrary manner and, of course, in a non-corrupt manner. This implies that any resources which States Parties to the CRPD have at their disposal should be used in the most efficient and effective way possible, including the identification by States of low cost alternative measures that can result in a similar facilitation of Convention rights. It is arguable that States should focus not only on increasing financial resources in the implementation of socio-economic rights. In addition, States will be expected to focus on the qualitative use of already available resources, such as natural, human, educational and regulatory resources.[197] In a similar vein to the duty to accommodate, additional resources may not even be required in certain instances and States may simply be required to utilise existing resources more efficiently. This type of review can be seen in the *TAC* case,[198] where the South African government argued that while the relevant medication itself could be provided at little or no cost, the true cost of the programme (in terms of counselling, testing, formula, and other administrative costs) would make a comprehensive roll-out too expensive. Notwithstanding the government's arguments, the High Court in *TAC* ordered the government to draw up a coherent plan, which would ensure efficient spending on priority areas and which would make it possible to obtain the further resources that were required for a nationwide programme (whether in the form of a reorganisation of priorities or by means of further budgetary allocations). The UNCESCR has also demonstrated this form of reasonableness review. In its concluding observations to Columbia, for instance, the Committee highlighted the practice of non-utilisation of budgeted items by the Colombian government in the field of social expenditure. The Committee expressed its concern at the disappointing results achieved by most governmental programmes to combat poverty and to improve living conditions, especially since funds allocated in the national budget for social expenditure had not been fully used for that purpose.[199]

---

195 M.M. Sepúlveda Carmona, *The Nature of the Obligations Under the International Covenant on Economic, Social and Cultural Rights*, School of Human Rights Research Series, Volume 18 (Intersentia, Antwerpen, 2003), at page 314.

196 Ibid.

197 On this point, see the article by Sigrun Skogly entitled 'The Requirement of Using the "Maximum Available Resources" for Human Rights Realisation: A Question of Quality as well as Quantity' (2012) 12(3) *Human Rights Law Review* 393.

198 The *TAC* case was discussed above in section 3.2.1.4.

199 In that regard, the Committee stated that 'it is anomalous that such levels of poverty should persist in a country with a steadily expanding economy.' [UNCESCR, Concluding observations to Colombia, adopted on 28 December 1995, UN Doc. E.C./1995/12, para. 9].

4.3.3. Equality Considerations

The CRPD Committee must view States' efforts in light of the balancing act which national authorities undertake between the rights and needs of all vulnerable and disadvantaged groups in terms of programme design and resource allocation. There is an innate relationship between the rights to equality and non-discrimination, on the one hand, and socio-economic rights, on the other hand. Inequality is both a cause and a manifestation of the lack of enjoyment of socio-economic rights by disadvantaged groups. In other words, the equality norm is a vital means by which socio-economic rights are realised to their fullest extent in the context of marginalised groups and socio-economic rights are an integral means by which systemic disadvantage and inequalities are addressed. Systemic inequalities have prevented, and continue to prevent, persons with disabilities from enjoying their rights on an equal basis with others. For instance, a lack of accessible buildings and transport (in the form of wheelchair ramps, for instance) impairs the realisation of many socio-economic rights for persons with disabilities. Failure to make transport accessible often results in denial of the rights to education and work for disabled people, who cannot access the workplace or school buildings without being able to use transport to get there. Even if transport is accessible, a lack of accessible buildings causes further disadvantage as it means that persons with disabilities are prevented from entering the building in question. Moreover, disability discrimination is exacerbated by the high incidence of poverty amongst disabled individuals,[200] who usually lack the financial resources to counteract the disadvantage which they suffer. The UNCESCR recognises the inextricable link between the principle of equality and the realisation of socio-economic rights.[201] The UNCESCR's 2007 statement outlining the guiding criteria for interpreting the reasonableness standard incorporated in Article 8(4) of the OP-ICESCR also emphasises the principles of non-discrimination and equality.[202] Despite the fact that equality and non-discrimination are a dominant theme generally in the UN system, the intersection of equality and socio-economic rights adjudication has been quite limited. Some of the South African cases under the reasonableness approach incorporate equality concerns, at least to some extent (as outlined above).[203] Sandra Liebenberg and Beth Goldblatt explore the potential for a greater interrelationship between equality and socio-economic rights under South Africa's transformative Constitution. The authors contend that:

> An approach to the interpretation of equality and socio-economic rights that acknowledges the interrelationship between these rights is [...] more likely to be responsive to the reality that the most severe forms of disadvantage are usually experienced as a result

---

[200] See generally, J. Braithwaite and D. Mont, *Disability and Poverty: A Survey of World Bank Poverty Assessments and Implications* (World Bank, February 2008), available at http://siteresources.worldbank.org/DISABILITY/Resources/280658-1172608138489/WBPovertyAssessments.pdf last accessed 12 January 2015.

[201] The UNCESCR has stated that non-discrimination and equality 'are essential to the exercise and enjoyment of economic, social and cultural rights.' [UNCESCR, General Comment 20: Non-Discrimination in Economic, Social and Cultural Rights (Article 2, para. 2) (2009), para. 2].

[202] See section 3.3 of this chapter.

[203] See generally section 3.2 of this chapter.

> of an intersection between group-based forms of discrimination and socio-economic marginalisation.[204]

The interdependence and interrelatedness of civil and political rights and economic, social and cultural rights is a fundamental tenet of international human rights law. Nowhere is this interdependence more obvious than in the context of the CRPD. Maintaining strict distinctions between civil and political rights and socio-economic rights is not helpful in the context of the CRPD as many of the substantive articles in the Convention contain elements of both types of rights and can be termed 'hybrid' rights. The right to education, for example, includes both an immediate dimension – in its requirement that persons with disabilities are not excluded from the general education system on the basis of disability[205] – and various progressive dimensions – in its requirement that persons with disabilities be given the opportunity to learn life and social development skills.[206] Many CRPD rights are a unique fusion of equality rights and traditional socio-economic rights. Several substantive rights which fall under the traditional category of economic, social and cultural rights (such as the rights to education and employment) contain reasonable accommodation requirements. This injects an element of immediacy into the realisation of those rights. On that basis, it is submitted that the right to equality – namely, the idea that all human beings are equal both in terms of substantive rights and in dignity – may provide an important key to advancing socio-economic claims under the CRPD.

In any analysis of the reasonableness of measures taken by States under the CRPD, it is important to bear in mind the overall objectives of the Convention, together with the underlying principles guiding realisation of the rights contained in the CRPD, as this will provide context for the implementation of the substantive rights and obligations in the Convention. This contextual approach to reasonableness would appear to be confirmed by the comments of the HRC, which has affirmed that any assessment of measures taken by States must be both purposive and contextual and that State policies must be consistent with the purpose of the Covenant read as a whole.[207] The contextual approach to assessing the reasonableness of State measures is also confirmed by Louise Arbour, United Nations High Commissioner for Human Rights. She observes that '[t]he role of an international quasi-judicial review mechanism is not to prescribe policy measures, but rather to assess the reasonableness of such measures in view of the object and purpose of the treaty.'[208]

---

204 S. Liebenberg and B. Goldblatt, 'The Interrelationship between Equality and Socio-Economic Rights under South Africa's Transformative Constitution' (2007) 23 *South African Journal on Human Rights* 335, at page 339.

205 UN CRPD, Article 24(2)(a).

206 UN CRPD, Article 24(3).

207 In the individual communication of *Sandra Lovelace v Canada*, the HRC was of the view that statutory restrictions affecting the right to residence on a reserve of a person belonging to a minority, must have both a reasonable and objective justification and be consistent with the other provisions of the Covenant, read as a whole [Human Rights Committee, *Sandra Lovelace v Canada* (1981) Communication No R.6/24, (Thirty-sixth session, 1981), U.N. Doc Supp. No. 40 A/36/40].

208 Louise Arbour, former United Nations High Commissioner for Human Rights, Opening statement, fourth session, 16 July 2007, available at www.ohchr.org/EN/NewsEvents/Pages/DisplayNews.aspx?NewsID=6011&LangID=E last accessed last accessed 10 December 2014.

Furthermore, as highlighted above, reasonableness review in the South African context constitutes an assessment of measures taken by States based on the values underlying the Constitution. The Court in *Khosa* pointed to the fact that:

> When the rights to life, dignity and equality are implicated in cases dealing with socio-economic rights, they have to be taken into account along with the availability of human and financial resources in determining whether the State has complied with the constitutional standard of reasonableness.[209]

Of course, in order to factor in equality considerations, one must designate a comparator. In the context of persons with disabilities, the comparator is clear. The overall aim of the CRPD is to ensure equalisation of opportunities for persons with disabilities, as well as *de facto* equality in the exercise and enjoyment of all rights[210] on an equal basis with others. The 'others' in this respect are made up of non-disabled people.[211] On this very point certain scholars have argued that, because equality is a comparative notion, it does not provide a substantive standard against which to measure the adequate fulfilment of socio-economic rights.[212] On the contrary, it is argued here that the overall framework of the CRPD makes it perfectly clear that equality can be a standard against which to measure the full and effective realisation of socio-economic rights. Most obviously, the inclusion of equality concerns in the Convention's socio-economic rights (via the duty to accommodate) mandates the consideration of equality as an integral part of the fulfilment process. One must, of course, be clear on what exactly is being equalised, whether in terms of resources, capabilities or other (such as welfare). Under the CRPD, persons with disabilities are entitled to measures to ensure equalisation of opportunities and also to ensure that *de facto* equality is realised. Reasonable accommodations seek to ensure equality of opportunity and also *de facto* equality, to varying extents. In addition to reasonable accommodation measures, States must also take other steps, within available resources, to ensure the facilitation of the capabilities of persons with disabilities and to ensure that the goal of *de facto* equality is realised. If a given State has available resources, then it must necessarily allocate those resources to disability rights and must balance this with equal consideration of the rights of other groups. As already noted at various junctures throughout this book, disability rights may require additional resources in many instances (over and above those required for other groups) and if that is the case then States must allocate those additional resources where they are available to the State. This is where the Committee's assessment of cost considerations and disproportionate burden will come into play. In many instances, the application of the equality norm in the disability context may not be prohibitively expensive for a State. Former UN Commissioner on Human Rights, Louise Arbour, points to the fact that 'many aspects of economic, social and cultural

---

209 See the *Khosa* judgment at para. 44.

210 See Article 1 of the CRPD.

211 In certain instances, disabled people may merely require equality with other disabled persons.

212 See, for instance, A. van der Walt, 'A South African Reading of Frank Michelman's Theory of Social Justice' in H. Botha, A van der Walt and J. van der Walt (eds.) *Rights and Democracy in a Transformative Constitution* (Sun Press Stellenbosch, 2003)163, at pages 174–176.

rights can be respected at little or no additional expense through simple regulatory changes or through the provision of a remedy to an aggrieved individual.'[213]

In its assessment of reasonableness, the Committee will have to monitor carefully the interaction between the application of the Convention's equality and non-discrimination norms and the implementation of socio-economic rights in particular. Among other things, the Committee will have to ask itself whether, in the implementation of socio-economic rights, disabled people have been granted equality before and under the law, equal benefit and equal protection of the law. The Committee will also have to investigate if, and to what extent, affirmative action has been taken to guarantee equal access for persons with disabilities to socio-economic rights. In addition, the Committee should keep a close eye on the provision of reasonable accommodations as a means to ensuring substantive equality via the socio-economic rights contained in the Convention. While equality considerations are vital in the context of such a disadvantaged group as persons with disabilities, that is not to say that equality concerns are not important in analysing socio-economic rights provision for other disadvantaged groups. However, the particular nature of impairment and the substantive disadvantage faced by disabled persons necessitates an approach which begins from an equality perspective. There are many recognised benefits to including equality as a relevant criterion in the assessment of measures taken by States.[214] Adopting an equality perspective would serve to enrich socio-economic claims and would mean that States will be required to provide heightened justifications for any alleged rights' violations. This is particularly so in circumstances where denying access to the right(s) in question would cause further entrenchment of inequalities or marginalisation for persons with disabilities. Integration of an equality perspective would also serve to ensure a deeper understanding of the actual rights' violations experienced by persons with disabilities and the multi-dimensional disadvantage which results in deprivation of the enjoyment and exercise of socio-economic rights at many levels in the disability context. Moreover, adopting an equality perspective would endeavour to ensure that disabled individuals benefit equally to their non-disabled counterparts in terms of access to socio-economic rights. As Sandra Liebenberg and Beth Goldblatt have argued:

> An approach to socio-economic rights that is blind to the disparate ways in which a lack of access to social services and economic resources affect different groups, and the consequent need for remedial programmes which take account of these differences, [would] curtail the transformative potential [of socio-economic rights jurisprudence].[215]

---

213 Statement by Ms. Louise Arbour, High Commissioner for Human Rights to the third session of the Open-Ended WG OP ICESCR, available at www.ohchr.org/EN/NewsEvents/Pages/DisplayNews.aspx?NewsID=6011&LangID=E last accessed 10 December 2014.

214 See generally S. Liebenberg and B. Goldblatt, 'The Interrelationship between Equality and Socio-Economic Rights under South Africa's Transformative Constitution' (2007) 23 *South African Journal on Human Rights* 335, at pages 351–352.

215 Ibid, at page 351.

In sum, it is argued here that there is increased scope to develop the interaction between equality and socio-economic rights adjudication generally, but in particular in the context of the CRPD, given the prominence of the duty to accommodate in the Convention's socio-economic provisions and the acute disadvantage encountered by disabled individuals. In any consideration of the core principle of equality, one must also factor into account dignity concerns as the two go hand in hand. An approach based on equality would renew the focus on the inherent dignity of persons with disabilities. This would help to overturn the countless stereotypes of disabled people as lacking capabilities which can be developed (if provided with sufficient resources or other assistance).

4.3.4. Dignity Considerations

The concept of human dignity forms an integral part of the South African Constitutional Court's reasonableness approach to socio-economic rights adjudication. In *Grootboom*, the Court confirmed that reasonableness must be read, not only in light of the Constitution as a whole, but also in light of the inherent dignity of individuals.[216] There has been some criticism of the use of what is perceived to be the rather vague notion of human dignity as a guiding value in the context of South African equality jurisprudence. Sandra Liebenberg classifies the critiques into three main categories.[217] The first 'relates to the alleged indeterminacy of human dignity as a normative concept'[218] and the fact that 'dignity is too vague and multifaceted a concept to serve us well as a guiding value in equality jurisprudence.'[219] The second critique, according to Liebenberg, relates to the fact that 'human dignity as a value is irrevocably linked with the protection of freedom and autonomy. As such, it serves to discourage the positive, redistributive measures needed to remedy conditions such as material inequality and disadvantage.'[220] Related to that is the third critique, which Liebenberg posits is encapsulated in Catherine Albertyn and Beth Goldblatt's argument that the use of dignity as a core concept promotes an individual, as opposed to, 'a group-based understanding of material advantage and disadvantage.'[221]

With regard to the first criticism of human dignity as a guiding value in socio-economic rights adjudication, it is argued here that rather than it being an indeterminate norm, it is quite clear what human dignity entails at the level of international human rights law, particularly under the CRPD. There are two strands

216 The Court stated that 'it is fundamental to an evaluation of the reasonableness of state action that account be taken of the inherent dignity of human beings [...] [*Grootboom*, para. 83].

217 S. Liebenberg, 'The Value of Human Dignity in Interpreting Socio-Economic Rights' (2005) 21 *South African Journal on Human Rights* 1, at page 5.

218 Ibid.

219 Ibid, referring to D. Davis, 'Equality: The Majesty of Legoland Jurisprudence' (1999) 116 *South African Law Journal* 398.

220 S. Liebenberg, 'The Value of Human Dignity in Interpreting Socio-Economic Rights' (2005) 21 *South African Journal on Human Rights* 1, at page 5.

221 Ibid, citing C. Albertyn and B. Goldblatt, 'Facing the Challenge of Transformation Difficulties in the Development of an Indigenous Jurisprudence of Equality' (1998) 14 *South African Journal of Human Rights* 248, at pages 257–258.

to the concept of human dignity in human rights law generally, and particularly dignity as a guiding value under the CRPD. The first strand of human dignity requires that consideration be given to the urgency of needs of different groups and that States respond accordingly. This interpretation can be garnered from the various pronouncements of the human rights treaty bodies relating to the necessity to cater for the needs of those in most dire circumstances. It is also confirmed by the *Grootboom* standard of reasonableness.[222] The second strand of human dignity at the international level, particularly in light of the entry into force of the CRPD, goes beyond catering to urgent needs and imposes a higher threshold on States. It involves an alignment with the equality norm and requires consideration of the equal worth of all human beings. This is similar to what Liebenberg terms 'treatment as an equal.'[223] She states that 'treatment as an equal requires full acknowledgment of the racial, gender, social, economic, cultural and other differences between groups in society.'[224] Accordingly, she observes that 'the quest for equal worth or dignity is not a quest for uniformity, but a quest to eliminate the disadvantages and inferior status that attach to membership of particular groups.'[225] In this sense, dignity is aligned with substantive and transformative equality. At the level of international human rights law, this interpretation of human dignity is justified, and clearly mandated, by the shift from a formal to a substantive, and later to a transformative approach, to equality (both in the core treaties themselves and also in the general comments and concluding observations of the human rights treaty bodies). In order to give effect to such approaches to equality, this requires consideration of the equal worth of all human beings, together with the particular contextual disadvantage faced by marginalised groups. Interestingly, some of the equality case law of the South African Constitutional Court also subscribes to this approach to human dignity. The Court affirms that equal moral worth requires treatment as an equal, as opposed to equal treatment.[226] Notwithstanding all of the above, it is important to note, as Sandra Fredman does, that the use of the notion of dignity in the application of the right to equality has 'in practice been highly problematic.'[227] This is because:

> Courts in several jurisdictions have tended to regard dignity as an independent element in discrimination law, requiring a claimant to prove not just that she has been disadvantaged, but that this signifies lack of respect of her as a person.[228]

---

222 In that case, the Court held that the Government's housing programme did not cater for groups in urgent need. In that regard, the Court stated that 'those whose needs are most urgent and whose ability to enjoy all rights therefore is most in peril, must not be ignored by the measures aimed at achieving the realisation of the right. [*Grootboom*, para. 44].

223 S. Liebenberg, 'The Value of Human Dignity in Interpreting Socio-Economic Rights' (2005) 21 *South African Journal on Human Rights* 1, at page 14.

224 Ibid.

225 Ibid.

226 Ibid, citing Prinsio v Van der Linde (1997) 3 SA 1012 (CC), at para. 32.

227 S. Fredman, 'Substantive Equality Revisited' Legal Research Paper Series, Paper No. 70/2014 (October 2014), at page 19, citing C. Albertyn and B. Goldblatt, *Facing the Challenge of Transformation: Difficulties in the Development of an Indigenous Jurisprudence on Equality* (1998) 14(2) South African Journal of Human Rights 248.

228 S. Fredman, 'Substantive Equality Revisited' Legal Research Paper Series, Paper No. 70/2014 (October 2014), at page 19.

Accordingly, Fredman notes that 'the right to equality cannot simply be collapsed into the right to dignity.'[229] It is therefore important to ensure that the notion of human dignity is applied carefully, in conjunction with the right to equality, in any assessment made by the CRPD Committee of measures adopted by States.

The other two interrelated criticisms of human dignity as a guiding norm in socio-economic rights adjudication are debunked by Liebenberg. Drawing on Nussbaum's capabilities approach, Liebenberg argues that the ambit of human dignity is 'by no means confined to subjective personality issues.'[230] She states that dignity derives from the 'central idea that we show respect for human potential and agency by creating an environment of basic liberties and material support which enables [disadvantaged groups] to flourish.'[231] Therefore, she argues that it can be used as a norm to tackle 'conditions of material disadvantage and its impact on different groups in our society.' Liebenberg puts forward an approach to dignity as a 'relational value,'[232] according to which 'we are interconnected human beings.'[233] She states that 'to value human dignity is not to create zero-sum trade-offs between negative liberty and welfare, but to constitute positive social relationships which both respect autonomy and foster the conditions in which it can flourish.'[234] By that token, she claims that 'dignity as a relational value can help us to perceive the limits of individual claims on social resources with reference to the needs and equal worth of others and the available resources of the society.'[235]

As demonstrated in previous chapters of this book, the CRPD is built around the central notion that persons with disabilities must be enabled to develop their capabilities and human potential. Responsibility lies on national authorities to provide the material support necessary to ensure that this is possible. On that basis, and in spite of the many criticisms of its use as a normative standard for human rights protection, it is submitted here that the core norm of human dignity can provide some insight into the realisation of the substantive rights and obligations contained in the CRPD. Of course, any consideration of the dignity interests of persons with disabilities must naturally be balanced against cost considerations (taking into account what constitutes a disproportionate burden for a particular State). Nonetheless, if we subscribe to Liebenberg's theory that human dignity is a relational value, which can help us to perceive the limits of individual claims on social resources with reference to the needs and equal worth of others and the available resources of the society, this should facilitate a balancing act between the rights of persons with disabilities and the rights of all other groups in society.

---

229 Ibid, at page 20.

230 S. Liebenberg, 'The Value of Human Dignity in Interpreting Socio-Economic Rights' (2005) 21 *South African Journal on Human Rights* 1, at page 9.

231 Ibid, at page 8.

232 Ibid, at page 11.

233 Ibid.

234 Ibid.

235 Ibid.

In the case of *Law v Canada (Minister of Employment and Immigration)*,[236] the Canadian Supreme Court notes that 'there can be different conceptions of what human dignity means.' The Court states that for the purpose of analysis under Section 15(1) of the Canadian Charter (whose equality guarantee has been interpreted in a substantive manner[237] and is concerned with the realisation 'of personal autonomy and self-determination'[238]), 'human dignity means that an individual or group feels self-respect and self-worth. It is concerned with physical and psychological integrity and empowerment.' The Court further observes that 'human dignity is harmed by unfair treatment premised upon personal traits or circumstances which do not relate to individual needs, capacities, or merits' and, furthermore, that 'it is enhanced by laws which are sensitive to the needs, capacities, and merits of different individuals, taking into account the context underlying their differences.'[239] All of this begs the question: what does dignity actually mean in the disability context and, in particular, with regard to the progressive realisation of CRPD rights? Dignity considerations under the CRPD must be examined from both perspectives outlined above. Firstly, the CRPD Committee must analyse measures taken by States relative to the urgency of needs in question. A consideration of human dignity requires, at its most basic level, that the needs of disabled persons who are in most dire circumstances must be catered for first and foremost (and of course that the needs of all other individuals who find themselves in dire circumstances must be catered for to the same extent). Thereafter, dignity should feature as an equality concern, whereby the full realisation of socio-economic rights under the CRPD takes account of the equal worth of persons with disabilities and their entitlement to enjoy rights on an equal basis with others. States must ensure to implement CRPD rights in a manner which respects the differential characteristics of persons with disabilities and gives sufficient consideration to their inherent dignity. Advancing this interpretation of human dignity does not alter the nature of State obligations or overly expand them. The obligations of States are laid out very clearly in the CRPD. The concept of human dignity lies at the core of the Convention. It features not only in the object and purpose of the CRPD, but also in the General Principles. General Principle 3(a) of the Convention mandates respect for the inherent dignity, individual autonomy (including the freedom to make one's own choices) and independence of persons with disabilities.[240] The focus on human dignity is carried through to General Principle 3(d) which mandates 'respect for difference and acceptance of persons with disabilities as part of human diversity and humanity.'[241] As outlined in chapter four of this book, the dignity interests of persons with disabilities can be deemed to form part of the outer limits of the duty to accommodate in the sense that an accommodation which is not effective (or indeed failure to provide any accommodation at all) will not cater for the inherent dignity of a disabled individual in terms of severe marginalisation and exclusion from the enjoyment of rights. The socio-economic provisions of the CRPD are effectively

236 *Law v Canada (Minister of Employment and Immigration)* [1999] 1 S.C.R. 497.
237 See chapter 3 of this book, section 4.2.2.
238 *Law v Canada (Minister of Employment and Immigration)* [1999] 1 S.C.R. 497, para. 53.
239 Ibid.
240 UN CRPD, General Principle 3(a).
241 UN CRPD, General Principle 3(d).

based on the foundational values of human dignity, equalisation of opportunities and *de facto* equality. That is not tantamount to saying that disabled people have an immediate right to all of the socio-economic guarantees contained in the Convention. It does mean, however, that in implementing the Convention's socio-economic provisions, disabled persons must not be granted a lesser enjoyment of human rights in comparison with non-disabled people. For instance, if an entity or a State is taking measures to ensure fulfilment of the right to education for children with disabilities, they must ensure that disabled children are treated with equal concern and respect as all other children. Children with disabilities should not be expected to exercise their rights in conditions which are degrading or humiliating. Another example concerns the implementation of the accessibility obligation in Article 9 of the CRPD. When States are implementing accessibility in the context of public buildings, they should ensure that disabled people can access physical structures by the same means as non-disabled people (in other words, disabled people should not be forced to resort to entering through the back entrance of buildings or otherwise be forced to use structures in a degrading manner). Indeed, guaranteeing *de facto* equality necessitates consideration of the inherent dignity of disabled individuals. Therefore, human dignity and the human rights model of disability in the CRPD should certainly feature in the Committee's assessment of the reasonableness of measures taken by States Parties to the Convention.

4.3.5. The Impact of Failure to Take Measures

As stated above, the effectiveness of measures taken by States should be a key criterion in any assessment of reasonableness. What then of failure on the part of States to take any measures at all? Traditionally, under international human rights law, a failure to take measures would not have qualified as a breach of State obligations under the relevant treaty. The introduction, in 1997, of the *Maastricht Guidelines*[242] altered that traditional view by distinguishing between State violations through acts of commission[243] and violations through acts of omission.[244] With respect to the latter type of violations, the Guidelines provide that violations of economic, social, cultural rights can also occur through the omission or failure of States to take necessary measures stemming from legal obligations. Examples of such violations include: (i) the failure to take appropriate steps as required under the Covenant;[245] (ii) the failure to enforce legislation or put into effect policies designed to implement provisions of the Covenant;[246] and; (iii) the failure to implement without delay a right which it is required by the Covenant to provide immediately.[247] If a failure to take measures in one context leads to depriving persons with disabilities of what may be essential to enable them to enjoy other rights vested in them under the Convention (as

242 *Maastricht Guidelines on Violations of Economic, Social and Cultural Rights, Maastricht,* January 22–26, 1997.

243 Ibid, Guideline 14.

244 Ibid, Guideline 15.

245 Ibid, Guideline 15(a).

246 Ibid, Guideline 15(c).

247 Ibid, Guideline 15(h).

was the case in the *Khosa* judgment), then this might lead to a finding that national authorities acted unreasonably or unfairly in the circumstances and consequently this may lead to a breach of the Convention. In the *Khosa* case, the exclusion of non-nationals from social security provisions was found to have had a grave effect on the life and dignity of the individuals concerned, as well as on the right to equality. As a result, it was deemed not to constitute a reasonable measure under the South African Constitution.

It was shown in chapter four of this book that the benefits of inclusion and the stigmatisation costs of not providing a requested accommodation to a disabled person should be taken into account as a relevant consideration under the outer limits of the duty to accommodate. In a similar vein, the benefits of inclusion and participation (as a guiding principle of the CRPD)[248] and the stigmatisation costs of failure to take measures should be included as a consideration in any analysis of the measures taken by States Parties to the CRPD. The overall substantive and transformative equality framework of the Convention seeks to target the exclusion and systemic disadvantage experienced by persons with disabilities. If a given State fails completely to take measures, one must necessarily examine the impact of this on the further entrenchment of inequality for persons with disabilities. As always, this consideration will be subject to an examination of cost – whether the particular measures impose a disproportionate burden on a State. Nonetheless, it is arguable that where inequality becomes even more embedded by a State's failure to take any measures at all, there must at least be an obligation incumbent on the State concerned to find low-cost alternative solutions to avoid or mitigate such inequality.

4.3.6. Participatory Processes/Accountability

The model of reasonableness review adopted by the South African Constitutional Court has been criticised for 'failing to give adequate weight to the perspective and voice of rights claimants and their communities in the application of human rights norms to particular contexts and in the implementation of appropriate remedies.'[249] Bruce Porter quotes Marius Pieterse, who has raised important concerns that the model of reasonableness review, as currently formulated by the South African Constitutional Court:

> Appears to divert the bulk of the dialogue over the meaning of socio-economic rights to the political process, to silence the voices of certain vital participants to the dialogue and to restrict the judicial role in the overarching societal discussion over the means and ends of transformation.[250]

---

248 See General Principle 3(c) of the CRPD which mandates 'full and effective participation and inclusion in society.'

249 B. Porter, 'The Reasonableness of Article 8(4) – Adjudicating Claims from the Margins' (2009) 27(1) *Nordisk Tidsskrift for Menneskerettigheter* 39, at page 52.

250 Ibid, citing Marius Pieterse: 'On "Dialogue," 'Translation' and 'Voice': Reply to Sandra Liebenberg' in S. Woolman & M. Bishop (eds.) *Constitutional Conversations* (Pretoria University Law Press, Pretoria, 2008) at page 33.

Any form of reasonableness review at the international level should respect the fundamental notion of participatory processes, both in the context of interpreting and applying Article 8(4) of the OP-ICESCR and in any analysis by the CRPD Committee of the reasonableness of measures adopted by States. Indeed, this element of participatory processes is even more fundamental in the context of a human rights treaty such as the CRPD. This is because General Obligation 4(3) of the Convention recognises the pivotal importance of participation of persons with disabilities and their representative organisations in every aspect of implementation of the Convention.[251] In addition, a review of 'process' will be particularly important in the context of the equality dimension of reasonableness review under the CRPD. Substantive and transformative equality frameworks require that efforts are made by States to involve affected groups to an adequate degree.

It will be essential to ensure that the participatory mandate of the CRPD is taken into account in any assessment by the Committee of the measures taken by States. The Committee will have to ask whether the State has, for instance, consulted with disabled people and their representative organisations and involved them actively in a participatory process of reform of social structures? Of course, the individualised duty to accommodate already mandates a constructive dialogue between the particular entity and the disabled individual in question. In implementing the other provisions of the Convention, disabled persons themselves are best placed to inform national authorities regarding the appropriateness of measures taken in realising the Convention's provisions. A consultative process of exchange of views would be much more likely to evidence the fact that measures taken by States are appropriate in conception and implementation and, moreover, are in compliance with the Convention. By undertaking a participatory process of reform, transparency and accountability will be enhanced. Participatory processes of reform will also seek to ensure that the views of disabled persons are taken into account in the assessment of the likely human rights impact of the proposed measures. Involving disabled people in the reform process will also facilitate ideas for alternative measures (perhaps even low-cost alternatives). It should also help governments in weighing up the various governmental priorities and necessary trade-offs (when balancing the various interests and burdens at stake). Importantly, it would also serve to ensure that remedies are moulded to address the particular needs and contextual background against which claims have been advanced. As noted above, when States are choosing between various options to achieve policy goals, they must choose the option which is both effective and which least inhibits the human rights of disabled people as laid down in the Convention. Therefore, a participatory process of reform would facilitate the effective implementation of human rights, by seeking to ensure that the measures adopted by States represent the least restrictive alternative for persons with disabilities, taking into account their inherent dignity.

251 General Obligation 4(3) of the Convention mandates that persons with disabilities should be consulted closely and actively involved, through their representative organisations, 'in the development and implementation of legislation and policies to implement the present Convention, and in other decision-making processes concerning issues relating to persons with disabilities.'

4.3.7. *Third-Party Benefits*

As well as considering the costs imposed by particular measures on States or private entities, another potentially relevant (albeit tangential) consideration is the issue of the benefits of the requested measures accruing to persons other than the disabled individual in question. In chapter four above, it was highlighted that the issue of third-party benefits was a relevant consideration in some national jurisdictions with regard to the duty to accommodate. It was also noted that the benefits of requested accommodation measures to other persons with impairments was deemed to be a positive criterion which could be used to assess requested measures in a joint dissenting opinion issued by five CRPD Committee members in a 2014 decision on an individual communication.[252]

Translating this to the wider context of progressive realisation, one could argue that the CRPD Committee might also consider whether undertaking particular measures would have benefits to persons with comparative disabilities or even to a wider cohort of individuals, beyond disabled persons. This may be a factor mitigating against cost arguments advanced by States. In the context of the right to education, for instance, ensuring accessibility of the educational curriculum arguably benefits other students in terms of learning outcomes (both disabled students and non-disabled students). Therefore, measures taken to ensure accessibility of the curriculum could contribute to the implementation of the right to education for all. While the Committee will only be directly concerned with the rights of disabled people (and therefore the potential benefits to other individuals with comparative disabilities), it may factor such issues into the overall consideration of whether a measure constitutes a disproportionate burden for a State. Admittedly, this may be a difficult criterion for the Committee to weigh up in practice and it may choose to focus only on benefits accruing to individuals with comparative disabilities (if it chooses to incorporate third-party benefits into its analysis at all, that is).

5. Conclusion

There is no denying the fact that the implementation of socio-economic rights will be a heavy burden for States Parties to the CRPD and that overseeing this will be an onerous task for the CRPD Committee. Among other things, this chapter has outlined the balancing act that will take place regarding the burdens and interests of duty-bearers, on the one hand, and persons with disabilities, on the other hand. The

[252] The dissenting Committee members stated that even if reasonable accommodations are in principle an individual measure, 'the benefit for other employees with disabilities must also be taken into account when assessing reasonableness and proportionality' under the substantive articles of the Convention. [See paragraph 5 of the Joint opinion of Committee members Mr. Carlos Rios Espinosa, Ms. Theresia Degener, Mr. Munthian Buntan, Ms. Silvia Judith Quan-Chang and Ms. Maria Soledad Cisternas Reyes (dissenting) in the individual communication of *Marie-Louise Jungelin (represented by the Swedish Association of Visually Impaired Youth (US) and the Swedish Association of the Visually Impaired (SRF) v Sweden*, Communication No. 5/2011, views adopted by the Committee at its twelfth session (15 September–3 October 2014), decision adopted 2 October 2014].

overall aim of this chapter was to outline a framework for review of State measures, tailored to the underlying purposes and values in the CRPD.

This chapter began by highlighting the outer limits of the concept of progressive realisation, taking into account the fact that States must take steps to realise CRPD rights progressively to the maximum of their available resources. This chapter demonstrated the fact that while a minimum threshold approach for the assessment of socio-economic rights is essential in determining the normative content of rights and consequent State obligations, it is not sufficient, on its own, to guarantee the full and effective realisation of rights for marginalised groups, such as persons with disabilities. Other considerations are necessary in the assessment by human rights treaty bodies of the types of measures adopted by States to fulfil their obligations under the relevant treaty. Several frameworks of 'reasonableness review' at the national and international levels were therefore outlined. Reasonableness review seeks to ensure that any analysis of the content of the right or rights at issue is adjudicated upon not in relation to mechanical and abstract indicators but rather in relation to the disadvantaged group at issue. It was argued above that the types of criteria inherent in existing frameworks of reasonableness review would fit well in the assessment of measures taken by States to fulfil their obligations under the CRPD. In that regard, the criteria inherent in existing review frameworks were drawn on and tailored to the specific context of the CRPD.

The interconnectedness of the equality norm with the implementation of socio-economic rights was also the focus of attention throughout this chapter. The realisation of socio-economic rights is characterised by and, moreover, impaired substantially by high levels of inequality. The socio-economic provisions in the CRPD are linked intrinsically to the equality norm via the duty to accommodate. That duty seeks to ensure that all rights become available to persons with disabilities on an equal basis with others so that they can have meaningful fulfilled lives. Therefore, the outer limits of the duty to accommodate were drawn on in order to inject an additional equality perspective into socio-economic review of CRPD rights.

The review framework proposed in this chapter seeks to preserve some discretion for States to choose policies which give effect to socio-economic rights, while at the same time retaining the overall supervision of the CRPD Committee in deciding whether the measures taken are in compliance with the Convention. In its assessment, the Committee must balance cost-related factors against many other considerations. Limited resources and institutional constraints may allow entities or States to justify, to a certain extent, the lack of measures taken with regard to the realisation of socio-economic rights and obligations. However, there is also a duty incumbent on entities and States to give effect to CRPD rights by utilising whatever resources and capacity they have in a non-arbitrary and non-discriminatory manner – one which accords a sufficient degree of priority to the dignity rights of claimants, to the values underlying the Convention as a whole and to the overall object and purpose of the CRPD.

The CRPD is a progressive human rights treaty endorsing a substantive and transformative model of equality. Bruce Porter argues that 'substantive equality requires a recognition that to realise an equal right to effective remedies for all, [economic, social and cultural rights] adjudication may have to meet different needs and develop new approaches.'[253] It is submitted that the approach outlined in this chapter would provide a realistic framework for the CRPD Committee in its adjudication mandate. Such a framework could provide the Committee with the opportunity to merge considerations of individual rights' violations with broader issues of socio-economic inequalities. Of course, the Committee itself will ultimately draw the line in the sand as to the criteria that might satisfy the progressive implementation of rights contained in the Convention and whether measures adopted by States Parties actually comply with the obligations delineated in the CRPD. It is essential that the Committee would approach this review from the perspective of informed adjudication. States Parties to the CRPD will play an important role in providing the Committee with objective, transparent and reliable evidence of the broader socio-economic contextual factors which led to decision-making in any given case. This will include evidence regarding competing claims on resources and institutional limitations. States must justify the measures taken by them in accordance with defined criteria and measureable indicators set by the Committee. Most importantly of all, the Committee's review framework must be grounded in the normative content of the rights contained in the Convention (including the minimum core), together with an analysis of the broader object and purpose of the Convention. Equality should move to centre stage in socio-economic claims. This is particularly so where the claim has as its ultimate aim the achievement of positive benefits, as opposed to preventing negative deprivations of rights. It is only in this way that the spirit and tenor of the CRPD can become a reality for persons with disabilities, as the CRPD links explicitly States' obligations to eliminate disability discrimination with guarantees for the full realisation of socio-economic rights.

In the next chapter of this book, one particular obligation of progressive effect will be explored, namely the accessibility obligation under Article 9 of the CRPD. One of the objectives of that chapter will be to examine the relationship between equality and accessibility. The normative content of Article 9 of the Convention will also be outlined and the various criteria proposed in the present chapter will be applied to the progressive realisation of disability accessibility.

---

253 B. Porter, 'The Reasonableness of Article 8(4) – Adjudicating Claims from the Margins' (2009) 27(1) *Nordisk Tidsskrift for Menneskerettigheter* 39, at page 41.

Chapter 6
The Accessibility Obligation in the CRPD

'Article 9 of the Convention clearly enshrines accessibility as the precondition for persons with disabilities to live independently, participate fully and equally in society, and have unrestricted enjoyment of all their human rights and fundamental freedoms on an equal basis with others.'[1]

1. Introduction

This chapter will explore the Convention's accessibility obligation, contained in Article 9 of the CRPD. The accessibility obligation is a key underlying principle which spans the substantive rights in the Convention. It requires the removal of discriminatory barriers that prevent disabled people from gaining access to various social spheres – the physical environment, information and communications technology, goods, services and facilities, among others. The duty imposed on States to guarantee accessibility is integral to ensuring equalisation of opportunities for persons with disabilities and to increasing their participation and inclusion in society. Alongside the equality and non-discrimination norms, accessibility is a vital facilitator of the substantive rights in the Convention. Accessibility and equality are therefore closely interconnected in the disability context. However, there are also clear lines of distinction to be drawn between these core norms and the exact nature of the link between them requires further exploration.

The first objective of this chapter is to delineate the interrelationship between the accessibility obligation and the equality and non-discrimination norms in the CRPD. Another related objective of this chapter is to outline the normative content of Article 9 and to tease out States' obligations to realise progressively disability accessibility. In order to explore those issues, this chapter will be broken down into five principal sections. In section two of this chapter the general contours of Article 9 will be traced. Section three will contain an analysis of the nature of the interrelationship between accessibility and equality, including the duty to accommodate. In that respect, section three of this chapter will contain an overview of the commonalities and key differences between the accessibility obligation, on the one hand, and the equality and non-discrimination obligations, on the other hand. That section will also explore the issue as to whether there are circumstances in which inaccessible social structures might be deemed to be in violation not only of Article 9, but also

1 UN Committee on the Rights of Persons with Disabilities, General Comment No. 2 on Article 9 (Accessibility), adopted at the eleventh session of the Committee (30 March–11 April 2014) on 11 April 2014, UN Doc. CRPD/C/GC/2, para. 14.

to constitute a breach of the Convention's non-discrimination norm. In section four of this chapter the normative content of Article 9 will be highlighted and States' obligations of progressive realisation will be delineated. Also in section four of this chapter the various criteria for assessment of measures taken by States will be applied to Article 9 of the Convention. Finally, section five will contain concluding remarks.

2. The Accessibility Obligation: Article 9 of the CRPD

In this section of the chapter the accessibility obligation contained in Article 9 of the CRPD will be introduced. In addition, the principal objectives of Article 9 will be reflected upon, as well as the interaction between accessibility and access to rights generally.

2.1. Introduction to Accessibility under Article 9 of the CRPD

The CRPD's accessibility obligation requires States Parties to take:

> Appropriate measures to ensure to persons with disabilities access, on an equal basis with others, to the physical environment, to transportation, to information and communications, including information and communications technologies and systems, and to other facilities and services open or provided to the public, both in urban and in rural areas.[2]

The concept of accessibility is not completely new to international human rights law. In fact, in its General Comment 14 (on the right to health), the UNCESCR has delineated the obligations inherent in the notion of accessibility and, by that token, States' positive duties to provide access. The Committee laid out four overlapping dimensions of accessibility as follows:

i. Non-discrimination – which enshrines the idea that facilities, goods and services must be accessible to all people (in particular persons belonging to marginalised groups) on an equal basis or without discrimination.
ii. Physical accessibility – which encompasses the notion that facilities, goods and services should be physically accessible, within safe physical reach for all sections of the population, especially vulnerable or marginalised groups.
iii. Economic accessibility – which expresses the concept that facilities, goods and fees for essential services must be based on the principle of equity, such that they are affordable for all persons, including socially disadvantaged groups.
iv. Information accessibility – expressing the idea that accessibility includes the right to seek, receive and impart information and ideas.[3]

---

2 UN CRPD, Article 9.

3 UNCESCR, General Comment 14, The right to the highest attainable standard of health (Article 12 of the ICESCR), adopted on 11 August 2000 Twenty-second session, 2000, U.N. Doc. E/C.12/2000/4 (2000), para. 12.

The foregoing components of accessibility (as enumerated by the UNCESCR) clearly do not comprise a disability-specific understanding of the term 'accessibility,' unlike that enshrined in Article 9 of the CRPD. The various elements of accessibility outlined by the UNCESCR do however find themselves mirrored in the components of accessibility contained in Article 9. The CRPD's accessibility obligation requires States to ensure both physical and information accessibility for persons with disabilities and it is expected that the Convention's broad-ranging accessibility obligations can add considerable value to human rights law in that regard and that the CRPD Committee can contribute significantly to previous articulations by treaty bodies on such aspects of accessibility. The non-discrimination component of accessibility is enshrined in Article 9 via the obligation to ensure accessibility to persons with disabilities 'on an equal basis with others.' Finally, the economic dimension of accessibility is also relevant to the CRPD framework, considering that preambular paragraph (t) of the Convention highlights the fact that the majority of persons with disabilities live in conditions of poverty. In that regard, the Convention recognises the critical need to address the negative impact of poverty on persons with disabilities.

There has been much debate about the nature of accessibility as defined in Article 9 of the CRPD. The question arises as to whether it is a principle, a right or an obligation of the Convention or rather a precondition for full and equal participation of persons with disabilities in society? One might ask whether it is all of the above? It is submitted that the CRPD's accessibility provisions constitute both a general principle contained in Article 3(f) of the Convention, as well as a substantive obligation in Article 9. Accessibility is also a precondition for ensuring full and effective participation and inclusion in society of persons with disabilities. Both Articles 3 and 9 of the Convention have transversal application. This indicates the overarching role of accessibility in achieving the object and purpose of the CRPD – to promote, protect and ensure the full and equal enjoyment of all human rights and fundamental freedoms by all persons with disabilities, and to promote respect for their inherent dignity.[4] Accessibility also appears throughout the Convention on numerous other occasions, such as in preambular paragraph (v),[5] in several of the substantive rights,[6] as well as in some of the Convention's specific implementation measures.[7]

4 UN CRPD, Article 1.

5 UN CRPD, Preamble para.(v) recognises 'the importance of accessibility to the physical, social, economic and cultural environment, to health and education and to information and communication, in enabling persons with disabilities to fully enjoy all human rights and fundamental freedoms.'

6 See, for instance, CRPD, Article 21 on Freedom of Expression and Opinion and Access to Information.

7 See, for example, CRPD Article 31(3) which provides that States Parties shall assume responsibility for the dissemination of any statistics collected under that article and ensure their accessibility to persons with disabilities and others; See also CRPD, Article 32(1)(a) which provides that States will undertake appropriate and effective measures to ensure, *inter alia*, that international cooperation, including international development programmes, is inclusive of and accessible to persons with disabilities.

2.2. The Objective of Article 9 of the CRPD

The objective of Article 9 is stated expressly as being to enable persons with disabilities to live independently and to participate fully in all aspects of life.[8] Accessibility is interconnected very clearly with the concepts of participation and inclusion in society. Inaccessibility, owing to numerous barriers (legislative, environmental, technological and so forth) hinders full and effective participation and inclusion for persons with disabilities in society and hence the capacity to live independently. The concepts of independent living and participation are not defined in the CRPD. Independent living is a general principle,[9] as well as being a substantive right of the Convention.[10] The Preamble of the CRPD recognises the importance of individual autonomy, independence and the freedom of people with disabilities to make their own choices.[11] Under Article 19 (on the right to live independently and be included in the community), States are required to guarantee that persons with disabilities have the opportunity to choose their place of residence, where and with whom they live on an equal basis with others and that they are not obliged to live in a particular living arrangement.[12] Notably, Article 19 requires that persons with disabilities have access to a range of in-home, residential and other community support services and does not exclude the concept of personal assistance necessary to support living and inclusion in the community.[13] Article 19 also requires that community services and facilities for the general population are available on an equal basis to persons with disabilities and that they are responsive to their needs.[14] All of these requirements link to the overall obligation of accessibility imposed on States by Article 9. The duties imposed by the Convention's independent living provisions require the elimination of barriers to participation and inclusion in society, just like the accessibility obligation. Beyond the objective of ensuring independent living, Article 9 has the distinct aim of ensuring that persons with disabilities can participate fully in all aspects of life. While the concept of participation is not defined expressly by the Convention, chapter two of this book demonstrates the fact that participation is linked inextricably to inclusionary structures which comprise, among other things, the guarantee of access to participation in every area of life and the facilitation of people with disabilities to limit the impact of disability.[15] From a brief examination of the specific objectives of Article 9, it becomes very clear that the Convention's accessibility obligation requires the removal of obstacles and barriers to ensure equal access to, and enjoyment of, human rights for persons with disabilities. As Janet Lord observes:

---

8 UN CRPD, Article 9.

9 UN CRPD, Article 3(a).

10 UN CRPD, Article 19.

11 UN CRPD, Preamble para.(n).

12 UN CRPD, Article 19(a).

13 UN CRPD, Article 19(b).

14 UN CRPD, Article 19(c).

15 M. Jones, 'Inclusion, Social Inclusion and Participation' in M.H. Rioux, L.A. Basser and M. Jones (eds.), *Critical Perspectives on Human Rights and Disability Law* (Martinus Nijhoff, The Hague, 2011) at page 58.

> Accessibility is clearly inextricably linked to all the rights in the Convention, howsoever we may wish to characterize it as a free standing right, duty, set of obligations or a general principle or implementation measure or rights facilitator.[16]

This raises the important question as to the exact nature of the link between accessibility in Article 9 and access to rights for persons with disabilities.

2.3. Accessibility and Access to Rights

It is important to draw a clear distinction between the terms 'accessibility of' and 'access to' in the disability context.[17] As demonstrated above, the implementation of disability accessibility means guaranteeing the removal of discriminatory barriers which hinder independent living and full participation and inclusion of persons with disabilities in all aspects of society. Guaranteeing accessibility contributes to ensuring access to, as well as substantive enjoyment of rights, for persons with disabilities. The CRPD Committee conceptualises the link between 'accessibility' and 'access to' when it observes that 'the right to access for persons with disabilities is ensured through strict implementation of accessibility standards.'[18] However, it must be noted that while ensuring access to human rights for persons with disabilities includes the implementation of accessibility obligations, it is not limited to this. In other words, accessibility is a precondition for persons with disabilities to live independently, participate fully and equally in society. It is a vital means of ensuring access to, and enjoyment of rights, for persons with disabilities. However, it is not the only means of ensuring such and, furthermore, it does not result in the full enjoyment of rights in all cases. Beyond the adoption of accessibility measures, ensuring access to, and enjoyment of, rights is also linked closely with the provision of reasonable accommodations and other individualised measures, as well as positive action measures. In order for disabled individuals to be able to access and enjoy their right to independent living, for example, this may require the provision of individualised measures, such as reasonable accommodations, residential and community support services and personal assistance, as well as the adoption of accessibility measures. Making school buildings physically accessible will not result in the full enjoyment of the right to education in many cases – by simply being able to enter a building, this does not mean that all persons with disabilities will be able to access the right to education and to benefit from education provided. Students

---

16 J.E. Lord, 'Accessibility and Human Rights Fusion in the CRPD: Assessing the Scope and Content of the Accessibility Principle and Duty under the CRPD' Presentation for the General Day of Discussion on Accessibility, Un CRPD Committee, UN – Geneva, October 7, 2010, at page 18. available at www2.ohchr.org/SPdocs/CRPD/DGD7102010/.../JanetELord.doc last accessed 22 October 2014.

17 It is notable that in its General Comment 14, the UNCESCR speaks of accessibility generally and does not regard accessibility as being a disability-specific obligation. Accessibility in that context refers to the various means by which all individuals are granted access to human rights (such as through economic accessibility, information accessibility etc.).

18 UN Committee on the Rights of Persons with Disabilities, General Comment No. 2 on Article 9 (Accessibility), adopted at the eleventh session of the Committee (30 March–11 April 2014) on 11 April 2014, UN Doc. CRPD/C/GC/2, para. 14.

with disabilities may need other measures, such as reasonable accommodations and other individualised supports and assistance to ensure full access to, and enjoyment of, the right to education. Notably Article 9 of the CRPD does envisage some forms of individualised supports. Article 9(2)(e) requires States:

> To provide forms of live assistance and intermediaries, including guides, readers and professional sign language interpreters, to facilitate accessibility to buildings and other facilities open to the public.[19]

Furthermore, Article 9(2)(f) requires States 'to promote other appropriate forms of assistance and support to persons with disabilities to ensure their access to information.' However, these provisions do not cover the entire range of possible measures that can be taken to ensure access to rights by persons with disabilities. Ensuring access and enjoyment of rights on an equal basis with others may also require positive action measures. For instance, ensuring the equal participation of persons with disabilities in political life may necessitate positive action measures to remedy past and present discrimination and to militate against the long history of exclusion of persons with disabilities in that area. Moreover, ensuring access to, and enjoyment of, human rights for persons with disabilities may include general positive measures such as social benefits designed to ensure increased access for persons with disabilities to social protection, including social security, social assistance and healthcare, education and certain goods or services available to the general public.

On an examination of the Convention as a whole, the term 'access to' appears throughout many of the substantive rights in the Convention. It appears, *inter alia*, in Article 13 of the CRPD[20] (on access to justice), Article 19 of the CRPD[21] (on the right to live independently and be included in the community) and Article 27 of the CRPD[22] (on employment). The relationship between 'accessibility' and 'access to' can be seen in Article 30 of the CRPD (on participation in cultural life, recreation, leisure and sport).[23] That article requires States to recognise the right of persons with disabilities to take part on an equal basis with others in cultural life, and in that regard, it requires States to take *all appropriate measures* to ensure, *inter alia*, that persons with disabilities 'enjoy *access* to cultural materials in *accessible*

---

19 CRPD, Article 9(2)(e).

20 See Article 13(1) of the CRPD which requires States Parties to 'ensure effective access to justice for persons with disabilities on an equal basis with others, including through the provision of procedural and age-appropriate accommodations, in order to facilitate their effective role as direct and indirect participants, including as witnesses, in all legal proceedings, including at investigative and other preliminary stages.'

21 See Article 19(b) of the CRPD which requires States Parties to ensure that 'persons with disabilities have access to a range of in-home, residential and other community support services, including personal assistance necessary to support living and inclusion in the community, and to prevent isolation or segregation from the community.'

22 See Article 27(1)(d) of the CRPD which requires States Parties to 'enable persons with disabilities to have effective access to general technical and vocational guidance programmes, placement services and vocational and continuing training.'

23 See Article 30 (1) (a) of the CRPD which requires States Parties to ensure that people with disabilities 'enjoy access to cultural materials in accessible formats.'

formats'[24] and that they 'enjoy *access to* television programmes, films, theatre and other cultural activities, in *accessible* formats.'[25] Ensuring access to cultural materials and television programmes can be achieved through the implementation of the accessibility obligation. In conjunction with other measures, this would entail States Parties monitoring the implementation of disability accessibility standards in respect of media services in order to ensure that cultural material is provided in accessible formats. In its General Comment 2 the CRPD Committee makes a clear distinction[26] between the concept of accessibility in the CRPD and the right of access when it states that 'accessibility should be viewed as a disability-specific reaffirmation of the social aspect of the right of access.'[27] Accessibility is therefore clearly viewed by the Committee as an underlying principle and a vital precondition for ensuring equal access to human rights for persons with disabilities. This interrelationship becomes relevant when exploring the link between accessibility and other core concepts contained in the CRPD, specifically the equality and non-discrimination norms.

3. The Interrelationship Between Accessibility and Equality in the CRPD

In considering the nature and scope of disability accessibility under the CRPD, it is vital to consider the link between accessibility and other core concepts contained in the Convention as this will provide some insight into the progressive nature of the accessibility obligation. In this section of the chapter, the interrelationship between accessibility and the equality and non-discrimination norms in the CRPD will be delineated, including the interaction between accessibility and reasonable accommodation measures. The CRPD Committee had the opportunity to shed some light on the nature of States Parties' accessibility obligations under the Convention in its General Comment 2, in particular the manner in which disability accessibility relates to the Convention's equality and non-discrimination norms and, furthermore, whether there are any circumstances in which inaccessibility may amount to a breach of the non-discrimination norm. That general comment will be drawn on as an aid to interpretation throughout the sub-sections which follow.

---

24 UN CRPD, Article 30(1)(a).

25 UN CRPD, Article 30(1)(b) [emphasis added].

26 Notwithstanding the clear distinction between the terms 'accessibility of' and 'access to,' the nature of the difference between the two concepts is not always clear and they are often used interchangeably. This is evident from the *travaux préparatoires* of the CRPD, in which the terms 'access to' and 'accessibility of' were used interchangeably to address the obligation to ensure disability accessibility. During the negotiation sessions, National Human Rights Institutions confounded the two notions, by referring to a 'definition of access *or* accessibility.' [emphasis added] [Ad Hoc Committee on the Disability Convention, Daily Summaries, Sixth Session, Evening Session, 5 August 2005].

27 UN Committee on the Rights of Persons with Disabilities, General Comment No. 2 on Article 9 (Accessibility), adopted at the eleventh session of the Committee (30 March–11 April 2014) on 11 April 2014, UN Doc. CRPD/C/GC/2, para. 4.

3.1. The Nature of the Link between Accessibility and Equality

The interrelationship between the fundamental norms of accessibility and equality is evident from the text of Article 9 itself. Under Article 9(1), States are required to take 'appropriate measures' to ensure that persons with disabilities have 'access' to the built environment, to information, technology and other types of facilities and services. Importantly, States must ensure that access is provided 'on an equal basis with others.'[28] While the link between accessibility and equality clearly exists, the exact nature of that link is much less explicit. Persons with disabilities are denied equal enjoyment of their human rights owing, *inter alia*, to a lack of accessibility. Without accessible means of transport, for example, disabled individuals are not in a position to carry out meaningful work because they will not be able to gain access to the workplace in the first instance. The accessibility obligation in the CRPD can be viewed as a vital tool for ensuring the equalisation of opportunities for persons with disabilities. Rule 5 of the *United Nations Standard Rules on the Equalization of Opportunities for Persons with Disabilities* highlights the significance of the accessibility of the physical environment, transport, information and communications to the equalisation of opportunities and to effective participation of persons with disabilities in society.[29] The CRPD Committee also points to the fact that:

> Without access to the physical environment, to transportation, to information and communication, including information and communications technologies and systems, and to other facilities and services open or provided to the public, persons with disabilities would not have *equal opportunities for participation* in their respective societies.[30]

Accessibility and equality of opportunity are listed side-by-side[31] as general principles of the CRPD. Both accessibility and equality of opportunity have an overarching role to play in the implementation of the rights and obligations contained in the Convention. The question arises as to how the accessibility obligation relates to other facets of the CRPD's equality paradigm? The CRPD's substantive and transformative equality paradigm is premised on the notion that disabled people should not only have equal opportunities to their non-disabled peers but that they should have equality in fact. Accessibility clearly contributes to ensuring transformative equality for persons with disabilities, as it seeks to ensure fundamental changes in social structures. Article 9 of the CRPD is built on the social model of disability and the accessibility measures imposed on States Parties to the Convention are aimed at the removal of discriminatory barriers to independent living and full and effective

---

28 UN CRPD, Article 9(1).

29 Rule 5, *United Nations Standard Rules on the Equalization of Opportunities for Persons with Disabilities*, Resolution adopted by the General Assembly at the 48th Session [on the report of the Third Committee (A/48/627)], UN Document A/RES/48/96, 4 March 1994, available at http://www.un.org/esa/socdev/enable/dissre00.htm last accessed 18 July 2014.

30 UN Committee on the Rights of Persons with Disabilities, General Comment No. 2 on Article 9 (Accessibility), adopted at the eleventh session of the Committee (30 March–11 April 2014) on 11 April 2014, UN Doc. CRPD/C/GC/2, para. 1 [emphasis added].

31 Equality of opportunity is listed as a general principle in Article 3(e) UN CRPD and accessibility is listed as a general principle in Article 3(f) UN CRPD.

participation in society. Article 9 enumerates several positive duties designed to ensure equal access to the environment, technology etc. and, hence, enjoyment of a host of different human rights. On that basis, one could argue that the overall objective of Article 9 is to contribute to ensuring *de facto* equality. The accessibility obligation also relates to the Convention's substantive equality paradigm, including the duty to accommodate. It must be borne in mind that ensuring substantive equality in the disability context sometimes goes beyond the implementation of accessibility measures *per se* as the implementation of accessibility standards will not always result in *de facto* equality for every disabled individual. As an example of this, the CRPD Committee speaks of 'individuals who have rare impairments that were not taken into account when the accessibility standards were developed or do not use the modes, methods or means offered to achieve accessibility,'[32] such as those individuals who do not read Braille print, for example. While failure to cater for every rare disability in the implementation of accessibility standards may not mean that Article 9 has been breached, it may mean that the equality norm has been breached if other measures mandated by the Convention are not taken to ensure that persons with disabilities can exercise rights on an equal basis with others. An individualised substantive equality measure, such as reasonable accommodation, may be required to ensure equal access to rights and to allow the disabled individual in question to benefit from the human rights guarantees contained in the Convention. As outlined above, other forms of individualised assistance are envisaged under Article 9 of the Convention itself.[33] Individualised measures might include assistance provided by others, whether in the form of personal care, communication or advocacy support, learning support, therapeutic interventions and aids or adaptations to the physical environment, to equipment and so forth. All of these approaches may fall within either accessibility or reasonable accommodations, depending on the circumstances in which they are provided (whether of an individualised nature or a broad and generalised nature) and this demonstrates the interconnectedness of both types of measures in ensuring *de facto* equality. The CRPD Committee notes that:

> Part of the task of encompassing the diversity of persons with disabilities in the provision of accessibility is recognizing that some persons with disabilities need human or animal assistance in order to enjoy full accessibility (such as personal assistance, sign language interpretation, tactile sign language interpretation or guide dogs).[34]

Such forms of individualised assistance may therefore be used to bolster disability accessibility and, ultimately, equality. A related point is that accessibility measures are not designed to remedy all past or present inequalities experienced by disabled people. Even when accessibility standards are implemented by States, there will

[32] UN Committee on the Rights of Persons with Disabilities, General Comment No. 2 on Article 9 (Accessibility), adopted at the eleventh session of the Committee (30 March–11 April 2014) on 11 April 2014, UN Doc. CRPD/C/GC/2, para. 25.

[33] UN CRPD, Article 9(2)(e) and Article 9(2)(f).

[34] UN Committee on the Rights of Persons with Disabilities, General Comment No. 2 on Article 9 (Accessibility), adopted at the eleventh session of the Committee (30 March–11 April 2014) on 11 April 2014, UN Doc. CRPD/C/GC/2, para. 29.

often remain additional barriers for persons with disabilities in accessing and enjoying CRPD rights and, thereby, achieving equality in fact. Such instances of inequality may need to be remedied, for example, by the types of positive action measures envisaged under Article 5(4) of the Convention. Historical and ongoing disadvantage in schools might mean that persons with disabilities have not attained the same level of education as their non-disabled counterparts and therefore cannot progress in education or in the workplace. This disadvantage cannot be remedied fully by putting in place accessibility standards. Therefore, employers may need to offer access to training facilities for persons with disabilities or other forms of positive action to bolster equality.

It is clear that accessibility contributes greatly to the achievement of *de facto* equality for persons with disabilities and it is a central provision of the Convention. However, as shown above, it is not the only form of positive measure that can be taken to ensure true equality in every instance. It is important that States bear this in mind in the implementation of Article 9. Indeed, the CRPD Committee notes that the duty on States to provide accessibility 'is an essential *part* of the new duty to respect, protect and fulfil equality rights.'[35] Accessibility may therefore be viewed as one part of ensuring fulfilment of the right to equality but it does not complete the whole picture.

Having traced the general contours of the link in the CRPD between the accessibility obligation and the equality and non-discrimination norms, further discrete aspects of that link will be considered in the subsections which follow.

3.2. Inaccessibility as a Breach of the Non-Discrimination Norm?

Article 9 itself does not elaborate on the circumstances in which inaccessible social structures may amount to a breach of Article 5 of the Convention. The CRPD Committee had the opportunity, in its General Comment 2, to clarify the nexus between accessibility and equality in order to assist States in meeting their obligations under the Convention. In that general comment, the Committee stated that the:

> Denial of access to the physical environment, transportation, information and communication, and services open to the public constitutes an act of disability-based discrimination that is prohibited by article 5 of the Convention.[36]

Presumably, denial of access means instances of systemic or deliberate discrimination. A simple example of such might arise where a disabled individual is denied access to a restaurant or to a bus service on the ground of disability *per se*. The Committee's comments certainly do not appear to equate denial of access with inaccessibility or to indicate that every instance of inaccessibility of the physical environment, technology, transportation etc. should be viewed as a prohibited act of

[35] Ibid, para. 14 [emphasis added].
[36] Ibid, para. 34.

discrimination. Taken in the context of the progressive realisation of States Parties' obligations, such a reading of Article 9 would not tally with the overall framework of the Convention. As Gerard Quinn points out:

> There is some elusive line beyond which the non-discrimination principle will not generate the more robust obligations contained in Article 9. Put another way, failure to have an [accessible] environment is clearly a form of discrimination. Using the non-discrimination tool it is possible to craft some limited positive obligations on States to undo this discrimination. But failure to achieve all the positive obligations outlined in Article 9 is probably not in itself a form of discrimination [...] Where this line falls is very hard to say – but it does exist.[37]

The progressive realisation of the accessibility obligation will be expanded upon in the next section of this chapter. For the moment, it suffices to note that failure to fulfil accessibility obligations resulting in unequal access to, and enjoyment of rights, may constitute discrimination in certain very limited circumstances. The CRPD Committee elaborates on the circumstances in which inaccessibility of structures and facilities may amount to a breach of the equality and non-discrimination norms in the Convention. The Committee observes that:

> *As a minimum,* the following situations in which lack of accessibility has prevented a person with disabilities from accessing a service or facility open to the public should be considered as prohibited acts of disability-based discrimination: [emphasis added]
> a. Where the service or facility was established after relevant accessibility standards were introduced;[38]
> b. Where access could have been granted to the facility or service (when it came into existence) through reasonable accommodation.[39]

On that basis, it can be argued that States have an absolute obligation to prevent the unjustifiable emergence of new barriers to accessibility and that failure to do so might amount to discrimination. Creating new barriers (in other words, setting up a new and inaccessible service or facility after the introduction of relevant accessibility standards) would be at variance with the obligation to eliminate inequalities for persons with disabilities, including the duty to prevent discrimination. In addition, it

[37] G. Quinn, *The Interaction of Non-Discrimination with Article 9: Added Reasonment* (unpublished paper, September 2010), cited by J.E. Lord, 'Accessibility and Human Rights Fusion in the CRPD: Assessing the Scope and Content of the Accessibility Principle and Duty under the CRPD' Presentation for the General Day of Discussion on Accessibility, UN CRPD Committee – Geneva, October 7, 2010, available at www2.ohchr.org/SPdocs/CRPD/DGD7102010/.../JanetELord.doc last accessed 15 July 2014 (unpublished paper on file with J.E. Lord).

[38] UN Committee on the Rights of Persons with Disabilities, General Comment No. 2 on Article 9 (Accessibility), adopted at the eleventh session of the Committee (30 March–11 April 2014) on 11 April 2014, UN Doc. CRPD/C/GC/2, para. 31.

[39] Ibid.

is important that research and technologies are used in such a way as to ensure that new barriers to accessibility do not emerge in States Parties to the CRPD.[40]

The second instance which potentially amounts to a breach of the non-discrimination norm (as outlined above by the CRPD Committee) arises where a State fails to provide reasonable accommodations as a complementary measure to ensure access to, and enjoyment of, rights in circumstances where facilities or services etc. are inaccessible. The exact parameters of the duty to accommodate expounded by the Committee in its General Comment 2 are not clear (although presumably it is similar to the general duty to accommodate under the Convention). Notably, the Committee points to the fact that a ban on guide dogs from entering a particular building or open space would constitute a prohibited act of disability-based discrimination.[41] It is also envisageable that disabled individuals could mount a claim arguing that failure to provide accommodations (involving a physical adaptation to a facility) in such instances of inaccessibility would be unreasonable, in light of the fact that many States Parties to the CRPD (at least all EU Member States) already have in place laws and policies designed to guarantee accessibility for disabled people to specified facilities.

3.3. Accessibility and Reasonable Accommodation Measures

This subsection of the chapter will reflect on the distinctions which can be drawn between accessibility and reasonable accommodation measures, before looking at the mutually reinforcing role that both of those measures have in ensuring the fulfilment of CRPD rights.

The most obvious difference between accessibility obligations and the duty to accommodate is that a failure to provide reasonable accommodation will result in a violation of the equality and non-discrimination norms, unlike a failure to ensure accessibility.[42] As already outlined in chapter three above, negotiations on Article 5(3) of the CRPD (which contains the duty to accommodate) resulted in heated arguments about the progressive implementation of rights. Several delegates had difficulty disentangling individualised reasonable accommodation requirements from the general obligation on States to provide accessibility. The International Disability Caucus (IDC) highlighted the distinction between the two types of measures when it stated that 'reasonable accommodation in this context refers to

---

40 In the words of the CRPD Committee, 'new technologies can be used to promote the full and equal participation of persons with disabilities in society, but only if they are designed and produced in a way that ensures their accessibility.' The Committee provides some examples of technological advancements designed to ensure accessibility and equality as follows: 'The use of hearing enhancement systems, including ambient assistive systems to assist hearing aid and induction loop users, and passenger lifts pre-equipped to allow use by persons with disabilities during emergency building evacuations.' [Ibid, para. 22].

41 Ibid, para. 29.

42 Subject to the remarks made by the CRPD Committee in its General Comment 2 and outlined in the preceding section of this chapter.

individual cases, such as for an employee or a student requiring an accommodation for a specific purpose.'[43] The IDC was at pains to point out that accommodations should be achievable immediately, whereas making the entire environment accessible immediately would indeed be impossible.[44]

This captures the essence of the distinction between the two types of measures. Accessibility measures have a generalised group-based dimension, whereas the duty to accommodate is noteworthy on account of its individualised and contextual nature. The duty to ensure accessibility is a proactive one. The CRPD Committee has termed it 'an ex ante duty,'[45] in so far as States Parties to the Convention 'have the duty to provide accessibility before receiving an individual request to enter or use a place or service.'[46] In that regard, States must establish accessibility standards, which should be 'adopted in consultation with organizations of persons with disabilities' and which must 'be specified for service-providers, builders and other relevant stakeholders.'[47] Furthermore, accessibility measures must be 'broad and standardized'[48] (subject to the exceptions contained in Articles 9(2)(e) and 9(2)(f) of the CRPD which envisage individualised measures of support for persons with disabilities as part of the duty to ensure accessibility). By way of comparison, the CRPD Committee terms the duty to accommodate an 'ex nunc duty,'[49] which means that 'it is enforceable from the moment an individual with an impairment needs it in a given situation [...] in order to enjoy her or his rights on an equal basis in a particular context.'[50] It is deemed generally to be a reactive duty.[51] It only arises upon specific request by a disabled individual and it is provided on foot of an interactive dialogue between the individual and the entity in question.

A further important distinction concerns the nature of the two types of measures. Accessibility measures may require significant expenditure on the part of States and private entities. As a result, the Convention's accessibility obligation is progressively realisable (subject, of course, to the outer limits and obligations of immediate effect inherent in the notion of progressive realisation). Reasonable accommodations, on the other hand, may often be low cost or no cost at all (such as the provision of a ramp or changing procedures at a workplace). Reasonable accommodations are deemed

---

43 Seventh Session of the Ad Hoc Committee, volume 8(1), January 16, 2006, available at www.un.org/esa/socdev/enable/rights/ahc7sum16jan.htm, accessed 16 October 2014.

44 Seventh Session of the Ad Hoc Committee, volume 8(1), January 16, 2006, available at www.un.org/esa/socdev/enable/rights/ahc7sum16jan.htm, accessed 16 October 2014.

45 UN Committee on the Rights of Persons with Disabilities, General Comment No. 2 on Article 9 (Accessibility), adopted at the eleventh session of the Committee (30 March–11 April 2014) on 11 April 2014, UN Doc. CRPD/C/GC/2, para. 25.

46 Ibid.

47 Ibid.

48 Ibid.

49 Ibid, para. 26.

50 Ibid.

51 In the UK, the duty to accommodate is an anticipatory duty, meaning that entities must anticipate in advance the types of individualised measures which will be required by disabled people with a range of impairments. On this point, see generally A. Lawson (ed.), *Disability and Equality Law in Britain: The Role of Reasonable Adjustments* (Hart Publishing, Oxford, 2008).

to be immediately enforceable and, furthermore, justiciable as they form part of the non-discrimination norm. Of course, it is also possible that, in some instances, reasonable accommodations may impose significant cost burdens on entities and that accessibility measures may, in certain circumstances, be low cost, particularly when accessibility is implemented by a State at an early stage in design or construction. However, it is generally the case that, in practice, ensuring accessibility of existing structures will be more costly than providing accommodations, as the duty to accommodate is subject to the disproportionate burden defence.

While there are many differences between generalised accessibility and individualised reasonable accommodations, there are also many overlaps. The CRPD Committee states that 'reasonable accommodation can be used as a means of ensuring accessibility for an individual with a disability in a particular situation.' For instance, the Committee notes that 'a person with a rare impairment might ask for accommodation that falls outside the scope of any accessibility standard.'[52] Of course, individuals who do not have so-called 'rare' impairments may also require the specifically tailored solution offered by the duty to accommodate, in lieu of standardised accessibility measures or other individualised measures envisaged by Article 9 of the Convention. Anna Lawson points to the fact that there is a 'strong and mutually reinforcing relationship'[53] between the duty to accommodate and accessibility measures. The more accessible the environment and information technologies etc. become, the less reasonable accommodations will be required. That is not to say that reasonable accommodations will become redundant once accessibility is ensured – indeed some individuals with disabilities may still need individualised accommodation measures even when the environment is accessible. The flip side of the relationship between the two types of measures is that the duty to accommodate sometimes contributes to improving access beyond the case of one particular disabled individual – the provision of accommodations may have the (often unintended) effect of improving access for other disabled people with comparative disabilities and also non-disabled people. For instance, widening the entrance to a workplace upon request by a wheelchair-user may result in increased access not only for the disabled person in question but also for people with comparative disabilities and for non-disabled people, such as older people or parents with buggies.

The interrelationship between accessibility and equality must be viewed in the overall context of the progressive realisation of Convention rights. In the next section of this chapter, the focus will be maintained on the progressive realisation of Article 9 of the CRPD.

52 UN Committee on the Rights of Persons with Disabilities, General Comment No. 2 on Article 9 (Accessibility), adopted at the eleventh session of the Committee (30 March–11 April 2014) on 11 April 2014, UN Doc. CRPD/C/GC/2, para. 26.

53 A. Lawson, 'Reasonable Accommodation and Accessibility Obligations: Towards a More Unified European Approach,' (2010) 11 *European Anti-Discrimination Law Review* 11, at page 21.

4. The Progressive Realisation of Article 9 of the CRPD

This section of the chapter will begin with an analysis of the tripartite obligations of States Parties under Article 9 of the CRPD. Thereafter, the minimum core of Article 9 will be examined, together with other relevant considerations in the progressive realisation of disability accessibility. Finally, the various criteria for assessment of measures adopted by States in the progressive realisation of Article 9 will be laid out.

4.1. The Tripartite Obligations of States Parties under Article 9 of the CRPD

States Parties to the CRPD are expected to take 'appropriate measures' to ensure disability accessibility. Article 9 specifies the types of measures which States must take in order to ensure accessibility for individuals with varying forms of disability in different contexts. The specific measures that States will be expected to take are listed in Article 9(2) of the Convention and they include the following:

- The development and monitoring of implementation of minimum accessibility standards and guidelines;
- Ensuring that private entities that offer facilities and services which are open or provided to the public take into account all aspects of accessibility for persons with disabilities;
- The provision of training on accessibility for all relevant stakeholders;
- The provision in buildings and other facilities open to the public of signage in Braille and in easy-to-read and easy-to-understand forms;
- The provision of live assistance and intermediaries, including guides, readers and professional sign language interpreters, to facilitate accessibility to buildings and other facilities open to the public;
- Promoting access to new information and communications technologies and systems, including the internet;
- The promotion of other appropriate forms of assistance and support to ensure access for persons with disabilities to information; and
- The promotion, design, development, production, and distribution of accessible information and communications technologies and systems at an early stage, so that these technologies and systems become accessible at minimum cost.[54]

States Parties to the CRPD have obligations to respect, protect and fulfil with regard to the realisation of the accessibility obligation. This tripartite framework is helpful in analysing and clarifying the nature and scope of State obligations under Article 9. The obligation to respect is a negative one, which requires States not to take any measures that might hinder the realisation of disability accessibility, such as to refrain from enacting legislation creating barriers to accessibility. The obligation to protect, on the other hand, is a positive obligation, which requires States to prevent violations

[54] UN CRPD, Article 9(2).

by third parties of the rights of persons with disabilities. In the context of Article 9(2)(b) of the CRPD, this would involve, among other things, monitoring and regulating the conduct of entities in the private sector (for instance, in the development of new products and services and also in the construction of buildings) to ensure that they are taking into account all aspects of accessibility for persons with disabilities and are not hindering the realisation of the accessibility obligation. The obligation to protect would also entail the setting up of effective monitoring mechanisms towards ensuring disability accessibility, as well as effective means of redress for disabled people in circumstances where Article 9 has been breached.

The obligation to fulfil will require States Parties to the CRPD to adopt 'appropriate legislative, administrative, budgetary, judicial, promotional and other actions'[55] towards the full realisation of the rights of persons with disabilities, including the implementation of Article 9. In order to ensure the implementation of disability accessibility, States must enact legislation mandating accessibility and they must repeal existing legislation which creates discriminatory barriers to the implementation of Article 9. The obligation to fulfil will also entail the removal of other barriers to the enjoyment of accessibility by people with disabilities and the adoption of positive measures towards ensuring full accessibility over time. It will also require States to raise awareness among national authorities and all relevant stakeholders about the disability accessibility obligations contained in the CRPD.[56] Under Article 9(2)(g) of the CRPD, States have a specific duty to 'promote access for persons with disabilities to new information and communications technologies and systems, including the Internet.'[57] This might be achieved, for example, through research and public education campaigns on information and communications technology (ICT). Finally, it is arguable that the obligation to promote also includes a duty to ensure that disability accessibility is part of the curriculum of both formal and non-formal education, particularly in higher education courses relating to infrastructure design and the production of goods.

4.2. The Progressive Implementation of Disability Accessibility under the CRPD

The obligation to take appropriate measures to implement Article 9 of the Convention will require national authorities to set aside significant financial and human resources and to implement widespread systematic changes to laws, policies and procedures

[55] UNCESCR, General Comment No. 14 (2000) on the right to the highest attainable standard of health (article 12 of the International Covenant on Economic, Social and Cultural Rights), UN Document E/C.12/2000/4, adopted on 11 August 2000, para. 33.

[56] The CRPD Committee notes that 'in order to introduce policies that allow better accessibility for persons with disabilities, it is necessary to change attitudes towards persons with disabilities in order to fight against stigma and discrimination, through ongoing education efforts, awareness-raising, cultural campaigns and communication.' [UN Committee on the Rights of Persons with Disabilities, General Comment No. 2 on Article 9 (Accessibility), adopted at the eleventh session of the Committee (30 March–11 April 2014) on 11 April 2014, UN Doc. CRPD/C/GC/2, para. 3].

[57] UN CRPD, Article 9(2)(g).

in order to comply with Convention requirements. In light of the resource-intensive nature of the duties imposed on States, Article 9 is clearly an obligation of progressive implementation.[58] This is confirmed by the drafting history of the Convention.[59] The progressive realisation norm should not be used as an excuse by States to evade their obligations to realise disability accessibility. Implementation of Article 9 will occur over the medium-to-long term. This does not mean that States can delay in the implementation of the Convention's accessibility obligation. As with all rights and obligations subject to progressive realisation, certain elements of disability accessibility should be capable of immediate realisation. National authorities will be required to identify, without delay, discriminatory barriers to accessibility and to take deliberate, concrete and targeted steps towards ensuring elimination of those barriers as expeditiously and efficiently as possible. The CRPD Committee points to the fact that 'barriers should be removed in a continuous and systematic way, gradually yet steadily.'[60] Of course, States must also ensure a minimum level of access to the essential material components of the accessibility obligation.

Anna Lawson describes Article 9 as 'an intriguing and somewhat bewildering provision, the exact scope and implications of which are not yet settled.'[61] Many questions remain about the reach of the accessibility obligations of States Parties to the CRPD. For instance, it is not yet settled law exactly which obligations in Article 9 can be deemed to constitute short-to-mid-term duties and which obligations may be implemented by States over the longer term. The CRPD Committee has given some guidance on that very issue in its General Comment 2, which guidance will be drawn on, where relevant, in the subsections which follow. Linking those subsections to chapter five of this book, the focus will be maintained, in the first instance, on the minimum core of disability accessibility under the CRPD (as this will be the starting point of the CRPD Committee's enquiry into the reasonableness of measures adopted by States). Thereafter, the minimum core approach will be combined with the criteria outlined in chapter five as being the most appropriate for assessing the progressive realisation of CRPD rights.

---

58 Like many of the Convention's substantive rights and obligations, Article 9 can be deemed to be a hybrid duty as elements of the accessibility obligation impact on civil and political rights. Inaccessible communication systems, for instance, have the potential to hinder the right to freedom of expression for certain disabled people.

59 The Chair of the Working Group, Mr. Ron Mc Callum, notes that there was clear agreement among delegates at the negotiation sessions that disability accessibility is subject to progressive realisation [Ad Hoc Committee on the Disability Convention, Daily Summaries, Seventh Session, Morning Session, 17 January 2006].

60 UN Committee on the Rights of Persons with Disabilities, General Comment No. 2 on Article 9 (Accessibility), adopted at the eleventh session of the Committee (30 March–11 April 2014) on 11 April 2014, UN Doc. CRPD/C/GC/2, para. 27.

61 A. Lawson, 'Reasonable Accommodation and Accessibility Obligations: Towards a More Unified European Approach,' (2010) 11 *European Anti-Discrimination Law Review* 11, at page 14.

4.3. The Obligation to Ensure Satisfaction of the Minimum Core of Article 9 of the CRPD

In the context of disability accessibility, the minimum core seeks to define that essential and basic level of provision, without which persons with disabilities cannot begin to enjoy and exercise the guarantees contained in Article 9. The minimum core of disability accessibility will no doubt be elaborated upon by the CPRD Committee in future general comments. In the subsections which follow, the key elements of what I propose to consist of the minimum core of Article 9 will be delineated, before moving on to various other aspects of implementation of disability accessibility, followed by a consideration of the criteria that might be used by the CRPD Committee in assessing the measures taken by States to realise progressively their Article 9 obligations.

4.3.1. Priority Areas of Disability Accessibility

Many difficult policy choices will arise in the process of implementing Article 9 of the CRPD. States will have to decide, for instance, whether to concentrate on making infrastructural investments designed to contribute towards full accessibility or whether they should provide assistive technology or devices allowing individuals to navigate inaccessible environments. Of course, one must recognise that the accessibility obligation will often entail costly investments and therefore States that lack resources must start from the core of the right and build from there towards ensuring full accessibility over time. Since the minimum core approach 'is a means of specifying priorities,'[62] it will provide a basic foundation for Article 9 implementation. Implementing the minimum core of disability accessibility under the Convention will entail the identification of priorities by States in relation to the core elements of the obligation. In circumstances where a government is experiencing financial and other constraints, priority should be given to ensuring that programmes and policies are implemented which provide immediate enjoyment of the minimum core of the normative content of Article 9. It is submitted that priority should be given to those goods, services and facilities which are essential to independent living and participation in society, as they are the key objectives of Article 9. Accessible housing and transportation have been recognised specifically by both the ILO[63] and the UNCESCR[64] as being pivotal to the realisation of other socio-economic

[62] D. Bilchitz, 'Towards a Reasonable Approach to the Minimum Core: Laying the Foundations for Future Socio-Economic Rights Jurisprudence' (2003) 19 *South African Journal on Human Rights* 1, at page 15.

[63] The ILO takes account of the fact that it is very often the physical barriers that society has erected in areas such as transport, housing and the workplace which are then cited as the reason why persons with disabilities cannot be employed. [See A/CONF.157/PC/61/Add.10, p. 12, cited by the UNCESCR, General Comment No. 5 (on persons with disabilities), para. 22].

[64] The UNCESCR acknowledges the importance of accessible means of transport in ensuring adequate levels of socio-economic rights provision. In its General Comment 5 (1994), the UNCESCR notes that '[...] the failure of Governments to ensure that modes of transportation are accessible to persons with disabilities greatly reduces the chances of such persons finding suitable, integrated jobs, taking advantage of educational and vocational training, or commuting to facilities of all types.' [UNCESCR, General Comment No. 5 (on persons with disabilities), para. 23].

rights. The CRPD Committee also recognises the importance of accessible means of transport when it observes that persons with disabilities would not have the opportunity to exercise the right to education without (among other things) accessible transport to schools.[65] Of course, many other rights, such as the rights to health and, in particular, primary education can also be deemed to be priority areas for States, in light of their importance to the facilitation of other socio-economic rights in the Convention.

While satisfying the minimum core is a good starting point for States with very limited resources, it is essential that national authorities do not use the minimum core as an excuse to justify inaction with respect to the more comprehensive obligations contained in Article 9. Accordingly, a crucial priority area of disability accessibility pertains to the drafting of an integral governmental policy for promoting and ensuring the full realisation of disability accessibility over time. States should draw up a clear strategy so that all organs of the State and private entities are working towards the same goals and objectives. As noted in chapter five of this book, many complex questions arise under the overall heading of priority-setting. While it is clear that States Parties to the Convention cannot make all priority areas accessible immediately, the CRPD Committee will need to apply defined criteria to States' efforts to designate priorities specific to local contexts and to allocate resources in that regard to satisfy, at the very least, the minimum core of Article 9 of the Convention. Thereafter, States will be required to work towards full implementation of disability accessibility over time.

4.3.2. The Obligation not to Create New Barriers

States Parties to the Convention will not be required to make the existing environment, information and communications systems, as well as goods and services accessible overnight. However, States should not create new barriers to disability accessibility and they should, furthermore, monitor the emergence of new barriers in the private sphere. Article 9(2)(a) requires States Parties to the CRPD to take appropriate measures 'to develop, promulgate and monitor the implementation of minimum standards and guidelines for the accessibility of facilities and services open or provided to the public.'[66] In circumstances where accessibility standards exist in a given State Party, the emergence of new barriers would be so contrary to the spirit and tenor of the Convention that it is almost certain that the Committee would find a given State to have breached Article 9. As already mentioned in the previous section of this chapter,[67] the Committee has already hinted that the setting up a new and inaccessible service or facility after the introduction of relevant

[65] UN Committee on the Rights of Persons with Disabilities, General Comment No. 2 on Article 9 (Accessibility), adopted at the eleventh session of the Committee (30 March–11 April 2014) on 11 April 2014, UN Doc. CRPD/C/GC/2, para. 39.

[66] UN CRPD, Article 9(2)(a).

[67] See section 3.2 of this chapter.

accessibility standards may even be deemed to be in violation of the Convention's non-discrimination norm.[68]

The foregoing considerations arguably make up part of the minimum core of Article 9 and they will no doubt be expanded upon by the CRPD Committee in its future pronouncements. The minimum core of disability accessibility must be accorded priority by States in their policy-making and budgetary allocations. Failure to do so will most certainly be taken into account by the Committee in its assessment of the measures taken by States to ensure implementation of Article 9. Other considerations will also be relevant for States in implementing Article 9. Such considerations will be outlined below, before turning to the various criteria which might be employed by the CRPD Committee in assessing the reasonableness of State action or inaction in the implementation of disability accessibility.

4.4. Relevant Considerations in the Implementation of Article 9 of the CRPD

Aside from implementing the minimum core requirements of Article 9 of the CRPD, States must also look to the following aspects of implementation of disability accessibility:

4.4.1. The Requirement to Adopt Legislation to Ensure Implementation of Article 9 of the CRPD and the Drafting of Accessibility Standards

One of the first steps to be taken by States in their efforts to implement Article 9 will be the adoption of national legislation that will address barriers to accessibility and the overarching issue of inequality of access to rights under the CRPD. States should also modify or abolish existing laws, regulations, customs and practices which are contrary to their accessibility obligations under the Convention. The CRPD Committee observes that States Parties 'should undertake a comprehensive review of the laws on accessibility in order to identify, monitor and address gaps in legislation and implementation.'[69] With regard to the content of accessibility legislation, the Committee notes that 'legislation should provide for the mandatory application of accessibility standards and for sanctions, including fines, for those who fail to apply them.'[70] States should also ensure that any legislative and policy measures adopted by them are implemented effectively. Importantly, domestic legal guarantees of equality and non-discrimination should be linked to accessibility legislation and the former should be interpreted in a manner which promotes States Parties' accessibility obligations under the Convention. The Committee notes that 'accessibility should be encompassed in general and specific laws on equal opportunities, equality and

68 UN Committee on the Rights of Persons with Disabilities, General Comment No. 2 on Article 9 (Accessibility), adopted at the eleventh session of the Committee (30 March–11 April 2014) on 11 April 2014, UN Doc. CRPD/C/GC/2, para. 31.

69 Ibid, para. 28.

70 Ibid.

participation in the context of the prohibition of disability-based discrimination.'[71] Furthermore, national governments should, without delay, begin to draft accessibility standards as this standardisation is so fundamental to the full realisation of Article 9 over time.

4.4.2. The Obligation to Monitor the Realisation of Disability Accessibility

One of the most important obligations which States Parties to the CRPD will have is to set up a mechanism that will monitor implementation of Article 9 by collecting data, establishing benchmarks and designing indicators to measure progress in the implementation of disability accessibility. States are required explicitly under Article 9(2)(a) of the Convention to 'monitor the implementation of minimum standards and guidelines for the accessibility of facilities and services open or provided to the public.'[72] The Committee notes in that connection that States should 'monitor sanctions against anyone who fails to implement accessibility standards.[73] Capacity-building for monitoring bodies concerned with the application and implementation of accessibility standards is an important issue according to the Committee.[74] In order to ensure implementation of the minimum core of disability accessibility, States will be expected to monitor the design of new products, services, infrastructure, facilities and so forth by private entities to ensure that they are being designed in a way that makes them fully accessible for persons with disabilities. Furthermore, States will be under an obligation to monitor the emergence of new barriers to accessibility.

4.4.3. The Provision of Effective Legal Remedies

Another vital element of Article 9 implementation is the provision of effective means of redress for any disabled individual who has been the subject of a breach of State obligations under Article 9, including actions or omissions by private parties. It is particularly important for domestic authorities to provide effective legal remedies in respect of the elements of Article 9 which overlap with equality considerations, as outlined by the CRPD Committee and detailed above – namely, the obligation not to create new barriers to accessibility and the obligation to grant access by means of reasonable accommodation where full accessibility is not feasible. The Committee also recognises the importance of effective legal remedies in instances of a denial of access when it confirms that 'persons with disabilities who have been denied access to the physical environment, transportation, information and communication, or services open to the public should have effective legal remedies

---

71 Ibid, para. 27.

72 UN CRPD, Article 9 (2)(a).

73 UN Committee on the Rights of Persons with Disabilities, General Comment No. 2 on Article 9 (Accessibility), adopted at the eleventh session of the Committee (30 March–11 April 2014) on 11 April 2014, UN Doc. CRPD/C/GC/2, para. 24.

74 In that regard, the Committee notes that 'States parties are under an obligation to develop an effective monitoring framework and set up efficient monitoring bodies with adequate capacity and appropriate mandates to make sure that plans, strategies and standardization are implemented and enforced.' [Ibid, para. 33].

at their disposal.'[75] Any barriers to accessing justice or effective remedies should therefore be dismantled. A lack of effective legal remedies at the domestic level would hinder the full realisation of Article 9.

4.4.4. The Provision of Disability Accessibility Training for Stakeholders

Another pivotal component of Article 9 implementation stems from State obligations to provide training for stakeholders on accessibility issues facing persons with disabilities. There is often a distinct lack of know-how, and even some degree of ignorance, among the general public and relevant stakeholders, regarding, in particular, the scope of accessibility obligations and the fact that accessibility does not cover merely the built environment. In terms of the content of disability accessibility training for stakeholders, the Committee observes that 'the all-encompassing nature of accessibility should be addressed, providing for access to the physical environment, transportation, information and communication, and services.'[76] In addition, the Committee notes that the awareness-raising efforts of States should draw attention to the fact that 'the duty to observe accessibility standards applies equally to the public and to the private sector.'[77] Disability accessibility training should be given priority on national policy and legislative agendas and it should be put in place as soon as possible as it is essential to the full realisation of Article 9 over time and to the improvement of the design of goods, services and accessibility policies.

Article 9 does not enumerate the relevant stakeholders to whom accessibility training should be provided. The CRPD Committee has clarified that training should be provided to the following non-exhaustive list of stakeholders, namely:

> The authorities that issue building permits, broadcasting boards and ICT licences, engineers, designers, architects, urban planners, transport authorities, service providers, members of the academic community and persons with disabilities and their organizations.[78]

The Committee specifies that 'training should be provided not only to those designing goods, services and products, but also to those who actually produce them.'[79] In order to ensure implementation of Article 9, it is particularly important that States would also engage in education campaigns and training programmes for all those involved in the enforcement of accessibility standards and obligations, such as public officials and the judiciary. Those enforcing accessibility standards should be trained on the manner in which accessibility relates to equality/non-discrimination and the overall requirement to ensure access to rights for persons with disabilities on an equal basis with others. Furthermore, staff employed to monitor implementation of Article 9 should be trained.

---

75 Ibid, para. 29.
76 Ibid, para. 35.
77 Ibid.
78 Ibid, para. 19.
79 Ibid.

4.4.5. *Accessibility as Part of the Educational Curriculum*

In addition to the duty imposed on States to ensure the provision of disability accessibility training to relevant stakeholders, it is arguable that there is also an obligation on States to incorporate accessibility training as part of the educational curriculum in higher education in those facilities providing education related to the design of infrastructure and the production of goods. There is arguably also a duty on States to incorporate some element of human rights education in their national systems, with a view to informing individuals from a young age about the importance of accessible structures and how the implementation of the accessibility obligation in Article 9 of the CRPD can contribute towards advancing the human rights of persons with disabilities. This will contribute towards combatting the widespread ignorance which exists in that regard.

4.4.6. *The Continuous Obligation to Improve Conditions of Accessibility*

States have a 'specific and continuing obligation'[80] to improve levels of accessibility in their territory. Failure by a State Party to take appropriate measures to address any decline in disability accessibility levels would be in violation of their obligations under the Convention. States must ensure that they increase not only levels of accessibility in terms of the range of disabled people who enjoy accessibility but that they also improve continuously the quality of accessible infrastructure, facilities, goods and services.[81]

4.4.7. *The Obligation to Abstain from Taking Deliberately Retrogressive Measures in Realising Disability Accessibility*

In implementing Article 9 of the CRPD, States will be required to ensure that they do not adopt deliberately retrogressive measures. In circumstances where the adoption of retrogressive measures is absolutely necessary, States will be required to justify the adoption of such measures to the CRPD Committee.[82] In assessing the extent to which such measures may be justifiable (or alternatively in breach of Article 9), it is likely that the Committee will take into account the identification by States of low-cost alternatives and also whether the State in question sought cooperation and assistance or rejected offers of resources from the international community for the purpose of implementing the Convention's accessibility provisions.

---

80 UNCESCR, General Comment No. 14 on the right to the highest attainable standard of health (Article 12 ICESCR), adopted at the twenty-second session on 11 August 2000, UN Doc. EC 12/2000/4, para. 31.

81 Subject to the very limited circumstances in which retrogressive measures may be permitted.

82 The UNCESCR has stated that any deliberate measures taken by States require 'the most careful consideration' and that they must be justified fully 'by reference to the totality of rights provided for in the Covenant and in the context of the full use of the maximum available resources.' [UNCESCR, General Comment 3 on the nature of States Parties' obligations (Article 2, para. 1, of the Covenant) (1990), adopted at the fifth session of the Committee on 14 December 1990, UN Doc. E/1991/23].

4.4.8. Privatisation of Goods, Products and Services: The Impact on States Parties' Accessibility Obligations

In any consideration of the privatisation of goods and services, it is vital to consider the manner in which such privatisation may affect the accessibility of those goods and services. There has been much debate about the impact which the privatisation of education services has had on the core elements of general accessibility of educational structures for everyone.[83] In the context of general accessibility measures under Article 9, it is very clear that the privatisation of goods and services does not affect States Parties' obligations to ensure that they are accessible to persons with disabilities on an equal basis with others. This is evident from Article 9(2)(b) of the Convention. Moreover, the CRPD Committee points to the fact that 'as long as goods, products and services are open or provided to the public, they must be accessible to all, regardless of whether they are owned and/or provided by a public authority or a private enterprise.'[84]

4.5. The Criteria for Assessment of Measures taken by States in the Progressive Realisation of Article 9 of the CRPD

Ensuring accessibility for disabled people cannot take priority over the needs of other disadvantaged groups and, in particular, those who are in dire circumstances. However, disability accessibility is a vital obligation falling on States under the CRPD and governments will be required to adhere to certain criteria in the adoption of measures to realise progressively this obligation (as they will in the realisation of all CRPD rights and obligations) in order to ensure that the needs of disabled people are met to the same extent as the needs of other disadvantaged groups. Bearing that in mind, the criteria which have already been set down in chapter five of this book will be applied to Article 9 of the CRPD below. Those criteria were drawn from the types of considerations that are taken into account in assessing the reasonableness of State measures at the national and international levels – specifically under Article 8(4) of the OP-ICESCR and under South African Constitutional jurisprudence. The outer limits of the duty to accommodate were also considered in order to tailor the various criteria to the specific purpose and values underlying the CRPD. By virtue of this, an equality perspective was added to bolster the already existing reasonableness criteria.

---

83 See, for example, the Right to Education project. Available at www.right-to-education.org/blog/civil-society-organisations-discussed-privatisation-and-right-education-during-human-rights last accessed 31 July 2014.

84 UN Committee on the Rights of Persons with Disabilities, General Comment No. 2 on Article 9 (Accessibility), adopted at the eleventh session of the Committee (30 March–11 April 2014) on 11 April 2014, UN Doc. CRPD/C/GC/2, para. 13.

4.5.1. Disproportionate Burden/Cost Considerations

States must introduce legislation and policies that are capable of realising the rights of all individuals in that State equally. Resources must be allocated carefully, taking account of the fact that the rights of vulnerable and disadvantaged groups must be realised to an equal degree. The CRPD Committee will have to consider the measures taken by States in light of resource and institutional constraints and also the needs of non-disabled people. In assessing whether particular accessibility measures place a disproportionate burden on a State, the Committee should consider, among other things, the extent to which the given State has realised their obligations relating to socio-economic rights in an economically efficient manner. In order to ensure that the rights of persons with disabilities are realised to the same extent as other groups, States must consider their accessibility obligations at a very early stage in the development of strategies and policies. The same applies to entities in the private sphere, which will be required to consider disability accessibility needs at an early stage in the design and development of products and services. Article 9(2)(h) of the Convention calls on States Parties 'to promote the design, development, production and distribution of accessible information and communications technologies and systems *at an early stage*, so that these technologies and systems become accessible at minimum cost.'[85]

The duty to ensure accessibility is often perceived by entities and States as being extremely costly. However, one must remember that creating accessible infrastructure, goods and services etc. from the very outset costs no more than creating inaccessible ones. Notably, studies[86] on the implementation of the ADA[87] have demonstrated the fact that the cost of making new goods and services or related infrastructure accessible is very low (less than 1% in the case of buildings) and quite limited in the case of retrofitting (between 1 and 3%).[88] On the other hand, it is quite expensive and onerous to create accessible infrastructure, goods and services at a later stage. The CRPD Committee recognises this fact in it observation that:

> Making a building accessible from the outset might not increase the total cost of construction at all in many cases, or only minimally in some cases. On the other hand, the

85 UN CRPD, Article 9(2)(h) [emphasis added].

86 Information taken from EDF submission to the UN Committee on the Rights of Persons with Disabilities on Article 9 'Accessibility' UNCRPD, 15 March 2012, available at www.edffeph.org/Page_Generale.asp?DocID=13854&thebloc=29617, last accessed 28 July 2014, at page 5, citing a study of New York University at Buffalo on estimated costs of accessible buildings.

87 See www.ada.gov/, last accessed 3 August 2014.

88 See article by David M Capozzi, 'Fifty Years of American Accessibility Experience,' in EDF, 'Freedom Guide: Paving the Way Towards Free Movement for Persons with Disabilities,' December 2011, at page 31; available at http://cms.horus.be/files/99909/MediaArchive/library/Freedom%20Guide.pdf [Information taken from EDF submission to the UN Committee on the Rights of Persons with Disabilities on Article 9 'Accessibility' UNCRPD 15 March 2012, available at www.edffeph.org/Page_Generale.asp?DocID=13854&thebloc=29617, last accessed 28 July 2014, at page 5].

> cost of subsequent adaptations in order to make a building accessible may be considerable in some cases, especially with regard to certain historical buildings.[89]

Cost considerations have already been factored into the Committee's remarks on States' accessibility obligations with regard to training relevant stakeholders. The Committee observes that accessibility training 'should promote [...] the idea that designing and building in an accessible way from the earliest stages is cost-effective and economical.'[90] The Committee also notes that 'accessibility of information and communication, including ICT, should also be achieved from the outset because subsequent adaptations to the Internet and ICT may increase costs.'[91]

Just like the disproportionate burden defence under the duty to accommodate (whereby larger entities with more resources will be expected to provide greater accommodations), larger States with more resources at their disposal will be expected to take more advanced steps early on in the realisation of disability accessibility for persons with disabilities. Nonetheless, all States Parties to the CRPD will be expected to take steps that minimise the cost burden of providing accessible structures. Thus, for instance, a small State with limited resources will surely be found to be in breach of its accessibility obligations under the Convention if it does not incorporate accessibility considerations at least into legislation, policy and design from an early stage in order to ensure that structures become accessible at a lower cost than would be the case if the same State delayed in implementing Article 9.

4.5.2. The Obligation to Use the Maximum of Available Resources: Resource Prioritisation and Resource Optimisation Efforts of States

In assessing compliance with Article 9 obligations, and in determining whether particular measures impose a so-called disproportionate burden on States, the CRPD Committee will have to adjudicate on the resource prioritisation and resource optimisation efforts of States, including determining whether the State in question sought to augment its available resources through international cooperation and assistance. Governments must secure as much revenue as is reasonably possible in order to meet their obligations under the CRPD to realise disability accessibility. States can also increase their technical capacity through international cooperation. The text of the CRPD itself acknowledges the fact that States must recognise the importance of 'international cooperation and its promotion, in support of national efforts for the realization of the purpose and objectives [of the Convention] and will undertake appropriate and effective measures in this regard,'[92] including 'by facilitating access to and sharing of accessible and assistive technologies [...].'[93]

---

[89] UN Committee on the Rights of Persons with Disabilities, General Comment No. 2 on Article 9 (Accessibility), adopted at the eleventh session of the Committee (30 March–11 April 2014) on 11 April 2014, UN Doc. CRPD/C/GC/2, para. 15.

[90] Ibid, para. 35.

[91] Ibid, para. 15.

[92] UN CRPD, Article 32.

[93] UN CRPD, Article 32(1)(d).

The requirement to prioritise and to optimise available resources will apply equally at the beginning of Article 9 implementation as it will as time goes on. The creation of accessible infrastructure, goods and services will result in less need for State authorities to provide individualised services, as disabled people will be enabled to live independently through the implementation of the Convention's accessibility obligation. Individualised services are often quite costly and therefore the progressive implementation of Article 9 will result in resources for such individualised services being freed up from budgets within a given State, at least up to a certain point. Of course, the impairment aspect of disability will not negate the need for individualised services altogether, irrespective of how accessible social structures become. Nonetheless, the implementation of accessibility will certainly reduce the need for individualised services and, to that extent, it is imperative that resources which are freed up within national budgets for individualised services are prioritised and optimised by public authorities for the further implementation of Article 9 obligations.

States Parties to the CRPD must also ensure that sufficient priority is allocated to disability accessibility in national, regional and local budgets, in accordance with available resources and that public spending in that connection is not inefficient or corrupt. States must put in place evaluation mechanisms which ensure that funds allocated for a specific purpose are reaching the intended beneficiaries. As part of their review of accessibility legislation, States Parties 'must also consider their laws on public procurement to ensure that their public procurement procedures incorporate accessibility requirements.'[94] In that respect, the CRPD Committee notes that 'it is unacceptable to use public funds to create or perpetuate the inequality that inevitably results from inaccessible services and facilities.'[95] States will also be required to engage in principled decision and policy-making processes related to disability accessibility, particularly with regard to resource allocation. Finally, when choosing between measures to facilitate their accessibility obligations under Article 9, States will be required to consider the least restrictive options and to identify low-cost alternative measures which can result in a similar facilitation of Convention rights, perhaps even reasonable accommodation measures which ensure wider accessibility.

4.5.3. The Necessity and the Effectiveness of Measures Taken by States

It has been shown in chapter five above that two relevant considerations in the progressive implementation of CRPD rights are the necessity and effectiveness of the actual measures adopted and of the outcomes achieved. The necessity criterion means that States must take those measures which are required to ensure compliance with the CRPD. The criterion of effectiveness implies that States Parties to the CRPD should, on a regular basis, assess whether the measures adopted by them are contributing towards fulfilling the objectives of the substantive right or obligation

94 UN Committee on the Rights of Persons with Disabilities, General Comment No. 2 on Article 9 (Accessibility), adopted at the eleventh session of the Committee (30 March–11 April 2014) on 11 April 2014, UN Doc. CRPD/C/GC/2, para. 32.

95 Ibid.

in question, as well as the object and purpose of the Convention on the whole. One of the most important duties of States in the progressive implementation of Article 9 will be the obligation to monitor effectively the extent to which measures taken in the context of disability accessibility are actually contributing to both the objectives of Article 9 (participation and independent living) and to the overall realisation of the right to equality. States should allocate resources carefully in that regard and any monitoring mechanisms put in place by national authorities should be connected closely to budgetary and programmatic revisions in order to ensure the use of the maximum of available resources. The extent to which measures taken by States impede or facilitate the requirement of effectiveness already appears to have been a relevant consideration for the CRPD Committee in assessing measures taken by national authorities under Article 9. This can be seen from the individual communication brought before the Committee by Hungarian citizens Szilvia Nyusti and Péter Takács.[96] The State Party in question was called upon to ensure that persons with visual and other types of impairments have unimpeded access to automatic teller machines on an equal basis with other clients of a particular financial institution. The Committee duly recognised the initial measures taken by the State Party to enhance the accessibility of the machines operated by the bank in question and other financial institutions. Notwithstanding this, the Committee observed that none of the measures taken had resulted in ensuring accessibility in practice (for the authors or other persons in a similar situation) to the banking card services provided by the machines operated by the particular institution in question. Accordingly, the Committee found that the State Party had failed to comply with its obligations under Article 9(2)(b) of the Convention to ensure that private entities that offer facilities and services which are open or provided to the public take into account all aspects of accessibility for persons with disabilities.

This is an interesting finding as it demonstrates that States are expected to take concrete measures that will result in outcomes consistent with Convention obligations. In the instant case, none of the measures taken by the State Party led to the effective realisation of Article 9. At least, they did not lead to a sufficient degree of realisation of Article 9. As a result, the Committee enjoined the State to adopt measures to remedy the lack of accessibility and noted that Hungary was under an obligation to take steps to prevent similar violations in the future. The Committee made numerous specific recommendations to Hungary as follows:[97] The Committee recommended firstly that Hungary should establish minimum standards for the accessibility of banking services provided by private financial institutions for persons with visual and other types of impairments. The Committee also recommended that the State Party should create a legislative framework with concrete, enforceable and time-bound benchmarks for monitoring and assessing the gradual modification and adjustment by private financial institutions of previously inaccessible banking services provided by them into accessible ones. In addition,

---

96 UN Committee on the Rights of Persons with Disabilities, Individual Communication taken by Szilvia Nyusti and Péter Takács (represented by counsel, Tamás Fazekas, Hungarian Helsinki Committee), Communication No. 1/2010, views adopted by the Committee at its ninth session (15–19 April 2013).

97 Ibid, at para. 9.6.

the Committee recommended that the Hungarian authorities should ensure that all newly procured ATMs and other banking services were fully accessible for persons with disabilities. This demonstrates the approach taken by the Committee to State obligations regarding pre-existing inaccessible infrastructure, on the one hand, and the obligation to ensure that newly designed infrastructure is fully accessible for disabled individuals. Furthermore, it is in line with the comments made throughout this chapter that there will be stringent obligations on States to ensure the prevention of newly emerging barriers to accessibility.

4.5.4. Equality Considerations

Under a framework of review designed to assess the compliance of national authorities with their obligations to realise rights progressively in the disability context, equality considerations should be paramount. Obviously not every product or service which emerges on the market will be accessible. However, there will be an obligation on States to ensure that there are accessible versions of products and services available to persons with disabilities at the same time as the launch of a standard (inaccessible) product or service so as to prevent the exclusion of persons with disabilities from market participation. Of course, the accessible products or services must be made available to persons with disabilities at no extra cost. States Parties to the Convention must also oversee that private entities create an accessible version of a given product or service that has the same functionality as the standard one. It would be inequitable to create one fully functional product and a so-called 'lighter' version of the product with fewer capacities for people with disabilities to use. In that regard, Yahoo Mail Classic, Outlook Web Access 2007 Light, and the basic hyper text mark-up language (HTML) version of Gmail are cited by Wentz et al. as examples of such inequality.[98] The authors point to the fact that Yahoo recommends that users of assistive technology revert to the Yahoo Mail Classic version of its web-based email interface rather than the current version of the Yahoo Mail interface, even though the two web-based interfaces do not have all of the same features. In addition, due to accessibility problems with its standard web-based interface for accessing corporate emails, Microsoft recommends that users who are blind, have low vision, or require screen magnification use a different interface called Outlook Web Access 'light.' The authors state that this version of the web-based email interface is not consistent with the features provided by the standard version of Outlook Web Access. Finally, Wentz et al. refer to Google's recommendation that its 'basic HTML' version of Gmail is the best version, having compatibility for screen readers. However, the authors note that this version is missing certain features incorporated into the standard version, including spell check and the ability to manage contacts.[99] Examples such as these demonstrate the fact that ensuring accessibility for persons with disabilities on an equal basis with others will require not only the mere provision of accessible

---

98 B. Wentz, P.T. Jaeger, and J. Lazar, 'Retrofitting Accessibility: The Legal Inequality of After-the-Fact Online Access for Persons with Disabilities in the United States' (May 2012), available at https://nfb.org/images/nfb/publications/bm/bm12/bm1205/bm120504.htm last accessed 5 August 2014.

99 Ibid.

products, services etc. but also the eradication of all discriminatory barriers to ensure true equality.

In essence, the CRPD Committee must ensure that measures taken by States under Article 9 meet the standards of accessibility guaranteed to non-disabled people. The relevant question to be asked by the Committee is whether persons with disabilities are guaranteed 'equivalent access' to non-disabled people by virtue of the measures adopted by States? In that regard, the European Disability Forum (EDF) draws attention to the fact that 'some individuals with disabilities may not necessarily use or access a product, a service, a facility or an infrastructure in the same manner as everyone else.'[100] EDF points to the fact that disabled people may require assistive technologies and/or alternative modes of use and that, in this context, two elements appear important to ensure equivalent access.[101] The first issue is the interoperability and compatibility between mainstream goods and services, on the one hand, and assistive technologies, on the other hand, as this is key to ensuring access for disabled individuals on an equal basis with others. Secondly, the idea of 'functionally equivalent access' must be considered. EDF cites EU e-communication legislation[102] in that respect. Those laws use the concept of 'functionally equivalent access' as meaning that persons with disabilities are entitled to the same usability of services as other end-users, but by different means, if necessary. For instance for a hard-of-hearing person who uses text and/or video-relay services instead of vocal telephony services, text and video services are considered as services which offer 'functionally equivalent access.'[103] Balancing its assessment with a consideration of resource and institutional constraints, the CRPD Committee should investigate the extent to which measures taken under Article 9 result in opportunities and outcomes for persons with disabilities which are equivalent to those guaranteed to their non-disabled peers.

[100] EDF submission to the UN Committee on the Rights of Persons with Disabilities on Article 9 'Accessibility' UNCRPD 15 March 2012, available at www.edffeph.org/Page_Generale.asp?DocID=13854&thebloc=29617, last accessed 28 July 2014, at page 5.

[101] Ibid.

[102] Directive 2009/136/EC of the European Parliament and of the Council of 25 November 2009 amending Directive 2002/22/EC on universal service and users' rights relating to electronic communications networks and services OJ L 337, 18.12.2009, p. 11–36; Directive 2002/58/EC concerning the processing of personal data and the protection of privacy in the electronic communications sector OJ L 201, 31.07.2002; Regulation (EC) No 2006/2004 of the European Parliament and of the Council of 27 October 2004 on cooperation between national authorities responsible for the enforcement of consumer protection laws OJ L 364, 9.12.2004; Directive 2009/140/EC of the European Parliament and of the Council of 25 November 2009 amending Directives 2002/21/EC on a common regulatory framework for electronic communications networks and services OJ L 337, 18.12.2009, p. 37–69; Directive 2002/19/EC on access to, and interconnection of, electronic communications networks and associated facilities OJ L 108, 24.4.2002; Directive 2002/20/EC on the authorisation of electronic communications networks and services OJ L 108, 24.4.2002; Regulation (EC) No 1211/2009 of the European Parliament and of the Council of 25 November 2009 establishing the Body of European Regulators for Electronic Communications (BEREC) and the Office OJ L 337, 18.12.2009, p. 1–10.

[103] EDF submission to the UN Committee on the Rights of Persons with Disabilities on Article 9 'Accessibility' UNCRPD 15 March 2012, available at www.edffeph.org/Page_Generale.asp?DocID=13854&thebloc=29617, last accessed 28 July 2014, at page 5.

Finally, it is important that States ensure a coherent implementation of accessibility and equality through national legislation. Interestingly, this consideration was referred to by the CRPD Committee in the individual communication brought before the Committee by Hungarian citizens Szilvia Nyusti and Péter Takács.[104] The Committee recommended that Hungary should ensure that its accessibility legislation and the manner in which it is applied by domestic courts is consistent with the State Party's obligations to ensure that legislation does not have the purpose or effect of impairing or nullifying the recognition, enjoyment or exercise of any right for persons with disabilities on an equal basis with others.[105] This demonstrates the complementary nature of States' accessibility obligations, on the one hand, and equality and non-discrimination norms, on the other hand. It also confirms the fact that it will be vital for States to ensure a structured implementation of Article 9, which accords with their obligations under the CRPD's equality and non-discrimination provisions.

4.5.5. Dignity Considerations

According to the CRPD's substantive and transformative approach to equality and to socio-economic rights, any accessibility measures adopted by States should ensure respect for individual difference and dignity and this should form part of the CRPD Committee's assessment. The importance of human dignity as a relevant consideration has already been highlighted in chapter four above in the context of the duty to accommodate, where it was shown that measures taken by entities under the duty to accommodate should result in the facilitation of the dignity of the disabled individual in question. The reasonableness approach under South African constitutional jurisprudence also demonstrates the importance of human dignity in socio-economic rights adjudication. In order to ensure that the CRPD's equality paradigm is realised fully in the context of Article 9, the inherent dignity of persons with disabilities should be taken into account in all aspects of Article 9 implementation, beyond implementation of the minimum core. Indeed, the Committee has already recognised the importance of dignity considerations in the implementation of Article 9. The Committee observes that 'persons with disabilities should have equal access to all goods, products and services that are open or provided to the public in a manner that ensures their effective and equal access and respects their dignity.'[106] A disabled individual should not be required to use or access goods, services, infrastructure or other facilities in a manner which compromises his/her inherent dignity. To take a simple example, a person with a disability should not be required to use the back entrance to a building when all other individuals can access the building using the front entrance. In that regard, it is important to weigh

[104] UN Committee on the Rights of Persons with Disabilities, Individual Communication taken by Szilvia Nyusti and Péter Takács (represented by counsel, Tamás Fazekas, Hungarian Helsinki Committee), Communication No. 1/2010, views adopted by the Committee at its ninth session (15–19 April 2013).

[105] Ibid, para. 10(2)(c).

[106] UN Committee on the Rights of Persons with Disabilities, General Comment No. 2 on Article 9: (Accessibility), adopted at the eleventh session of the Committee (30 March–11 April 2014) on 11 April 2014, UN Doc. CRPD/C/GC/2, para. 13.

up dignity interests against costs and burdens for States and private entities. In other words, the reasonableness of costs must be balanced against respect for the inherent dignity of persons with disabilities.

States should also ensure consideration of dignity interests in the design of accessibility standards by respecting the diverse impairments that persons with disabilities have. The fact that the inherent dignity of persons with disabilities should be taken into consideration in socio-economic rights adjudication is also evident from the Committee's remarks in its individual communication concerning disability accessibility in Hungary. In that decision, the Committee recommended that the Hungarian authorities should provide appropriate and regular training on the scope of the Convention and its Optional Protocol to judges and other judicial officials in order to encourage them to adjudicate cases in a disability-sensitive manner.[107]

Inclusive design approaches can be deemed to be the most respectful of the inherent dignity of persons with disabilities. Therefore, when States or entities are constructing new buildings, undertaking renovations or launching new products and services, they should take into account the inherent dignity of persons with disabilities by not making design choices that create barriers for disabled people and, thereby, hinder the participation and inclusion of persons with disabilities in society.

4.5.6. Participation and Inclusion: The Requirement to Involve Persons with Disabilities in all Aspects of the Implementation and Monitoring of Disability Accessibility

States must ensure participatory processes in the implementation and monitoring of Article 9, as disabled persons can provide important information on established or novel solutions to the various issues which they face in enjoying disability accessibility. In its assessment of the measures taken by States in implementing Article 9, the CRPD Committee will undoubtedly have regard to the extent to which national authorities have ensured participatory processes in fulfilling their accessibility obligations, as required under Article 4(3) of the Convention.[108] This will allow the Committee to determine whether governments have adopted the most appropriate measures which are least restrictive of the rights of persons with disabilities.

In the review and adoption of legislation, States will also be expected to involve persons with disabilities, among other stakeholders, such as members of the academic community and expert associations of architects, urban planners, engineers and

[107] UN Committee on the Rights of Persons with Disabilities, Individual Communication taken by Szilvia Nyusti and Péter Takács (represented by counsel, Tamás Fazekas, Hungarian Helsinki Committee), Communication No. 1/2010, views adopted by the Committee at its ninth session (15–19 April 2013), para. 10(2)(b).

[108] Article 4(3) of the CRPD specifically requires States Parties to consult with and involve persons with disabilities in developing and implementing legislation and policies and in decision-making processes, including in the formulation of accessibility standards concerning UN CRPD rights.

designers.[109] Close consultation with disabled people and other relevant stakeholders would demonstrate to the CRPD Committee that national disability laws take account of all aspects of accessibility and that efforts have been made to ensure effective implementation of Convention obligations. This is particularly important, according to the Committee, which observes that:

> Disability laws often fail to include ICT in their definition of accessibility, and disability rights laws concerned with non-discriminatory access in areas such as procurement, employment and education often fail to include access to ICT and the many goods and services central to modern society that are offered through ICT.[110]

In assessing whether private entities have taken into account all aspects of accessibility for persons with disabilities, as mandated under Article 9(2)(b), the Committee will undoubtedly deem it relevant whether persons with disabilities were consulted closely in the development of products, services or facilities. The Committee has stated, for example, that 'strengthening the direct involvement of persons with disabilities in product development would improve the understanding of existing needs and the effectiveness of accessibility tests.'[111] South Africa provides a good example of a jurisdiction which has engaged in participatory processes in ensuring the roll-out of an accessible transport system. DPOs contributed significantly to the South African Universal Access Policy which seeks to guide the implementation of accessibility obligations under the Cape Town's MyCiti integrated Rapid Transport system.[112] Persons with disabilities and their representative organisations should also be involved in the development, promulgation and monitoring of minimum standards for the accessibility of different facilities and services provided by public and private enterprises for persons with different types of impairments.[113] They should also be involved closely in defining the criteria for assessment of how accessible given products, services and facilities are.[114]

---

109 UN Committee on the Rights of Persons with Disabilities, General Comment No. 2 on Article 9: Accessibility), adopted at the eleventh session of the Committee (30 March–11 April 2014) on 11 April 2014, UN Doc. CRPD/C/GC/2, para. 28.

110 Ibid.

111 Ibid, para. 19.

112 Information taken from zeroproject.org, last accessed 24 October 2014.

113 In addition to developing the relevant accessibility standards in conjunction with disabled persons and their representative organisations, the CRPD Committee also recommends that they can be 'developed in collaboration with other States parties and international organizations and agencies through international cooperation, in accordance with article 32 of the Convention.' [UN Committee on the Rights of Persons with Disabilities, General Comment No. 2 on Article 9: Accessibility), adopted at the eleventh session of the Committee (30 March–11 April 2014) on 11 April 2014, UN Doc. CRPD/C/GC/2, para. 30].

114 EDF maintains that, in defining the criteria to be used for assessing the accessibility of goods, services and infrastructures, there must be close involvement of persons with disabilities. EDF further asserts that these criteria may include, but are not limited to, the following:

- Safety
- Affordability, i.e. whether the price of an accessible product is the same or comparable to the price of an ordinary product;
- Interoperability, i.e. compatibility with assistive devices or accompanying services;

In addition, disabled people and their representative organisations must be involved fully and enabled to participate in any monitoring mechanisms set up by national authorities. States will be required to design indicators to measure progress in the implementation of disability accessibility. Appropriate indicators and benchmarks should be devised in conjunction with persons with disabilities and their representative organisations in order to assess how key structures, activities, programmes, interventions and outcomes can contribute to Article 9 implementation. In addition, awareness-raising on the Convention's accessibility obligation should be carried out in cooperation with persons with disabilities, their representative organisations and technical experts.[115] If a given State fails to carry out such awareness-raising through participatory processes, the Committee might well find that it is in breach of its Article 9 obligations as persons with disabilities are best placed to inform relevant stakeholders of their accessibility requirements.

4.5.7. The Impact of Failure to Take Measures to Ensure Disability Accessibility

In its assessment of the effectiveness of measures taken in a particular context to ensure implementation of Article 9, the CRPD Committee might also take account of the impact of State inaction on the exercise by persons with disabilities of both the accessibility obligation, as well as other substantive rights in the Convention. This is particularly important in light of the fact that Article 9 is of transversal and overarching application. A failure to take measures in the context of disability accessibility will have a knock-on effect on access to many other CRPD rights. It is important that governments assess the likely costs to society of their failure to take measures and to support projects and programmes which have been designed specifically for the implementation of disability accessibility obligations under the Convention. In particular, the Committee should assess the impact of failure to take measures on the exercise of the non-discrimination norm for persons with disabilities and the guarantee that persons with disabilities should be able to enjoy Convention guarantees on an equal basis with others. It is arguable that the Committee should incorporate the inherent dignity of persons with disabilities into its analysis of a States' failure to take measures (subject, as always, to available resources) by analysing the extent to which failure to take necessary and appropriate measures to fulfil Article 9 obligations impacts on the further marginalisation and stigmatisation of persons with disabilities in society.

- Autonomy, i.e. the extent to which the user needs to be accompanied to be able to manipulate the product or use the service alone;
- User-friendliness;
- Choice, i.e. the ability to choose from a range of accessible products and services available, as such healthy competition makes products more affordable.

[Information taken from EDF submission to the UN Committee on the Rights of Persons with Disabilities on Article 9 'Accessibility' UNCRPD, 15 March 2012, available at www.edffeph.org/Page_Generale.asp?DocID=13854&thebloc=29617, last accessed 28 August 2014, at page 7].

115 UN Committee on the Rights of Persons with Disabilities, General Comment No. 2 on Article 9: Accessibility), adopted at the eleventh session of the Committee (30 March–11 April 2014) on 11 April 2014, UN Doc. CRPD/C/GC/2, para. 35.

4.5.8. Benefits to Third Parties

Chapter four of this book highlighted the fact that the issue of third-party benefits can be deemed to be one of the outer limits of the accommodation duty, via the notion of disproportionate burden. Third-party benefits may also be a relevant consideration for the CRPD Committee in the context of Article 9 implementation. In addition to considering the costs imposed by particular measures on States or private entities, another potentially relevant consideration for the Committee may be the issue of whether undertaking particular accessibility measures would have benefits to a wider group of individuals, such as the duty-bearer or people with a comparative disability or even non-disabled persons. This may be a factor mitigating, to some extent, against cost arguments advanced by States. Of course, the CRPD Committee is charged with the task of overseeing the implementation of disability rights alone. However, part of that task involves a consideration of the resource constraints facing a given State. Therefore, in considering the burden imposed by a given disability measure on a State, the Committee may have to weigh up the competing interests involved. Thus, for example, if a disabled person brings an individual complaint alleging inaccessibility of the physical environment, the Committee might consider the extent to which requiring measures of that particular entity or State will have tangential benefits for the entity or State concerned (such as increased revenue) or will have benefits for other citizens (such as ensuring easy access for persons with a comparative disability, older persons, parents with children and so forth). Jenny Goldschmidt has stated that a clear example of third party benefits can be seen in the US context under the ADA. In that regard, she states that when the Metropolitan Transport Agency in Washington, DC was under an obligation to make the public transport system (including platforms, exits and trains) accessible for people with disabilities, 'they subsequently noticed that the metro was used much more by fathers and mothers with prams, and this led to far more profit than expected.'[116]

In the individual communication taken by Szilvia Nyusti and Péter Takács against Hungary[117] regarding the inaccessibility of banking facilities, the CRPD Committee did not comment on the criterion of third-party benefits. However, as outlined above,[118] in the individual communication of *Jungelin v Sweden*, the dissenting members of the Committee took into account the issue of third-party benefits (accruing to persons with comparative disabilities) in its overall assessment of cost. Therefore, this criterion may acquire some degree of importance in the Committee's assessment over time. In may respects, the issue of third-party benefits would require a broader consideration of the progressive realisation of socio-economic rights by

---

116 J. Goldschmidt (interviewed by J. Anderson and J. Philips), 'Shifting the Burden of Proof: How the CRPD is Transforming our Understanding of Discrimination, Intersectionality and Priorities' in J. Anderson and J. Philips (eds.), *Disability and Human Rights: Legal, Ethical and Conceptual Implications of the Convention on the Rights of Persons with Disabilities* (Netherlands Institute of Human Rights, SIM Special 35, 2012), at page 52.

117 UN Committee on the Rights of Persons with Disabilities, Individual Communication taken by Szilvia Nyusti and Péter Takács (represented by counsel, Tamás Fazekas, Hungarian Helsinki Committee), Communication No. 1/2010, views adopted by the Committee at its ninth session (15–19 April 2013).

118 See chapter 4, section 4.5.2.

States relative to other groups in society. While this will be a difficult criterion for the CRPD Committee to weigh up in practice, the Committee has already commented on the obligation to design structures universally. In its General Comment 2, the Committee has drawn attention to the fact that implementation of Article 9 should be carried out in accordance with the principles of universal design contained in the Convention. The Committee took into account the criterion of third-party benefits when it noted that 'the application of universal design makes society accessible for all human beings, not only persons with disabilities.'[119] The Committee further observes that:

> The strict application of universal design to all new goods, products, facilities, technologies and services should ensure full, equal and unrestricted access for *all* potential consumers, including persons with disabilities, in a way that takes full account of their inherent dignity and diversity.[120] [emphasis added]

Universal design is defined in Article 2 of the Convention as meaning 'the design of products, environments, programmes and services to be usable by all people, to the greatest extent possible, without the need for adaptation or specialized design.'[121] It seeks to reduce the need for individualised measures, such as reasonable accommodations.[122] It recognises the inherent limitations of various inaccessible environments in promoting access for the general population, including disabled people. Such inaccessible environments relate not only to physical accessibility but also access to educational curricula, access to information and so forth. The concept of universal design evolved from accessible design features and it is therefore linked to the overall concept of accessibility but it goes further in requiring consideration of the whole spectrum of human diversity – from persons with disabilities to older people, parents and children, among others. The obligation to design structures universally, together with the observations of the Committee regarding the third-party benefits of accessibility measures, demonstrates the fact that such benefits may be a relevant tangential consideration in assessing the types of measures adopted by States to ensure progressive implementation of Article 9. Notwithstanding the promotion by the CRPD Committee of concepts of universal design in the overall implementation of Article 9, one must resist the temptation to view universal design as a utopian solution because that certainly is not the case. Colin Barnes notes that the emergence of universal design:

> Has generated considerable debate amongst academics and practitioners. Critics argue that the definition and principles of universal design are too general and lack clarity. The generality and lack of bench marking in the definition and principles of universal design

[119] UN Committee on the Rights of Persons with Disabilities, General Comment No. 2 on Article 9: Accessibility), adopted at the eleventh session of the Committee (30 March–11 April 2014) on 11 April 2014, UN Doc. CRPD/C/GC/2, para. 16.

[120] Ibid, para. 15.

[121] UN CRPD, Article 2.

[122] However, Article 2 also states that the concept of universal design shall not exclude assistive devices for particular groups of persons with disabilities where this is needed.

> are said to be too broad and contradictory [...] Concerns have also been raised about issues such as cost, participation outcomes and social change.[123]

In spite of the many complexities that remain in the design of infrastructure according to a universal design mandate, States Parties to the Convention are, at the very least, under a duty (pursuant to Article 4(1)(f) of the Convention) to undertake research into the development of universally designed goods, services, equipment and facilities, as defined under Article 2 of the CRPD. It is interesting to note that Norway is one of the few European countries[124] which requires the application of universal design and which promotes universally designed features actively in practice. Norway's Anti-Discrimination and Accessibility Act[125] is a disability-specific nationwide non-discrimination act which contains the legally enforceable standard of universal design. In addition, Norway amended its Planning and Building Act in 2010 to include an obligation to design features universally. Norwegian legislation also provides that a failure to design accessible information and communications technology (ICT) constitutes discrimination.[126]

5. Conclusion

This chapter has outlined the link between the accessibility and equality/non-discrimination norms under the Convention, as well as delineating the normative content of States' accessibility obligations and applying defined criteria to Article 9 in the overall assessment of the progressive realisation of Convention rights. The Convention's accessibility obligations breathe new life into the equality norm. The obligations imposed on States Parties to the CRPD under Article 9 aim to guarantee equal life opportunities for persons with disabilities in line with those that their non-disabled peers enjoy. The effective implementation of the Convention's accessibility provisions is a precondition for full participation and inclusion in society. While accessibility standards and measures may facilitate access to human rights and, in some cases, may ensure *de facto* equality, this will not always be the case. In such circumstances, States must go further in their endeavours to ensure effective implementation of both Article 5 and Article 9 of the Convention in tandem, including monitoring implementation of measures such as reasonable accommodations and positive action.

The CRPD Committee will have the difficult task of adjudicating the efforts of States to ensure disability accessibility, while at the same time ensuring the realisation of other socio-economic rights and obligations in the CPRD. The Committee must be

---

123 C. Barnes, 'Understanding Disability and the Importance of Design for All' (2011) 1(1) *Journal of Accessibility and Design for All* 55, at pages 71–72.

124 Certain Spanish laws and policies also promote universally designed features.

125 Act (No. 61 of 2013) prohibiting discrimination on grounds of disability (Anti-Discrimination and Accessibility Act) [Lov (Nr 61 av 2013) om forbud mot diskriminering på grunn av nedsatt funksjonsevne (diskriminerings- og tilgjengelighetsloven)].

126 Information taken from zeroproject.org, last accessed 24 October 2014.

realistic in its assessment – all States will have a duty to ensure the fulfilment of the rights of all marginalised groups and therefore the Committee must, in assessing the issue of disproportionate burden, take account of the fact that there will be many different constraints on a given country's resources. Nonetheless, States have a duty to ensure that whatever limited resources they have are used wisely and in a non-discriminatory manner. It will be the Committee's task to monitor the actions of States in that regard. The criteria outlined in this chapter are merely intended to guide the CRPD Committee in its assessments. The Committee must assess the extent to which the particular human rights gaps in a given country are being measured reliably and effectively by appropriate indicators (structural, process and outcome) and benchmarks. The Committee must also assess whether the measures taken on foot of those indicators and benchmarks are tailored appropriately to respond to the requirements identified in the specific national context. Most importantly, the Committee will have to assess States' compliance with Article 9 in a coherent manner, according to defined and realistic criteria and, furthermore, in a manner which does justice to the overall objective of *de facto* equality which guides Article 9 implementation.

The CRPD's equality, non-discrimination and accessibility norms form the backbone of a human rights-based approach to disability and their complementary nature cannot be overlooked. Any measures taken to guarantee that persons with disabilities can enjoy the accessibility guarantees in the Convention must be structured coherently as part of an overall schema for ensuring fulfilment of the Convention's equality and non-discrimination norms. Moreover, legal guarantees of equality and non-discrimination should be interpreted by State institutions in a manner which facilitates and promotes the Convention's accessibility requirements, as part of the overall goal of ensuring the full and effective realisation of socio-economic rights, as well as the civil and political guarantees contained in the CRPD.

Charlotte McClain Nhlapo describes accessibility as 'a continuum and a process.'[127] This rings true in the context of Article 9. Implementation of that article by States will be a lengthy process. Notwithstanding this, the drafters of the Convention did not intend that the concept of progressive realisation would run roughshod over States Parties' obligations. In order to operationalise the CRPD's accessibility obligations, national strategies and policies must go beyond a list of vague commitments to set specific and feasible objectives, with realistic timelines and adequate resource allocation.

[127] Remarks of Charlotte McClain Nhlapo, General Day of Discussion on Accessibility, Palais des Nations, Geneva, October 7, 2010, cited by J.E. Lord, 'Accessibility and Human Rights Fusion in the CRPD: Assessing the Scope and Content of the Accessibility Principle and Duty under the CRPD' (Presentation for the General Day of Discussion on Accessibility, UN CRPD Committee – Geneva, October 7, 2010, at page 1, available at www2.ohchr.org/SPdocs/CRPD/DGD7102010/.../JanetELord.doc last accessed 15 July 2014).

Chapter 7
The Right to Education for Persons with Disabilities

'Education is a human right with immense power to transform.'[128]

1. Introduction

The right to education in international human rights law is both an end in itself as well as a means towards attaining all other human rights. Former UN Special Rapporteur on Education, Katarina Tomasevski, has described education as 'a bridge to all human rights.'[129] Tomasevski observes that 'education is indispensible for effective political participation and for enabling individuals to sustain themselves; [...] it is the foundation for eliminating discrimination. It is the key to unlocking other human rights'[130] The proper enjoyment of the right to education is of fundamental importance for persons with disabilities. It is linked intrinsically with empowerment and participation and inclusion of disabled people in society on an equal basis with others. As an empowerment right, education has been described as 'the primary vehicle by which economically and socially marginalized adults and children can [...] obtain the means to participate fully in their communities.'[131] Without an appropriate education, persons with disabilities are denied the exercise and enjoyment of many other rights, including the right to work and the right to independent living, as without a formative education disabled individuals will be deprived of essential life and social skills necessary to ensure full and effective participation in society.[132]

There are huge gaps in the protection of the right to education for persons with disabilities. In many developing countries, in particular, an overwhelming majority of disabled children are excluded from the mainstream education system at every level. In a 2007 report,[133] former UN Special Rapporteur on Education succeeding

128 Kofi A. Annan, former Secretary-General of the United Nations, foreword in United Nations Children's Fund, *The State of the World's Children* (1999).

129 K. Tomasevski, *Education Denied: Costs and Remedies* (Zed Books Ltd, London, 2003), at page 172.

130 Ibid.

131 Committee on Economic, Social and Cultural Rights, General Comment 13 on The Right to Education (Article 13 of the Covenant) (1999), UN Doc. E/C.12/1999/10, 8 December 1999, para. 1.

132 The Committee on the Rights of the Child has recognised this fact in its General Comment 9, in which it notes that 'the lack of appropriate education and vocational training discriminates against [children with disabilities] by denying them job opportunities in the future.' [UN Committee on the Rights of the Child, General Comment 9 on Children with Disabilities (2006), adopted by the Committee at its Forty-third session Geneva, 11–29 September 2006, UN Doc. CRC/C/GC/9, para. 8].

133 Report of the Special Rapporteur on the Right to Education, Vernor Muñoz Villalobos, *The Right to Education of Persons with Disabilities,* UN Doc. A/HRC/4/29, 19 February 2007 available at http://ap.ohchr.org/documents/alldocs.aspx?doc_id=12900 last accessed 14 October 2014.

Ms. Tomasevski, Mr. Vernor Muñoz Villalobos, highlighted the fact that while the net enrolment rate in primary education in the developing world had increased to 86 per cent over all regions,[134] 'estimates of the number of children with disabilities attending school in developing countries range from less than 1 per cent to 5 per cent.'[135] The vast majority of persons with hearing or visual impairments in developing nations lack basic literacy skills.[136] In addition, many individuals with intellectual and psychiatric disabilities are often grossly neglected within the mainstream education system.[137] In the past, and indeed up to the present day, persons with disabilities have largely been segregated from their non-disabled peers in so-called 'special schools.' Until the adoption of the CRPD, international human rights law did not recognise a right to inclusive education within the mainstream school system. Inclusive education has been described by the CRC Committee as:

> A set of values, principles and practices that seeks meaningful, effective, and quality education for all students, that does justice to the diversity of learning conditions and requirements not only of children with disabilities, but for all students [...].[138]

While inclusive education seeks to benefit all learners, it is particularly important for persons with disabilities, as disabled learners have been subject to acute marginalisation and exclusion from mainstream society. Article 24 of the CRPD contains the first explicit legal enunciation of the right to inclusive education for persons with disabilities and it imposes wide-ranging duties on States Parties to the Convention. The primary objective of this chapter is to interpret and analyse the right to education contained in Article 24 from a legal perspective and to delineate the normative content of that right. To aid in the interpretation of Article 24, recourse will be had to the rules of treaty interpretation codified in the VCLT.[139] As a subsidiary source of interpretation, reference will be made primarily to the observations and recommendations of the CRPD Committee. The present chapter relates to the other chapters in this book by elaborating on the meaning of equality in the context of the right to education and by focusing on the progressive realisation of CRPD rights. To that end, the key criteria that might be employed by the CRPD Committee in assessing compliance by States with their obligations under Article 24 will be considered in this chapter. Those criteria are reflective of the factors outlined

---

134 Ibid, para. 8, citing United Nations, *The Millennium Goals Development Report* (2006), at page 6, available at http//mdgs.un.org/unsd/mdg/Resources/Static/Products/Progress2006/MDGReport2006.pdf last accessed 7 November 2014.

135 Ibid, citing S.J. Peters, *Inclusive Education: An EFA Strategy for All Children,* World Bank (November 2004), available at www.worldbank.org; See also the United Nations Educational, Scientific and Cultural Organization (UNESCO), Guidelines for Inclusion: Ensuring Access to Education for All (United Nations Educational, Scientific and Cultural Organization, France, 2005), at page 11.

136 UNESCO, *The Flagship on Education for All and the Right to Education for Persons with Disabilities: Towards Inclusion*, available at www.unesco.org/education/efa/know_sharing/flagship_initiatives/disability last accessed 10 November 2014.

137 Ibid.

138 UN Committee on the Rights of the Child, General Comment 9 on Children with Disabilities (2006), adopted by the Committee at its Forty-third session Geneva, 11–29 September 2006, UN Doc. CRC/C/GC/9, para. 67.

139 The interpretative tools contained in the VCLT have been outlined in detail in chapter one of this book.

in chapter five above as being pertinent to the assessment by the Committee of measures adopted by States under the Convention. One of the primary criterion of import for the Committee will be the Convention's equality and non-discrimination norms and, in particular, their impact on the interpretation of the right to education for disabled people.

This chapter will be broken down into six sections. In section two of this chapter, the normative framework securing the right to education in international human rights law will be outlined, together with the development of the right to inclusive education at the international level. Section three of this chapter will contain an outline of the concept of inclusive education generally, as well as an interpretation and analysis of the duties imposed on States under Article 24 of the CRPD. In section four of this chapter, the various criteria that might be employed by the CRPD Committee in assessing compliance by States with their obligations pursuant to Article 24 will be considered. In section five of this chapter, the emerging trends in the provision of inclusive education in States Parties to the CRPD will be highlighted. Finally, section six of this chapter will contain some concluding remarks.

2. The Right to Education in International Human Rights Law

In this section, the enunciation of the right to education in international human rights law will be traced, as well as the development of the right to inclusive education. The normative content of the right to education at the international level will then be reflected upon, according to the pronouncements of the UNCESCR and the observations of the former UN Special Rapporteur on Education, Ms. Katarina Tomasevski.

2.1. The Right to Education in International Human Rights Law and the Development of the Right to Inclusive Education

The right to education is a long established right at the level of international human rights law. It was first introduced in the Universal Declaration of Human Rights,[140] which affirmed a right to education for all individuals. The right to education has been expanded upon and strengthened considerably in subsequent international instruments. It is contained, *inter alia*,[141] in Articles 13[142] and 14 of

140 Universal Declaration on Human Rights, Article 26.

141 See also United Nations Convention on the Elimination of Discrimination against Women, Article 10; United Nations Convention on the Rights of the Child, Articles 28 and 29; United Nations Convention on the Rights of Persons with Disabilities, Article 24.

142 Article 13 of the ICESCR obliges States Parties to the Covenant to ensure that: (a) Primary education shall be compulsory and available free to all; (b) Secondary education in its different forms, including technical and vocational secondary education, shall be made generally available and accessible to all by every appropriate means, and in particular by the progressive introduction of free education; and

the ICESCR.[143] Notably, the right to education for disabled children is mentioned specifically in Article 23 of the Convention on the rights of the child.[144] In addition to its prominence in the binding core international human rights treaties, the right to education has been addressed in several internationally approved conventions and declarations. The *United Nations Educational, Scientific and Cultural Organization (UNESCO) Convention against Discrimination in Education*,[145] adopted in 1960, lays down comprehensive standards pertaining to non-discrimination and equal treatment of individuals in education. In 1990, the *World Declaration on Education for All* (WEA)[146] was adopted. It emanated from an important conference entitled the World Conference on Education for All (WCEFA) which was convened in Jomtien, Thailand by the World Bank, UNESCO and UNICEF, among others. The conference was organised in response to pervasive concerns about the deterioration of education systems on a global scale.[147] The Conference concluded with the unanimous adoption of the WEA and it also endorsed a *Framework for Action to Meet Basic Learning Needs*. Those texts are essentially policy documents which do not use rights language as such. Rather, they serve to renew the commitment of the world community in respect of the right to 'Education for All' (EFA),[148] which represents a global commitment designed to ensure the provision of basic and quality education for all children, youth and adults alike.[149] With regard to the rights of persons with disabilities, the Declaration affirmed the fact that 'the learning needs of the disabled demand special attention' and that 'steps need to be taken to provide equal access to education to every category of disabled persons as an integral part of the education system.'[150] However, the objectives of the WEA were not mandated specifically for persons with disabilities. Rather, the aim of the Declaration was to renew the global commitment to education, regardless of physical, social, economic and psychological

that (c) Higher education shall be made equally accessible to all, on the basis of capacity, by every appropriate means, and in particular by the progressive introduction of free education.

143 Article 14 of the ICESCR imposes an obligation on States to work out and adopt (within two years) a detailed plan of action for the progressive implementation, within a reasonable number of years (to be fixed in the plan) of the principle of compulsory education free of charge for all where, at the time of becoming a Party, the State has not been able to secure compulsory primary education, free of charge.

144 The content of Article 23 of the Convention of the Rights of the Child will be expanded upon briefly in section 3.2 below.

145 UNESCO, Convention against Discrimination in Education, adopted at the General Conference of the United Nations Educational, Scientific and Cultural Organization, meeting in Paris, 14 November to 15 December 1960, at its eleventh session.

146 UNESCO, The World Declaration on Education for All: Meeting Basic Learning Needs (1990), adopted by the UNESCO World Conference on Education for All of 9 March 1990, available at www.unesco.org/education/wef/en-conf/jomtien%20declaration%20eng.shtm last accessed 10 November 2014.

147 It brought together in the region of 1500 individuals representing 155 governments, 33 intergovernmental bodies and 125 non-governmental organisations, among other institutes and foundations.

148 For more information on Education for All, see www.un.org/en/globalissues/briefingpapers/efa/, last accessed 12 December 2014.

149 The Preamble of the WEA acknowledges the fact that, overall, the provision of education at that time was seriously deficient and that it must be made more relevant, qualitatively improved and must also be made universally available.

150 UNESCO, The World Declaration for Education for All: Meeting Basic Learning Needs (1990), adopted by the UNESCO World Conference on Education for All of 9 March 1990, available at www.unesco.org/education/wef/en-conf/jomtien%20declaration%20eng.shtm last accessed 10 November 2014.

condition. Following from the more general provisions on education contained in the WEA, the *UN Standard Rules on the Equalization of Opportunities for Persons with Disabilities*, adopted in 1993, dealt (among other things) with the right to education for disabled individuals. The Rules provide that 'States should recognize the principle of equal primary, secondary and tertiary educational opportunities for children, youth and adults with disabilities, in integrated settings.'[151] They also urge States to ensure that education for persons with disabilities forms 'an integral part of national educational planning, curriculum development and school organization.'[152] As we saw in chapter two above, the Standard Rules constitute the most comprehensive international instrument protecting the rights of disabled people before the adoption of the CRPD.

The next important instrument protecting the right to education arose out of the 'UNESCO World Conference on Special Needs Education: Access and Equality,' which was held in Salamanca, Spain in 1994. *The Salamanca Statement and Framework for Action on Special Needs Education*[153] resulted from the negotiations which took place during that conference. The Salamanca Statement and Framework was the first major international human rights document to recognise the diversity of learners and the need for accommodations. It marked the beginnings of the acknowledgment at the international level of the importance of educating children in inclusive learning environments.[154] Article 3 of the Statement urges States to 'include all children regardless of individual differences or difficulties [... and to ...] adopt as a matter of law or policy the principle of inclusive education, enrolling all children in regular schools, unless there are compelling reasons for doing otherwise.'[155] The Statement proclaims that 'every child has unique characteristics, interests, abilities and learning needs' and that 'education systems should be designed and educational programmes implemented to take into account the wide diversity of these characteristics and needs.'[156] It also recognises the specific needs of disabled children, noting that 'those with special educational needs must have access to regular schools which should accommodate them within a child-centred pedagogy capable of meeting these needs.'[157] The Salamanca Statement and Framework for Action clearly introduced the concept of 'inclusion' in education for persons with disabilities. It proclaims that 'regular schools with this inclusive orientation are the most effective means of combating discriminatory attitudes, creating welcoming

151 Rule 6, UN Standard Rules on the Equalization of Opportunities for Persons with Disabilities (adopted by the United Nations General Assembly, forty-eighth session, resolution 48/96, annex, of 20 December 1993), available at www.un.org/disabilities/default.asp?id=26 last accessed 3 September 2014.

152 Ibid.

153 The Salamanca Statement and Framework for Action on Special Needs Education (adopted at the World Conference on Special Needs Education: Access and Quality, Salamanca, Spain, 7–10 June 1994).

154 The Salamanca Statement defines inclusive education as follows: [...] schools should accommodate all children regardless of their physical, intellectual, social, emotional, linguistic or other conditions. This should include disabled and gifted children, street and working children, children from remote or nomadic populations, children from linguistic, ethnic or cultural minorities and children from other disadvantaged or marginalised areas or groups. Ibid, para. 3.

155 Ibid, para. 3.

156 Ibid, at page viii.

157 Ibid.

communities, building an inclusive society and achieving education for all.'[158] The Salamanca Statement and Framework for Action on Special Needs Education can be described as representing a human rights-based approach to education, not only for persons with disabilities but also for other disadvantaged groups with special educational needs, on account of the fact that it calls for empowerment and equality/non-discrimination for disabled persons (and indeed all disadvantaged groups). It also calls for the increased accountability of national governments in the provision of educational supports for such groups. Despite intermittent references to the right to education for persons with disabilities under the binding and non-binding UN instruments,[159] there were still major gaps to be filled in ensuring education in the mainstream for disabled persons. Article 24 of the CRPD seeks to redress such anomalies by enshrining the cornerstone principle of inclusive education in international human rights law. Before outlining the types of obligations incumbent on States under Article 24 in section three of this chapter, the next subsection of this chapter will reflect briefly on the normative content of the right to education generally at the level of international human rights law as this will also aid in the interpretation of Article 24.

2.2. The Normative Content of the Right to Education in International Human Rights Law

The right to education falls within the category of economic, social and cultural rights and is therefore subject to progressive realisation. This section will explore the normative content of the right to education set forth in the ICESCR and corresponding State obligations, as the education provisions of the ICESCR lay the foundations for the right to education generally in international human rights law.

158 Ibid, at page ix.

159 Another international instrument protecting the right to education – *The Dakar Framework for Action* – reaffirms the fact that education is a fundamental human right and highlights the importance for national authorities of adopting a rights-based approach to the implementation of EFA. The overall objective of the Dakar Framework is to ensure the realisation of EFA goals by 2015. The Dakar Framework contains only vague references to the educational rights of persons with disabilities. It states, for example, that the 'the inclusion of children with special needs [...] and others excluded from education, must be an integral part of strategies to achieve [universal primary education] by 2015' [at para. 32]. It also provides that 'education systems must be inclusive, actively seeking out children who are not enrolled, and responding flexibly to the circumstances and needs of all learners' [at para. 33]. Furthermore, the Dakar Framework urges States to ensure 'that the learning needs of all young people and adults are met through equitable access to appropriate and life-skills programmes' [at para. 7(iii)]. [See *The Dakar Framework for Action - Education for All: Meeting Our Collective Commitments* (adopted by the World Education Forum Dakar, Senegal, 26–28 April 2000), available at www.unesco.org/education/wef/en-conf/dakframeng.shtm last accessed 10 November 2014].

The core content[160] of a right has been deemed to define 'that essential element without which a right loses its substantive significance as a human right.'[161] Fons Coomans argues that the 'essence of the right to education means that no one shall be denied a right to education.'[162] This equates to an 'individual right of access to available education,'[163] namely the right to access on an equal basis with others the existing education system. In particular, access must be ensured for all individuals to the most basic forms of education. Coomans notes that the core content of education must include free and compulsory primary education.[164] He asserts that 'primary education is so fundamental for the development of a person's abilities that it can be rightfully defined as a minimum claim.'[165] The UNCESCR affirms that States are 'obliged to prioritise the introduction of compulsory, free primary education.'[166] The obligation to provide free primary education for all is deemed to be an immediate duty of States[167] and therefore must be addressed as a matter of priority.

The features of the right to education as a human right and the legal obligations of governments stemming from the right to education have been set down in the 4-A scheme developed by former UN Special Rapporteur on Education, Katarina Tomasevski, and adopted by the UNCESCR in its General Comment 13. In that general comment, the Committee expands on the various components of the progressive realisation of the right to education. It states that education in all its forms and on all levels should be available, accessible, acceptable, and adaptable.[168] According to the Committee, the availability of education implies that States must create and maintain functional educational facilities, which include all the materials and resources necessary for the education of the learners.[169] Tomasevski highlights the fact that availability refers to three different kinds of governmental obligation. In the first instance, she states that 'education as a civil and political right requires governments to permit the establishment of schools respecting freedom *of* and *in* education.' Secondly, she argues that 'education as a social and economic right requires governments to ensure that free and compulsory education is available to

---

160 For further analysis of the core content of the right to education, see K. Tomasevski, *Education Denied: Costs and Remedies* (Zed Books Ltd., London, 2003), at pages 51–52; See also K. Tomasevski, *Manual on Rights-Based Education: Global Human Rights Requirements Made Simple* (Collaborative project between the UN Special Rapporteur on the Right to Education and UNESCO Asia and Pacific Regional Bureau for Education) UNESCO Bangkok, 2004.

161 See F. Coomans, *De Internationale Bescherming van het Recht op Onderwijs* [The International Protection of the Right to Education], thesis, Leiden 1992, at pages 38–39.

162 F. Coomans, "Clarifying the Core Element to the Right to Education," *SIM Special 18,* 7 available at http://aihr-resourcescenter.org/administrator/upload/documents/core.pdf, last accessed 11 November 2014. last accessed 24 November 2014.

163 Ibid.

164 Ibid. Coomans also refers to free choice as being a core element of the right to education, stating that this element includes, but is not limited to, religious or philosophical convictions.

165 Ibid.

166 UNCESCR, General Comment No. 13 on the right to education (1999) (adopted at the twenty-first session, 1999), U.N. Doc. E/C.12/1999/10, para. 51.

167 Ibid.

168 Ibid, para. 6.

169 Ibid, para. 6(a).

all school-age children.' Finally, 'education as a cultural right [...] requires respect of diversity, expressed in particular through minority and indigenous rights.'[170]

The second criterion outlined by the UNCESCR in its General Comment 13 is the accessibility of education.[171] According to the Committee, accessible education has three overlapping dimensions. Firstly, it must be provided on a non-discriminatory basis. Secondly, it must be physically accessible and within safe physical reach for all. Thirdly, it must be economically accessible or affordable to all, especially vulnerable or marginalised groups.[172] Tomasevski underlines the fact that 'accessibility relates to the primary, secondary and tertiary levels of education in different ways' – in other words 'governments are only obliged to provide access to free and compulsory education for all children in the compulsory age range [...]'[173] She states that 'the right to education should be realized progressively, ensuring all-encompassing, free and compulsory education is available as soon as possible, and facilitating access to post-compulsory education as circumstances permit.'[174] The 2007 report drafted by Vernor Muñoz Villalobos maintains that ensuring access in the disability context encompasses 'physical access, communication access (sign language and Braille), social access (to peers) [... and ...] economic access (affordability).'[175]

The next criterion outlined by Ms. Tomasevski (and adopted by the UNCESCR in its General Comment 13) is the acceptability of education. This translates into the requirement that the form and substance of education, including curricula and teaching methods, should be acceptable to students (e.g. relevant, culturally appropriate and of good quality).[176] Tomasevski highlights the fact that 'acceptability requires minimum guarantees regarding the quality of education [...] but it is much wider in scope that this.' She states that acceptability 'has been considerably broadened through the development of international human rights law [...] to include the contents of educational curricula and textbooks, which are increasingly considered from the perspective of human rights.'[177]

---

170 K. Tomasevski, *Manual on Rights-Based Education: Global Human Rights Requirements Made Simple* (Collaborative project between the UN Special Rapporteur on the Right to Education and UNESCO Asia and Pacific Regional Bureau for Education) UNESCO Bangkok, 2004, at page 7.

171 UNCESCR, General Comment No. 13 on the right to education (1999) (adopted at the twenty-first session, 1999), U.N. Doc. E/C.12/1999/10, para. 6(b).

172 Ibid.

173 K. Tomasevski, *Manual on Rights-Based Education: Global Human Rights Requirements Made Simple* (Collaborative project between the UN Special Rapporteur on the Right to Education and UNESCO Asia and Pacific Regional Bureau for Education) UNESCO Bangkok, 2004, at page 7.

174 Ibid.

175 Report of the Special Rapporteur on the Right to Education, Vernor Muñoz Villalobos, *The Right to Education of Persons with Disabilities,* UN Doc. A/HRC/4/29, 19 February 2007, para. 28, available at http://ap.ohchr.org/documents/alldocs.aspx?doc_id=12900 last accessed 14 October 2014.

176 UNCESCR, General Comment No. 13 on the right to education (1999) (adopted at the twenty-first session, 1999), U.N. Doc. E/C.12/1999/10, para. 6(c).

177 K. Tomasevski, *Manual on Rights-Based Education: Global Human Rights Requirements Made Simple* (Collaborative project between the UN Special Rapporteur on the Right to Education and UNESCO Asia and Pacific Regional Bureau for Education) UNESCO Bangkok, 2004.

The final criterion is that of adaptability. This means that learning systems must be flexible and must adapt according to the changing needs of societies and communities and must respond to the needs of students within their diverse social and cultural settings.[178] In other words, education must not be provided according to a 'one-size-fits-all' approach. The best interests and the individual learning and support needs of each child must necessarily be taken into account. The adaptability of education is particularly relevant in the context of children with disabilities and it reflects a rights-based approach to education, entailing the provision of reasonable accommodations and other individualised supports. Tomasevski highlights the fact that, 'as human rights are indivisible, adaptability requires safeguards for all human rights within education as well as enhancing human rights through education.'[179]

Having considered the various components of the right to education generally in international human rights law, the next section of this chapter will explore the right to inclusive education and the corresponding State obligations under Article 24 of the CRPD.

3. The Right to Inclusive Education: Article 24 of the CRPD

This section of the chapter will reflect firstly on the concept of inclusive education generally and the various components of an inclusive learning system, before moving on to interpret and analyse Article 24 of the CRPD according to the rules of treaty interpretation contained in the VCLT. Thereafter, the normative content of Article 24 and corresponding State obligations will be outlined.

3.1. The Concept of Inclusive Education

Outside the context of the CRPD, inclusive education refers not only to the education of persons with disabilities but to all disadvantaged groups. It has been described as a:

> Process of addressing and responding to the diversity of needs of all learners by increasing participation in learning, cultures and communities, and reducing exclusion within and from education.[180]

The goals of inclusive learning can be summarised as including the core principles of non-discrimination and equality of opportunities, as well as accessibility of structures, facilities and processes and individualised learning methods. Diversity can be seen as a key value underlying inclusive educational systems. The benefits of

178 UNCESCR, General Comment No. 13 on the right to education (1999) (adopted at the twenty-first session, 1999), U.N. Doc. E/C.12/1999/10, para 6(d).

179 K. Tomasevski, *Education Denied: Costs and Remedies* (Zed Books Ltd. London, 2003), at page 52.

180 UNESCO, *Overcoming Exclusion through Inclusive Approaches in Education: A Challenge and a Vision, Conceptual Paper* (UNESCO 2003), at page 7.

inclusive education have been documented widely.[181] The World Report on Disability recognises that inclusion in mainstream schools 'promotes universal primary completion, is cost-effective and contributes to the elimination of discrimination.'[182] Former UN Special Rapporteur on the Right to Education, Mr. Vernor Muñoz Villalobos, acknowledges that the inclusion of learners with disabilities in mainstream schools 'confers significant psychological advantages, as well as greater fulfilment of intellectual and, especially social and emotional needs through regular and natural interaction with a diverse group of learners.'[183] In spite of its reported benefits, certain representative organisations of persons with disabilities have voiced concerns that education in inclusive settings may not cater fully to the diverse needs of all individuals with disabilities, owing to a lack of sufficient supports for disabled learners. For instance, the World Federation of the Deaf (WFD) has advocated for the option of separate schooling for students who are deaf, blind or deaf-blind. WFD expresses its concern that inclusion might become 'a simple placement in a regular school without meaningful interaction with classmates and professionals [... which is ...] tantamount to exclusion of the deaf learner from education and society.'[184] Article 24(3)(c) of the CRPD seeks to ensure that those types of fears are mitigated. It maintains the option for disabled individuals, particularly those who are blind, deaf or deaf-blind to attend specialised schools as long as it is in an environment which 'maximizes academic and social development.'[185]

In order to ensure fully inclusive educational systems, it is vital that proper supports are available to individuals. This raises the important distinction between mere integration in mainstream schools and full and effective participation and inclusion for persons with disabilities. In its concluding observations, the CRPD Committee has drawn attention to the fact that there is 'some confusion' between inclusive education and integrated education.[186] As outlined in chapter two of this book, an integrationist approach seeks merely to ensure that the disabled learner fits in with

---

181 For instance, Phil Smith observes that 'inclusive practices bring clear, unequivocal academic and social benefits for students with and without disabilities, across a variety of age ranges and education disciplines [P. Smith, 'Defining Inclusion. What Is It? Who Does it Benefit?' in P. Smith (ed.), *Whatever Happened to Inclusion? The place of students with intellectual disabilities in education,* at page 41 (Peter Lang Publishing, Inc., New York, 2010)]; See also, R. Morrison and I. Burgman, 'Friendship Experiences Among Children with Disabilities who Attend Mainstream Schools' (2009) 76 *Canadian Journal of Occupational Therapy* 145. [Information taken from L. Waddington and C. Toepke, 'Moving Towards Inclusive Education as a Human Right: An Analysis of International Legal Obligations to Implement Inclusive Education in Law and Policy' (December 8, 2014) Maastricht Faculty of Law Working Paper No. 2014-, available at http://papers.ssrn.com/sol3/papers.cfm?abstract_id=2535198 last accessed 7 January 2014].

182 World Health Organization & World Bank, World Report on Disability (2011), at page 206.

183 Report of the Special Rapporteur on the Right to Education, Vernor Muñoz Villalobos, *The Right to Education of Persons with Disabilities,* UN Doc. A/HRC/4/29, 19 February 2007, para. 39, available at http://ap.ohchr.org/documents/alldocs.aspx?doc_id=12900 last accessed 14 October 2014.

184 See World Federation of the Deaf, *Education rights for deaf children: A policy statement of the World Federation of the Deaf* (2007), available at www.wfdeaf.org/databank/policies, last accessed 11 November 2014.

185 UN CRPD, Article 24(3)(c).

186 UN Committee on the Rights of Persons with Disabilities, Concluding Observations of the on the initial report of Austria (2013), UN Doc. CRPD/C/AUT/CO/1, para. 40.

the 'norm.' Mr. Villalobos has outlined the fact that 'the "integration" of learners with disabilities without full inclusion can lead to isolation of the learner and ultimately, [can be] an obstacle to meeting the education needs of all learners.'[187] Integrationist systems can therefore be exclusionary in themselves. By way of contrast, an inclusive learning system is designed to ensure that persons with disabilities can participate fully and access the right to education on an equal basis with others, entailing the elimination of barriers restricting participation and the provision of material support where necessary. Inclusive education accords with the tenets of the social model of disability to the extent that it requires fully accessible structures. On the other hand, systems of segregated or special education mirror the out-dated medical model of disability, in the sense that they focus on the functional limitations of the child in question and require the disabled learner to adapt to inaccessible educational institutions.

Article 24 of the CRPD does not define what is meant by the principle of inclusive education. However, it does give some indication of the types of measures which might make an education system inclusive, such as reasonable accommodations and individualised supports. These measures will be expanded upon in the next subsection of this chapter. The UN organs have elaborated on the requirements of an inclusive education system for persons with disabilities in the handbook for parliamentarians entitled *From Exclusion to Equality*, in which the following tenets of inclusive education are put forward:

- The provision of suitable equipment and teaching materials for persons with disabilities;
- The adoption of teaching methods and curricula that embrace the needs of all children and students, including those with disabilities, and promote acceptance of diversity;
- The training of teachers to teach in an inclusive classroom and encouragement for them to support each other;
- The provision of a range of supports that meets the diverse needs of all students, including students with disabilities, to the greatest extent possible.[188]

The handbook has also put forward a number of suggestions to ensure that education becomes more inclusive, as follows:

- Disseminating inclusive education methodologies as an integral part of teacher-training syllabuses;
- Using pyramid training techniques whereby teachers, once trained in inclusive-education methodologies, teach other teachers;

---

187 Report of the Special Rapporteur on the Right to Education, Vernor Muñoz Villalobos, *The Right to Education of Persons with Disabilities*, UN Doc. A/HRC/4/29, 19 February 2007, para. 40, available at http://ap.ohchr.org/documents/alldocs.aspx?doc_id=12900 last accessed 14 October 2014.

188 United Nations, *From Exclusion to Equality: Realizing the Rights of Persons with Disabilities: Handbook for Parliamentarians on the Convention on the Rights of Persons with Disabilities and its Optional Protocol* (2007, Inter-Parliamentary Press, Geneva), at page 82.

- Promoting peer-tutoring programmes, whereby higher-level students assist junior students;
- Ensuring reasonable accommodation is provided in child assessment;
- Turning existing special schools into resource centres and setting up a reporting mechanism to monitor school registration and completion by children with disabilities.[189]

Having considered the general components of an inclusive learning environment, the specific obligations contained in Article 24 of the CRPD will be interpreted below, having recourse to the rules contained in the VCLT, as well as the observations and recommendations of the CRPD Committee as a subsidiary source of interpretation.

3.2. A Legal Interpretation of Article 24 of the CRPD

Article 24 of the CRPD cements the principle of inclusive education in international human rights law. It endorses a strong mandate for States Parties to the Convention to ensure participation and inclusion for persons with disabilities in education. Before the adoption of the CRPD, the right to inclusive education had not been mentioned explicitly in an international human rights treaty. The CRC did, however, contain references to many of the objectives of inclusive education, in particular the importance of ensuring adaptability in learning systems. Article 23(3) of the CRC recognises the special needs of disabled children. It outlines the requirement to accord assistance designed to ensure that children with disabilities have effective access to and receive education and training (among other things) in a manner which is conducive to the child's achieving the fullest possible social integration and individual development, including his or her cultural and spiritual development.[190] Article 28(1)(b) of the CRC requires that secondary education should be available and accessible[191] and Article 28(1)(c) requires that higher education must be accessible to all on the basis of capacity by every appropriate means.[192] The aims of education outlined in Article 29 of the CRC (including development of the child's potential, talents and abilities to their fullest potential and development of respect for human rights) also endorse an inclusive philosophy and are reflective of a rights-based approach to education. Notwithstanding this, the CRC does not mention explicitly a right to inclusive education for disabled children.

---

189 Ibid, at page 84.

190 UN Convention on the Rights of the Child, Article 23(3).

191 Under Article 28(1)(b) of the Convention on the Rights of the Child, States undertake to 'encourage the development of different forms of secondary education, including general and vocational education, make them available and accessible to every child, and take appropriate measures such as the introduction of free education and offering financial assistance in case of need.'

192 Under Article 28(1)(c) of the Convention on the Rights of the Child, States undertake to 'make higher education accessible to all on the basis of capacity by every appropriate means' and Article 28(1)(d) requires states to 'make educational and vocational information and guidance available and accessible to all children.'

Before the adoption of the CRPD, the maintenance of segregated educational systems was allowed under the *UNESCO Convention Against Discrimination in Education* in certain circumstances (outside of the disability context).[193] Interestingly, the *travaux préparatoires* of the CRPD reveal that there was some debate during the negotiation sessions as to whether segregated education should be prohibited explicitly under the Convention or whether it should be allowed in certain circumstances.[194] The original draft Article 17(3) of the CRPD provided as follows: 'Where the general education system does not adequately meet the needs of persons with disabilities, special and alternative forms of learning should be made available.'[195] The phrase 'effective alternative support measures' was generally understood as referring to special education or a mixed form of educational provision.[196] On foot of proposals put forward by the EU and Australian delegates, this stance was altered, and under the new draft Article 17(1), States Parties to the Convention undertook to ensure 'the goal of inclusiveness of their general education systems.'[197] Many delegates believed

193 Article 2 of the UNESCO Convention against Discrimination in Education states that the following situations shall not be deemed to constitute discrimination, within the meaning of Article 1 of this Convention:
(a) The establishment or maintenance of separate educational systems or institutions for pupils of the two sexes, if these systems or institutions offer equivalent access to education, provide a teaching staff with qualifications of the same standard as well as school premises and equipment of the same quality, and afford the opportunity to take the same or equivalent courses of study; (b) The establishment or maintenance, for religious or linguistic reasons, of separate educational systems or institutions offering an education which is in keeping with the wishes of the pupil's parents or legal guardians, if participation in such systems or attendance at such institutions is optional and if the education provided conforms to such standards as may be laid down or approved by the competent authorities, in particular for education of the same level; and (c) The establishment or maintenance of private educational institutions, if the object of the institutions is not to secure the exclusion of any group but to provide educational facilities in addition to those provided by the public authorities, if the institutions are conducted in accordance with that object, and if the education provided conforms with such standards as may be laid down or approved by the competent authorities, in particular for education of the same level.

194 For instance, the Canadian delegate argued that persons with disabilities should 'always [be] educated within the general education system.' On the other hand, the Japanese delegate maintained that 'the use of general or special schools should be decided according to the best interests of the child.' [Seventh Session of the Ad Hoc Committee (16/01/06–03/02/06), Daily summary of discussion at the seventh session 24th January 2006, www.un.org/esa/socdev/enable/rights/ahc7sum24jan.htm, last accessed 10 November 2014].

195 Draft Article 17(3) of the CRPD, Report of the Working Group to the Ad Hoc Committee (2004), UN Doc. A/AC.265/2004/WG/1, Annex 1, available at www.un.org/esa/socdev/enable/rights/ahcwgreortax1.htm last accessed 12 November 2014.

196 G. De Beco, 'The Right to Inclusive Education According to Article 24 of the UN Convention on the Rights of Persons with Disabilities: Background, Requirements and (Remaining) Questions,' (2014) 285 *Netherlands Quarterly of Human Rights* 32(3), at page 285, citing O. Arnardóttir, 'The Right To Inclusive Education For Children With Disabilities – Innovations In The CRPD' in A. Eide, J. Möller, and I. Ziemele (eds), *Making Peoples Heard. Essays on Human Rights in Honour of Gudmundur Alfredsson* (Martinus Nijhoff Publishers 2011) 197, at page 217.

197 See the proposals put forward by the Australian delegate in the negotiation sessions leading to the adoption of the CRPD – 'Draft Article 17 EDUCATION,' available at www.un.org/esa/socdev/enable/rights/ahc6australia.htm last accessed 7 November 2014; See also the proposal put forward by the EU delegate – 'European Union Proposal for Article 17,' www.un.org/esa/socdev/enable/rights/ahc6eu.htm last accessed 12 November 2014.

that the focal point of the right to education should be on inclusion.[198] It is noteworthy that Article 24 of the CRPD does not prohibit segregated education explicitly.[199] It allows for special educational systems in limited circumstances – where necessary to cater for individuals who are blind, deaf or deaf-blind.[200] As Gauthier de Beco notes, the consequence of that particular provision is that persons with sensory or communication impairments 'should be allowed to be educated in special schools, although this option should not prevent them from asking to be able to participate in the general education system.'[201] Doubts remain regarding the extent to which special educational systems are permitted under Article 24(2)(e) of the CRPD in circumstances where the individual in question does not fall under the exception for blind, deaf or deaf-blind students. Article 24(2)(e) provides that effective individualised support measures may be provided in 'environments that maximize academic and social development, consistent with the goal of full inclusion.'[202] This would appear to give some leeway to States, in terms of educational provision, where fully inclusive education is not yet feasible. Of course, many States Parties to the CRPD retain a robust system of segregated educational settings. It would be unrealistic to expect those special schools to be closed overnight. Moreover, doing so would lead to a discriminatory gap in education for many disabled children, who would not have access to any educational provision. What is required in those States Parties is that there is a gradual shift away from segregation towards inclusive education systems. As de Beco observes:

> Such a transition can be achieved by establishing a mixed form of education. One of the solutions is to bring the two systems to the same campus so that the knowledge and

198 The Centre for Studies on Inclusive Education (CSIE) noted that inclusive education 'should be the thrust of Article 24.' The CSIE defined inclusion broadly to mean 'education in mainstream schools with a full range of support and accommodations necessary to facilitate effective education for all students with disabilities, including those who are blind, deaf and deafblind.' [Seventh Session of the Ad Hoc Committee (16/01/06–03/02/06), daily summary of discussion at the seventh session 24th January 2006, www.un.org/esa/socdev/enable/rights/ahc7sum24jan.htm, last accessed 10 November 2014].

199 Some States Parties have made specific reservations to Article 24 regarding inclusive education. For instance, Mauritius made a reservation with regard to Article 24(2)(b) because, although the State Party had a policy of inclusive education, it wanted to keep its special education system also. [Mauritius Reservation to the CRPD, Article 24 https://treaties.un.org/Pages/ViewDetails.aspx?src=TREATY&mtdsg_no=IV-15&chapter=4&lang=en accessed 10 November 2014]. Similarly, the United Kingdom made a reservation to Articles 24(2)(a) and 24(2)(b) regarding the right for disabled children to be educated outside their local community where more appropriate educational provision is available elsewhere. Nevertheless, the UK made clear that parents of disabled children have the same opportunity as other parents to state a preference for the school at which they wish their child to be educated. including in both mainstream and segregated or so-called special schools. [United Kingdom Reservation to the CRPD, Article 24 https://treaties.un.org/Pages/ViewDetails.aspx?src=TREATY&mtdsg_no=IV-15&chapter=4&lang=en accessed 10 November 2014].

200 See Article 24(3) of the CRPD.

201 G. De Beco, The Right to Inclusive Education According to Article 24 of the UN Convention on the Rights of Persons with Disabilities: Background, Requirements and (Remaining) Questions,' (2014) 285 *Netherlands Quarterly of Human Rights* 32(3), 286.

202 CRPD, Article 24(2)(e).

> materials from special schools can be used in regular schools. Special schools will then be transformed as learning resource centres.[203]

De Beco notes, however, that this must remain 'a temporary solution, considering that bringing these two systems together can still mean a segregated education system in reality.'[204] Thus, he posits that 'the learning resource centres should be incorporated into mainstream schools. Resources have likewise to be transferred from the special schools to the mainstream schools.'[205]

One vital question that might be asked is how to align the CRPD's mandate of inclusion with providing effective education for persons with severe or profound disabilities. Indeed, there are a limited number of individuals for whom reasonable accommodations may not be possible or for whom supports may not be effective. In those cases where the eloquent theory of inclusive education is not (yet) achievable, what then? As de Beco notes, 'Article 24 does not prevent States from establishing special schools for these children.'[206] 'Nor, however, does it compel them to be equipped with special schools.'[207] De Beco contends that providing special education to such learners with disabilities is permissible 'as long as this is not done on the basis of their impairments but on the basis of the barriers to their participation in society.'[208] States will therefore 'have a certain leeway' in the provision of education, although they should 'provide a strong CRPD-based justification if they keep a partially-segregated education system.'[209] In addition, de Beco highlights the fact that the 'special' forms of education provided to these disabled children 'must not be of lesser quality than normal education, because this would again lead to discrimination.'[210]

Aside from the foregoing 'deviations' from inclusive education systems, the CRPD lays down the principle of inclusion very clearly in Article 24 and States should therefore aim for full inclusion where that is feasible. On a textual, systematic and teleological reading of the Convention, there is no doubt but that States Parties to the CRPD are obliged to ensure that education for persons with disabilities is provided

---

203 G. De Beco, The Right to Inclusive Education According to Article 24 of the UN Convention on the Rights of Persons with Disabilities: Background, Requirements and (Remaining) Questions,' (2014) 285 *Netherlands Quarterly of Human Rights* 32(3), at page 285 citing OHCHR, 'Thematic study on the right of persons with disabilities to education' (2013) UN Doc A/HRC/25/29, at page 13.

204 G. De Beco, The Right to Inclusive Education According to Article 24 of the UN Convention on the Rights of Persons with Disabilities: Background, Requirements and (Remaining) Questions,' (2014) 285 *Netherlands Quarterly of Human Rights* 32(3), at page 285.

205 Ibid.

206 Ibid, citing A. Kanter, 'The Right to Inclusive Education for Students with Disabilities under International Law' [forthcoming], at page 24 (paper on file with G. De Beco).

207 Ibid, citing O. Arnardóttir, 'The Right To Inclusive Education For Children With Disabilities – Innovations In The CRPD' in A. Eide, J. Möller, and I. Ziemele (eds.), *Making Peoples Heard. Essays on Human Rights in Honour of Gudmundur Alfredsson* (Martinus Nijhoff Publishers 2011) 197, at page 210.

208 Ibid, at page 285.

209 Ibid.

210 Ibid.

in an inclusive learning environment. As outlined in chapter one of this book, the VCLT contains the rules of treaty interpretation that are widely accepted as being the most appropriate rules for interpreting the norms contained in international human rights treaties. The interpretative tools set forth in Articles 31 and 32 of the VCLT are as follows: literal (textual) interpretation, systematic (contextual) interpretation, teleological (functional) interpretation and historical interpretation. These interpretative tools will be relied on throughout this section of the chapter to aid in the analysis of Article 24 of the CRPD.

On a textual reading of the Convention, States are required to 'ensure an inclusive education system at all levels.'[211] The Human Rights Committee has stated that an obligation 'to ensure' requires States Parties to adopt 'legislative, judicial, administrative, educative and other appropriate measures in order to fulfil their legal obligations.'[212] Therefore States Parties to thc CRPD are under a particularly strong onus to take wide-ranging measures to guarantee inclusive education. Article 24(2)(b) of the Convention refers to inclusive primary education. It requires States to ensure that 'persons with disabilities can access an inclusive, quality and free primary education on an equal basis with others in the communities in which they live.'[213] Article 24 of the CRPD also underlines the goals to be achieved by education in the context of disabled persons. First and foremost, education should be directed towards 'the full development of human potential and sense of dignity and self-worth, and the strengthening of respect for human rights, fundamental freedoms and human diversity.'[214] Article 24 also highlights the fact that education should aim at the 'development by persons with disabilities of their personality, talents and creativity, as well as their mental and physical abilities, to their fullest potential.'[215] The third goal to be achieved by education under the Convention is to enable 'persons with disabilities to participate effectively in a free society.'[216] All of these goals are clearly reflective of an inclusive education mandate – they seek to ensure that the innate capabilities of persons with disabilities are nurtured and given room to develop and to guarantee the removal of barriers to full and effective participation in society.

The object and purpose of the Convention is stated in Article 1 as being to promote, protect and ensure the full and equal enjoyment of all human rights and fundamental freedoms by all persons with disabilities, and to promote respect for their inherent dignity.[217] Article 1 of the Convention also acknowledges the fact that the participation in society of persons with disabilities is hindered through interaction with various barriers.[218] This reflects the social model of disability which underlies

---

211 UN CRPD, Article 24(1).

212 Human Rights Committee, General Comment 31 on the nature of the general legal obligation on States Parties to the Covenant (2004), U.N. Doc. CCPR/C/21/Rev.1/Add.13, para. 7.

213 UN CRPD, Article 24(2)(b).

214 UN CRPD, Article 24(1)(a).

215 UN CRPD, Article 24(1)(b).

216 UN CRPD, Art. 24 (1)(c).

217 UN CRPD, Article 1.

218 Ibid.

the Convention as a whole, including Article 24. The application of the social model to the right to education seeks to ensure full participation and inclusion of persons with disabilities in mainstream learning systems. The Preamble of the CRPD evidences a rights-based approach to children. It requires States to ensure that children with disabilities 'have full enjoyment of all human rights and fundamental freedoms on an equal basis with other children.'[219] In addition, the general principles of the Convention, contained in Article 3, mirror this rights-based approach by seeking to ensure '[r]espect for the evolving capacities of children with disabilities and respect for the right of children with disabilities to preserve their identities.'[220] The object and purpose and general principles of the Convention are cross-cutting, applying *inter alia* to Article 24. By recognising the diversity of children with disabilities, the Convention endorses the principles of accessibility and adaptability, including in the context of the right to education. Once again, this demonstrates that the Convention as a whole seeks to ensure that children with disabilities can develop their talents and abilities in the mainstream, through the provision of material support where necessary.

The concluding observations of the CRPD Committee can be used as a subsidiary aid to interpretation of Article 24. The Committee has confirmed that full inclusion of persons with disabilities in the general education system will be the ultimate goal of States. In its 'List of Issues' to the Tunisian government, the Committee includes a request for 'information about the progress achieved toward ensuring *full scholastic inclusion* of children with disabilities.'[221] [emphasis added] On the basis of all of the above, it is beyond doubt that full inclusion of persons with disabilities is the ultimate aim of the CRPD. Having established this much, the various obligations incumbent on States under Article 24 of the Convention will be discerned below.

3.3. The Obligations of States under Article 24 of the CRPD

The subsections which follow will delineate the specific obligations imposed on States under Article 24 of the CRPD. The concluding observations and recommendations of the CRPD Committee will be drawn on in order to clarify the steps to be taken by States to ensure that persons with disabilities are guaranteed the right to education on an equal basis with others.

3.3.1. Non-Discrimination in Education

The observations of the core international human rights treaty bodies make it very clear that the non-discrimination principle is not subject to the overall concept of progressive realisation. States Parties to the CRPD will be required to ensure non-

219 UN CRPD, Preamble (r).

220 UN CRPD, General Obligation 3(h).

221 UN Committee on the Rights of Persons with Disabilities, *List of Issues to be Taken up in Consideration of the Initial Report of Tunisia* (adopted at the fourth session of the Committee, 4-8 October 2010), para. 20 www.ohchr.org/en/hrbodies/crpd/pages/crpdindex.aspx last accessed 14 October 2014.

discrimination in access to, and in the exercise of, the right to education by persons with disabilities. Discrimination in education has been defined as including the treatment of any student in a way that separates him or her from the other students and negatively impacts on his or her ability to participate in and receive education.[222] This includes depriving a person or a group from access to education,[223] limiting a person or group to an inferior education,[224] establishing or maintaining separate educational systems for certain groups,[225] or inflicting on any person or group conditions which are against their dignity.[226]

The right of non-discriminatory access to education for persons with disabilities is set out in Articles 24(2)(a) and 24(2)(b) of the CRPD. Article 24(2)(a) of the Convention requires States to ensure that 'persons with disabilities are not excluded from the general education system on the basis of disability, and that children with disabilities are not excluded from free and compulsory primary education, or from secondary education, on the basis of disability.'[227] Under Article 24(2)(b) of the CRPD, States undertake to ensure that persons with disabilities 'can access an inclusive, quality and free primary and secondary education on an equal basis with others in the communities in which they live.'[228] During the negotiation sessions, the Chair of the Ad-Hoc Committee, Mr. Ronald Mc Callum, explained the parameters of that obligation by stating that if free and compulsory primary education is available to non-disabled people, it should be made available to disabled people without discrimination based on disability.[229] The same logic applies in respect of secondary and university-level education.[230] States should make greater efforts to enable students with disabilities to study at universities and other tertiary institutions. Indeed, the CRPD Committee has drawn attention to the fact that States should focus on inclusion at all levels, including adult education.[231]

Lack of access to education has been recognised as a 'dominant problem in the disability field'[232] for both children and adults with disabilities. Susan Peters

---

222 UNESCO Convention against Discrimination in Education, Paris (1960), Article 1.

223 Ibid, Article 1(a).

224 Ibid, Article 1(b).

225 Ibid, Article 1(c). Article 2 of the Convention against Discrimination in Education elaborates that separate educational systems are allowed if the separate systems offer equivalent access to education with teachers of the same qualifications, quality school premises and equipment, and equivalent courses.

226 Ibid, Article 1(d).

227 UN CRPD, Article 24(2)(a).

228 UN CRPD, Article 24(2)(b).

229 Quoting the words of Ronald Mc Callum, CRPD Ad-Hoc Committee, daily summaries, sixth session, 3 August 2005 www.un.org/esa/socdev/enable/rights/ahc6sum3aug.htm last accessed 14 June 2014.

230 Ibid.

231 UN Committee on the Rights of Persons with Disabilities, Concluding Observations of the UN Committee on the Rights of Persons with Disabilities, Costa Rica, U.N. Doc. CRPD/C/CRI/CO/1 (2014), para. 48.

232 S.J. Peters, 'Inclusive Education: An EFA Strategy for All Children' (World Bank 2004), 5, citing the United Nations Special Rapporteur on Human Rights and Disability, Bengt Lindqvist, 'Education as a fundamental right' in UNICEF, *Education Update* (1999) 2(4), page 7, available at www.unicef.org/education/files/vol2disabileng.pdf last accessed 14 November 2014.

points to the fact that 'in a majority of countries, there is a dramatic difference in the educational opportunities provided for disabled children and those provided for non-disabled children [...].[233] In particular, it is concerning to note that there are still major anomalies in access to free and compulsory primary education for disabled children. This is revealed by the shadow report submitted to the CRPD Committee during the State examination of China, which highlights the fact that, while the proportion of disabled children entering compulsory education in China is increasing,[234] 'there is still a clear gap compared with the national level of school-age children in compulsory education.'[235] Likewise, attention has been drawn to the fact that, in Peru, 87.1% of school-age children with disabilities remain outside of the education system.[236] The CRPD Committee has emphasised that States Parties to the Convention must intensify their efforts to ensure that disabled children benefit to the same extent as non-disabled children from any system of compulsory education established by domestic authorities.[237] The Committee voices its concern throughout its concluding observations that access to mainstream education is being blocked for a large proportion of disabled individuals. The Committee has outlined in its concluding observations that, in many countries, disabled learners are being placed in segregated education and not in inclusive educational settings.[238] This discriminatory practice has also been highlighted in the shadow reports submitted to the Committee. For instance, the shadow report submitted to the Committee by a Spanish NGO criticises the legislative framework in that country. The report claims that the relevant legislation,[239] although apparently based on inclusive education and equal opportunities, still permits individuals with certain disabilities or high support

---

233 Ibid.

234 Reaching 71.4% in 2010 as a result of the implementation of education aid policies. [Information taken from the Alternative Report of One Plus One Beijing, *Implementation in China of the United Nations Convention on the Rights of Persons with Disabilities* (March 2012), para. 87, available at www.ecoi.net/file_upload/1930_1373293379_oneplusonebeijing-report-eng.pdf last accessed 14 November 2014, citing the China Disabled People's Federation, 2010 Report on the Progress of the Well-being of Disabled People in China].

235 Alternative Report of One Plus One Beijing, *Implementation in China of the United Nations Convention on the Rights of Persons with Disabilities* (March 2012), para. 87, available at www.ecoi.net/file_upload/1930_1373293379_oneplusonebeijing-report-eng.pdf last accessed 14 November 2014.

236 See the Alternative Report on the Compliance with the Convention on the Rights of Persons with Disabilities submitted by the Peruvian National Confederation of People with Disabilities, available at www2.ohchr.org/SPdocs/CRPD/6thsession/CONFENADIP_Peru_en.doc last accessed 15 November 2014.

237 UN Committee on the Rights of Persons with Disabilities, Concluding Observations to Argentina, U.N. Doc. CRPD/C/ARG/CO/1 (2012), para. 38.

238 See, for instance, UN Committee on the Rights of Persons with Disabilities, Concluding Observations to China, U.N. Doc. CRPD/C/CHN/CO/1 (2012), para. 35; Concluding Observations to Spain, U.N. Doc. CRPD/C/ESP/CO/1 (2011), para. 43; Concluding Observations to Costa Rica, U.N. Doc. CRPD/C/CRI/CO/1 (2014), para. 45; Concluding Observations to Austria, U.N. Doc. CRPD/C/AUT/CO/1 (2013), para. 40; Concluding Observations to Australia, U.N. Doc. CRPD/C/AUS/CO/1 (2013), para. 45; Concluding Observations to Hungary, U.N. Doc. CRPD/C/HUN/CO/1 (2012), para. 39.

239 The General Organisation of the Education System Act of 1990 (Ley Organica de Ordenacion General del Sisterna Educativo).

needs to be referred to special education centres.[240] In that regard, it was highlighted above[241] that there may be instances in which fully inclusive education is not yet feasible for States Parties. In those circumstances, States must demonstrate that they are making every effort to ensure that resources tied into special educational centres are being harnessed towards ensuring full inclusion over time.

Ensuring access to inclusive education will begin with States Parties to the CRPD drawing up a clear definition of what is meant by inclusive education and including this in national legislation.[242] It has been acknowledged that while:

> There is almost universal recognition of the need to promote inclusive education practices [...] the concept of inclusive education does not seem to be clearly recognized in all countries, many of which identify it with integrated education.[243]

In other words, 'there does not appear to be a consensus on the meanings and implications of the two pedagogical approaches or methods.'[244] Guaranteeing access to inclusive education will also require the removal of discriminatory barriers to participation and inclusion.[245] True access to education has been deemed to implicate 'factors both external and personal to each student.'[246] Mr. Vernor Muñoz Villalobos maintains that to overcome external factors limiting access to education, this will include 'altering the physical environment, such as the design of hallways and classrooms, desks, widening entrances, building ramps, installation of elevators, altering or reconsidering geographical locations, adapting rules and admission standards.'[247] Overcoming personal factors will require such measures as 'the provision of supplementary classes, alternative/additional forms of communication, special tutors or support staff [...].'[248]

In view of the clear duties falling on States to remove discriminatory barriers, the next subsection of this chapter will consist of an examination of the types of measures that must be put in place by States under Article 24 of the CRPD in order to remove discriminatory barriers to accessing education on an equal basis with others.

---

240 Alternative Report of the Comité Espanol de Representantes de Personas Con Discapacidad (CERMI State Delegation) (2010), *Human Rights and Disability*, at para. 99, available at www2.ohchr.org/SPdocs/CRPD/.../CERMI_Spain_5thSession_en.doc. last accessed 15 November 2014.

241 See section 3.2 of this chapter.

242 See Concluding Observations of the UN Committee on the Rights of the Child, Cyprus, U.N. Doc. CRC/C/CYP/CO/3-4 (2012), paras. 38 and 39.

243 Report of the Special Rapporteur on the Right to Education, Vernor Muñoz Villalobos, *The Right to Education of Persons with Disabilities*, UN Doc. A/HRC/4/29, 19 February 2007, para. 53, available at http://ap.ohchr.org/documents/alldocs.aspx?doc_id=12900 last accessed 14 October 2014.

244 Ibid.

245 See generally UN Committee on the Rights of Persons with Disabilities, Concluding Observations to Argentina, U.N.Doc. CRPD/C/ARG/CO/1 (2012), para. 37.

246 Report of the Special Rapporteur on the Right to Education, Vernor Muñoz Villalobos, *The Right to Education of Persons with Disabilities*, UN Doc. A/HRC/4/29, 19 February 2007, para. 14.

247 Ibid.

248 Ibid.

3.3.2. Reasonable Accommodations and Other Individualised Support Measures

Experience has shown that 'as many as 80 to 90 per cent of children with special education needs, including children with intellectual disabilities, can easily be integrated into regular schools and classrooms, as long as there is basic support for their inclusion.'[249] Educational systems must adapt to the individual needs of disabled learners. In order to contribute to ensuring adaptability and accessibility in education for persons with disabilities, Article 24 of the CRPD imposes several positive obligations on States, including the duty to provide reasonable accommodations and other individualised measures of support. This reflects the human-rights based approach to educational provision. Under Article 24(2)(c) of the CRPD, States are required to 'ensure that reasonable accommodation of the individual's requirements is provided.'[250] The provision of reasonable accommodations seeks to ensure disability equality in the context of the right to education. The Salamanca Statement and Framework of Action recognises that inclusive education requires of States the accommodation of 'both different styles and rates of learning.'[251] The CRPD Committee has reiterated the importance of the provision of reasonable accommodations to inclusive education in its concluding observations.[252] The Committee observes that the provision of inclusive education, through reasonable accommodations and other measures, will include such measures as assistive technology, accessible and adapted educational materials and curricula as well as accessible school environments.[253] It is important to note that the duty to accommodate falls on the State (in the case of public education) and on private providers (in circumstances where education has been privatised) and the CRPD Committee has emphasised the fact that States must 'ensure that the parents of children with disabilities are not obliged to pay [...] for the measures of reasonable accommodation in mainstream schools.'[254]

In tandem with the provision of reasonable accommodations, Articles 24(2)(d) and 24(2)(e) of the Convention impose a duty on States to provide other forms of

249 United Nations, *From Exclusion to Equality: Realizing the Rights of Persons with Disabilities: Handbook for Parliamentarians on the Convention on the Rights of Persons with Disabilities and its Optional Protocol* (2007, Inter-Parliamentary Press, Geneva), at page 85.

250 UN CRPD, Article 24(2)(c).

251 The Salamanca Statement and Framework for Action on Special Needs Education (adopted at the World Conference on Special Needs Education: Access and Quality, Salamanca, Spain, 7–10 June 1994), para. 7.

252 For instance, in its recommendations to Spain, the Committee urged the Spanish government to 'increase its efforts to provide reasonable accommodation in education by allocating sufficient financial and human resources to implement the right to inclusive education.' [UN Committee on the Rights of Persons with Disabilities, Concluding Observations to Spain, U.N. Doc. CRPD/C/ESP/CO/1 (2011), para. 43, para. 44(a)]. In its concluding observations on the Hungarian State report, the Committee further emphasised that the provision of reasonable accommodations must be based on the student's individual requirements. UN Committee on the Rights of Persons with Disabilities, Concluding Observations to Hungary, U.N.Doc. CRPD/C/HUN/CO/1 (2012), para 41].

253 UN Committee on the Rights of Persons with Disabilities, Concluding Observations to Azerbaijan, U.N.Doc. CRPD/C/AZE/CO/1 (2014), para 41(a).

254 UN Committee on the Rights of Persons with Disabilities, Concluding Observations to Spain, UN Doc. CRPD/C/ESP/CO/1 (2011), para. 44.

individualised supports to persons with disabilities in the education system. Examples of this might be personal assistance and material supports, as well as Braille and sign language supports. According to Article 24(2)(d) of the CRPD, any support provided within mainstream education must facilitate the 'effective education'[255] of disabled persons. Where education is deemed necessary in 'environments that maximize academic and social development'[256] (in other words, where education is provided in segregated settings for certain individuals with a view to achieving full inclusion progressively), Article 24(2)(e) requires the provision of 'effective individualized support measures.'[257] The main point arising from both of these sub-articles is the requirement that any education provided is effective for the disabled learner. This is 'very much in line with the principles of adaptability and accessibility' as set out in the 4 A's framework above and 'reinforces the notion that individuals should be in a position to actually draw benefit from the education provided.'[258]

Unlike the provision of reasonable accommodations, which is an immediate obligation, the provision of supports under Article 24 falls within the obligations of progressive realisation incumbent on States and is therefore subject to the 'maximum of available resources' criterion. As de Beco notes:

> Support measures are general measures which must gradually achieve inclusive education. They do not aim to provide for particular adjustments but to adapt the general education system in order to include all children. Although they are general in nature, they have still to be tailored to the special needs of the child.[259]

Where the resources of a given State are constrained, the implementation of adequate supports to ensure the effective education of people with disabilities will be a difficult challenge and there will therefore be some leeway for States to ensure that supports are put in place gradually with a view to achieving fully inclusive systems over the medium-to-long term. No longer is it acceptable to pour all resources into segregated learning environments, special classes or special units in mainstream schools.

3.3.3. Appropriate Forms of Communication, Training for Teachers and Lifelong Learning

Article 24(3) of the CRPD recognises the fact that certain disabled individuals will require specific forms of support in terms of alternative modes of communication etc. in order to ensure 'full and equal participation in education and as members of the

---

255 UN CRPD, Article 24(2)(d).

256 UN CRPD, Article 24(2)(e).

257 Ibid.

258 A. Broderick and S. Quinlivan, 'The Right to Education: Article 24 of the CRPD' in G. Quinn and C. O' Mahony (eds.), *The UN Convention on the Rights of Persons with Disabilities: Comparative, Regional and Thematic Perspectives* (Intersentia Publishers forthcoming 2015).

259 G. De Beco, The Right to Inclusive Education According to Article 24 of the UN Convention on the Rights of Persons with Disabilities: Background, Requirements and (Remaining) Questions,' (2014) 285 *Netherlands Quarterly of Human Rights* 32(3), at page 282.

community.'[260] Article 24(3) requires States to ensure that persons with disabilities 'learn life and social development skills'[261] by taking appropriate measures, including by facilitating the learning of 'Braille, alternative script, augmentative and alternative modes, means and formats of communication and orientation and mobility skills, and facilitating peer support and mentoring'[262] and by 'facilitating the learning of sign language and the promotion of the linguistic identity of the deaf community.'[263]

Article 24(4) of the CRPD gives concrete examples of the types of measures that will be necessary in order to help ensure the realisation of the right to education for persons with disabilities. It highlights the fact that it is not just financial resources that will be determinant in the proper implementation of Article 24. Human resources will be particularly important in ensuring the realisation of the right to inclusive education. To that end, Article 24(4) provides that States Parties 'shall take appropriate measures to employ teachers, including teachers with disabilities, who are qualified in sign language and/or Braille, and to train professionals and staff who work at all levels of education.'[264] It further provides that such training shall 'incorporate disability awareness and the use of appropriate augmentative and alternative modes, means and formats of communication, educational techniques and materials to support persons with disabilities.'[265] The CRPD Committee has drawn attention to the importance of human resources in implementing Article 24[266] and has advised States to put in place policies designed to train education professionals in inclusive education.[267] The Committee has also emphasised the fact that teachers and all other educational staff, as well as school administrators, must be trained to work in inclusive educational settings.[268] Training of teachers and other educational professionals is essential in facilitating proper communication between the disabled student and educators and in ensuring full and effective participation and inclusion for persons with disabilities in mainstream education.

---

260 UN CRPD, Article 24(3).

261 UN CRPD, Article 24(3).

262 UN CRPD, Article 24(3)(a).

263 UN CRPD, Article 24(3)(b).

264 UN CRPD, Article 24(4).

265 Ibid.

266 See, for instance, UN Committee on the Rights of Persons with Disabilities, Concluding Observations to Spain, U.N Doc. CRPD/C/ESP/CO/1 (2011), para. 44(a); Concluding Observations to Tunisia, U.N. Doc. CRPD/C/TUN/CO/1 (2011), para. 32(d); Concluding Observations to Azerbaijan, U.N. Doc. CRPD/C/AZE/CO/1 (2014), para. 41(b); Concluding Observations to Hungary, U.N. Doc. CRPD/C/HUN/CO/1 (2012), para. 41; Concluding Observations to Tunisia, U.N. Doc. CRPD/C/TUN/CO/1 (2011), para. 32(c).

267 UN Committee on the Rights of Persons with Disabilities, Concluding Observations to Costa Rica, U.N.Doc. CRPD/C/CRI/CO/1 (2014), para. 46; See also UN Committee on the Rights of Persons with Disabilities, Concluding Observations to Azerbaijan, U.N.Doc. CRPD/C/AZE/CO/1 (2014), para. 41(c).

268 See, for example, UN Committee on the Rights of Persons with Disabilities, Concluding Observations to Hungary, U.N.Doc. CRPD/C/HUN/CO/1 (2012), para. 41; UN Committee on the Rights of Persons with Disabilities, Concluding Observations to Tunisia, U.N.Doc. CRPD/C/TUN/CO/1 (2011), para. 32(c); See also UN Committee on the Rights of Persons with Disabilities, Concluding Observations to Costa Rica, U.N.Doc. CRPD/C/CRI/CO/1 (2014), para. 45.

Article 24(5) of the Convention highlights the fact that it is not just children with disabilities who must benefit from inclusive educational settings. States must also ensure that adults with disabilities are guaranteed the right to inclusive education on an equal basis with others, as many individuals with disabilities have been deprived of a basic formative education. Article 24(5) of the Convention provides that 'States Parties shall ensure that persons with disabilities are able to access general tertiary education, vocational training, adult education and lifelong learning without discrimination and on an equal basis with others.'[269] In order to give teeth to the principle of lifelong learning and adult education, States are required to ensure the provision of reasonable accommodations,[270] as well as other effective supports.

4. Assessment by the CRPD Committee of the Measures Taken by States under Article 24 of the CRPD

This section of the chapter will consider the key criteria that might be employed by the CRPD Committee in assessing compliance by States with their obligations under Article 24. As outlined in chapter five of this book, the criteria below are drawn from several sources. In the first instance, they are based on reasonableness review frameworks at the national and international levels – namely, South African jurisprudence, as well as the standard of review contained in Article 8 of the OP-ICESCR (together with the statements emanating from the UNCESCR in that regard). The criteria below have also been tempered to fit the specific context of the CRPD, in particular its focus on the notion of disproportionate burden and on equality and dignity concerns via the outer limits of the duty to accommodate. Bearing all of this in mind, the most relevant factors to be taken into account by the CRPD Committee in its assessment of measures adopted by States to secure the right to inclusive education will be outlined below.

4.1. Disproportionate Burden/Cost Considerations

During the drafting of the CRPD, the concept of progressive realisation was deemed to be 'particularly contentious with regard to the right to education, for fear that it may be invoked by states, particularly developing states, as an 'escape clause' from the obligations of the CRPD.'[271] The current Special Rapporteur on the right to education, Mr. Kishore Singh (India), took office on 1st August 2010 following his appointment at the 14th session of the Human Rights Council. In his Interim Report on the Right to Education,[272] Mr. Singh highlights the fact that 'resource

---

269 UN CRPD, Article 24(5).

270 Ibid.

271 School of Oriental and African Studies, *The Convention on the Rights of Persons with Disabilities: The Right to Education and the Obligations of States* (2011) 44, SOAS International Human Rights Clinic Project – Research Paper No. 06/2011, at page 6, available at http://papers.ssrn.com/sol3/papers.cfm?abstract_id=1895726, last accessed 10 October 2014.

272 Interim Report of the United Nations Special Rapporteur on the right to education, Mr. Kishore Singh, *Financing Education and Update on Education in Emergencies* (5th August 2011), UN Doc. 66/269,

constraints remain a major barrier to the realisation of the right to education.'[273] The costs of providing inclusive education will of course be a factor to be taken into account by the CRPD Committee in its assessment of measures taken by States. In any discussion about costs, it is important to note that inclusive education is often perceived wrongly to be prohibitively expensive. This is not always the case and many positive educational measures are not extremely costly. In fact, it has been recognised that 'inclusive educational settings are generally less expensive than segregated systems [...]'[274] when appropriately implemented.[275] Having one centralised education system usually entails cost savings, at least over the medium-to-long term. It has been observed that 'a single system lowers management and administration costs. Transport, too, is less expensive, since segregated settings usually involve individuals from a larger geographical area.'[276] Inclusion International has estimated that inclusive education may be seven to nine times cheaper than segregated education.[277] The Salamanca Statement and Framework for Action also recognises the cost-effectiveness of inclusive education systems.[278] That is not to say that resource implications will not be a major concern for many States in implementing Article 24 of the CRPD, particularly developing States. The transitional period that States will go through in ensuring the transformation of special educational systems to fully inclusive systems may incur significant outlays in terms of resources. However, the cost benefits in the long term are assured. In the interim, States will be required to allocate resources to ensure the provision of sufficient supports for persons with disabilities within mainstream education. In many of its concluding observations, the CRPD Committee has emphasised the importance of including sufficient budgetary allocations in inclusive education policies drawn up by States.[279] While some support measures may be expensive, ensuring inclusive education may not require additional

available at www.ineesite.org/uploads/files/resources/SR_Education_GA_report_2011.pdf last accessed 13 October 2014.

273 Ibid, page 3 at para. 5.

274 United Nations, *From Exclusion to Equality: Realizing the Rights of Persons with Disabilities: Handbook for Parliamentarians on the Convention on the Rights of Persons with Disabilities and its Optional Protocol* (Inter-Parliamentary Press, Geneva, 2007), at page 85.

275 Research suggests that 'States that have appropriately implemented the inclusive education model have found it to be less costly to implement and operate than segregated special education services.' [Report of the Special Rapporteur on the Right to Education, Vernor Muñoz Villalobos, *The Right to Education of Persons with Disabilities,* UN Doc. A/HRC/4/29, 19 February 2007, para. 37, available at http://ap.ohchr.org/documents/alldocs.aspx?doc_id=12900 last accessed 14 October 2014].

276 United Nations, *From Exclusion to Equality: Realizing the Rights of Persons with Disabilities: Handbook for Parliamentarians on the Convention on the Rights of Persons with Disabilities and its Optional Protocol* (Inter-Parliamentary Press, Geneva, 2007), page 85.

277 Inclusion International, *Better education for all when we are included too: A Global Report – People with an Intellectual Disability and their Families Speak out on Education for All, Disability and Inclusive Education* (INICO 2009) 41, available at http://ii.gmalik.com/pdfs/Better_Education_for_All_Glonal_Report_October_2009.pdf last accessed 12 November 2014.

278 It proclaims that inclusive systems 'improve the efficiency and ultimately the cost-effectiveness of the entire education system.' [The Salamanca Statement and Framework for Action on Special Needs Education. adopted at the World Conference on Special Needs Education: Access and Quality, Salamanca, Spain (7–10 June 1994), section 2].

279 See generally, UN Committee on the Rights of Persons with Disabilities, Concluding Observations to Argentina, UN Doc. CRPD/C/ARG/CO/1 (2012), para. 38; Concluding Observations to Hungary, U.N.Doc. CRPD/C/HUN/CO/1 (2012), para. 41; Concluding Observations to Peru, UN Doc. CRPD/C/

resources but merely a cost-effective reallocation of existing resources which have been poured into special educational facilities.[280] Of course, many practical and challenging issues lie ahead for States in harnessing existing resources from special educational facilities into resources designed to assist the mainstream provision of education. National authorities must therefore draw up a plan of action with concrete benchmarks for addressing such challenges in order to enable the full and effective realisation of the right to education within a reasonable timeframe. In all States, but particularly in developing States, resources should be used optimally. States will be required to ensure that they maximise existing resources through international assistance, where necessary. It will be particularly important to ensure rights-based and performance-based budgeting in order to identify the areas where resources are being wasted and where existing resources can be more efficiently targeted to implement the right to inclusive education (among other rights) for persons with disabilities. In States where new schools are being built, the most important thing will be to identify and implement appropriate cost-effective measures from the outset. In that regard, the Convention's universal design mandate will be critical. Diane Richler states that the CRPD can promote system change by encouraging State Parties to ensure 'universal design in educational provision, including curriculum, instructional and teaching methods.'[281] As we saw already in chapter six above, the cost of including accessible features from the very outset, at the time of construction, can be low or minimal. However, costs increase substantially if accessibility features are introduced at a later stage. States Parties to the Convention should therefore ensure that schools are made as physically accessible, and therefore as inclusive as possible, from an early stage.

Many States are turning to private providers of education as a means of economic reform. Privatisation has been identified as an obstacle to 'the expansion of [the right to education].'[282] On account of this nascent trend, States should ensure to weigh up the detrimental consequences which the private provision of education will have on the rights of persons with disabilities and should, furthermore, take measures to counteract this detrimental impact. In particular, privatisation of educational facilities may impact on access to education, owing mainly to the fact that private providers hinder the economic accessibility of education. This is particularly relevant

PER/CO/1 (2012), para. 37; Concluding Observations to Spain, U.N.Doc. CRPD/C/ESP/CO/1 (2011), para. 44(a); Concluding Observations to Tunisia, U.N.Doc. CRPD/C/TUN/CO/1 (2011), para. 32(d).

280 Mr. Villalobos acknowledges that 'much can be done to work towards inclusive education either at little additional costs or through the more efficient and effective use of existing resources.' [Report of the Special Rapporteur on the Right to Education, Vernor Muñoz Villalobos, *The Right to Education of Persons with Disabilities*, UN Doc. A/HRC/4/29, 19 February 2007, para. 83, available at http://ap.ohchr.org/documents/alldocs.aspx?doc_id=12900 last accessed 14 October 2014]. See also UN Committee on the Rights of Persons with Disabilities, Concluding Observations to China, UN Doc. CRPD/C/CHN/CO/1 (2012), para. 36.

281 D. Richler, 'Inclusive Education and Systemic Reform' (Presentation at the Conference on Inclusive Education, Moscow, September 27 2011), available at www.unicef.org/ceecis/Diane.pptx, last accessed 4 December 2014.

282 Report of the Special Rapporteur on the Right to Education, Vernor Muñoz Villalobos, *The Right to Education of Persons with Disabilities*, UN Doc. A/HRC/4/29, 19 February 2007, para. 60, available at http://ap.ohchr.org/documents/alldocs.aspx?doc_id=12900 last accessed 14 October 2014.

in the context of persons with disabilities.[283] The provision of adequate supports in private educational systems also remains a major concern. Private providers are often unwilling, or are not in a position, to provide elaborate support measures for persons with disabilities. This has the potential to hinder greatly the realisation of inclusive education under Article 24 of the CRPD. States must therefore ensure to collect data on the effects of privatisation and they must monitor this aspect of the right to education carefully to ascertain what the consequences of privatisation might be on the exercise and enjoyment by persons with disabilities of the right to inclusive education.

4.2. Equality Considerations

It was highlighted above in chapter five that equality considerations could be more effectively integrated into frameworks of reasonableness review in order to ensure greater enjoyment of socio-economic rights for marginalised groups. The non-discrimination and equality norms are of paramount importance in implementing Article 24 of the CRPD. As demonstrated earlier in this chapter, the CRPD Committee must continue to focus sharply on the current inequalities in education for persons with disabilities, including instances of discriminatory access and segregation from the mainstream. It is vitally important that inclusive education is not viewed as a 'policy of differentiation'[284] – in other words, that it is not transformed 'into a process that, once again, singles out persons considered to be different from the rest',[285] as 'this contradicts the very spirit of the shift in education towards inclusion.'[286] While the provision of education to persons with disabilities should naturally respect their differential characteristics, it should not serve to alienate them in the mainstream. Persons with disabilities should not be placed in special classes or special units within mainstream schools. Disabled individuals are entitled to exercise the right to education on an equal basis with others. This implies that differences must be incorporated into the 'norm' rather than distinguished from it. In other words, the 'norm' must be widened to include the vast array of impairments which the education system will have to cater for. This will mean fundamental changes in the processes of learning, educational curricula and so forth to accommodate different learning styles and means of communication. Ensuring equality for disabled learners means granting such learners entitlements which will guarantee that they can benefit

283 The Committee on the Rights of the Child has noted that, in the context of decentralisation and privatisation of services 'it should not be forgotten that it is the State Party's ultimate responsibility to oversee that adequate funds are allocated to children with disabilities along with strict guidelines for service delivery. Resources allocated to children with disabilities should be sufficient – and earmarked so that they are not used for other purposes – to cover all their needs [...]' [UN Committee on the Rights of the Child, General Comment 9 on the rights of children with disabilities (2006), adopted by the Committee at its Forty-third session Geneva, 11–29 September 2006, UN Doc. CRC/C/GC/9, para. 20].

284 Report of the Special Rapporteur on the Right to Education, Vernor Muñoz Villalobos, *The Right to Education of Persons with Disabilities*, UN Doc. A/HRC/4/29, 19 February 2007, para. 64, available at http://ap.ohchr.org/documents/alldocs.aspx?doc_id=12900 last accessed 14 October 2014.

285 Ibid.

286 Ibid.

from education to the same extent as their non-disabled peers. Of course, this will entail an allocation of financial resources. This may simply mean a re-structuring of existing processes and facilities and the transfer of resources from segregated education to mainstream systems. However, there is no denying the fact that the human resources required to implement the right to inclusive education and to ensure *de facto* equality for persons with disabilities will be costly. It will require specialised teaching capabilities and additional allocations of teaching time on the part of educational providers. This may prove to be a difficult task for many States Parties to the Convention and that must be taken into account by the Committee in its assessment of disproportionate burden.

4.3. Dignity Considerations

Dignity considerations for persons with disabilities are linked intrinsically to the equality norm and must necessarily be taken into account by the CRPD Committee in its assessment of measures adopted by States. The outer limits of the duty to accommodate can be deemed to include a consideration of the inherent dignity of persons with disabilities. Dignity also featured as a central concern in the *Grootboom* standard of reasonableness. In the context of education, the link between equality and human dignity is affirmed by the Convention against Discrimination in Education, wherein it is stated that discrimination includes inflicting on any person or group conditions which are against their dignity.[287] Persons with disabilities must be respected as equals and consideration must be given to their inherent dignity in all matters concerning the provision of education. They must not be made to feel 'different' and they must not be required to endure conditions in education which are degrading or humiliating, when compared with the conditions afforded to their non-disabled peers. One of the main challenges that lies ahead for States in the implementation of the right to inclusive education is the elimination of discrimination and stigmatisation of the capabilities of persons with disabilities in terms of learning outcomes and so forth. These prejudices are prevalent not only among the wider community but also among teachers and school authorities. This is where the awareness-raising obligations of States come into play. Article 8 of the CRPD requires States to foster 'at all levels of the education system, including in all children from an early age, an attitude of respect for the rights of persons with disabilities.'[288] A UNESCO report highlights the fact that 'teacher attitudes and tolerance are the vehicles for the construction of an inclusive and participatory society.'[289] If the inherent dignity and capabilities of disabled learners are not respected, this will hinder significantly the provision of education that is fully inclusive.

---

287 Article 1(d) of the Convention against Discrimination in Education.

288 UN CRPD, Article 8(2)(b).

289 UNESCO, *Guidelines for Inclusion: Ensuring Access to Education for All* (United Nations Educational, Scientific and Cultural Organization France, 2005), at page 17.

4.4. The Necessity and Effectiveness of Measures Taken to Ensure the Right to Inclusive Education

As with all other CRPD rights, necessity and effectiveness in implementation will be vital criteria for consideration by the Committee. States will be required to ensure implementation of the minimum core of the right to education (particularly compulsory primary education) and to ensure that basic necessities for inclusive education are prioritised. After that, States should work towards full and effective implementation of the right to education contained in Article 24. It is not sufficient for States to merely put in place inclusive education policies and practices. These policies and practices must actually be implemented and their implementation must be effective.[290] In its concluding observations to Australia, the CRPD Committee recommended that the Australian authorities should conduct research into the effectiveness of current inclusive education policies, including the extent to which the relevant disability standards in education are being implemented in each State and territory.[291] The Committee also urged States to 'set targets to increase participation and completion rates by students with disabilities in all levels of education and training.'[292] The collection of data and the establishment of national educational benchmarks and indicators will allow States Parties to the CRPD to monitor the effectiveness of measures taken by them under Article 24.[293] As mentioned earlier in this chapter, the criterion of effectiveness is actually contained in Article 24 itself.[294] It is vitally important to ensure that individualised or more generalised supports provided within the mainstream school system do not constitute token measures of support. Rather, they must be sufficient to enable the disabled learner to participate fully and to be included. In order to ensure that education is effective for children with disabilities, States will be required to tailor programmes and curricula to the needs of disabled students.[295] In addition, national authorities will be required to identify and reduce illiteracy among children with disabilities.[296]

4.5. Participation of Persons with Disabilities in the Provision of Inclusive Education

As outlined in chapter five above, participation of persons with disabilities is essential in ensuring accountability and the effectiveness of rights implementation. Article 4(3)

---

290 UN Committee on the Rights of Persons with Disabilities, Concluding Observations to Australia, UN Doc. CRPD/C/AUS/CO/1 (2013), para. 46.

291 Ibid, para. 46(b).

292 Ibid, para. 46(c).

293 UN Committee on the Rights of Persons with Disabilities, Concluding Observations to Azerbaijan, UN Doc. CRPD/C/AZE/CO/1 (2014), para. 41(d).

294 According to Article 24(2)(d), any support provided to disabled individuals within the general education system must be sufficient to facilitate their 'effective education.'

295 UN Committee on the Rights of Persons with Disabilities, Concluding Observations to Argentina, UN Doc. CRPD/C/ARG/CO/1 (2012), para. 37.

296 UN Committee on the Rights of Persons with Disabilities, Concluding Observations to Peru, UN Doc. CRPD/C/PER/CO/1 (2012), para. 37.

of the CRPD highlights the obligation on States to ensure that individuals, *including children with disabilities* and their representative organisations, are consulted closely and involved actively in the development and implementation of legislation and policies related to the CRPD.[297] The Convention recognises children with disabilities as holders of rights. Children must therefore be respected and consulted (through their representative organisations, where necessary) in the implementation of rights that concern them. The CRPD Committee has also acknowledged this in its assertion that persons with disabilities, including children with disabilities and their representative organisations should be involved 'in the day-to-day implementation'[298] of inclusive education models. The involvement of civil society, including local and international DPOs and non-governmental organisations (NGOs) concerned with children's' rights has been deemed to not only strengthen advocacy but also to enable people with disabilities to secure their own rights and support.[299]

The 2007 report of the former Special Rapporteur on education, Vernor Muñoz Villalobos, advises States to 'invest in inclusive early childhood care and education (ECCE) programmes, which can lay the foundation for lifelong inclusion of children with disabilities in both education and society.'[300] In that connection, the report notes that 'States may need to undertake a consultative process, including disabled people's organizations and groups for parents of disabled children, to develop a national ECCE policy.'[301] The report also urges States 'to support civil organizations, including those of parents of children with disabilities, to build capacity on the right to education and how to influence effective policy and practice.'[302] The effective implementation of the right to inclusive education will require not only the participation of persons with disabilities and their representative organisations, but also teachers and school administrators, as well as the wider community, in order to ensure that all of these actors understand the complex processes involved in providing fully inclusive education which caters to the needs of all individuals with disabilities.

4.6. Third-Party Benefits

The issue of third-party benefits can be deemed to be one of the outer limits of the duty to accommodate. With regard to the right to education, the needs of disabled people cannot be given priority over the educational needs of all other individuals in a given State, especially those who are vulnerable and marginalised. Therefore,

---

297 UN CRPD, Article 4(3) [emphasis added].

298 UN Committee on the Rights of Persons with Disabilities, Concluding Observations to Austria, UN Doc. CRPD/C/AUT/CO/1 (2013), para. 43.

299 Social Transition Team, Office of Democracy, Governance and Social Transition of the United States Agency for International Development (USAID), *Best Practice in Inclusive Education for Children with Disabilities: Applications for Program Design in the Europe & Eurasia Region* (2010), at page x.

300 Report of the Special Rapporteur on the Right to Education, Vernor Muñoz Villalobos, *The Right to Education of Persons with Disabilities*, UN Doc. A/HRC/4/29, 19 February 2007, para. 84(f), available at http://ap.ohchr.org/documents/alldocs.aspx?doc_id=12900 last accessed 14 October 2014.

301 Ibid, para. 84(f).

302 Ibid, para. 84(g).

a delicate balancing act must ensue. Inclusive education has been recognised as benefiting all learners, not only individuals with disabilities. The 2007 report of Mr. Villalobos acknowledges the fact that 'creating an inclusive learning environment will assist all children in learning and achieving their potential.'[303] While the CRPD Committee is concerned with the rights of persons with disabilities, it can take into account (in its overall consideration of whether measures impose a disproportionate burden on States), the fact that the implementation of inclusive education can assist in the realisation of the right to education for non-disabled children also. Furthermore, while ensuring universal design in education is a complex task, the Committee can potentially take into account, in weighing up the various burdens and interests, the fact that States' efforts to universally design educational structures will also benefit other learners.

It is submitted that the foregoing criteria provide a good starting point from which to assess the reasonableness of measures taken by States Parties to the Convention to ensure compliance with Article 24 of the CRPD. Of course, the CRPD Committee will exercise its own competence and will undoubtedly expand on these criteria. In the next section of this chapter, the emerging trends in the provision of inclusive education will be highlighted.

5. Emerging Trends in Inclusive Education Provision in States Parties to the CRPD

The full and effective implementation of the right to inclusive education for persons with disabilities will be a challenge for many States Parties to the Convention. To date, progress has generally been slow in ensuring that disabled individuals are educated in fully inclusive settings. Notwithstanding the lofty guarantees enshrined in Article 24 of the CRPD, many disabled people are still educated in segregated educational structures. Additionally, in many countries that have recognised the right to inclusive education and have granted access to mainstream education for persons with disabilities, more often than not sufficient supports are not being provided to ensure that persons with disabilities can benefit from the right to education on an equal basis with others. However, there are also many examples of good practice in inclusive education provision. Below some examples of good and bad practice emerging from research conducted in States Parties to the Convention will be highlighted.

5.1. Good Practices in Inclusive Education Provision

The European Association of Service Providers (EASPD) has conducted research with regard to the varying levels of progress attained in European countries in the implementation of Article 24 of the CRPD. That research demonstrates both

---

303 Ibid, citing World Health Organization & World Bank, *World Report on Disability* (2011) 206.

positive and negative trends in the provision of inclusive education for persons with disabilities. There are clear indications emerging from the EASPD research that in all ten participating countries[304] there has been an increase in awareness 'both of the educational potential and the citizen's rights dimension of inclusive education for children with [special educational needs].'[305] The EASPD report highlights the fact that 'this is reflected in positive statements towards inclusive education formulated by governments, parents' organisations, teacher unions and other relevant public actors.'[306] It is also reflected 'in legal developments for support of inclusive education'[307] through educational laws. In two out of the ten participating countries – Finland and France – legislation was rated as being 'fully supportive of inclusive education.'[308]

Portugal has been characterised as a country that is demonstrating 'significant'[309] progression in inclusive education practices. The Portuguese government undertook a seismic shift in education laws and policy in 2008, with the adoption of Decree Law No. 3/2008,[310] which is intended to ensure the implementation of the right to inclusive education for persons with special educational needs. It defines specialised supports to be provided in pre-school, primary and secondary education, in the public, private and cooperative sectors. According to the EASPD report, the principle of inclusion has now been deemed 'the predominant answer'[311] to pupils with special educational needs. In Portugal, inclusion for children with special educational needs 'increased dramatically'[312] after the enactment of the 2008 Decree Law and segregated education is being maintained only for students who were already educated in segregated environments prior to 2008. The only special education schools available are at primary level and they are all private facilities. There are no public special education schools and no secondary special schools (private or public).[313] The Swedish government has also demonstrated concerted efforts in implementation of the right to inclusive education. The CRPD Committee has recognised this in its concluding observations, where the Committee has commended Sweden for its education system, in which only 1.5% of children are instructed outside inclusive, mainstream schools.[314] In its 'Study on the Challenges and Good Practices in the

304 The ten participating countries were Austria, Belgium (Flanders), Finland, France, Germany, Hungary, Ireland, Netherlands, Portugal, Slovenia.

305 European Association of Service Provider, *Barometer of Inclusive Education in Selected European Countries* (ZPE-Schriftenreihe Nr. 31), at page 37, available at www.investt.eu/sites/default/files/barometerreport.pdf last accessed 9 November 2014.

306 Ibid, at page 37.

307 Ibid.

308 Ibid.

309 Ibid, at page 122.

310 Portuguese Decree Law No. 3/2008 (adopted 7 January 2008), available at https//dre.pt/application/dir/pdf1s/2008/01/00400/0015400164.pdf last accessed 13 October 2014.

311 European Association of Service Provider, Barometer of Inclusive Education in Selected European Countries (ZPE-Schriftenreihe Nr. 31), at page 122, available at www.investt.eu/sites/default/files/barometerreport.pdf last accessed 9 November 2014, at page 117.

312 Ibid, page 118.

313 Ibid, page 117.

314 UN Committee on the Rights of Persons with Disabilities, Concluding Observations to Sweden, U.N.Doc. CRPD/C/SWE/CO/1 (2014), para. 4.

Implementation of the UN Convention on the Rights of Persons with Disabilities,' the European Foundation Centre maintains that the Cypriot experience 'reveals positive ways of implementing Article 24 of the CRPD' and can thus be considered as 'good practice in this area.'[315] The study draws attention to the fact that the Cypriot government has made considerable progress in integrating disabled children into a common learning environment,[316] primarily as a result of the 1999 Act of Parliament on the Education and Training of Children with Special Needs,[317] which is directed towards early identification of children with special educational needs. That law also requires the implementation of a robust support system, whereby local district committees (charged with overseeing special education and training) must provide necessary measures in terms of curriculum adaptation, technical and staffing support, or other, for the effective education of the child in an ordinary school.[318] Furthermore it requires evaluation of a child's progress at least once every year.[319]

5.2. Bad Practices in Inclusive Education Provision

Notwithstanding the positive trends outlined above, there are also many examples of bad practice emerging from research conducted in States Parties to the Convention. The EASPD report highlights the fact that, apart from Finland and France, in all other participating countries 'legislation has not been accompanied with the allocation of necessary resources to provide inclusive arrangements for all persons with [special educational needs] in regular schools or other educational facilities.'[320] The report notes that 'efforts to make new resources available or to shift resources from the special system to mainstreaming have been of limited success so far.'[321] Another worrying issue highlighted by the EASPD report is the fact that the general increase in the provision of inclusive education 'has not caused a general decrease of persons with [special educational needs] in special schools or other segregating facilities.'[322] On the contrary, the report draws attention to the fact that:

---

315 European Foundation Centre, *Study on challenges and good practices in the implementation of the UN Convention on the Rights of Persons with Disabilities* VC/2008/1214, at page 127, available at www.inclusive-education.org/system/files/publications-documents/European%20Foundation%20 Centre%20Report%20good%20practices%20UNCRPD.pdf last accessed 26 October 2014.

316 Ibid.

317 Act of Parliament on the Education and Training of Children with Special Needs 113(1)/1999 available at www.moec.gov.cy/eidiki/nomothesia/Number 113(1)_1999.pdf. last accessed 14 November 2014.

318 Ibid, Part II, Section 3(1) of the Law 113(1)/1999 [Information taken from the European Foundation Centre, Study on challenges and good practices in the implementation of the UN Convention on the Rights of Persons with Disabilities VC/2008/1214, at page 127].

319 Information taken from the European Foundation Centre, Study on challenges and good practices in the implementation of the UN Convention on the Rights of Persons with Disabilities VC/2008/1214, page 127.

320 European Association of Service Provider, *Barometer of Inclusive Education in Selected European Countries* (ZPE-Schriftenreihe Nr. 31), at page 37, available at www.investt.eu/sites/default/files/ barometerreport.pdf last accessed 9 November 2014.

321 Ibid.

322 Ibid, page 38.

> Especially in countries with a traditional special education system the number of children and youngsters in special schools has also been increasing [and as a consequence] persons with more severe educational needs [are still] mostly excluded from inclusive education.[323]

These negative trends are also evident when one examines the State and Shadow reports submitted to the CRPD Committee. In Hungary, for instance, only a number of persons with disabilities are being educated in inclusive settings.[324] The situation in Tunisia is also concerning. While the Tunisian authorities are in the process of implementing a phased inclusion policy for students with certain disabilities, the report of the Tunisian government refers to the planned construction and extension of alternative education centres.[325] In its concluding observations to Tunisia, the Committee notes 'with deep concern'[326] the fact that, in practice, the national authorities' inclusion strategy was not equally implemented in schools. The Committee also voices its disquiet that rules relating to the number of children in mainstream schools and to the management of inclusive classes were commonly breached.[327] Even in seemingly progressive and wealthy countries, segregated education is still a common feature. For instance, in its concluding observations to Australia, the CRPD Committee expresses disconcertion regarding the fact that, despite the establishment of Disability Standards for Education designed to ensure access to education for persons with disabilities on an equal basis with others, 'students with disabilities continue to be placed in special schools and many of those who are in regular schools are largely confined to special classes or units.'[328] Apart from the worrying issue of continued segregation of persons with disabilities, there are currently major anomalies in the provision of sufficient and effective supports for persons with disabilities within mainstream education, hindering completion of education. In Spain, for instance, the fact remains that while approximately 80% of pupils with disabilities are educated in mainstream schools,[329] 11.5% of the population with disabilities have not completed primary education, in comparison with 2.1% of the overall population.[330] In its concluding observations to Australia, the Committee draws attention to the fact that 'students with disabilities enrolled in regular schools receive a substandard

---

323 Ibid.

324 UN Committee on the Rights of Persons with Disabilities, Report submitted by Hungary, *National report on the basis of Article 35 (1) of the Convention on the Rights of Persons with Disabilities*, CRPD/C/HUN/1, (2010).

325 UN Committee on the Rights of Persons with Disabilities, Report submitted by Tunisia, *Implementation of the Convention on the Rights of Persons with Disabilities: Initial Report of State Parties Submitted Under Article 35 of the CRPD* (July 2010), http://tbinternet.ohchr.org/_layouts/treatybodyexternal/TBSearch.aspx?Lang=en&TreatyID=4&DocTypeID=29.

326 UN Committee on the Rights of Persons with Disabilities, Concluding Observations to Tunisia, UN Doc. CRPD/C/TUN/CO/1, para. 30.

327 Ibid.

328 UN Committee on the Rights of Persons with Disabilities, Concluding Observations to Australia, UN Doc. CRPD/C/AUS/CO/1 (2013), para. 45.

329 Alternative Report of the Comité Espanol de Representantes de Personas Con Discapacidad (CERMI State Delegation) (2010), *Human Rights and Disability*, at para. 105, available at www2.ohchr.org/SPdocs/CRPD/.../CERMI_Spain_5thSession_en.doc. last accessed 14 October 2014.

330 Ibid, at para. 104.

education due to a lack of reasonable accommodation.'[331] In addition, the EASPD report highlights the difficulties inherent in implementation of inclusive education from the perspective of human resources. In its assessment of progress made by the Austrian authorities in implementing education in the mainstream, the report notes that 'there is a strong tendency of teachers against individual curricula, didactical adaptations and teaching methods.'[332] Moreover, there is 'no guidance and support, parents are not involved [...]'[333] and there are 'huge regional variations'[334] in terms of teacher training. The CRPD Committee has already observed that, in many States Parties to the Convention, there is a distinct lack of teachers trained in disability awareness working in mainstream schools. In Tunisia, for instance, many integrated schools are not equipped to receive children with disabilities and the Committee has stated that the training of teachers and administrators with regard to disability-related matters remains a concern.[335] As a result, the Committee has urged States to adopt a policy of teacher training in the inclusive model and to provide support for trained teachers, such as Braille, alternative means and modes of communication, easy-reading texts and other auxiliary equipment and media.[336] In addition to all of these examples of bad practices, Mr. Vernor Muñoz Villalobos has drawn attention to the fact that participatory processes are often not followed in implementation of the right to education for persons with disabilities.[337] He remarks that 'in most countries, neither persons with disabilities nor their relatives or representatives take part in designing specific education programmes and curriculum guidelines, or else, their participation is essentially reduced to orientation courses or to collective learning or recreational activities.'[338]

331 UN Committee on the Rights of Persons with Disabilities, Concluding Observations to Australia, U.N.Doc. CRPD/C/AUS/CO/1 (2013), para. 45.

332 European Association of Service Provider, *Barometer of Inclusive Education in Selected European Countries* (ZPE-Schriftenreihe Nr. 31), at page 48, available at www.investt.eu/sites/default/files/barometerreport.pdf last accessed 9 November 2014.

333 Ibid.

334 Ibid.

335 UN Committee on the Rights of Persons with Disabilities, Concluding Observations to Tunisia, CRPD/C/TUN/CO/1, para. 31.

336 UN Committee on the Rights of Persons with Disabilities, Concluding Observations to Costa Rica, U.N. Doc. CRPD/C/CRI/CO/1 (2014), para. 46.

337 Notwithstanding the overall lack of participation of persons with disabilities and their representative organisations in decision-making in respect of the right to education, there are some examples of best practices. For instance, 'in some regions of Latin America, parents are made aware of the importance of their cooperation in developing pedagogical proposals in regular schools.' In addition, some European countries have implemented programmes and policies calling for the active participation of parents in decisions concerning their children's' right to education. In Finland, for example, 'parents' participation in special education is obligatory.' [Report of the Special Rapporteur on the Right to Education, Vernor Muñoz Villalobos, *The Right to Education of Persons with Disabilities*, UN Doc. A/HRC/4/29, 19 February 2007, para. 79, available at http://ap.ohchr.org/documents/alldocs.aspx?doc_id=12900 last accessed 14 October 2014].

338 Report of the Special Rapporteur on the Right to Education, Vernor Muñoz Villalobos, *The Right to Education of Persons with Disabilities*, UN Doc. A/HRC/4/29, 19 February 2007, para. 79, available at http://ap.ohchr.org/documents/alldocs.aspx?doc_id=12900 last accessed 14 October 2014.

6. Conclusion

This chapter has traced the evolution of the right to education at the level of international human rights law, as well as the development of the cornerstone principle of inclusive education for persons with disabilities. Article 24 of the CRPD cements the principle of inclusion as an indispensible element of the provision of education for disabled people. Article 24 is an important facilitator of full and effective participation and inclusion in society for persons with disabilities. During the negotiation sessions leading to the adoption of the CRPD, education was described aptly as 'the vector for all human development [... a right which is ...] foundational to society.'[339] It was also described as 'a predicate to the full enjoyment of a wide range of civil, political, economic, social and cultural rights, including political participation, freedom of expression, and access to employment.'[340] The provision of education to persons with disabilities on an equal basis with others is particularly important in ensuring that the fundamental principles of the Convention are realised.

The UNCESCR has pointed to the fact that 'the right to education epitomises the indivisibility and interdependence of all human rights.'[341] It has been variously classified as 'an economic right, a social right and a cultural right. It is all of these. It is also, in many ways, a civil right and a political right, since it is central to the full and effective realisation of these rights as well.'[342] The indivisibility and interdependence of all human rights is reflected explicitly in the CRPD[343] and can be seen in the hybrid nature of many of the rights contained in the Convention. Article 24 is clearly such a hybrid right. It is primarily a social right. However, as with all rights subject to progressive implementation, elements of the right to inclusive education are realisable immediately (in particular the non-discrimination norm, including the provision of reasonable accommodations). It is within that context that the obligations of States under Article 24 must be monitored by national authorities and ultimately by the CRPD Committee. While existing educational systems will not be transformed overnight, States will be required to 'plan and develop their capacity in line with the [CRPD] from the moment of adoption.'[344] One of the primary tasks which States will have under Article 24 of the CRPD is to 'develop a comprehensive

339 Remarks by Judith Heumann, Special Advisor for International Disability Rights the United States Delegation, at Round Table 2: CRPD Article 24 – Inclusion and the Right to Education Third Conference of States United Nations, New York (September 2010), available at usun.state.gov › the Briefing Room › Statements › 2010, last accessed 14 November 2014.

340 Ibid.

341 UNCESCR, General Comment 11 on plans of action for primary education (Article 14 of the Covenant) (1999) adopted at the twentieth Session of the Committee on 10 May 1999, UN Doc. E/C.12/1999/4, para. 2.

342 Ibid.

343 See, in particular, UN CRPD, preamble para. (c).

344 R. Rieser, *Implementing Inclusive Education: A Commonwealth Guide to Implementing Article 24 of the UN Convention on the Rights of People with Disabilities* (Commonwealth Secretariat, UK, 2008), available at www.worldofinclusion.com/res/internat/Commonwealth_Guide.doc last accessed 17 October 2014.

State education policy that guarantees the right to inclusive education.'[345] In this policy, States should identify minimum standards in relation to the right to education itself and the underlying determinants of education. Of course, it is not sufficient to merely put in place inclusive education policies. These policies must be implemented effectively. According to the CRPD Committee, domestic policies must include, among other things, implementation strategies.[346] If States wish to guarantee meaningful content to the right to education for persons with disabilities, they must remove any discriminatory legislative, physical and economic barriers to accessing mainstream educational systems. Domestic authorities will be required to amend their laws in line with the CRPD. The effective realisation of Article 24 will also require States to provide reasonable accommodations to disabled learners and to adopt concrete, targeted and positive measures towards the provision of individualised supports, with a view towards ensuring full inclusion. Implementation of the right to education must actually be assured and this is contingent, among other things, on the establishment of effective monitoring mechanisms. Domestic authorities will be required to allocate sufficient resources – financial, human and other – to ensure the full realisation of the right to education.[347] The CRPD Committee has drawn attention to the fact that States must monitor the progression of inclusive education through indicators.[348]

The progressive norms contained in Article 24 of the Convention go a long way towards seeking to ensure full and effective participation and inclusion of persons with disabilities in society. It is clear that States Parties to the Convention are demonstrating both positive and negative trends in the provision of inclusive education for persons with disabilities. Many States Parties to the Convention have begun to evidence shifts in their laws and policies in line with the mandate set down by the CRPD. Despite the positive trends highlighted in this chapter, the fact remains that Article 24 of the Convention is far from being realised effectively in the majority of States Parties to the Convention. The right of children with disabilities to education is being violated consistently through the maintenance, and even the expansion, of segregated educational structures in some States. There is also clear evidence of unequal educational opportunities and the denial of reasonable accommodations for persons with disabilities.

While many countries are understandably facing resource constraints, this cannot be allowed to hinder the attainment and expansion of the right to education for persons with disabilities. Financial resources must be mobilised and used efficiently in order to create equal opportunities for persons with disabilities in the education system

---

345 UN Committee on the Rights of Persons with Disabilities, Concluding Observations to Argentina, UN Doc. CRPD/C/ARG/CO/1 (2012), para. 38.

346 UN Committee on the Rights of Persons with Disabilities, Concluding Observations to Spain, U.N. Doc. CRPD/C/ESP/CO/1 (2011), para. 43; UN Committee on the Rights of Persons with Disabilities, Concluding Observations to Tunisia, UN Doc. CRPD/C/TUN/CO/1 (2011), para. 30.

347 See, for example, UN Committee on the Rights of Persons with Disabilities, Concluding Observations to Tunisia, U.N. Doc. CRPD/C/TUN/CO/1 (2011), para. 32(d).

348 UN Committee on the Rights of Persons with Disabilities, Concluding Observations to Costa Rica, U.N.Doc. CRPD/C/CRI/CO/1 (2014), para. 47.

and to foster a spirit of inclusion. States will be required to improve conditions continuously and to ensure that already existing levels of educational provision for persons with disabilities are maintained. They should ensure that cutbacks due to economic crises do not impact negatively on the right to inclusive education. Aside from the obligation to allocate sufficient financial resources, human resources are pivotal in ensuring an inclusive education system. The manner in which children with disabilities are taught is essential and therefore training for educators is imperative. All of these components of an inclusive education system are vital if the right to education for persons with disabilities is to be realised effectively. The CRPD Committee will be the ultimate arbitrator on the reasonableness of measures adopted by States and it will apply its own defined set of criteria to Article 24. It is hoped that the types of criteria outlined in this chapter can provide the building blocks for effective monitoring by the Committee of the right to inclusive education. There is a long road ahead in the fulfilment of the right to education for disabled individuals. Nonetheless, it is hoped that the CRPD 'can help to close the gap between the theory of inclusive education and reality.'[349]

[349] Inclusion International, 'The Implications of the CRPD for Education for All' (2009), available at www.inclusion-international.org/wp.../ImplicationsCRPD_dr2_X2.pd... last accessed 20 November 2014.Similar.

Chapter 8
Case Study: The Influence of the CRPD on the Council of Europe

'It is hard to quarrel with the claim that international law scholars should pay attention to all of the effects of international law.'[1]

1. Introduction

This chapter will contain a case study on the impact which the CRPD (hereafter UN Convention) is having on the legal and policy mechanisms in the Council of Europe. The case study will focus primarily on disability equality issues and on the wider issues of participation and inclusion in society for persons with disabilities.

The Council of Europe was founded in 1949 in the aftermath of the Second World War. It has 47 Member States, covering virtually the entire continent of Europe. 28 of its Member States are also members of the European Union – in other words, all EU Member States are members of the Council of Europe. It is the leading human rights organisation in Europe and it seeks to promote harmony between European countries in the areas of human rights, legal standards and democratic development, among others.[2] The primary judicial body within the Council of Europe is the European Court of Human Rights (ECtHR or Strasbourg Court), a supra-national court that sits in Strasbourg, France, and was established to monitor compliance by Member States with the European Convention on Human Rights (ECHR). The Strasbourg Court hears applications alleging that a contracting state has breached one or more of the human rights provisions relating to the civil and political rights set out in the ECHR and its various protocols. Alongside the ECHR, another important instrument within the Council of Europe is the European Social Charter (original Charter), which is a treaty guaranteeing social and economic rights. The original Charter was adopted in 1961. In 1996, the Revised European Social Charter (revised Charter) was adopted. The European Committee of Social Rights (ECSR) is a quasi-judicial body that is tasked to rule on the conformity of Member States' actions with the original Charter, the 1988 Additional Protocol and the revised Charter.

1 E.A. Posner, 'Evaluating the Effects of International Law: Next Steps' (A response to 'Beyond Compliance: Rethinking Why International Law Really Matters) 1(3) *Journal of Global Policy* (October 2010) 334.

2 Article 1(a) of the Statute of the Council of Europe states that 'the aim of the Council of Europe is to achieve a greater unity between its members for the purpose of safeguarding and realising the ideals and principles which are their common heritage and facilitating their economic and social progress.'

The first part of this chapter will contain an analysis of the impact to date of the CRPD on the case law of the ECtHR related to disability equality. The principal aim of that case study will be to determine the extent to which the Strasbourg Court is already taking cognisance of the provisions of the UN Convention in its judgments concerning disability equality. Based on those observations and findings, the influence which the CRPD might have in the future on the interpretation by the Strasbourg Court of the provisions contained in the ECHR will be considered. A secondary part of this chapter will involve a consideration of the impact of the CRPD on the general disability policy of the Council of Europe, as well as on the case law of the ECSR in its interpretation of the provisions of the revised Charter. While the CRPD has potential to influence both the original and the revised Charter, this chapter will only analyse the Convention's impact on the revised Charter, as it is submitted that the CRPD's wide-ranging rights have increased relevance to the more progressive disability provisions of the revised Charter.

This chapter fits into the overall framework of this book in several ways. Having already analysed the theoretical framework of the CRPD (in terms of its conceptualisation of disability and its theoretical model(s) of equality), it is appropriate to determine by way of case study the manner in which the progressive norms in the Convention are influencing regional sources of disability law and policy. This will allow an assessment of the potential influence that the provisions of the CRPD may have in practice, going beyond the theory of its substantive norms. A case study on the Council of Europe has been chosen, among other reasons, to draw attention to the legal and policy impediments that may exist in terms of translating the rights and obligations contained in the CRPD into practice. It is also important to highlight the potential which policy and legislative regimes have in ensuring effective implementation of CRPD rights. Another reason for selecting the Council of Europe as the relevant organisation for this case study stems from the fact that the wide-ranging provisions of the CRPD have relevance to the Council's legal and policy mechanisms. The judicial and quasi-judicial bodies of the Council of Europe – the ECtHR and the ECSR – regard their respective treaties as living instruments and aim to apply a contextual approach to interpretation, taking into account principles of international law, among others. Thus, there is potential for the CRPD to exert its influence over these mechanisms, albeit admittedly at a very slow pace. It is also envisaged that any influence which the CRPD might have in changing the direction of disability law and policy in the Council of Europe may trickle down slowly into national legislation and policy.

This chapter will be broken down into six sections. Sections two, three and four of this chapter comprise the case study on the ECHR. Section two provides an overview of the relevance of the CRPD to the interpretation by the Strasbourg Court of the ECHR. It also contains an introduction to the equality norm in the ECHR. In section three of this chapter the jurisprudential trends in the case law of the ECtHR since the coming into force of the CRPD will be highlighted. Section four outlines the potential future impact which the CRPD might have on the interpretation of the ECHR. In section five of this chapter, the second part of the case study on the Council of Europe will be carried out. This will consist of an analysis of the influence to date of the UN Convention on the general disability policy of the Council of Europe, as well as its impact on the ECSR in its interpretation of the provisions of the revised Charter. Finally, in section six of this chapter concluding remarks will be penned.

2. Case Study Part 1: The Influence of the CRPD on the Interpretation of the ECHR

2.1. Introduction to the Case Study (Part I)

In part 1 of this case study, the impact which the CRPD is having to date, and its potential influence, on disability equality judgments of the ECtHR will be analysed. The legal reasoning of the Strasbourg Court will be traced, in its examination of the merits of relevant cases. This will allow a determination as to whether the CRPD is already having an impact on the manner in which the Court interprets the provisions of the ECHR or applies those provisions. The principal question that will be addressed is whether the Court is evidencing a shift in its approach to disability equality on foot of the entry into force of the UN Convention? The main factor that will be taken into account in assessing if there has been such a shift in approach is whether the Court is showing signs of adopting a more substantive model of equality, signalled by such indicators as *de facto* reasonable accommodation duties and a social model of disability. The subsections which follow will contain a reflection on the relevance of the CRPD to the interpretation of the ECHR and also a general reflection on the interpretation of the equality norm in the ECHR. Sections 3 and 4 of this chapter will comprise the substantive case study on the ECHR.

2.2. The Relevance of the CRPD to the Interpretation by the European Court of Human Rights of the ECHR

The ECHR is the primary legal instrument in the Council of Europe. The Strasbourg Court was established under the ECHR to hear complaints of violations of the human rights which are contained therein. At the outset, it is vital to shed some light on the relevance of the CRPD to the Strasbourg Court in its interpretation of ECHR provisions, in light of the fact that (unlike the European Union) the Council of Europe is not a party to the UN Convention. It is well established that the ECHR is a 'living instrument,'[3] which must be interpreted in accordance with present-day conditions. This dynamic or evolutive approach to interpretation reflects the approach that is most appropriate in the context of the CRPD also.[4] Françoise Tulkens, Section President of the ECtHR, has stated that, because the interpretation of the ECHR should not be static, the Court has had to come up with 'methods of

---

3 See, for example, *Tyrer v United Kingdom*, application no. 5856/72, judgment 25 April 1978 (1978) 2 EHRR 1, para. 31.

4 See generally chapter 3 of this book.

interpretation.'[5] In order to do so, it has been guided by the VCLT, particularly the purposive/teleological approach to interpretation that is contained in Article 31(1) of the VCLT. According to Article 31(2) of the VCLT, the Preamble of the treaty provides important context for its interpretation. Tulkens draws attention to the fact that the Preamble to the ECHR refers not only to the 'maintenance' but also to the 'further realisation' of human rights and fundamental freedoms. She states that 'maintenance' requires the Court 'to ensure in particular that the rights and freedoms set out in the Convention continue to be effective in changing circumstances' and that 'this concern for effectiveness is the main driving force behind the interpretative methods developed by the Court.' She observes that the concept of 'further realisation' allows for 'a degree of innovation and creativity, extending the reach of the Convention guarantees, especially when it is necessary to protect the substance of the rights and freedoms.'[6]

The evolutive approach to interpretation has featured heavily in the jurisprudence of the Strasbourg Court since its early days.[7] The evolutive approach was first emphasised by the ECtHR in the case of *Tyrer v United Kingdom*,[8] wherein the Court stated that 'the Convention is a living instrument which [...] must be interpreted in the light of present-day conditions.[9] In recent years, the ECtHR has shown an increased readiness to draw on other international instruments as interpretative aids to the construction of the ECHR. This can be seen in the case of *Opuz v Turkey* (2010).[10] Additionally, in *Kiyutin v Russia*,[11] the ECtHR remarked as follows:

> The Court has consistently held that it takes into account relevant international instruments and reports in order to interpret the guarantees of the Convention and to establish whether there is a common standard in the field. It is for the Court to decide which international instruments and reports it considers relevant and how much weight to attribute to them.[12]

In *Demir and Baykara v Turkey*,[13] the Strasbourg Court elaborated on the relevant criteria according to which it had developed its contextual approach to interpretation

5 F. Tulkens, Section President of the European Court of Human Rights, Seminar 'What are the limits to the evolutive interpretation of the Convention?' (Strasbourg, January 2011), at page 6, available at http://echr.coe.int/Documents/Dialogue_2011_ENG.pdf last accessed 14 November 2014.

6 Ibid, at page 7.

7 See, for instance, *Tyrer v United Kingdom*, application no. 5856/72, judgment 25 April 1978 (1978) 2 EHRR 1; *Marckx v Belgium*, application no. 6833/74, judgment 13 June 1979; and *Dudgeon v United Kingdom*, application no. 7525/76, judgment 24 February 1983.

8 *Tyrer v United Kingdom*, application no. 5856/72, judgment 25 April 1978 (1978) 2 EHRR 1.

9 Ibid, para. 31.

10 When considering the definition and scope of discrimination against women, in addition to the more general meaning of discrimination as determined in its case-law [...] the Court has to have regard to provisions of more specialised legal instruments and the decisions of international legal bodies [...]. [*Opuz v Turkey*, application no. 33401/02, judgment 9 September 2009 (2010), 50 EHRR 28, at para. 185].

11 *Kiyutin v Russia*, application no. 2700/10, judgment 10 March 2011, at footnote 164.

12 Ibid, para. 67.

13 *Demir and Baykara v Turkey*, application no. 34503/97, judgment 12 November 2008 (2009) 48 EHRR 54.

of the ECHR.[14] In that regard, it stated that 'it will be sufficient for the Court that the relevant international instruments denote a continuous evolution in the norms and principles applied in international law and show, in a precise area, that there is common ground in modern societies.'[15] Moreover, the ECtHR held that:

> The consensus emerging from specialised international instruments and from the practice of contracting States may constitute a relevant consideration for the Court when it interprets the provisions of the Convention in specific cases.[16]

Lisa Waddington argues that 'the Court's interpretation of ECHR provisions is [...] influenced by emerging international consensuses'[17] expressed, *inter alia*, through treaty law. She further contends that the CRPD 'reflects such an emerging consensus,'[18] by virtue of the high number of signatures and ratifications that the UN Convention attracted within a short period of time, both within the Council of Europe[19] and on a global stage.[20] Of course, it is important to point out that the dynamic or evolutive approach to interpretation of the ECHR cannot be unlimited or without boundaries. In particular, it has been acknowledged that while the ECHR and its Protocols 'must certainly be interpreted in light of present-day conditions [...] the Court cannot, by means of an evolutive interpretation, derive from [other] instruments a right which was not included [in the ECHR and its Protocols] at the outset' and this is 'particularly so where the omission was deliberate.'[21] That observation is certainly true. However, it is also true that the interpretation of the right to equality under the ECHR should evolve somewhat to cover the true disadvantage experienced by marginalised groups in the exercise of ECHR rights. The CRPD represents a genuine consensus between States Parties and a change in approach to disability equality. Most States Parties to the CRPD are also members of the Council of Europe. There will therefore be significant changes in the laws and policies of those States and this should be reflected in a dynamic interpretation of the rights of persons with disabilities under the ECHR. As Tulkens notes, 'a decisive element of

---

14 In the case of *Demir and Baykara v Turkey*, the ECtHR was interpreting Article 11 of the ECHR (on freedom of expression) by reference to the International Labour Organisation Conventions and the European Social Charter.

15 *Demir and Baykara v Turkey* (2009) 48 EHRR 54, para. 86.

16 Ibid, para. 85.

17 L. Waddington, Europees Hof voor de Rechten van de Mens, 21 December 2010, nr. 45744/08, "Jasinskis tegen Letland", *European Human Rights Cases*, Aflevering 4, april 2011, Jaargang 12, 556–567, 566.

18 Ibid.

19 Of the 47 Council of Europe States, 45 have signed the CRPD (Switzerland and Liechtenstein have not yet signed) and 41 have ratified the CRPD (Finland, Iceland, Ireland, Liechtenstein, Monaco and The Netherlands have not yet ratified), available at www.un.org/disabilities/countries.asp?id=166 last accessed 19 April 2014.

20 As at December 2014, the UN Enable website shows that the CRPD has 153 ratifications and accessions, while the Optional Protocol (OP) has 85 ratifications. The number of signatories to the CRPD is 159 while the OP has 91 signatures, available at www.un.org/disabilities/countries.asp?id=166 last accessed 19 January 2014.

21 F. Tulkens, Section President of the European Court of Human Rights, Seminar 'What are the limits to the evolutive interpretation of the Convention?' (Strasbourg, January 2011), at page 7, available at http://echr.coe.int/Documents/Dialogue_2011_ENG.pdf last accessed 14 November 2014.

evolutive interpretation results from the convergence between domestic laws'[22] of States Parties to the ECHR. Without doubt, the Strasbourg Court cannot incorporate all of the progressive CRPD provisions into its jurisprudence. It is constrained *inter alia* by the nature and scope of the ECHR itself (a point which will be elaborated on later in this chapter). Nonetheless, it will be argued throughout this chapter that the equality norm in the ECHR applies equally to disabled people as it does to all other individuals and, in order to give full effect to the ECHR's equality norm in the context of persons with disabilities, some regard must be had to the provisions of the CRPD, as well as to its overall spirit and tenor.

Since the coming into force of the CRPD in May 2008, the Strasbourg Court has cited[23] the UN Convention on numerous occasions in the context of relevant international law in interpreting the provisions of the ECHR. In the case of *Pleso v Hungary*,[24] for example, the ECtHR referred to Article 12 of the CRPD (on the right to legal capacity), in finding that the plaintiff was deprived unlawfully of his liberty in contravention of Article 5(1) of the ECHR.[25] Furthermore, in *Jasinskis v Latvia*,[26] the Strasbourg Court again referred to the CRPD in the context of the international legal framework which the Court deems relevant to the interpretation of ECHR rights. While it is encouraging to note that the ECtHR is referring to the UN Convention, it is important to determine whether it is taking the spirit and tenor of the CRPD into account as an aid to interpretation in reaching its conclusions in individual judgments on disability equality or whether the UN Convention is merely being cited by the Court in the context of relevant international law. That question will be addressed, among others, in the next substantive section of this chapter.

2.3. The Interpretation of the Equality Norm in the ECHR

The prohibition on discrimination in the ECHR is contained in Article 14, as well as in Protocol No. 12.[27] This chapter will focus on Article 14, as it provides a richer source of case law regarding the substantive issues to be addressed. Article 14 ECHR provides as follows:

---

22 Ibid.

23 See, among others: *Glor v. Switzerland*, application no. 13444/04, judgment 30 April 2009, para. 53; *Jasinskis v. Latvia*, application no. 45744/08, judgment 21 December 2010 para. 40; *Seal v the United Kingdom*, application no. 50330/07, judgment 7 December 2010, paras. 41–43; *Kiyutin v Russia*, application no. 2700/10, judgment 10 March 2011; *Kiss v. Hungary*, application no. 38832/06, judgment 20 May 2010, para. 14; *Stanev v. Bulgaria*, application no. 36760/06, judgment 17 January 2012, para. 72; *D.D. v. Lithuania*, application no. 13469/06, judgment 14 February 2012, para. 84.

24 *Pleso v Hungary*, application no. 41242/08, judgment 2 October 2012.

25 The plaintiff in that case had been hospitalised against his will and forced to undergo treatment for schizophrenia, notwithstanding the fact that the plaintiff's guardian *ad litem* had argued in an earlier hearing that the plaintiff posed no danger to himself or others.

26 *Jasinskis v. Latvia*, application no. 45744/08, judgment 21 December 2010.

27 The prohibition of discrimination in Protocol 12 is not limited to the enjoyment of the rights set forth in the ECHR, unlike Article 14 ECHR.

> The enjoyment of the rights and freedoms set forth in this Convention shall be secured without discrimination on any ground such as sex, race, colour, language, religion, political or other opinion, national or social origin, association with a national minority, property, birth or *other status*.[28]

The ECHR does not contain any specific rights for the protection of disabled people,[29] nor does it mention disability as a ground of discrimination. The ECHR was adopted at a time when disability was not even seen as a likely ground of discrimination. In other words, disadvantage relating to disability was explained according to the individual or medical model. In spite of the fact that disability is not mentioned explicitly in Article 14, the list of grounds of discrimination in Article 14 ECHR is clearly not exhaustive and it is noteworthy that, in 2009, disability was recognised by the Court as coming within the term 'other status' in Article 14 in the case of *Glor v Switzerland*.[30]

The ECHR was adopted at a time when the formal approach was the dominant theoretical model of equality. For many years, the Strasbourg Court failed to endorse a substantive model of equality. In other words, it failed to deal with equality issues under the ECHR in a manner which could address within its framework issues of disadvantage and inequality.[31] The Court tended to examine formal distinctions between individuals in analogous situations. Rory O'Connell has described the Court's earlier jurisprudence on equality as 'uninspiring.'[32] Since the 1980s, however, the Court has shown itself to be disposed increasingly to recognising exceptions to formal equality.[33] O'Connell points to the fact that the approach taken by the ECtHR to equality law is now 'focused not merely on the rationale behind formal distinctions, but has the potential to tackle the discrimination, disadvantage and oppression faced by vulnerable and disadvantaged groups.'[34]

---

28 ECHR, Article 14 [emphasis added].

29 With the exception of Article 5(1)(e) which refers (in outdated terminology) to 'persons of unsound mind.'

30 *Glor v. Switzerland*, application no. 13444/04, judgment 30 April 2009.

31 Rory O' Connell states that 'during the first decades of its existence, the ECtHR saw discrimination solely through a lens of formal equality.' [R. O'Connell, *Substantive Equality in the European Court of Human Rights?* 107 *Michigan Law Review First Impressions* 129 (2009), 129, available at www.michiganlawreview.org/firstimpressions/vol107/oconnell.pdf, last accessed 18 September 2014].

32 Ibid.

33 See, for instance, the following contributions which trace the developments in the ECtHR's Article 14 jurisprudence towards a more substantive conception of equality: R. O'Connell, 'Cinderella Comes to the Ball: Article 14 and the Right to Non-discrimination in the ECHR'(2009) 29 *Legal Studies: The Journal of the Society of Legal Scholars* 211; C. Danisi, 'How Far Can the European Court of Human Rights Go in the Fight Against Discrimination? Defining New Standards in Its Non-discrimination Jurisprudence' (2011) 9 *International Journal of Constitutional Law* 793; and A. Timmer, 'Toward an Anti-Stereotyping Approach for the European Court of Human Rights' (2011) 11 *Human Rights Law Review* 707.

34 R. O'Connell, 'Cinderella Comes to the Ball: Article 14 and the right to non-discrimination in the ECHR' (2009) 29 (2) *Legal Studies: The Journal of the Society of Legal Scholars* 211, 229.

There are some examples outside of the disability context which demonstrate the fact that the ECtHR has moved towards a more substantive approach to equality. In *Thlimmenos v Greece*, for instance, the Court stated that:

> The right not to be discriminated in the enjoyment of the rights guaranteed under the Convention is also violated when States without objective and reasonable justification fail to treat differently persons whose situations are significantly different.[35]

Additionally, in *Stec v United Kingdom*,[36] the ECtHR stated that 'the failure to take steps to address factual inequalities might itself be a violation of Article 14.'[37] In addition, the case of *D.H. v Czech Republic*[38] is significant in terms of the Court's extension of the ambit of its Article 14 jurisprudence. That case concerned the segregation of Roma children in education on the basis of allegedly biased aptitude tests. The Court in *D.H.* confirmed that indirect discrimination falls within the ambit of Article 14 ECHR and repeated its remarks from *Stec* that 'in certain circumstances a failure to attempt to correct inequality through different treatment may in itself give rise to a breach of [Article 14 ECHR].'[39] In a subsequent ruling on segregated educational structures in the context of Roma children, *Horváth and Kiss v. Hungary*,[40] the Strasbourg Court once again found indirect discrimination contrary to Article 14 ECHR. The novel feature of the *Horváth* judgment lies in the Court's analysis of the State's positive obligations in addressing long-standing discrimination with regard to the rights of Roma children to education. In considering the State's margin of appreciation in the education sphere, the ECtHR examined the procedural safeguards that were put in place for the benefit of the applicants and took into account the special needs of Roma children as members of a disadvantaged class.[41] The Court stated that the applicants had 'received an education which did not offer the necessary guarantees stemming from the positive obligations of the state to undo a history of racial segregation in special schools.'[42] The Court noted that in light of the 'recognised bias in past placement procedures,'[43] the State had 'specific positive obligations to avoid the perpetuation of past discrimination or discriminative practices disguised in allegedly neutral tests.'[44] The ECtHR in *Horváth* acknowledged the fact that the structural disadvantage and discrimination affecting vulnerable groups must be tackled by means of positive measures, in the context of the right to education at least.[45]

---

35 *Thlimmenos v Greece*, application no. 34369/97, judgment 6 April 2000, at paragraph 44.

36 *Stec* v *United Kingdom*, application nos. 65731/01 and 65900/01, judgment 12 April 2006 (2006) 43 EHRR 47.

37 Ibid, paras. 51–64.

38 *D.H.* v. *Czech Republic*, application no. 57325/00, judgment 13 November 2007 (2007) 47 EHRR 3.

39 Ibid, para. 175.

40 *Horváth and Kiss v. Hungary*, application no. 11146/11, judgment 29 January 2013.

41 Ibid, para. 127.

42 Ibid.

43 Ibid, para. 116.

44 Ibid.

45 In that regard, the Court stated that 'structural deficiencies call for the implementation of positive measures in order, *inter alia*, to assist the applicants with any difficulties they encountered in following

It is refreshing to note that the Strasbourg Court has moved towards a more substantive conceptualisation of equality in the context of minority rights. The term 'minority rights' is generally deemed to embody two separate notions. The first is that it denotes individual rights as they are applied to members of certain groupings, such as racial, ethnic or sexual minorities for instance. The second meaning attributed to the term is that of collective rights, as accorded to minority groups such as those listed above.[46] While the rights of persons with disabilities have sometimes been examined through a minority group (or civil rights) lens,[47] disabled people do not fall within the legal category of minority rights *per se* for the purposes of UN law and policy.[48] Indeed, the term 'minority' as used in the UN human rights system refers generally to national or ethnic, religious and linguistic minorities, as established by the United Nations Minorities Declaration.[49] Furthermore, the ECtHR has not classified persons with disabilities as falling within the category of minority rights and, of course, disabled persons themselves would not welcome being labelled as a minority in the traditional sense of the word. Nonetheless, developments in the ECtHR's approach to minority rights are of great significance in the disability context as they leave wide open the potential to move towards a more substantive approach to instances of discrimination against persons with disabilities.

As well as demonstrating a substantive conceptualisation of the equality norm in the context of minority groups, the ECtHR has also begun to demonstrate some signs of a move towards substantive equality in the field of disability rights. The Court has evidenced a trend in recent years towards considering the social context of the disadvantage experienced by disabled people. As part of the analysis that will be undertaken in the next section of this chapter, the key trends related to disability equality which are evident in the case law of the ECtHR since the coming into force of the CRPD will be explored. The aim of that analysis will be to determine the extent to which those developments are linked to the CRPD. In other words, to what extent is the UN Convention influencing the Court to move towards a more substantive approach to equality in the context of the rights of disabled people? Moreover, is the ECtHR having regard to the relevant standards contained in the CRPD in its

the school curriculum.' [*Horváth and Kiss v. Hungary*, application no. 11146/11, judgment 29 January 2013, para. 104].

46 According to a definition put forward in 1977 by Francesco Capotorti, former Special Rapporteur of the United Nations Sub-Commission on Prevention of Discrimination and Protection of Minorities, a minority is: 'A group numerically inferior to the rest of the population of a State, in a non-dominant position, whose members – being nationals of the State – possess ethnic, religious or linguistic characteristics differing from those of the rest of the population and show, if only implicitly, a sense of solidarity, directed towards preserving their culture, traditions, religion or language.' [See UN Doc. E/CN.4/Sub.2/384/Rev.1, para. 568].

47 See, for instance, J.E. Bickenbach, 'Minority Rights or Universal Participation: The Politics of Disablement' in M. Jones and L.A. Basser Marks (eds.), *Disability, Divers-Ability and Legal Change* (Springer, The Hague, 1999).

48 For an elaboration on this point, see T. Degener and Y. Koster-Dreese, *Human Rights and Disabled Persons: Essays and Relevant Human Rights Instruments* (Martinus Nijhoff, London, 1995), at page 12.

49 UN Declaration on the Rights of Persons Belonging to National or Ethnic, Religious and Linguistic Minorities A/RES/47/135 (adopted at the 92nd plenary meeting on 18 December 1992), available at www.un.org/documents/ga/res/47/a47r135.htm, last accessed 7 August 2014.

interpretation of ECHR rights, according to its self-professed evolutive approach to interpretation? On the basis of those findings, I will put forward my views (in section four of this chapter) regarding the influence that the CRPD may have on the future interpretation by the Strasbourg Court of the provisions contained in the ECHR.

3. Case Study Part I: The Influence of the CRPD on the Interpretation of ECHR Rights

The sub-sections which follow will provide an overview of the key trends related to disability equality which are evident in the case law of the ECtHR since the coming into force of the CRPD. The assessment by the Strasbourg Court of the merits of various judgments will be examined in order to establish whether the provisions of the CRPD, in particular its equality and non-discrimination norms, are exerting any influence on the Strasbourg Court's case law.

3.1. A Heightened Standard of Scrutiny of Disability Rights at the ECtHR: The 'Vulnerable Groups Approach'

The Strasbourg Court appears to be increasingly aware of the historical discrimination to which persons with disabilities have long been subjected and the need to prevent discrimination against disabled people generally. In recent cases (discussed below), the Court has ruled that persons with disabilities (specifically persons with psychosocial/mental disabilities) constitute a particularly vulnerable and marginalised group in society on account of past discrimination. The concept of vulnerability does not sit particularly well with the disability rights agenda. In particular, there is the fear that it may lead to further stigmatisation of persons with disabilities.[50] The notion of group vulnerability is also at odds with the fact that the CRPD views persons with disabilities as anything but vulnerable. Therefore, classifying persons with disabilities as a vulnerable group certainly does not reflect the empowering approach taken to disability under the CRPD. Nonetheless, it is interesting to note that the insertion of this concept in the Court's legal reasoning appears to be having some positive effects on the Court's judgments related to disability equality. This is primarily due to the fact that the consequences of applying a group vulnerability approach are a heightened standard of scrutiny and a somewhat more substantive approach to equality.

The 'vulnerable groups approach' or the 'vulnerability approach'[51] may be viewed as providing a potential means of addressing structural inequalities. Lourdes Peroni

[50] See L. Peroni and A. Timmer, 'Vulnerable Groups: The Promise of an Emergent Concept in European Human Rights Convention Law' 11 *International Journal of Constitutional Law* 1056.

[51] For a detailed examination of group vulnerability in the ECtHR's case law, see the following articles: A. Timmer, 'Toward an Anti-Stereotyping Approach for the European Court of Human Rights' (2011) 11(4) *Human Rights Law Review* 707; See also L. Peroni and A. Timmer, 'Vulnerable Groups: The Promise of an Emergent Concept in European Human Rights Convention Law' 11 *International*

and Alexandra Timmer are of the opinion that the Court's use of the notion of group vulnerability is an important step in the direction of a more substantive model of equality.[52] The vulnerability approach is not new to the ECtHR's legal reasoning. In the past, the Court has identified a number of vulnerable groups that suffered differential treatment on account, *inter alia*, of sex,[53] sexual orientation[54] and race or ethnicity.[55] The vulnerability approach has, for instance, been applied to Roma rights in many cases.[56] The application of the concept of group vulnerability to disability is a very recent development in the ECtHR's case law. As a result of its categorisation of persons with (psychosocial) disabilities as a vulnerable and disadvantaged group, the Court acknowledges disability as a suspect ground of discrimination and has stated that it will apply a strict standard of scrutiny in respect of alleged violations of the rights of disabled people under the ECHR, in particular instances of discriminatory treatment. The acknowledgement that disability is a suspect ground of discrimination coincides with the entry into force of the CRPD. Therefore, it is important to determine whether the UN Convention is linked to the Court's increased awareness of the disadvantage experienced by persons with disabilities and its use of the vulnerable groups approach. Moreover, it is important to explore whether the Strasbourg Court is harnessing the spirit and purpose of the CRPD in its interpretation of the ECHR's equality norm for persons with disabilities under the evolutive approach to interpretation which it professes to apply.

Journal of Constitutional Law 1056; In addition, see A. Timmer, 'A Quiet Revolution: Vulnerability in the European Court of Human Rights' in M. Fineman and A. Grear (eds.) *Vulnerability: Reflections on a New Ethical Foundation for Law and Politics* (Ashgate Publishing Ltd, UK, 2013), at pages 147–170.

52 The authors argue that the Court's use of the notion of group vulnerability: 'Represents a crucial step towards an enhanced anti-discrimination case law and a more robust idea of equality. The Court's use of the term "vulnerable groups" is therefore not mere rhetorical flourish. The term *does* something: it addresses and redresses different aspects of inequality in a more substantive manner.' [emphasis in original] [L. Peroni and A. Timmer, 'Vulnerable Groups: The Promise of an Emergent Concept in European Human Rights Convention Law,' (2013) 1 *International Journal of Constitutional Law* 1074].

53 See, for instance, *Abdulaziz, Cabales and Balkandali v United Kingdom*, application nos. 9214/80, 9473-81, 9474-81, judgment 28 May 1985, para. 78; See also *Burghartz v. Switzerland*, application no. 16213/90, judgment 22 February 1994, para. 27.

54 See, for example, *Schalk and Kopf v. Austria*, application no. 30141/04, judgment 22 November 2010, para. 97; See *Smith and Grady v. United Kingdom*, application nos. 33985/96 and 33986/96, judgment 27 December 1999, para. 90.

55 See *D.H.* v. *Czech Republic*, application no. 57325/00, judgment 13 November 2007 (2007) 47 EHRR 3, para. 182; See also *Timishev v. Russia*, application nos. 55762/00 and 55974/00, judgment 13 March 2006, para. 56.

56 See, for example, the cases of *Chapman v United Kingdom* (GC), application no. 27238/95, judgment 18 January 2001 (2001) EHRR18, 96; *D.H.* v *Czech Republic*, application no. 57325/00, judgment 13 November 2007 (2007) 47 EHRR 3; *Sampanis and Others v Greece*, application no. 32526/05, judgment 5 June 2008; *Oršuš and Others v Croatia* (GC), application no. 15766/03, 52 EHHR 7; *Horváth and Kiss v Hungary*, application no. 11146/11, judgment 29 January 2013; *M.S.S. v Belgium and Greece* [GC], application no. 30696/09, judgment 21 January 2011; and *V.C. v Slovakia*, application no. 18968/07, judgment 8 November 2011.

3.1.1. A Positive Step in the Direction of Substantive Equality

The first ground-breaking case in which the ECtHR found a violation of the right to non-discrimination on the basis of disability was *Glor v Switzerland*,[57] decided after the entry into force of the CRPD. The Court in *Glor* found disability discrimination contrary to Article 14, in conjunction with Article 8 ECHR, by virtue of the fact that the State had failed to carve out exemptions to a rule that imposed a penalty tax on persons deemed unfit to perform military service on grounds other than severe disability. The applicant in *Glor* had a minor disability and he alleged discrimination on account of the fact that he was subject to the aforementioned penalty tax on the basis of said disability. The primary relevance of the *Glor* case lies in the fact that the Strasbourg Court showed an increased awareness of the importance of the non-discrimination norm in protecting the rights of persons with disabilities. The Court adopted a heightened standard of scrutiny, ruling that States have a 'considerably reduced'[58] margin of appreciation in establishing different legal treatment for disabled people, on account of the 'need to prevent discrimination against people with disabilities and foster their full participation and integration in society.'[59] The adoption of a stricter standard of scrutiny stemmed from the Court's recognition of the considerable discrimination faced by persons with disabilities. Moreover, it appears to have been influenced, in large part, by the entry into force of the CRPD.[60] This assertion is based on the fact that the Court referred to the CRPD as an example of a 'European and worldwide consensus on the need to protect people with disabilities from discriminatory treatment.'[61] In narrowing the margin of appreciation to the State concerned, the Court commented that it was 'fully aware that where the organisation and operational effectiveness of the armed forces are concerned [...] States enjoy a certain margin of appreciation [...].'[62] It nevertheless enquired as to what prevented the authorities from 'setting in place special forms of service for people in a situation comparable to that of the applicant.'[63] The ECtHR gave examples of what it considered to be viable alternatives for the applicant, namely 'activities which, although carried out within the armed forces, required less physical effort and could therefore be performed by people like the applicant.'[64] This passage can be seen as an implicit recognition of the inclusion of some form of duty to accommodate within Article 14 ECHR. At the very least, it demonstrates the Court's willingness to consider the potential special measures that States can take

---

57 *Glor v. Switzerland*, application no. 13444/04, judgment 30 April 2009.

58 Ibid, para. 84.

59 Ibid.

60 The import of the *Glor* case also lies in the fact that the State Party in question had not even signed the CRPD at the time the judgment was handed down and, in fact, is still not a signatory to the UN Convention.

61 *Glor v. Switzerland*, application no. 13444/04, judgment 30 April 2009, para. 53.

62 Ibid, para. 94.

63 Ibid.

64 The ECtHR noted that, in certain States, 'the law provides for alternative forms of military service, in the armed forces, for people with partial disabilities. In practice these people are recruited to posts suited to their degree of disability and their occupational skills.' [Ibid, para. 94].

in order to accommodate the needs, and facilitate the rights, of disabled applicants. This illustrates some understanding of the social model of disability by the Court.[65]

3.1.2. A Heightened Standard of Scrutiny of Disability Rights

Following in the wake of the *Glor* judgment, in which the Court stated that national authorities have a considerably reduced margin of appreciation with regard to disability discrimination, the ECtHR confirmed explicitly for the first time in *Alajos Kiss v Hungary*[66] the application of a standard of 'strict scrutiny'[67] in the context of disability and, furthermore, adopted the vulnerability approach. The Court categorised persons with psychosocial disabilities ('the mentally disabled'[68]) as a 'particularly vulnerable group,'[69] basing this categorisation on the 'considerable discrimination'[70] which they have suffered in the past.

The *Alajos Kiss* case related to the automatic disenfranchisement of a man on account of the fact that he had manic depression and was under partial guardianship. Although the case was not decided under Article 14 ECHR, it essentially concerns disability discrimination. As a result of the treatment in question, the Court found a violation of Article 3, Protocol 1 ECHR (on the right to free elections).[71] In the course of reaching its decision, the Court made explicit reference to Articles 12 and 29 of the CRPD, which concern the rights to legal capacity and participation in political and public life, respectively. It would appear that the UN Convention influenced the Court's assessment of the merits of the case, to some extent at least. The applicant had submitted that any exclusion of people with disabilities from public life must be subject to scrutiny as to whether it was compatible with relevant international human rights requirements, including the CRPD.[72] It would seem that this submission was taken on board by the Court in narrowing the margin of appreciation in the matter. The Government had argued, relying on the doctrine of the margin of appreciation, that it must be permissible for the legislature to establish rules ensuring that only those who are capable of assessing the consequences of their decisions and making conscious and judicious decisions should participate in public affairs. In response, the Court drew attention to the fact that restrictions to participation in public affairs would normally warrant the granting of a wide margin of appreciation to Member States.[73] It ruled, however, that:

---

65 A hint of the social model of disability is also evident in the Court's conclusion that 'obliging the applicant to pay the disputed tax after denying him the opportunity to do his military (or civilian) service might prove to be in contradiction with the need to prevent discrimination against people with disabilities and foster their full participation and integration in society.' [Ibid, para. 84].

66 *Alajos Kiss v Hungary*, application no. 38832/06, judgment 20 May 2010.

67 Ibid, para. 44.

68 Ibid, para. 42.

69 Ibid.

70 Ibid.

71 Article 3, Protocol 1 ECHR provides as follows: 'The High Contracting Parties undertake to hold free elections at reasonable intervals by secret ballot, under conditions which will ensure the free expression of the opinion of the people in the choice of the legislature.'

72 *Alajos Kiss v Hungary*, para. 28.

73 Ibid, para. 41.

> An indiscriminate removal of voting rights, without an individualised judicial evaluation and solely based on a mental disability necessitating partial guardianship, cannot be considered compatible with the legitimate grounds for restricting the right to vote.[74]

It further stated that 'the treatment as a single class of those with intellectual or mental disabilities is a questionable classification, and the curtailment of their rights must be subject to strict scrutiny.'[75] The Court based this finding partly on the approach taken in instruments of international law which it had cited earlier in the judgment (including the CRPD).[76] Referring to the UN Convention and employing the concept of group vulnerability to narrow the margin of appreciation, the Court in *Alajos Kiss* concluded unanimously that a blanket denial of the right to vote to people with disabilities or to a category of persons with certain forms of disabilities was in contravention of Article 3, Protocol 1 ECHR and was therefore not within a State's margin of appreciation.

3.1.3. A Failure to Recognise Systemic Disadvantage

As shown in the preceding subsections, the UN Convention appears to be at the cornerstone of an increased awareness by the Court of the importance of the non-discrimination norm in protecting the rights of persons with disabilities. It also appears to be the basis for a heightened standard of scrutiny in recent disability equality judgments of the ECtHR. Another question altogether is whether, in adopting this stricter standard of scrutiny, the Court is actually taking account of the standards which are contained in the CRPD as a guiding tool under the evolutive approach to interpretation which it professes to follow. If we apply that question to the *Alajos Kiss* case, the answer appears to be that the Court is not yet taking the spirit and purpose of the CRPD into account in interpreting the provisions of the ECHR.

The *Alajos Kiss* ruling appears, at first glance, to be more promising than it is in reality. The reason for this is that the Court seems to have based its finding primarily on the absolute nature of the ban in question rather than on a consideration of the wider systemic disadvantage faced by disabled applicants in participating in the political process. In that case, both the third party intervener[77] (the Harvard Law School Project on Disability) and the applicant[78] argued that the rights under the ECHR of persons with disabilities should be interpreted in light of the CRPD. The applicant contended that the restriction imposed on him was incompatible with the CRPD's spirit and text, in particular Articles 12 and 29 thereof.[79] Those articles require support for persons with disabilities in exercising their legal capacity and reasonable accommodations to enable disabled people to participate in political

74 Ibid, para. 44.
75 Ibid, para. 44.
76 Ibid, para. 44.
77 Ibid, para. 34.
78 Ibid, para. 35.
79 Ibid, para. 35.

life, respectively. While it is commendable that the ECtHR narrowed the margin of appreciation in the case and conveyed its disapproval of a blanket ban on the rights of disabled individuals, it is the starting point of the Court's reasoning with which one might take issue. Anna Lawson contends that the ECHR's non-discrimination provision 'appears to affirm the view that human rights must be enjoyed by all on an equal basis.'[80] She states that, in order to ensure that this occurs in the context of disability, 'some notion of reasonable accommodation is required.'[81] The Court in *Alajos Kiss* blindly accepted the fact that an individualised assessment of a person's fitness to vote could legitimately lead to that person being denied the right to vote.[82] It is of course a legitimate aim to ensure that only persons fit to vote can exercise that right. However the Court did not consider (in its general remarks in the case) that *de facto* differential treatment of persons with disabilities may be required in order to ensure that they can exercise their rights on an equal basis with others.[83] The Court should have deliberated on the potential measures which could be put in place to assist disabled persons in exercising the right to vote, if so required. The Court's approach is out of step with the provisions of the CRPD invoked by the applicant and, in particular, the social model of disability which underlies the UN Convention, since individualised assessments of a person's fitness to vote measure functional deficiencies rather than addressing attitudinal and environmental barriers.[84] The Court's failure to consider alternative measures for disabled people is also out of step with Article 29 of the CRPD, which calls on States to secure full participation of persons with disabilities in political and public life, if necessary by accommodating their specific needs. Indeed, in the aftermath of the *Kiss* decision, the former Council of Europe Commissioner for Human Rights, Thomas Hammarberg, issued a Human Rights Comment[85] in which he critiques the judgment. Mr. Hammarberg emphasises the fact that instead of helping persons with disabilities to adjust to existing conditions, 'our societies should seek to adapt to and accommodate everyone, including those with special needs.'[86] Of course, that sentiment is in line with the CRPD. As Theresia Degener points out, the CRPD Committee's recommendations[87] demonstrate the fact that States Parties:

---

80 A. Lawson, 'the UN Convention on the Rights of Persons with Disabilities and European Disability Law: A Catalyst for Cohesion?' in O.M. Arnardóttir and G. Quinn, *The UN Convention on the Rights of Persons with Disabilities: European and Scandinavian Perspectives* (Martinus Nijhoff, Leiden, 2009) 94.

81 Ibid.

82 *Alajos Kiss v Hungary*, para. 44.

83 While the applicant – a man with psychosocial disability – merely required the same treatment as others, namely, exercise of the right to vote, and while a reasonable accommodation was not actually needed or requested in this case, the Court in *Alajos Kiss* allows for a legitimate denial of the right to vote in circumstances where a disabled person is assessed as being unfit to vote.

84 It is ironic that the Strasbourg Court actually cited Article 1 of the CRPD (which endorses the social model of disability) in the course of its judgment when referring to relevant provisions of international law. [*Alajos Kiss v Hungary*, para. 14].

85 T. Hammarberg, Council of Europe Commissioner for Human Rights, Human Rights Comment, 'Persons with Disabilities must not be Denied the Right to Vote,' available at http://commissioner.cws.coe.int/tiki-view_blog_post.php?postId=127 last accessed 12 December 2013.

86 Ibid.

87 In that regard, Degener cites the UN CRPD Committee's Concluding Observations to Tunisia (UN Doc. CRPD/C/TUN/CO/1, 2011, at para. 35), together with the Committee's Concluding Observations to

> Should review their voting laws and ensure inclusion of all persons with disabilities, regardless of their impairments, legal capacity status and institutional placement, as well as abolish the *de facto* denial of the right to political participation by making the political process accessible and providing reasonable accommodation to persons with disabilities.[88]

3.1.4. Further Evidence of a Heightened Standard of Scrutiny

Following the *Alajos Kiss* judgment, the endorsement of a rigorous level of scrutiny was replicated in the case of *Kiyutin v Russia*.[89] The applicant in *Kiyutin* had argued that the rejection of his application for a residency permit violated his right to respect for family life, in conjunction with his right to non-discrimination on the basis of his HIV status contrary to Articles 8 and 14 ECHR. Categorising HIV as a form of disability might be controversial in some quarters. However, the Court itself in *Kiyutin* made a link between HIV and disability in its judgment and therefore in the subsections below HIV will be equated with disability in order to maintain consistency with the Court's approach. The third party intervener in the case, Interights, argued for the applicability of the disability anti-discrimination framework established under the CRPD to people living with HIV/AIDS, contending that this had been endorsed by the United Nations Office of the High Commissioner for Human Rights, the World Health Organization and UN AIDS in their joint report, *Disability and HIV Policy Brief*.[90] The intervener also argued that the disability-based approach to HIV was further supported by the legislation and practice of many countries,[91] which had expressly or implicitly extended their disability laws to include HIV status. The ECtHR appears to have taken the submissions of the intervener on board in that regard. The Court cited a resolution[92] of the UN Commission on Human Rights to the effect that the term 'other status' in non-discrimination provisions in international legal instruments can be interpreted to cover health status, including HIV-infection. The Court also cited the general prohibition of disability-based discrimination contained in the CRPD in its deliberations.[93] On that basis, the Court concluded that a distinction made on account of one's health status, including such conditions as

---

Spain (UN Doc. CRPD/C/ESP/1, 2011, paras 47 and 48) and the Committee's Concluding Observations to Peru (UN Doc. CRPD/C/PER/CO/1, 2012, para 45(a)).

88 T. Degener, 'The Right to Political Participation: From Exclusion to Universality' in International Disability Alliance Publication Series, Issue 1: The Right to Vote and to Stand for Election (March 2013), available at www.internationaldisabilityalliance.org/sites/disalliance.e-presentaciones.net/files/public/files/Theresia%20Degener_The%20right%20to%20political%20participation_from%20exclusion%20to%20universality.pdf, last accessed 14 October 2014.

89 *Kiyutin v Russia*, application no. 2700/10, judgment 10 March 2011.

90 [2009]. Available at www.who.int/disabilities/jc1632_policy_brief_disability_en.pdf last accessed 12 December 2014.

91 Namely, Canada, Germany, Norway, the United Kingdom and the United States of America [*Kiyutin v Russia*, Application no. 2700/10, judgment 10 March 2011, para. 44].

92 United Nations Commission on Human Rights, Resolution no. 1995/44, 'The protection of human rights in the context of HIV and AIDS' (adopted at its 53rd meeting on 3 March 1995).

93 *Kiyutin v Russia*, para. 57.

HIV infection, should be covered – either as a form of disability or alongside with it – by the term 'other status' in the text of Article 14 ECHR.[94]

The main influence exerted by the UN Convention in *Kiyutin* can be viewed in terms of the seeming applicability by the ECtHR of the disability anti-discrimination framework established under the CRPD to people living with HIV/AIDS and also the increased awareness within the Court of the importance of preventing discrimination on the basis of disability (including health-related HIV grounds). The Court in *Kiyutin* carried out a separate and thorough examination of the alleged violation of Article 14, noting that the 'focal point'[95] of the application was the difference in treatment to which the applicant was subjected on account of his health status when applying for a residence permit.[96] In the course of its judgment, the ECtHR cited several articles of the CRPD in the context of relevant international law, namely Article 5 (on the right to equality/non-discrimination), Article 18 (liberty of movement and nationality), together with Article 23 of the CRPD (on respect for home and family).[97] The ECtHR also showed itself open to a social-contextual approach to discrimination/disadvantage in *Kiyutin* by examining in great detail the manner in which the stigmatisation and exclusion of HIV-positive persons manifests itself and its consequences for persons with HIV.[98] Alexandra Timmer observes that the Court made 'a real effort to address the sources of prejudice against people living with HIV.'[99] The Court employed the vulnerable groups approach, classifying HIV-positive individuals as 'a vulnerable group with a history of prejudice and stigmatisation.'[100] This resulted in the ruling by the Court that the State should only be afforded a narrow margin of appreciation in choosing measures which single out that group for differential treatment on the basis of their HIV status.[101]

The Government in *Kiyutin* had put forward health-related concerns as a major justification for the legal measure in question and posited that the refusal of the residence permit was 'a necessary measure directed at preventing and combating

94 Ibid.

95 Ibid, para. 39.

96 Ibid.

97 The Court cited the paragraphs of those articles that deal with non-discrimination on the basis of disability. With regard to Article 5, the Court cited paragraph 2 of that article, which provides that 'States Parties shall prohibit all discrimination on the basis of disability and guarantee to persons with disabilities equal and effective legal protection against discrimination on all grounds.' In relation to Article 18, the focus of the Court was again on the equal rights of persons with disabilities. In that regard, the Court cited Article 18(1), which provides that 'States Parties shall recognize the rights of persons with disabilities to liberty of movement, to freedom to choose their residence and to a nationality, *on an equal basis with others.*' [emphasis added] Finally, with regard to Article 23 of the CRPD, the Court cited the obligation incumbent on States to take 'effective and appropriate measures to eliminate discrimination against persons with disabilities in all matters relating to marriage, family, parenthood and relationships, *on an equal basis with others.*' [emphasis added]. [Ibid, para. 32].

98 *Kiyutin v Russia*, para. 64.

99 A. Timmer, 'Toward an Anti-Stereotyping Approach for the European Court of Human Rights' (2011) 11(4) *Human Rights Law Review* 707, 713.

100 *Kiyutin v Russia*, para. 64.

101 Ibid.

HIV infection.'[102] While the Court in *Kiyutin* did consider this a legitimate aim in principle, it scrutinised the justification advanced by the State. In applying a strict standard of proportionality, the Court noted that the Government had proceeded from a generalised assumption that the applicant represented a grave threat to the health of the nation and had not analysed his individual circumstances.[103] The Court also expressed its concern regarding the 'blanket and indiscriminate nature of the impugned measure'[104] and stated that the measure did not leave 'any room for an individualised assessment based on the facts of a particular case.'[105] The applicant was deemed to be a victim of discrimination on account of his health status, in violation of Article 14, taken in conjunction with Article 8 ECHR.[106]

In *Kiyutin*, as in *Alajos Kiss* before it, the Court employed the notion of group vulnerability in order to narrow the margin of appreciation accorded to the State concerned. By that token, the Court adopted a social-contextual approach to the disadvantage suffered by the particular vulnerable group at issue. It is notable, however, that (just like in *Alajos Kiss*), the concept of group vulnerability is not the only factor at play in *Kiyutin* in influencing the Court's legal reasoning. Yet again, 'the blanket and indiscriminate nature of the impugned measure,'[107] together with a European consensus militating against the types of measures at issue,[108] appears to have influenced the Court to narrow the margin in *Kiyutin*. Overall, it would seem that the CRPD has had some influence with respect to the ECtHR's increased awareness of the importance of preventing disability-based discrimination (as shown in *Glor* above) and its consequent classification of persons with disabilities (specifically, those with psychosocial disabilities and those with HIV) as a vulnerable and disadvantaged group. By virtue of the vulnerable groups approach, the Court appears to be identifying some of the root causes of the disadvantage experienced by persons with disabilities, leading to their social exclusion.

3.1.5. The Social-Contextual Approach – Steps in the Direction of the Social Model of Disability?

In both the *Alajos Kiss* and *Kiyutin* cases above, the Court placed great emphasis on the social context of the disadvantage experienced by the applicants. Oddný Mjöll Arnardóttir claims that a social-contextual approach:

> Can be seen as denoting the general idea that non-discrimination analysis should be conscious of how structural patterns of social disadvantage and exclusion function to keep marginalised groups in the margins. It is, therefore, a perspective on the interpretation and

---

102 Ibid, para. 40.
103 Ibid, para. 68.
104 Ibid, para. 72.
105 Ibid.
106 Ibid, para. 74.
107 Ibid, para. 72.
108 Ibid, para. 65.

> application of Article 14 that keeps in mind the object and purpose of eliminating such structures, or at least minimising their effect on individuals.[109]

The Court has placed emphasis on social context in other recent judgments. For instance, in the Grand Chamber judgment of *Konstantin Markin v Russia*[110] (related to the issue of parental leave allowances for fathers), the Court referred to the evolution in the legislation of Member States towards granting parental leave entitlements to men. Significantly, the ECtHR noted that gender stereotypes cannot be used to justify different treatment 'any more than similar stereotypes based on race, origin, colour or sexual orientation.'[111] Arnardóttir is of the opinion that the *Konstantin Markin* judgment:

> In a sense exhibits at the same time the general logic of the 'common ground' approach, but this time coupled with an express moral compass that gives clearer normative content to Article 14 through focussing on the negative effects of stereotyping.[112]

She claims that recent trends in the Strasbourg Court's case law appear to indicate that the Court is 'beginning to integrate an express focus on social context into its analysis under Article 14' but cautions that the Court is 'still at an early stage of development' in this regard as other cases[113] involving the relevant discrimination grounds 'continue to be decided without any reference to membership in vulnerable groups, social exclusion, stigma or stereotyping.'[114]

In both the *Alajos Kiss* and *Kiyutin* cases outlined above, the Court elaborated on its reasoning for applying a strict standard of scrutiny and acknowledged the extent to which socially constructed stereotypes[115] have in the past perpetuated, and indeed continue to, perpetuate the social exclusion of persons with psychosocial disability and those with HIV, respectively.[116] By showing itself open to the social context of the alleged violation and, therefore, to the social construction of disability/health-

---

109 O.M. Arnardóttir, 'The Differences that Make a Difference: Recent Developments on the Discrimination Grounds and the Margin of Appreciation under Article 14 of the European Convention on Human Rights' (2014) 14 *Human Rights Law Review* 647, 664.

110 *Konstantin Markin v Russia*, application no. 30078/06, judgment 22 March 2012.

111 Ibid, at para. 143.

112 O.M. Arnardóttir, 'The Differences that Make a Difference: Recent Developments on the Discrimination Grounds and the Margin of Appreciation under Article 14 of the European Convention on Human Rights' (2014) 14 *Human Rights Law Review* 647, 654.

113 In that regard, Arnardóttir cites *Kurić and Others v Slovenia*, application no. 26828/06, 26 June 2012 (race) and *Vallianatos and Others v Greece*, applications nos. 29381/09 and 32684/09, judgment 7 November 2013 (sexual orientation).

114 O.M. Arnardóttir, 'The Differences that Make a Difference: Recent Developments on the Discrimination Grounds and the Margin of Appreciation under Article 14 of the European Convention on Human Rights' (2014) 14 *Human Rights Law Review* 647, 654.

115 See generally the comments of J. Gerards regarding the Court's anti-stereotyping approach – J. Gerards, 'The Discrimination Grounds of Article 14 of the European Convention on Human Rights' (2013) 31 *Human Rights Law Review* 99; See also A. Timmer, 'Toward an Anti-Stereotyping Approach for the European Court of Human Rights' (2011) 11(4) *Human Rights Law Review* 707.

116 *Alajos Kiss v. Hungary*, application no. 38832/06, judgment 20 May 2010, para. 42 and *Kiyutin v Russia,* application no. 2700/10 judgment 10 March 2011, para. 63.

related grounds, the Court recognises implicitly that the disabling factors in those cases resulted from attitudinal and legislative barriers to participation. In spite of this positive development in the Court's approach, it is important to bear in mind that the Court in *Alajos Kiss* clearly failed to consider the fact that the substantive disadvantage encountered by persons with disabilities may need to be remedied by accommodation measures in some instances.

In the subsequent case of *I.B. v Greece*,[117] the ECtHR showed positive trends in its understanding of disability equality and more affinity with the social construction of disability (HIV). The Court in *I.B.* made a further ruling on the issue of HIV-based discrimination, this time in the employment context. However, the Strasbourg Court shows inconsistency in its approach to using the CRPD as an interpretative guide to ECHR rights. In *I.B.*, the Court fails completely to mention the UN Convention in its judgment. This is inconsistent when compared with previous cases in which it mentions the Convention as a relevant source of international law for the interpretation of ECHR rights and particularly after the Court acknowledged in *Kiyutin* the link between HIV health-related grounds and disability.

The *I.B.* case concerned a man who had been diagnosed with HIV and who was subsequently fired from his employment, following complaints by fellow employees that they may be exposed to the HIV virus as a result of the applicant's presence in the workplace. The applicant alleged that his dismissal violated his right to private life under Article 8 ECHR. The applicant also alleged discriminatory treatment, contrary to Article 14 ECHR, on account of the dismissal itself and also in view of the fact that the reason given by the Greek Supreme Court for justifying the dismissal (namely, his HIV status and the necessity to preserve an amicable work environment) constituted unjustified discrimination under Article 14.[118] In finding a violation of both Articles 8 and 14 ECHR, the Court in *I.B.* followed a similar line of legal reasoning to the *Kiyutin* case outlined above. Once again, the Court spoke extensively about the difficulties faced by persons diagnosed with HIV in terms of stigmatisation and discrimination.[119] The ECtHR adopted the vulnerability approach and repeated its pronouncements from the *Kiyutin* case that, by virtue of the fact that people living with HIV are a 'vulnerable group with a history of prejudice and stigmatisation, States should only be afforded a narrow margin of appreciation in choosing measures that single out that group for differential treatment on the basis of their HIV status.'[120] By that token, the Court focused again on the social-contextual approach to disadvantage. In the course of its judgment, the ECtHR referred to

[117] *I.B. v Greece*, application 552/10, judgment 3 October 2013.
[118] In considering the merits of the application, the Strasbourg Court found that the Greek Supreme Court did not analyse sufficiently the interests of both sides (employer and employee) and, furthermore, that the Supreme Court had gone along with the discriminatory attitude of the employer and the applicant's co-workers.
[119] See, in particular, paragraphs 72, 80 and 81 of the *I.B.* judgment.
[120] *I.B. v Greece*, paras. 79 and 81.

Recommendation No. 200 of the International Labour Organization (ILO)[121] and relevant pronouncements of the UNCESCR[122] which link HIV to discrimination. Employing a comparative approach, the Court recognised that decisions of domestic courts and other bodies for human-rights protection in some States 'show that they grant protection against dismissal to HIV-positive persons through the prohibition imposed on other grounds of discrimination, such as health or disability.'[123] While the applicant did not invoke the provisions of the CRPD, the UN Convention has obvious relevance to the facts of the case and it is surprising that the Court made no mention of it in its consideration of the merits of the *I.B.* case, in light of its comparative and evolutive approach to interpretation of ECHR rights. In spite of its failure to mention the CRPD, the social model of disability appears to have infiltrated the Court's legal reasoning in several ways. In the first instance, the ECtHR took the social model of disability into account in its analysis of the scope of application of the right to private life under Article 8 ECHR. In that regard, the Court stated that there is no question but that situations involving persons with HIV come within the ambit of the right to private life under Article 8, on account of the fact that the HIV epidemic cannot be considered solely as a medical problem. Rather, its consequences reverberate through all spheres of one's private life.[124] The Court noted that the treatment in question, namely the dismissal of the applicant, resulted in his stigmatisation and that this treatment inevitably had serious repercussions on his personality, on the level of respect which others showed him and, eventually, on his private life.[125] Furthermore, in deciding that there was no objective and reasonable justification for the treatment in question, the Strasbourg Court again adopted the social model of disability. The Court acknowledged the fact that HIV-positive persons 'have to face up to a whole host of problems, not only medical, but also professional, social, personal and psychological ones, and above all to sometimes deeply rooted prejudices even among the most highly educated people.'[126] The ECtHR was of the view that the discriminatory treatment in question originated in the attitude of rejection adopted

---

121 International Labor Organisation, Recommendation 200: Recommendation concerning HIV and AIDS and the world of work/La Recommandation (no 200) de l'OIT concernant le VIH et le sida et le monde du travail (2010).

122 UNCESCR, General Comment No. 20 (2009) on Non-Discrimination in Economic, Social and Cultural Rights (ICESCR: Article 2, para. 2), adopted at the forty-second session of the Committee on 25 May 2009, UN Doc. E/C.12/GC 20.

123 *I.B. v Greece*, para. 39.

124 At paragraph 70 of the *I.B.* judgment, the Court states as follows: 'It is therefore now established that both employment matters and situations involving HIV-infected persons fall within the scope of private life. The Court cannot but conclude thus, since the HIV epidemic cannot be considered only as a medical problem as its effects are felt in every sphere of private life.'

125 At paragraph 72 of *I.B. v Greece*, the Court states that: 'It is clear that the applicant's dismissal resulted in the stigmatisation of a person who, even if they were HIV positive, had not shown any symptoms of the disease. That measure was bound to have serious repercussions for his personality rights, the respect owed to him and, ultimately, his private life. To that must be added the uncertainty surrounding his search for a new job, since the possibility of finding one could reasonably have appeared remote having regard to his previous experience. The fact that the applicant did find a new job after being dismissed does not suffice to erase the detrimental effect of his dismissal on his ability to lead a normal personal life.'

126 See paragraph 80 of *I.B. v Greece*.

by the applicant's colleagues when faced with his HIV-positive status.[127] On that basis, it concluded that the applicant was a victim of discrimination in breach of Article 8, taken together with Article 14 ECHR.

It is clear that the Court applied a social model of disability to the disadvantage encountered by the applicant in *I.B.* and this shows some promise for the further application of the social model of disability which underlies the CRPD in future cases. In spite of these positive trends in the *I.B.* judgment, Alexandra Timmer is of the opinion that the legal reasoning in that case 'does not provide much support for cases that concern questions of reasonable accommodation.'[128] She contends that *I.B* essentially concerns a negative interference with the applicant's private life. She bases this assertion on the fact that the Strasbourg Court refers extensively to the domestic Court of Appeal, which had emphasised the fact that 'the applicant's health status had in no way diminished his work capacity.'[129] Timmer questions what the ECtHR might have ruled in this case if the applicant's health status had in fact hindered his ability to work?[130] In other words, she questions whether, if the applicant had 'been required to take some time off work to deal with his health' or if he had become 'somewhat less efficient in his job,' could his dismissal not then raise an issue of discrimination?[131] Of course, the CRPD includes a failure to reasonably accommodate within the definition of discrimination on the basis of disability in Article 2. As it stands, it is difficult to discern what influence the substantive provisions of the Convention might have on the Court's case law, in particular in relation to the duty to accommodate. All we can say at this point is that the Court's case law is showing promising trends. In particular, the Court in *I.B.* shows positive signs of a social construction of disability/health-related HIV grounds. However, by failing to mention the provisions of the CRPD in its judgment, the question still hangs in the air as to whether the CRPD is really impacting on the Court's approach to equality. In other words, it is unclear whether the Court is truly cognisant of the substantive disadvantage faced by persons with disabilities in society, beyond prejudices and stereotypes and whether this will influence the interpretation of Article 14 in future cases.

3.1.6. Conclusion: Two Steps Forward – One Step Back

It would appear from the cases outlined above that the ECtHR is more cognisant than before of the fact that persons with disabilities face considerable barriers in their everyday lives. The CRPD appears to have influenced the Court to condemn discrimination on the basis of disability, including health-related HIV grounds. This

---

127 At paragraph 77 of *I.B. v Greece*, the Court noted that 'the employer's concern was admittedly to restore peace in the company, but that that concern was rooted in the situation created by the attitude of the applicant's colleagues towards his HIV status.'

128 A. Timmer, 'HIV-based employment discrimination: the ECtHR takes a strong stance in I.B. v. Greece' October 21, 2013, available at http://strasbourgobservers.com/2013/10/21/hiv-based-employment-discrimination-the-ecthr-takes-a-strong-stance-in-i-b-v-greece/ last accessed 8 December 2013.

129 Ibid.

130 Ibid.

131 Ibid.

has served as the basis for the adoption by the Court of a heightened standard of scrutiny in recent disability equality judgments. As shown above, the Strasbourg Court has moved away from a formal approach to equality and closer to the core of the substantive equality model in many respects. For example, the *Glor* case demonstrates the fact that the Court may now be willing to incorporate reasonable accommodation duties into its non-discrimination analysis, implicitly at least. However, more precedent would be needed in that regard to establish a trend in the Court's case law and subsequent cases of the Court do not provide much hope in that regard (as illustrated above). Outside of the disability context, the ECtHR does seem to be demonstrating an increasing willingness to view some form of positive obligations as an element of its substantive equality analysis, as demonstrated, for instance, by the *Horváth* case. While not a disability-specific case, *Horváth* is significant from the perspective of the Court's increased awareness of the needs of marginalised groups. Again more precedent would be needed to establish a definitive trend in the Court's approach. The social-contextual approach which the ECtHR has adopted in several cases appears to have drawn the attention of the Court to the discriminatory barriers faced by persons with disabilities in their everyday lives. This has served to widen the scope of application of certain rights (as seen in the *I.B.* case above) and to heighten the scrutiny of defences raised by States. Encouragingly, the Court has linked the impact of historical discrimination on persons with psychosocial disabilities and those with HIV to the applicable margin of appreciation in both *Alajos Kiss* and *Kiyutin*. As a result, the ECtHR will not allow any blanket curtailment of the rights of disabled people and has ruled that indiscriminate differential treatment of persons with disabilities cannot be justified.

While these trends are largely positive, the ECtHR is not following through in its legal reasoning with the spirit of the model of equality which underlies the UN Convention. In other words, the Court is not taking into account the substantive disadvantage experienced by persons with disabilities in its interpretation of ECHR rights. This can be seen by the fact that, while the Court in *Alajos Kiss* stated its intention to apply a strict standard of scrutiny and condemned the considerable discrimination suffered by persons with psychosocial disabilities in the context of the right to vote, it gave no consideration to the potential positive obligations that might arise in the context of accommodating a disabled person to participate in the political sphere. The Strasbourg Court therefore still has a long way to go in its interpretation of ECHR rights if it is to contribute, to a greater extent, towards increasing the enjoyment of human rights for persons with disabilities on an equal basis with others. It will be necessary to await a case in which the question of reasonable accommodations falls squarely before the Court to see what approach the Court will take. Since the ECtHR professes to take an evolutive approach to interpretation of ECHR rights, any interpretation of Article 14 in the disability context must necessarily involve some level of accommodations so that persons with disabilities can enjoy their rights on an equal basis with others. The Court must bear in mind the fact that protection of the rights of disadvantaged groups involves not only scrutiny of differential treatment but also scrutiny of instances in which States fail to take into account differential characteristics. *Glor* illustrates the potential of the CRPD to act as an interpretative guide to the rights of persons with disabilities under the ECHR. It also demonstrates the potential which exists for a fusion of ECHR disability discrimination jurisprudence with the norms contained in the CRPD. Whether the Strasbourg Court chooses to act on that potential is another question altogether. One would certainly hope that the tenets of international human rights law will find their way into the case law of the ECtHR to a greater extent in the coming years and that this will deepen the Court's conception of substantive disadvantage and, therefore substantive equality, for persons with disabilities.

Apart from case law decided by the ECtHR under Article 14 since the coming into force of the CRPD, the Court has also considered many cases relating to persons with disabilities in institutional settings under Article 2 ECHR (on the right to life) and Article 3 ECHR (which contains the prohibition on torture and inhuman and degrading treatment or punishment). Those cases demonstrate further scope for the development of reasonable accommodation duties under the ECHR. That line of the Court's case law will be examined below, from an equality perspective.

3.2. *De Facto* Reasonable Accommodation Duties under the ECHR in Limited Circumstances

To date the ECtHR has not recognised an explicit right to be reasonably accommodated under the ECHR's non-discrimination provision in the context of disability. Outside of the disability context, certain case law of the ECtHR has arguably contributed to the development of the notion of reasonable accommodation in the Court's jurisprudence. The judgment of *Thlimmenos v Greece*[132] is particularly significant in that connection. That case concerned a Jehovah's witness who wished to become a chartered accountant but was refused access to the profession on account of a criminal conviction that he held for refusing to serve in the armed forces for religious reasons. As noted above,[133] the Court famously stated that the right not to be discriminated under Article 14 of the ECHR was not only violated when States treat differently persons in analogous situations without providing an objective and reasonable justification but also 'when States without an objective and reasonable justification fail to treat differently persons whose situations are significantly different.'[134] The Court essentially held that the Greek authorities had discriminated against the applicant by failing to 'introduce appropriate exceptions to the rule barring persons convicted of a serious crime from the profession of chartered accountants.'[135] The *Thlimmenos* case is important on account of its potential links to disability accommodations. Oliver de Schutter notes that 'although the expression, as such, does not appear in the judgment, the language used by the Court is reminiscent

[132] *Thlimmenos v Greece*, application no. 34369/97, judgment of 6 April 2000.
[133] See section 2.3 of this chapter.
[134] *Thlimmenos v Greece*, para. 44.
[135] Ibid para. 48.

of the notion of reasonable accommodation.'[136] He states that the Court's judgment demonstrates the fact that:

> A failure to take account of certain specific needs of an individual may now amount to discrimination; it may be unjustified to *refuse to create an exception to the general norm*, even where that norm is justifiable as reasonably related to a legitimate aim and proportionate to fulfillment of that aim.[137]

On that basis, de Schutter notes that the reasoning in Thlimmenos is 'immediately useful to disability rights advocates.'[138]

The ECtHR has also shown a trend towards locating a *de facto* duty to accommodate persons with disabilities within certain substantive rights of the ECHR. *De facto* reasonable accommodation duties have, for instance, been acknowledged by the Court in many cases which invoke, in particular, articles 2 and 3 of the ECHR in limited circumstances, most notably in institutional or prison settings. The reason for the Court's insistence on *de facto* accommodation duties in those settings appears to relate to the grave nature of the potential breaches of rights involved and the particularly vulnerable situation of the applicants in question, leaving aside the issue of disability. The circumstances in which the Court has pronounced *de facto* reasonable accommodation duties to date will be examined below, as well as the extent to which the CRPD is having an influence on the Court's perception of the duty to accommodate disabled persons. In other words, does the UN Convention appear to be influencing the ECtHR to move towards greater recognition of the equal rights of persons with disabilities via the duty to accommodate?

3.2.1. De Facto Reasonable Accommodation Duties in Prison Settings: Pre-CRPD

Disabled prisoners are confronted with numerous barriers which hinder their inherent dignity and which impair their right to life. As such, they often require reasonable accommodations to ensure that these rights are preserved on an equal basis with others. Article 3 ECHR contains the prohibition on torture and inhuman and degrading treatment. The link between reasonable accommodation and ill-treatment in institutional settings has been recognised explicitly by Manfred Nowak (former UN Special Rapporteur on Torture), who observes that 'the lack of reasonable accommodation in detention facilities may increase the risk of exposure to neglect, violence, abuse, torture and ill-treatment.'[139] Article 15(1) of the CRPD contains a similar prohibition to that contained in Article 3 ECHR. It provides that 'no one shall be subjected to torture or to cruel, inhuman or degrading treatment

---

136 O. de Schutter, 'Reasonable Accommodation and Positive Obligations in the European Convention on Human Rights' in A. Lawson and C. Gooding (eds.), *Disability Rights in Europe: From Theory to Practice* (Hart Publishing, Oxford and Portland, Oregon, 2005), at page 53.

137 Ibid.

138 Ibid.

139 M. Nowak, *Interim report of the Special Rapporteur on Torture and Other Cruel, Inhuman or Degrading Treatment or Punishment*, A/63/175, 28 July 2008, para. 38 available at www.un.org/disabilities/images/A.63.175.doc. last accessed 15 January 2014.

or punishment.'[140] In addition, Article 15(2) of the CRPD requires States Parties 'to take all effective legislative, administrative, judicial or other measures to ensure that persons with disabilities are prevented from being subjected to torture, inhuman or degrading treatment or punishment *on an equal basis with others*.'[141] Furthermore, Article 14(2) of the UN Convention requires States to ensure that:

> If persons with disabilities are deprived of their liberty through any process, they are, *on an equal basis with others*, entitled to guarantees in accordance with international human rights law and shall be treated in compliance with the objectives and principles of the present Convention, *including by provision of reasonable accommodation*.[142]

It is clear that the CRPD perceives reasonable accommodations as an essential element of disability equality in the context of deprivation of liberty. Without such accommodations, persons with disabilities are unable to enjoy their human rights on an equal basis with other individuals who are subject to detention. In order to satisfy the threshold for inhuman or degrading treatment and thereby to fall within the ambit of Article 3 ECHR, a victim must be in a position to show that his/her suffering attains a certain minimum level of severity. In assessing whether this level has been attained, the ECtHR takes into account all the circumstances of the case, including the duration of the treatment, its physical and mental effects and, in some cases, the sex, age and state of health of the victim.[143] Anna Lawson points to the fact that:

> This emphasis on the circumstances of the particular victim has been relied on by the ECtHR and other supranational adjudicatory bodies to rule that the level of suffering endured by particular detainees with physical, sensory or other impairments, for whom adjustments were not made, has exceeded this minimum level of severity.[144]

In several cases that have come before it, the ECtHR has not hesitated in finding a violation of Article 3 ECHR in circumstances where the special needs and circumstances of a disabled detainee were not taken into account by the authorities in institutional settings. For instance, in the case of *Price v United Kingdom*,[145] (which was decided before the coming into force of the CRPD), the Strasbourg Court ruled that the State in question had inflicted degrading treatment on the applicant (a disabled woman in state custody) contrary to Article 3 ECHR, by virtue of the fact that it had failed to accommodate her particular needs arising from her impairment. The Court found that the detention conditions of the applicant, including inaccessible toilets and bed, amounted to degrading treatment under Article 3, notwithstanding the lack of any evidence of an intention to humiliate Ms. Price. As Olivier de

140 UN CRPD, Article 15(2).
141 Ibid [emphasis added].
142 UN CRPD, Article 14(2) [emphasis added].
143 *Z.H. v Hungary*, application no. 28973/11, judgment 8 November 2012, para. 28.
144 A. Lawson, "Disability Equality, Reasonable Accommodation and the Avoidance of Ill-Treatment in Places of Detention: The Role of Supranational Monitoring and Inspection Bodies" 16(6) *International Journal of Human Rights* (August 2012) 845, at page 851.
145 *Price v United Kingdom*, application no. 33394/96, judgment 10 July 2001 (2002) 34 EHRR 53.

Schutter points out, 'it was the lack of any consideration of Ms. Price's special needs which led to the Court's finding that degrading treatment had taken place.'[146] The Court in *Price* did not use the language of reasonable accommodations and it did not take the opportunity to frame the rights of the disabled applicant in terms of non-discrimination or equality. One could argue that this could not have been expected of the Court as far back as 2001 when the concept of reasonable accommodation was relatively new and unknown in international and European law at that point. The *de facto* duty to accommodate established in *Price* is a limited one, confined to institutional settings and also to the substantive right at issue. It certainly did not translate to a wider duty to accommodate disabled people under the ECHR in diverse social situations and, in particular, under Article 14 ECHR. The subsections below will examine the extent to which this situation has changed (if at all) following the entry into force of the CRPD. In other words, is the Strasbourg Court more inclined to recognise the duty to accommodate as an inherent part of the exercise of equal rights for persons with disabilities in institutional and other settings on foot of the norms contained in the CRPD?

3.2.2. *Post-CRPD Case Law on Disabled Prisoners*

Since the coming into force of the CRPD the Strasbourg Court has evinced a similar trend to its pre-CRPD case law in locating *de facto* reasonable accommodation duties within Article 3 ECHR, on account of the fact that the specific circumstances of disabled detainees were not taken into account by the relevant authorities. In some cases, the Court refers to the CRPD. In many cases, however, the Court does not refer to the CRPD at all or to the concept of reasonable accommodation contained in the UN Convention. Both sets of cases will be discussed in the subsections which follow.

3.2.2.1. A Marked Absence of Reference to the CRPD in the ECtHR's Case Law on Disabled Prisoners

Several cases relating to *de facto* accommodation duties have come before the Court since the entry into force of the CRPD in the specific context of disabled prisoners. Many of these cases are marked by a lack of reference to the CRPD. In *Vincent v France*,[147] for example, the Court held that detaining a disabled person in a prison where he could not move around and, in particular, could not leave his cell independently, amounted to degrading treatment, without referring once to the concept of reasonable accommodations under the CRPD. In a similar vein, in *Engel v Hungary*,[148] the Court ruled that leaving a person with a serious physical disability to rely on his cellmates for assistance with using the toilet, bathing and getting dressed or undressed, was sufficient for a finding that the conditions of detention amounted

[146] O. de Schutter, 'Reasonable Accommodation and Positive Obligations in the European Convention on Human Rights' in A. Lawson and C. Gooding (eds.), *Disability Rights in Europe: From Theory to Practice* (Hart Publishing, Oxford and Portland, Oregon, 2005), at page 55.

[147] *Vincent v. France*, application no. 6253/03, judgment 24 October 2006, paras. 94–103.

[148] *Engel v. Hungary*, application no. 46857/06, judgment 20 May 2010, paras. 27–30.

to degrading treatment. The Court again made this ruling without referring to the CRPD. Findings of *de facto* reasonable accommodation duties have been made in numerous other cases of a similar nature since the entry into force of the UN Convention.[149] Once again, it is interesting to note that the ECtHR does not refer to the CRPD at all in any of these cases. In other cases related to disabled individuals in institutional settings, there seems to be a greater emphasis by the Court on the concept of reasonable accommodation as enshrined in the CRPD. The important point to note however is that the Court's approach is ad-hoc. Some of the cases outlined above (in which the Court does not refer to the CRPD or to the concept of reasonable accommodation contained therein) were decided around the same time as the handful of cases in which the Court places greater emphasis on the concept of reasonable accommodation. Notwithstanding this inconsistency in approach, it is worth examining the selection of case law in which the ECtHR appears to be showing increased cognisance of relevant provisions of the CRPD in interpreting the rights of disabled persons in institutional settings.

3.2.2.2. Increased Recognition of the CRPD in the ECtHR's Case Law on Disabled Prisoners

The first case of significance in this regard is *Jasinskis v Latvia*.[150] That case concerned the failure of the domestic authorities to provide medical assistance to and also to communicate properly with the applicant, a seriously injured deaf man who was also unable to speak. The applicant died after being held in police custody for 14 hours. Relying mainly on Article 2 and secondarily on Article 3 ECHR, Mr Jasinskis' father alleged that the Latvian police had been responsible for his son's death and that the investigation which ensued had been ineffectual. The Court in *Jasinskis* showed itself once again to be conscious of the needs and special requirements of persons with disabilities, noting that where the authorities decide to place and maintain in detention a person with disabilities, 'they should demonstrate special care in guaranteeing such conditions as correspond to his special needs resulting from his disability.'[151] Of course that finding had already

[149] See, for example, the cases of *Khudobin v Russia*, application no. 59696/00, judgment 26 October 2006; *Rupa v Romania*, application no. 58478/00, judgment 16 December 2008; *Kupczak v Poland*, application no. 2627/09, judgment 25 January 2009; *Xiros v Greece*, application no. 1033/07, judgment 9 September 2010; *Grori v Albania*, application no. 25336/04, judgment 7 July 2009; *Raffrey Taddei v France*, application no. 36435/07, judgment 21 December 2010; *Logvinenko v Ukraine*, application no. 13448/07, judgment 14 October 2010; *Vasyukov v Russia*, application no. 2974/05, judgment 5 April 2011; *Vladimir Vasilyev v Russia*, application no. 28370/05, judgment 10 January 2012; *Artyunyan v Russia*, application no. 48977/09, judgment 10 January 2012; *Grzywaczewski v Poland*, application no 18364/06, judgment 31 May 2012.

[150] *Jasinskis v Latvia*, application no. 45744/08, judgment 21 December 2010 (2010) ECHR 2095.

[151] Ibid.

been made in earlier cases, such as *Price v UK*,[152] among others.[153] The novelty in the *Jasinskis* case relates to the fact that, in the context of relevant international law, the ECtHR referred explicitly to the CRPD, which Latvia signed on 18 July 2008 and ratified on 1 March 2010. The Court cited[154] Article 14(2) of the UN Convention, which requires States to provide reasonable accommodations where persons are deprived of their liberty. The ECtHR also quoted from[155] the Interim Report[156] of the then Special Rapporteur (Manfred Nowak) on the question of torture and other cruel, inhuman or degrading treatment or punishment. That report outlines the disadvantaged situation of disabled prisoners, when compared with their non-disabled counterparts.[157] The Court cited, *inter alia*, paragraph 54 of the report, which highlights the fact that the obligation inherent in Article 14(2) of the CRPD implies a duty to ensure equality by making 'appropriate modifications in the procedures and physical facilities of detention centres [...] to ensure that persons with disabilities enjoy the same rights and fundamental freedoms as others [...].'[158] In considering the substantive aspects of the merits of the *Jasinskis* case, the ECtHR did not refer specifically to the UN Convention. However, in outlining the particular duties[159] owed by national authorities to disabled individuals, the Court did refer[160] back to the international standards which it had quoted earlier in its judgment[161] and those included Article 14(2) of the CRPD. Thus, it is implicit in the judgment that the UN Convention, among other legal sources, inspired the Strasbourg Court's reading of some form of reasonable accommodation duty into the substantive rights at issue in this case. The Court in *Jasinskis* recognised the disadvantage suffered by persons with disabilities in detention by noting with regard to the alleged violation of Article 2 ECHR that 'persons in custody are in a vulnerable position and that the authorities are under a duty to protect them.'[162] The ECtHR further ruled that States 'have an obligation to take particular measures to provide effective protection of vulnerable persons from ill-treatment of which the authorities had or ought to have

---

152 In *Price v UK*, it was held that: 'To detain a severely disabled person in conditions where she is dangerously cold, risks developing sores because her bed is too hard or unreachable, and is unable to go to the toilet or keep clean without the greatest of difficulty, constitutes degrading treatment contrary to Article 3 of the Convention.' [*Price v United Kingdom*, application no. 33394/96, judgment 10 July 2001 (2002) 34EHRR53, para. 30].

153 See also *Farbtuhs v. Latvia*, application no. 4672/02, judgment 2 December 2004, para. 56.

154 *Jasinskis v Latvia*, para. 40.

155 Ibid, para. 41.

156 M. Nowak, *Interim Report of the Special Rapporteur on the question of torture and other cruel, inhuman or degrading treatment or punishment*, submitted on 28 July 2008 by the Office of the United Nations High Commissioner for Human Rights to the 63rd session of the General Assembly of the UN (A/63/175), available at www.un.org/disabilities/images/A.63.175.doc. last accessed 15 January 2014.

157 The Court cited paragraph 50 of the Report which provides as follows: 'Persons with disabilities often find themselves in [...] situations [of powerlessness], for instance when they are deprived of their liberty in prisons or other places[...] In a given context, the particular disability of an individual may render him or her more likely to be in a dependant situation and make him or her an easier target of abuse.'

158 Ibid, para. 54.

159 For an outline of those duties, see paragraphs 59, 61, 66 and 67 of the *Jasinskis* judgment.

160 *Jasinskis v Latvia*, para. 59.

161 Ibid, paras. 39 to 41.

162 Ibid, para. 59.

had knowledge.'[163] In light of the fact that the applicant's son was deaf and unable to speak, the Court held that the police had a clear obligation, arising, *inter alia*, from the above-mentioned international standards, to at least provide him with a pen and a piece of paper to enable him to communicate his concerns.[164] In sum, the Court concluded that the Latvian police were in violation of the substantive and procedural aspects of Article 2 ECHR.[165] The ECtHR also held that the investigation into the circumstances of the death of Mr Jasinskis' son had not been effective, in further violation of Article 2.[166] Lisa Waddington notes that the *Jasinskis* case 'reflects two positive trends in the case law of the European Court of Human Rights in cases concerning persons with disabilities.'[167] The first trend which she identifies concerns the 'willingness of the Court to refer to the [CRPD].'[168] The second trend she picks up on:

> Relates to the willingness of the Court to recognise that states may be under certain additional (positive) obligations, which amount to *de facto* reasonable accommodation duties, when it comes to protecting the rights of individuals with disabilities, in recognition of the different, and sometimes particularly vulnerable, situation such individuals are in, in comparison with persons without disabilities.[169]

Waddington contends that, even though the Court did not use the terminology of 'reasonable accommodation' specifically in its considerations on Article 2 ECHR, *Jasinskis* demonstrates that 'the ECHR includes a duty to make a reasonable accommodation for people with disabilities, at least with regard to some rights.'[170] Her reason for arguing as such is based on the fact that the Court quoted 'relevant international legal provisions which do use [the language of accommodations], and then [found] such a *de facto* accommodation obligation to apply in the case in question.'[171]

---

163 Ibid.

164 Ibid, para. 66.

165 The Court ruled that the police had failed to fulfil their duty to safeguard the life of the applicant's son by providing him with adequate medical treatment, taking into account their knowledge about his fall and his sensory disability, their failure to seek a medical opinion about his state of health, coupled with their failure to react to his knocking on the doors and walls of the sobering-up cell and to call an ambulance for almost seven hours after he could not be woken up on the morning of his death. [*Jasinskis v Latvia*, para. 66].

166 Ibid, para. 82. In light of this finding, the Court considered that there was no need to examine Mr Jasinskis' complaint under Article 3 ECHR.

167 L. Waddington, *European Human Rights Cases*, Aflevering 4, april 2011, Jaargang 12, 556–567, at page 564.

168 Ibid.

169 Ibid, at pages 564 and 565.

170 Ibid, at page 567.

171 Ibid.

3.2.2.3. The Vulnerable Groups Approach: An Obligation to Take 'Reasonable Steps'

In the subsequent case of *Z.H. v Hungary*,[172] the ECtHR came even closer than it had done in *Jasinskis* to recognising a duty to reasonably accommodate persons with disabilities under the ECHR – this time in the context of an alleged violation of Article 3 ECHR, taken in conjunction with Article 5(2) ECHR.[173] The applicant in *Z.H.* was a Hungarian national who was deaf and unable to speak, to use sign language or to read or write. He also had an intellectual disability. The applicant complained that, on account of his disabilities, he could not understand the reasons for his arrest on a charge of mugging in breach of Article 5(2) ECHR. The applicant further alleged that his ensuing detention had amounted to inhuman and degrading treatment, in breach of Article 3 ECHR.

In *Z.H.*, the Strasbourg Court once again referred to the CRPD in the context of relevant international law in interpreting the provisions of the ECHR. Importantly, the Court cited[174] the definition of reasonable accommodation in Article 2 of the CRPD. This, in itself, is significant as it is the first time that the Court has cited this definition in its case law relating to the provision of accommodations in police detention. The Court also cited Article 14(2) of the CRPD which, as outlined above, requires the provision of reasonable accommodations to persons with disabilities in detention. In addition, the Court cited Article 13 of the UN Convention, which requires States Parties to provide 'procedural and age-appropriate accommodations'[175] to persons with disabilities in accessing justice. The Court also employed the vulnerable groups approach, stating that any interference with the rights of persons 'belonging to particularly vulnerable groups – such as those with mental disorders – is required to be subject to strict scrutiny, and only very weighty reasons could justify any restriction.'[176] The Court quoted the decision of *Alajos Kiss v. Hungary* in that regard[177] and employed the notion of group vulnerability to read into Article 3 a *de facto* obligation to provide reasonable accommodations in the context of persons with disabilities. This can be seen from the Court's remarks as follows:

> Given that the applicant undoubtedly belongs to a particularly vulnerable group [...] as such he should have benefited from *reasonable steps* on the side of the authorities to prevent situations likely to result in inhuman and degrading treatment.[178] [emphasis added]

The notion of 'reasonable steps' in this instance was linked firmly by the Court to the concept of reasonable accommodations in the CRPD. Indeed, later on in its judgment

---

172 *Z.H. v Hungary*, application no. 28973/11, judgment 8 November 2012.

173 Article 5(2) of the ECHR provides that everyone who is arrested shall be informed promptly, in a language which he understands, of the reasons for his arrest and of any charge against him.

174 *Z.H. v Hungary*, para. 19.

175 UN CRPD, Article 13.

176 Ibid.

177 Ibid.

178 Ibid, para. 31.

the Court stated explicitly that the concept of 'reasonable steps' is 'quite akin to that of "reasonable accommodation" in Articles 2, 13 and 14 of the UNCRPD.'[179] It is interesting to note that the ECtHR scrutinised the arguments advanced on behalf of the State quite strictly. The national authorities had argued that they had taken sufficient measures to satisfy the requirement to reasonably accommodate the applicant's disabilities.[180] The Court ruled, however, that these measures were insufficient to remove the applicant's treatment from the scope of Article 3 ECHR.[181] Importantly, the Court also redistributed the burden of proof in the context of Article 3 and considered that it was incumbent on the Government to prove that the authorities had taken the requisite measures to prevent situations likely to result in inhuman and degrading treatment[182] and to provide a plausible explanation with regard to the manner in which the applicant's injuries were caused, failing which a clear issue would arise under Article 3 of the Convention.[183] Redistribution of the burden of proof in instances such as this is an important means by which to bring structural disadvantages to light. As the third party intervener in the case, MDAC, pointed out, the Court thereby establishes that a person with a disability 'does not have to prove that he or she has suffered; it is enough for the State to fail to prove that they have provided necessary reasonable accommodation for that person to be exposed to inhuman and degrading treatment.'[184]

With respect to the alleged violation of Article 5(2) ECHR, MDAC made a third party intervention submitting that, when interpreting the guarantees enshrined in Article 5(2), the provisions of the CRPD should be taken into account.[185] MDAC argued that the UN Convention requires States to provide reasonable accommodations to persons with disabilities in order to ensure their effective access to justice.[186] MDAC explained that, in the present case, reasonable accommodation would have required the presence of a person who could have communicated effectively with the applicant and assisted him during the interrogation.[187] In the Court's view, 'if the condition of a person with intellectual disability is not given due consideration in this process,' it cannot be said that he was provided with the requisite information enabling him to make effective and intelligent use of the right ensured by Article 5(4) to challenge the lawfulness of detention, unless a lawyer or another authorised person was informed in his stead.[188]

179 Ibid, para. 43.

180 For instance, half-way through his detention, the authorities had moved the applicant to a cell with one of his relatives and other inmates were asked to help him write letters.

181 *Z.H. v Hungary*, para. 31.

182 Ibid.

183 Ibid.

184 Mental Disability Advocacy Center, 'European Court: Hungary Neglected Prisoner with Multiple Disabilities,' 19 November 2012, available at www.mdac.info/en/19/11/2012/european-court-hungary-neglected-prisoner-with-multiple-disabilities, last accessed 2 August 2014.

185 *ZH v Hungary*, Application no. 28973/11, para. 40.

186 Ibid.

187 Ibid.

188 Ibid, para. 41.

In the course of its deliberations on Article 5(2) ECHR, the Court referred specifically to the CRPD. As outlined above, the Court noted that it was regrettable that the authorities 'did not take any truly "reasonable steps"– a notion quite akin to that of "reasonable accommodation" in Articles 2, 13 and 14 of the CRPD – to address the applicant's condition, in particular by procuring for him assistance by a lawyer or another suitable person.'[189] The Court was of the opinion that the police officers interrogating him must have realised that no meaningful communication was possible in the situation and they therefore should have sought assistance in the first place from the applicant's mother (who could have at least informed the officers about the magnitude of the applicant's communication problems) – rather than making the applicant simply sign the minutes of the interrogation. These considerations were sufficient to enable the Court to conclude that there had been a violation of Article 5(2) ECHR. In other words, it was the failure to procure appropriate assistance or to provide suitable accommodation for the applicant which led to a finding of a violation of the substantive right at issue.

Overall, the Court in *Z.H.* demonstrates a growing awareness of the individual provisions of the CRPD related to disability equality and, specifically, of the duty to accommodate under the CRPD. The *Z.H.* case is an important step forward in the Court's perception of reasonable accommodation duties. As demonstrated above, the ECtHR links the alleged violations under Articles 3 and 5(2) ECHR to the duty to accommodate in the CRPD. By that token, the Court draws explicitly on the individual provisions of the UN Convention (related to reasonable accommodations) to inform its interpretation of the specific rights at issue under the ECHR. In spite of these positive trends, the Court confines its allocation of *de facto* reasonable accommodation duties in each case to the substantive right in question, rather than locating the failure to provide reasonable accommodation within the non-discrimination norm in Article 14 ECHR. This demonstrates that the Court still does not perceive the right to equality for persons with disabilities as requiring differential treatment. By refusing to view the disadvantage in these cases as sufficient to merit a finding of disability-based discrimination, the Court declines to view reasonable accommodations as an integral means by which to remedy the factual inequalities experienced by persons with disabilities, as is the case under the CRPD. In the cases outlined above, while the Court is clearly drawing on the CRPD to inform its interpretation of ECHR rights for persons with disabilities, the UN Convention has not had an impact in terms of influencing the Court to move towards recognition of the discriminatory effects of failing to provide reasonable accommodations to persons with disabilities in institutional settings (and consequently in wider social settings). Therefore, the situation essentially remains as it was in its pre-CRPD case law, such as *Price v UK*.

---

189 Ibid, para. 43.

3.2.2.4. An Inconsistent Approach to International Law as an Interpretative Guide to ECHR Rights

In the case of *D.G. v Poland*,[190] the Strasbourg Court shows inconsistency, vis-à-vis the previous case of *Z.H.*, with regard to using the CRPD as a potential guide for the interpretation of ECHR rights by failing completely to mention the UN Convention in the course of its judgment. In the *D.G.* case, the Court found a violation of Article 3 ECHR on account of the fact that the applicant, a paraplegic man who used a wheelchair, had been detained in conditions which were not suitable for persons with physical disabilities and that sufficient efforts had not been made to reasonably accommodate his special needs. The third-party interveners in the case – the Helsinki Foundation for Human Rights, EDF and IDA –submitted that Poland had failed to meet basic international standards for the protection of the rights of persons with disabilities, in particular the standards of accessibility and reasonable accommodation, and that this raised a serious issue under Article 3 of the ECHR.[191] While not actually referring to the CRPD, the Court did use the language of reasonable accommodations in its judgment and appeared to take on board the submissions of the third-party interveners, at least implicitly. The Court conducted a thorough review[192] of the failure of the relevant authorities to provide accessible or adapted facilities. It concluded that detaining the applicant for eighteen months in a prison that was 'unsuitable for the incarceration of persons with physical disabilities'[193] and 'not making sufficient efforts to *reasonably accommodate* his special needs'[194] raised 'a serious issue under the Convention.'[195] In the instant case, the Court still did not locate the duty to accommodate within the non-discrimination provision (locating it instead within the substantive rights of the ECHR). Moreover, it is unfortunate that the Court in *D.G.* failed to mention the CRPD. This casts doubt on the Court's willingness to engage with the spirit and text of the UN Convention in its judgments related to disability equality. It could also be taken as a sign of the Court's uncertainty as to the relevance of CRPD reasonable accommodation duties in the interpretation of ECHR rights. Overall, however, it is submitted that the most important aspect of the case is that the Court did actually use the language of reasonable accommodations.

Following on from its failure to refer to the CRPD in *D.G. v Poland*, in the subsequent case of *Grimailovs v Latvia*[196] the ECtHR again referred back to the UN Convention in the context of relevant international law. The Court cited the definition of reasonable accommodation in Article 2 of the CRPD, together with the obligation to provide reasonable accommodations in detention contained in Article 14(2) of the UN Convention. The applicant in *Grimailovs* had alleged

190 *D.G. v Poland,* application no. 45705/07, judgment 17 September 2014.
191 Ibid, para. 138.
192 See, in particular, paras. 144–158.
193 Ibid, para. 176.
194 Ibid.
195 Ibid [emphasis added].
196 *Grimailovs v Latvia*, application no. 6087/03, judgment 25 September 2013.

that there was a violation of Article 3 ECHR. The Court noted that the crux of the applicant's complaint related to the material conditions of his detention in view of his physical disability and the lack of any organised assistance in that regard.[197] The applicant complained that the prison facilities were unsuitable for him as he used a wheelchair. In support of his allegations, he submitted that there had been no social care or assistance in the prison to help him with his everyday activities and, as a result, he had to rely on the voluntary assistance of his cellmate.[198] While the Court did not refer explicitly to the CRPD during its consideration of the merits of the case, it did refer[199] to the international legal materials which it had quoted at the beginning of its judgment in outlining the State's duty to demonstrate special care in guaranteeing such conditions as correspond to the special needs of the applicant. As outlined above, those materials included the CRPD and specifically the definition of reasonable accommodation contained therein, together with the obligation to provide reasonable accommodations in detention under Article 14(2) of the UN Convention. With regard to the applicant's claim that the authorities' failure to provide appropriate assistance constituted a violation of Article 3 ECHR, the Court held that while the ECHR does not guarantee a right to social assistance *per se*, the applicant's special needs were not sufficiently attended to by the State.[200] It ruled that 'the help offered by the applicant's cellmate did not form part of any *organised assistance* by the State to ensure that the applicant was detained in conditions compatible with respect for his human dignity.'[201] It could not therefore be considered 'suitable or sufficient in view of the applicant's physical disability.'[202] By recognising that a lack of *organised assistance* in respect of the applicant's mobility reached the threshold of severity required to constitute degrading treatment contrary to Article 3 of the Convention,[203] the Court again read a *de facto* reasonable accommodation duty into that same article. However, it is still unclear how the Court actually perceives this duty and what relevance the CRPD's accommodation duty holds for the Court's future interpretation of the non-discrimination norm in Article 14 ECHR.

It is interesting to note that the Court showed itself conscious of the fact that the prison had many barriers hindering the participation of disabled detainees and once again conducted a thorough review of the inaccessibility of the relevant facilities.[204] In its conclusions, the Court found, *inter alia*, that the applicant's inability to have access

197 Ibid, para. 154.
198 Ibid, para. 121.
199 Ibid, para. 151.
200 Ibid, para. 161.
201 Ibid [emphasis added].
202 Ibid.
203 Ibid, para. 162.
204 See, in particular paras. 157–159 of the *Grimailovs v Latvia* judgment. The Court noted that while the applicant had been placed in a special unit for inmates with health problems, the facilities did not appear to have had 'less architectural or technical barriers than the facilities in the ordinary wings of that prison.' The Court observed that a ramp had been installed to facilitate the applicant's access to the outdoor yard. Yet other areas, such as the canteen, toilets, sauna, library, shop, gym, meeting room and telephone room, remained inaccessible for persons who used a wheelchair, a fact which the Government did not deny. The Court found that the inaccessibility of the sanitation facilities raised a particular cause for concern under Article 3 ECHR and that the applicant's special needs were further

to various prison facilities amounted to degrading treatment contrary to Article 3 ECHR. However, as Waddington points out, 'the Court made no direct or implied reference to the aforementioned "reasonable accommodation" obligation as a means of alleviating the applicant's suffering'[205] in the context of this inaccessibility.

3.2.3. Conclusion on De Facto Reasonable Accommodations in Institutional Settings

The Strasbourg Court has, from the beginning of its case law in this area, endeavoured to give special consideration to the particular needs of persons with disabilities in institutional settings. The cases outlined in this section demonstrate that the ECtHR is cognisant of the fact that some form of reasonable accommodations are required by disabled prisoners in order to ensure that their human dignity is preserved, to counteract ill-treatment and also to protect the right to life. In view of this, the Court is interpreting certain provisions of the ECHR (most notably Articles 2, 3 and 5 ECHR) to include a duty to accommodate disabled persons in institutional settings. However, as far back as *Price* (decided before the coming into force of the CRPD), the Court had integrated *de facto* accommodation duties into its case law. The novelty in the Court's case law since the entry into force of the CRPD is the fact that the Court is drawing on the CRPD in some instances to read accommodation duties into the substantive rights of the ECHR and that the Court has actually used the language of reasonable accommodation in its case law. The Strasbourg Court's approach is not consistent however. In some cases, the Court does not reference the CRPD at all or its accommodation duties. In other cases, the ECtHR refers quite extensively to the CRPD and also shows increased awareness of the individual provisions of the CRPD related to reasonable accommodations. This is particularly clear in the *Z.H.* case, in which the Court stated that the duty which emerged from the case law was akin to the duty to provide reasonable accommodations contained in Articles 2, 5 and 14 of the CRPD.

In spite of these positive trends in the ECtHR's case law, the Court appears reluctant to specify the exact duty to accommodate which States bear in the disability context. In addition, the ECtHR's case law to date related to disabled prisoners has focused on the substantive rights at issue (most notably the right to life and the right to be free from torture or cruel, inhuman or degrading treatment or punishment). In the cases outlined in this section, the ECtHR concludes that the national authorities failed to take the requisite measures to ensure that the needs of the disabled prisoners were catered for in terms of accessible or adapted facilities or access to medical care. This, in turn, led the Court in each case to rule that the treatment in question surpasses the minimum level of severity necessary to satisfy the Article 3 threshold for inhuman and degrading treatment. However, the ECtHR has not yet recognised a general duty to accommodate persons with disabilities under Article 14 ECHR. By that token,

---

disregarded as no measures were adopted to alleviate the hardship caused by the inaccessibility of the sanitation facilities while meeting his wife for conjugal visits.

205 L. Waddington, Noot bij: European Court of Human Rights. (25-06-2013), EHRC 2013-, (Europees Hof voor de Rechten van de Mens, 25 juni 2013, nr. 6087/03, Grimailovs tegen Letland), 2286/2305, 2305.

the Court has failed to take into account the substantive disadvantage suffered by disabled people on account of their impairments. In its case law, the Court has noted that Article 3 ECHR requires States:

> To ensure that prisoners are detained in conditions which are compatible with respect for human dignity, [and] that the manner and method of the execution of the measure do not subject them to distress or hardship of an intensity exceeding the unavoidable level of suffering inherent in detention.[206]

A lack of accessibility and reasonable accommodations results in a level of suffering and hardship for disabled prisoners over and above the suffering which is experienced by their non-disabled counterparts in detention and this, in turn, impairs the dignity and integrity of persons with disabilities in institutional settings. Furthermore, it impacts on their right to equality. The ECtHR must begin to view individualised accommodations through the lens of non-discrimination. By not recognising that a failure to reasonably accommodate, in the exercise of ECHR rights, is a form of discrimination (as prescribed by the CRPD) the Court ignores the entrenched disadvantage encountered by disabled individuals in all aspects of their lives. In contrast to the Court's restricted case law in this regard, Janet Lord and Rebecca Brown note that the CRPD 'offers a legal framework which can embrace both the substantive rights involved in these cases, and, crucially, adequately address the underlying discrimination, which has created or exacerbated the violations.'[207] In other words, the UN Convention provides a framework for ensuring substantive equality for disabled detainees and, indeed, for disabled people in wider social settings. It is important that the Strasbourg Court begins to engage with the CRPD on a deeper level, in order to ensure Article 14 protection for persons with disabilities on an equal basis with others.

Following on from the observations contained in this section, the next section of this chapter will consider the potential future influence which the UN Convention might have on the Court's case law related to disability equality.

4. Case Study Part I: The Potential Influence of the CRPD on the Interpretation of the Right to Equality for Persons with Disabilities under the ECHR

This section of the chapter will consider the potential influence which the CRPD might have on the interpretation of the right to equality for persons with disabilities under the ECHR. At present, the approach of the Court remains rooted in the

206 See, for instance, *Grimailovs v Latvia*, para. 150.

207 J.E. Lord and R. Brown, 'The Role of Reasonable Accommodation in Securing Substantive Equality for Persons with Disabilities: The UN Convention on the Rights of Persons with Disabilities' in M.H. Rioux, L.A. Basser and M. Jones (eds.) Critical Perspectives on Human Rights and Disability Law (Martinus Nijhoff 2011), at page 292.

specific difference model of equality, to the extent that positive measures such as reasonable accommodation duties do not yet form an integral part of the Court's analysis of the potential applicability of the right to equality for persons with disabilities under the ECHR. It is hoped that, under the influence of the CRPD, the Court will move in the direction of the substantive disadvantage model of equality, whereby reasonable accommodation measures are perceived as a vital means by which to correct for the many inequalities faced by persons with disabilities. A move towards substantive disadvantage equality would mean that it would no longer be the differential treatment *per se* that would trigger non-discrimination analysis but the social disadvantage faced by disabled people. This would enable the Court to target more effectively long-standing discrimination issues and deep-seated barriers to participation through such measures as reasonable accommodation duties. Of course, the Strasbourg Court will not embrace the substantive disadvantage model of equality overnight. It is expected that any move in that direction will be the result of a protracted process.

As outlined at the outset of this chapter, the CRPD reflects an emerging consensus, which the Strasbourg Court may take into account in interpreting the provisions of the ECHR. However, it is not bound by the CRPD and the provisions of the UN Convention may be of interpretative value only. Nonetheless, it is important to outline the areas in which there may be further scope for the CRPD to influence the case law of the ECtHR related to disability equality. The subsections which follow will highlight those potential areas.

4.1. The Explicit Recognition of a Duty to Accommodate under the ECHR's Non-Discrimination Provision?

While sounding a note of caution against too much optimism, arguably the strongest potential avenue for the CRPD to exert its influence on the Strasbourg Court's jurisprudence lies in the area of reasonable accommodation duties. Reasonable accommodations are pivotal to removing disadvantage and increasing the participation of persons with disabilities in all areas of society. At present, the Court does not recognise a substantive right to be accommodated under the ECHR as part of the non-discrimination obligation in Article 14. We have seen that disability-related accommodation duties have been recognised by the Court in a series of cases relating to Article 2 and, in particular, Article 3 ECHR. Stepping outside of the institutional context, the ECtHR has also recognised *de facto* reasonable accommodation duties in other spheres. In the case of *Kutzner v Germany*,[208] for example, the Court found a violation of Article 8 ECHR (on the right to respect for private and family life) in circumstances where the national authorities had removed the children of a married couple and ordered their placement in a foster home, on the grounds that the parents did not have the requisite intellectual capacity to raise their children. The Court stated as follows:

208 *Kutzner v Germany*, Application No. 46544/99, Judgment of 26 February 2002 (2002) 35 EHRR 25.

> It is questionable whether the domestic administrative and judicial authorities have given sufficient consideration to additional measures of support as an alternative to what is by far the most extreme measure, namely separating the children from their parents.[209]

It seems that disability is still perceived by the Strasbourg Court as a specific difference, which may require accommodation in certain circumstances. The Court does not yet view reasonable accommodations as constituting an integral means by which to remedy the factual inequalities faced by disabled people in society. There are, however, recent indications that the ECtHR is moving towards a more holistic view of the importance of reasonable accommodation duties in ensuring substantive equality. The *Glor* case, outlined above, appears to provide some hope for the development of a reasonable accommodation duty within Article 14 ECHR. In language reminiscent of reasonable accommodation duties, the Court in *Glor* remarked that the Swiss authorities could have come up with alternatives to the imposition of a penalty tax on the applicant (a man who had diabetes), such as adapting the military service to his needs or requiring him to carry out civil service duties instead.[210] This is clear evidence of a deeper understanding of the equality norm for persons with disabilities. On foot of the *Glor* case, Lisa Waddington and Gerard Quinn have claimed that 'the Court has moved towards substantive jurisprudence on "reasonable accommodation" under the European Convention.'[211] Indeed, the Court's acknowledgment in *Glor* of the CRPD as an example of a European and worldwide consensus on the need to protect people with disabilities from discriminatory treatment signals the potential for the UN Convention to exert further influence on the Strasbourg Court's Article 14 case law. MDAC Executive Director Oliver Lewis recognises this potential. He asserts that the *Glor* case has 'paved the way for litigation which encourages a synthesis of European human rights jurisprudence with the principles and provisions of the [CRPD].'[212] In addition, he remarks that the *Glor* judgment represents 'the European Court's attempt to limit State discretion to establish different legal frameworks for persons with disabilities where this does not promote their full inclusion.'[213] It is unclear at present whether the Strasbourg Court will build on the approach taken in *Glor* in future judgments involving Article 14 ECHR, particularly in light of its failure to even mention potential reasonable accommodation duties in the *Alajos Kiss* case. Only time will tell the effect that the CRPD will have in encouraging the Court to interpret the non-discrimination provision in such a manner as to include an obligation to reasonably accommodate disabled people. In particular, the ECtHR may be reluctant to impose positive duties on States due to the nature of the rights contained in the ECHR, being civil and political rights, which are not associated traditionally with a redistribution of resources. On the other hand, the scope of the duty to accommodate is well-

[209] Ibid, para. 75.

[210] See *Glor v. Switzerland*, application no. 13444/04, judgment 30 April 2009, para. 95.

[211] L. Waddington and G. Quinn (eds.), *European Yearbook of Disability Law* (Intersentia, Antwerp, 2010) 256.

[212] O. Lewis, MDAC, 'Three Disability Firsts in a European Court of Human Rights Case,' 2 June 2009, available at http://www.mdac.info/ru/node/187 last accessed 10 January 2014.

[213] Ibid.

defined when compared with the potential financial implications of wholesale positive obligations, as it is subject to the proviso that the accommodation must not impose a disproportionate or undue burden on the accommodating party. This, in itself, could provide an incentive for incorporating reasonable accommodation duties into the Court's interpretation of Article 14 ECHR. Moreover, the comparative interpretative approach followed by the Court means that it should interpret the provisions of the ECHR in light of already existing common European standards. Lisa Waddington points to the fact that '[...] the obligations imposed on States Parties by the CRPD arguably create potential positive obligations for States within the context of the ECHR.'[214] In view of the fact that States are obliged under the CRPD to include a failure to accommodate as a form of discrimination in their laws, combined with the fact that the majority of Member States of the Council of Europe are also party to the UN Convention, it is enviseagable that the ECtHR might eventually take this into account in its interpretation of ECHR rights. On the other hand, one might also question whether this constitutes 'sufficient common ground' in the eyes of the Court. Nonetheless, it is submitted that the CRPD has some role to play in encouraging the ECtHR to interpret Article 14 in a disability-sensitive manner, one which allows persons with disabilities to enjoy and exercise ECHR rights on an equal basis with others. Finally it is important to note that there is increased scope across the substantive provisions of the ECHR for development of reasonable accommodation duties. Anna Lawson observes that Article 14 ECHR 'undoubtedly provides the most obvious site for the development of a concept of reasonable accommodation under the ECHR.'[215] However, she cautions against confining any consideration of reasonable accommodation duties to Article 14 and contends that 'it is entirely possible to interpret substantive ECHR rights in such a way to incorporate some notion of reasonable accommodation.'[216]

4.2. The Vulnerable Groups Approach as a Facilitator of Substantive Equality in the Context of Disability Rights?

On the whole, the application of the concept of group vulnerability to the rights of persons with disabilities is a positive development in the ECtHR's case law. Of course, the term itself is not the most appropriate one and there are several risks inherent in the use of the notion of 'vulnerability.'[217] One risk is that the concept of group vulnerability may further stigmatise and prejudice already disadvantaged

[214] L. Waddington, 'Unravelling the Knot: Article 8, Private Life, Positive Duties and Disability. Rewriting: *Sentges* v. *the Netherlands*' in E. Brems (ed.) *Diversity and European Human Rights: Rewriting Judgments of the ECHR* (Cambridge University Press, Cambridge, 2013) 349.

[215] A. Lawson, 'The UN Convention on the Rights of Persons with Disabilities and European Disability Law: A Catalyst for Cohesion? in Arnardóttir O M and Quinn G (eds.), *The UN Convention on the Rights of Persons with Disabilities: European and Scandinavian Perspectives* (Martinus Nijhoff Publishers 2009), at page 95.

[216] Ibid.

[217] For a thorough analysis of the drawbacks to the group vulnerability approach, see L. Peroni & A. Timmer, 'Vulnerable Groups: the Promise of an Emergent Concept in European Human Rights Convention Law,' (2013) 11 *International Journal of Constitutional Law* 1074.

individuals. In particular, the notion of vulnerability can have negative connotations in the disability context. Nonetheless, the group vulnerability approach, and the consequent acknowledgment that invidious differentiations on the basis of disability must be subject to strict scrutiny, has the potential to enhance the substantive equality of persons with disabilities. Jarleth Clifford recognises that, by applying a standard of strict scrutiny, the Court has indicated that 'a very high threshold must be met' in order to justify the curtailment of the rights of persons with disabilities.[218] It has been demonstrated above[219] that a heightened standard of scrutiny in the Court's case law appears to be linked to the CRPD in some respects and, furthermore, that this development has already heralded positive trends.

Lourdes Peroni and Alexandra Timmer refer to Sandra Fredman's multi-dimensional classification of substantive equality[220] in arguing that the Strasbourg Court's application of group vulnerability has addressed the four chief aims of substantive equality as set out by Fredman.[221] It is arguable that some of the aims contained in Fredman's classification overlap with what I have described (in chapter two of this book) as a transformative approach to equality rather than a substantive approach *per se*.[222] However, in order to avoid any confusion, I will also refer to Fredman's classification under a substantive equality approach. The four aims of substantive equality, as outlined by Fredman and summarised by Peroni and Timmer, are as follows:

i. Equality as participation: Participation, according to Fredman, is a 'multi-layered concept,'[223] which entails not only political participation but also 'taking part in decisions in a wide range of situations affecting individuals or groups, including at the workplace or in education, in healthcare and in community organization.'[224]
ii. Equality as transformation: The transformative dimension of substantive equality, according to Fredman's classification, refers to accommodations and seeks to 'remove the detriment which is attached to difference' rather than the difference itself.[225]

---

218 J. Clifford, 'The UN Disability Convention and its Impact on European Equality Law,' *The Equal Rights Review* (Volume 6 2011), at page 20.

219 See section 3.1 of this chapter generally.

220 See S. Fredman, Discrimination Law (Oxford University Press, Oxford, 2nd Edition 2011), at pages 25–33.

221 L. Peroni and A. Timmer, 'Vulnerable Groups: the Promise of an Emergent Concept in European Human Rights Convention Law,' 11 *International Journal of Constitutional Law* (2013) 1054.

222 See the distinction between substantive and transformative approaches to equality in chapter 2 of this book.

223 L. Peroni and A. Timmer, 'Vulnerable Groups: the Promise of an Emergent Concept in European Human Rights Convention Law,' 11 *International Journal of Constitutional Law* (2013), 1054, at page 1075, citing S. Fredman, *Human Rights Transformed: Positive Rights and Positive Duties* (Oxford University Press 2008) 180.

224 Ibid, at page 1075, citing S. Fredman, *Discrimination Law* (Oxford University Press, 2nd edition, 2011) at page 30.

225 Ibid.

iii. Equality as redistribution: The redistributive aspect of equality aims at 'breaking the cycle of disadvantage'[226] and this encompasses, among other things, the 'maldistribution of resources.'[227]
iv. Equality as recognition: Under Fredman's substantive equality framework, recognition involves promoting 'respect for dignity and worth, thereby redressing stigma, stereotyping, humiliation and violence because of membership of an identity group.'[228]

Peroni and Timmer demonstrate the fact that the group vulnerability approach tackles the foregoing dimensions of substantive equality by looking at case law in which the Court addresses each of the four aims of substantive equality in turn. For instance, in several Roma cases, such as *Chapman v United Kingdom*[229] and its sister cases,[230] the authors argue[231] that the Court has furthered the participative element of substantive equality by requiring States to facilitate the Gypsy way of life. Those cases, they contend,[232] also demonstrate a step towards ensuring fulfilment of the transformative aspect of substantive equality by recognising the importance of accommodating differences.[233] Peroni and Timmer also assert[234] that, in cases such as *Yordonava v Bulgaria*[235] and *M.S.S v Belgium and Greece*,[236] the Court endeavours to tackle the redistributive aspect of substantive equality by addressing issues of social disadvantage and material deprivation in the contexts of Articles 8 and 3 ECHR. They argue that this is clear from the socio-economic nature of the positive duty imposed on the State in those judgments.[237] Finally, in cases outlined in the previous section of this chapter, such as *Alajos Kiss v Hungary* and *Kiyutin v Russia,* the ECtHR aims to tackle the misrecognition dimension of substantive equality by redressing stigma and stereotyping of persons with psychosocial disabilities and those with HIV, respectively.

---

226 Ibid, at page 1075, citing S. Fredman, *Discrimination Law* (Oxford University Press, Oxford, 2nd Edition, 2011) at page 26.

227 Ibid.

228 Ibid.

229 *Chapman v. United Kingdom* (GC), application 27238/95, 18 January 2001 (2001) EHRR18, 96.

230 Four similar cases were decided on the same day as *Chapman*: *Beard v. the United Kingdom*, application no. 24882/94, *Coster v. the United Kingdom,* application no. 24876/94, *Jane Smith v. the United Kingdom*, application no. 25154/94 and *Lee v. the United Kingdom*, application no. 25289/94 (all judgments of 18 January 2001).

231 L. Peroni and A. Timmer, 'Vulnerable Groups: the Promise of an Emergent Concept in European Human Rights Convention Law,' 11 *International Journal of Constitutional Law* (2013) 1054, at page 1076.

232 Ibid, at page 1077.

233 Although, as the authors point out, the cases ultimately fall short of requiring the State to accommodate differences.

234 L. Peroni and A. Timmer, 'Vulnerable Groups: the Promise of an Emergent Concept in European Human Rights Convention Law,' 11 *International Journal of Constitutional Law*(2013) 1054, 1067.

235 *Yordanova v. Bulgaria*, application no. 25446/06, judgment 24 April 2012.

236 *M.S.S. v. Belgium and Greece*, application.no. 30696/09, judgment 21 January 2011, 53 EHHR 2.

237 L. Peroni and A. Timmer, 'Vulnerable Groups: the Promise of an Emergent Concept in European Human Rights Convention Law,' 11 *International Journal of Constitutional Law* (2013) 1054, 1077.

The Strasbourg Court has already based its conceptualisation of vulnerability in the disability context on the considerable discrimination suffered by persons with disabilities in the past and on the socially constructed stereotypes which exist regarding disabled people up to the present day. While this is encouraging, true equality in the disability context would need to go far beyond addressing discrimination in the form of prejudices and stereotypes to address the four crucial elements which Fredman has enunciated (outlined above). The group vulnerability approach has the potential to increase the Court's perception of substantive equality for persons with disabilities under the guiding influence of the progressive equality and non-discrimination norms contained in the CRPD. Through its application of the concept of vulnerability to the rights of persons with disabilities the ECtHR has already shown some signs of a contextual and asymmetrical approach to equality (as shown above).[238] An asymmetrical approach to equality considers the relevance of the actual group which suffers disadvantage on account of a particular measure. Peroni and Timmer observe that the notion of asymmetry is 'essential to substantive equality' and it 'implies that not all differentiations are problematic but only those that affect groups suffering disadvantage, prejudice and stereotyping.'[239] In other words, as Kristin Henrard points out:

> In so far as a particular measure disadvantages an already disadvantaged group, this would trigger heightened scrutiny. Conversely, if the measure concerned would disadvantage a privileged group, this would not necessarily trigger heightened scrutiny.[240]

The CPRD adopts both a contextual and asymmetrical approach to equality and is likely to encourage the ECtHR (at least to some extent) to examine the substantive disadvantage faced by persons with disabilities in society. Among other things, it is likely that the concept of group vulnerability and the model of equality contained in the UN Convention will lead the Court to examine more disability cases under Article 14 ECHR and to narrow the margin of appreciation even further. Indeed, it can be seen from the case law outlined in this chapter that the heightened standard of scrutiny adopted by the Court has already resulted in increased findings of discrimination on the basis of disability. Furthermore, cases such as *Horváth and Kiss v. Hungary*[241] have illustrated the role that the group vulnerability approach plays in increasing the positive obligations of States in the context of marginalised groups generally. Interestingly, in *Horváth and Kiss*, the Court referred to the vulnerability and marginalisation of persons with psychosocial disabilities[242] (alongside its consideration of Roma rights in that case). Peroni and Timmer highlight the fact

---

238 See generally section 3.1 of this chapter.

239 L. Peroni and A. Timmer, 'Vulnerable Groups: the Promise of an Emergent Concept in European Human Rights Convention Law,' 11 *International Journal of Constitutional Law* (2013) 1054, 1075.

240 K. Henrard, 'Asymmetrical Approach towards Non-Discrimination and Special Minority Rights (Max-Planck-Institut für ausländisches öffentliches Recht und Völkerrecht 2011), at page 389, available at www.zaoerv.de/71_2011/71_2011_2_a_379_418.pdf last accessed 14 October 2014.

241 *Horváth and Kiss v. Hungary*, Application no. 11146/11, judgment 29 January 2013, not yet reported.

242 Ibid, para. 128.

that the vulnerability approach acts as a 'magnifying glass,'[243] to the extent that the alleged violation of rights 'looks bigger through the vulnerability lens.'[244] It is submitted that this logic can be seen in the *Z.H.* case, outlined above. The Strasbourg Court in *Z.H.* ruled that the applicant should have benefited from reasonable steps on the side of the authorities to prevent situations likely to result in inhuman and degrading treatment by virtue of the very fact that he belonged to a particularly vulnerable group. By that token, the Court clearly weighed the applicant's disability and his special needs heavily in its analysis of the substantive rights at issue. Each of these examples demonstrates the potential of the vulnerability approach to lead to an increased enjoyment by persons with disabilities of ECHR rights on an equal basis with others. However, the effectiveness of the vulnerability approach is subject to the proviso that the Court, in its analysis of the rights contained in the ECHR, sees fit to take into account the substantive disadvantage which persons which disabilities face in society (in line with the CRPD).

4.3. Social-Contextual Analysis and the Social Model of Disability as a Potential Pre-Cursor to a Mainstreaming Approach in the Interpretation of the ECHR?

The final way in which the CRPD may influence the interpretation of the ECHR is through a greater incorporation by the Court of the social model of disability into its judgments. There is an increasing tendancy in the case law of the Strasbourg Court to place emphasis on the social construction of identity markers,[245] especially in the areas of discrimination on the grounds of sex and race. The Court is clearly showing increased emphasis on social-contextual analysis in its case law related both to disability rights and non-disability cases. In the case of *Horváth and Kiss*, the Court's focus on social context is clear. In that case, the Court clearly paid attention to the vulnerable situation of, and considerable discrimination experienced by, Roma children in its analysis of Article 14. Furthermore, in the case of *Konstantin Markin*, the Court highlighted the impacts of gender stereotyping. In the cases of

243 L. Peroni & A. Timmer, 'Vulnerable Groups: the Promise of an Emergent Concept in European Human Rights Convention Law,' 11 *International Journal of Constitutional Law* (2013) 1054, at page 1079.

244 Ibid.

245 See the comments of Oddný Mjöll Arnardóttir in 'Non-discrimination in International and European Law: Towards Substantive Models' (2007) 2 *Nordic Journal of Human Rights*, available at www.idunn.no/ntmr/2007/02/nondiscrimination_in_international_and_european_lawtowards_substantive_mod last accessed 12 December 2014. Arnardóttir states as follows: 'In recent years, the Court seems to be becoming increasingly aware of the social context of cases as evidenced in *Stec and Others v. The United Kingdom*. Related to this trend in the case law is a fairly fluid approach to the construction of the discrimination grounds themselves, complementing the focus on natural or immutable differences with awareness of the social construction of group identity.' Arnardóttir gives the example of the grounds of sex and gender, stating that 'it seems that the biologically construed category of sex in the approach of the Court should by now be replaced by the socially construed category of gender; *cf.* the *Christine Goodwin v. the United Kingdom* judgment of 2002 which clearly replaced sex with gender under Article 12 ECHR.' See also the comments of O.M. Arnardóttir, 'A Future of Multidimensional Disadvantage Equality,' in O.M. Arnardóttir and G. Quinn (eds.) *The UN Convention on the Rights of Persons with Disabilities: European and Scandinavian Perspectives* (Martinus Nijhoff, Leiden, 2009), at pages 57/58.

Alajos Kiss and *Kiyutin*, the Court drew attention to the fact that socially constructed stereotypes are a significant factor inhibiting the participation in society of persons with psychosocial disabilities and persons living with HIV. A social-contextual analysis of HIV also infiltrated the Court's legal reasoning in *I.B. v Greece*. The Court has used this social-contextual model of disadvantage, together with the concept of group vulnerability, to highlight the considerable discriminatory barriers faced by persons with disabilities and to justify strict scrutiny in the context of curtailments of the rights of disabled people. It is arguable that if the ECtHR takes more cognisance of the concrete provisions of the CRPD, then the social model of disability which underlies it has the potential to influence the Court to adopt a mainstreaming approach to disability. In turn, this might impact on the interpretation of the equality norm. In the context of judicial decision-making, Waddington argues that mainstreaming involves recognition of the fact that 'the application of seemingly neutral rules, which do not single out a particular group for disadvantage, such as people with disabilities, can in fact lead to unequal results and reinforce pre-existing disadvantage.'[246] Mainstreaming disability in the context of ECHR rights would involve the recognition that positive measures (including reasonable accommodations) are essential to removing the specific disadvantage experienced by disabled people in participating in society. It is worth noting that the Council of Europe's own Action Plan on Disability[247] (which will be outlined in detail in the next section of this chapter) emphasises the importance of mainstreaming disability within its human rights framework. Adopting a mainstreaming approach to ECHR rights, and in particular Article 14, would enable the Court to address participation issues for persons with disabilities and to uncover the manner in which judicial decision-making, and society in general, function to maintain disadvantage. Whether the Court will choose to move in that direction is debatable. Nonetheless, the potential remains.

To conclude this part of the case study, it is hoped that the ECtHR will take the evolutive interpretative approach to its fullest and that it will draw on the substantive provisions of the CRPD to a greater extent in the future. Of course, one must be cognisant of the limitations of judicial decision-making in the Council of Europe. Nonetheless, the ECHR does affirm the principle of equal rights for all persons. Thus, the Court is encouraged to take into account the substance and spirit of CRPD rights in its interpretation of the ECHR in order to ensure that human rights protection within the Council of Europe is effective for persons with disabilities on an equal basis with others. Of course, the case law of the ECtHR is not the only means by which CRPD provisions can infiltrate the mechanisms of the Council of Europe. There are many other avenues through which the CRPD can potentially exert some influence. With that in mind, the next section of this chapter will reflect

[246] L. Waddington, 'Unravelling the Knot: Article 8, Private Life, Positive Duties and Disability. Rewriting: *Sentges* v. *the Netherlands*' in E. Brems (ed.) *Diversity and European Human Rights: Rewriting Judgments of the ECHR* (Cambridge University Press, Cambridge, 2013), at page 347.

[247] The Council of Europe Action Plan to Promote the Rights and Full Participation of People with Disabilities in Europe: Improving the Quality of Life of People with Disabilities in Europe 2006–2015.

on the CRPD's influence to date, and its potential influence, on wider (quasi-)legal and policy mechanisms in the Council of Europe.

5. Case Study Part II: The CRPD, General Disability Policy of the Council of Europe and the Revised European Social Charter

The subsections below will focus on the influence that the CRPD is having on wider Council of Europe (quasi-)legal and policy mechanisms going beyond the ECHR. In a similar manner to the case study on the ECHR, the focus of this part of the case study will be on issues of disability equality and on broader issues of participation and inclusion for persons with disabilities in society. The first set of documents that will be examined relate to Council of Europe policy instruments in the field of disability. The primary research question to be addressed in that regard is whether the CRPD is having an influence on the direction taken on disability policy within the Council of Europe? The second area that will be examined below consists of the decisions of the ECSR under the revised Charter. A pivotal research question to be answered in that respect is whether the CRPD has already influenced, or can potentially influence, the ECSR to move towards more substantive equality analysis on foot of its entry into force?

5.1. The CRPD and Council of Europe Policy Instruments on Disability

The subsections which follow will outline the key developments in disability policy within the Council of Europe in the period directly before and after the entry into force of the CRPD.

5.1.1. Pre-CRPD: The Council of Europe Disability Action Plan

In order to reflect on the influence which the CRPD is having, or might have, on the general disability policy of the Council of Europe, it is necessary to take a step back in time to the period preceding the CRPD's adoption. The Council of Europe mechanisms first started to focus on disability issues in 1992 when *Recommendation No. R(92)(6) on a Coherent Policy for Persons with Disabilities*[248] was adopted by the Council of Europe's Committee of Ministers – the decision-making body of the Council of Europe and the guardian of its fundamental values. That pioneering recommendation proved influential and it had an impact on disability policy within the Council of Europe for more than ten years. However, disability policy changed immensely on a global scale in the period following that recommendation. There was therefore a need for the Council of Europe organs to revise their policies in

[248] Committee of Ministers, Recommendation No.R(92)6 to Member States on a Coherent Policy for People with Disabilities, adopted by the Committee of Ministers on 9 April 1992 at the 474th meeting of the Ministers' Deputies.

line with international changes. In April 2006, eight months before the UN General Assembly adopted the CRPD, the Council of Europe adopted its Disability Action Plan[249] on foot of a recommendation made in May 2003 at the second European Conference of Ministers responsible for Integration Policies for People with Disabilities, held in Malaga, Spain. Following from the recommendations made at that conference, the Committee of Ministers adopted the Council's Disability Action Plan[250] and launched it officially at a high-level National Conference on Disability entitled 'Social Protection of Persons with Disabilities: National and International Dimensions.' The Action Plan sought to replace the piecemeal approach to disability issues which had been the order of the day in the Council of Europe up until that point. Its adoption demonstrated the extent to which disability policy and discourse had changed in the period preceding the CRPD's adoption.

The CRPD entered into force two years after the adoption of the Council of Europe's Disability Action Plan. Notwithstanding the fact that the two instruments differ in their legal nature and geographical scope, many of the basic premises and key focus areas of the Action Plan are in line with the CRPD's foundational principles and substantive rights. The Action Plan has been described as a 'genuine toolkit to improve, throughout Europe, the participation of people with disabilities in active citizenship.'[251] It recommends specific actions in 15 key action lines,[252] covering nearly all areas of life of people with disabilities and corresponding largely with the substantive rights and obligations contained in the CRPD. The Action Plan states specifically that 'due account'[253] has been taken in its drafting of 'relevant existing European and international instruments, treaties and plans, particularly the developments in relation to the draft [CRPD].'[254] The fundamental principles on which the Plan is based mirror those contained in the CRPD.[255] Furthermore, the Disability Action Plan is based on several premises, which are also in line with

---

[249] Council of Europe Action Plan to promote the rights and full participation of people with disabilities in society: improving the quality of life of people with disabilities in Europe 2006–2015.

[250] The Council of Europe's Disability Action Plan was adopted pursuant to Recommendation (2006)5 of the Committee of Ministers to member states on the Council of Europe Disability Action Plan to promote the rights and full participation of people with disabilities in society: improving the quality of life of people with disabilities in Europe 2006–2015 (adopted by the Committee of Ministers on 5 April 2006 at the 961st meeting of the Ministers' Deputies).

[251] Council of Europe, Disability, A Citizenship Issue (2013), at page 7, available at www.coe.int/t/dg4/majorhazards/activites/2013/didrr/DisabilityACitizenshipIssue_EN.pdf, last accessed 4 October 2014.

[252] The Action lines are as follows: Action line No. 1: Participation in political and public life; Action line No. 2: Participation in cultural life; Action line No. 3: Information and communication; Action line No. 4: Education; Action line No. 5: Employment, vocational guidance and training; Action line No. 6: The built environment; Action line No. 7: Transport; Action line No. 8: Community living; Action line No. 9: Health care; Action line No. 10: Rehabilitation; Action line No. 11: Social protection; Action line No. 12: Legal protection; Action line No. 13: Protection against violence and abuse; Action line No. 14: Research and development; and Action line No. 15: Awareness-raising.

[253] Council of Europe Action Plan to promote the rights and full participation of people with disabilities in society: improving the quality of life of people with disabilities in Europe 2006–2015, at page 4.

[254] Ibid.

[255] They include the principles of non-discrimination, equality of opportunities, full participation in society of all persons with disabilities, respect for difference and acceptance of disability as part of human diversity, dignity and individual autonomy and the freedom to make one's own choices. [Ibid, at page 11].

the CRPD. The first premises underlying the Action Plan reflects the move from the deficit to the capabilities approach to disability. In other words, it incorporates a paradigm shift which reflects 'ability, referring to each individual's talents and aptitudes.'[256] Like the CRPD, another guiding value of the Action Plan is the human rights model of disability.[257] The Action Plan also reflects the shift from the concept of disability as being a medical one to a social model approach.[258] In a similar vein to the CRPD, the Action Plan acknowledges the cross-cutting aspects of disability discrimination in its recognition that there are people with disabilities who face specific barriers or multiple discrimination, for example, women, children, elderly persons, and migrants with disabilities or persons with disabilities in need of a high level of support. It is clear that the CRPD and the Disability Action Plan are intended to complement one another. The Action Plan has been described 'as a regional framework for the implementation of the commitments accepted under the UN Convention.'[259] It is intended to serve as a point of reference for all future policies and actions carried out within the field of disability and it should be used as a practical policy tool by States Parties to the CRPD in their efforts to implement the UN Convention in Europe.

While the Disability Action Plan preceded the coming into force of the CRPD, the Committee of Ministers of the Council of Europe has adopted many non-binding recommendations and issue papers on disability matters since the CRPD entered into force. An overview of some of those instruments will be provided below, in order to determine whether the CRPD is having a concrete influence on the general direction of disability policy within the Council of Europe.

5.1.2. Post-CRPD: Committee of Ministers' Recommendations[260] on Disability

The Committee of Ministers of the Council of Europe has the power to make recommendations to Member States on specific areas of concern. These recommendations are not legally binding. However, they do carry political weight. The Committee has made many disability-specific recommendations over the

256 Council of Europe, Disability, A Citizenship Issue, at page 7, available at www.coe.int/t/dg4/majorhazards/activites/2013/didrr/DisabilityACitizenshipIssue_EN.pdf, last accessed 4 October 2014.

257 The Action plan supports 'the legitimate assertion that people with disabilities are citizens like any other and that the authorities must facilitate, at all levels, their access to political and public life, education, training, employment, health care, social welfare, justice, information, culture and leisure.' [Ibid].

258 The Action Plan recognises that 'we have moved from seeing the disabled person as a patient in need of care who does not contribute to society to seeing him/her as a person who needs the present barriers removed in order to take a rightful place as a fully participative member of society.' [Council of Europe Action Plan to promote the rights and full participation of people with disabilities in society: improving the quality of life of people with disabilities in Europe 2006–2015, at page 8].

259 Welcome Address given by Ms Maud de Boer-Buquicchio, Deputy Secretary General of the Council of Europe, Swedish Conference on the UN Disability Convention and the Council of Europe Disability Action Plan, Strasbourg 29–30 October 2008, Conference Proceedings: Protecting and promoting the rights of persons with disabilities in Europe: towards full participation, inclusion and empowerment.

260 In this section, I will consider only the Recommendations on disability that have been adopted by the Committee of Ministers as there are no relevant resolutions of the Committee since the coming into force of the CRPD.

years.[261] More recent recommendations of the Committee reflect the distinct move from rehabilitation policy towards more inclusive disability policy, targeted at ensuring full and effective participation of persons with disabilities in society. Since the CRPD entered into force in 2008, the Convention's influence can be seen quite clearly on the substantive content of some of the Committee's recommendations.

The first recommendation that was adopted by the Committee of Ministers after the passage of the CRPD was *Recommendation CM/Rec(2009)6 on Ageing and Disability in the 21st century: Sustainable Frameworks to enable Greater Quality of Life in an Inclusive Society.*[262] The fundamental principles on which that recommendation is based are stated explicitly to be drawn from both the Council of Europe Disability Action Plan and the CRPD. Those principles are as follows: Equality of opportunity for all citizens, non-discrimination, respect for and acceptance of disability as part of human diversity, the rights of people with disabilities to be involved fully in all decision-making processes that affect them and the concept of universal design, (i.e. the notion that environments, products, services are designed to be accessible and usable by all). In line with Article 4(3) of the CRPD, the recommendation reiterates the need to involve ageing people with disabilities and older people with disabilities[263] in decisions affecting their lives. It notes that such individuals should be involved fully and directly throughout the process of designing, implementing and evaluating services.[264] The recommendation also reflects the principles of both Article 19 of the CRPD (the right to live independently and be included in the community) and Article 12 of the CRPD (the right to equal recognition before the law/legal capacity), in its assertion that 'living arrangements (at home, in supported accommodation or in residential placement) should take account of the individuals' wishes and needs.'[265]

The next recommendation adopted by the Committee of Ministers was *Recommendation CM/Rec(2010)2 on Deinstitutionalisation and Community Living*

[261] See, for instance, Recommendation on the Situation of the Mentally Ill (EC Recommendation No. 818) (1977); Recommendation on Rehabilitation Policies for the Disabled (EC Recommendation No. 1185) (1985); Recommendation on a Coherent Policy for the Rehabilitation of People with Disabilities (EC Recommendation No. (92) 6); Recommendation Towards full social inclusion of people with disabilities Recommendation 1592 (2003) Recommendation Towards concerted efforts for treating and curing spinal cord injury - Parliamentary Assembly 1560 (2002).

[262] Recommendation CM/Rec(2009)6 of the Committee of Ministers to member states on ageing and disability in the 21st century: sustainable frameworks to enable greater quality of life in an inclusive society (Adopted by the Committee of Ministers on 8 July 2009 at the 1063rd meeting of the Ministers' Deputies).

[263] According to the recommendation, the expressions 'ageing people with disabilities' and 'older people with disabilities' refer to two distinct but related groups of people. The first group refers to people who grow old having experienced a disability for much of their lives, sometimes from birth. For the second group, disability is first experienced at a relatively advanced age.

[264] Recommendation CM/Rec(2009)6 of the Committee of Ministers to member states on ageing and disability in the 21st century: sustainable frameworks to enable greater quality of life in an inclusive society, para. 2.2.

[265] Ibid, para. 1.4.

of Children with Disabilities.[266] That recommendation refers to the CRPD as stressing the right of children with disabilities to be treated on an equal basis with other children, including the right to express themselves on matters of concern to them and the essential need for fully accessible services. The recommendation also refers to the CRPD when it urges States to conduct public awareness campaigns that nurture receptiveness to the inclusion of disabled children and to collective responsibility for upholding their right to a life within the community. All of these themes can be seen quite clearly throughout the CRPD. Furthermore, the recommendation highlights the fact that it draws 'on basic principles enshrined in international legal instruments'[267] (without actually mentioning the CRPD) in its recognition of the equal rights of children with disabilities.[268] While the CRPD is not mentioned explicitly in that regard, it is likely that provisions of international human rights law are influencing the Committee's reasoning on issues of disability discrimination for children with disabilities and equal access to rights. Indeed, the CRPD, as well as the CRC, were quoted at the beginning of the recommendation as sources of relevant law.

In its *Recommendation CM/Rec(2009)9 to Member States on the Education and Social Inclusion of Children and Young People with Autism Spectrum Disorders*,[269] the Committee of Ministers again draws on the CRPD,[270] among other international instruments.[271] That recommendation demonstrates concrete attempts to adopt a cohesive approach to disability law and policy, one which draws on the strengths of the CRPD in seeking to influence the laws and policies of Member States. The recommendation also includes many suggestions for Member States, which reflect the principles enshrined in the CRPD. For instance, the Committee recommends inclusion of children with disabilities in mainstream education and urges States to put in place:

> A legal framework which ensures the rights of children and young people with disabilities, including people with autism spectrum disorders, to receive education – within general

---

266 Recommendation CM/Rec(2010)2 of the Committee of Ministers to member states on deinstitutionalisation and community living of children with disabilities (Adopted by the Committee of Ministers on 3 February 2010 at the 1076th meeting of the Ministers' Deputies).

267 Ibid.

268 The Recommendation notes that: 'All children have rights, hence disabled children have the same rights to family life, education, health, social care and vocational training as all children; long-term planning involving all stakeholders will be needed to ensure that children with disabilities are able to exercise the same rights as other children and to access social rights on the same basis as other children.' [Ibid, para. 1.1.].

269 Recommendation CM/Rec(2009)9 of the Committee of Ministers to member states on the education and social inclusion of children and young people with autism spectrum disorders (Adopted by the Committee of Ministers on 21 October 2009 at the 1068th meeting of the Ministers' Deputies).

270 It notes that: 'In line with other instruments of the Council of Europe, as well as the CRPD, member states should ensure not only that education, social welfare and other public policies do not discriminate against people with disabilities, including people with autism spectrum disorder, but that equality of opportunity and appropriate educational interventions are provided.'

271 The recommendation has regard to the United Nations Convention on the Rights of the Child (1989), the United Nations Standard Rules on the Equalisation of Opportunities for Persons with Disabilities (1993) and the United Nations Convention on the Rights of Persons with Disabilities (2006).

schemes wherever possible – that is appropriate to their needs, is non-discriminatory and works towards social inclusion.[272]

In its next recommendation to Member States – *Recommendation CM/Rec(2009)8 on Achieving Full Participation through Universal Design*[273] – the Committee mentions the CRPD in the context of relevant international documents but it does not draw specifically on any of the CRPD's provisions in elaborating its advices for States. The concept of universal design had been introduced previously as a strategy in accordance with the action lines of the *Council of Europe Disability Action Plan 2006–2015*[274] and had also been introduced in *Resolution ResAP(2001)1 of the Committee of Ministers*.[275] Additionally, the Committee had referred to the concept of Universal Design in its *Resolution ResAP(2001)3*.[276] In Recommendation CM/ Rec(2009)8, the Committee encourages governments to accept universal design 'as a philosophy and strategy supporting implementation of full citizenship and independent living of all people, including people with disabilities.'[277] While the Committee does not mention the CRPD's universal design provisions specifically in that connection, there is no doubt that the obligations contained in the CRPD have the potential to provide further support and guidance for the Committee's recommendations pertaining to universal design and for the laws and policies of Member States in that regard.

Recommendation CM/Rec(2011)14 of the Committee of Ministers to Member States on the Participation of Persons with Disabilities in Political and Public Life[278] demonstrates the clearest influence of the CRPD on Council of Europe disability policy relating to equality and inclusion. In that progressive recommendation, the Committee builds on the approach taken in the CRPD to increasing participation of persons with disabilities in political and public life and indeed draws explicitly on many of the provisions of the CRPD. At the very outset, the Committee has regard to the relevant provisions of the CRPD, particularly Article 29 which highlights the obligation to secure for persons with disabilities the enjoyment of their political rights on an equal basis with other members of society. The Committee also draws guidance from Article 2 of the CRPD, which includes the denial of reasonable accommodation in the definition of discrimination on the basis of disability. In addition, the

---

272 Ibid.

273 Recommendation CM/Rec(2009)8 of the Committee of Ministers to member states on achieving full participation through Universal Design(Adopted by the Committee of Ministers on 21 October 2009 at the 1068th meeting of the Ministers' Deputies).

274 See, for instance, Action Line 6 of the Disability Action Plan 2006–2015.

275 Resolution ResAP(2001)1 of the Committee of Ministers on the introduction of the principles of Universal Design into the curricula of all occupations working on the built environment ("Tomar Resolution").

276 Resolution ResAP(2001)3 of the Committee of Ministers entitled "Towards full citizenship of persons with disabilities through inclusive new technologies."

277 Recommendation CM/Rec(2009)8 of the Committee of Ministers to member states on achieving full participation through Universal Design.

278 Recommendation CM/Rec(2011)14 of the Committee of Ministers to member states on the participation of persons with disabilities in political and public life (Adopted by the Committee of Ministers on 16 November 2011 at the 1126th meeting of the Ministers' Deputies).

Committee draws on Article 12 (on equal recognition before the law), in its assertion that Member States of the Council of Europe should 'make support available to persons who may need assistance in exercising their legal capacity in various aspects of life, in particular when exercising their right to vote.'[279] The Committee focuses, among other things, on the accessibility of political processes and again draws on the provisions of the CRPD in that regard.[280] It also argues that 'failure to guarantee accessibility by means of universal design and reasonable accommodations would infringe the rights and the dignity of persons with disabilities and the principles of non-discrimination and equal opportunities'[281] and that the concepts of 'reasonable accommodation' and 'universal design' should be understood as defined in Article 2 [of the CRPD].'[282] The Committee also draws on Article 4(1) of the CRPD (which contains the general obligations of the Convention) and Article 9 of the CRPD (on accessibility) in its suggestions that Member States 'should ensure that all aspects of political and public life are accessible to persons with disabilities.'[283] The Committee also has regard to the CRPD in its advice that Member States 'should pay due attention to the importance of accessible rules and procedures before and during elections at all levels, as well as at other occasions when citizens are invited to participate in the conduct of public affairs.'[284] In that connection, the Committee suggests that Member States should make use, *inter alia*, of the provisions of the relevant articles of the CRPD, namely Article 9 (on Accessibility), Article 21 (on Freedom of expression and opinion, and access to information) and Article 13 (on Access to justice) as a guide to measures to be taken in pursuing the aims of total accessibility as described throughout the recommendation.[285] Furthermore, the Committee draws on the awareness-raising provisions of the CRPD, as well as those contained in the Council of Europe Disability Action Plan. It observes that combating stereotypes among all members of society in relation to the participation of persons with disabilities in political and public life 'is a task which should be tackled by means of training programmes and awareness-raising campaigns in accordance with the spirit of Article 8 of the UNCRPD and Action Line No. 15 of the Council of Europe Disability Action Plan.'[286] Finally, the Committee draws

---

[279] Ibid.
[280] Ibid, section 2.
[281] Ibid.
[282] Ibid.
[283] Ibid.
[284] Ibid, section 2.4.
[285] Ibid, section 2.4.
[286] Ibid, section 5.

on the CRPD (particularly Article 4(3),[287] Article 29(b)[288] and Article 33[289] thereof) and the spirit of the Council of Europe Disability Action Plan in support of its assertion that Member States should 'ensure that all their participatory processes are fully accessible to persons with disabilities and do not exclude them'[290] and that 'appropriate mechanisms should be adopted to ensure meaningful representation of persons with disabilities and/or [disabled persons' organisations] in relevant bodies of public authorities and advisory boards.'[291]

The recommendations outlined above, in particular the latest recommendation on participation in political and public life, demonstrate clearly that the Committee of Ministers of the Council of Europe is taking the spirit and tenor of the CRPD into account in drafting its advices to Member States. Apart from the various recommendations that have been adopted by the Committee of Ministers in the period after the CRPD's adoption, the Committee has also adopted other soft-law instruments on disability, which will be examined below.

5.1.3. Post-CRPD: Council of Europe Issue Papers on Disability

The former Council of Europe Commissioner for Human Rights, Mr. Thomas Hammarberg, has published two progressive issue papers on disability since the coming into force of the CRPD – one on legal capacity and one on independent living. Issue papers are published by the Commissioner with a view to contributing to debate and reflection on important current human rights issues. Many of them also include recommendations by the Commissioner addressing the concerns identified in the paper. In 2012, Mr. Hammarberg published an issue paper on legal capacity, entitled '*Who Gets to Decide? Right to Legal Capacity for Persons with Intellectual and Psychosocial Disabilities*.'[292] In that issue paper the Commissioner pays particular attention to the equality and participation dimensions of the right to legal capacity. Mr. Hammarberg notes that Article 12 of the CRPD 'provides a

[287] Article 4(3) of the CRPD provides as follows: 'In the development and implementation of legislation and policies to implement the present Convention, and in other decision-making processes concerning issues relating to persons with disabilities, States Parties shall closely consult with and actively involve persons with disabilities, including children with disabilities, through their representative organizations.'

[288] Article 29(b) of the CRPD provides that states should 'promote actively an environment in which persons with disabilities can effectively and fully participate in the conduct of public affairs, without discrimination and on an equal basis with others, and encourage their participation in public affairs, including: (i) Participation in non-governmental organizations and associations concerned with the public and political life of the country, and in the activities and administration of political parties; (ii) Forming and joining organizations of persons with disabilities to represent persons with disabilities at international, national, regional and local levels.'

[289] Article 33(3) of the CRPD provides that 'civil society, in particular persons with disabilities and their representative organizations, shall be involved and participate fully in the monitoring process.'

[290] Recommendation CM/Rec(2011)14 of the Committee of Ministers to member states on the participation of persons with disabilities in political and public life, section 6.

[291] Ibid.

[292] Council of Europe Commissioner for Human Rights, Thomas Hammarberg, Issue Paper, *Who Gets to Decide? Right to Legal Capacity for Persons with Intellectual and Psychosocial Disabilities*, CommDH/IssuePaper(2012)2, adopted on 20th February 2012.

paradigm shift in policies towards persons with disabilities'[293] and that 'it signals a deeper understanding of equality.'[294] In fact, an entire section of the recommendation is devoted to the understanding of equality espoused by the CRPD.[295] The issue paper acknowledges the fact that the paradigm shift embodied by the CRPD (from the medical model to the social model and the human rights-based approach to disability), together with the CRPD's equality/non-discrimination norms 'call for a new approach to legal capacity.'[296] Mr. Hammarberg then draws on Article 12 of the CRPD as demonstrating the best manner in which to put this new approach to legal capacity into practice.[297] The Commissioner urges Member States to ratify the CRPD and its Optional Protocol and goes on to outline several recommendations to Member States which can be aligned very clearly with the fundamental values enshrined in the CRPD, not least the principle of equality. Mr. Hammarberg recommends that States should review existing legislation on legal capacity in the light of current human rights standards, with particular reference to Article 12 of the CRPD.[298] The issue paper also recognises the importance of the duty to accommodate in the context of legal capacity reforms and reiterates the definition of reasonable accommodation according to Article 2 of the CRPD.[299]

The influence of the CRPD and its progressive equality and non-discrimination provisions are evidenced clearly in the issue paper on legal capacity. In 2012, Mr. Hammarberg also published an issue paper on independent living, which again exhibits a clear influence of the CRPD on the direction of Council of Europe disability policy related to equality and inclusion in society for persons with disabilities. That issue paper is entitled '*The Right of People with Disabilities to Live Independently and be Included in the Community.*'[300] It is stated explicitly to have been 'prompted by the opportunity that the CRPD affords for promoting the right to live in the community,

293 Ibid.

294 Ibid.

295 In that connection, Mr. Hammarberg notes that: 'The CRPD was developed on the basis of the recognition that the existing human rights framework had failed to protect the human rights of people with disabilities in an equal measure with others. Hence, the principle of equality underpins the entire convention [...] It presents a fully developed concept of equality in human rights terms. It moves beyond formal equality and creates an understanding of equality that is closely linked with the perception that disability is a disadvantage that occurs when persons with impairments meet an inaccessible environment and not a characteristic simply imputable to the individual.' [Ibid, section 3.2].

296 Ibid, section 4. In that regard, the paper notes that 'the demand for equality compels us to develop alternatives to accommodate and enable all persons with disabilities to be in charge of their lives.'

297 The paper states that Article 12 can be deemed 'to be the beating heart of the [CRPD]' as 'it is closely related to social inclusion, autonomy and equality, all core values of the instrument.' [Ibid, section 4.1].

298 Recommendation 9 of Thomas Hammarberg, Council of Europe Commissioner for Human Rights, Issue Paper: Who Gets to Decide? Right to Legal Capacity for Persons with Intellectual and Psychosocial Disabilities, CommDH/IssuePaper(2012)2, adopted on 20th February 2012.

299 In that connection, the Commissioner recommends that States should 'create a legal obligation for governmental and local authorities, the judiciary, health care, financial, insurance and other service providers to provide reasonable accommodation to persons with disabilities who wish to access their services.' [Ibid].

300 Council of Europe Commissioner for Human Rights, Thomas Hammarberg, Issue Paper: *The Right of People with Disabilities to Live Independently and be Included in the Community,* CommDH/IssuePaper(2012)3, adopted on 12 March 2012 (Council of Europe Publishing, France, June 2012).

on the one hand, and worrying trends in the implementation of this right, on the other hand.'[301] The primary aim of the issue paper is 'to draw out the guidance contained in international standards, and in particular Article 19 of the CRPD'[302] in order to promote an understanding of what the right to independent living looks like when implemented and when violated.[303] It draws on Article 19 of the CRPD 'to identify the various forms of violation and provides guidance on community-based responses governed by choice and on achieving inclusion and participation.'[304]

The 2012 issue paper on independent living acknowledges the fact that Article 19 of the CRPD embodies 'the most developed articulation for the right to live in the community of people with disabilities'[305] and that it 'embodies a positive philosophy, which is about enabling people to live their lives to the fullest within society.'[306] The issue paper notes that the Council of Europe Disability Action Plan 'foreshadows many CRPD provisions,'[307] including with regard to enabling persons with disabilities to live as independently as possible. It states that 'the content of Article 19 of the CRPD is [...] an articulation of equality and inclusion, and a declaration of independence and interdependence'[308] and goes on to draw guidance from Article 19 for Member States in their implementation of the right to independent living in the community. In that regard, the issue paper concludes with a sample of indicators and guidance questions directed towards Member States. These are designed to serve as a tool to monitor whether the vision of the right to independent living is being incorporated in implementation measures by States.[309]

It is clear that the general disability policy of the Council of Europe is being influenced by the substantive provisions and the spirit and tenor of the CRPD. Many of the instruments outlined above adopt the fundamental values and principles underlying the Convention, particularly in relation to equality/non-discrimination and participation and inclusion in society for persons with disabilities. Many of the documents draw specific guidance from the concrete provisions of the Convention and go on to use that guidance to formulate recommendations and suggestions to be employed by Member States in their implementation of disability rights. While the CRPD is certainly influencing Council of Europe mechanisms in its general disability policy, another question altogether is whether the values enshrined in the CRPD will filter down to Member State level to facilitate real change on the ground. Indeed, it is somewhat too early to answer that question definitively in light of the recency of the CRPD's adoption. Nonetheless, that question is still relevant to the

301 Ibid, at page 5.
302 Ibid, at page 9.
303 Ibid.
304 Ibid, at page 6.
305 Ibid, at page 14.
306 Ibid, at page 11.
307 Ibid, at page 24.
308 Ibid, at page 28.
309 The paper highlights the fact that the indicators and questions 'follow the core components of Article 19 relating to choice, access to individualised support services and equal availability of community services and facilities for the general public.' [Ibid, at page 45].

next subsection of this chapter, which will consider the influence of the CRPD on the interpretation of the disability provisions of the revised Charter by the ECSR.

5.2. The CRPD and the Revised European Social Charter

This section of the chapter will contain a brief case study on the interpretation of the revised Charter by the ECSR. As stated at the outset of this chapter, while the CRPD has potential relevance for the interpretation of the original Charter, the wide-ranging provisions of the CRPD bear increased relevance to the more progressive provisions of the revised Charter and therefore the focus will be maintained on the revised Charter in this section. Nonetheless, it is important to note that Member States of the Council of Europe can still be a party to the original Charter.

The role of the ECSR differs from that of the ECtHR (which is a judicial body). The ECSR can be termed a quasi-judicial body. Its role is to assess whether States are in conformity, in law and in practice, with the provisions of the original and revised European Social Charter. The Committee has the power to hear collective complaints alleging violations of the substantive rights contained in the original and revised charters.[310] The ECSR also has the power to examine national reports in order to decide whether or not the situations in the countries concerned are in conformity with the original and revised charters. Its decisions, known as 'conclusions,' are published every year. If a State takes no action on a Committee decision to the effect that it does not comply with the Charter, the Committee of Ministers addresses a recommendation to that State, urging it to change the situation in law and/or in practice. Due to time and space constraints, only the collective complaints submitted to the ECSR pertaining to disability will be considered and not the national reports.

The Council of Europe has not adopted any specific binding human rights instruments related to disabled persons. It must be remembered, however, that for a very long time the original Charter[311] was the first human rights treaty in which disabled persons were mentioned explicitly as holders of human rights. The original Charter lays down twenty-three fundamental rights. Pursuant to Article 15 of the original Charter, Contracting Parties undertake to adopt adequate measures for: (i) the provision of training facilities for disabled persons; and (ii) the placing of disabled persons in employment, such as specialised placing services, facilities for sheltered employment and measures to encourage employers to admit disabled persons to employment.[312] The concept of disability contained in the original Charter is based on the antiquated medical model or the traditional institutional approach. In line with changes at the international level, the Charter was revised in order to adapt the substantive contents of the Charter to take into account, in particular, the fundamental societal changes that had occurred since the text was adopted. The

310 As well as the 1988 Additional Protocol to the Charter.
311 European Social Charter of 1961, ETS no. 035.
312 Ibid, Article 15.

revised Charter[313] updated the provision on disability contained in the original Charter to reflect the human rights-based approach to disability. The explanatory report to the revised Charter highlights the fact that Article 15 of the revised Charter '[...] no longer applies only to vocational rehabilitation but to the right of persons with disabilities to independent social integration, personal autonomy and participation in the life of the community in general [...]'[314] In addition to the revised Article 15, Article 10 of the revised Charter requires States to ensure the effective exercise of the right to vocational training, including for persons with disabilities. Furthermore, Article 17 of the revised Charter relates to the right of children and young persons to social, legal and economic protection, including children with disabilities. Of added relevance to persons with disabilities is the cross-cutting Article E of the revised Charter on non-discrimination.[315]

In a similar vein to the various other elements of the case study undertaken throughout this chapter, this part of the case study on the Council of Europe aims to address the influence, and potential influence, of the CRPD on the interpretation of the revised Charter relating to issues of equality and participation and inclusion for persons with disabilities. At the outset it is important to consider whether the ECSR shows a willingness to take account of provisions of international law in its interpretation of the revised Charter. The answer to that question appears to be quite clear. Legal scholars have recognised the fact that the ECSR seems to be very open 'to be guided by other standards and treaty body jurisprudence (e.g., General Comments on the ICESCR) in its work.'[316] Janet Lord and Rebecca Brown point to the fact that the ECSR has a 'fairly strong record of looking to treaty body jurisprudence to guide its work' and they cite in that regard the collective complaint of *Mental Disability Advocacy Center (MDAC) v. Bulgaria*,[317] in which the ECSR refers to the UNCESCR[318] as an interpretative aid to the provisions of the revised Charter.[319]

313 European Social Charter (revised) of 1996, ETS no. 196.

314 Explanatory Report to the European Social Charter (revised) of 1996, ETS no. 196, available at http://conventions.coe.int/Treaty/EN/Reports/HTML/163.htm last accessed 12 October 2014, para. 63.

315 Article E of the European Social Charter (revised) states that the enjoyment of the rights set forth in the Charter 'shall be secured without discrimination on any ground such as race, colour, sex, language, religion, political or other opinion, national extraction or social origin, health, association with a national minority, birth or other status.' Article E, and in particular the notion of 'other status,' has been applied to the rights of persons with disabilities in numerous views adopted by the ECSR, as I will demonstrate below.

316 J.E. Lord and R. Brown, 'The Role of Reasonable Accommodation in Securing Substantive Equality for Persons with Disabilities: The UN Convention on the Rights of Persons with Disabilities' in M.H. Rioux, L.A. Basser and M. Jones (eds.) Critical Perspectives on Human Rights and Disability Law (Martinus Nijhoff 2011), at page 292.

317 *Mental Disability Advocacy Centre (MDAC) v Bulgaria*, Complaint No. 41/2007, European Committee of Social Rights (Decision on the Merits, 3 June 2007).

318 Ibid, at para. 37.

319 In that collective complaint, the ECSR was influenced by the UNCESCR's enunciation, in its General Comment 13 of the criteria to be taken into account by States in the provision of education. The UNCESCR noted that all education provided by States must fulfil the criteria of availability, accessibility, acceptability and adaptability. The ECSR considered that the UNCESCR's criteria of accessibility and adaptability were at stake (i.e. that educational institutions and curricula have to be accessible to everyone, without discrimination and teaching has to be designed to respond to children with special needs) and went on to assess the State's progress in line with the UNCESCR's

In light of the openness of the ECSR to take account of provisions of international law in its interpretation, in particular, of the revised Charter, it is submitted that the CRPD has the potential to influence the complaints brought before the ECSR. Indeed, there would appear to be more potential for the CRPD's mandate of full and effective participation and inclusion to exert influence on the interpretation of the revised Charter than there is for it to influence the interpretation of the ECHR, in light of the particular nature of the rights contained in the revised Charter. As outlined above, the original Charter and its revised version are concerned with social and economic rights. This contrasts with the provisions of the ECHR, which relate to civil and political rights. The full and effective realisation of socio-economic rights is particularly important for persons with disabilities as they contribute in important ways to increasing participation and inclusion of persons with disabilities in society. Many of the substantive provisions of the CRPD have potential relevance for the interpretation of both the original and revised Charters. Since the provisions of the revised Charter are more progressive, from a disability perspective, than those of the original Charter, it is likely that the ECSR will have more recourse to the CRPD in its interpretation of the revised Charter. Indeed, the wide-ranging provisions of the CRPD have clear relevance, in particular to Articles 15 and 17 of the Revised Charter. As outlined above, Article 15 of the revised Charter enshrines the right of persons with disabilities to independence, social integration and participation in the life of the community and Article 17 relates to children with disabilities. Article 19 of the CRPD (on independent living),[320] Article 24 (on education), Article 27 (on employment),[321] among many other CRPD provisions, are potentially relevant interpretative guides in this connection. For the purposes of analysing the influence to date, and the potential future influence, of the CRPD on the interpretation of the revised Charter, the most important line of collective complaints relates to the

---

criteria. [UNCESCR, General Comment No. 13 (on the right to education), UN Doc. E/C.12/1999/10 of 8 December 1999, at para. 6].

320 Article 15 of the revised Charter requires States to promote the 'full social integration and participation in the life of the community in particular through measures, including technical aids, aiming to overcome barriers to communication and mobility and enabling access to transport, housing, cultural activities and leisure.' It is evident that many provisions of the CRPD hold potential relevance here, not least its provisions on accessibility and independent living contained in Articles 9 and 19 of the CRPD, respectively.

321 Article 15 of the Revised Charter requires States to promote access to employment for persons with disabilities 'through all measures tending to encourage employers to hire and keep in employment persons with disabilities in the ordinary working environment and to adjust the working conditions to the needs of the disabled [...].' In a similar vein, Article 27 of the CRPD requires States to recognise the right of persons with disabilities 'to the opportunity to gain a living by work freely chosen or accepted in a labour market that is open, inclusive and accessible to persons with disabilities.' It also requires States 'to ensure that reasonable accommodation is provided to persons with disabilities in the workplace.' There are clear overlaps between the CRPD and the revised Charter on the issue of employment for persons with disabilities. On the other hand, Article 15 of the revised Charter is much less progressive than the CRPD, to the extent that it provides that where open labour market participation is not possible 'by reason of the disability,' States should arrange for 'creating sheltered employment according to the level of disability. In certain cases, such measures may require recourse to specialised placement and support services.' This is not in line with the CRPD's emphasis on open labour market participation. Thus the UN Convention has a potential role to play in ensuring that the ECSR interprets the provisions of the revised Charter in line with changing international norms for persons with disabilities.

inclusion of children with disabilities in mainstream educational settings, as the CRPD has been invoked in support of arguments for a right to inclusive education under the revised Charter. The next subsection of this chapter will explore that very issue.

5.2.1. The Right to Education for Persons with Disabilities under the Revised European Social Charter

Before the CRPD entered into force, several cases were taken before the ECSR regarding the ongoing widespread segregation of children with disabilities, contrary to Articles 15 and 17 of the revised Charter, as well as the non-discrimination principle contained in Article E thereof. Article 15(1) of the revised Charter requires States to 'take the necessary measures to provide persons with disabilities with guidance, education and vocational training in the framework of general schemes wherever possible or, where this is not possible, through specialised bodies, public or private.'[322] Article 17 of the revised Charter obliges States to provide for the establishment or maintenance of institutions and services sufficient and adequate for this purpose, providing all children with a free primary and secondary education.[323] The reason for focusing on the education line of case law is because it is the main area under the revised Charter in which the CRPD may be of potential influence in the future. This is particularly so because there is currently a collective complaint pending before the ECSR (the 2014 case of *Mental Disability Advocacy Center (MDAC) v. Belgium*),[324] in which the applicant invokes the provisions of the CRPD related to inclusive education. Before considering that case, the next subsection of this chapter will explore the collective complaints (related to the right to education) which came before the ECSR prior to the entry into force of the CRPD.

5.2.2. Pre-CRPD Collective Complaints on the Right to Education

Before the adoption of the CRPD, two important collective complaints came before the ECSR seeking to enforce the right of children with disabilities to non-discrimination and education within the mainstream under the revised Charter. The first complaint of relevance is *Autism Europe v France*,[325] which was decided by the ECSR in 2003. In that case, there was evidence that the proportion of autistic children being educated in either general or specialist schools was disproportionately low in comparison to non-disabled children. France had passed relevant legislation[326] in the area as far back as 1975. However, it had failed to enforce the legislation in the interim. In view of this, the Committee ruled that the relevant State Party had not made sufficient provision for the education of autistic children and, as a

322 Article 15(1) of the European Social Charter (revised).

323 See Article 17(1)(a) and Article 17(2) of the European Social Charter (revised).

324 *Mental Disability Advocacy Center (MDAC) v. Belgium*, European Committee of Social Rights, Complaint No.109/2014 (pending).

325 *Autism Europe v France*, Complaint No. 13/2002, European Committee of Social Rights (Decision on the Merits, 7 November 2003).

326 The Disabled Persons Policy Act (1975).

result, a high proportion of autistic children[327] were deemed not to have received an appropriate education. In other words, the right to education was not being realised effectively. The Committee ruled that the State Party was in breach of Article 15(1) and Article 17(1) of the revised Charter, relating to the right of persons with disabilities to education and the general right of children and young people to education, respectively. The Committee also found that France had violated the non-discrimination principle in the enjoyment of Charter rights.[328] The Committee made an important pronouncement with regard to the progressive realisation of the right to education. It stated that the Charter requires State Parties to take not merely legal action, but also practical action to give full effect to the rights recognised in the Charter.[329] It also asserted that when the achievement of a right is exceptionally complex and particularly expensive to resolve, State Parties must take measures to do so 'within a reasonable time with measurable progress and to an extent consistent with the maximum use of available resources.'[330]

Similarly, in the case of *MDAC v Bulgaria*,[331] the ECSR considered a collective complaint alleging that a group of children with disabilities who were residing in certain social care home institutions in Bulgaria received no education on account of their disabilities and that this constituted a violation of Article 17(2) of the revised Charter. In essence, the complaint alleged that legislation guaranteeing the right to education for all children was not implemented in respect of the children who resided in the social care institutions. In that regard, evidence was adduced which showed government data indicating that only 6.2% of children living in the relevant institutions were enrolled in schools. It was further alleged that mainstream schools were not adapted to accommodate the needs of the children with disabilities and that staff in those institutions provided either no education at all or inadequate education. The Committee found that the children in question were denied an effective right to education on account of disability discrimination. It held that, although the Bulgarian government had undertaken measures to respect the right to education for children with disabilities living in institutions by putting in place legislation and action plans, those laws and policies had not been implemented effectively. They also found that there were inadequate standards elaborating on the right to education and equality of educational opportunities. Specifically, the ECSR found that Bulgarian educational standards were inadequate because mainstream educational institutions and curricula were not accessible in practice.[332] It also held that there appeared to be insufficient evidence to show real attempts to integrate the children in question into mainstream education. The Committee considered therefore that the criterion of accessibility was not fulfilled.[333] Finally, the Committee found that mainstream schools were not

327 In the instant case, 80–90% of autistic children did not receive an adequate education.

328 Article E of the European Social Charter (revised).

329 *Autism Europe v France*, Complaint No. 13/2002, European Committee of Social Rights (Decision on the Merits, 7 November 2003), para. 53.

330 Ibid.

331 *Mental Disability Advocacy Centre (MDAC) v Bulgaria*, Complaint No. 41/2007, European Committee of Social Rights (Decision on the Merits, 3 June 2007).

332 Ibid, para. 43.

333 Ibid.

adapted to the specific needs of children with intellectual disabilities, teachers were not properly trained, and resources were not developed to cater for the educational needs of children with disabilities. The ECSR ruled that the schools were not suited to meet the needs of children with intellectual disabilities and that the criterion of adaptability of education was not met.[334] The Committee found that teachers had not been trained sufficiently to teach intellectually disabled children and that teaching materials were inadequate in mainstream schools. Moreover, due to the absence of primary educational opportunities, children with disabilities were ineligible to enter secondary education.[335] In view of this, the Committee determined that the government had failed to fulfil the three core criteria consistent with progressive realisation of rights, namely, (1) a reasonable timeframe; (2) measurable progress; and (3) financing consistent with the maximum use of available resources.

The two cases highlighted above raise many issues that have clear relevance to the types of concerns which the CRPD seeks to address related to inclusion and equality in education for persons with disabilities. The ECSR has interpreted the rights of children with disabilities progressively in these two cases.[336] While this is encouraging to note, it is submitted that the provisions of the CRPD could add further impetus to the ECSR's recommendations to States and could also serve to provide a more concrete vision of inclusive education for children with disabilities. Janet Lord and Rebecca Brown acknowledge the fact that:

> The framework for non-discrimination and equality and reasonable accommodation in education in the CRPD offers additional tools for the European Committee of Social Rights (and indeed other treaty monitoring bodies) to draw upon in such cases.[337]

The provisions of Article 24 of the CRPD are hugely detailed and outline the aims of education for persons with disabilities.[338] Article 24 of the CRPD also details the types of measures that States Parties to the CRPD should take in order to ensure inclusion for persons with disabilities in the mainstream. These measures include reasonable accommodations, effective individualised support measures and other specific measures for children who are blind and deaf. As Lord and Brown note,

---

334 Ibid, para. 44.

335 Ibid, para. 46.

336 Janet Lord and Rebecca Brown argue that *Autism Europe v France* and *MDAC v Bulgaria* 'reflect a progressive trend in recognizing and applying the right to an education for children with disabilities and, further, in animating the non-discrimination and equality provision of the Charter.' [J.E. Lord and R. Brown, 'The Role of Reasonable Accommodation in Securing Substantive Equality for Persons with Disabilities: The UN Convention on the Rights of Persons with Disabilities' in M.H. Rioux, L.A. Basser and M. Jones (eds.) Critical Perspectives on Human Rights and Disability Law (Martinus Nijhoff, The Hague, 2011), at page 292].

337 Ibid.

338 Article 24(1) of the CRPD states that education should be directed to: 'The full development of human potential and sense of dignity and self-worth, and the strengthening of respect for human rights, fundamental freedoms and human diversity; The development by persons with disabilities of their personality, talents and creativity, as well as their mental and physical abilities, to their fullest potential, Enabling persons with disabilities to participate effectively in a free society.'

Article 24 provides 'a highly contextualized, disability-specific understanding'[339] of the right to education. As such, they claim that 'it would be surprising if Article 24 did not serve as a prominent guide for regional and international human rights procedures.'[340] In particular, the OP-CRPD provides a further mechanism for disability advocates to find redress for frequent violations of the right to education. Moreover, the observations of the CRPD Committee may prove instructive for regional human rights mechanisms, such as the ECSR. Bearing all of this in mind, the next subsection of this chapter will consider the collective education complaints which have been brought before the ECSR since the coming into force of the CRPD.

5.2.3. Post-CRPD Collective Complaints on the Right to Education

Since the CRPD entered into force, two collective claims alleging violations of revised Charter rights relating to education for persons with disabilities have invoked the provisions of the CRPD. The first collective complaint of relevance is entitled *European Action of the Disabled (AEH) v France.*[341] In that complaint, the AEH alleged that, by failing to provide autistic children and adolescents with compulsory schooling, France had violated its obligations under Article 15(1) of the revised Charter. The AEH also claimed that by failing to foster access to vocational training for young adults with autism, France had failed to fulfil its obligation to 'promote, as necessary, the technical and vocational training of all persons, including the handicapped,' as laid down in Article 10(1) of the revised Charter. Furthermore, the complainant alleged that France had failed to provide or promote 'adequate and readily available training facilities for adult workers' as required by Article 10(3)(a) of the revised Charter. The complainant also argued that there was discrimination on the grounds of disability (in breach of Article E of the revised Charter), on account of the fact that French persons with autism did not enjoy the right to vocational education and training. Significantly, the complaint brought before the ECSR in *AEH* outlined the changing international context and the Committee was asked to examine the rights set out in the revised Charter in accordance with Article 24 of the UN Convention.[342] In its decision on the merits, adopted on September 11 2013, the ECSR refers[343] to the CRPD, and in particular to Article 24 thereof, in the context of relevant international standards and instrument. However, it does not go any further than this. It does not refer to the CRPD in the rest of its opinion and it does not invoke the provisions of Article 24 of the CRPD as an aid to interpretation. Notwithstanding

---

339 J.E. Lord and R. Brown, 'The Role of Reasonable Accommodation in Securing Substantive Equality for Persons with Disabilities: The UN Convention on the Rights of Persons with Disabilities' in M.H. Rioux, L.A. Basser and M. Jones (eds.) *Critical Perspectives on Human Rights and Disability Law* (Martinus Nijhoff, The Hague, 2011), at page 292.

340 Ibid.

341 *European Action of the Disabled (AEH) v France*, complaint no. 81/2012, decision on the merits adopted on 11 September 2013.

342 The complainant drew attention to the fact that France had ratified the CRPD on 9 March 2010 and therefore is 'committed to uphold non-discrimination, to adopt measures to protect the rights of persons with disabilities and to provide them with the services they need in order to participate fully in society.' [*European Action of the Disabled (AEH) v France*, European Committee of Social Rights, complaint no. 81/2012, decision on the merits adopted on 11 September 2013, para. 17].

343 Ibid, at para. 1.

its failure to refer further to the CRPD, the views adopted by the ECSR in *AEH* reflect a positive outcome for children with disabilities. The ECSR ruled that there was a violation of Article 15(1) of the revised Charter with regard to the right of children and adolescents with autism to be educated primarily in mainstream schools and with regard to the right of young persons with autism to vocational training, because the work done in specialised institutions caring for children and adolescents with autism was not predominantly educational in nature. The Committee also ruled that there was a violation of Article E of the Revised Charter, taken in conjunction with Article 15(1) because families had no other choice than to leave the national territory in order to educate their children with autism in a specialised school because France had failed to provide autistic children and adolescents with compulsory schooling. This was held to constitute direct discrimination against them.[344] In spite of the overall positive outcome of the judgment for disabled persons, it is regrettable that the ECSR did not take more cognisance of the detailed articulation of the right to education contained in Article 24 of the CRPD.

Following on from the *AEH* decision, another opportunity has arisen for the ECSR to consider the right to education under the CRPD as a means to providing a contextualised interpretation of the provisions of the revised Charter. MDAC has sent a collective complaint to the ECSR entitled *Mental Disability Advocacy Center v. Belgium*[345] alleging a violation of Article E in relation to Articles 15 and 17 of the revised Charter. The complaint focuses on the education system in Flanders, where there is a startlingly high rate of educational segregation. In that complaint, MDAC draws on the substantive provisions of the CRPD as a clear basis for its argumentation in support of the education of children with disabilities in the mainstream. In its complaint, MDAC cites the paragraphs of Article 24 of the CRPD which lay out the objectives of education for persons with disabilities and corresponding State responsibilities.[346] MDAC also quotes the concluding observations of the CRPD Committee, in which it stresses the importance of establishing education policy that guarantees the right to inclusive education for everyone, including people with disabilities. It remains to be seen the effect which MDAC's submissions will have on the interpretation by the ECSR of the provisions of the revised Charter related to the education of children with disabilities. However, it is likely that it is only a matter of time before the observations of the CRPD Committee and the detailed provisions of the CRPD find their way into the case law of the ECSR. In a recent collective complaint, the ECSR has acknowledged the CRPD as the relevant standard for the interpretation of disability rights. In that regard, the ECSR notes that the CRPD 'reflects existing trends in comparative European law in the sphere

[344] The Committee also found that there was a violation of Article E taken in conjunction with Article 15(1) of the revised Charter because the State had allocated limited funds in its budgets for the education of children and adolescents with autism, which the Committee deemed disadvantaged indirectly those persons with disabilities.

[345] *Mental Disability Advocacy Center v. Belgium*, European Committee of Social Rights, complaint no. 109/2014.

[346] Ibid, at paras. 64–66.

of disability policies.'[347] It is certainly to be expected that the ECSR will draw on the wide-ranging provisions of the CRPD in its future interpretation of the general human rights obligations contained in the revised Charter in the specific context of persons with disabilities. However, it is by no means clear how long we will have to wait to witness this type of development.

6. Conclusion

The case study conducted in this chapter has sought to demonstrate the influence which the CRPD is having to date and the potential future impact of the CRPD on Council of Europe mechanisms – primarily ECtHR jurisprudence but also on the general disability policy of the Council of Europe, as well as on the interpretation of the revised European Social Charter by the ECSR.

This case study has shown that the CRPD is exerting some influence on the relevant organs in the Council of Europe by guiding the general direction of disability policy via recommendations and issue papers. The impact of the CRPD to date on the case law of both the ECtHR and the ECSR is less consistent. The CRPD is certainly proving to be of potential significance to the Strasbourg Court in its interpretation of ECHR rights for persons with disabilities. At the very least, the UN Convention is acting as a reference point for the Strasbourg Court, although the Court has not always been consistent in referring to the CRPD. In its short lifespan thus far, the CRPD has begun to have an impact on the judgments of the ECtHR with regard to disability discrimination.[348] To date, however, the potential influence of the UN Convention has been tempered, among other things, by the self-imposed constraints which the Court has placed on the interpretation of ECHR rights – in other words, the fact that the ECtHR is a judicial body that is extremely cautious about the imposition of positive duties on States Parties to the ECHR.[349] The CRPD is still in its infancy and it is too early to predict with any degree of accuracy the extent to which the Strasbourg Court will draw on its provisions in the future in its case law related to disability equality. Notwithstanding this, Anna Lawson asserts that 'the ECtHR is by no means impervious to the influences of international law.'[350] It is abundantly clear that the ECHR is never the sole frame of reference for the interpretation of the provisions contained therein. The fact remains that many of the rights contained in the CRPD are relevant to the interpretation of the human rights of persons with

[347] *International Federation for Human Rights (FIDH) v. Belgium*, European Committee of Social Rights, complaint No. 75/2011, para. 112.

[348] See, in particular, section 3.2 of this chapter.

[349] For further analysis on this point, see C. O'Cinneide, 'Extracting Protection for the Rights of Persons with Disabilities from Human Rights Frameworks: Established Limits and New Possibilities' in O.M. Arnardottir and G. Quinn, The UN Convention on the Rights of Persons with Disabilities European and Scandinavian Perspectives (Martinus Nijhoff, Leiden, 2009).

[350] A. Lawson, 'The UN Convention on the Rights of Persons with Disabilities and European Disability Law: A Catalyst for Cohesion?' in O.M. Arnardóttir and G. Quinn G (eds.), *The UN Convention on the Rights of Persons with Disabilities: European and Scandinavian Perspectives* (Martinus Nijhoff, Leiden, 2009), at page 93.

disabilities under the ECHR, if the Court decides to taken them into account. In particular, the CRPD's non-discrimination norm has the potential to enhance the substantive equality of persons with disabilities under the ECHR. In that respect, Lawson observes that 'the appearance of the CRPD is likely to add considerable weight to arguments that including disabled people in society's mainstream is a matter of equality and human rights with which the ECtHR should be concerned.'[351]

The interpretation by the ECSR of the rights of persons with disabilities under the revised European Social Charter is likely to be influenced by the CRPD, in particular in the area of inclusive education. To date, the ECSR appears only to be referring to the CRPD in the context of relevant international law. However, the wide-ranging rights contained in the CRPD are clearly relevant to the rights of persons with disabilities under the original and revised Charters. It is submitted that there is even more potential for the CRPD to influence the ECSR's interpretation of the revised Charter than there is for it to influence the interpretation of the ECHR by the Strasbourg Court. This stems from the fact that the revised Charter aims at the protection of social rights (which are essential to increasing participation and inclusion of persons with disabilities in society) and that the revised Charter contains specific provisions for disabled individuals. This is in contrast to the ECHR, whose fundamental aim is to protect civil and political rights and which does not contain any specific provisions for the protection of the rights of persons with disabilities. It is likely that the Strasbourg Court will be much slower to show signs of change when compared with other bodies in the Council of Europe. On the basis of the evidence presented in this chapter, it would seem logical to assert that the standards contained in the UN Convention will continue to exert their influence on the general disability policy of the Council of Europe and will weave their way slowly into the interpretation of the ECHR and the Revised European Social Charter in the coming years.

[351] Ibid, at page 92.

Chapter 9
Concluding Chapter: Findings, Conclusions and Recommendations

'If we are to achieve a richer culture, rich in contrasting values, we must recognize the whole gamut of human potentialities, and so weave a less arbitrary social fabric, one in which each diverse human gift will find a fitting place.'[1]

1. Summary of Book's Objectives

The research carried out for this book emerged amidst a number of research gaps identified in the introductory chapter relating, *inter alia*, to the lack of a comprehensive legal interpretation of the equality and non-discrimination norms in the CRPD. While many scholars have written about various aspects of the right to equality under the Convention, there was considerable scope for a more integral approach to its interpretation. This book has bridged the research gaps which existed in several respects. In the first instance, this research has provided the first comprehensive legal interpretation of all aspects of Article 5 of the CRPD and related articles. The aim of that interpretation was twofold. Firstly, the interpretation of the equality and non-discrimination norms contained in the CRPD had the objective of teasing out the specific nature of States' obligations under the Convention. Secondly, the research conducted for this book aimed to define the precise theoretical model(s) of equality endorsed by the CRPD, as well as establishing the extent to which the Convention's equality and non-discrimination norms fit in comparatively with already existing norms at the international level. With a view to providing a backdrop to the interpretation of the CRPD's equality and non-discrimination provisions, the state of the law was analysed at the international level preceding the adoption of the CRPD. This helped to demonstrate the necessity for the adoption of an integral binding human rights treaty to protect the rights of persons with disabilities.

After having interpreted the CRPD's equality and non-discrimination norms from a theoretical and comparative legal standpoint, the research in this book then moved from theory to practice. In that regard, this research has proposed a framework for review of measures adopted by States to ensure the progressive realisation of CRPD rights, drawing lessons from existing frameworks of reasonableness review at the national and international levels and from the balancing of interests and burdens inherent in the duty to accommodate persons with disabilities. That information was collated into a framework of review criteria, tailored to the specific context of

1 M. Mead, *Sex and Temperament in Three Primitive Societies* (W. Morrow and Company, New York, 1935), at page 322.

the CRPD. Those review criteria were then applied to the rights and obligations of progressive implementation in the Convention, namely the accessibility obligation in Article 9 and the right to education contained in Article 24 of the CRPD. The research on Article 9 defined the normative content of the accessibility obligation and it applied various 'reasonableness' criteria to the measures to be adopted by States to ensure compliance with Article 9. With regard to Article 24 of the Convention, the normative content of the right to education was also defined and the criteria that the CRPD Committee might employ in assessing measures taken by States to ensure the right to inclusive education for persons with disabilities were elaborated upon. Consistent with the overarching theme of equality in this book, the link between the accessibility obligation and the equality norm was explored, as well as the impact of the Convention's equality paradigm on the right to education for persons with disabilities. The final part of the research conducted for this book related to the impact, and potential impact, of the CRPD on the interpretation of the equality norm in the Council of Europe, under both the case law of the ECtHR and in the views adopted by the ECSR, as well as in the general disability policy of the Committee of Ministers of the Council of Europe. By that token, the progressive norms contained in the CRPD were taken outside of their theoretical box, in order to analyse whether they have had an impact to date, or whether they can potentially have a substantive impact in the future, on the disability rights agenda at the level of law-making and policy at the regional level.

2. Main Findings and Conclusions

2.1. Introduction

In this section of the chapter, the main findings and conclusions emanating from my research will be elaborated upon. In that connection, the research questions that were pinpointed in the introductory chapter to this book will be reiterated and answered below. Firstly, the methodology that was used throughout this book will be summarised briefly below.

2.2. Methodology

The primary research methodology that was employed throughout this book consisted of a normative analytical framework. For the most part, that comprised an analysis of the normative content of rights and obligations, specifically the rights and obligations contained in the CRPD. The specific research methodology that was employed to interpret the obligations of States Parties under the CRPD was that of treaty interpretation. The primary point of reference in all aspects of treaty interpretation in this book was the text of the CRPD itself and the VCLT. In that regard, the wording of the provisions under interpretation was considered, as well as the terms of the treaty in their context and the object and purpose of the CRPD. Recourse was also had to the *travaux préparatoires* of the Convention as a subsidiary source of interpretation, as well as the general comments and concluding observations of the CRPD Committee (and those of the other core human rights treaty bodies as they relate to equality provisions in the respective treaties).

The research conducted for this book did not entail a normative *de lege ferenda* element in the usual sense of the word. This research has not proposed what the law 'should be' and it has not suggested legislative improvements. Rather, this research enters within the realm of *lex lata*, in that it sets out and analyses the law as it exists, interpreting such law according to an established and reliable framework of interpretation. At various junctures throughout this book, my own opinions on the meaning of the rights and obligations contained in the CRPD are put forward, at all times adhering to the strict interpretative criteria set out in the VCLT. Furthermore, suggestions are proposed for the CRPD Committee as to the correct interpretation (in my view) of the rights and obligations contained in the Convention, according to the VCLT methodology. However, that does not amount to proposing 'new' law.

As well as engaging in normative analysis, this book also contains a descriptive methodology. The classic form of legal scholarship – namely, a traditional legal doctrinal approach was used to describe, evaluate and critically analyse legal sources (legislative provisions, *travaux préparatoires*, case law and academic sources) in order to clarify the current state of the law. That methodology was used, for instance, in the consideration of various theoretical models of disability and equality, and in the delineation of the protection of disability rights in key documents which preceded the adoption of the CRPD. Descriptive methodology was also used in the case study on the legal reasoning of the ECtHR, the ECSR and the disability policy of the Council of Europe. Finally, a comparative analytical approach was used in analysing the evolution of the equality norm at the international level and in outlining the various frameworks for review of measures taken by States in realising progressively human rights, as well as in conducting the case study on the Council of Europe legal and policy mechanisms.

2.3. Findings and Conclusions

By way of reminder, the overall research question formulated at the outset of this book was as follows: To what extent has the CRPD advanced disability equality in theory and how can this potentially advance the participation and inclusion in society of persons with disabilities in practice? Taking that research question as a vital starting point, various sub-research questions were delineated and answered in each chapter of the book. Hereunder those sub-questions and pertinent findings will be elaborated upon:

2.3.1. *The Gaps in the Protection of the Rights of Persons with Disabilities Pre-CRPD*

The first set of findings emanating from the research in this book relates to the background leading up to the adoption of the CRPD. In that regard, the sub-research question that was answered was as follows: What gaps existed in relation to the protection of the rights of persons with disabilities, which necessitated the adoption of a binding international human rights treaty for disabled people?

While persons with disabilities were covered under a multitude of soft-law instruments and they were also protected in principle under the core international human rights treaties, a number of problems existed with regard to the protection of their rights in practice. Before the adoption of the CRPD, the human rights instruments addressing disability issues were not binding and therefore States were not legally obliged to follow the recommendations contained in those documents. Another concern with the existing corpus of human rights law was the fact that many of the existing instruments conceptualised disability according to a medical model approach. This hindered the advancement of the rights of persons with disabilities, in particular impairing their full and effective participation and inclusion in society. Thus, while in theory persons with disabilities were protected under the core binding international human rights treaties, there were huge gaps in practice. The core treaties did not contain disability-specific provisions and many of them also contained universal equality norms, which were not tailored to the specific needs and circumstances of disabled people. As a result of the foregoing deficiencies, there was consensus among the international human rights community regarding the fact that a binding international human rights instrument was required, which would reflect the social model and a human rights-based approach to disability. Hence the emergence of the CRPD to plug those gaps.

2.3.2. *The Legal Meaning of Equality in the CRPD – A Theoretical and Comparative Framework*

The second set of findings emanating from this research relates to the legal meaning of the equality norm, as well as the theoretical models of disability and equality which the CRPD endorses. In that connection, the following sub-research questions were laid out:

i. What is the legal meaning of the equality and non-discrimination norms in the CRPD?; and
ii. How do the concepts of equality and non-discrimination contained in the CRPD fit within the various theoretical models of disability and conceptions of equality which have been elaborated to date by scholars?

The goal of this part of the research was to provide a comprehensive legal interpretation of the CRPD's equality provisions in order to delineate States' obligations under the Convention and to demonstrate the novelties introduced by the CRPD at the international level. Having analysed the theoretical framework of equality under the CRPD, the equality provisions were then compared to those contained in other human rights treaties which preceded the Convention. In that regard, the following sub-research questions were answered:

i. To what extent does the non-discrimination obligation contained in the CRPD go further than previous non-discrimination norms at the international level; and
ii. How can this potentially advance the rights of persons with disabilities to participate and be included in society?

It was demonstrated in chapter three of this book that the CRPD can be described as embodying substantive and transformative models of equality. The substantive model of equality seeks to target covert forms of discrimination, as well as ensuring that differential characteristics are accommodated within the equality norm. Article 5(1) of the CRPD focuses primarily on formal equality in its guarantee of equality before and under the law. An examination of the guarantee of 'equal benefit of the law' under Article 5(1) leads to the conclusion that it can be construed as endorsing a substantive conception of equality, which will require the adoption of positive measures in certain circumstances in order to ensure that persons with disabilities can exercise their rights on the basis of equality with others. With regard to Article 5(2) of the CRPD, the prohibition of discrimination on the basis of disability which is mandated by that article is broad in several respects. States will be required to cover multiple forms of discrimination, such as direct and indirect discrimination, a denial of reasonable accommodation, as well as discrimination by association, among others. States will also be required to regulate not only the public sphere of society but also the private sphere and this will include tackling discrimination by individuals. In addition, the requirement to guarantee equal and effective legal protection against discrimination imposes a positive duty of protection on States Parties to take active measures to combat discrimination. This brings Article 5(2) of the CPRD in line with a substantive conception of equality. Article 5(3) of the Convention consolidates the substantive approach to equality, imposing an obligation on States to take positive measures to ensure that entities provide reasonable accommodations to disabled people, with a view to increasing equality of opportunities, as well as *de facto* equality, and thereby increasing participation and inclusion in mainstream society. The accommodation duty brings a redistributive element into the non-discrimination norm under the CRPD. Finally, it has been illustrated in chapter three of this book that there is no absolute duty on the face of the Convention for States to take positive action measures. However, Article 5(4) of the CPRD clearly legitimates such measures and, indeed, the interpretation of Article 5(4) which has been presented in chapter three establishes that States must take temporary or permanent positive action measures whenever the circumstances so require in order to accelerate or achieve *de facto* equality for persons with disabilities. Positive action can be linked intrinsically to the substantive equality paradigm to the extent that it seeks to increase participation and inclusion in the mainstream by targeting historical and ongoing unequal power relations between persons with disabilities and their non-disabled counterparts. Overall, Article 5 of the CRPD does not merely enunciate a hazy notion of substantive equality. Rather, it underscores its vision of substantive equality with positive measures aimed at accelerating the concrete fulfilment of the principle of equality in the context of persons with disabilities.

The CRPD also goes beyond a pure substantive equality model to endorse a transformative equality model. This finding was underlined by the fact that the Convention's overall mandate seeks to target deep-rooted structural inequalities, systemic prejudices and institutional biases. The provisions of the CRPD on the whole aim at ensuring a reallocation of resources in favour of persons with disabilities. They are designed to guarantee empowerment of disabled people and to foster their inherent abilities in order that persons with disabilities can participate and be included fully in mainstream society on an equal basis with others. The transformative model of equality can be seen quite clearly by means of the CRPD's accessibility obligations, its universal design provisions and its awareness-raising duties, as well as in the Convention's application of the equality norm (via the reasonable accommodation duty) to each of the substantive rights contained in the Convention, particularly socio-economic rights. The transformative model of equality in the CRPD is underpinned by its social-contextual understanding of disability and its human-rights based approach to disability. These far-reaching models of disability aim at creating inclusive structures and ensuring that persons with disabilities are provided with the material support necessary to achieve equality in fact, thereby reaching their full potential and capabilities. The CRPD's endorsement of the social model of disability has resulted in the reconfiguration of the equality norm for persons with disabilities – it acknowledges that the full and effective participation and inclusion of people with disabilities can only be achieved through the realisation of a barrier-free society.

The understanding of the equality norm has evolved greatly in recent years, both at the level of international human rights law and in the disability context, from embodying a formal model of equality to endorsing a more substantive and even transformative conception of equality. Oddný Mjöll Arnardóttir highlights the fact that in the era of 'universal sameness,'[2] there was no accommodation for difference. The open-ended non-discrimination provisions and the universal equality norm applied to everyone in the same manner, regardless of difference. This is evidenced by such instruments as the ICCPR and the ICESCR. Over time, international human rights law began gradually to recognise differential characteristics in the quest for true equality. The next era that can be detected at the level of international human rights law has been termed the 'specific difference'[3] equality era. The substantive difference model of equality, which is characteristic of that era, forms the basis of the non-discrimination provisions in both CERD and CEDAW.[4] Those two treaties view discrimination based on specific identity markers or biological and immutable

2 O.M. Arnardóttir, 'A Future of Multidimensional Disadvantage Equality' in O.M. Arnardóttir and G. Quinn, *The UN Convention on the Rights of Persons with Disabilities: European and Scandinavian Perspectives* (Martinus Nijhoff, Leiden, 2009), at page 47.

3 Ibid, at page 49.

4 Ibid.

characteristics as worthy of special attention, but only in certain circumstances. Both treaties incorporate the notion of indirect discrimination in their non-discrimination clauses and they also permit the adoption of special measures or positive action wherever necessary. However, the focus under the specific difference era remained with differential characteristics rather than with wider disadvantage in mainstream society. Before the CRPD, the emphasis was largely on differential characteristics as an exception to the rule of equal treatment. The CRPD can be deemed to represent the culmination of previous steps in the direction of substantive and transformative models of equality. Oddný Mjöll Arnardóttir characterises the era culminating with the adoption of the CRPD as embracing 'multidimensional disadvantage'[5] equality. The substantive disadvantage model of equality underlying the CRPD displays a true understanding of structural inequalities. It mandates that legal mechanisms no longer look to differential characteristics but rather to the broader structural disadvantage encountered by persons with disabilities in society. The substantive disadvantage model advocates legal tools such as indirect discrimination, positive action, reasonable accommodations and other positive measures as integral means by which to eradicate barriers which maintain or perpetuate disadvantage. As outlined in chapter three of this book, the CRPD strengthens the non-discrimination norm in many respects. The inclusion of the duty to accommodate within the non-discrimination provision guarantees an individualised application of the equality paradigm and has increased the potential for ensuring *de facto* equality. The CRPD recognises the fact that the universal equality norm must be tailored to the specific needs of disabled people. It breathes new life into the Convention's guarantees in accordance with the lived realities of disabled people. Furthermore, the CRPD adopts a contextual approach to equality – it seeks to target asymmetrical structures of disadvantage and oppression and shifts the target of non-discrimination laws to deeply unequal structures in society. Finally, the CRPD embraces a multidimensional or intersectional approach to non-discrimination, recognising the fact that discrimination arising from a number of grounds in combination produces a unique discriminatory experience for the individual concerned. In that regard, the CRPD goes further than the other core human rights treaties, which do not mention multiple or intersectional discrimination explicitly within their text.

The CRPD certainly goes beyond any of the other core human rights treaties in seeking to ensure a transformative approach to equality. While Article 5(a) CEDAW requires States to take all appropriate measures to eliminate prejudices, as well as customary and other practices which are based on the idea of the inferiority or the superiority of either of the sexes or on stereotyped roles for men and women, the CRPD requires States to target, in addition, all socially constructed barriers which hinder *de facto* equality and full and effective participation and inclusion in society for disabled people. It is clear that this will require the adoption of a wide variety of positive measures in all spheres of society and a significant reallocation of resources to ensure equality of opportunity and equality in fact. On the basis of the foregoing, there is no doubt that the CRPD holds enormous promise for the future application

[5] Ibid.

of the equality and non-discrimination norms in relation to the rights of persons with disabilities. Among other things, it is hoped that the interaction of the equality norm and socio-economic rights in the Convention may provide the key to unlocking the structural inequalities faced by disabled people, in order to bring them fully into the mainstream. Notwithstanding this, the realisation of *de facto* equality for persons with disabilities will be a significant challenge for many States, not only on account of obvious resource and institutional constraints, but also because the Convention requires widespread attitudinal change regarding the inherent capabilities of persons with disabilities and the potential contribution which they can make in mainstream society.

2.3.3. Lessons Drawn from the Outer Limits of the Duty to Accommodate

After having analysed the theoretical and comparative framework within which the Convention's equality norm operates, chapter four of this book examined a specific component of the equality norm, namely the duty to accommodate persons with disabilities. The sub-research question to be answered in that regard was as follows: What are the outer limits of the duty to accommodate? More precisely, whether the balancing and sharing of interests and burdens inherent in the accommodation duty (namely, the fact that the covered party is obliged to accommodate the needs of a disabled individual, unless this would amount to a disproportionate burden for the entity concerned) can teach us lessons about the overall balancing of burdens and interests implicit in many Convention rights subject to progressive realisation?

Three principal lessons were drawn from an examination of the outer limits of the duty to accommodate. The first of these is that any requested accommodation must be necessary and appropriate in the circumstances of a particular, individualised case. Translating the concept of necessity to the context of progressive realisation, this implies that States will be required to take all essential measures towards ensuring that persons with disabilities can begin to enjoy CRPD rights and towards ensuring the full realisation over time of CRPD rights. The criterion of appropriateness translates to the requirement that measures taken by States must be effective in allowing the disabled person in question to participate in the required activity and in contributing towards realisation of the substantive rights and obligations contained in the CRPD. Linked to the notion of effectiveness of measures is the concept of human dignity and the equality norm. The duty to accommodate is based on the core values of human dignity and respect for difference. These values, taken together with a consideration of the object and purpose of the duty to accommodate (the promotion of equality and the elimination of discrimination), will be essential to any determination of whether measures taken by private entities or States are effective. The third lesson drawn from the outer limits of the duty to accommodate rests on an underlying proportionality test. That test endeavours to balance the rights of, and burdens and benefits to, all persons affected by the proposed accommodation. Burdens or costs will not be merely financial in nature but will also extend to a consideration of the level of difficulty for a particular entity in terms, for instance, of the manner in which the accommodation affects the entity's business. It was also argued that third-party benefits should be considered in the provision of accommodations under the CRPD. In deciding whether a measure constitutes a disproportionate burden for an entity, regard should be had to the manner in which a requested accommodation has knock-on effects, not only for the entity concerned, but also for other individuals, such as individuals with comparative disabilities or potentially even consumers of an entity. All of these elements of the duty to accommodate have the potential to map over to the context of progressive realisation. In a similar vein to the accommodation duty, the realisation of the Convention's substantive rights and obligations is characterised by an implicit balancing of burdens and interests between the duty-bearer and the rights-holder. In order to ensure an appropriate balancing of needs and interests between States (and entities), on the one hand, and disabled individuals, on the other hand, it is necessary to place a normative framework around the progressive realisation of CRPD rights, both in terms of resource allocation and programme and policy design. Chapter five of this book put forward such a framework of review, incorporating many of the criteria outlined above into that framework.

2.3.4. A Proposed Framework for the Progressive Realisation of Rights in the CRPD

In chapter five of this book the outer limits of the concept of progressive realisation were highlighted and various criteria were put forward, which can potentially be used to assess the measures adopted by States within those outer limits. In a similar vein to some of the outer limits of the duty to accommodate (which apply to entities), the outer limits of the progressive realisation norm will be adjudicated on by the CRPD Committee in accordance with the resources available to States, as well as priorities set by national authorities, among other considerations. In that regard, the Committee will be tasked with assessing State action or inaction based, not only on the needs of persons with disabilities, but also in light of resource and institutional or capacity constraints in a given State. The Committee must acknowledge the fact that the needs and interests of others, including other marginalised groups in society, will be a relevant consideration for national authorities when they allocate resources. It was argued in chapter five of this book that the measures adopted by States within available resources should be adjudged according to their reasonableness. Accordingly, several frameworks of reasonableness review at the national and international levels were explored – specifically, the criteria adopted under South African Constitutional jurisprudence and the emerging notion of reasonableness review envisaged under the OP-ICESCR. The sub-research question in that regard was as follows: What are the criteria inherent in already existing frameworks of reasonableness review and how can those criteria be tailored to the specific context of the CRPD in order to advance its equality paradigm? It was argued in chapter five that the types of criteria inherent in already existing frameworks of reasonableness review would fit well in the assessment of measures taken by States to fulfil their obligations under the CRPD. By virtue of the fact that the socio-economic provisions in the CRPD are linked intrinsically to the equality norm via the duty to accommodate, the outer limits of that duty were drawn on in order to inject an additional equality dimension into the review of CRPD rights realisation. In sum, the research outcomes were as follows:

In realising disability rights progressively, national authorities are required to adopt all necessary measures to give effect, at the very least, to the minimum core of the right(s) in question in order to ensure that the basic needs and capabilities of persons with disabilities are catered for. States are also required to take essential measures to ensure that the totality of CRPD rights will be realised in the fullness of time. In line with the criterion of effectiveness, any steps adopted by governments to realise progressively CRPD rights must produce tangible outcomes, which are compatible with the requirements of the Convention. States must also ensure that the least restrictive measures are put in place to facilitate the realisation of socio-economic rights. In deciding whether measures taken by States are in compliance with the Convention, the CRPD Committee must balance cost-related factors against many other considerations. States will make policy choices regarding priority-setting in their own national contexts. This raises very difficult issues, to which there is no definitive solution. Nonetheless, it was argued in chapter five of this book that the types of policy choices made by States must be justified and thereafter judged according to their reasonableness. In spite of the resource and institutional constraints weighing on national authorities, there is a duty incumbent on those authorities to utilise whatever resources and capacity they have in a manner which accords a sufficient degree of priority to the values underlying the Convention as a whole. The Committee's review framework must be grounded in the normative content of the right(s) at issue (including the minimum core), together with an analysis of the broader object and purpose of the Convention. Minimum thresholds for assessment of socio-economic rights are important, but not sufficient on their own, to guarantee the full and effective realisation of the rights of disadvantaged groups, such as persons with disabilities. As such, it was argued in chapter five that equality should be a paramount consideration in any framework of reasonableness review, as the CRPD links States' obligations to eliminate disability discrimination with guarantees for the full realisation of socio-economic rights. Incorporating equality into a review framework under the CRPD would serve to ensure that States Parties to the Convention put forward heightened justifications for any alleged rights violations and to overturn the entrenchment of inequalities or marginalisation for persons with disabilities. An approach to socio-economic rights adjudication based on equality would bolster the human-rights based approach to disability which underlies the Convention as a whole and would seek to avoid the misguided stereotypes which exist regarding the capabilities of disabled persons.

Another related criterion that will be important in any assessment of socio-economic rights under the CRPD is the underlying core norm of the inherent dignity of persons with disabilities. The research conducted for chapter five of this book provided counter-arguments against criticisms of the use of human dignity as a normative guide to human rights implementation. Moreover, it was contended in chapter five that there are two strands to the concept of human dignity that have particular relevance to the CRPD. The first of these requires that consideration be given to the urgency of needs of different groups. States must respond accordingly to ensure that those urgent needs are catered for. The second of these involves an alignment with the equality norm and requires consideration of the equal worth of all human beings. It involves treatment as an equal. In the context of the CRPD, dignity considerations must be examined relative to both strands of human dignity. The needs of disabled persons who are in most dire circumstances must be catered for first and foremost. Once this basic level of provision has been satisfied, dignity should feature thereafter as an equality concern, whereby the full realisation of socio-economic rights under the CRPD takes account of the equal worth of persons with disabilities and their entitlement to enjoy rights on an equal basis with others. Of course, national authorities will not have limitless resources to spend on disability rights and therefore the Committee will be required to balance the right to equality and also dignity considerations against an assessment of costs in order to determine if particular measures constitute a disproportionate burden on States. Having said that, it is important to bear in mind that the equality norm (including dignity considerations) is a vital means by which systemic disadvantage can be addressed in the context of socio-economic rights enjoyment for persons with disabilities and this must also factor in the Committee's balancing act.

In the overall assessment of what constitutes a disproportionate burden on States, the CRPD Committee will have to ask whether national authorities have used all powers at their disposal to ensure resource prioritisation and resource optimisation, including through international assistance. In that connection, the Committee must ensure that States do not act in a discriminatory or arbitrary manner. States must ensure that any resources they have are used efficiently in order to implement fully (within available resources) disability rights, as well as the rights of all marginalised groups in society. In addition to the foregoing, the Committee should look to the impact of failure to take measures in implementing socio-economic rights for persons with disabilities. Thus, for instance, if a failure to take measures in one context leads to depriving persons with disabilities of what may be essential to enable them to enjoy other rights vested in them under the Convention, this may be a relevant factor in the CRPD Committee's assessment of the reasonableness of State measures. Participatory processes will also be essential to ensure accountability in the implementation of Convention rights. In deciding on priorities in realising socio-economic rights in the context of limited resources, input from disabled persons organisations and civil society groups will be vital in determining the greatest needs of citizens. It will also facilitate the effective implementation of rights, by identifying the measures that are most suited to the realisation of rights in various contexts.

Another potentially relevant (albeit tangential) consideration is the issue of third-party benefits. This may be a difficult criterion for the CRPD Committee to factor into its assessment of State measures. Nonetheless, it is arguable that measures taken by States to ensure compliance with the Convention may result in benefits to other individuals with similar impairments or even to a wider cohort of individuals than persons with disabilities. This may be a relevant consideration in weighing up the burden imposed by particular measures on governments (taking into account the various interests at stake).

After having explored the concept of progressive realisation of disability rights generally, the relationship between the CRPD's equality provisions and certain substantive rights and obligations in the Convention which are subject to progressive realisation was traced, namely the accessibility obligation and the right to education. In that section of the research, the following sub-research questions were answered:

i. What kind of criteria might be applied to determine the reasonableness of State action or inaction in the context of the accessibility obligation and the right to education?; and
ii. Can the Convention's equality paradigm advance the realisation of socio-economic rights for persons with disabilities?

2.3.5. The Interrelationship between the Accessibility Obligation and the Equality Norm

In chapter six of this book the link between the CRPD's accessibility obligation (contained in Article 9) and the equality and non-discrimination norms in the Convention was delineated, including the overlaps and key differences between the two. After having deliberated on the normative content of the accessibility obligation and States' obligations in that regard, the various criteria outlined in chapter five of this book as being pertinent to the assessment by the CRPD Committee of the reasonableness of State measures were applied to Article 9 implementation.

In light of the fact that Article 9 is a resource-intensive obligation, the CRPD Committee will have to consider the issue of what constitutes a disproportionate burden for a particular State. National authorities will be required to justify their policy choices to the Committee, which will have to ask itself whether such authorities have taken measures that ensure the most cost-effective implementation of Article 9 by, for instance, considering accessibility issues at the beginning of the design of products, services and buildings. If States have not taken reasonable cost-effective measures (not imposing a disproportionate burden), this may lead to a finding by the Committee of a potential violation of Convention obligations. Of course, not all measures required to ensure disability accessibility will, by definition, be cost-effective (especially those taken to retrofit facilities or infrastructure). In that regard, the Committee should investigate whether States have ensured an optimal use of (limited) resources targeted at realising disability accessibility and whether they have prioritised resources in that regard. If a given State has not done so, this may lead to a finding by the Committee that the State has not taken all reasonable measures to implement CRPD rights. A further relevant consideration is whether States have consulted closely with and involved persons with disabilities in all aspects of implementation of disability accessibility. This will allow a determination of whether States have adopted measures which are most effective and least restrictive of the rights of persons with disabilities. To that end, disabled persons and their representative organisations should be consulted closely in the development of products, services and facilities, as well as in the development, promulgation and monitoring of minimum standards for the accessibility of different facilities and services provided by public and private enterprises. In the overall assessment of whether measures impose a disproportionate burden on a State, the Committee may evaluate the extent to which particular accessibility measures would have benefits to a wider cohort of individuals, beyond disabled persons, and thereby the extent to which such measures contribute to the Convention's universal design provisions.

One of the primary factors that should feature in the CRPD Committee's assessments is that of equality. As always, equality arguments must be balanced with the notion of disproportionate burden. In that vein, one must acknowledge the impact of limited resources and respect the sovereignty of a State to make appropriate choices in its national context. Notwithstanding this, the Convention clearly mandates accessibility of the environment, structures, and so forth, for disabled persons on an equal basis with others. Thus, the Committee will have to judge whether, in setting priorities, States have had regard to the extent to which measures adopted by them to ensure accessibility will actually contribute to achieving the overall goals of equalising opportunities and outcomes for persons with disabilities. A fundamental premise of accessibility measures adopted by States is that persons with disabilities should be guaranteed equivalent or functionally equivalent access to non-disabled people. Closely related to equality issues is the fact that disabled people should not be required to use or access goods, services, infrastructure or other facilities in a manner which compromises their human dignity. States should therefore ensure consideration of dignity interests in all aspects of the implementation and monitoring of Article 9, including in the design of accessibility standards.

There is no doubt that the equality and non-discrimination norms in the CRPD are closely linked to the accessibility obligation. By applying equality and dignity considerations as key criteria in the implementation of Article 9, this can serve to ensure that disabled people are treated as true equals in the enjoyment of socio-economic rights. States must therefore ensure effective implementation of both Article 5 and Article 9 of the Convention in tandem. Guarantees of equality and non-discrimination should be interpreted by national judicial authorities in a manner which facilitates and promotes the Convention's accessibility requirements.

2.3.6. The Right to Education for Persons with Disabilities

Chapter seven of this book examined the right to education for persons with disabilities, as contained in Article 24 of the CRPD. That chapter related to the overall theme underlying the book as a whole, namely the advancement of *de facto* equality by means of increased participation and inclusion in society of persons with disabilities. In that vein, the meaning of equality in the context of the right to education was elaborated on and the potential value which the equality and non-discrimination norms in the CRPD can add to the right to education for persons with disabilities was teased out. In addition, several criteria were highlighted, which may be employed by the CRPD Committee in assessing compliance with Article 24.

In the first instance, attention was drawn to the fact that the costs of providing inclusive education will be an obvious factor to be taken into account by the CRPD Committee in its assessment of State action or inaction. In that regard, it is noteworthy that inclusive education is often mistakenly viewed as being prohibitively costly. However, research has highlighted the fact that many positive educational measures are not very expensive. Indeed, it was shown in chapter seven of this book that inclusive educational settings are generally less expensive than segregated systems when appropriately implemented and that maintaining segregated educational systems is costly. Nonetheless, resource implications will be a concern for many States in implementing Article 24 of the CRPD, particularly developing States. The transformation of special educational systems into fully inclusive systems may incur significant outlays in terms of resources (both human and financial), at least in the transitional phase. On the other hand, the CRPD Committee must bear in mind the fact that the cost benefits of inclusive education are assured in the long term and that the implementation of inclusive education can assist in the realisation of the right to education for non-disabled children also in certain circumstances. The Committee will be required to assess whether States are ensuring an efficient and effective use of existing resources (including resources that are being poured into special educational systems), as those resources can potentially be harnessed to assist the mainstream provision of education. It will be particularly important to ensure rights-based and performance-based budgeting in order to identify the areas where existing resources can be more efficiently targeted to implement the right to inclusive education, among other rights, for persons with disabilities.

As with all other rights contained in the Convention, the non-discrimination and equality provisions are of paramount importance in implementing Article 24 of the CRPD. In many cases, access to mainstream education is being hindered for a large proportion of disabled individuals who are being placed in segregated educational settings. Ensuring access to inclusive education and equal educational opportunities for disabled people will involve fundamental changes in physical structures and facilities, educational curricula and in the processes of learning, in order to accommodate different learning styles and means of communication. In tandem with equality considerations, dignity concerns will be paramount to the CRPD Committee's assessment of the measures taken by States to ensure implementation of Article 24 of the CRPD. One of the main challenges which lies ahead for States in the implementation of the right to inclusive education is the elimination of discrimination and stigmatisation of the capabilities of persons with disabilities in terms of learning outcomes and so forth. Under the CRPD, States must undertake awareness-raising campaigns and persons with disabilities must be given the material support to ensure that their inherent potential is allowed to develop in education, as in all other areas.

According to Article 24, any support provided within mainstream education must facilitate the effective education of disabled persons. States should conduct research into the effectiveness of current inclusive education policies. The CRPD Committee should keep a close watch on the collection of data and the establishment of national educational benchmarks and indicators. These will allow States Parties to the CRPD to monitor the effectiveness of measures taken in the realisation of the right to education for persons with disabilities. In order to ensure enjoyment of the right to education for disabled persons on a truly equal basis as others, their input, through participatory processes, is vital as this is the key to unlocking structural inequalities which have hindered the right to inclusive education for far too long now.

On the basis of all of the above, it is abundantly clear that the Convention's equality and non-discrimination norms have huge potential to impact on the implementation of socio-economic rights for persons with disabilities. However, this potential must be realised through the application of defined and equitable criteria to the rights and obligations contained in the Convention.

2.3.7. The Influence of the CRPD on Council of Europe Disability Law and Policy

The final part of this research entailed a case study on the Council of Europe. The first part of that case study related to the influence to date, and the potential influence, of the CRPD on the disability equality case law of the ECtHR. The sub-research question answered in that regard was as follows: Is the Strasbourg Court evidencing a shift in its approach to disability equality on foot of the entry into force of the Convention, in terms of adopting a more substantive model of equality, signalled by such indicators as *de facto* reasonable accommodation duties and a social model of disability? Based on the outcomes of the first part of the case study, the research conducted in chapter eight of this book reflected on the influence which the CRPD might have in the future on the interpretation by the Strasbourg Court of the provisions contained in the ECHR. In the second part of the case study, the provisions of the Revised European Social Charter were considered, as well as the views of the ECSR and the general disability policy of the Council of Europe. The sub-research question addressed in that connection was as follows: What influence is the CRPD having on those Council of Europe legal and policy mechanisms?

The CRPD is exerting some degree of influence on the relevant organs in the Council of Europe. However, the extent of its impact varies quite considerably between the various legal and policy mechanisms. The CRPD is certainly guiding the general direction of disability policy through the recommendations and issue papers of the Committee of Ministers. Those non-binding instruments are drawing quite heavily on relevant elements from the substantive provisions of the CRPD as an interpretative guide for Member States in their implementation of disability rights. Many of the instruments adopt the fundamental values and principles underlying the Convention, particularly in relation to equality/non-discrimination and inclusion in society for persons with disabilities. Many of the documents also draw specific guidance from the concrete provisions of the Convention in formulating recommendations and suggestions to be employed by Member States in their implementation of disability rights.

In terms of tangible effects of the CRPD on the case law of the ECtHR, the Strasbourg Court has cited the Convention on numerous occasions in the context of relevant international law. However, the Court is not always consistent in referring to the Convention and the reasons for its failure to refer to the CRPD are not always clear from one case to another. One can only surmise that the Court is not quite sure of the relevance of CRPD provisions to ECHR rights. Notwithstanding the Court's inconsistent approach, the CRPD appears to be having some positive influence on judgments of the ECtHR with regard to disability discrimination and also on the standard of scrutiny adopted by the Court. It was shown in chapter eight of this book that the Court has included some form of implicit duty to accommodate within Article 14 and has begun to incorporate a social-contextual or social model reasoning in certain selected judgments. It has also referred to the CRPD as an example of a European and worldwide consensus on the need to protect people with disabilities from discriminatory treatment. In addition, the ECtHR has demonstrated an increased awareness of the impact of historical discrimination on persons with disabilities and links this to the applicable margin of appreciation of States. On the other hand, the Court has not yet recognised an explicit right to be accommodated under Article 14 as an essential means of ensuring disability equality in the enjoyment of ECHR rights. It is hoped that the social-contextual approach which the Court is beginning to adopt, together with the evolutive interpretative approach which it professes to employ will play a greater role in the future. In light of the fact that the majority of Member States of the Council of Europe are also party to the CRPD and will, thus, be incorporating reasonable accommodation duties into their national legislative frameworks (where they have not already done so), this might encourage the Court to recognise the substantive disadvantage experienced by persons with disabilities in society and to incorporate this into its analysis of ECHR rights.

Not many disability-related collective complaints have been taken before the ECSR since the coming into force of the CRPD. Therefore, it is difficult to measure the Convention's impact or potential impact in that respect. To date, the ECSR is referring to the CRPD in the context of relevant international law but the Convention has not actually had a concrete influence on the Committee's reasoning. Nonetheless, the provisions of the revised Charter overlap, to a large degree, with many substantive rights contained in the CRPD, including the right to education and the right to independent living. It was argued in chapter eight of this book that the education line of case law appears to provide most scope for the interpretation of rights under the revised Charter in a manner which is compatible with the CRPD.

It is evident that there will be significant challenges ahead in translating the progressive approach to equality contained in the CRPD into legislation and policy at the European level and, specifically, in the Council of Europe. In particular, the process of change will be a slow and arduous one at the level of the judicial system, especially in the ECtHR. There will also be many barriers ahead for persons with disabilities in their efforts to turn the aspirations of the Convention into individually justiciable rights. In spite of the challenges inherent in the process of change, the CRPD still holds great promise for the future application of the equality and non-discrimination norms, provided of course that this potential is realised and utilised by policy-makers and the judiciary.

3. Main Recommendations

3.1. Recommendations for the CRPD Committee

The ultimate role of the CRPD Committee is to oversee implementation of the CRPD and to elaborate on the obligations of States as contained in the Convention. The Committee will be required to determine if national authorities are living up to their commitments under the Convention. In that regard, it will have to delineate set criteria for assessing State action or inaction in the progressive realisation of the rights and obligations under the Convention. The Committee must be realistic in its assessments. All States will have an obligation to ensure the fulfilment of the rights of all marginalised groups and therefore the Committee must, in assessing cost considerations and, in particular, the issue of disproportionate burden, take account of the fact that there are many different constraints (both resource and institutional) on a given country's resources.

Throughout this book, it has been argued that the CRPD Committee should be particularly mindful of the equality and non-discrimination norms contained in the Convention in any assessment which it makes regarding implementation of the substantive rights and obligations in the CRPD. If the Committee ensures that equality is a key criterion in its assessments, this should help to tackle multidimensional disadvantage in the exercise of socio-economic rights for persons with disabilities. The Committee will be required to ensure that States take many active measures to promote *de facto* equality and, thereby, contribute towards increasing participation and inclusion of persons with disabilities in society. To ensure the realisation of this objective, the Committee should merge considerations of individual rights violations with broader issues of socio-economic inequalities, particularly where the claim has as its objective the achievement of tangible positive benefits, when compared with the prevention of negative deprivations of rights.

The Committee should approach its assessment of State measures from the perspective of informed adjudication. States Parties to the CRPD will play a vital role in providing the Committee with transparent, objective and reliable evidence of the wider contextual factors which led to decision-making in any given case, including competing claims on resources and institutional limitations. States must justify the measures taken by them, in accordance with defined and realistic criteria set by the Committee. The most important task that the CRPD Committee has is to ground its assessments in the normative content of the right or rights at issue, while at the same time explicating the values which underlie Convention rights and which guide implementation of those rights – *inter alia*, the equality and non-discrimination norms, full and effective participation and inclusion for persons with disabilities and the core norm of the inherent dignity of disabled persons.

3.2. Recommendations at the National Level (EU and beyond)

There is much work to be done at the national level in order to bring States' laws and policies in line with their obligations under the CRPD. States Parties to the Convention will have to consider the impact of the CRPD's progressive equality and non-discrimination provisions when enacting reforms of existing legislation and policies. For instance, national authorities will have to incorporate the expansive understanding of disability-based discrimination contained in the CRPD for all individuals who are not protected by non-discrimination statutes at present. National laws and policies must be expanded in order to ensure that the prohibition of disability-based discrimination is broad enough to cover multiple disabilities, perceived disability and discrimination by association with a disabled person. States should ensure that the prohibition of discrimination on the basis of disability under the CRPD is included not only in general non-discrimination laws, but in all laws governing the substantive rights of persons with disabilities, such as in laws governing education, health, transport and electoral procedures, among others.

States would be well advised to ensure that sufficient consideration is given to equality matters in the adoption of action plans and strategies to identify existing barriers which affect the exercise and enjoyment of rights by persons with disabilities on an equal basis with others. National authorities must establish fixed time frames for the removal of existing barriers to equality and they must allocate sufficient financial and other resources in order to ensure implementation of the substantive rights and obligations contained in the Convention. National authorities must also set up mechanisms to ensure that the right to non-discrimination is monitored effectively by appropriate indicators and benchmarks. In addition, the equality and non-discrimination norms must be considered carefully in the implementation of each and every one of the substantive rights in the Convention, particularly the accessibility obligation, which is so fundamental in ensuring increased participation and inclusion of persons with disabilities in society. Finally, at EU Member State level, it is vital that the provisions of the Employment Equality Directive are interpreted consistently with the CRPD. The Directive is not explicit in recognising a failure to provide a reasonable accommodation as a form of discrimination, unlike the CRPD. At Member State level, those States that have ratified the CRPD should ensure that their national laws define a failure to reasonably accommodate as a form of discrimination (where they have not done so already).

3.3. Recommendations for the Council of Europe Mechanisms

The primary recommendation which emerges from the case study conducted on the Council of Europe concerns the manner in which the Council mechanisms are interpreting disability rights at present. The policy mechanisms of the Council of Europe are showing a marked tendency to draw on and incorporate the spirit and tenor, and substantive rights of the CRPD, into their policy documents. On the other hand, the Council of Europe's main judicial and quasi-judicial organs – the ECtHR and the ECSR – have yet to open up fully to the provisions of the CRPD to guide their interpretation of disability rights.

The CRPD bears clear relevance to the interpretation of the rights of persons with disabilities in the Council of Europe, particularly in light of the fact that the majority of Council of Europe Member States are also party to the CRPD. In order to ensure consistency and legal certainty, it would be advisable that all of the Council's judicial/quasi-judicial organs would take the spirit and tenor of the CRPD fully into account in their interpretation of disability rights. Of course, it is evident why the ECSR should take the provisions of the CRPD into account – the revised Charter is, after all, a social rights treaty with specific provisions aimed at protecting persons with disabilities. On the other hand, one might question why the ECtHR should concern itself with disability as a matter of equality and human rights. The answer to that is simple – the provisions of the ECHR apply to disabled people to the same extent as they apply to any other marginalised group. In order to ensure the exercise and enjoyment of rights for persons with disabilities on an equal basis with others, differential treatment is often required. The Strasbourg Court should take more cognisance of reasonable accommodation duties as a means to ensure the exercise of Article 14 ECHR for persons with disabilities on an equal basis with others. The Court should have further regard to the contextual and asymmetrical model of equality contained in the CRPD and it should scrutinise alleged violations of disability rights more closely, in particular by examining alleged violations under Article 14, where appropriate.

There is increased scope for disability rights to be mainstreamed to a greater extent within judicial decision-making in the Council of Europe, particularly in light of the fact that the Council of Europe's own Action Plan on Disability urges the mainstreaming of disability in Member States. The Strasbourg Court should also place more emphasis on the social construction of disability in its analysis of ECHR rights. This would serve to facilitate a mainstreaming approach to disability. Such an approach would enable the Court to move closer to the substantive disadvantage model of equality by uncovering the manner in which disadvantage is maintained and perpetuated in the disability context. Again this is a tentative recommendation and it is important to guard against too much optimism in that regard, particularly in light of the slow pace of change at the level of the ECtHR.

4. Concluding Remarks

The research carried out for this book has demonstrated the fact that the human rights of persons with disabilities have evolved significantly at the international level in recent decades. The evolving interpretation of the equality and non-discrimination norms in international human rights law has also been traced. These changes foreshadowed the adoption of the CRPD, which represents the most comprehensive legal framework for the protection of the rights of persons with disabilities. The path towards the adoption of the Convention was long and arduous. The many challenges and impediments encountered along the way, in seeking to ensure an integral framework for the protection of disability rights, did not end upon the adoption of the CRPD. While the equality and non-discrimination norms in the CRPD are extremely progressive and have the potential to effect real change in practice, structural barriers to reform exist, particularly at the level of judicial decision-making, but also at the level of policy-making at both the national and the European level. In order for the provisions of the Convention to come alive, such barriers must be eradicated. The substantive rights and obligations contained in the CRPD must be translated into practical strategies to achieve true reform for persons with disabilities. It is hoped that this reform will reach into the everyday lives of disabled individuals, slowly but surely.

The full enjoyment of human rights for disabled people will be realised progressively by States Parties to the CRPD. Nonetheless, the obligation to ensure non-discrimination in the exercise of Convention rights is an obligation of immediate effect. Its application, via the accommodation duty, to the socio-economic rights in the Convention may provide the key to unlocking part of the substantive disadvantage encountered by persons with disabilities in their everyday lives. Amartya Sen argues that 'equal consideration for all may demand very unequal treatment in favour of the disadvantaged'[6] and, furthermore, that 'the demands of substantive equality can be particularly exacting and complex when there is a good deal of antecedent inequality to counter.'[7] This rings true in the context of persons with disabilities. Of course, the situation is even more complex when one factors in the impairment dimension in ensuring full and effective participation and inclusion in society on an equal basis with others. The substantive and transformative approach to equality forms the backbone of the CRPD and the implementation of the equality and non-discrimination norms must be assured as a matter of priority by States Parties to the Convention.

Without a doubt, the CRPD represents a bright light at the end of a long and winding road, paved with discrimination and marginalisation. The CRPD provides renewed hope for disabled persons everywhere that full and effective participation and inclusion in mainstream society is a golden promise within their reach. In spite of the many challenges and stumbling blocks that we will encounter on the homeward journey of implementation of the Convention, let us hold strongly to the hope that this golden promise will come to pass.

6 A. Sen, *Inequality Re-examined* (Oxford University Press 1992) 1.
7 Ibid.

Summary in English

The research conducted for this book has been triggered by the establishment of the DREAM (Disability Rights Expanding Accessible Markets) network of research, which had as its primary objective to educate the next generation of disability entrepreneurs and to take the norms of the CRPD out of their theoretical box to promote substantive change for persons with disabilities in practice.

This book examines several aspects of the equality and non-discrimination norms in the CRPD. In the first instance, this book provides an interpretation and critical analysis of the legal meaning of the principles of equality and non-discrimination in the context of the CRPD. It analyses the extent to which the concepts of equality and non-discrimination contained in the Convention fit within the various theoretical models of disability and conceptions of equality that have been elaborated to date by scholars and compares the theoretical framework of equality in the CRPD to that contained in other international human rights treaties which preceded the Convention. The aim of that interpretation is both to tease out States' obligations under the Convention and to facilitate a demonstration of how the non-discrimination tool contained in the CRPD can potentially be leveraged to promote lasting reforms and true equality for people with disabilities. A particular focus throughout this book is on the manner in which the equality and non-discrimination norms in the CRPD can increase participation and inclusion in society of persons with disabilities. This book also examines in detail an integral component of the equality norm under the CRPD, namely the duty to reasonably accommodate persons with disabilities and, in particular, its outer limits. In that regard, the research conducted for this book analyses whether the balancing and sharing of burdens inherent in the accommodation duty (namely, the fact that the covered party is obliged to accommodate the needs of a disabled individual, unless that would amount to a disproportionate burden for the entity concerned) can teach us lessons about the overall balancing of burdens and interests implicit in many Convention rights subject to progressive realisation? Following on from that, this book devises a framework for review of measures taken by States in the overall context of the progressive realisation of disability rights, with a particular emphasis on how the CRPD's equality norm might strengthen the realisation of socio-economic rights for disabled people. That framework of review criteria is then applied to the right to education and the accessibility obligation incumbent on States under the CRPD. Finally, this book investigates how the equality and non-discrimination norms in the Convention have already influenced, and can potentially influence, the crucial shape of disability equality case law and policy. It identifies the challenges which lie ahead in the implementation of the Convention. In that connection, a case study is carried out on the Council of Europe mechanisms, in order to assess whether the CRPD is having an influence on disability law and policy at the regional level. This facilitates an analysis of whether the equality and non-discrimination norms in the CRPD can be used to expand disability discrimination claims in the Council of Europe.

Interpretation of the Equality and Non-Discrimination Norms in the CRPD

The non-discrimination norm in the CRPD can be described as embodying substantive and transformative models of equality. The substantive model of equality seeks to target covert forms of discrimination, as well as ensuring that differential characteristics are accommodated within the equality norm. In particular, the duty to accommodate under the Convention consolidates the substantive approach to equality, imposing an obligation on States to take positive measures to ensure that entities provide reasonable accommodations to disabled people, with a view to increasing equality of opportunities, as well as *de facto* equality. The accommodation duty brings a redistributive element into the non-discrimination norm under the CRPD. In addition, the legitimation of temporary and permanent positive action under the CPRD seeks to accelerate and achieve *de facto* equality for persons with disabilities. Positive action can be linked intrinsically to the substantive equality paradigm by virtue of the fact that it seeks to increase participation and inclusion in the mainstream by targeting historical and ongoing unequal power relations between persons with disabilities and their non-disabled counterparts. Overall, the CRPD underscores its vision of substantive equality with positive measures aimed at accelerating the concrete fulfilment of the principle of equality in the context of persons with disabilities.

The CRPD goes beyond a pure substantive equality model to endorse a transformative equality model. The Convention's overall mandate seeks to target deep-rooted structural inequalities, systemic prejudices and institutional biases. The provisions of the CRPD on the whole aim at ensuring a reallocation of resources in favour of persons with disabilities. They are designed to guarantee empowerment of disabled people and to foster their inherent abilities in order that persons with disabilities can participate and be included fully in mainstream society on an equal basis with others. The transformative model of equality can be seen quite clearly by means of the CRPD's accessibility obligations, its universal design provisions and its awareness-raising duties, as well as in the Convention's application of the equality norm (via the reasonable accommodation duty) to each of the substantive rights contained in the Convention, particularly socio-economic rights. The transformative model of equality in the CRPD is underpinned by its social-contextual understanding of disability and its human-rights based approach to disability. Those far-reaching models of disability aim at creating inclusive structures and ensuring that persons with disabilities are provided with the material support necessary to achieve equality in fact, thereby reaching their full potential and capabilities. The CRPD's endorsement of the social model of disability has resulted in the reconfiguration of the equality norm for persons with disabilities – it acknowledges that the full and effective participation and inclusion of people with disabilities can only be achieved through the realisation of a barrier-free society.

The understanding of the equality norm has evolved greatly in recent years, both at the level of international human rights law and in the disability context, from embodying a formal model of equality to endorsing a more substantive and even transformative conception of equality. Oddný Mjöll Arnardóttir highlights the fact that in the era of 'universal sameness,'[1] there was no accommodation for difference. The open-ended non-discrimination provisions and the universal equality norm applied to everyone in the same manner, regardless of difference. This is evidenced by such instruments as the ICCPR and the ICESCR. Over time, international human rights law began gradually to recognise differential characteristics in the quest for true equality. The next era that can be detected at the level of international human rights law has been termed the 'specific difference'[2] equality era. The substantive difference model of equality which is characteristic of that era forms the basis of the non-discrimination provisions in both CERD and CEDAW.[3] Those treaties view discrimination based on specific identity markers or biological and immutable characteristics as worthy of special attention, but only in certain circumstances. Both treaties incorporate the notion of indirect discrimination in their non-discrimination clauses and they also permit the taking of special measures or positive action, wherever necessary. However, the focus under the specific difference era remained with differential characteristics rather than with wider disadvantage in mainstream society. Before the CRPD, the emphasis was largely on differential characteristics as an exception to the rule of equal treatment. The CRPD can be deemed to represent the culmination of previous steps in the direction of substantive and transformative models of equality. Oddný Mjöll Arnardóttir characterises the era culminating with the adoption of the CRPD as embracing 'multidimensional disadvantage'[4] equality. The substantive disadvantage model of equality underlying the CRPD displays a true understanding of structural inequalities. The substantive disadvantage model advocates legal tools such as indirect discrimination, positive action, reasonable accommodations and other positive measures as integral means by which to eradicate barriers which maintain or perpetuate disadvantage. The CRPD strengthens the non-discrimination norm in many respects. The inclusion of the duty to accommodate within the non-discrimination provision guarantees an individualised application of the equality paradigm and has increased the potential for ensuring *de facto* equality. The CRPD recognises the fact that the universal equality norm must be tailored to the specific needs of disabled people. It breathes new life into the Convention's guarantees in accordance with the lived realities of disabled people. Furthermore, the CRPD adopts a contextual approach to equality – it seeks to target asymmetrical

1 O.M. Arnardóttir, 'A Future of Multidimensional Disadvantage Equality' in O.M. Arnardóttir and G. Quinn, *The UN Convention on the Rights of Persons with Disabilities: European and Scandinavian Perspectives* (Martinus Nijhoff, Leiden, 2009), at page 47.

2 Ibid, at page 49.

3 Ibid.

4 Ibid.

structures of disadvantage and oppression and shifts the target of non-discrimination laws to deeply unequal structures in society. Finally, the CRPD embraces a multidimensional or intersectional approach to non-discrimination, recognising the fact that discrimination arising from a number of grounds in combination produces a unique discriminatory experience for the individual concerned. In that regard, the CRPD goes further than the other core human rights treaties, which do not mention multiple or intersectional discrimination explicitly within their text.

In addition, the CRPD goes beyond any of the other core human rights treaties in seeking to ensure a transformative approach to equality. CEDAW requires States to take all appropriate measures to eliminate prejudices, customary and other practices, which are based on the idea of the inferiority or the superiority of either of the sexes or on stereotyped roles for men and women. The CRPD requires States to target, in addition, all socially constructed barriers which hinder *de facto* equality and full and effective participation and inclusion in society for disabled people. It is clear that this will require the adoption of a wide variety of positive measures in all spheres of society and a significant reallocation of resources to ensure equality of opportunity and equality in fact. On the basis of the foregoing, there is no doubt that the CRPD holds enormous promise for the future application of the equality and non-discrimination norms in relation to the rights of persons with disabilities. Among other things, it is hoped that the interaction of the equality norm and socio-economic rights in the Convention may provide the key to unlocking the structural inequalities faced by disabled people, in order to bring them fully into the mainstream. Notwithstanding this, the realisation of *de facto* equality for persons with disabilities will be a significant challenge for many States, not only on account of obvious resource and institutional constraints, but also because the Convention requires widespread attitudinal change regarding the inherent capabilities of persons with disabilities and the potential contribution which they can make in mainstream society.

The Outer Limits of the Duty to Accommodate

This book also examines the outer limits of the duty to accommodate persons with disabilities. Three principal lessons can be drawn from an examination of the outer limits of the duty to accommodate. The first of these is that any requested accommodation must be necessary and appropriate in the circumstances of a particular, individualised case. Translating the concept of necessity to the context of progressive realisation, this implies that States will be required to take all essential measures towards ensuring that persons with disabilities can begin to enjoy CRPD rights and towards ensuring the full realisation over time of Convention rights. The criterion of appropriateness translates to the requirement that measures adopted by States must be effective in allowing the disabled person in question to participate in the required activity and in contributing towards realisation of the substantive rights and obligations contained in the CRPD. Linked to the notion of effectiveness of measures is the concept of human dignity and the equality norm.

The duty to accommodate is based on the core values of human dignity and respect for difference. These values, taken together with a consideration of the object and purpose of the duty to accommodate (the promotion of equality and the elimination of discrimination), will be essential to any determination of whether measures taken by private entities or States are effective. The third lesson drawn from the outer limits of the duty to accommodate rests on an underlying proportionality test. That test endeavours to balance the rights of, and burdens and benefits to, all persons affected by the proposed accommodation. Burdens or costs will not be merely financial in nature but will also extend to a consideration of the level of difficulty for a particular entity in terms, for instance, of the manner in which the accommodation affects the entity's business. It was also argued that third-party benefits should be considered in the provision of accommodations under the CRPD. In deciding whether a measure constitutes a disproportionate burden for an entity, regard should be had to the manner in which a requested accommodation has knock-on effects, not only for the entity concerned, but also for other individuals, such as individuals with comparative disabilities or potentially even consumers of an entity. All of these elements of the duty to accommodate have the potential to map over to the context of progressive realisation. In a similar vein to the accommodation duty, the realisation of the Convention's substantive rights and obligations is characterised by an implicit balancing of burdens and interests between the duty-bearer and the rights-holder. In order to ensure an appropriate balancing of needs and interests between States (and entities), on the one hand, and disabled individuals, on the other hand, it is necessary to place a normative framework around the progressive realisation of CRPD rights, both in terms of resource allocation and programme and policy design. This book went on to propose such a framework, based on 'reasonableness review' criteria, incorporating the outer limits of the duty to accommodate and drawing on frameworks of reasonableness review under South African constitutional jurisprudence and the OP-ICESCR.

A Proposed Framework for the Progressive Realisation of CRPD Rights

In a similar vein to some of the outer limits of the duty to accommodate (which apply to entities), the outer limits of the progressive realisation norm will be adjudicated on by the CRPD Committee in accordance with the resources available to States, as well as priorities set by national authorities, among other considerations. In that regard, the Committee will be tasked with assessing State action or inaction based not only on the needs of persons with disabilities, but also in light of resource and institutional or capacity constraints in a given State. The Committee must acknowledge the fact that the needs and interests of others, including other marginalised groups in society, will be a relevant consideration for national authorities when they allocate resources. It was argued in this book that the measures adopted by States within available resources should be adjudged according to their reasonableness. Accordingly, several frameworks of reasonableness review at the national and international levels were explored – specifically, the criteria adopted under South African Constitutional jurisprudence and the emerging notion of reasonableness review envisaged under the OP-ICESCR. The research conducted for this book sought to explore the criteria inherent in already existing frameworks of reasonableness review to tailor them to the specific context of the CRPD in order to advance its equality paradigm. It was demonstrated that the types of criteria inherent in already existing frameworks of reasonableness review would fit well in the assessment of measures taken by States to fulfil their obligations under the CRPD. By virtue of the fact that the socio-economic provisions in the CRPD are linked intrinsically to the equality norm via the duty to accommodate, the outer limits of the duty to accommodate were also drawn on in order to inject an additional equality dimension into the review of CRPD rights realisation. In sum, the outcomes for this portion of the research project were as follows:

In realising disability rights progressively, national authorities are required to take necessary measures to give effect, at the very least, to the minimum core of the right(s) in question in order to ensure that the basic needs and capabilities of persons with disabilities are catered for. States are also required to take essential measures to ensure that the totality of CRPD rights will be realised in the fullness of time. In line with the criterion of effectiveness, any steps taken by governments to realise progressively CRPD rights must produce tangible outcomes, which are compatible with the requirements of the Convention. States must also ensure that the least restrictive measures are put in place to facilitate the realisation of socio-economic rights. In deciding whether measures taken by States are in compliance with the Convention, the CRPD Committee must balance cost-related factors against many other considerations. States will make policy choices regarding priority-setting in their own national contexts. This raises very difficult issues, to which there is no definitive solution. Nonetheless, the types of policy choices made by States must be justified and thereafter judged according to their reasonableness. In spite of the resource and institutional constraints weighing on national authorities, there is a duty incumbent on those authorities to utilise whatever resources and capacity they have in a manner which accords a sufficient degree of priority to the values underlying the Convention as a whole. The Committee's review framework must be grounded in the normative content of the right(s) at issue (including the minimum core), together with an analysis of the broader object and purpose of the Convention. Minimum thresholds for assessment of socio-economic rights are important, but not sufficient on their own, to guarantee the full and effective realisation of the rights of disadvantaged groups, such as persons with disabilities. As such, equality should be a paramount consideration in any framework of reasonableness review, as the CRPD links States' obligations to eliminate disability discrimination with guarantees for the full realisation of socio-economic rights. Incorporating equality into a review framework under the CRPD would serve to ensure that States Parties to the Convention put forward heightened justifications for any alleged rights violations. This, in turn, would serve to highlight instances in which the denial of access to the socio-economic right in question results in the entrenchment of inequalities or marginalisation for persons with disabilities. An approach to socio-economic rights adjudication based on equality would bolster the human-rights based approach to disability, which underlies the Convention as a whole, and would seek to overturn the misguided stereotypes which exist regarding the capabilities of disabled persons.

Another related criterion that will be important in any assessment of socio-economic rights under the CRPD is the underlying core norm of the inherent dignity of persons with disabilities. While there are several criticisms of the use of human dignity as a normative guide to human rights implementation, the research in this book provided counter-arguments to that. Moreover, it argued that there are two strands to the concept of human dignity which have particular relevance to the CRPD. The first of these requires that consideration be given to the urgency of needs of different groups. States must respond accordingly to ensure that those urgent needs are catered for. The second strand of human dignity in international human rights law involves an alignment with the equality norm and requires consideration of the equal worth of all human beings. It involves treatment as an equal. In the context of the CRPD, dignity considerations must be examined relative to both strands of human dignity. In the first instance, the needs of disabled persons who are in most dire circumstances must be catered for. Once this basic level of provision has been satisfied, dignity should feature thereafter as an equality concern, whereby the full realisation of socio-economic rights under the CRPD takes account of the equal worth of persons with disabilities and their entitlement to enjoy rights on an equal basis with others. Of course, national authorities will not have limitless resources to spend on disability rights and therefore the Committee will be required to balance the right to equality (including dignity considerations) against an assessment of costs in order to determine if particular measures constitute a disproportionate burden on States.

In the overall assessment of what constitutes a disproportionate burden on States, the CRPD Committee will have to ask whether national authorities have used all powers at their disposal to ensure resource prioritisation and resource optimisation, including through international assistance. In that connection, the Committee must ensure that States do not act in a discriminatory or arbitrary manner. States must ensure that any resources they have are used efficiently in order to implement fully (within available resources) disability rights, as well as the rights of all marginalised groups in society. In addition to the foregoing, the Committee should look to the impact of failure to take measures in implementing socio-economic rights for persons with disabilities. Thus, for instance, if a failure to take measures in one context leads to depriving persons with disabilities of what may be essential to enable them to enjoy other rights vested in them under the Convention, this may be a relevant factor in the CRPD Committee's assessment of State measures.

Participatory processes will also be essential to ensuring accountability in the implementation of Convention rights. In deciding on priorities for the realisation of socio-economic rights in the context of limited resources, input from disabled persons organisations and civil society groups will be vital to determining the greatest needs of citizens. It will also facilitate the effective implementation of rights, by identifying the measures that are most suited to the realisation of rights in various contexts. Another potentially relevant (albeit tangential) consideration is the issue of the benefits accruing to persons other than the disabled individual in question (such as persons with a comparative disability or even non-disabled persons).

Having considered the overall link between progressive realisation and equality, the research carried out for this book went on to examine two substantive rights and obligations subject to progressive realisation, namely the accessibility obligation and the right to education under the CRPD.

The Interrelationship between the Accessibility Obligation and the Equality Norm

The link between the CRPD's accessibility obligation contained in Article 9 and the equality and non-discrimination norms in the Convention is delineated in this book, including the overlaps and key differences between the two. The Convention's accessibility obligation breathes new life into the equality norm. The obligations imposed on States Parties to the CRPD under Article 9 aim to guarantee equal life opportunities for persons with disabilities in line with those enjoyed by their non-disabled peers. The effective implementation of the Convention's accessibility provisions is a precondition for full participation and inclusion in society. While accessibility standards and measures may facilitate access to human rights and, in some cases, may ensure *de facto* equality, this will not always be the case. In such circumstances, States must go further in their endeavours to ensure effective implementation of both Article 5 and Article 9 of the Convention in tandem, including monitoring implementation of measures such as reasonable accommodations and positive action.

The CRPD Committee will have the difficult task of adjudicating the efforts of States to ensure disability accessibility, while at the same time ensuring the realisation of other socio-economic rights and obligations in the CPRD. In light of the fact that Article 9 is a resource-intensive obligation, the Committee will have to consider the issue of what constitutes a disproportionate burden for a particular State. States will be required to justify their policy choices to the Committee, which will have to ask itself whether national authorities have taken measures that ensure the most cost-effective implementation of Article 9 by, for instance, considering accessibility issues at the beginning of the design of products, services and buildings. If States have not taken reasonable cost-effective measures (not imposing a disproportionate burden), this may lead to a finding by the Committee of a potential violation of Convention obligations. Of course, not all measures required to ensure disability accessibility will, by definition, be cost-effective (especially those taken to retrofit facilities or infrastructure). In that regard, the Committee should ask itself whether States have ensured an optimal use of (limited) resources targeted at realising disability accessibility and whether they have prioritised resources in that regard. If a given State has not done so, this may lead to a finding by the Committee that the State has not taken all reasonable measures to implement CRPD rights. A further relevant consideration is whether States have consulted closely with and involved persons with disabilities in all aspects of implementation of disability accessibility, as required under Article 4(3) of the Convention. This will allow a determination of whether States have adopted measures which are most effective and which are least restrictive of the rights of persons with disabilities. To that end, disabled persons and their representative organisations should be consulted closely in the development of products, services and facilities, as well as in the development, promulgation and monitoring of minimum standards for the accessibility of different facilities and services provided by public and private enterprises. In the overall assessment of whether measures impose a disproportionate burden on a State, the Committee may evaluate the extent to which particular accessibility measures would have benefits to a wider cohort of individuals, beyond disabled persons, and thereby the extent to which such measures contribute to the Convention's universal design provisions. The issue of third-party benefits may be fraught with difficulties and any assessment in that regard would have to be considered cautiously by the Committee.

One of the primary factors that should feature in the CRPD Committee's assessments is that of equality. As always, equality arguments must be balanced against the notion of disproportionate burden. In that vein, one must acknowledge the impact of limited resources and respect the sovereignty of a State to make appropriate choices in its national context. Notwithstanding this, the Convention clearly mandates accessibility of the environment, structures, and so forth, for disabled persons on an equal basis with others. Thus, the Committee will have to judge whether, in setting priorities, States have had regard to the extent to which measures adopted by them to ensure accessibility will actually contribute to achieving the overall goals of equalising opportunities and outcomes for persons with disabilities. A fundamental premise of accessibility measures adopted by States is that persons with disabilities should be guaranteed equivalent or functionally equivalent access to non-disabled people. Closely related to equality issues is the fact that disabled people should not be required to use or access goods, services, infrastructure or other facilities in a manner which compromises their human dignity. States should therefore ensure consideration of dignity interests in all aspects of the implementation and monitoring of Article 9, including in the design of accessibility standards.

There is no doubt that the equality and non-discrimination norms in the CRPD are closely entwined with the accessibility obligation. By applying equality and dignity considerations as key criteria in the implementation of Article 9, this can serve to ensure that disabled people are treated as true equals in the enjoyment of socio-economic rights. States must therefore ensure effective implementation of both Article 5 and Article 9 of the Convention in tandem. Guarantees of equality and non-discrimination should be interpreted by national judicial authorities in a manner which facilitates and promotes the Convention's accessibility requirements. Accessibility and equality measures should be coherent and coordinated with a view to ensuring that the overall objective of the CRPD – namely the achievement of *de facto* equality for persons with disabilities – is realised in the most efficient and effective manner possible.

The Right to Education for Persons with Disabilities

This book also elaborates on the meaning of equality in the context of the right to education and teases out the potential value which the equality and non-discrimination norms in the CRPD can add to the right to education for persons with disabilities. In addition, this book applies the various criteria that may be employed by the CRPD Committee in assessing compliance with Article 24.

The costs of providing inclusive education will be an obvious factor to be taken into account by the CRPD Committee in its assessment of State action or inaction. In that regard, it is noteworthy that inclusive education is often mistakenly viewed as being prohibitively costly. However, research has demonstrated the fact that many positive educational measures are not very expensive. Inclusive educational settings are generally less expensive than segregated systems, when appropriately implemented. Nonetheless, resource implications will be a concern for many States in implementing Article 24 of the CRPD, particularly developing States, and the transformation of special educational systems to fully inclusive systems may incur significant outlays in terms of resources (both human and financial), at least in the transitional phase. On the other hand, the CRPD Committee must bear in mind the fact that the cost benefits of inclusive education are assured in the long term and that the implementation of inclusive education can assist in the realisation of the right to education for non-disabled children also. In that vein, the CRPD Committee will be required to assess whether States are ensuring an efficient and effective use of existing resources (including resources which are being poured into special educational systems), as existing resources can potentially be harnessed to assist the mainstream provision of education. It will be particularly important to ensure rights-based and performance-based budgeting in order to identify the areas where existing resources can be more efficiently targeted to implement the right to inclusive education, among other rights, for persons with disabilities.

As with all other rights contained in the Convention, the non-discrimination and equality provisions are of paramount importance in implementing Article 24 of the CRPD. In many cases, access to mainstream education is being hindered for a large proportion of disabled individuals who are being placed in segregated educational settings. Ensuring access to inclusive education and equal educational opportunities for disabled people will require the removal of barriers to participation and inclusion. This will involve fundamental changes in physical structures and facilities, educational curricula and in the processes of learning to accommodate different learning styles and means of communication. Overall, it must be emphasised that Article 24 reflects the human rights-based approach to educational provision. Article 24 of the CRPD mandates truly inclusive and accessible educational structures. In tandem with equality considerations, dignity considerations for persons with disabilities will be paramount to the CRPD Committee's assessment of the measures taken by States to ensure implementation of Article 24 of the CRPD. One of the main challenges which lies ahead for States in the implementation of the right to inclusive education is the elimination of discrimination and stigmatisation of the capabilities of persons with disabilities in terms of learning outcomes and so forth. Under the CRPD, States must undertake awareness-raising campaigns and persons with disabilities must be given the material support to ensure that their inherent potential is allowed to develop in education, as in all other areas.

According to Article 24, any support provided within mainstream education must facilitate the effective education of disabled persons. States should conduct research into the effectiveness of current inclusive education policies. The CRPD Committee will have to keep a close watch on the collection of data and the establishment of national educational benchmarks and indicators, which will allow States Parties to the CRPD to monitor the effectiveness of measures taken in the realisation of the right to education for persons with disabilities. In order to ensure enjoyment of the right to education for persons with disabilities on a truly equal basis as others, their input, through participatory processes, is vital as this is the key to unlocking structural inequalities which have hindered the right to education for disabled people for far too long now.

On the basis of all of the above, it is abundantly clear that the Convention's equality and non-discrimination norms have huge potential to impact on the implementation of socio-economic rights for persons with disabilities. However, this potential must be realised properly through the application of defined and equitable criteria to the rights and obligations contained in the Convention.

The Influence of the CRPD on Council of Europe Disability Law and Policy

The final part of the research for this book entails a case study on the Council of Europe. The first part of that case study relates to the influence to date, and the potential influence, of the CRPD on the disability equality case law of the European Court of Human Rights (ECtHR). In the second part of the case study, the provisions of the Revised European Social Charter (revised Charter) are considered, as well as the views of the European Committee of Social Rights (ECSR) and the general disability policy of the Council of Europe. The aim of that second part of the case study is to explore the influence which the CRPD is having on those Council of Europe legal and policy mechanisms.

The CRPD is exerting some degree of influence on the relevant organs in the Council of Europe. However, the extent of its impact varies quite considerably between the various legal and policy mechanisms in the Council. The CRPD is certainly guiding the general direction of disability policy through the recommendations and issue papers of the Committee of Ministers. Those non-binding instruments are drawing quite heavily on relevant elements from the substantive provisions of the CRPD as an interpretative guide for Member States in their implementation of disability rights. Many of the instruments adopt the fundamental values and principles underlying the Convention, particularly in relation to equality/non-discrimination and inclusion in society for persons with disabilities. Many of the documents also draw specific guidance from the concrete provisions of the Convention in formulating recommendations and suggestions to be employed by Member States in their implementation of disability rights.

In terms of tangible effects of the CRPD on the case law of the ECtHR, the Court has cited the Convention on numerous occasions in the context of relevant international law since the coming into force of the CRPD. However, the Court is not always consistent in referring to the Convention and the reasons for its failure to refer to the CRPD are not always clear from one case to another. One can only surmise that the Court is not quite sure of the relevance of CRPD provisions to ECHR rights. Notwithstanding the Court's inconsistent approach, the CRPD appears to be having some positive influence on judgments of the ECtHR with regard to disability discrimination and also on the standard of scrutiny adopted by the Court. The Court has included some form of implicit duty to accommodate within Article 14 and has begun to incorporate a social-contextual or social model reasoning in certain selected judgments. It has also referred to the CRPD as an example of a European and worldwide consensus on the need to protect people with disabilities from discriminatory treatment. In addition, the ECtHR has demonstrated an increased awareness of the impact of historical discrimination on persons with disabilities and links this to the applicable margin of appreciation of States. On the other hand, the Court has not yet recognised an explicit right to be accommodated under Article 14 as an essential means of ensuring disability equality in the enjoyment of ECHR rights. It is envisaged that the social-contextual approach which the Court is beginning to adopt, together with the evolutive interpretative approach that it professes to employ, will play a greater role in the future. In light of the fact that the majority of Member States of the Council of Europe are also party to the CRPD and will, thus, be incorporating reasonable accommodation duties into their national legislative frameworks (where they have not already done so), this might encourage the Court to recognise the substantive disadvantage experienced by persons with disabilities in society and to incorporate this into its analysis of ECHR rights.

Not many disability-related collective complaints have been taken before the ECSR since the coming into force of the CRPD. Therefore, it is difficult to measure the Convention's impact or potential impact in that regard. To date, the ECSR is referring to the CRPD in the context of relevant international law but the Convention has not actually had a concrete influence on the Committee's reasoning. Nonetheless, the provisions of the revised Charter overlap, to a large degree, with many substantive rights contained in the CRPD, including the right to education and the right to independent living. The education line of case law appears to provide most scope for the interpretation of rights under the revised Charter in a manner which is compatible with the CRPD.

It is evident that there will be significant challenges ahead in translating the progressive approach to equality contained in the CRPD into legislation and policy at the European level and, specifically, in the Council of Europe. In particular, the process of change will be a slow and arduous one at the level of the judicial system, especially in the ECtHR. There will also be many barriers ahead for persons with disabilities in their efforts to turn the aspirations of the Convention into individually justiciable rights. In spite of the challenges inherent in the process of change, the CRPD still holds great promise for the future application of the equality and non-discrimination norms, provided of course that this potential is realised and utilised by policy-makers and the judiciary.

Valorisation Addendum

This book emerged from a unique collaborative research project entitled the DREAM (Disability Rights Expanding Accessible Markets) network. DREAM was a training network for early stage researchers and it was funded by the Marie Curie FP7 project of the European Commission. The primary objective of the DREAM project was to develop professionally and educate the next generation of disability policy researchers and entrepreneurs to assist the EU and its Member States in their efforts to implement the CRPD at the national and EU levels. The DREAM network (within which this research was born) had both a human rights and an economic impetus. It was premised on the insight that respecting the rights of persons with disabilities is not only a good objective, in and of itself, but that this helps to create economic opportunities for over 60 million European citizens with disabilities and that it also expands markets for European business. Thus, it is evident that the research undertaken for this book was not intended to result in mere words on paper, but to move outside a theoretical framework in order to enable legal and policy makers to identify areas for legal and policy reform on the ground.

This book is an academic piece of research, which is directed primarily at scholars in the arena of international human rights law. However, it also has direct relevance to other groups in society. Most notably, it is an important piece of work for the very group whose rights it examines – persons with disabilities. The research conducted for this book seeks, among other things, to clarify and analyse the newly emerging rights at the level of international human rights law as they pertain to disabled people. In that regard, persons with disabilities and their representative organisations can potentially use this research to educate themselves on their entitlements and to campaign for those entitlements. In particular, the research carried out in chapter eight of this book, related to the rights of persons with disabilities in the Council of Europe legal and policy mechanisms, and especially the research on disability rights in the European Court of Human Rights, might be of interest to advocacy networks and organisations of persons with disabilities that have as their objective the furtherance of disability litigation.

This research undoubtedly also has relevance to legal and policy makers at the EU and national levels. This book contains the first comprehensive legal interpretation of Article 5 of the CRPD (the equality provision) and related articles. To that end, this research illuminates the various legal and policy avenues which have been opened up since the entry into force of the CRPD, in terms of advocacy and implementation of disability rights. The legal and policy recommendations that are developed in chapter nine of this book can be of potential use to law and policy makers at the national and EU levels in the adoption of action plans, strategies and legislation and in furthering the debate surrounding the rights of persons with disabilities. The analysis of disability rights in the Council of Europe also has relevance for the institutions in the Council itself. In that regard, the recommendations in chapter eight of this book can go some way towards bringing the policy and legal mechanisms of the Council of Europe more in line with the CRPD.

The research outcomes emerging from this book, and especially the framework of reasonableness review devised in chapter five, are also of particular relevance to the CRPD Committee (the Committee responsible for overseeing compliance with the Convention in the various States Parties to the Convention). The Committee might be inclined to take some aspects of my proposed reasonableness review framework into account in its work on the rights of persons with disabilities. In chapters six and seven of this book, I demonstrated how the reasonableness review framework might work in practice with respect to two substantive rights and obligations in the Convention (namely, the accessibility obligation and the right to education). That analysis might serve to aid the Committee in its general comments and concluding observations to the various States Parties to the CRPD.

In addition to contributing to the work of the above-mentioned groups and institutions, the research results emerging from this research project can also be of interest to the European Commission, which initiated the DREAM project in the first instance. The European Commission has established various high-profile projects on disability rights, particularly with regard to ensuring the implementation of the CRPD at the EU level, as well as throughout the 28 Member States. In light of the fundamental importance of the equality norm to the implementation of all the other rights and obligations in the CRPD at the EU level, this research will be of particular interest to the Commission in its analysis of the equality framework in the EU (when compared with the CRPD).

The DREAM project had as one of its aims to take the knowledge gained through doctoral research outside of its theoretical box in order to disseminate it to a wider audience and to contribute to the broader debate on disability rights. As part of the DREAM network, and as an integral part of my Ph.D. research, I had the opportunity to gain invaluable work experience with a leading European civil society organisation, the European Disability Forum (EDF), in Brussels. Throughout my time there, I gained valuable knowledge regarding the means by which disability rights advocacy can be strengthened and the various channels which can be used to achieve that objective, something which I plan to use in the dissemination of my own work. Working with EDF greatly enriched my research in numerous ways. In the first instance, I was exposed to the daily challenges of those who are fighting for the human rights of persons with disabilities. The internship enabled me to see first-hand the various policy and bureaucratic challenges that are part and parcel of the fight for change and the ways in which these challenges can be averted and overcome. By virtue of my presence at EDF, I believe that the organisation also benefited from a unique insight into the interpretation of the equality and non-discrimination norms in the CRPD, through discussions about the various ways in which litigation strategies and advocacy can be strengthened for the benefit of persons with disabilities.

By virtue of my work with the various partner institutes in the DREAM project, and through the many interactions I have had with the European Commission (both in the DREAM project, as Rapporteur for the annual disability Work Forum at the EU level and in writing reports for the Commission on disability rights), I have gained a platform for my own research, which I plan to utilise into the future. To date, my research has been publicised through the DREAM webblog, through academic publications in leading international journals and through many conferences that took place within the framework of the DREAM project. Copies of this book will be distributed to relevant NGO's. The results emerging from my research project can potentially be transformed into litigation strategies by those campaigning for the rights of persons with disabilities. In addition, they can be transformed into proposals for law reform at the level of States Parties to the Convention. It is envisaged that there may also be some opportunity for me to engage in the review process of the draft general comments of the CRPD Committee on issues related to non-discrimination/equality. In that regard, I have already contributed (with other researchers) to one draft comment on accessibility obligations under the CRPD. The close network of researchers that I have liaised with right throughout my research project will no doubt present future opportunities for collaboration on disability issues, including dissemination of my research results. In addition, the training activities provided in the DREAM network events also exposed me to leading agents of change in the disability field. This enabled me to observe disability policy entrepreneurship in action. Each event brought together different generations of policy entrepreneurs and scholars, which enabled me to situate my own work within that scholarship, to identify the gaps and to highlight areas in which to move forward in the process of change.

The aim of this research as a whole was to provide a platform to translate the general rights and obligations of the CRPD into practical strategies to achieve substantive reform and change that can reach into the everyday lives of persons with disabilities. I believe that the research results emerging from this book can contribute to doing just that.

Curriculum Vitae

Andrea Broderick holds a B.A. International (Law and French) degree with First Class Honours from the National University of Ireland, Galway (NUIG). She also graduated from NUIG with a Bachelor of Laws (LL.B.). Andrea has also completed an LL.M. in International and Comparative Disability Law and Policy at NUIG, with First Class Honours. In addition, Andrea is a qualified Solicitor, having graduated from the Law Society of Ireland, Dublin. Andrea is currently a full-time lecturer at the Department of International and European Law at Maastricht University and has previously worked as a legal officer in the area of banking law and as a trainee Solicitor in a general practice firm.

Bibliography

I. International Law Sources

A. International Treaties

International Convention on the Elimination of All Forms of Discrimination against Women adopted and opened for signature, ratification and accession by General Assembly resolution 34/180 of 18 December 1979, entry into force 3 September 1981.

International Convention on the Elimination of All Forms of Racial Discrimination, adopted and opened for signature and ratification by General Assembly resolution 2106 (XX) of 21 December 1965, entry into force 4 January 1969.

International Covenant on Civil and Political Rights, resolution adopted by the UN General Assembly, Resolution 2200A (XXI) of 16 December 1966 entry into force 23 March 1976.

International Covenant on Economic, Social and Cultural Rights, resolution adopted by the UN General Assembly, Resolution 2200A (XXI) of 16 December 1966, entry into force 3 January 1976.

UN Convention on the Rights of Persons with Disabilities, resolution adopted by the UN General Assembly, 13 December 2006, UN Doc. A/RES/61/106, entry into force 3 May 2008.

UN Convention on the Rights of the Child, adopted and opened for signature, ratification and accession by General Assembly resolution 44/25 of 20 November 1989, entry into force 2 September 1990.

UNESCO Convention against Discrimination in Education, Paris (1960), adopted by the UNESCO General Conference of 14 December 1960.

Universal Declaration of Human Rights, resolution adopted by the UN General Assembly, 10 December 1948, Paris, Resolution 217 A (III).

B. International Soft-Law Instruments

Beijing Declaration on the Rights of People with Disabilities (2000), adopted on 12 March 2000 at the World NGO Summit on Disability, Beijing, People's Republic of China.

Dakar Framework for Action - Education for All: Meeting Our Collective Commitments, adopted by the World Education Forum Dakar, Senegal, 26–28 April 2000.

Declaration on the Rights of Disabled Persons, proclaimed by General Assembly resolution 3447 (XXX) of 9 December 1975).

Declaration on the Rights of Mentally Retarded Persons, proclaimed by General Assembly resolution 2856 (XXVI) of 20 December 1971.

Declaration on the Rights of Persons Belonging to National or Ethnic, Religious and Linguistic Minorities A/RES/47/135, adopted at the 92nd plenary meeting on 18 December 1992.

Guidelines for Inclusion: Ensuring Access to Education for All, United Nations Educational, Scientific and Cultural Organization, France, 2005.

Guidelines for the Establishment and Development of National Coordinating Committees on Disability or Similar Bodies (2000) UN Doc. A/C.3/46/4.

International Classification of Functioning, Disability and Health, World Health Organisation, Geneva, Switzerland, 2001 (endorsed by all 191 WHO Member States in the Fifty-fourth World Health Assembly on 22 May 2001 - resolution WHA 54.21).

International Classification of Impairments, Disease and Handicaps: A Manual of Classification Relating to the Consequences of Disease (WHO, Geneva, Switzerland, 1980) published in accordance with resolution WHA 29.35 of the Twenty-ninth World Health Assembly, May 1976.

Limburg Principles on the Implementation of the International Covenant on Economic, Social and Cultural Rights, adopted by the Commission on Human Rights at the 43rd session, UN doc. E/CN.4/1987/17, reprinted as the Limburg Principles on the Implementation of the International Covenant on Economic, Social and Cultural Rights (1987) 9 *Human Rights Quarterly* 121–135.

Maastricht Guidelines on Violations of Economic, Social and Cultural Rights, Maastricht, January 22–26, 1997, reprinted as the Maastricht Guidelines on Violations of Economic, Social and Cultural Rights 1998 20(3) *Human Rights Quarterly* 691–704.

Office of the High Commission of Human Rights, Resolution 1994/27 on Human Rights and Disability.

Office of the High Commission of Human Rights, Resolution 1996/27 on the Human Rights of Persons with Disabilities.

Principles for the Protection of Persons with Mental Illness and the Improvement of Mental Health Care, UN Document A/RES/46/119, adopted at the 75th plenary meeting, 17 December 1991.

Salamanca Statement and Framework for Action on Special Needs Education. adopted at the World Conference on Special Needs Education: Access and Quality, Salamanca, Spain (7–10 June 1994).

Standard Rules on the Equalization of Opportunities for Persons with Disabilities, adopted by the United Nations General Assembly, forty-eighth session, resolution 48/96, annex, of 20 December 1993.

Tallinn Guidelines for Action on Human Resources Development in the Field of Disability, UN Doc.A/RES/44/70, adopted at the 78th plenary meeting, 8 December 1989.

UN Commission on Human Rights, Resolution 1998/31, Human Rights of Persons with Disabilities, 17 April, 1998 (Geneva).

UN Nations Commission on Human Rights, Resolution no. 1995/44, The protection of human rights in the context of HIV and AIDS, adopted at its 53rd meeting on 3 March 1995).

UN General Assembly, Resolution 56/168 of 19 December 2001 on a Comprehensive and integral international convention to promote and protect the rights and dignity of persons with disabilities.

Vienna Declaration and Programme of Action, adopted by the World Conference on Human Rights in Vienna on 25 June 1993, UN Doc. A/CONF.157/24.

World Declaration for Education for All: Meeting Basic Learning Needs (1990), UNESCO, adopted by the UNESCO World Conference on Education for All of 9 March 1990.

World Programme of Action Concerning Disabled Persons, adopted by the General Assembly on 3 December 1982, by its resolution 37/52, UN Doc. A/RES/37/52.

C. General Comments/General Recommendations of the Core Human Rights Treaty Bodies

Human Rights Committee

Human Rights Committee, General Comment 4 on equality between the sexes (Article 3) (adopted at the thirteenth Session of the Committee in 1981), U.N. Doc. HRI/GEN/1/Rev.6 at 126 (2003).

Human Rights Committee, General Comment No. 8 on Liberty and security of the person (Article 9) (1982) (adopted at the sixteenth session of the Committee on 30 June 1982).

Human Rights Committee, General Comment No. 18 on non-discrimination (1989), adopted at the thirty-seventh session of the Committee, 1989), U.N. Doc. HRI/GEN/1/Rev.1 at 26 (1994).

Human Rights Committee, General Comment 28 on Equality of rights between men and women (article 3), adopted on 29 March 2000, U.N. Doc. CCPR/C/21/Rev.1/Add.10 (2000).

Human Rights Committee, General Comment No. 31 on the Nature of the General Legal Obligation on States Parties to the Covenant, adopted on 29 March 2004, U.N. Doc. CCPR/C/21/Rev.1/ Add.13 (2004).

UN Committee on Economic, Social and Cultural Rights

UN Committee on Economic, Social and Cultural Rights, General Comment No. 1 on *Reporting by State Parties* (1989), adopted at the third session of the Committee, 1989, UN Doc. E/1989/22.

UN Committee on Economic, Social and Cultural Rights, General Comment No. 3 on The nature of States parties obligations (Article 2, para. 1), adopted at the fifth session of the Committee on 14 December 1990, UN Doc. E/1991/23.

UN Committee on Economic, Social and Cultural Rights, General Comment No. 4 on The Right to Adequate Housing (1991), adopted at the sixth session of the Committee, 1991, U.N. Doc. E/1992 /23.

UN Committee on Economic, Social and Cultural Rights, General Comment No. 5 on Persons with disabilities, adopted at the eleventh session of the Committee, 1994), U.N. Doc E/1995/22 at 19 (1995).

UN Committee on Economic, Social and Cultural Rights, General Comment No. 11 on Plans of Action for Primary Education (Article 14), adopted at the twentieth session of the Committee, 1999, UN Doc. E/2000/22 (1999).

UN Committee on Economic, Social and Cultural Rights, General Comment No. 13 on the right to education, adopted at the twenty-first session of the Committee on 8 December 1999, UN Doc. E/C.12/1999/10.

UN Committee on Economic, Social and Cultural Rights, General Comment 14 (2000) on The right to the highest attainable standard of health (Article 12), adopted at the twenty-second session of the Committee, 2000, UN Doc. E/C.12/2000/4.

UN Committee on Economic, Social and Cultural Rights, General Comment No. 15 on the Right to Water (Article 11 and 12) on twenty ninth session of the Committee, 2003, U.N. Doc E/C.12/2002/11 (2003).

UN Committee on Economic, Social and Cultural Rights, General Comment No. 16 (2005) on the equal right of men and women to the enjoyment of all economic, social and cultural rights (Article 3), adopted at the thirty-fourth session of the Committee, 2005, UN Doc. E/C.12/2005/4.

UN Committee on Economic, Social and Cultural Rights, General Comment No. 19 (2008) on The Right to Social Security adopted at the thirty-ninth session of the Committee, UN doc E/C12/GC/19.

UN Committee on Economic, Social and Cultural Rights, General Comment No. 20 *(2009) on Non-Discrimination in Economic, Social and Cultural Rights (Article 2, para. 2),* adopted at the forty-second session of the Committee on 25 May 2009, UN Doc. E/C.12/GC 20.

UN Committee on the Elimination of all Forms of Discrimination against Women

UN Committee on the Elimination of all Forms of Discrimination against Women, General Recommendation No. 18 on disabled women, adopted at the tenth session of the committee, 1991 (contained in Document A/46/38), 1991, UN Doc. A/46/38.

UN Committee on the Elimination of Discrimination against Women, General Recommendation 23 on Political and Public Life (1997), adopted at the 16th session of the Committee, 1997.

UN Committee on the Elimination of all Forms of Discrimination Against Women, General Recommendation No. 24 on Article 12 of the Convention (Women and Health), adopted at the twentieth session of the Committee, 1999, UN Doc. A/54/38/Rev.1.

UN Committee on the Elimination of All Forms of Discrimination Against Women, General Recommendation 25, on article 4, paragraph 1, of the Convention on the Elimination of All Forms of Discrimination against Women, On Article 4, Paragraph 1, – Temporary Special *Measures* (2004), UN Doc. HRI/GEN/1/Rev.7.

UN Committee on the Elimination of all Forms of Discrimination against Women, General Recommendation 28 on The Core Obligations of States Parties under Article 2 of the Convention on the Elimination of All Forms of Discrimination against Women (2010), UN Doc. CEDAW/C/GC/28.

UN Committee on the Elimination of Racial Discrimination

UN Committee on the Elimination of Racial Discrimination, General Recommendation No. 14 on the definition of discrimination (Article 1, para. 1)(1993), adopted on 22 March 1993 at the forty-second session of the Committee, U.N. Doc. A/48/18 at 114 (1994).

UN Committee on the Elimination of Racial Discrimination, General Recommendation 32 on The meaning and scope of special measures in the International Convention on the Elimination of Racial Discrimination (2009), adopted at the seventy-fifth session of the Committee on 24 September 2009, UN Doc. CERD/C/GC/32.

UN Committee on the Rights of Persons with Disabilities

UN Committee on the Rights of Persons with Disabilities, General Comment No. 2 on Article 9: Accessibility, adopted at the eleventh session: 30 March–11 April 2014, UN Doc. CRPD/C/11/3.

UN Committee on the Rights of the Child

UN Committee on the Rights of the Child, General Comment 9 on the Rights of Children with Disabilities (2006), adopted by the Committee at the forty-third session of the Committee, Geneva, 11–29 September 2006, U.N. Doc. CRC/C/GC/9.

D. Concluding Observations of the Core Human Rights Treaty Bodies

Human Rights Committee

Human Rights Committee, Concluding Observations to United Kingdom, UN Doc. CCPR/C/79/Add.55 (1995).
Human Rights Committee, Concluding Observation on Ireland, UN Doc.A/55/40 (2000).
Human Rights Committee, Concluding Observations to Togo, UN Doc. CCPR/CO/76/TGO (2002).
Human Rights Committee, Concluding Observations to Georgia, UN Doc. CCPR/CO/74/GEO (2003).
Human Rights Committee, Concluding Observations to Philippines, UN Doc. CCPR/CO/79/PHL (2003).

UN Committee on Economic, Social and Cultural Rights

UN Committee on Economic, Social and Cultural Rights, Concluding Observations to Norway, UN Doc. E/C.12/1/Add.109 (2005).
UN Committee on Economic, Social and Cultural Rights, Concluding Observations to Serbia and Montenegro, UN Doc. E/C.12/1/Add.108 (2005).

UN Committee on the Elimination of Racial Discrimination

UN Committee on the Elimination of Racial Discrimination, Concluding Observations to Nepal, UN Doc. CERD/C/304/Add.108 (2000).
UN Committee on the Elimination of Racial Discrimination, Concluding Observations to Liberia, UN Doc.A/56/18 (2001).
UN Committee on the Elimination of Racial Discrimination, Concluding Observations to Ukraine, UN Doc.A/56/18 (2001).
UN Committee on the Elimination of Racial Discrimination, Concluding Observations to Saudi-Arabia, UN Doc. CERD/C/62/CO/8 (2003).

UN Committee on the Rights of Persons with Disabilities

UN Committee on the Rights of Persons with Disabilities, Concluding Observations to Spain, UN Doc. CRPD/C/ESP/CO/1 (2011).
UN Committee on the Rights of Persons with Disabilities, Concluding Observations to Tunisia, U.N.Doc. CRPD/C/TUN/CO/1 (2011).
UN Committee on the Rights of Persons with Disabilities, Concluding Observations to Argentina, U.N. Doc., UN Doc. CRPD/C/ARG/CO/1 (2012).
UN Committee on the Rights of Persons with Disabilities, Concluding Observations to China, UN Doc. CRPD/C/CHN/CO/1 (2012).
UN Committee on the Rights of Persons with Disabilities, Concluding Observations to Hungary, U.N. Doc. CRPD/C/HUN/CO/1 (2012).
UN Committee on the Rights of Persons with Disabilities, Concluding Observations to U.N. Doc. CRPD/C/PER/CO/1 (2012).
UN Committee on the Rights of Persons with Disabilities, Concluding Observations to Austria, U.N. Doc. CRPD/C/AUT/CO/1 (2013).
UN Committee on the Rights of Persons with Disabilities, Concluding Observations to Australia, UN Doc. CRPD/C/AUS/CO/1 (2013).

UN Committee on the Rights of Persons with Disabilities, Concluding Observations to Azerbaijan, U.N. Doc. CRPD/C/AZE/CO/1 (2014).
UN Committee on the Rights of Persons with Disabilities, Concluding Observations to Rica, U.N. Doc. CRPD/C/CRI/CO/1 (2014).
UN Committee on the Rights of Persons with Disabilities, Concluding Observations to Sweden, U.N. Doc. CRPD/C/SWE/CO/1 (2014).

E. Decisions of the Core Human Rights Treaty Bodies

Human Rights Committee

Human Rights Committee, *Althammer et al. v. Austria*, Communication No. 998/2001, U.N. Doc. CCPR/C/78/D/998/2001 (2003).
Human Rights Committee, *C v Australia*, Communication No. 900/1999, views adopted 13 November 2002.
Human Rights Committee, *Guido Jacobs v Belgium*, Communication No. 943/2000, UN Doc. CCPR/C/81/D/943/2000.
Human Rights Committee, *Hamilton v Jamaica*, Communication No. 616/1995, views adopted 28 July 1999.
Human Rights Committee, *Sandra Lovelace v Canada* (1981), Communication No. R.6/24, (1981), U.N. Doc Supp. No. 40 A/36/40.
Human Rights Committee, *Simunek et al. v. the Czech Republic*, Communication No. 516/1992, views adopted 19 July 1995.
Human Rights Committee, *Stalla Costa v Uruguay*, Communication No. 198/1985, U.N. Doc. Supp. No. 40 (A/42/40) 170 (1987), UN Doc. CCPR/C/30/D/198/1985.
Human Rights Committee, *Wackenheim v France*, Communication No. 854.1999, views adopted 26 July 2002.

UN Committee on the Rights of Persons with Disabilities

UN Committee on the Rights of Persons with Disabilities, *HM v Sweden*, Communication no. 3/2011, UN Doc CRPD/C/7/D/3/2011, views adopted 21 May 2012.
UN Committee on the Rights of Persons with Disabilities, *Marie-Louise Jungelin (represented by the Swedish Association of Visually Impaired Youth (US) and the Swedish Association of the Visually Impaired (SRF) v Sweden*, Communication No. 5/2011, views adopted 2 October 2014.
UN Committee on the Rights of Persons with Disabilities, *S.C. v Brazil*, communication no. 10/2013, UN Doc. CRPD/C/12/D/10/2013, views adopted 2 October 2014.

II. Council of Europe and Regional Law Sources

A. Council of Europe and Regional Treaties/Charters

Additional Protocol to the American Convention on Human Rights in the Area of Economic, Social and Cultural Rights "Protocol of San Salvador" Adopted in San Salvador on November 17, 1988.
Convention for the Protection of Human Rights and Fundamental Freedoms, Rome, 4.XI.1950.

European Social Charter, CETS No.35 (1961).
European Social Charter (Revised), CETS No. 163 (1996).
Inter-American Convention on the Elimination of All Forms of Discrimination against Persons with Disabilities, O.A.S. AG/Res. 1608, 7 June 1999, entered into force 14 September 2001.
International Labour Convention No. 159 Concerning Vocational Rehabilitation and Employment (Disabled Persons), adopted in Geneva at the 69th ILC Session (20 June 1983).
Protocol No. 12 to the Convention for the Protection of Human Rights and Fundamental Freedoms, Explanatory Report, CETS No. 177 (2000).

B. Council of Europe Soft-Law Instruments

Commissioner for Human Rights, Hammarberg T., *Who Gets to Decide? Right to Legal Capacity for Persons with Intellectual and Psychosocial Disabilities,* CommDH/IssuePaper(2012)2, adopted on 20th February 2012.
Commissioner for Human Rights, Hammarberg T., *The Right of People with Disabilities to Live Independently and be Included in the Community,* CommDH/IssuePaper(2012)3, adopted on 12 March 2012 (Council of Europe Publishing, France, June 2012).
Committee of Ministers, Recommendation No.R(92)6 of the Committee of Ministers to Member States on a Coherent Policy for People with Disabilities (adopted by the Committee of Ministers on 9 April 1992 at the 474th meeting of the Ministers' Deputies).
Committee of Ministers, Recommendation Rec(2006)5 to member states on the Council of Europe Action Plan to promote the rights and full participation of people with disabilities in society: improving the quality of life of people with disabilities in Europe 2006–2015 (adopted by the Committee of Ministers on 5 April 2006 at the 961st meting of the Ministers' Deputies).
Committee of Ministers Recommendation CM/Rec(2009)6 to member states on ageing and disability in the 21st century: sustainable frameworks to enable greater quality of life in an inclusive society (adopted by the Committee of Ministers on 8 July 2009 at the 1063rd meeting of the Ministers' Deputies).
Committee of Ministers, Recommendation CM/Rec(2009)9 to member states on the education and social inclusion of children and young people with autism spectrum disorders (adopted by the Committee of Ministers on 21 October 2009 at the 1068th meeting of the Ministers' Deputies).
Committee of Ministers, Recommendation CM/Rec(2009)8 to member states on achieving full participation through Universal Design (adopted by the Committee of Ministers on 21 October 2009 at the 1068th meeting of the Ministers' Deputies).
Committee of Ministers, Recommendation CM/Rec(2010)2 to member states on deinstitutionalisation and community living of children with disabilities (adopted by the Committee of Ministers on 3 February 2010 at the 1076th meeting of the Ministers' Deputies).
Committee of Ministers, Recommendation CM/Rec(2011)14 to member states on the participation of persons with disabilities in political and public life (adopted by the Committee of Ministers on 16 November 2011 at the 1126th meeting of the Ministers' Deputies).
Committee of Ministers, Resolution ResAP(2001)1 on the introduction of the principles of Universal Design into the curricula of all occupations working on the built environment ('Tomar Resolution').
Committee of Ministers, Resolution ResAP(2001)3 Towards full citizenship of persons with disabilities through inclusive new technologies.
Council of Europe Action Plan to promote the rights and full participation of people with disabilities in society: improving the quality of life of people with disabilities in Europe 2006–2015.

International Labour Organization, Recommendation No. 99 Concerning Vocational Rehabilitation (Disabled) (1995).

International Labour Organization, Recommendation No. 168 Concerning Vocational Rehabilitation and Employment (Disabled Persons) (1983), adopted in Geneva, 69th ILC session (20 June 1983).

International Labour Organization, Recommendation 200: Recommendation concerning HIV and AIDS and the world of work/La Recommandation (no 200) de l'OIT concernant le VIH et le sida et le monde du travail (2010).

Parliamentary Assembly, Recommendation on the Situation of the Mentally Ill (EC Recommendation No. 818) (1977), text adopted by the Assembly on 8 October 1977 (12th Sitting).

Parliamentary Assembly, Recommendation on Rehabilitation Policies for the Disabled (EC Recommendation No. 1185) (1985), text adopted by the Assembly on 7 May 1992 (6th Sitting).

Parliamentary Assembly, Recommendation *Towards concerted efforts for treating and curing spinal cord injury*, 1592 (2003), *Text adopted by the Assembly* on 26 April 2002 (16th Sitting).

Parliamentary Assembly, Recommendation Towards full social inclusion of people with disabilities 1592 (2003), text adopted by the Assembly on 29 January 2003 (5th Sitting).

C. European Court of Human Rights Case Law

Abdulaziz, Cabales and Balkandali v UK, application nos. 9214/80, 9473-81, 9474-81, judgment 28 May 1985.

Alajos Kiss v Hungary, application no. 38832/06, judgment 20 May 2010.

Artyunyan v Russia, application no. 48977/09, judgment 10 January 2012.

Beard v. the United Kingdom, application no. 24882/94, judgment 18 January 2001.

Burghartz v. Switzerland, application no. 16213/90, judgment 22 February 1994.

Chapman v. United Kingdom (GC), application no. 27238/95, judgment 18 January 2001 (2001) EHRR18.

Coster v. the United Kingdom, application no. 24876/94, judgment 18 January 2001.

D.D. v Lithuania, application no. 13469/06, judgment 14 February 2012.

D.G. v Poland, application no. 45705/07, judgment 17 September 2014.

D.H. v. Czech Republic, application no. 57325/00, judgment 13 November 2007 (2007) 47 EHRR 3.

Demir and Baykara v Turkey, application no. 34503/97, judgment 12 November 2008 48 EHRR 54.

Dudgeon v United Kingdom, application no. 7525/76, judgment 24 February 1983.

Engel v Hungary, application no. 46857/06, judgment 20 May 2010.

Farbtuhs v. Latvia, application no. 4672/02, judgment 2 December 2004.

Glor v Switzerland, application no. 13444/04, judgment 30 April 2009.

Grori v Albania, application no. 25336/04, judgment 7 July 2009.

Grzywaczewski v Poland, application no. 18364/06, judgment 31 May 2012.

Horváth and Kiss v. Hungary, application no. 11146/11, judgment 29 January 2013.

I.B. v Greece, application no. 552/10, judgment 3 October 2013.

Jasinskis v Latvia, application no. 45744/08, judgment 21 December 2010.

Khudobin v Russia, application no. 59696/00, judgment 26 October 2006.

Kiyutin v Russia, application no. 2700/10, judgment 10 March 2011.

Konstantin Markin v Russia, application no. 30078/06, judgment 22 March 2012.

Kupczak v Poland, application no. 2627/09, judgment 25 January 2009.

Kurić and Others v Slovenia, application no. 26828/06, judgment 26 June 2012.

Kutzner v Germany, Application No. 46544/99, Judgment of 26 February 2002 (2002) 35 EHRR 25.
Logvinenko v Ukraine, application no. 13448/07, judgment 14 October 2010.
Marckx v Belgium, application no. 6833/74, judgment 13 June 1979.
M.S.S. v Belgium and Greece (GC), application no. 30696/09, judgment 21 January 2011.
Oršuš and Others v. Croatia (GC), application no. 15766/03, 52 EHHR 7.
Pleso v Hungary, application no. 41242/08, judgment 2 October 2012.
Price v United Kingdom, application no. 33394/96, judgment 10 July 2001 (2002) 34 EHRR 53.
Raffrey Taddei v France, application no. 36435/07, judgment 21 December 2010.
Rupa v Romania, application no. 58478/00, judgment 16 December 2008.
Sampanis and Others v. Greece, application no. 32526/05, judgment 5 June 2008.
Schalk and Kopf v. Austria, application no. 30141/04, judgment 22 November 2010.
Seal v the United Kingdom, application no. 50330/07, judgment 7 December 2010.
Smith and Grady v. the United Kingdom, application nos. 33985/96 and 33986/96, judgment 27 December 1999.
Stanev v Bulgaria, application no. 36760/06, judgment 17 January 2012.
Stec v. United Kingdom, application nos. 65731/01 and 65900/01, judgment 12 April 2006 (2006) 43 EHRR 47.
Thlimmenos v Greece, application no. 34369/97, judgment 6 April 2000.
Timishev v. Russia, application nos. 55762/00 and 55974/00, judgment 13 March 2006.
Tyrer v. United Kingdom, application no. 5856/72, judgment 25 April 1978 (1978) 2 EHRR 1.
V.C. v Slovakia, application no. 18968/07, judgment 8 November 2011.
Vallianatos and Others v Greece, applications nos. 29381/09 and 32684/09, judgment 7 November 2013.
Vasyukov v Russia, application no. 2974/05, judgment 5 April 2011.
Vladimir Vasilyev v Russia, application no. 28370/05, judgment 10 January 2012.
Vincent v France, application no. 6253/03, judgment 24 October 2006.
Wemhoff v. Germany, application no. 2122/64, 27 June 1968,1 EHRR 55.
Xiros v Greece, application no. 1033/07, judgment 9 September 2010.
Yordanova v. Bulgaria, application no. 25446/06, judgment 24 April 2012.
Z.H. v Hungary, application no. 28973/11, judgment 8 November 2012.

D. Decisions of the European Committee of Social Rights

Autism Europe v France, Complaint No. 13/2002, European Committee of Social Rights, decision on the Merits, adopted 7 November 2003.
European Action of the Disabled (AEH) v France, European Committee of Social Rights, complaint no. 81/2012, decision on the merits adopted on 18 November 2013.
International Federation for Human Rights (FIDH) v. Belgium, European Committee of Social Rights, complaint No. 75/2011.
Mental Disability Advocacy Centre (MDAC) v Bulgaria, Complaint No. 41/2007, European Committee of Social Rights (Decision on the Merits, 3 June 2007).
Mental Disability Advocacy Center (MDAC) v. Belgium, European Committee of Social Rights, complaint no. 109/2014.

III. European Union Law Sources

A. European Union Legislation

Charter of Fundamental Rights of the European Union (2000) OJ C 364/01.
Directive 2000/78/EC of the Council of 27 November 2000 establishing a general framework for equal treatment in employment and occupation OJ L 303, 02/12/2000 P. 0016–0022.
Directive 2002/19/EC of the European Parliament and of the Council of 7 March 2002 on access to interconnection of, electronic communications networks and associated facilities OJ L 108, 24.4.2002.
Directive 2002/20/EC of the European Parliament and of the Council of 7 March 2002 on the authorisation of electronic communications networks and services, OJ L 108, 24.4.2002.
Directive 2002/58/EC of the European Parliament and of the Council of 12 July 2002 concerning the processing of personal data and the protection of privacy in the electronic communications sector OJ L 201, 31.07.2002.
Directive 2009/136/EC of the European Parliament and of the Council of 25 November 2009 amending Directive 2002/22/EC on universal service and users' rights relating to electronic communications networks and services OJ L 337, 18.12.2009, p. 11–36.
Directive 2009/140/EC of the European Parliament and of the Council of 25 November 2009 amending Directives 2002/21/EC on a common regulatory framework for electronic communications networks and services.
Regulation (EC) No 2006/2004 of the European Parliament and of the Council of 27 October 2004 on cooperation between national authorities responsible for the enforcement of consumer protection laws OJ L 364, 9.12.2004.
Regulation (EC) No 1211/2009 of the European Parliament and of the Council of 25 November 2009 establishing the Body of European Regulators for Electronic Communications (BEREC) and the Office OJ L 337, 18.12.2009, p. 1–10.
Resolution of the Council of 6 February 2003 on 'eAccessibility' - improving the access of people with disabilities to the knowledge based society, OJ C 39, 18.2.2003.

B. European Union Case Law

European Court of Justice, Case C-303/06, *Coleman v. Attridge Law and Law* [2008] ECR I-5603.
European Court of Justice, Joined Cases C-335/11 and C-337-11, *HK Danmark, acting on behalf of Jette Ring v Dansk almennyttigt Boligselskab and HK Danmark, acting on behalf of Lone Skouboe Werge v Dansk Arbejdsgiverforening acting on behalf of Pro Display A/S*, Judgment of the Court (Second Chamber) of 11 April 2013.

IV. National Sources

A. National Legislation

Americans with Disabilities Act (ADA) [1990], as amended by the Amendments Act of 2008 (P.L. 110–325), which became effective on January 1, 2009.
Australian Disability Discrimination Act [1992], Act No. 135 of 1992 as amended.
Austrian Act on the Employment of People with Disabilities (effective as of 1 January 2006).
Belgian Guide to Reasonable Accommodations for Persons with a Disability at Work [March 2005].

Bulgarian Protection Against Discrimination Act (effective as of 1 January 2004).
Cypriot Act of Parliament on the Education and Training of Children with Special Needs [113(1)/1999].
Finnish Non-Discrimination Act 21 [2004] [including Preparatory Works to the Finnish Non-Discrimination Act, HE 44/2003 [Government Proposal 44/2003] concerning Section 5 of the Act].
German Social Law Code, Book Nine 9 (SGB IX), Rehabilitation and Participation of Disabled Persons [19 June 2001].
Israeli Equal Rights for People with Disabilities Law 5758 [1998].
Norwegian Act (No. 61) [2013] prohibiting discrimination on grounds of disability (Anti-Discrimination and Accessibility Act) [Lov (Nr 61 av 2013) om forbud mot diskriminering på grunn av nedsatt funksjonsevne (diskriminerings- og tilgjengelighetsloven)].
Portuguese Decree Law No. 3/2008 [adopted 7 January 2008].
Slovakian Anti-Discrimination Act No. 365/2004 Coll. On Equal Treatment in Certain Areas and Protection against Discrimination, amending and supplementing certain other laws (Anti-Discrimination Act) [20 May 2004].
South African Employment Equality Act No. 55 [1998].
Spanish General Organisation of the Education System Act [1990] (Ley Organica de Ordenacion General del Sisterna Educativo).
UK Disability Discrimination Act [1995].
UK Equality Act [2010].

B. National Case Law

Australian Human Rights Commission, *Woodhouse v Wood Coffill Funerals Pty Ltd* [1998] HREOCA 12.
Constitutional Court of South Africa, *Soobramoney v Minister of Health (Kwazulu-Natal)* (CCT32/97) [1997] ZACC 17; 1998 (1) SA 765 (CC); 1997 (12) BCLR 1696 (27 November 1997).
Constitutional Court of South Africa, *Government of the Republic of South Africa and Others v Grootboom and Others* [2001] (1) SA 46 (CC). 2000 (11) BCLR 1169 (CC).
Constitutional Court of South Africa, *Minister of Health and Others v Treatment Action Campaign and Others (No 2) (CCT8/02)* [2002] ZACC 15; 2002 (5) SA 721; 2002 (10) BCLR 1033 (5 July 2002).
Constitutional Court of South Africa, *Khosa and Others v Minister of Social Development and Others, Mahlaule and Another v Minister of Social Development* (CCT 13/03, CCT 12/03) [2004] ZACC 11; 2004 (6) SA 505 (CC); 2004 (6) BCLR 569 (CC) (4 March 2004).
Constitutional Court of South Africa, *Occupiers of 51 Olivia Road, Berea Township and 197 Main Street Johannesburg v City of Johannesburg and Others* [2008] ZACC 1.
Federal Court of Australia, *Daghlian v Australia Post* [2003] FCA 759.
Federal Magistrates Court of Australia, *Hills Grammar School v Human Rights and Equal Opportunity Commission* [2000] 100 FCR 206.
Federal Magistrates Court of Australia, *Access for All Alliance (Hervey Bay) v Hervey Bay City Council* [2004] FMCA 915 [87].
High Court of South Africa, *Treatment Action Campaign and Other v Minister of Health and Others* [2002] 4 BCLR 356.
Supreme Court of Canada, *Central Alberta Dairy Pool v Alberta (Human Rights Commission)* [1990] 72 D.L.R. 4th 417.
Supreme Court of Canada, *Eldridge v. British Columbia (A.G.)*, [1997] 3 S.C.R. 624.
Supreme Court of Canada, *Eaton v Brant County Board of Education* [1998] 1 S.C.R. 24.

Supreme Court of Canada, *Vriend v. Alberta* [1998] 132 D.L.R. (4th) 595 (Alta. C.A.).
Supreme Court of Canada, *British Columbia (Public Service Employee Relations Commission) v. British Columbia Government Service Employees' Union* [1999] 3 S.C.R. 3, 1999 SCC 48
Supreme Court of Canada, *Law v Canada (Minister of Employment and Immigration)* [1999] 1 S.C.R. 497.
United States Court of Appeals, *Nelson v. Thornburgh*, Third Circuit, 732 F.2d 146 3/6/84567 F. Supp. 369 (E.D.Pa. 1983).

V. Secondary Academic Sources

A. Books/Book Chapters

Abberley P., 'Work, Utopia and Impairment' in Barton L. (ed.), *Disability and Society: Emerging Issues and Insights* (Longman Publishing, New York, 1996).
Arnardóttir O.M., 'A Future of Multidimensional Disadvantage Equality' in Arnardóttir O.M. and Quinn G. (eds.), *The UN Convention on the Rights of Persons with Disabilities: European and Scandinavian Perspectives* (Martinus Nijhoff, Leiden, 2009).
Aust A., *Modern Treaty Law and Practice* (Cambridge University Press, Cambridge, 2nd edition, 2007).
Barnes C. and Mercer G., 'Theorising and Researching Disability from a Social Model Perspective' in Barnes C. and Mercer G. (eds.) *Implementing the Social Model of Disability: Theory and Research* (The Disability Press, Leeds, 2004).
Bickenbach J.E., 'Minority Rights or Universal Participation: The Politics of Disablement' in Jones M. and Basser L.A. (eds.) *Disability, Divers-Ability and Legal Change* (Martinus Nijhoff, London, 1999).
Broderick A. and Quinlivan S., 'The Right to Education: Article 24 of the CRPD' in Quinn G. and O' Mahony C. (eds.), *The UN Convention on the Rights of Persons with Disabilities: Comparative, Regional and Thematic Perspectives* (Intersentia, 2015).
Byrne B., 'Minding the Gap? Children with Disabilities and the United Nations Convention on the Rights of Persons with Disabilities in Freeman M. (ed.), *Law and Childhood Studies* (Oxford University Press, Oxford, 2012).
Cali B., 'Specialised Rules of Treaty Interpretation: Human Rights' in Hollis D.B. (ed.), *The Oxford Guide to Treaties* (Oxford University Press, Oxford, 2012).
Chapman A. and Russell S. (eds.), *Core Obligations: Building a Framework for Economic, Social and Cultural Rights* (Intersentia, Antwerp, 2002).
Coomans F., *De Internationale Bescherming van het Recht op Onderwijs* [The International Protection of the Right to Education], thesis, Leiden 1992.
Coomans F., 'In Search of the Core Content of the Right to Education' in Brand D. and Russell S. (eds.) *Exploring the Core Content of Socio-Economic Rights: South African and International Perspectives* (Protea Book House, Pretoria, 2002).
Cook R., 'Obligations to Adopt Temporary Special Measures under the Convention on the Elimination of All Forms of Discrimination Against Women' in I. Boerefijn, F. Coomans, J. Goldschmidt, R. Holtmaat and R. Wolleswinkel (eds.), *Temporary Special Measures: Accelerating de facto Equality of Women under Article 4(1) UN Convention on the Elimination of All Forms of Discrimination Against Women* (Intersentia, Antwerp, 2003).
Crocker D.A. and Robeyns I., 'Capability and agency' in Morris C. (ed.), *The Philosophy of Amartya Sen* (Cambridge University Press, Cambridge, 2009).
Daw R. (ed.), *The Impact of the Human Rights Act on Disabled People* (Disability Rights Commission, London, 2003).

De Schutter O., 'Reasonable Accommodation and Positive Obligations in the European Convention on Human Rights' in Lawson A. and Gooding C. (eds.), *Disability Rights in Europe: From Theory to Practice* (Hart, Oxford, 2005).

De Schutter O., 'Positive Action' in Schiek D., Waddington L., Bell M. (eds.), *Cases, Materials and Text on National, Supranational and International Non-Discrimination Law* (Hart, Oxford, 2007).

Dixon M. (ed.), *Textbook on International Law* (Oxford University Press, Oxford, 7th edition, 2013).

Donnelly J. (ed.), *Universal Human Rights in Theory and Practice* (Cornell University Press, Ithaca, NY, 2003).

Eide A., 'Economic, Social and Cultural Rights as Human Rights' in Eide A., Krause C and Rosas (ed.), *Economic, Social and Cultural Rights: A Textbook* (Martinus Nijhoff, Dordrecht/London, 2nd edition, 2001).

Fitzmaurice M., 'The Practical Working of the Law of Treaties' in Evans M. (ed.) International Law (Oxford University Press, 2nd edition, 2006).

Fredman S., 'Beyond the Dichotomy of Formal and Substantive Equality: Towards a New Definition of Equal Rights' in Boerefijn I., Coomans F., Goldschmidt J., Holtmaat R. and Wolleswinkel R. (eds.), *Temporary Special Measures: Accelerating de facto Equality of Women under Article 4(1) UN Convention on the Elimination of All Forms of Discrimination Against Women* (Intersentia, Antwerp, 2003).

Fredman S., 'Disability Equality, A Challenge to the Existing Anti-Discrimination Paradigm?' in Lawson A. and Gooding C. (eds.), *Disability Rights in Europe: From Theory to Practice* (Hart Publishing, Oxford, 2005).

Fredman S., 'Disability Equality and the Existing Anti-Discrimination Paradigm –European Discrimination Law,' in Lawson A. and Gooding C. (eds), *Disability Rights in Europe: From Theory to Practice* (Hart Publishing, Oxford, 2005).

Fredman S. (ed.), *Human Rights Transformed: Positive Rights and Positive Duties* (Oxford University Press, Oxford, 2008).

Fredman S. (ed.), *Discrimination Law* (Oxford University Press, Oxford, 2nd edition, 2011).

Freeman M.A., Chinkin C. and Rudolf B. (eds.), *The UN Convention on the Elimination of All Forms of Discrimination Against Women* (Oxford University Press, New York, 2012).

Gardiner R. K. (ed.), *Treaty Interpretation* (Oxford University Press, Oxford, 2008).

Hendriks A., 'The Significance of Equality and Non-Discrimination for the Protection of the Rights and Dignity of Disabled Persons' in Degener T. and Koster-Dreese Y. (eds.) *Human Rights and Disabled Persons Essays and Relevant Human Rights Instruments* (Martinus Nijhoff, Dordrecht, 1995).

Hendriks A., '*Disabled Persons and their Right to Equal Treatment: Allowing Differentiation while Ending Discrimination*' in Maan J.M., Gruskin S., Grodin M.J. and Anna G.J., *Health and Human Rights: A Reader* (Routledge 1999).

Hendriks A., 'The UN Disability Convention and (Multiple) Discrimination: Should EU Non-Discrimination Law Be Modelled Accordingly?' in Quinn G. and Waddington L. (eds.), *European Yearbook of Disability Law*, Volume 2 (Intersentia, Antwerp, 2010).

Hunt P. and Mac Naughton G., 'A Human Rights-Based Approach to Health Indicators', in Baderin M. and McCorquodale R. (eds.), *Economic, Social and Cultural Rights in Action* (Oxford University Press, Oxford, 2007).

Jones M., 'Inclusion, Social Inclusion and Participation' in Rioux M.H., Basser L.A. and Jones M. (eds.), *Critical Perspectives on Human Rights and Disability Policy* (Martinus Nijhoff, The Hague, 2011).

Joseph S., Schultz J. and Castan M. (eds.), *The International Covenant on Civil and Political Rights: Cases, Materials, and Commentary* (Oxford University Press, Oxford, 2nd edition, 2005).

Kälin W. and Künzli J. (eds.), *The Law of International Human Rights Protection* (Oxford University Press, Oxford, 2009).

Kimber C.J.M., 'Equality or Self-Determination' in Grearty C. and Tomkins A. (eds.), *Understanding Human Rights* (Mansell Publishing, London, 1996).

Koch I.E., 'From Invisibility to Indivisibility: The International Convention on the Rights of Persons with Disabilities' in Arnardóttir O.M. and Quinn G. (eds.) *The UN Convention on the Rights of Persons with Disabilities: European and Scandinavian Perspectives* (Martinus Nijhoff, Leiden, 2009).

Lawson A., 'The UN Convention on the Rights of Persons with Disabilities and European Disability Law: A Catalyst for Cohesion?' in Arnardóttir O.M. and Quinn G. (eds.), *The UN Convention on the Rights of Persons with Disabilities: European and Scandinavian Perspectives* (Martinus Nijhoff, Leiden, 2009).

Liebenberg S., 'Adjudicating Social Rights Under a Transformative Constitution' in Langford M. (ed.), *Social Rights Jurisprudence: Emerging Trends in International and Comparative Law* (Cambridge University Press, Cambridge, 2008).

Liebenberg S. (eds.), *Socio-economic rights: Adjudication under a Transformative Constitution* (Juta & Co Ltd Publishers, Claremont, 2010).

Liisberg M.V., *Disability and Employment: A Contemporary Disability Human Rights Approach Applied to Danish, Swedish and EU Law and Policy* (Intersentia, The Netherlands, 2011).

Lord J.E. and Brown R., 'The Role of Reasonable Accommodation in Securing Substantive Equality for Persons with Disabilities: The UN Convention on the Rights of Persons with Disabilities' in Rioux M.H., Basser L.A. and Jones M. (eds), *Critical Perspectives on Human Rights and Disability Policy* (Martinus Nijhoff, The Hague, 2011).

Lord Lester of Herne Hill QC and Joseph S., 'Obligations of Non-Discrimination' in Harris D. and Joseph S. (eds.), *The International Covenant on Civil and Political Rights and United Kingdom Law* (Clarendon Press, Oxford, 1995).

Mc Naughton G., 'Beyond a Minimum Threshold: The Right to Social Equality' in Minkler L. (ed.) *The State of Economic and Social Human Rights: A Global Overview* (Cambridge University Press, Cambridge, 2013).

Minow M. (ed.), *Making All the Difference: Inclusion, Exclusion and American Law* (Cornell University Press, Ithaca, 1990) 20.

Moeckli D., 'Equality and Non-Discrimination' in Moeckli D., Shah S., Sivakumaran S. and Harris D. (eds.), *International Human Rights Law* (Oxford University Press, Oxford, 2014).

Morris J. (ed.), *Pride Against Prejudice: Transforming Attitudes to Disability: A Personal Politics of Disability* (Women's Press, London, 1991).

Morris J. (ed.), *Independent lives? Community Care and Disabled People* (The Macmillan Press, London, 1993).

Nowak M. (ed.), *UN Covenant on Civil and Political Rights: CCPR commentary* (N.P. Engel, Kehl, 2nd edition, 2005).

Nussbaum M.C. (ed.), *Women and Human Development* (Cambridge University Press, Cambridge, 2001).

Nussbaum M.C. (ed.), *Frontiers of Justice* (Harvard University Press, Cambridge/London, 2006).

Nussbaum M.C. (ed.), *Creating Capabilities: The Human Development Approach* (Harvard University Press, Cambridge/Oxford, 2011).

O'Cinneide C., 'Extracting Protection for the Rights of Persons with Disabilities from Human Rights Frameworks: Established Limits and New Possibilities,' in Arnardóttir O.M. and

Quinn G. (eds.), *The UN Convention on the Rights of Persons with Disabilities: European and Scandinavian Perspectives* (Martinus Nijhoff, Leiden, 2009).

O'Elias T. (ed.), *The Modern Law of Treaties* (Sijthoff Publishing Company B.V., Leiden, 1974).

Oliver M., 'If I had a Hammer' in Barnes C. and Mercer G. (eds.) *Implementing the Social Model of Disability: Theory and Research* (The Disability Press, Leeds, 2004).

Pieterse M., 'On Dialogue, Translation and Voice: Reply to Sandra Liebenberg' in S. Woolman & M. Bishop (eds.) *Constitutional Conversations* (Pretoria University Law Press, Pretoria, 2008).

Quinn G., 'The International Covenant on Civil and Political Rights and Disability: A Conceptual Framework,' in Degener T. and Koster-Dreese Y. (eds.), *Human Rights and Disabled Persons: Essays and Relevant Human Rights Instruments* (Martinus Nijhoff, Dordrecht, 1995).

Quinn G., 'The European Social Charter and EU Anti-discrimination Law in the Field of Disability: Two Gravitational Fields with One Common Purpose' in de Búrca G., de Witte B. and Ogertschnig L. (eds.) *Social Rights in Europe* (Oxford University Press, Oxford, 2005).

Quinn G., 'A Short Guide to the United Nations Convention on the Rights of Persons with Disabilities,' in G. Quinn and L. Waddington (eds.), *European Yearbook of Disability Law* (Intersentia, Antwerp, 2009).

Reyes M.S.C., 'Standard Rules on Equality of Opportunities for Persons with Disabilities: Legal View of Provisions on Support Services, Auxiliary Resources and Training/View from Latin America' in Rioux M.H., Basser L.A. and Jones M. (eds.), *Critical Perspectives on Human Rights and Disability Policy* (Martinus Nijhoff, The Hague, 2011).

Rioux M.H. and Riddle C.A., 'Values in Disability Policy and Law: Equality' in Rioux M.H., Basser L.A. and Jones M. (eds.), *Critical Perspectives on Human Rights and Disability Policy* (Martinus Nijhoff, The Hague, 2011).

Robinson M. (ed.), *Performance Budgeting: Linking Funding and Results* (Palgrave Macmillan, New York, November 2007).

Sen A.K., 'Development as Capability Expansion' in Griffin K. and Knight J. (eds.), *Human Development and the International Development Strategy for the 1990s* (Macmillan, London, 1990).

Sen A.K. (ed.), *Inequality Re-examined* (Oxford University Press, Oxford, 1992).

Sen A.K. (ed.), *Development as Freedom* (Oxford University Press, Oxford, 1999).

Sepúlveda Carmona M.M., *The Nature of the Obligations Under the International Covenant on Economic, Social and Cultural Rights* (School of Human Rights Research Series, Volume 18, Intersentia, Antwerpen, 2003).

Shakespeare T. (ed.), *Disability rights and wrongs* (Routledge, London, 2006).

Shue H., *Basic Rights, Substinence, Affluence and U.S. Foreign Policy* (Princeton University Press, Princeton, 2nd edition, 1996) 160.

Sinclair I. (ed.), *The Vienna Convention on the Law of Treaties*, (Manchester University Press, Manchester, 1984).

Smith P., 'Defining Inclusion. What Is It? Who Does it Benefit?' in P. Smith (ed.), *Whatever Happened to Inclusion? The place of students with intellectual disabilities in education*, (Peter Lang Publishing Inc., New York, 2010).

Timmer A., 'A Quiet Revolution: Vulnerability in the European Court of Human Rights' in Fineman M. & Grear A. (eds.) *Vulnerability: Reflections on a New Ethical Foundation for Law and Politics* (Ashgate Publishing Ltd, UK, 2013).

Tomasevski K., *Education Denied: Costs and Remedies* (Zed Books Ltd., London, 2003).

Trömel S., 'A Personal Perspective on the Drafting History of the United Nations Convention on the Rights of Persons with Disabilities' in Quinn G. and Waddington L. (eds.) *European Yearbook of Disability Law: Volume 1* (Intersentia, Antwerp, 2009) 121.

Van der Walt A., 'A South African Reading of Frank Michelman's Theory of Social Justice' in Botha H., Van der Walt A. and Van der Walt J. (eds.) *Rights and Democracy in a Transformative Constitution* (Sun Press Stellenbosch, 2003) 163.

Vandenhole W., *Non-Discrimination and Equality in the View of the UN Human Rights Treaty Bodies* (Intersentia, Antwerp/Oxford, 2005).

Villiger M.E., 'The Rules on Interpretation: Misgivings, Misunderstandings, Miscarriage? The 'Crucible' Intended by the International Law Commission' in Cannizzaro E. (ed.), *The Law of Treaties: Beyond the Vienna Convention* (Oxford University Press, Oxford, 2011).

Waddington L., 'Unravelling the Knot: Article 8, Private Life, Positive Duties and Disability. Rewriting: *Sentges v. the Netherlands'* in Brems E. (ed.) *Diversity and European Human Rights: Rewriting Judgments of the ECHR* (Cambridge University Press, Cambridge, 2013) 349.

Waddington L., 'Reasonable Accommodation' in Schiek D., Waddington L. and Bell M. (eds.), *Cases, Materials and Text on National, Supranational and International Non-Discrimination Law* (Hart Publishing, Oxford, 2007).

Weller P. (ed.), *New Law and Ethics in Mental Health Advance Directives: The Convention on the Rights of Persons with Disabilities and the Right to Choose* (Routledge, New York, 2013).

Yuill C., 'The Social Model of Health' in Yuill C., Crinson I., and Duncan E. (eds.), *Key Concepts in Health Studies* (Sage Publications, CA, 2010).

B. Journal Articles

Albertyn C. and Goldblatt B., 'Facing the Challenge of Transformation: Difficulties in the Development of an Indigenous Jurisprudence of Equality' (1998) 14 *South African Journal on Human Rights* 248.

Albertyn C., 'Substantive Equality and Transformation in South Africa' (2007) 23 *South African Journal on Human Rights* 253.

Arnardóttir O.M., 'The Differences that Make a Difference: Recent Developments on the Discrimination Grounds and the Margin of Appreciation under Article 14 of the European Convention on Human Rights' (2014) 14 *Human Rights Law Review* 647.

Barnes C., 'Understanding Disability and the Importance of Design for All' (2011) 1(1) *Journal of Accessibility and Design for All* 55.

Barmes L., 'Equality law and experimentation: The positive action challenge' (2009) 68 *Cambridge Law Journal* 623.

Bickenbach J.E., Chatterji S., Badley E.M., & Üstün T.B. 'Models of disablement, universalism and the international classification of impairments, disabilities and handicaps,' (1999) 48 *Social Science & Medicine* 1173.

Bilchitz D., 'Giving socio-economic rights teeth: the minimum core and its importance' (2002) 119 *South African Law Journal* 484.

Bilchitz D., 'Towards a Reasonable Approach to the Minimum Core: Laying the Foundations for Future Socio-Economic Rights Jurisprudence' (2003) *South African Journal of Human Rights* 1.

Clifford J., 'The UN Disability Convention and its Impact on European Equality Law,' (2011) 6 *The Equal Rights Review*.

Coate S. and Loury G.C., 'Will Affirmative-Action Policies Eliminate Negative Stereotypes?' (1993) 83(5) *The American Economic Review* 1220.

Coomans F., 'Reviewing Implementation of Social and Economic Rights: An Assessment of the "Reasonableness" Test as Developed by the South African Constitutional Court (2005) 65 *Max-Planck-Institut für ausländisches öffentliches Recht und Völkerrecht* 167.

Coomans F., 'Clarifying the Core Element to the Right to Education,' *SIM Special 18*, 7 available at www.uu.nl/faculty/leg/EN/organisation/schools/schooloflaw/organisation/departments/studieeninformatiecentrummensenrechten/publications/simspecials/18/Pages/default.aspx.

Danisi C., 'How Far Can the European Court of Human Rights Go in the Fight Against Discrimination? Defining New Standards in Its Non-discrimination Jurisprudence' (2011) 9 *International Journal of Constitutional Law* 793.

Day S. and Brodsky G., 'The Duty to Accommodate: Who Will Benefit?' (1996) 75 *Canadian Bar Review* 433.

De Beco G., The Right to Inclusive Education According to Article 24 of the UN Convention on the Rights of Persons with Disabilities: Background, Requirements and (Remaining) Questions,' (2014) 285 *Netherlands Quarterly of Human Rights* 32(3).

De Campos Velho Martel L., 'Reasonable Accommodation: The New Concept from an Inclusive Constitutional Perspective' (2007) *International Journal on Human Rights* available at www.surjournal.org/eng/conteudos/getArtigo14.php?artigo=14.

De Vos P., 'Grootboom, The Right of Access to Housing and Substantive Equality as Contextual Fairness' (2001) 17 *South African Journal of Human Rights* 258.

Degener T., 'International Disability Law – A New Legal Subject on the Rise: The Interregional Experts' Meeting in Hong Kong, December 13–17, 1999' (2000) 18 *Berkley Journal of International Law* 180.

Doyle B., 'Enabling Legislation or Dissembling Law? The Disability Discrimination Act 1995,' (1997) 60 *Modern Law Review* 64.

Eberle E.J., 'The methodology of comparative law' (2011) 16(1) *Roger Williams University law review* 51.

Eide A., 'Realisation of Social and Economic Rights and the Minimum Threshold Approach' (1989) 10(1–2) *Human Rights Law Journal* 36.

Emens E.F., 'Integrating Accommodation' (2008) 156(4) *University of Pennsylvania Law Review* 839.

Fredman S., 'Changing the Norm: Positive Duties in Equal Treatment Legislation' (2005) 12(4) *Maastricht Journal of European and Comparative Law* 369.

Gerards J., 'The Discrimination Grounds of Article 14 of the European Convention on Human Rights' (2013) 31 *Human Rights Law Review* 99.

Goldschmidt J. (interviewed by Anderson J. and Philips J.), 'Shifting the Burden of Proof: How the CRPD is Transforming our Understanding of Discrimination, Intersectionality and Priorities' in Anderson J. and Philips J., *Disability and Human Rights: Legal, Ethical and Conceptual Implications of the Convention on the Rights of Persons with Disabilities* (Netherlands Institute of Human Rights, SIM Special 35, 2012).

Griffey B., 'The "Reasonableness" Test: Assessing Violations of State Obligations under the Optional Protocol to the International Covenant on Economic, Social and Cultural Rights' (2011) 11(2) *Human Rights Law Review* 275.

Hammel J., Magasi S, Heinemann A., Whiteneck G., Bogner J. and Rodriguez E., 'What does Participation Mean: An Insider Perspective from People with Disabilities' (2008) 30(19) *Disability and Rehabilitation* 1445.

Harnacke C., 'Disability and Capability: Exploring the Usefulness of Martha Nussbaum's Capabilities Approach for the UN Disability Rights Convention' (2013) 41 *Journal of Law, Medicine & Ethics* 768.

Harnacke C., 'Capability and Disability: The CRPD from the Perspective of the Capabilities Approach' in J. Anderson and J. Philips (eds.), *Disability and Universal Human Rights: Legal, Ethical, and Conceptual Implications of the Convention on the Rights of Persons with Disabilities*, available at http://sim.rebo.uu.nl/wp-content/uploads/2013/10/SIMspecial35.pdf.

Hughes B. and Paterson K., 'The Social Model of Disability and the Disappearing Body: Towards a Sociology of Impairment,' (1997) 12(3) *Disability & Society* 325.

Jonas D.S. and Saunders T.N., 'The Object and Purpose of a Treaty: Three Interpretive Methods' (2010) 43(3) *Vanderbilt Journal of Transitional Law* 565.

Karlan P.S. and Rutherglen G., 'Disabilities, Discrimination, & "reasonable accommodation"' (1996) 46(1) *Duke Law Journal* 1.

Kayess R. and French P., 'Out of Darkness Into Light? Introducing the Convention on the Rights of Persons with Disabilities' (2008) 8(1) *Human Rights Law Review* 1.

Klare K., 'Legal Culture and Transformative Constitutionalism' (1998) 14 *South African Journal of Human Rights* 146.

Koch I.E., 'Dichotomies, Trichotomies or Waves of Duties?' (2005) 5 *Human Rights Law Review* 81.

Lacy W., 'Equality Under and Before the Law' (2011) 61(3) *University of Toronto Law Journal* 411.

Lawson A., 'The EU Rights Based Approach to Disability: Strategies for Shaping an Inclusive Society,' (2005) 6(4) *International Journal of Discrimination and the Law* 269.

Lawson A., 'Reasonable Accommodation and Accessibility Obligations: Towards a More Unified European Approach,' 11 *European Anti-Discrimination Law Review* (December 2010) 11.

Lawson A., 'Disability Equality, Reasonable Accommodation and the Avoidance of Ill-Treatment in Places of Detention: The Role of Supranational Monitoring and Inspection Bodies' 16(6) *International Journal of Human Rights* (August 2012) 845.

Liebenberg S., 'The value of human dignity in interpreting socio-economic rights' (2005) 21 *South African Journal on Human Rights* 1.

Liebenberg S., 'Needs, Rights and Transformation: Adjudicating Social Rights' (2006) 17 *Stellenbosch Law Review* 5.

Liebenberg S., 'Towards a transformative adjudication of socio-economic rights,' (2007) 21 *Speculum Juris* 41.

Liebenberg S. and Goldblatt B., 'The Interrelationship between Equality and Socio-Economic Rights under South Africa's Transformative Constitution' (2007) 23 *South African Journal on Human Rights* 359.

Lixinski L., 'Treaty Interpretation by the Inter-American Court of Human Rights: Expansionism at the Service of the Unity of International Law' (2010) 21(3) *European Journal of International Law* 585.

Mac Kinnon C.A., 'Substantive Equality: A Perspective' 96 Minnesota Law Review 1.

Marks D., 'Dimensions of Oppression: Theorising the Embodied Subject,' (1999) 14(5) *Disability & Society* 661.

Mégret F., 'The Disabilities Convention: Human Rights of Persons with Disabilities or Disability Rights?' (2008) 30 *Human Rights Quarterly* 494.

Mégret F., 'The Disabilities Convention: Towards a Holistic Concept of Rights' (2008) *The International Journal of Human Rights* 261.

Michel K., 'Treaty Bodies and the Interpretation of Human Rights' (2009) 42 *Vanderbilt Journal of Transitional Law* 905.

Minow M., Learning to Live with the Dilemma of Difference: Bilingual and Special Education' (1985) *Law and Contemporary Problems* 202.

Moellendorf D., 'Reasoning About Resources: Soobramoney and the Future of Socio-Economic Rights Claims' (2008) 14 *South African Journal on Human Rights* 327.

Morrison R. and Burgman I., 'Friendship Experiences Among Children with Disabilities who Attend Mainstream Schools' (2009) 76 *Canadian Journal of Occupational Therapy* 145

Nussbaum M.C., 'Capabilities and Human Rights' (1997) 66(2) *Fordham Law Review* 273.

O' Brien J., 'Affirmative Action, Special Measures and the Sex Discrimination Act' (2004) 27(3) *University of New South Wales Law Journal* 840.

O' Connell R., *Substantive Equality in the European Court of Human Rights?*, 107 *Michigan Law Review First Impressions* 129 (2009), 129, available at www.michiganlawreview.org/firstimpressions/vol107/oconnell.pdf.

O' Connell R., 'Cinderella Comes to the Ball: Article 14 and the Right to Non-discrimination in the ECHR'(2009) 29 *Legal Studies*: *The Journal of the Society of Legal Scholars* 211–229.

Perenboom R.J.M. and A.M.J. Chorus, 'Measuring participation according to the International Classification of Functioning, Disability and Health (ICF)' (2003) 25 *Journal of Disability Rehabilitation* 577.

Peroni L. & Timmer A., 'Vulnerable Groups: the Promise of an Emergent Concept in European Human Rights Convention Law,' (2013) 11 *International Journal of Constitutional Law* 1054.

Peters B., 'Aspects of Human Rights Interpretation by the UN Treaty Bodies,' available at http://ssrn.com/abstract=2013298.

Porter B., Reasonableness and Article 8(4) in M. Langford, B. Porter, R. Brown and J. Rossi (eds.), The Optional Protocol to the International Covenant on Economic, Social and Cultural Rights: A Commentary (2014), available at http://papers.ssrn.com/sol3/papers.cfm?abstract_id=2481712.

Porter B., 'The Reasonableness of Article 8(4) – Adjudicating Claims from the Margins' (2009) 27(1) *Nordisk Tidsskrift for Menneskerettigheter*, 39.

Posner E.A., 'Evaluating the Effects of International Law: Next Steps' (A response to 'Beyond Compliance: Rethinking Why International Law Really Matters) (October 2010) 1(3) *Journal of Global Policy* 334.

Redish M.H., 'The Federal Courts, Judicial Restraint, and the Importance of Analyzing Legal Doctrine' (1985) 85 *Columbia Law Review* 1378.

Rogers C., Inclusive education and intellectual disability: a sociological engagement with Martha Nussbaum, (2013) 17(9) *International Journal of Inclusive Education* 988.

Samuel G., 'Comparative Law and Jurisprudence' (1998) 47(4) *International and Comparative Law Quarterly* 817.

Scott C. and Alston P., 'Adjudicating Constitutional Priorities in a Transnational Context: A Comment on *Soobramoney's* Legacy and *Grootboom's* Promise' (2000) 16 *South African Journal of Human Rights* 206.

Sen A.K., 'Development as Capability Expansion,' (1989) 19 *Journal of Development Planning* 41.

Skogly S., 'The Requirement of Using the "Maximum Available Resources" for Human Rights Realisation: A Question of Quality as well as Quantity' (2012) 12(3) *Human Rights Law Review* 393.

Stein M.A., 'The Law and Economics of Disability Accommodations' (2003) 53(1) *Duke Law Journal* 79.

Stein M.A., 'Disability Human Rights' (2007) 95 *California Law Review* 75.

Stein M.A. & Stein P.J.S., 'Beyond Disability Civil Rights' (2007) 58 *Hastings Law Journal* 1203.

Sunstein C.R., 'Social and Economic Rights? Lessons from South Africa' 11(4) *Constitutional Forum* (2001).

Tiller E.H. and Cross F.B., 'What is Legal Doctrine,' 100(1) *Northwestern University Law Review* 517.

Timmer A., 'Toward an Anti-Stereotyping Approach for the European Court of Human Rights' (2011) 11(4) *Human Rights Law Review* 707.

Tobin J., 'Seeking to Persuade: A Constructive Approach to Human Rights Treaty Interpretation' (2010) 23(1) *Harvard Human Rights Journal* 1.

Tucker B.P., 'The ADA's Revolving Door: Inherent Flaws in the Civil Rights Paradigm' (2001) 62 *Ohio State Law Journal* 335.
Waddington L., 'When it is Reasonable for Europeans to Be Confused: Understanding When a Disability Accommodation is "Reasonable" from a Comparative Perspective (2008) 29(3) *Comparative Labor Law & Policy Journal* 317.
Waddington L. and Bell M., 'Exploring the Boundaries of Positive Action under EU Law: A Search for Conceptual Clarity' (2011) 48(5) *Common Market Law Review* 1503.
Waddington L., *European Human Rights Cases*, Aflevering 4, april 2011, Jaargang 12, 556.
Waddington L., Noot bij: European Court of Human Rights. (25-06-2013), EHRC 2013-, (Europees Hof voor de Rechten van de Mens, 25 juni 2013, nr. 6087/03, Grimailovs tegen Letland), 2286/2305.
Wells K., The Impact of the Framework Employment Directive on UK Disability Discrimination Law (December 2003) 32(4) *Industrial Law Journal* 253.
Westen P., 'The Empty Idea of Equality,'(1982) 95(3) *Harvard Law Review*, 537.
Woodward W.R. and Barbour L., 'Beyond Universalism: Capabilities Approach for Improving Women's Quality of Life' (2009) 3(2) *Journal of Human Ontogenetics* 75.
Young K., 'The Minimum Core of Economic and Social Rights: A Concept in Search of Content' (2008) 33(1) *Yale Journal of International Law* 113.
Young R.D., 'Performance-Based Budget Systems' *Public Policy and Practice USC Institute for Public Service and Policy Research* (2003).

VI. Miscellaneous Sources (Reports and Other)

Ad Hoc Committee on a Comprehensive and Integral International Convention on Protection and Promotion of the Rights and Dignity of Persons with Disabilities (New York), 16–27 June 2003 Compilation of proposals for a Comprehensive and Integral International Convention to Promote and Protect the Rights and Dignity of Persons with Disabilities.
Alternative Report of the Comité Espanol de Représentantes de Personas Con Discapacidad (CERMI State Delegation) to the CRPD Committee, *Human Rights and Disability* (2010).
Alternative Report of One Plus One Beijing (March 2012).
Alternative Report on the Compliance with the Convention on the Rights of Persons with Disabilities submitted by the Peruvian National Confederation of People with Disabilities (2010).
Annan K., Official Statement of the UN Secretary-General, 'Secretary General Hails Adoption of Landmark Convention on Rights of People with Disabilities,' (13 December 2006)
Arbour L., former United Nations High Commissioner for Human Rights, Statement to the third session of the Open-Ended WG OP ICESCR (2006).
Arbour L., former United Nations High Commissioner for Human Rights, Opening statement to the fourth session of the Open-Ended WG OP ICESCR (16 July 2007).
Australian Human Rights Commission, *Guidance and Information, Employment and the Disability Discrimination Act: Part 1.*
Bell M. and Waddington L., Annotation to the Legal Definition of Positive Action used in the PAMECUS Project (International perspectives on positive action measures: a comparative analysis in the European Union, Canada, the United States and South Africa, Office for Official Publications of the European Communities, 2009).
Blanck P.D., *Communicating the Americans with Disabilities Act, Transcending Compliance: 1996 Follow-up Report on Sears, Roebuck and Co* (Iowa City, Iowa, 1996).

Bossuyt M., Special Rapporteur, *The Concept and Practice of Affirmative Action*, Final Report, in accordance with resolution 1998/5 of the Sub-Commission for the Promotion and Protection of Human Rights, UN Doc. E/CN.4/Sub.2/2002/21, 17 June 2002.

Capozzi D.M., 'Fifty Years of American Accessibility Experience,' in EDF, 'Freedom Guide: Paving the Way Towards Free Movement for Persons with Disabilities,' December 2011, available at http://cms.horus.be/files/99909/MediaArchive/library/Freedom%20Guide.pdf.

Council of Europe, *Disability, A Citizenship Issue* (2013).

Crow L., 'Renewing The Social Model of Disability' (Published in Coalition News, Greater Manchester Coalition of Disabled People, July 1992).

De Búrca G., 'The EU in the Negotiation of the Disability Convention' *Fordham Law Legal Studies Research* (Paper No. 1525611).

Degener T., 'The Right to Political Participation: From Exclusion to Universality' in International Disability Alliance Publication Series, Issue 1: The Right to Vote and to Stand for Election (March 2013), available at www.internationaldisabilityalliance.org/sites/disalliance.e-presentaciones.net/files/public/files/Theresia%20Degener_The%20right%20to%20political%20participation_from%20exclusion%20to%20universality.pdf.

Despouy L., former Special Rapporteur appointed by the UN Sub-Commission on Prevention of Discrimination and Protection of Minorities, *Human Rights and Disabled Persons* (1993), UN Sales No. E.92.XIV.4.

EDF and IDA, Joint Third Party Intervention in the case of *DG v Poland* (application no. 45705/07), judgment 12 February 2013.), available at www.internationaldisabilityalliance.org/en/third-party-interventions.

EDF submission to the UN Committee on the Rights of Persons with Disabilities on Article 9 'Accessibility' UNCRPD, 15 March 2012, available at www.edffeph.org/Page_Generale.asp?DocID=13854&thebloc=29617.

E.U. Network of Experts on Disability Discrimination, *Implementing and Interpreting the Reasonable Accommodation Provision of the Framework Employment Directive: Learning from Experience and Achieving Best Practice* (Report Prepared by Lisa Waddington in collaboration with Basser L.A., Burgdorf R.L., Cooper J., Quinlivan S., and members of the European Commission Expert Group on Disability Discrimination) 2004.

European Association of Service Provider, *Barometer of Inclusive Education in Selected European Countries* (ZPE-Schriftenreihe Nr. 31), available at www.investt.eu/sites/default/files/barometerreport.pdf.

European Foundation Centre, *Study on challenges and good practices in the implementation of the UN Convention on the Rights of Persons with Disabilities* VC/2008/1214.

Explanatory Report to the European Social Charter (revised) of 1996, ETS no. 196, available at http://conventions.coe.int/Treaty/EN/Reports/HTML/163.htm.

Fredman S., 'Substantive Equality Revisited' Legal Research Paper Series, Paper No. 70/2014 (October 2014).

Hammarberg T., former Council of Europe Commissioner for Human Rights, *Human Rights in Europe: No Grounds for Complacency* (Council of Europe Publishing, Strasbourg, April 2011).

Hammarberg T., former Council of Europe Commissioner for Human Rights, Human Rights Comment, 'Persons with Disabilities must not be Denied the Right to Vote,' available at http://commissioner.cws.coe.int/tiki-view_blog_post.php?postId=127.

Henrard K., 'Asymmetrical Approach towards Non-Discrimination and Special Minority Rights (Max-Planck-Institut für ausländisches öffentliches Recht und Völkerrecht 2011), available at http://www.zaoerv.de/71_2011/71_2011_2_a_379_418.pdf.

Hunt P., *State Obligations, Indicators, Benchmarks and the Right to Education* (Background paper submitted to the Committee on Economic, Social and Cultural Rights), 16 July 1998, E/C. 12/1998/11].

Hunt P., *Report of the Special Rapporteur on the Right of Everyone to the Enjoyment of the Highest Attainable Standard of Physical and Mental Health*, 3 March 2006, E/CN.4/2006/48.

Inclusion International, *Better education for all when we are included too: A Global Report – People with an Intellectual Disability and their Families Speak out on Education for All, Disability and Inclusive Education* (INICO 2009), http://ii.gmalik.com/pdfs/Better_Education_for_All_Glonal_Report_October_2009.pdf.

Inclusion International, *The Implications of the CRPD for Education for All* (2009), available at www.inclusion-international.org/wp.../ImplicationsCRPD_dr2_X2.pd...

International Disability Alliance, Interactive Roundtable on Legislative Measures to Implement the CRPD, with a Focus on Accessibility and Reasonable Accommodation, available at www.un.org/.../IDA%20Draft%20Background%20Note_Roundtable.

International Law Commission, Report of the Commission to the General Assembly, Volume 2, *Yearbook of the International Law Commission* (1966).

Jackson R.M., *National Centre on Accessing the General Curriculum, Curriculum Access for Students with Low-Incidence Disabilities: The Promise of Universal Design for Learning* (2011), available at http://aim.cast.org/learn/disabilityspecific.

Kitching K. (ed.), *International Discrimination Law: A Handbook for Practitioners* (Interights, London, January 2005).

Lewis O., MDAC, 'Three Disability Firsts in a European Court of Human Rights Case,' 2 June 2009, available at www.mdac.info/ru/node/187

Lindqvist B., *Final Report of the Special Rapporteur of the UN Commission on Social Development on the application and oversight activities of the Standard Rules on the Equalisation of Opportunities for Persons with Disabilities.*

Lord J.E., 'Accessibility and Human Rights Fusion in the CRPD: Assessing the Scope and Content of the Accessibility Principle and Duty under the CRPD' Presentation for the General Day of Discussion on Accessibility, UN CRPD Committee UN – Geneva October 7, 2010, available at www2.ohchr.org/SPdocs/CRPD/DGD7102010/.../JanetELord.doc.

Lord Lester of Herne Hill QC, 'Non Discrimination in International Human Rights Law,' in *Developing Human Rights Jurisprudence* (Volume 6: Sixth Judicial Colloquium on the Domestic Application of International Human Rights Norms: Bloemfontein, South Africa, 3–5 September 1993).

Mental Disability Advocacy Center, *Building the Architecture for Change: Guidelines on Article 33 of the UN Convention on the Rights of Persons with Disabilities* (March 2011).

Mental Disability Advocacy Center, 'European Court: Hungary Neglected Prisoner with Multiple Disabilities,' 19 November 2012, available at www.mdac.info/en/19/11/2012/european-court-hungary-neglected-prisoner-with-multiple-disabilities.

Mokhiber C., Chief of Development and Economic and Social Issues Branch at the Office of the High Commissioner for Human Rights, Opinion cited at http://globalaccessibilitynews.com/2012/09/12/ohchr-says-the-core-crpd-obligations-to-be-immediately-implemented-not-implemented-only-as-money-becomes-available.

National Council on Disability, *Understanding the Role of an International Convention on the Human Rights of Persons with Disabilities* (2002), available at www.ncd.gov/policy/CRPD.

Nowak M., *Interim Report of the former UN Special Rapporteur on the question of torture and other cruel, inhuman or degrading treatment or punishment*, submitted on 28 July 2008 by the Office of the United Nations High Commissioner for Human Rights to the 63rd session of the General Assembly of the UN (A/63/175), available at www.un.org/disabilities/images/A.63.175.doc.

Office of the High Commissioner of Human Rights, *From Vision to Action: The Road to Implementation of the Convention* (2007).

Office of the High Commissioner for Human Rights, *The United Nations Human Rights Treaty System: An Introduction to the Core Human Rights Treaties and the Treaty Bodies*, available at www.ohchr.org/Documents/Publications/FactSheet30en.pdf.

Office of the High Commissioner for Human Rights, *Report of the United Nations High Commissioner for Human Rights on progress in the implementation of the recommendations contained in the study on the human rights of persons with disabilities* (14 January 2003), UN Doc. E/CN.4/2003/88, available at www.un.org/disabilities/default.asp?id=147.

Office of the High Commissioner of Human Rights, *Frequently Asked Questions on Economic, Social and Cultural Rights: Factsheet 33*, available at www.ohchr.org/Documents/Publications/FactSheet33en.pdf.

People with Disability Australia (Incorporated) and the Australian National Association of Legal Centres, Position Paper, available at www.un.org/esa/socdev/enable/rights/ahc8docs/ahc8naclc2.do.

Peters S.J., Inclusive Education: An EFA Strategy for All Children, World Bank (November 2004), available at www.worldbank.org.

Porter B. and Liebenberg S., *Consideration of Merits under the OP-ICESCR: Reasonableness Review under 8(4) and the Maximum of Available Resources Standard* (Notes for Discussion at the Workshop on Strategic Litigation under the OP-ICESCR), available at www.escr-net.org/sites/default/files/Porter_and_Liebenberg,_Reasonableness_0.pdf.

Position Paper of People with Disability Australia (Incorporated) and the Australian National Association of Legal Centres, Eighth Session of the Ad Hoc Committee on a Comprehensive and Integral International Convention on the Protection and Promotion of the Rights and Dignity of Persons with Disabilities, available at www.un.org/esa/socdev/enable/rights/ahc8docs/ahc8naclc2.doc, last accessed 14 October 2014.

Quinn G. and Degener T., *Human Rights and Disability: The Current Use and Future Potential of the United Nations Human Rights Instruments in the Context of Disability* (Office of the High Commissioner for Human Rights, United Nations, Geneva 2002).

Quinn G., The UN Convention on the Human Rights of Persons with Disabilities, Presentation to the Irish Human Rights Commission (Dublin, 19th April, 2007), available at www.ihrc.ie/download/doc/gquinn.doc.

Richler D., 'Inclusive Education and Systemic Reform' (Presentation at the Conference on Inclusive Education, Moscow, September 27 2011), available at www.unicef.org/ceecis/Diane.pptx.

Rieser R., *Implementing Inclusive Education: A Commonwealth Guide to Implementing Article 24 of the UN Convention on the Rights of People with Disabilities* (Commonwealth Secretariat, UK, 2008), available at www.worldofinclusion.com/res/internat/Commonwealth_Guide.doc.

School of Oriental and African Studies, *The Convention on the Rights of Persons with Disabilities: The Right to Education and the Obligations of States* (2011), *SOAS International Human Rights Clinic Project* – Research Paper No. 06/2011, available at http://papers.ssrn.com/sol3/papers.cfm?abstract_id=1895726.

Schulze M., *Understanding The UN Convention On The Rights Of Persons With Disabilities: A Handbook on the Human Rights of Persons with Disabilities* (July 2010), at page 39, available at www.hrea.org/erc/Library/display_doc.php?url=http%3A%2F%2Fwww.hiproweb.org%2Fuploads%2Ftx_hidrtdocs%2FHICRPDManual2010.pdf&external=N.

Segal G. and Summers A., *Citizens' Budget Reports: Improving Performance and Accountability in Government, Reason Public Policy Institute* (Policy Study No. 292, March 2002).

Sen A.K., *Equality of What?* Stanford University: Tanner Lectures on Human Value, delivered at Stanford University, May 22, 1979, available at http://tannerlectures.utah.edu/_documents/a-to-z/s/sen80.pdf.

Sheikha Hissa Khalifa bin Ahmed al-Thani, Statement by the former Special Rapporteur on Disability, *Convention on the Rights of Persons with Disabilities: A Progressive Human Rights Instrument*, September 2006, available at www.un.org/esa/socdev/enable/srstathrc2006.html.

Singh K., Interim Report of the United Nations Special Rapporteur on the right to education, *Financing Education and Update on Education in Emergencies,* UN Doc. A66/269, 5 August 2011, available at www.ineesite.org/uploads/files/resources/SR_Education_GA_report_2011.pdf.

Social Transition Team, Office of Democracy, Governance and Social Transition of the United States Agency for International Development (USAID), *Best Practice in Inclusive Education for Children with Disabilities: Applications for Program Design in the Europe & Eurasia Region* (2010).

The Disability Rights Commission (in collaboration with Skill and The Learning and Skills Network), *Understanding the Disability Discrimination Act: A guide for colleges, universities and adult community learning providers in Great Britain* (2007).

The Irish Equality Authority, Department of Justice, *Equality and Law Reform, Positive Action for People with Disabilities: Assisting Public Sector Bodies to Achieve the 3% Employment Target*, available at www.equality.ie/Files/Positive%20Action%20for%20People%20with%20Disabilities.pdf.

Timmer A., 'HIV-based employment discrimination: the ECtHR takes a strong stance in I.B. v. Greece' October 21, 2013, available at http://strasbourgobservers.com/2013/10/21/hiv-based-employment-discrimination-the-ecthr-takes-a-strong-stance-in-i-b-v-greece/.

Tomasevski K., *Manual on Rights-Based Education: Global Human Rights Requirements Made Simple* (Collaborative project between the UN Special Rapporteur on the Right to Education and UNESCO Asia and Pacific Regional Bureau for Education) UNESCO Bangkok, 2004.

Tulkens F., Section President of the European Court of Human Rights, Seminar 'What are the limits to the evolutive interpretation of the Convention?' (Strasbourg, January 2011), available at http://echr.coe.int/Documents/Dialogue_2011_ENG.pdf.

UK Parliament, Joint Committee On Human Rights Twenty-First Report (2004), available at www.publications.parliament.uk/pa/jt200304/jtselect/jtrights/183/18307.html.

UNCESCR, *Statement on Poverty and the ICESCR*, UN Doc. E/C.12/2001/10, 4 May 2001.

UNCESCR, *Statement: An Evaluation of the Obligation to Take Steps to the 'Maximum of Available Resources' Under an Optional Protocol to the Covenant*, UN Doc. E/C.12/2007/1, adopted at the thirty-eighth session of the Committee on 10 May 2007.

UNESCO, *Overcoming Exclusion through Inclusive Approaches in Education: A Challenge and a Vision: Conceptual Paper* (UNESCO 2003).

UNESCO, *The Flagship on Education for All and the Right to Education for Persons with Disabilities: Towards Inclusion,* available at www.unesco.org/education/efa/know_sharing/flagship_initiatives/disability last accessed 10 November 2014.

UN, *From Exclusion to Equality: Realizing the Rights of Persons with Disabilities: Handbook for Parliamentarians on the Convention on the Rights of Persons with Disabilities and its Optional Protocol* (2007 Inter-Parliamentary Press Geneva).

United Nations, *The Millennium Goals Development Report* (2006), available at http//mdgs.un.org/unsd/mdg/Resources/Static/Products/Progress2006/MDGReport2006.pdf last accessed 7 November 2014.

UN Committee on the Rights of Persons with Disabilities, Report submitted by Hungary, *National report on the basis of Article 35 (1) of the Convention on the Rights of Persons with Disabilities,* CRPD/C/HUN/1, (2010).

UN Committee on the Rights of Persons with Disabilities, Report submitted by Tunisia, *Implementation of the Convention on the Rights of Persons with Disabilities: Initial Report of State Parties Submitted Under Article 35 of the CRPD* (July 2010).

UN Committee on the Rights of Persons with Disabilities, *List of Issues to be Taken up in Consideration of the Initial Report of Tunisia* (October 2010).

UN Committee on the Rights of Persons with Disabilities, Seventh Session, Shadow Report of the Democratic Party of Hong Kong (September 2011).

UN General Assembly, *Human Rights Council Annual report of the United Nations High Commission for Human Rights and reports of the Office of the High Commission and the Secretary-General: Thematic study on the right of persons with disabilities to education*, UN Doc. A/HRC/25/29 (18 December 2013).

UN Press Releases, 'Chairman says draft convention sets out 'detailed code of implementation and spells out how individual rights should be put into practice, 15 August 2005, SOC/4680, available at www.un.org/News/Press/docs/2005/soc4680.doc.htm.

U.S. Federal Equal Employment Opportunities Commission's (EEOC) ADA Enforcement Guidelines: *Reasonable Accommodation and Undue Hardship Under the Americans with Disabilities Act*, available at www.eeoc.gov/policy/docs/accommodation.html.

Villalobos V.M., Report of the former Special Rapporteur on the Right to Education, *The Right to Education of Persons with Disabilities*, UN Doc. A/HRC/4/29, 19 February 2007.

Waddington L. and C. Toepke, *Moving Towards Inclusive Education as a Human Right: An Analysis of International Legal Obligations to Implement Inclusive Education in Law and Policy* (December 8, 2014) Maastricht Faculty of Law Working Paper No. 2014, available at http://papers.ssrn.com/sol3/papers.cfm?abstract_id=2535198.

Weiwei L., 'Equality and Non-Discrimination under International Human Rights Law' (Norwegian Centre for Human Rights, University of Oslo, 2004), available at www.mittendrinundaussenvor.de/fileadmin/bilder/0304.pdf.

Working Group to the Ad Hoc Committee, *Annex I: Draft articles for a Comprehensive and Integral International Convention on the Protection and Promotion of the Rights and Dignity of Persons with Disabilities,* available at www.un.org/esa/socdev/enable/rights/wgcontrib-chair1.html.

World Federation of the Deaf, *Education rights for deaf children: A policy statement of the World Federation of the Deaf* (2007), available at www.wfdeaf.org/databank/policies.

World Health Organization & World Bank, *World Report on Disability* (2011).

School of Human Rights Research Series

The School of Human Rights Research is a joint effort by human rights researchers in the Netherlands. Its central research theme is the nature and meaning of international standards in the field of human rights, their application and promotion in the national legal order, their interplay with national standards, and the international supervision of such application. The School of Human Rights Research Series only includes English titles that contribute to a better understanding of the different aspects of human rights.

For previous volumes in the series, please visit http://shr.intersentia.com.

Published titles within the Series:

65. Gustavo Arosemena, *Rights, Scarcity and Justice. An Analytical Inquiry into the Adjudication of the Welfare Aspects of Human Rights* ISBN 978-1-78068-275-4.
66. Etienne Ruvebana, *Prevention of Genocide under International Law. An analysis of the obligations of states and the United Nations to prevent genocide at the primary, secondary and tertiary levels* ISBN 978-1-78068-273-0.
67. Evgeni Moyakine, *The Privatized Art of War. Private Military and Security Companies and State Responsibility for Their Unlawful Conduct in Conflict Areas* ISBN 978-1-78068-281-5.
68. Esther Janssen, *Faith in Public Debate. On Freedom of Expression, Hate Speech and Religion in France and The Netherlands* ISBN 978-1-78068-309-6.
69. Stefanie Jansen-Wilhelm, *Accepting Assistance in the Aftermath of Disasters* ISBN 978-1-78068-329-4.
70. Helen Beckmann-Hamzei, *The Child in ICC Proceedings* ISBN 978-1-78068-339-3.
71. Karel De Meester, *The Investigation Phase in International Criminal Procedure: In Search of Common Rules* ISBN 978-1-78068-305-8.
72. Nelleke Koffeman, *Morally sensitive issues and cross-border movement in the EU. The cases of reproductive matters and legal recognition of same-sex relationships* ISBN 978-1-78068-349-2.
73. Roland Moerland, *The Killing of Death. Denying the Genocide against the Tutsi* ISBN 978-1-78068-351-5.

www.ingramcontent.com/pod-product-compliance
Ingram Content Group UK Ltd.
Pitfield, Milton Keynes, MK11 3LW, UK
UKHW051918100926
8556IPUK00021B/1249

9 781780 683584